The Sports Junkie's Book of Trivia, Terms, and Lingo

Books by Harvey Frommer

SPORTS

Old Time Baseball
The Sports Junkie's Book of Trivia, Terms, and Lingo
Red Sox vs. Yankees: The Great Rivalry (with Frederic J. Frommer)
A Yankee Century
The New York Yankee Encyclopedia
New York City Baseball: The Last Golden Age, 1947-1957
Rickey and Robinson: The Men Who Broke Baseball's Color Line
Throwing Heat: The Autobiography of Nolan Ryan
Red on Red: The Autobiography of Red Holzman
Running Tough: The Autobiography of Tony Dorsett
Basketball My Way: Nancy Lieberman
Shoeless Joe and Ragtime Baseball
Growing Up at Bat: The 50th Anniversary Book of Little League Baseball
A Baseball Century: The First Hundred Years of the National League

ORAL HISTORIES (WITH MYRNA KATZ FROMMER)

It Happened in the Catskills
It Happened in Brooklyn
Growing Up Jewish in America
It Happened on Broadway
It Happened in Manhattan

The Sports Junkie's Book of Trivia, Terms, and Lingo

What They Are, Where They Came from, and How They're Used

Harvey Frommer

TAYLOR TRADE PUBLISHING
Lanham • New York • Dallas • Toronto • Oxford

Published by Taylor Trade Publishing
An imprint of The Rowman & Littlefield Publishing Group, Inc.
4501 Forbes Boulevard, Suite 200
Lanham, Maryland 20706

Distributed by National Book Network

Library of Congress Cataloging-in-Publication Data

Frommer, Harvey.
  The sports junkie's book of trivia, terms, and lingo : what they are, where they came from, and how they're used / Harvey Frommer—1st Taylor Trade Publishing ed.
      p. cm.
  ISBN 1-58979-255-6 (pbk. : alk. paper)
  1. Sports—Dictionaries. I. Title.
  GV567.F75 2005
  796'.03—dc22
2005009903

To
Arielle Cecelia
"A.C."
the newest Frommer
with much love

Contents

Acknowledgments

A work of this sort would never have surfaced without the many helpers and supporters who were there for me throughout this project. At the top of the list is my son (and sometimes sports coauthor) Frederic J. Frommer whom I especially thank for his careful review of the baseball section. Then there is the team on the bench—Myrna, Jennifer and Jeff, Ian and Laura, and Michele—a big thank you to all.

Special thanks to Christopher Strouthopoulos and Kristen M. Getchell for their interest, suggestions, and reading of sections of the manuscript.

At Taylor, genial Rick Rinehart was enthusiastic about this book from the start and was helpful in its progress through all the stages.

Introduction

Sports language comes and goes with the times. It is a language that grows each year, and changes and attempts to adjust to the ever expanding world of athletics that it describes. It is technical yet colorful, simple yet tremendously involved—a language for those who are inside sports and at the same time an important part of the general cultural vocabulary.

Some expressions live out their time because of the popularity of the figures who used them. Mel Allen's "How about that?" and Red Barber's "In the catbird seat"—phrases that marveled at a baseball player's accomplishments—departed the sports language scene when Mr. Allen and Mr. Barber left their play-by-play announcing roles. Other expressions live on much past their time like *"Say It Ain't So, Joe"*—a comment attributed to a small boy wanting to hear from "Shoeless Joe" Jackson that he was not guilty.

Within the clubhouses and in their private conversations with each other, athletes use another level of language. This sports speech, this special language, provides another view of sports. Some of these terms are also included in this almanac.

A baseball player who hits the ball hard and with straight force is one who manufactures a *frozen rope.* A basketball player who shoots *in your face* is one who attempts to show up another player who is guarding him. A loose and relaxed basketball player *shakes and bakes.* One who *picks someone's pockets* is able to steal the basketball from another player. Such terms and expressions no longer are "inside." Each time a sportscaster or sportswriter hears them, there's a good chance that they become public, part of the culture, and part of the sports language at large.

How many know the differences among the following: *penalty* (football), *penalty kick* (soccer), *penalty killer* (hockey), *penalty shot* (basketball), *penalty box* (hockey), *penalty goal* (soccer), *penalty kick mark* (soccer), *penalty shot* (hockey), *penalty timekeeper* (hockey)?

How many can explain the differences among these terms from basketball: *free throw, bonus free throw, free-throw area, free-throw circle, free-throw lane, free-throw line, freewheeling offense*?

How many know the sports meanings and the sports they belong to of each of the following: *own goal, goal area, goal-area line, goal-line stand, goal average, goal crease, goalie, goal judge, goalkeeper, goal kick, goal-less, goal light, goal mouth, goal post, goaltender, goaltending*?

Can you identify the sports and the meanings of the following colorful terms: *gold, yellow card, red card, black flag, checkered flag, red flag, body in white, greens fee, gold* or *red handkerchief, red-dog, blue line, red line, black belt, blueprint, yellow light*?

Individual sports have a language personality all their own. A lot of fencing is spoken in the accents of Italian and French. The racquet sports are all related, and there is a good deal of inbreeding of language among them. Football has a military aura surrounding its language, while soccer—or what the world outside the United States refers to as "football"—is characterized by an international flavor and many British expressions. Bowling's language contains a quaint and colorful application of this sport's reliance on words taken from the general cultural vocabulary—*Cincinnati, Christmas tree,* and *mother in-law,* for example. Skateboarding, with its origins in surfing (in fact, the sport is called sidewalk surfing), is filled with expressions borrowed from surfing.

And if there were a championship trophy awarded for the richest and most varied sports language, baseball would win it easily. More than one hundred years old, played over a very long season in all sections of the United States, baseball's language is aimed at explaining and describing the nuances of our national game.

It is fascinating to survey the sports lingo that lives and dies depending on developments in sports. The *set shot* (a stationary, two-handed shot at the basket) in basketball was replaced with the *jump shot* as the game evolved. The *three-point shot* (awarding three points for a basket made from twenty-six or more feet out) and the *30-second rule* (mandating that an offensive team shoot within thirty seconds of change of possession), and the red, white, and blue basketball all vanished with the end of the American Basketball Association. But, as all sports fans know, the *three-point shot,* alias *trey, three, triple,* came back to be a significant part of NBA scoring.

The *spitter,* or *spitball,* was supposed to die as a term as a result of a rule in major league baseball that outlawed this type of pitch. The *designated hitter* was born as a result of an American League decision.

Some sports terms belong to all sports. A player-manager is a team member who both plays and manages. A player-coach performs the same role no matter the sport. All sports have *home teams* (the ones that play at their home site) and *visiting teams* (the ones that travel to play at the home team's location). The *bleachers* (those seats beyond the outfield in baseball) are generally the same in all sports, although the Los Angeles Dodgers give their bleacher seats a touch of class by referring to them as *pavilion seats.*

To be *up* (ahead) or *down* (behind) or to *rally* (come from behind) or to be *in the lead* (to be winning) or to *trail* (to be losing) or to *falter* (to fall behind) or to *clinch* (to assure victory)—these are all general words that apply to all sports.

Sometimes the same word or phrase varies greatly in meaning from sport to sport. *Dribbling* in soccer is done with the feet, while in basketball it is performed with the hands. *Fan* in football is a pass pattern; in baseball, to *fan* means to strike out. *Down* in baseball means out, whereas in football it signifies one of a series of four attempts to gain ten yards. To *center a ball* in football is to have the center hike the ball back to the quarterback; in hockey, a meaning of the word *center* is to get the puck back to the center of the rink.

To *trap* a baseball is to gain control of it after it has bounced. To *trap* a soccer ball is to gain control of it by cushioning it with any part of the body except for the arms or hands. To *trap* in football is to block off a defensive lineman in order to allow an offensive ball carrier to have ease of movement. To *trap* in basketball is the act of two players tightly guarding the player with the ball in an attempt to take the ball away. The *pocket* as used in baseball and lacrosse refers to the part of the glove or the head of the stick most useful for gaining control of the ball. *Pocket* in football is a field location a few yards behind the line of scrimmage that a quarterback stays in for protection in his passing attempts.

Sports analogies have infiltrated our nonsports culture as well. To *quarterback* (football) is to lead, to be a *backup quarterback* (football) is to wait to lead, to be a *Monday-morning quarterback* (football) is to second-guess. To *pinch hit* (baseball) is to take someone's place, while *hit a foul ball* (baseball) is to make a mistake. To *throw a curveball* (baseball) is to attempt to trick someone, while to be *thrown a curveball* (baseball) is to have someone attempt to trick you. To get a *rain check* (baseball) is to have an opportunity to do something again. To *get to first base* (baseball) and to *kick off* (football) is to begin . . . the examples go on into sudden death, overtime, extra innings . . . *kissoff* (archery), *ace* (racquet sports), *dunk* (basketball), *mod* (auto racing), *hairy* (auto racing), *bomb* (football), *mag wheels* (auto racing), *raunchy* (auto racing), *zop* (motorcycling), *bull's-eye* (archery), *hot hand* (basketball), *K.O.* (boxing), *take a dive* (boxing), *split* (bowling), *belly whopper* (diving), *caddy* (golf), *duffer* (golf), *in the soup* (surfing), *wiped out* (surfing), *hacker* (tennis), *pug* (boxing), *on guard and parry* (fencing), *dead heat* (track and field), *gun lap* (track), *half-nelson* (wrestling).

There is even a sports language of letters with a symbolism all its own. Here's a sampling:

A	*assist* (basketball)
BA	*batting average* (baseball)
BB	*base on balls* (baseball)
BK	*balk* (baseball)
C	*catcher* (baseball)
CC	*cubic centimeters* (auto racing)
D	*defense* (basketball)
DH	*designated hitter* (baseball)
DOHC	*double overhead camshaft* (auto racing)
E	*error* (baseball); *end* (football)
FG	*field goal* (basketball)
G	*goaltender* (hockey)
H	*the shape of the goalposts* (football)

I	*a type of formation* (football)
JV	*junior varsity* (all sports)
K	*strike out* (baseball)
L	*loss* (baseball pitcher)
M	*a type of formation* (soccer)
MX	*moto-cross* (motorcycling)
N	*novice slope* (skiing)
O	combined with X to diagram football plays
P	*pitcher* (baseball)
PH	*pinch hitter* (baseball)
QB	*quarterback* (football)
R	*run* (baseball)
RBI	*run batted in* (baseball)
S	*sacrifice* (baseball)
SB	*stolen base* (baseball)
SF	*sacrifice fly* (baseball)
T	*technical foul* (basketball); a type of *formation* (football); time-out
U	*utility player* (baseball)
V	*victory* (all sports)
W	*a type of formation* (soccer); *win* (baseball)
WFO	*wide-open throttle* (motorcycling)
WP	*wild pitch* (baseball)
X	combined with O to diagram football plays
X	Former NBA star Xavier McDaniel who had some moments of glory for several different NBA teams
Y	another shape of football goalposts
Z	*zig-zag pattern* (football)
Z	Zydrunas Ilgauskas of the Cleveland Cavaliers, a 7-foot-3, $60 million investment with a name that for some is tough to pronounce

Nicknames have power. Would former boxing great *Jersey Joe Walcott* have been as dynamic if he went by his real name, Arnold Cream? How super would the *Super Bowl* be if it had a different name? Jerome Hannah Dean was never as exciting as *Dizzy Dean*. And *Clyde* was always more glamorous than Walt Frazier, former New York Knickerbockers star.

In writing this guide I attempted to fuse the common with the exotic, the arcane with the ordinary, the old with the new, and the poignant with the matter-of-fact. There are many, many words here. But this is not at all the last word on this fascinating subject.

Archery

AMO Archery Manufacturers and Merchants Organization, which generally sets standards.

Anchor Spot on the archer's face or neck where the string hand rests at time of release.

Armguard Piece of leather wrapped around the forearm protecting it from string slap.

Arrow A thin shaft shot from a bow.

Arrow Plate Vertical section of the bow against which the arrow rests before release.

Arrow Rest A projection on the side of the bow which supports the arrow.

Arrowhead Point or head of the arrow (Pile).

Back The side of the bow that faces the target.

Backed Bow A layer of material bonded to the back of a bow for reinforcement.

Barreled Arrow An arrow that is tapered at each end and thicker in the middle.

Belly The side of the bow that faces the archer.

Blank The old name for the bull's-eye on an archery target.

Blunt An arrow that has a flat tip.

Bolt A short arrow that is shot from a crossbow.

Bow An instrument that is used to shoot arrows. A bow consists of a flexible strip that is tapered at either end and connected to an arc.

Bow Arm The supporting arm for a bow.

Bow Hand The hand that grasps the bow.

Bowbender An archer, a term more appropriate for traditional archery shooters.

Bowsight An aiming device fastened to a bow.

Bowstring A string used to propel an arrow.

Bowyer One who makes or deals with bows.

Brace The act of stringing a bow.

Brace Height Indication of the correct distance between the bow and the bowstring at the handle.

Bracer An arm guard.

Broadhead Triangular soft-shaped flat and sharp arrowhead used in hunting.

Buck Fever/Target Panic Losing control due to a target or a buck.

Bull's-Eye The centermost ring in a target.

Butt A backstop behind a target.

Cams Pulleys at the end of the limbs of compound bows. They vary in shape and size.

Cast The distance a bow can propel an arrow. The speed at which a bow can shoot; the privilege of shooting first in a competition.

Chested Arrow An arrow that is thickest near the nock.

Clearance (Arrow) The way to verify if an arrow clears the bow without any contact.

Clout Target One twelve-times-standard four-foot target. A clout target is laid flat on the ground and used for distance shooting up to 180 yards.

Cock Feather A feather that is set at a ninety-degree angle to a string and is of a different color from the other feathers to facilitate locating the nock.

Creep The edging forward of an arrow during the aiming process.

Crest Colored marks placed near the nock of an arrow for identification purposes.

Deflexed Shape of the riser.

Double Round A round that is shot two times in succession, with the scores of both added together.

Draw The act of pulling back the bowstring.

Drawing Hand The hand that pulls back the bowstring.

Drawing Weight The specific power needed for pulling the bow all the way back.

Drift An arrow's movement sideways because of crosswinds.

End In target competition, the number of arrows shot and scored as a group.

Eye Loop at the bowstring's end.

Face Front of a target.

Fast Flight Different string style used on modern bows.

Field Archery Competitive events held in forestlike areas to approximate bow-hunting conditions.

Field Arrow An arrow used in field archery.

Field Point A tapered arrowhead.

Field Round A round in field archery.

Field Roving Course A course set in forestlike areas to approximate bow-hunting conditions.

Finger Stall Protective coverings for the draw fingers.

Finger Tab Protective leather coverings for the string fingers.

Fistmele The distance from the belly of a bow to the string.

Fletch The act of putting feathers on an arrow.

Fletcher An arrowsmith.

Fletching The vanes or feathers attached to an arrow.

Flick A change in direction of an arrow in flight.

Flight Arrow An arrow designed for distance shooting.

Flight Shooting Distance shooting.

Flirt A flickering of an arrow just after it is shot from the bow.

Flu-Flu An arrow with a broad point, designed for bird hunting.

FOC Front of center, the balance point of the arrow, generally 60 percent of the weight in the back and 40 percent in the front.

Foot Bow A bow placed against the feet and drawn with both hands.

Footed Arrow An arrow with strong material inserted behind the pile for greater strength.

Freestyle Competition that allows various kinds of bows, aiming devices, and types of shooting.

Gold A bull's-eye in a target.

Grains Standard measurement of weight in archery.

Grip The bow handle.

Handle Center of the bow, the part which the archer uses in gripping the bow (Riser).

Head The point of the arrow.

Hen Feathers Two out of three feathers of a three-feather bow that are colored alike.

Hold The pause at full draw.

Hunter's Round A field-archery round on a roving course.

Hunting Bow A bow used for hunting game.

IBO International Bowhunters Organization, which sets standards.

In The second unit in a field-archery round.

Kick Jolt when a bow is let go.

Kinetic Energy Energy being transferred from the archer to the bow, and then on to the arrow.

Kisser A button or knot located on the bowstring, against which the lips are pressed to fix draw and arrow elevation.

Kissoff Arrow that bounces off one already in the target and lodges in a lesser scoring area or misses the target altogether.

Let Down The loss of bow weight.

Limb Bow ends.

Longbow A long, straight bow, such as those used in medieval England.

Loose The act of releasing the drawstring and shooting the arrow.

Matt The straw or grass coil on which the target is placed.

Nock The grooves on an arrow or on limb tips into which the bowstring fits.

Nocking Point The place on the bowstring where the arrow nock fits.

Out The first unit shot in a round of field archery.

Overbowed A bow that requires greater strength to draw than the archer has.

Overdraw The act of drawing an arrow back too much.

Pass Through The clearing of the bow by the arrow while having nominal contact, affording improved accuracy and consistency.

Peep Sight Placed on string to help seeing through it, used for better consistency and easier use of sights.

Petticoat White rim of a target.

Pile The metal tip of the arrow.

Pin Hole A point in the center of a target that aids aiming.

Point Pile.

Point Blank The distance from the target at which the point-of-aim and the gold coincide.

Point-of-Aim The object an archer sights on to get proper elevation.

Popinjay Shooting A shooting competition in which blunt arrows are shot at artificial birds; scoring values are attached to high overhead perches.

Power Form A stance used for target shooting that is aimed at increasing body muscle tension. In the power form, the feet are turned out more toward the target than ordinarily, and the upper body is twisted to some degree away from the target while the archer aims.

Projectile Arrow released from the bow.

Pull Act of pulling the bowstring to full draw.

Quiver A carrying device to hold arrows, usually a long leather bag worn over the shoulder.

Range Finder An aid in estimating the distance to a target or in determining the point-of-aim.

Recurved Bow A bow whose tips are formed with a reverse bend.

Reflex Bow A bow with limbs that curve away from the archer when unstrung and held in shooting position.

Release To loose an arrow by releasing the bowstring.

Riser Additional stripping glued to the bow handle's belly side for depth or reinforcement.

Round A specific number of arrows shot at given distances; in field shooting, a two-unit or twenty-eight-target course.

Rover An individual who engages in the old method of field archery by shooting progressively at casual, or random, targets.

Self A bow or arrow made from a single kind of material; an arrow with no footing; a bow created from only one type of wood.

Serving Additional wrapping around the bowstring to prevent chafing and making for longer wear.

Shaft An arrow's cylindrical body from the nock to the pile.

Shaftment The part of the shaft at which feathers are attached.

Sight Window Cutout area of the riser.

Spine Arrow-shaft stiffness, firmness, elasticity; the arrow's ability after being released from the bow to resume its original shape.

Stacked Bow A narrow-limbed bow whose limbs are not as thick as they are wide.

Stake A shooting position in field archery.

Stick Bows Recurves and longbows, the more "primitive" bows.

String To get set for shooting the arrow by bending the bow (see Brace).

String Arm The string-pulling arm.

String Dampener A device that helps cut down the twanging sound made when an arrow is released. It is composed of rubber or plastic and is fitted on the bowstring to cushion vibrations (String Slencer).

String Hand The bowstring-pulling hand.

Tab Leather covering for the fingers that pull the bowstring.

Tackle Archery equipment.

Takedown Bows A recurve with removable limbs.

Target A circular outline positioned on a backing of straw and having concentric rings representing scoring areas of different values. The bull's-eye in the center has the highest scoring value.

Target Archery Competitive events where archers shoot at a target from specific distances.

Target Arrow The target-shooting arrow composed of a fairly small fletching, an equal-diameter shaft, and a pile that is pointed.

Target Point A cone-shaped pile that is pointed.

Target Round A target-shooting round.

Tear Drops Attachment at the end of cable used to attach the string.

The target-shooting arrow composed of a fairly small fletching, an equal-diameter shaft, and a pile that is pointed.

Tiller To find a bow's curvature at all bends and to adjust unequal bending.

Torque The act of the bow twisting due to improper twisting of the string by an improper hold.

Toxophilite A word derived from the Greek *toxon* ("bow") and *philos* ("loving") and meaning an archer or someone who is a fan of archery.

Underbowed An archer with a bow that is too weak for his strength.

Underdraw To draw back just shy of full draw, diminishing shot power.

Unit Half of a full field course; a fourteen-target loop.

Unlimited A category of shooters and their bows, that can be simply stated as one who shoots with a trigger and has a stabilizer bar longer than 15 inches.

Unstring To take the bowstring off the nock(s) of a bow.

Vane Fletching; generally refers to plastic types.

Velocity Speed at which the arrow travels measured in feet per second.

Walk-Up Progressively placed shooting stakes.

Wand A long, narrow target stuck into the ground.

Wand Shooting Competitive events where thirty-six arrows are shot at a wand.

Weight The force necessary to pull a bow all the way back (Bow Weight).

Whip The act of putting a serving (wrapping) around a bowstring.

Badminton

Ace A winning point.

Alley Extension of the court by 1½ feet on both sides for doubles play.

Back Alley Area located between back boundary line and long service line for doubles.

Backcourt The court's back third, in the area of the back boundary lines.

Backhand Stroke hit by right-handed players on the left side of the body or by left-handed players on the right side of the body.

Backswing Movement of the racquet backward in anticipation of the forward swing.

Badminton A game called *poona* was developed in India and then allegedly came to Great Britain by way of British army officers who had played it during their leisure hours. In 1873 the Duke of Beaufort staged a party at his country manor, Badminton. Poona, or the English version of the sport, was played with slightly rearranged rules. The streamlined version of poona played at Badminton was the root of the sport as we know it today.

Balk (Feint) Deceptive movement disconcerting to an opponent before or during the service.

Base A spot on the middle line, a bit closer to the net than the baseline, where players in singles games should attempt to return after most shots.

Baseline Back boundary line at each end of the court, parallel to net.

Bird A cone-shaped missile with rounded cork at one end and fourteen to sixteen feathers at the other end (Shuttle; Shuttlecock).

Carry Illegally, shuttle is caught and held on the racquet, then slung during the execution of a stroke (see Sling).

Center Line One that is perpendicular to net separating left and right service courts.

Center (Base) Position Location in the center of the court to which a singles player after each shot tries to return.

Clear A lofting stroke that projects the bird to the back of the opponent's court (Lob).

Court Area of play, as defined by the outer boundary lines.

Crosscourt A stroke that gets the bird to go diagonally across court.

Drive A flat, fast stroking of the bird.

Drop Shot The bird barely clears the net and descends almost vertically as a result of this stroke, which may be hit underhanded or overhanded.

Fault A foul that costs the server the serve.

Feint (Balk) Deceptive movement disconcerting to opponent before or during the service.

Flick Rapid wrist-movement shot, performed with little motion in the player's arm, that gets the bird high in the air and to the rear of the opponent's court.

Follow-Through After racquet contact, smooth continuance of the stroke in the direction of the bird.

Forecourt Front court.

Forehand Right-handed players' natural stroking of the bird from a position to the right of the body, or a stroke hit on the left side of the body by left-handed players.

Front Service Line The forward boundary of the service courts; a line parallel to and 6 feet from the net on each side of the court (Short Service Line).

Game In singles, 15 points for men and 11 for women; 15 points in the different types of doubles play.

Half Court The serving court for one player, which is diagonally opposite the receiving court of his opponent.

Halfcourt Shot A shot struck low and to midcourt, used effectively in doubles against the up-and-back formation.

High Serve A serve delivered high and deep into the half court of the receiver (Lob Serve).

Kill A hard and quick shot that is virtually impossible to return (Put-Away).

Let Point played over; an expression indicating that because play has been interfered with, a point has to be played over.

Long Service Line In singles, the back boundary line. In doubles, line 2½ feet inside the back boundary line.

Loose Shot A poorly hit, weak shot.

Love A scoring term that indicates zero.

Love-All No score.

Low Serve A serve that is softly hit and just skims over the net (Short Serve).

Match A three-game set; the first player to win two games wins the match.

Midcourt Court's middle third, halfway between net and the back boundary line.

Mixed Doubles A pairing of a man and woman as partners against another man and woman.

Net Shot A shot played from close to the net; a type of drop shot.

Overhead Stroke hit from a level above a player's head.

Placement Stroking the bird to a part of the court where the opponent will have difficulty in returning the shot.

Position During a rally, the point occupied by a player on the court at a particular time.

Push Shot Gentle shot played by pushing shuttle with little wrist motion, generally from net or midcourt to opponent's midcourt.

Racquet (Racket) Used by the player to hit the shuttlecock. Weight about ninety grams (three ounces), length 680 mm (27 inches), and made from metal alloys (steel/aluminum) or from ceramic, graphite, or boron composites. Strung with synthetic strings generally or natural gut.

Rally Exchanges of the bird over the net between players or teams prior to the finishing of a point.

Receiver The player designated to receive a serve.

Reply The stroking back of an opponent's shot (Return).

Round-the-Head A stroke executed from the area of the left shoulder, utilizing the forehand grip, that results in an overhead shot smashed with some degree of force.

Serve To put the bird into play at the start of a rally.

Server The player who serves.

Service Courts The half courts designated as areas to which players must serve.

Setup An easy chance at a winning shot.

Short Service Line To be legal, serve must reach to a line 6½ feet from the net.

Shuttlecock (Shuttle) The object players must hit. Composed of sixteen goose feathers attached to a cork base covered with leather. Synthetic shuttles are sometime used.

Sling The act of not hitting the shuttle cleanly but carrying it on the racket, which is a fault (Throw).

Smash A powerful downward stroke hit with much speed.

Stroke The hitting of the bird with the racquet.

Wood Shot One that results when the base of the shuttle is hit by the frame of the racket.

Baseball

Advance The moving ahead of a base runner to the next base as a result of a hit, error, sacrifice, balk, and so forth.

Advanced Rookie Baseball Minor league baseball league just above rookie baseball.

AERA Adjusted earned run average. Formula for pitcher's ability to prevent runs from being scored—adjusted for league and home park factors.

"All-American Boy" Superstar slugger Dale Murphy had a long career with the Atlanta Braves and had many nicknames including: "Murph," "Gentle Giant," "John Boy," "Lil' Abner."

Alley The space between the center fielder and right fielder or between the center fielder and left fielder.

All-Star Game The idea was conceived in 1933 by Arch Ward, *Chicago Tribune* sports editor. To give the fans a real rooting interest, Ward suggested that they be allowed to vote for their favorite players via popular ballot. In perhaps no other game do fans have such a rooting interest, although there have been a few periods when voting by fans has been abandoned. Today it appears that Ward's original principle will remain permanently in effect. The American League won twelve of the first sixteen All-Star games but went on to lose twenty of the next twenty-three to the National League through 1978. Some memorable moments have taken place in the contest often referred to as the Midsummer Dream Game. In the first game ever played, Babe Ruth slugged a towering home run. The next year, New York Giants immortal Carl Hubbell struck out Babe Ruth, Lou Gehrig, Jimmy Foxx, Al Simmons, and Joe Cronin in succession to make for some more baseball history.

Amazin' Mets The first run the Mets ever scored came in on a balk. They lost the first nine games they ever played. They finished last their first four seasons. Once they were losing a game, 12-1, and there were two outs in the bottom of the ninth inning. A fan held up a sign that said "PRAY!" There was a walk and, ever hopeful, thousands of voices chanted, "Let's go Mets." They were 100-1 underdogs to win the pennant in 1969 and incredibly came on to finish the year as World Champions. They picked the name of the best pitcher in their history (Tom Seaver) out of a hat on April Fools' Day. They were supposed to be the replacement for the Brooklyn Dodgers and the New York Giants. They could have been the New York Continentals or Burros or Skyliners or Skyscrapers or Bees or Rebels or NYBs or Avengers or even Jets (all runner-up names in a contest to tab the National League New York team that began playing ball in 1962). They've never been anything to their fans but amazing—the Amazin' New York Mets.

American League Silver Slugger Award Presented to the best offensive player in the American League for each position.

Anaheim Angels The franchise began play as the Los Angeles Angels in 1961, became the California Angels when it moved to Anaheim in 1966, and has been the Anaheim Angels since 1997, after the team negotiated a thirty-year lease with Anaheim. "Angels" derives from Los Angeles, the "City of Angels," where the team started.

"Apollo of the Box" Hurler Tony Mullane, a tribute to his handsome appearance and playing position. Mullane was also called "The Count" or "Count."

Appeal Play An appeal play occurs when a defensive player claims a runner did not touch a base and urges the umpire to call the player out. The defensive player must tag the runner or the base to get the appeal considered.

"Arizona Diamondbacks" Team nickname derived from the diamondback rattlesnakes that are in the Arizona desert.

"Arkansas Hummingbird" Lon Warneke, a pitcher for the Chicago Cubs and St. Louis Cardinals from 1930–1945, hailed from Mt. Ida, Arkansas.

"A-Rod" A shortening of Yankee third baseman Alex Rodriguez's name.

Around the Horn A phrase describing a ball thrown from third base to second base to first base, generally in a double-play situation.

Assist A player's throw to another player on his team that results in a putout.

AstroTurf Not all of the artificial carpets that have now taken root in ball parks and stadiums in the United States and around the world are produced by the Monsanto Chemical Company. AstroTurf was the first, however, having been installed when the Houston Astrodome opened in 1965, and that's why the term has almost become a generic one for artificial sod. There is also Tartan Turf (made by Minnesota Mining and Manufacturing) and Poly-Turf (a product of American Bilt-Rite). Resistant to all types of weather, more efficient to keep up than grass, better for traction than most other surfaces, synthetic "grass" has continued to "grow" throughout the world of sports, despite complaints that it results in more injuries for players. Studies focused on injuries are still in progress, while other research is under way aimed at improving the quality of the artificial carpets.

At Bat An official time up at the plate as a hitter.

Athletic Hose White socks worn under stirrup socks as part of a baseball uniform.

Atlanta Braves The franchise began in 1871 known as the Boston Red Stockings and then by several other names including Beaneaters through 1906, then Doves when the Dovey family owned the franchise, 1907–1910. In 1911, the nickname changed for new owner James Gaffney, a Tammany Hall "Brave." From 1936 to 1940, the team was called Rustlers, Braves, and Bees. In 1941, the Braves nickname returned and has stuck with the franchise through moves to Milwaukee in 1953 and Atlanta in 1966.

Away A pitch out of the reach of a batter. A side retired in its half of an inning.

Away Uniform Distinctive gray (nonwhite) clothing worn by a team when playing "away" games.

"Babe" George Herman Ruth probably leads the list for most nicknames acquired. First called "Babe" by teammates on the Baltimore Orioles, his first professional team because of his youth, Ruth was also called "Jidge" by Yankee teammates, short for George. They also called him "Tarzan." He called most players "Kid," because he couldn't remember names, even of his closest friends. Opponents called him "The Big Monk" and "Monkey."

Many of Babe Ruth's nicknames came from overreaching sports writers who attempted to pay tribute to his slugging prowess: "The Bambino," "The Wali of Wallop," "The Rajah of Rap," "The Caliph of Clout," "The Wazir of Wham," "The Sultan of Swat," "The Colossus of Clout," "The Maharajah of Mash," "The Behemoth of Bust," "The King of Clout." His main nickname was rooted in President Grover Cleveland's Baby Ruth.

Perhaps the greatest slugger of all time and also one of baseball's most colorful characters, Ruth set some fifty records in his twenty-two years as a player. His accomplishments, his personality, his nickname—all combined to rocket major league baseball firmly into the nation's psyche.

Babe and Ruth In spring training 1927, Babe Ruth bet pitcher Wilcy Moore $100 that he would not get more than three hits all season. A notoriously weak hitter, Moore somehow managed to get six hits in seventy-five at bats. Ruth paid off his debt and Moore purchased two mules for his farm. He named them "Babe" and "Ruth."

Babe Ruth's Legs Sammy Byrd, sometimes used as a pinch runner for Ruth.

"Baby Doll Jacobson" Allegedly, in Mobile (in the Southern League) in 1912, the grandstand band played "Oh, You Beautiful Doll" after Jacobson's opening day homer.

Backstop Another name for the position of catcher, area behind home plate at base of stands.

Back-to-Back Jacks Two home runs hit in the same inning one after another.

"Bad Vlad" Shortening of Vladimir Guerrero's name and a compliment to how good "Bad Vlad" was as a member of the Expos and now with the Angels.

Bail Out The movement of a batter away from a pitched ball as a result of fear of being hit by the pitch.

Balk Illegal movement by a pitcher that, when executed with runner(s) on base, allows the runner(s) to advance one base; with the bases empty, a ball is added to the count of the batter.

Ballantine Blast Expression in deference to beer sponsor that legendary Yankee announcer Mel Allen used to describe a home run.

Baltimore Chop A hard-smashed ball in or just beyond the home plate area that bounces high in the air and gives the runner a good chance to beat the fielder's throw to first base.

Baltimore Orioles The St. Louis Browns moved to Baltimore in 1954 and a traditional Baltimore team nickname, the Orioles, named for the state bird of Maryland, was brought back. The nineteenth-century version of the team became the New York Yankees.

"Bam-Bam" Hensley Meulens could speak about five languages and had a difficult name to pronounce.

Banjo Hitter A "Punch and Judy," or weak batter.

"Banty Rooster" Casey Stengel's nickname for Whitey Ford because of his style and attitude.

"The Barber" Sal Maglie had the unique distinction of pitching for the Brooklyn Dodgers, the New York Yankees, and the New York Giants in the 1950s. A curveballing clutch pitcher, his nickname came from two sources. A swarthy 6'2" right-hander who always seemed to need a shave, he was a master at "shaving" or" barbering" the plate. His pitches would nick the corner, and he wasn't too shy about nicking a batter if the occasion demanded it.

Base The white canvas bags, set 90 feet apart in professional baseball, and designated as first base, second base, and third base. The size of a base is 15 inches by 15 inches (see Home Plate, Sack, Bag).

Baseball The weight of the ball is not less than five ounces nor more than five and one-quarter ounces. Its circumference is not less than 9 inches or more than 9¼ inches.

Baseball Cards About twenty years before the American League was organized in 1901, the first baseball cards appeared. Photographs were taken in an artist's studio. Action was simulated to approximate game conditions: the baseballs that players apparently were hitting were suspended from the ceiling by a string, and the bases that players were shown sliding into were actually set into a wooden floor. These early baseball cards were printed on paper with sepia tone and included in packs of cigarettes from the leading companies of that era: Old Judge, Piedmont, Sweet Caporal, Polar Bear, and Recruit. Bubblegum baseball cards originated in 1933 with cards made of heavy cardboard. Their popularity grew until World War II caused a halt in their production. In 1951 Topps entered the baseball card field and has continued to innovate and dominate the market.

    The most valuable baseball card in existence is a 1910 Honus Wagner that was issued by the Sweet Caporal Tobacco Company. Wagner did not smoke and objected to the use of his name and image on a card; therefore, all the Wagner cards were removed from circulation except for the seven known to exist today. The largest collection of baseball cards is housed in New York City's Metropolitan Museum of Art—over 200,000 cards make up the collection.

Baseball Shoe Shoe for baseball, having metal or plastic projections on the sole for enhanced traction.

Baseball Uniform Uniforms worn by players, managers, and coaches while on the field.

Base Hit Any fair hit that results in a player reaching a base safely; generally refers to a single (Bingle).

Base on Balls The yielding of a fourth pitch outside the strike zone to a batter, which allows him to move to first base (Walk; Pass; Free Ticket).

Bases-Empty Home Run One hit without runners on base.

Bases Loaded A situation where there are runners on first, second, and third base.

"Bash Brothers" Mark McGwire and Jose Canseco were once sluggers paired on Oakland.

Basket Catch A ball catch by an outfielder with glove at waist level, palm side up; made famous by Willie Mays.

Bat Requirements include that it must be one piece of solid wood, round, not over 2¾ inches in diameter at the thickest part, nor more than 42 inches in length.

Bat Around A situation where each batter in the lineup receives a chance to hit in the same inning.

Bat Boy/Girl Generally, a youngster who takes care of bats and other baseball equipment.

Bat Day In 1951 Bill Veeck ("as in wreck") owned the St. Louis Browns, a team that was not the greatest gate attraction in the world. (It's rumored that one day a fan called up Veeck and asked, "What time does the game start?" Veeck's alleged reply was, "What time can you get here?") Veeck was offered six thousand bats at a nominal fee by a company that was going bankrupt. He took the bats and announced that a free bat would be given to each youngster attending a game accompanied by an adult. That was the beginning of Bat Day. Veeck followed this promotion with Ball Day and Jacket Day and other giveaways. Bat Day, Ball Day, and Jacket Day have all become virtually standard major league baseball promotions.

Batter The player who is up at bat, hitting (Batsman).

Batter's Box A rectangle on either side of home plate in which the batter must stand in order to hit; it is 4 feet by 6 feet.

Batter's Wheelhouse That part of the plate from which the batter hits most effectively.

Battery The pitcher and catcher.

Batting Average A means of indicating the effectiveness of a hitter; to compute the average, the number of hits is divided by the number of official times at bat, displayed with three decimal points.

Batting Categories

C Catcher
1B First Baseman
2B Second Baseman
3B Third Baseman
SS Short Stop
LF Left Fielder
CF Center Fielder
RF Right Fielder
P Pitcher

Batting Order The sequence in which hitters on a team come to bat in a game.

Batting Terms

AB At Bat (Does not include walks or sacrifice hits)
AVG Batting Average, H/AB
BB Base on Balls
CS Caught Stealing
H Hit
HBP Hit by Pitch
HR Home Run
IBB Intentional Base on Balls
K Strikeouts
OBP On-Base Percentage, (H+BB+HBP) / (AB+BB+HBP+Sacrifice Flies)
R Run
RBI Run Batted In
SB Stolen Base
SB% Stolen Base Percentage, SB / (SB+CS)
SF Sacrifice Fly
SH Sacrifice Hit
SLG Slugging Percentage, TB/AB
TB Total Bases, H + 2B + (2 x 3B) + (3 x HR)

Battle of the Biltmore 1947 World Series celebration in Manhattan's Biltmore Hotel was a time and place where Larry MacPhail drunkenly fought with everyone and ended his Yankee ownership.

Bean To strike a batter in the head with a pitched ball.

Beanball A pitched ball aimed generally at the head of a batter.

Bedford Avenue Blast Red Barber, Brooklyn Dodger legendary announcer, used this expression to describe a home run hit onto a famous Brooklyn street.

Belt The hitting of a ball with much force by a batter.

Bench Jockey A loud-mouthed player who teases the opposition from his position on the bench in the dugout.

Berra-isms Yogi Berra had a way with words; herewith, a sampler:

"Congratulations on breaking my record last night. I always thought the record would stand until it was broken."—to Johnny Bench, who broke his record for career home runs by a catcher.

"I didn't say the things I said."

"If you don't know where you are going, you will wind up somewhere else."

"If you come to a fork in the road, take it."

"He must have made that before he died."—on a Steve McQueen movie, 1982.

"A nickel ain't worth a dime anymore."

"It's tough to make predictions, especially about the future."

"The future ain't what it used to be."

"A home opener is always exciting, no matter if it's home or on the road."

"I take a two-hour nap between 1:00 p.m. and 3:00 p.m."

"Ninety percent of the putts that are short don't go in."

"Baseball is 90 percent mental. The other half is physical."

"You have to give 100 percent in the first half of the game. If that isn't enough, in the second half, you have to give what is left."

"Nobody goes there any more. It's too crowded."

"It gets late out there early," referring to the bad sun conditions in left field at the stadium.

"He is a big clog in their machine."

"I've been with the Yankees seventeen years, watching games and learning. You can see a lot by observing."

"Baseball is the champ of them all. Like somebody said, the pay is good and the hours are short."

"All pitchers are liars and crybabies."

"Bill Dickey learned me all his experience."

"I want to thank you for making this day necessary."—to fans in hometown St. Louis for giving him a day in 1947 at Sportsman's Park.

"I've known this guy so long. Can't he spell my name right?"—after receiving a check that said "Pay to the order of bearer."

"I think Little League is wonderful. It keeps the kids out of the house."

"If the people don't want to come out to the ballpark, nobody's going to stop them."

"Pair off in threes."

"The other teams could make trouble for us if they win."—as Yankee manager.

"Always go to other people's funerals, otherwise they won't come to yours."

"We have very deep depth!"

"It was impossible to get a conversation going, everybody was talking too much."

When asked what time it is—"Do you mean now?"

When asked what he would do if he found a million dollars—"If the guy was poor, I'd give it back."

When asked by a waitress how many pieces she should cut his pizza into—"Four. I don't think I could eat eight."

When asked why the Yankees lost the 1960 series to Pittsburgh—"We made too many wrong mistakes."

When told by Yankee manager Bucky Harris to think about what was being pitched to him—"Think? How
   the hell are you gonna think and hit at the same time?"
When told Ernest Hemingway was a great writer—"Yeah, for what paper?"
When asked what his cap size was at the beginning of spring training—"I don't know, I'm not in shape."
"It's dèjá vu all over again."
"It ain't over 'til it's over."

"Bidge" Craig Biggio (pronounced "Beedge"), long time star for Houston Astros.

"Big Cat" Johnny Mize, former New York Giant and St. Louis Cardinal standout earned the name for his
   agility around first base.

"Big D" His playing weight was 210 pounds and he stood 6'5". That partially accounted for former Dodger
   pitcher Don Drysdale's nickname. The rest stemmed from his nearly 2,500 career strikeouts, his more than
   two hundred games won, and the power pitching he was capable of during a fourteen-year career. Perhaps
   Drysdale's finest accomplishment was a string of 58.2 consecutive scoreless innings pitched.

"Big Ed" Five Irish brothers excited the sporting world around the turn of the century. The brothers Delahanty
   were paced by Edward James Delahanty, better known as Ed, best known as Big Ed; he was over 6 feet tall
   and weighed 170 pounds—large proportions for his time. On a July afternoon in 1896, he became the second player in history to hit four home runs in one game. In a sixteen-year major league career, the Hall of
   Famer recorded 2,597 hits and a lifetime batting average of .346. Delahanty batted .410 to lead the National
   League in 1899, when he was a member of the Philadelphia Phillies, and his .376 average in 1902, when he
   was a member of the Washington team in the American League, was second only to Napoleon Lajoie's .378.
   Collectively, the brothers Delahanty (Joe, Jim, Frank, Tom, and Ed) played in the majors for thirty-eight
   years—two years more than the lifetime of the most accomplished Delahanty, Ed, who died at the age of
   thirty-six.

"Big Hurt" First baseman Frank Thomas, White Sox, given this nickname for his size and slugging ability.

"Big Mac" Name given to Mark McGwire, a shortening of his surname and a nod to his size.

"Big Poison," "Little Poison" Paul Waner's rookie year with the Pittsburgh Pirates was 1926, when he batted .336 and led the league in triples. In one game he cracked out six hits using six different bats. In 1927
   the second Waner arrived, brother Lloyd. For fourteen years, the Waners formed a potent brother combination in the Pittsburgh lineup. Paul was 5' 8½" and weighed 153 pounds. Lloyd was 5' 9" and weighed
   150 pounds. Paul was dubbed Big Poison even though he was smaller than Lloyd, who was called Little
   Poison. An older brother even then had privileges. But both players were pure poison for National League
   pitchers. Slashing left-handed line-drive hitters, the Waners collected 5,611 hits between them. Paul's lifetime batting average was .333, and he recorded three batting titles. Lloyd posted a career average of .316.
   They played a combined total of thirty-eight years in the major leagues.

"Big Red Machine" The Cincinnati Reds of the 1960s and middle 1970s were an offensive powerhouse. Sparked by Johnny Bench, Pete Rose, Tony Perez, and others, in one six-year span the club, with machinelike precision, produced an average of ninety-five wins a year.

"Big Six" Christy Mathewson, seventeen years a pitcher for the New York Giants (he also pitched one game for the Cincinnati Reds), was almost 6' 2" and weighed nearly two hundred pounds. He wore uniform number 6. His fabled fadeaway pitch enabled the Hall of Famer to win twenty or more games twelve years in a row and thirty games in each of four years, three of those years in succession. The big blond with the number 6 on his back was one of the greatest pitchers in all of baseball history.

"Big Train" Hall of Famer Walter Johnson led the majors in strikeouts twelve of his twenty-one years as a pitcher, notching a record 3,508. He pitched 113 shutout games, including a string of fifty-six straight scoreless innings from April 10 to May 14, 1913. Part of the reason for his nickname was his seven shutout wins in seven opening-day games, which moved his Washington Senator team off down the track. Another reason for his nickname was the almost mechanical precision of the 6' 1," 200-pound right-hander, who harnessed durability to power in becoming one of baseball's immortals.

A traveling salesman watched in awe as a big right-handed pitcher struck out batter after batter on an Idaho sandlot. The salesman, a loyal fan of the Washington Senators, contacted manager Joe Cantillon and raved, and Cantillon dispatched his injured catcher Cliff Blankenship to see the pitcher.

"Take along your bat, Cliff," said the Washington skipper. "And if you can get a loud foul off him, leave him where he is," joked Cantillon to his light-hitting backstop.

A few days later Cantillon received a telegram.

"You can't hit what you can't see. I've signed him and he is on his way," Blankenship wrote.

His name was Walter Perry Johnson. He joined the Washington Senators in 1907 and remained with the team known as "first in war, first in peace, and last in the American League" until 1927. Literally carrying the Washington team year after year, Johnson was selected fourteen times to pitch the Senators season opener. A nonsmoker and nondrinker, Johnson's strongest expression was "Goodness gracious sakes alive." Batters had choicer words for the side-arming, whip-lashing right-hander with the blinding speed. Although Johnson holds the record for the most hit batsmen in history (206), he was too nice a man to ever dust off a batter on purpose.

"It was a disgrace the way I took advantage of him," Ty Cobb had said. "Knowing he would not throw at me, I crowded the plate outrageously and hit the outside pitch from him more often than I was entitled to."

Baseball records are made to be broken, and Johnson's career strikeout mark of 3,508 was shattered by Nolan Ryan. But the "Big Train's" record of 113 career shutouts should stand for a long time, especially the way complete game hurlers have become a vanishing breed these days. Johnson's career win-loss record was 416-279.

Once Johnson hurled a shutout on a Friday, another one on Saturday, and another one on Monday—three shutouts in four days. He probably would have had four shutouts in four days, but there was no game scheduled for the Sunday.

Twelve of Johnson's career shutouts were hurled in his high-water year of 1913, a season when he posted a gaudy 36-7 won-lost record and a glittering 1.09 earned run average. His fifty-six straight scoreless innings pitched that year was a record at the time.

The "Big Train" achieved some other remarkable career stats, including most 1-0 wins (thirty-eight), most 1-0 losses (twenty-seven), and most shutout losses (sixty-five). In 1909 alone he had the misfortune of losing ten games when opposing hurlers pitched shutouts against his weak hitting Washington Senators team.

Many argue that Walter Johnson was the greatest pitcher who ever lived. It is an argument with a great deal of merit, especially when one considers who he pitched for and what he accomplished. He was also called "Sir Walter" and the "White Knight" because of his gentlemanly gamesmanship.

"Big Unit" Longtime star hurler Randy Johnson can throw a fastball close to 100 miles per hour and is 6' 10" tall.

"Big Wheel" Lance Parrish was a member (a very important one) of the Detroit Tigers from 1977 to 1986.

Billyball Aggressive style of play utilized by Billy Martin.

"Billy Buck" Billy Buckner was the toast of Wrigley Field as a master batsman in the late 1970s and early 1980s, an even .300 hitter as a Cub. The fans of the Boston Red Sox were not too enamored with him after 1986 because of an error in Game Six of the World Series.

"Bird" Because of his resemblance to "Big Bird" of *Sesame Street*, Detroit pitcher Mark Fidrych earned this tag.

"Biscuit Pants" Reference to the well filled-out trousers of Lou Gehrig.

"Black Babe Ruth" His name was Josh Gibson, and he played at approximately the same time as Babe Ruth. A catcher in the Negro Leagues (1930–1946), Gibson once hit a ball 580 feet in Yankee Stadium—the longest clout ever recorded there. In one four-year period, Gibson notched 278 homers—and that was a major reason for his nickname.

"Black Honus Wagner" John Henry "Pop" Lloyd and Honus Wagner were baseball contemporaries in the years 1906–1917. Lloyd was a shortstop in the Negro Leagues who had few equals, while Wagner played the same role with the Pittsburgh Pirates of the National League. Not only did Lloyd and Wagner play at about the same time (Lloyd continued playing until 1931), but the way they played was similar. Both men were big powerful hitters, excellent fielders, and smart base runners.

Black Sox In 1919 eight members of the Chicago White Sox were accused of conspiring to fix the World Series of that year. They were Shoeless Joe Jackson, Lefty Williams, Chick Gandil, Swede Risberg, Fred McMullin, Happy Felsch, Buck Weaver, and Eddie Cicotte. Williams won twenty-three games during the regular season; Cicotte won twenty-nine. In the World Series Williams lost three games and Cicotte two as the Reds defeated the White Sox in five of the eight games played. Cicotte later admitted he was given $10,000 to "dump" the World Series. A 1920 grand jury investigation indicted the eight players, but before they had even been brought to trial they were banned for life from playing major league baseball. By 1921 seven of the players had been acquitted of the charges but the tarnishing and potentially damaging effect the allegations of a "fixed" World Series carried, resulted in this nickname for a whole team.

"Black Ty Cobb" Oscar Charleston, superstar of the Negro Leagues, was said to resemble Ty Cobb in baseball abilities.

Blank To shut out; to hold the opposition scoreless (Whitewash).

Blast A very powerfully hit ball that travels for distance.

Bleacher Bums A self-named phenomenon of the late 1960s and early 1970s at Wrigley Field in Chicago, these were yellow-hard-hatted fans who swizzled beer and taunted opposing players while swearing allegiance to the Cubs. They functioned for a time as the tenth man on the Chicago Cubs team.

Bleachers Rows and rows of wooden bench-seats located in the most distant outreaches of stadiums, bleachers took their name from the effect that a dazzling summer sun can have on the bodies and clothes of diehard fans.

"Blind Ryne" Pitcher Ryne Duren of Yankee fame. His name came from his very poor vision, uncorrected -20/70 and 20/200.

Block the Plate The act of a catcher straddling the baseline between home plate and an oncoming base runner in an attempt to be in a good position to tag out the runner.

Bloody Angle In the 1923 season the space between the bleachers and right-field foul line at Yankee Stadium was very asymmetrical causing crazy bounces. It was eliminated in 1924, causing the plate to be moved 13 feet and the deepest left-center corner to be changed from 500 to 490 feet.

Blooper A softly hit ball that generally has some backspin and which barely drops in beyond the infield. A lobbed pitch.

Bobble A fielder's fumbling of a ball.

"Bob the Gob" Yankee Bob Shawkey spent most of 1918 in the Navy as a yeoman petty officer aboard the battleship *Arkansas.*

"Boily" A shortening of the given name of Burleigh Grimes who pitched for the Pirates, Dodgers, and Giants. "Ol' Stubblebeard" was another name for the look of his facial hair.

"Bonehead Merkle" The phrase "pulling a bonehead play," or "pulling a boner," is not only part of the language of baseball, but of all sports and, in fact, of the language in general. Its most dramatic derivation goes back to September 9, 1908. Frederick Charles Merkle, a.k.a. George Merkle, was playing his first full game at first base for the New York Giants. It was his second season in the majors; the year before, he had appeared in fifteen games. The Giants were in first place and the Cubs were challenging them. The two teams were tied, 1-1, in the bottom of the ninth inning. With two outs, the Giants' Moose McCormick was on third base and Merkle was on first. Al Bridwell slashed a single to center field, and McCormick crossed the plate with what was apparently the winning run. Merkle, eager to avoid the Polo Grounds crowd that surged onto the playing field, raced directly to the clubhouse instead of following through on the play and touching second base. Amid the pandemonium, Johnny Evers of the Cubs screamed for the baseball, obtained it somehow, stepped on second base, and claimed a forceout on Merkle. When things subsided, umpire Hank O'Day agreed with Evers. The National League upheld O'Day, Evers, and the Cubs, so the run was nullified and the game not counted. Both teams played out their schedules and completed the season tied for first place with ninety-eight wins and fifty-five losses. A replay of the game was scheduled, and Christy Mathewson, seeking his thirty-eighth victory of the season, lost, 4-2, to Three-Finger Brown (q.v.). The Cubs won the pennant. Although Merkle played sixteen years in the majors and had a lifetime batting average of .273, he will forever be rooted in sports lore as the man who made the "bonehead" play that lost the 1908 pennant for the Giants, for had he touched second base there would have been no replayed game and the Giants would have won the pennant by one game.

"Boo" Name for a day in 1979 of Giants shortstop Johnnie LeMaster, who heard the boo-birds in San Francisco. He took his field position wearing "Boo" on his back. LeMaster switched back to his regular jersey after one game.

"Boomer" David Wells, for his in-your-face personality.

Boot A fielder's mishandling of a ground ball.

"The Boss" An apt description of Yankee owner, George Steinbrenner.

The Boston Massacre A four-game sweep of the Red Sox by the Yankees in September 1978. The series ended with the teams tied for first place.

Boston Red Sox (1901) In the early years of the American League, the team was known as the Pilgrims or Puritans. They were later briefly known as the Somersets—a reference to owner Charles Somers. The team was then known as the Red Stockings, which was shortened to Red Sox by sports writers.

Bottom of the Inning Part of the inning when the home team bats.

Boudreau Shift Named after Cleveland Indians manager Lou Boudreau, this was a radical shifting of four infielders to the right side of the infield to counteract the left-handed pull-hitting of Boston Red Sox star Ted Williams.

"Bow Wow" Henry Irven Arft played five years with the St. Louis Browns in the late 1940s and early 1950s and was a journeyman ballplayer. His nickname came from the onomatopoeic sound of his last name.

"The Brat" Eddie Stanky was a protégé of Leo Durocher. An infielder with limited skills, Stanky played eleven years in the major leagues with five different teams and compiled a lifetime batting average of .268. He was also known as Muggsy, in tribute to his tough-guy, loud-mouthed playing characteristics (see "The Lip").

Breaking Pitch A pitch that does not come in straight to a batter but moves about, such as a curve or a slider.

Brew Crew Used to characterize Milwaukee Brewer teams—playing in a city some would say beer made famous.

"Broadway" Shortstop Lyn Lary was married to Broadway star Mary Lawler.

Bronx Bombers New York Yankees nickname, for their borough and home run power.

Bronx Cheer Another term for booing or razzing or raspberry, this sound allegedly originated in the Bronx in the 1920s.

Bronx Zoo A derogatory reference to Yankee off-color behavior on and off the playing field through the years and especially in the 1970s.

Brooklyn Cyclones A name-the-team contest for the return of baseball to Brooklyn after forty-four years resulted in seven hundred names, including "Hot Dogs," "Bums," "Mets," "Dodgers," and "Cyclones." The latter won hands down for the minor league team of the New York Mets located in Coney Island. The stadium is located right near the beach and the Cyclone—one of the oldest roller coasters in the USA.

Brooklyn Dodger Sym-Phony From 1938 to 1957 a group of unlikely musicians serenaded Dodger fans at Ebbets Field in Brooklyn. Sometimes they sat in seats 1-8, row 1, section 8. Sometimes they sauntered up and down the aisles, tooting and rooting on their beloved Bums. Sometimes they climbed on top of the Dodger dugout and played their original form of jazz through the long summer days and nights. A special feature of the group was a tune they performed known as the "Army Duff." Fans referred to the song as "The Worms Crawl In." The little band would razz a visiting-team strikeout victim back to his bench with this song. As the player would sit down on his bench, the Sym-phony would accentuate the touchdown of his derriere with a blasting beat of the bass drum. There were many games of cat-and-mouse between the Sym-phony and strikeout victims who would feign seating themselves to avoid the last, razzing bass-drum beat. The Sym-phony always managed to time the touchdown and accentuate it musically to the delight of Dodger fans and to the dismay of the visiting players. Brooklyn broadcaster Red Barber originated the nickname for the group.

"Brooklyn Schoolboy" Waite Hoyt, for his time as a star pitcher at Erasmus High School in Brooklyn.

Brooklyn Tip-Tops Played in the Federal League 1914–1915 and were named after the Wonder Bread Company's top selling "Tip Top Bread."

Brushback Pitch As opposed to a beanball, a pitch not thrown at the batter, but thrown close enough to him to make him move back from a too choice position in the batter's box.

B-12 Shots Clubhouse code for steroids.

"Bucky" Dent Millions watched the 1978 World Series and saw the man they call Bucky Dent star in the field and at bat. The Yankee shortstop was voted the series Most Valuable Player award. But most people did not realize that "Bucky" was Dent's nickname. His real name is Russell Earl. The nickname Bucky was given to him by his grandmother—the word means a "small Indian boy."

"Bugs" Raymond Arthur Lawrence Raymond was a major league pitcher for parts of six seasons in the early 1900s. He really had an apt nickname, as the following anecdote reveals. One day he was quietly eating his lunch in a restaurant. The waiter recognized him as a major league ball player and asked Bugs what the trick was in throwing the spitter. Bugs replied, "The whole thing is in the break." He then proceeded to demonstrate. Using a water glass for a baseball, he told the waiter to watch how his two fingers, which he had wet with water, gripped the glass. Then Bugs moved into his pitching motion, smilingly saying, "Watch the break." He threw the glass through a restaurant window and shouted, "See the break? That's how it's done."

"The Bull" Orlando Cepeda was a first baseman for various teams. His nickname was a tribute to his strength and determination. Greg Luzinski was born the year of the "Whiz Kids," 1950, a time when a team of young Philadelphia Phillies amazed baseball by winning the National League pennant. Twenty years later, Luzinski became a member of the Philadelphia team. A 6' 1," 220-pounder, his muscles and girth and power hitting earned Greg his nickname.

"Bulldog" Jim Bouton, for his tenacity.

Bullet A hard-thrown fastball. A powerfully hit ball.

"Bullet Bob" Former Yankee hurler Bob Turley, for the pop on his fastball.

Bullpen An area, generally in the left- or right-field vicinity, where relief pitchers are allowed to warm up during a game in case they are needed to come in and pitch (Pen).

Bunt To tap at, but not swing at, a ball to get it to roll just a bit onto the playing field. Bunters can try to make it to first safely in order to get a bunt hit, or they may place the ball in such a way as to sacrifice or give themselves up while moving a teammate up to another base.

Bush Leagues The low minor leagues or not well-known leagues.

"Bye-Bye" Steve Balboni, the primary designated hitter of the 1990 Yankees, had seventeen homers but hit just .192.

Cactus League Spring training schedule of major league teams in the Southwest.

Call Announcement of an umpire, or the keeping track of balls and strikes.

The Called Shot A heavier, slower, and older Babe Ruth had much more to prove in 1932. And prove he did! Batting .341, driving in 137 runs, slugging forty-one homers, the Sultan of Swat pushed the New York Yankees to another pennant. The Cubs of Chicago were the opposition in the World Series.

There was bad recent history between the two teams. Joe McCarthy had been let go as Chicago manager in 1930. He wanted payback. Ruth's old buddy, Mark Koenig, now a Cub, had helped his new team win the pennant. His Chicago teammates voted Ruth's old buddy only a half–World Series share. The Babe was not happy about that.

On October 1 in Chicago during batting practice, Ruth shouted: "Hey, you damn bum Cubs, you won't be seeing Yankee Stadium again. This is going to be all over Sunday." The Babe was referring to the fact that the Yanks had won the first two games in New York. The game got underway before 49,986 fans. Lemons from the stands and curses from the Cubs were heaped upon the Yankees. Chicago fans showered Ruth with fruits and vegetables and other projectiles when he was on defense in the outfield. The Babe smiled, doffed his cap, felt the fire.

When he came to bat in the fifth inning, Ruth had already slugged a three-run homer into the bleachers in right centerfield. He had more in store. Right-hander Charlie Root got a strike on Ruth, who as accounts go raised up one big finger and yelled "strike one!" Another fast ball strike. Ruth, as the story continues, raised two fingers and bellowed "strike two!"

Then as the story has been handed down, the thirty-eight-year-old Yankee legend stepped out of the batter's box and pointed. Some said he pointed at Root; others said the pointed at the Chicago bench, others said at the centerfield bleachers. "To tell the truth," Joe McCarthy said, "I didn't see him point anywhere at all. But maybe I turned my head for a moment." "The Babe pointed out to right field," said George Pipgras who pitched and won that game, "and that's where he hit the ball."

The count was 2-2 when Babe swung from his heels. Johnny Moore, the Chicago centerfielder started back, then stopped. The ball disappeared into the right-field bleachers, 436 feet from home plate, the fifteenth and last World Series home run for Babe Ruth, the longest home run ever hit to that point in time in Wrigley Field. "As I hit the ball," Ruth would say later, "every muscle in my system, every sense I had, told me that I had never hit a better one, that as long as I lived nothing would ever feel as good as this one."

Chicago fans cheered and applauded the Babe as he rounded the bases yelling out a different curse for each Cub infielder. When the "Sultan of Swat" reached third base, he paused. Then he bowed toward the Chicago dugout. Then he came across home plate.

Through the years the debate has continued. Did he or did he not call the home run? Babe Ruth explained: "I didn't exactly point to any spot like the flagpole. I just sorta waved at the whole fence, but that was foolish enough. All I wanted to do was give the thing a ride . . . outta the park . . . anywhere. Every time I went to the bat the Cubs on the bench would yell 'Oogly googly.' It's all part of the game, but this particular inning when I went to bat there was a whole chorus of Oogly googlies. The first pitch was a pretty good strike, and I didn't kick. But the second was outside and I turned around to beef about it. As I said, Gabby Hartnett said 'Oogly googly.' That kinda burned me and I said 'All right, you bums, I'm gonna knock this one a mile.' I guess I pointed, too."

Called Strike A strike that a batter does not swing at but which is announced as a strike by the umpire.

"Candy" In 1939, William Arthur Cummings was elected to the Hall of Fame, for his alleged invention of the curveball more than his talent. His nickname came from fans—as a sign of affection.

"Cannon" Jimmy Wynn, for his power at bat.

Can of Corn A lazy fly ball.

"Can't Anybody Here Play This Game?" In 1960 Casey Stengel managed the New York Yankees to a first-place finish, on the strength of a .630 percentage compiled by winning ninety-seven games and losing fifty-seven. By 1962 he was the manager of the New York Mets, a team that finished tenth in a ten-team league. They finished sixty games out of first place, losing more games (120) than any other team in the twentieth century. Richie Ashburn, who batted .306 for the Mets that season and then retired, remembers those days: "It was the only time I went to a ball park in the major leagues and nobody expected you to win."

A bumbling collection of castoffs, not-quite-ready-for-prime-time major league ballplayers, paycheck collectors, and callow youth, the Mets underwhelmed the opposition. They had Jay Hook, who could talk for hours about why a curveball curved (he had a master's degree in engineering) but couldn't throw one consistently. They had "Choo-Choo" Coleman, an excellent low-ball catcher, but the team had very few low-ball pitchers. They had "Marvelous Marv" Throneberry, a Mickey Mantle look-alike in the batter's box—and that's where the resemblance ended. Stengel had been spoiled with the likes of Mantle, Maris, Ford, and Berra. Day after day he would watch the Mets and be amazed at how they could find newer and more original ways to beat themselves. In desperation—some declare it was on the day he witnessed pitcher Al Jackson go fifteen innings yielding but three hits, only to lose the game on two errors committed by Marvelous Marv—Casey bellowed out his plaintive query, "Can't anybody here play this game?"

"Cap" Adrian Constantine Anson, a shortening of his managerial title. He was also known as "Big Swede" for his size and Nordic extraction.

"Captain Hook" Manager Sparky Anderson never hesitated to use his Cincinnati bullpen.

"Carnesville Plowboy" Spud Chandler was raised on a farm in Carnesville, Georgia, hence the nickname. Spurgeon "Spud" Chandler was better known during his collegiate days at the University of Georgia as a football player who also played baseball. Chandler had a career mark of 109-43 with the Yankees from 1937 to 1947. He was a part of seven World Series teams.

Casey at the Bat The title of the Ernest Thayer poem, written in 1888, about the legendary hero of the Mudville baseball team. The final stanzas are especially famous:

> The sneer is gone from Casey's lip; his teeth are clenched with hate;
> He pounds with cruel violence his bat upon the plate;
> And now the pitcher holds the ball, and now he lets it go,
> And now the air is shattered by the force of Casey's blow.
> Oh, somewhere in this favored land, the sun is shining bright;
> The band is playing somewhere, and somewhere hearts are light;
> And somewhere men are laughing, and somewhere children shout;
> But there is no joy in Mudville—mighty Casey has struck out!

"Cat-a-lyst" name given to Mickey Rivers by Howard Cosell for his ability to trigger Yankee team offense.

Catcher (Backstop) The player positioned behind home plate who catches the ball thrown by the pitcher.

"Catfish" Hunter James Augustus Hunter was his real name but the world knew him as "Catfish," primarily because of Oakland A's owner Charles O. Finley. Actually Hunter ran away from home when he was a child and returned with two catfish. His parents called him "Catfish" for a while, and then the name was dropped. Finley decided that Jim Hunter was too bland a name for such a star pitcher. To add color and imagery, Finley revived Hunter's childhood nickname and it stuck.

"Cece" Pronounced "Sess," was the nickname for Cecil Travis who had a solid career for the old Washington Senators in the late 1930s and a couple of years in the 1940s.

"Chairman of the Board" Whitey Ford pitched for the New York Yankees for sixteen seasons, winning 236 games, losing 106, and notching an earned-run average of 2.75. His .690 winning percentage places him second on the all-time list. Ford knew how to win, knew how to take charge, knew how to preside over the Yankee fortunes—and all of these factors helped earn him his nickname given to him by Elston Howard.

"Champ" James Champlin Osteen played in Hendersonville, North Carolina, in 1898 in the infield with a team called "Champions of South Carolina." It was from that experience that he got his nickname. Champ played several years in the majors.

Chance A fielder's opportunity to catch a ball.

Channel Ted Turner, owner of the Atlanta Braves, overstepped his bounds by having pitcher Andy Messersmith wear "Channel" and uniform number "17," a sort of ad for his cable TV station. Commissioner Bowie Kuhn stopped the shameless commercialism.

Charley Horse There are a couple of legends as to how this term associated with the muscular cramps in the legs of athletes originated. Seventeenth-century English policemen—constables, or Charleys, as they were called—complained a good deal about leg and foot strain. The reference survived into nineteenth-century America. Ball players who complained about weary and tired legs claimed they were "riding Charley's horse." The other theory for the origin of the term points to an incident in the 1890s at the Chicago White Sox ball park, where a horse strained to pull a roller across the infield. The pulling was done stiffly by Charley the horse.

"Charlie Hustle" It was Yankee hurler Whitey Ford who allegedly and scornfully gave Pete Rose the nickname after seeing him in a spring training game in 1963 race down to first base after being walked.

Chase To cause a pitcher to leave a game because a team scores quite a few runs off him. An umpire forcing a player, coach, or manager to leave the game because of what the umpire deems to be misconduct.

Check the Runner When the pitcher eyes the base runner to try to keep him close to the base.

Chest Protector A stuffed pad worn over the chest by catchers and umpires to ward off damage from thrown or batted balls.

Chicago Cubs Previously known as White Stockings in the 1870s, Colts in the late 1890s, Orphans in 1898 after the firing of longtime manager Cap Anson, and Remnants in 1901 after a number of players deserted the team for the American League, the nickname Cubs was coined in 1902 when manager Frank Selee arrived and rebuilt the club with young, inexperienced players.

Chicago White Sox Originally team was known as "Invaders" because they "invaded" Chicago before the opening of the 1900 season. Franchise adopted the Chicago White Stockings name used by the National League team in the late 1880s. Sportswriters shortened name to White Sox.

"Chick" Nickname bestowed upon Charles James Hafey because the female fans loved him so much.

"Chief" Bender Charles Albert Bender won 210 games and compiled a 2.45 lifetime earned-run average in sixteen years of pitching. He was admitted to baseball's Hall of Fame in 1953. His nickname came from the fact that he was a Chippewa Indian.

"Chili" When he was about twelve years old, Charles Davis was given a not too attractive haircut which led to his getting the nickname "Chili Bowl," later shortened to "Chili" as the boy became the man and the baseball player "Chili" Davis.

Chinese Home Run A home run that barely clears the outfield wall.

Chin Music Euphemism for pitch thrown at batter.

Choke Up To grip the bat nearer to the middle than down at the handle in order to get better bat control. To panic in stress situations.

"Choo-Choo" Coleman A catcher for the New York Mets during their early struggling years, Coleman is a case in point of the fact that not all things can be traced back to their origins. Once during a television interview, Coleman was asked how he got his nickname. He responded, "I don't know." He followed this up some time later with another gem. Casey Stengel, a bit frustrated by the ineptitude of the Mets, decided to return to basics. He held up a baseball during a locker room meeting and said, "This is a baseball." Coleman interrupted, "Wait, you're going too fast."

Chop To smash the ball down onto the ground.

Cincinnati Reds Known as the Reds since 1961, Cincinnati is baseball's first professional club. The franchise was created on March 15, 1869, and known as the Red Stockings. In 1944 and 1945, the nickname was Red Legs. Redlegs was the nickname of choice briefly in the 1950s because of the negative connotation of Communism. It was not until 1959 that "Reds" was officially used by team.

Clean-Up Hitter The fourth man in the batting order.

Cleat Projecting piece of plastic, rubber, or metal at the bottom of an athletic shoe to improve traction.

Cleveland Indians The franchise originated in 1901 as an American League charter team. They were the Blues (for the uniform color). Players did not like reporters calling the team "Bluebirds" when they were defeated so the name was changed to Broncos (1902). The team was known as the Naps (1903–1914) honoring star player Napoleon Lajoie. From 1912 to 1915, the team was called the Molly McGuires because of the large number of Irish players it fielded. In 1915 the Indians nickname was introduced for Louis Frances Sockalexis, believed to be the first Native American major leaguer. He played for the Cleveland Spiders in the 1880s.

Closer Relief pitcher who is consistently used to get the final outs in games.

"Clown Prince of Baseball" Al Schacht performed for only three seasons as a member of the Washington Senators (1919–1921), but he still was able to make a mighty reputation on the baseball field. Schacht was a comic, and his routines centered on the foibles and eccentricities of the national pastime. It was said that nobody did it better, and that's why Schacht was dubbed the Clown Prince.

Coach's Boxes Rectangular boxes 8 feet outside first base and third base in which the coaches of the team at bat stand, giving signals and advice to the batters and base runners.

Colorado Rockies Since 1993, named after the Rocky Mountains in the area.

"Columbia Lou" Lou Gehrig because of his collegiate roots.

Comebacker A ground ball batted back toward the pitcher.

"Commerce Comet" Mickey Mantle burst onto the major league baseball scene with the New York Yankees in 1951 and called it a career after eighteen storied seasons. Four times he led the American League in home runs. He was a rare blend of raw power and blinding speed—tape-measure home runs and trackstar dashes down the baseline to first. He came from Commerce, Oklahoma, and lit up major league baseball.

Complete Game A game that a pitcher starts and finishes.

Computer Baseball Baseball played by using computer simulation.

Corner The inside and the outside portions of home plate.

Count The number of balls and strikes on a batter during his turn at bat.

"The Count" Sparky Lyle—handlebar mustache and lordy ways contributed to his look and nickname.

Cousin A player whom another player has luck performing against.

"The Crab" The middle man in the famed Tinker to Evers to Chance double-play combination, Johnny Evers was a pugnacious and combative ballplayer and manager. Admitted to the Hall of Fame in 1946, Evers had an eighteen-year playing career and managed for three other years. His introverted personality and bench-jockeying ability gave him his nickname on merit. Pitcher Jesse Burkett earned the name for his surly disposition and also the peculiar manner of his stride.

"Crime Dog" Fred McGriff was given this name by ESPN sportscaster Chris Berman, a play on McGruff, a cartoon dog developed for American police to raise children's awareness on crime prevention.

Crossfire A sidearm pitch that angles across the plate.

"The Crow" A fairly little man with a screechy voice, Frank Crosetti fit his nickname. He played shortstop for the New York Yankees for seventeen years and then had a long stint as a coach with the team.

Crowding the Plate A situation where a batter moves up close to home plate, either to increase his chances of walking or his ability to hit an outside pitch.

Cup of Coffee A very brief time as a player in the major leagues.

Curse of the Bambino Since the day Boston owner Harry Frazee sold Babe Ruth to the Yankees in 1920, the Yankees have won and won and won all those world championships. The Red Sox had won none—until 2004.

Curveball A pitch that breaks and curves as it crosses the plate.

Cut A batter's swing.

Cut Down A fielder's throw that results in a base runner being put out in the act of trying to reach the next base.

Cut Off A throw, usually from an outfielder to a catcher, that is stopped by an infielder on its way to the catcher or infielder.

Cut-off Man Infielder who cuts off the outfielder's throw to shorten it.

"Cy" His full name was Denton True Young. His nickname was given to him by a young catcher helping to warm him up. The backstop reported that Young pitched as fast as a "cyclone." Reporters shortened the nickname to Cy. Young was still in great pitching shape until he was forty-four years old. He credited his daily chores and farm work for giving him strength.

"Cy the Second" Irving Melrose Young pitched for six years in the major leagues concurrently with Denton True Young—the storied "Cy" Young who won 508 games in his career. Irving Young only won sixty-two, while losing ninety-four, but the fact that he had the same last name and pitched at the same time as the great Cy Young earned Irving his nickname (see Cy Young Award).

"Cy the Third" In 1908, a year in which Cy Young won twenty-one games and compiled a 1.26 earned-run average, Harley E. Young made it to the major leagues. He pitched only 75.2 plus innings, losing three games and winning none. But because his last name and the time he played reminded fans of the great Cy Young, Harley was called Cy the Third.

Cy Young Award Baseball's award to the top pitcher in each league originated in 1956. The rationale was that pitchers were at a disadvantage in Most Valuable Player balloting. The award gets its name from the Hall of Famer who pitched for twenty-two years, winning more games than any other performer in baseball history (508). Young also started more games, completed more games, and pitched more innings than any other pitcher in history. He is fourth on the all-time list in strikeouts and shutouts. His career accomplishments personified the value of a pitcher to a team and underlined the reason for naming the award for the top pitcher after him.

Cycle A batter achieving a single, double, triple, and home run in the same game (Hits for the Cycle).

"Daddy Longlegs" Dave Winfield, for his size and long legs.

"Daffiness Boys" Also known as "Dem Brooklyn Bums," the 1926 Brooklyn Dodgers wreaked havoc on friend and foe alike. The hotshot of the team was freeswinging, slump-shouldered Babe Herman, dubbed the "Incredible Hoiman," who bragged that among his stupendous feats was stealing second base with the bases loaded. Once Herman was one of a troika of Dodger base runners who found themselves all on third base at the same time. A Dodger rookie turned to Brooklyn manager "Uncle" Wilbert Robinson on the bench. "You call that playing baseball?" "Uncle" Robbie responded, "Leave them alone. That's the first time they've been together all year."

"Danish Viking" George Pipgras, for his size and ethnic roots.

Daylight Play An infielder gets position behind a base runner taking a lead; the pitcher then can attempt to pick off the runner if he sees "daylight" between the runner and the infielder.

"Dazzy" Vance A pitcher with mediocre Brooklyn Dodger teams for most of his sixteen years, the "Dazzler," as he was also known, did not publicize his full name—Clarence Arthur Vance. His nickname came from the blazing speed he put on his fastball. His big windup and dazzling fastball enabled him to lead the National League in strikeouts seven straight years. Vance, who recorded his first major league victory at the age of thirty-one, was characterized by former New York Giant great George "Highpockets" Kelly as follows: "Heck, you knew what he was going to throw—the dazzler—and you still couldn't hit him." At the age of thirty-seven, in 1928, he won twenty-two games and was the league ERA leader with a sixth-place team. That wasn't his best year. In 1924 the Hall of Famer put together a 28-6 record, 262 strikeouts, and a 2.16 earned-run average to really dazzle National League hitters.

Dead Ball A ball that does not carry far. A ball that is out of play either because play has been temporarily suspended or because the ball is outside the boundaries of play. Also refers to era in baseball when ball was "dead," not lively—early twentieth century.

Dead Fish Ball thrown with very little speed.

Death Valley The old deep centerfield in Yankee Stadium—a home run there was a mighty poke.

Delayed Steal A stolen base executed after the pitcher has thrown the ball to the catcher and not while the pitch is underway, as in a traditional stolen base.

"Dem Bums" When the Dodgers left Brooklyn in 1957, they left the "bums" behind. A beloved nickname in Flatbush, Gowns, Bensonhurst, and Williamsburg, "Bums" was deemed not quite appropriate for the

Dodgers of Los Angeles. The nickname originated during the Depression. There was an excitable Brooklyn fan who used to scratch and claw at the chicken wire screen behind home plate at Ebbets Field. One day he was moved to anger at what he perceived as the inadequacies of the home team. "Ya, bum, ya, yez, bums, yez!" he bellowed. From that moment on, "Bums" meant Brooklyn Dodgers. The term was pictorialized by such cartoonists as Willard Mullin, used in newspaper headlines and stories, and capitalized on by the Dodger organization in its image-making for the Brooklyn team.

Designated Hitter A rule in the American League that allows a team to designate a batter to hit for the pitcher; the designated hitter doesn't play in the field and the pitcher never comes to bat.

Detroit Tigers In 1901, players on Detroit wore yellow and black socks. Editor Philip Reid thought they were similar to those worn by the Princeton University Tigers football team.

Dial-a-Deal Gabe Paul earned this one for his telephone trading habits.

Diamond The baseball infield, whose four bases resemble the points of a diamond in the shape they outline.

Die A situation where a runner is left on base at the end of an inning because his batting teammates cannot score him. A situation where a baseball drops abruptly in its flight.

Dig In The act of a batter getting firmer footing in the batter's box by using the spikes on his shoes to loosen the ground. Metaphorically, a situation where a batter bears down in his concentration against a pitcher.

Dinger Home run, homer, round-tripper.

Division Winner Team that completes the regular season with the best win-loss record in its division.

"Dizzy" and "Daffy" Dean Perhaps the most famous of all brother acts in the history of sports was "Me and Paul," the dazzling Dean brothers of the St. Louis Cardinals. Jerome Hannah Dean, also known as Jay Hannah Dean and best known as Dizzy, and his kid brother Paul, also known as Daffy, beguiled National League batters in the 1930s and at times drove their own teammates to despair with their madcap antics.

The brothers were born in a rickety shack on a plot of Arkansas ground that their destitute sharecropper parents worked. Dizzy picked cotton for fifty cents a day, and although he later bragged that he learned how to pitch while attending Oklahoma State Teachers College, he only went as far as the second grade in school. In Dizzy, and to a lesser extent Paul, was the sadness and brashness of the American Depression experience. "Some of the things I seen in this here life," Dizzy recalled, "almost cause my ol' heart to bust right through my sweatshirt."

Dizzy grew to be a 6' 2", slope-shouldered right hander, a little bigger than his younger brother. Both of them had arms and hands toughened and shaped by the cotton fields. "I never bothered what those guys could hit and couldn't hit," he said. "All I knowed is that they weren't gonna get a-holt of that ball ol' Diz was throwin'."

In 1934, Dizzy and Daffy won forty-nine games between them. Dizzy won thirty—more than any Cardinal pitcher ever. In a doubleheader against Brooklyn, Diz one-hit the Dodgers in the first game and Paul no-hit them in the second game. "If I'd a knowed Paul was gonna do that," Diz said, "I'd a done the same."

Dizzy was actually the zanier brother. Paul went along with his antics and thus was labeled Daffy. Dizzy once wrapped himself in a blanket and made a fire in front of the Cardinal dugout on a day when the temperature was over one hundred degrees. Dizzy once led Daffy and a couple of other Cardinals into a staid hotel and announced to the manager that he was under orders to redecorate the place. Armed with ladders, buckets of paint, and brushes, the baseball players proceeded to splash red paint with wild abandon all over the walls of the hotel lobby. Dizzy also once made more than a mild commotion when he told scouts and newspapermen that there was a third Dean "who was throwin' real good at Tulsa." When the tip was checked out, it turned out that the third Dean brother who was "throwing real good" was throwing bags of peanuts—he was a peanut vendor at the Tulsa ballpark.

The Deans had bright but relatively brief careers. Paul won nineteen games in both 1934 and 1935 and then lapsed into a journeyman pitcher role, the victim of arm trouble. In the 1937 All-Star Game, Dizzy had a line shot off the bat of Earl Averill carom off his right foot. They found out later that his toe was broken. Diz pitched again and again during the 1937 season, but he was not what he was; the fluid, cotton picking pitching motion was gone. He finished the year with a 13-10 record, and in 1938 he was sent to the Cubs for two pitchers and $200,000. He won seven, lost one, and had an ERA of 1.81, but that was his last year of pitching effectiveness. They were Dizzy and Daffy, but in their time they beguiled baseball fans and intimidated National League hitters.

"Dr. K" When he performed for the New York Mets, Dwight Gooden was a hurler proficient in the art of the strikeout.

"Dr. Strangeglove" Dick Stuart, known especially for his time as a Red Sox player, had many adventures in the field.

Dodgers The early years of the Brooklyn National League baseball team saw it called by many different nicknames. They were called "Brooklyns" and "Brooks." At one point in their history, quite a few of the players happened to get married at about the same time, and "Bridegrooms" became the new nickname. They were also called "Superbas," after a famed vaudeville act, and "Robins," in tribute to the manager of that era, Wilbert Robinson. The borough of Brooklyn circa 1900 was an area linked by trolleys. To Manhattan residents, it appeared that the citizens of Brooklyn were always dodging these trolleys. The contemptuous reference to those living in Brooklyn was the term "trolley dodgers." Eventually, since the area where the Brooklyn team played was near a web of trolley tracks, the team was called the "Trolley Dodgers." This was ultimately shortened to "Dodgers." Even in 1958, when Walter O'Malley moved the team to Los Angeles, he was able to leave Brooklyn behind but the "Dodgers" went along.

"Donnie Baseball" Don Mattingly was the only player in any sport to have a nickname with the actual name of his or her sport in it. Some say it was coined by Yankee broadcaster Michael Kay; others say it came from Kirby Puckett. Kay takes the credit; Mattingly gives the credit to Puckett.

"Don't Look Back. Something Might Be Gaining on You." This line of homespun wisdom formed the sixth rule of a recipe attributed to former baseball pitching great Leroy "Satchel" Paige. The other five rules were 1) avoid fried meats which angry up the blood; 2) if your stomach disputes you, lie down and pacify it with cool thoughts; 3) keep your juices flowing by jangling around gently as you move; 4) go very gently on the vices, such as carrying on in society—the social ramble ain't restful; 5) avoid running at all times. It seems that most of us have managed to break all of Mr. Paige's rules more than once. As for rule 5—don't tell it to your neighborhood jogger.

Double A hit that allows a player to run from the batter's box to second base (Two-Base Hit; Two-Bagger).

Doubleheader Two games played on the same day.

Double No-Hitter It's almost a baseball cliché. A no-hitter is tossed. And the next time that pitcher takes the mound, there is all the talk and speculation about the possibility of a second straight no-no taking place. And always what Johnny Vander Meer did comes back into the public consciousness.

On June 11, 1938, the Cincinnati hurler no-hit the Boston Bees, 3-0. Four nights later, he was tabbed to start against the Brooklyn Dodgers in the first night game ever in the New York City metropolitan area. To that point in time, only two pitchers had ever recorded two career no-hitters. No one had ever posted two no-hitters in a season. No one had probably even contemplated back-to-back no-hitters.

More than forty thousand (fire department rules notwithstanding) jammed into Ebbets Field to see the first night game in that tiny ballpark's history and also bear witness to Vander Meer questing after his second straight no-hitter. Utilizing a one-two-three-four pitching rhythm that saw him cock his right leg in the air before he delivered the ball to the plate, "Vandy" featured a fastball that was always moving and a curveball that broke ever so sharply. Inning after inning, the Dodgers went down hitless. In the seventh inning, Vander Meer walked two batters. But the fans of "Dem Bums" cheered the Cincinnati pitcher on, sensing they were witnessing baseball history. The ninth inning began with Cincinnati holding a 6-0 lead. Buddy Hasset was retired on a grounder. Then suddenly, Vander Meer lost control of the situation. He loaded the bases on walks. Reds manager Bill McKechnie came out to the mound to talk to his beleaguered pitcher.

"Take it easy, Johnny," he said, "but get the no-hitter." Vander Meer got Ernie Koy to hit a grounder to infielder Lou Riggs, who conservatively elected to go to the plate for the force-out for the second out. The bases were still loaded, though. Leo "Lippy" Durocher, the Dodger player-manager and a veteran of many wars, stepped into the batter's box.

Only the "Lip" stood between Vander Meer and the double no-hitter. Durocher took a lunging swing and smashed the ball down the right-field line. But it went foul into the upper deck. Bedlam and tension intermingled at Ebbets Field as Vander Meer's left arm came around and delivered the pitch to Durocher, who swung and popped up the ball into short center field. Harry Craft clutched the ball. Johnny Vander Meer had made baseball history.

Fans leaped out onto the playing field, but Vander Meer's Cincinnati teammates had formed a protective shield around the exhausted hurler as he scurried into the relative calm of the dugout. His mother and father, who had come to see their son pitch with about five hundred others from their hometown, were not as lucky. Swarms of well-wishers and autograph hunters milled about Vandy's parents. It took about half an hour before they could be extricated from the mob of admirers. The event remains in memory as the miracle of 1938, consecutive no-hitters spun by John Samuel Vander Meer, the man they called the "Dutch Master." President Franklin D. Roosevelt sent congratulations. Newspapers and magazines featured every detail of the event for months. For Vander Meer, the double no-hitters were especially sweet coming against Boston and Brooklyn—teams he had tried out for and been rejected by.

Vander Meer performed for thirteen big-league seasons, winning 119 games and losing 121. He perhaps would be remembered as a southpaw pitcher who never totally fulfilled his promise if it had not been for the epic moments of June 11 and June 15, 1938.

Double Play The retiring of two players for two outs on the same play.

Double Steal A situation where two base runners each steal a base on the same play.

"Double X" Hall of Famer Jimmie Foxx had two nicknames. His main one was derived from the last two letters of his name. He was also known as "The Beast," which indicated the way his rivals viewed his baseball-playing ability. Foxx averaged better than a hit a game in a twenty-year career, compiling a .325 batting average and a .609 slugging percentage. He hit 534 homers, scored over 1,700 runs, and drove in almost 2,000 runs.

Down Losing or out ("one man down in the top of the ninth"), or trailing in the score ("down by three runs").

Down the Line On the field near the foul lines, often used to describe the location of batted balls.

Down the Middle Over the middle portion of home plate, used to describe the location of pitches.

"Downtown" Ollie Brown's nickname earned for his home run hitting.

Drag Bunt A ball purposely hit slowly by a batter facing away from the pitcher to give himself a head start in his run to first base in pursuit of a hit. The ball is generally placed between the pitcher and first baseman.

Drive A batted ball hit for distance.

Drive In To bat a run in, to cause a run to score.

Drop off the Table Characterizes extreme break of a curveball.

"Ducky" ("Ducky-Wucky") Joe Medwick despised the name and teammates were careful not to call him the fan-given characterization in his presence. "Ducky" made fun of the way Medwick walked. "Muscles" he did not mind—that was a tribute to his physique.

Dugout An area on each side of home plate where players stay while their team is at bat. There is a visitor's dugout and a home-team dugout. They were originally dug out trenches at the first and third base lines allowing players and coaches to be at field level and not blocking the view of the choice seats behind them.

"Duke" There have been many athletes dubbed Duke, but Edwin Donald "Duke" Snider, the man also known as the "Silver Fox" because of the color of his hair, has a lock on the nickname. Snider had this regal nickname from the day he first entered school. His father said, "Well, here comes his majesty, the Duke" after the youngster came home that first day.

From 1947 to 1957 he starred in center field for the old Brooklyn Dodgers. Although the New York Giants had Willie Mays and the New York Yankees had Joe DiMaggio and then Mickey Mantle playing the same position, to Brooklyn fans Snider was the Duke—their royalty. He fit the name well. A handsome, tempestuous left-handed slugger, Snider was a vital part of the Dodger machine. "Somebody once asked me if I wanted to be twenty-five years old again," he said. "Not if I had to trade those Brooklyn Dodger days. It was something special."

"Duke of Tralee" Roger Bresnahan refers to Tralee, Ireland, where Bresnahan's ancestors were from.

"Dummy" William Ellsworth Hoy, a major league baseball player in the years 1888–1902, was only 5' 4" tall and weighed only 148 pounds. Yet his lifetime batting average was .288. His nickname was a little more than insensitive, for Bill Hoy was a deaf mute.

Duster A pitch thrown high and inside to a batter and intended to make him "hit the dust" or jump out of the way to avoid being hit by the pitch.

Earned Run A run scored without the aid of an error.

Earned-Run Average (ERA) The average number of earned runs scored against a pitcher for every nine innings he pitches; the average is obtained by dividing the total number of earned runs by the number of innings pitched and multiplying this figure by nine. A low ERA is preferred.

Ebbets Field On April 9, 1913, the Brooklyn Dodgers played their first game in their new ballpark against the Philadelphia Phillies. An account of the event read: "A cold, raw wind kept the attendance down to about 12,000 but did not affect the players, who put up a remarkable battle. Both Tom Seaton (Philadelphia) and Nap Rucker (Brooklyn) pitched brilliant ball, the former just shading the noted southpaw in a 1 to 0 shutout. The opening ceremonies were impressive, the two teams parading across the field headed by a band. . . . Casey Stengel made a sensational catch."

The site of the ballpark was 4½ acres on the lower slope of Crown Heights in Brooklyn, a filled-in tract of marshy land that the neighborhood people called Pigtown. Ebbets Field originally seated eighteen thousand, with another three thousand standees able to watch the games. The park had a double-decked grandstand that extended around the right-field foul line virtually to the fence in left field. A small, open bleacher section with concrete seats was located in left field between the stands and the field. Beyond right field was Bedford Avenue. It was a confined, intimate, tiny, odd-shaped ballpark—and it was a place that on the day it opened became obsolete and needed architectural and seating changes. The man the park was named for was Charles H. Ebbets, who moved from selling peanuts and scorecards to the presidency and primary ownership of the Brooklyn National League franchise. It was his vision that created the fabled ball park.

Eephus Ball (Eephus Pitch) A specialty of Pittsburgh Pirate pitcher Truett "Rip" Sewell, this pitch sort of sailed to the plate in a high, lazy arc that tantalized overeager hitters. With his trick pitch, Sewell won a grand total of forty-two games in 1943 and 1944. Sewell explained that he developed the pitch after a war injury made him change his windup. He adopted an overhand delivery because he was not able to pivot on his right foot.

Eighth Wonder of the World On what was once Texas swampland and a wind-swept prairie, the Houston Astros once played baseball in the Astrodome, which many nicknamed the Eighth Wonder of the World. Built at a cost of $38 million, the colossal complex sprawled over 260 acres six miles from downtown Houston. The facility had the biggest electric scoreboard and the largest dome ever constructed. It was the largest clear-span building ever built and the largest air-conditioned stadium ever. The Astrodome had forty-five thousand plush opera-type seats, from which fans viewed athletic events in the additional comfort supplied by a six-thousand-ton air-conditioning system that maintained the temperature in the stadium at seventy-two degrees. The inspiration for the Astrodome was the Roman Colosseum, built circa 80 AD, which prodded Judge Roy Hofheinz, president of the Houston Sports Association, the owners of the team, to press for the creation of a domed stadium.

"I knew with our heat, humidity and rain, the best chance for success was in the direction of a weather-proof, all-purpose stadium," said Hofheinz. Buckminster Fuller, media-famed ecologist and inventor of the geodesic dome, served as consultant to the project. Hofheinz said, "Buckminster Fuller convinced me that it was possible to cover any size space so long as you didn't run out of money." They didn't run out of money and even had $2 million to spare for the three-hundred-ton scoreboard, with 1,200 feet of wiring that stretched 474 feet across the brown pavilion seats in center field.

"El Duque" Pitcher Orlando Hernandez, for his lordly ways.

"El Duquecito" Adrian Hernandez because of a pitching style similar to Orlando "El Duque." Hernandez, the younger Cuban, is not related to his elder countryman.

"$11,000 Lemon" In 1908, Rube Marquard was purchased by John McGraw of the New York Giants from the minor league Indianapolis team. The $11,000 paid for Marquard was a record sum paid for a minor leaguer at that time. Since Marquard's record during his first three years with the Giants was nine wins and eighteen losses, McGraw's judgment was criticized and Marquard was labeled the "$11,000 Lemon." However, in 1911 the left-handed pitcher rewarded McGraw's patience and showed that the Giants manager's judgment was correct by achieving a record of 24-7. The next year his record nineteen consecutive victories powered the Giants to the National League pennant. And there were those who then called him the "$11,000 Wonder."

"Ellie Affectionate" Abbreviation of former Yankee catching great Elston Howard's first name.

"El Maestro" Charleston Martin Dihigo was skilled enough to play all nine positions well. He was a master. The native of Cuba starred in Mexico, Venezuela, and Puerto Rico. A twelve-year veteran of the Negro Leagues, he was elected to the Baseball Hall of Fame in 1977 and is also a member of halls of fame in Mexico and Cuba.

"El Presidente" Dennis Martinez, pitcher, played for the Baltimore Orioles (1976–1986) and the Montreal Expos (1986–1993). He had a commanding manner about him.

"El Tiante" Luis Tiant pitched for the Cleveland Indians (1964–1969), Minnesota Twins (1970), Boston Red Sox (1971–1978), and New York Yankees (1979). His name was a tribute to his Cuban roots.

English This term, denoting spin, twist, or movement on a baseball, tennis ball, or billiard ball, was allegedly derived from body English—all those hand, shoulder, and posture moves used when words are not sufficient to describe something as accurately, colorfully. The popular theory that the word as used in sports is derived from the offbeat or tricky ways of Englishmen is just a case—or so the story goes—of Americans getting back at the Mother Country.

Error A misplay of a ball by a fielder.

Even the Count A situation where a batter or pitcher is able to get the count even—that is, a like number of balls and strikes.

Extra-Base Hit Any hit other than a single.

Extra Inning Any inning beyond the regulation nine.

Eye Black A black substance applied under the eyes to reduce glare.

Fallaway Slide Used to avoid a tag, a slide to one side of a base, catching the base with the foot of a bent leg (Fall-Away Slide, Fade-Away Slide, Fade-Away).

Father of the Emory Ball Rookie right-hander Russ Ford posted a 26-6 record with eight shutouts in 1910.

Fenway Park The Boston Red Sox moved into their new home in 1912 on the property of the Fenway Realty Company at Landsdowne and Jersey streets. Although it was rebuilt in 1934, it is essentially the way it was at the time of its birth. Its "Green Monster"—the 37-foot-high wall extending from the foul pole in left field 315 feet from home plate to the flagpole 388 feet from home well past left-center—is its most distinctive feature.

Fielding Terms

A Assists

CERA Earned-Run Average when Catching

Ch Chances (Balls hit to a position)

CS Caught Stealing (on throws by catchers or pickoffs by pitchers)

CS% Caught Stealing Percentage

DP Double Play

E Error

FPct Fielding Percentage, (PO+A) / (PO+A+E)

G Game Played

GS Game Started

INN Inning

PB Passed Ball

PO Puout

SBA Stolen Base Attempt

Fireballer A fastball-throwing pitcher (Hard Chucker).

"Fireman" Johnny Murphy, the first great relief pitcher, who put out fires. Joe Page picked up this nickname for his top relief work later on. A relief pitcher.

First Refers to first base.

First Baseman A player whose position is first base (First Sacker).

First Televised Sports Event On May 17, 1939, over station W2XBS, a sixteen-man NBC crew with equipment costing $100,000 sent out the first televised sports coverage. The subject was the Princeton-Columbia baseball game from Baker Field in New York. A single camera was used, and the total cost of transmittal was $3,000. There were no close-ups of action. The players on the television screen looked like white flies. The single camera was stationed near the third-base line, and it swept back and forth across the diamond. Instant replay, "slo-mo," split screen, Zoomar lens, handheld cameras, instant isolates, overhead blimps, graphics, Monday Night Football, and Super Bowl were not even dimly perceived by the average fan, but on June 5, 1939, an editorialist for *Life* magazine showed some vision: No fuzziness (in the telecast) could hide what television will mean for American sports. . . . Within ten years an audience of 10,000,000 sitting at home or in the movie theaters will see the World Series or the Rose Bowl game. . . . Thousands of men and women who have never seen a big-time sports event will watch the moving shadows on the television screen and become excited fans."

First World Series Back in the 1880s for a period of seven years there had been play-offs between the winners in the National League and the American Association. Once the play-offs went to fifteen games—in 1887 between St. Louis and Detroit. Pittsburgh won its third straight National League pennant in 1903. Boston won the brand new American League title by fourteen and one-half games over the Philadelphia Athletics. The Pirates bragged about Honus Wagner whose .355 average earned him the batting title. Their swashbuckling manager Fred Clarke was runner-up with a .351 average. Boston boasted about two twenty-game winners in Deacon Phillippe and Sam Leever.

The first modern World Series came about at the suggestion of Boston owner Henry J. Killilea and Pittsburgh's owner Barney Dreyfuss. It was called "Championship of the United States" and it was a five-of-nine-games affair. The first game was October 1, 1903, at Boston's Huntington Avenue Grounds before 16,242 fans. Deacon Phillippe pitched Pittsburgh to a 7-3 win over Boston's Cy Young.

Throughout the game and the series Boston's rabid fans serenaded Pittsburgh players with a popular song of the day, "Tessie," but they substituted their own vulgar words for the regular lyrics. The routine definitely had a negative impact on the Pittsburgh players. "It was that damn song that caused us problems," grumbled Buc player Tommy Leach afterwards.

Deacon Phillippe won three of the first four games of the series for Pittsburgh but then faltered. Boston then swept the next four games. Bill Dinneen and Cy Young won all five games for Boston in the series. On October 13, only 7,455 fans showed up—the smallest crowd of the series. Phillippe pitched his fifth complete game of the series but lost 3-0 to Dinneen and Boston had the championship.

Right after the game ended, players from both clubs lined up for a combination team photo. It was a remarkable display of good sportsmanship considering the bitterness that had existed between the junior American League and senior National League.

An oddity of the World Series was that the losing players received more money than the winners. Owner Dreyfuss put his club's share of the gate receipts into the players' pool. Each Pittsburgh player netted $1,316 while each Boston player netted $1,182.

Deacon Phillippe—heroic in his efforts in the series with five decisions and forty-four innings pitched, still World Series records—was given a bonus and ten shares of stock in the Pirates.

There was no World Series played in 1904. Boston was ready, willing, and able. But the National League pennant-winning New York Giants were not. Their manager, John J. McGraw snarled: "We are the champions of the only major league." In 1905, the World Series resumed, fitted itself into its best-of-seven format, and has been with us ever since.

Five o'Clock Lightning Back in the 1920s to attract school kids and the Wall Street crowd, baseball games at Yankee Stadium began at 3:30 p.m. At five o'clock, a whistle from a nearby factory blew signaling the end of the workday and often a typical late-inning home team rally and triumph, earning the Yankees that colorful nickname.

Flare A hit that is part fly-ball and part pop-up and that drops between the infielders going out for it and the outfielders coming in for it (Texas Leaguer).

Flip-Downs Sunglasses allowing fielders to "flip" the shaded lenses up or down to block out sun.

Florida Marlins Named after the large fish found off the Florida coast and also a minor league AAA team, the Miami Marlins. It was H. Wayne Huizenga, Blockbuster Video founder and owner of the team, who chose the name. "I chose Marlin," he said, "because the fish is a fierce fighter and an adversary that tests your mettle."

Fly A batted ball hit high in the air (Fly Ball).

"Flying Dutchman" Honus Wagner played for the Pittsburgh Pirates for twenty-one years, winning eight batting titles, collecting 3,430 hits, and establishing team records for most doubles, triples, and extra-base hits. He played every position except catcher, but he earned his fame as a shortstop. Of Dutch origin, he was a speedy base runner, leading the National League five times in stolen bases and recording a career total of 722 stolen bases. His speed and his Dutch heritage blended together to form his nickname, the "Flying Dutchman."

Force-Out The retiring of a runner on a force play.

Force Play A condition where a runner must leave his base and move to the next base because of a ground ball the batter has hit. The runner's failure to reach the next base before it is touched by a defensive player in possession of the ball creates a force-out.

"Fordham Johnny" Ace former Yankee relief pitcher Johnny Murphy attended Fordham University in the Bronx.

Forkball A pitch thrown by a pitcher who grips the ball with his index and middle fingers spread apart; this pitch dips downward as it crosses the plate.

Foul Ball A ball hit into foul territory.

"Foulkey" A nickname from Boston relief pitcher Keith Foulke's surname.

Foul Lines The boundary lines of fair territory that extend on a right angle from the back corner of home plate past the outside edges of first and third base and on into the outfield.

Foul Off To hit a pitched ball foul.

Foul Out To foul off a pitch and have it caught by a defensive player before it touches the ground, for an out.

Foul Poles Vertical extensions of the foul lines whose lower portions are generally painted on the outfield walls, above which extends the actual pole.

Foul Territory The opposite of fair territory.

Foul Tip A ball swung at and tipped back by the batter. If a batter hits a foul tip with two strikes and the catcher holds onto the ball, the batter is out on a strikeout. If the catcher can't hold the ball, it's considered a foul ball and the batter stays alive.

Four-Bagger A home run (Circuit Clout).

Four-Hour Manager A negative slap at former Yankee manager Bucky Harris, who put his time in at the game and was finished.

"Freshest Man on Earth" ("Clown Prince of Baseball") Arlie Latham played seventeen fun-filled major league seasons beginning in 1880. He delighted in setting off firecrackers and lighting candles in the dugout—a signal to the umpire of impending darkness.

Friday Night Massacre On April 26, 1974, Yankees Fritz Patterson, Steve Kline, Fred Beene, Tom Buskey, and half the pitching staff were traded to Cleveland for Chris Chambliss, Dick Tidrow, and Cecil Upshaw.

"F Robby" ("The Judge") Hall of Famer Frank Robinson played for the Cincinnati Reds (1956–1965), Baltimore Orioles (1966–1971), Los Angeles Dodgers (1972), California Angels (1973). His nicknames indicated an abbreviation of his name and some deference to his forceful ways.

Full Count Three balls and two strikes on a batter.

Fumble To bobble a ground ball.

Fungo A batting practice procedure in which a player throws up a ball and hits it with his bat as it drops down to strike-zone level.

Fungo Bat A specially designed bat with a long handle and a thin shape, used to practice hitting fungoes.

Fungo Circles Circular areas near the baselines on either side of home plate, from which fungoes are hit.

Game-Ending Home Run A home run by home team in the bottom of the ninth or extra inning that scores the winning run and ends the game.

Game of Inches Characterization of the game of baseball because a lot of it is decided by very small distances.

"Gashouse Gang" The St. Louis Cardinals of the mid-1930s earned this nickname because of their unique personalities and their spirited performances on and off the field. Mingled together to make baseball history were such competitors as "the Dazzling Deans," Dizzy and his brother Paul; Pepper Martin, who as a third baseman used his chest to stop ground balls; Joe "Ducky" Medwick, also known as the "Hungarian Rhapsody" because of his verve and drive and Hungarian origins; and a young shortstop named Leo Durocher, who some were already calling "Screechy" because of his nonstop chatter. On the field they played with wild abandon—stealing bases, taking chances, fighting with each other and the opposition, covering their uniforms with dirt so that it "appeared as if they worked in a gashouse and not a ball park," as one observer declared. And that was how the nickname was born.

In the 1934 World Series, Joe Medwick did more than astonish thousands and thousands of Detroit Tiger fans. The Cardinals were on their way to a seventh game 11-0 romp over Detroit. In the sixth inning of that game, Medwick tripled and allegedly spiked Tiger third baseman Marv Owen. Taking his left-field position the next inning, Medwick was bombarded with rotten fruit, beer bottles, raw eggs, and other missiles. Ducky did not duck but stuck out his jaw and called for more. Baseball Commissioner Landis called for Medwick and informed him that he was taking him out of the game for the good of baseball—and for the good of Medwick. The Gashousers earned their name for many things, but this was the first time one of them, one wit observed, was removed from a game because he smelled up the playing field (see Dizzy and Daffy Dean, and "Wild Horse of the Osage").

"Gator" Ron Guidry hailed from Louisiana alligator country.

"Gay Caballero" Yankee Hall of Famer hurler Lefty Gomez, for his Mexican roots and fun-loving ways.

"Gay Reliever" Name given to former Yankee relief pitcher Joe Page for his night-owl activity.

Gehrigville Bleachers in right-center at Yankee Stadium, a place where Lou Gehrig hit a few shots.

"Georgia Peach" Tyrus Raymond Cobb, baseball immortal, played twenty-two seasons for the Detroit Tigers and two more for the Philadelphia Athletics. He also managed Detroit in the years 1921–1926. Cobb compiled a lifetime batting average of .367, stole 892 bases, and won twelve batting titles in a span of thirteen years. By the time he retired, he had set ninety individual records. Cobb was born in Narrows, Georgia, and his nickname was partially derived from his native state, which is called the Peach State. His nickname is also rooted in the glorious but tempestuous talent of the man many claim to be the greatest baseball player of all time. Cobb was not one who fit the stereotype of the typical Southern gentleman. Once he almost demolished a baseball roommate as they jostled to get to the bathroom. "I just had to be first," was Cobb's response—and his way of life.

"Gerbil" For looks and behavior, the nickname fit Don Zimmer.

"Gettysburg Eddie" Eddie Plank starred for the Philadelphia Athletics (1901–1914) and got his nickname from his time as a student at Gettysburg College in Pennsylvania.

Giants One sultry summer's day in 1885, Jim Mutrie, the saber-mustached manager of the New York Gothams, was enjoying himself watching his team winning an important game. Mutrie screamed out with affection, "My big fellows, my giants." Many of his players were big fellows, and they came to be Giants. For that was how the nickname Giants came to be. And when the New York team left for San Francisco in 1958, Giants—Mutrie's endearing nickname—went along with it.

Give Oneself Up A sacrificing effort by a batter who hits the ball behind a runner on base in order to advance the runner, even though such an effort usually causes the batter to be thrown out.

Give Up Mental lapse or courage breakdown on the part of a player, allowing his opponent to gain an advantage.

Glove Man A fine fielder.

"The Godfather" Joe Torre, for his Italian roots and his leadership skills on the baseball field.

"Godzilla" Hideki Matsui was given this name for his prodigious home runs—fifty with the Yomiuri Giants in 2002. He signed with the Yankees in 2003.

Go for the Fences To consciously swing for a home run.

Go-Go Sox The 1959 Chicago White Sox won the team's first American League pennant in forty years, as they excited Windy City fans and others throughout the United States with their distinctive style of baseball. As a team, the Sox batted only .250, but their 113 stolen bases paced the majors and they parlayed speed and daring into a playing pattern good for ninety-four wins. Where there was an opportunity to take an extra base, the White Sox took it. Where there was a chance to use their speed or their bunting ability, they capitalized on it. Seemingly always on the move and using what ability they had to maximum advantage, the White Sox earned the nickname of Go-Go Sox, whose assets they inflicted on the opposition. Their siege gun was Luis Aparicio ("Little Looie"), a 5' 9," 160-pound speedster who led the majors in stolen bases with fifty-six. Aparicio also batted .332, walked fifty-two times, and scored ninety-eight runs to pace the "go" in the Go-Go Sox.

Going, Going, Gone Originated by former New York Yankee broadcaster Mel Allen, this phrase has become part of the popular language. Allen used the words to describe the suspense generated by balls hit to the distant reaches of Yankee Stadium, which traveled and traveled until they went out of the playing field and into home run territory. Sometimes just "Going, going" was uttered—as the ball would be caught before it was "gone."

"Golden Greek" Harry Agganis, of Greek ancestry, was born on April 20, 1930, and died, too young, on June 27, 1955. A powerfully built player, Agganis batted .251 his first year as a member of the Boston Red Sox, and .313 in his second and final year. The unrealized potential of Agganis makes his nickname especially poignant.

Golden Outfield Tris Speaker, Harry Hooper, and Duffy Lewis formed the outfield for the Boston Red Sox in the years 1910–1915. Speaker and Hooper are both in baseball's Hall of Fame. Lewis played Fenway Park's left field so well that the incline in front of the wall was known as "Duffy's Cliff." The trio, which earned its nickname because of its value to the Red Sox and its exceptional skills, really glittered in the 1915 World Series. Lewis batted .444, Hooper .350, Speaker .294, and collectively they accounted for twenty of Boston's forty-two hits. The storied outfield was broken up after the 1915 season, when Tris Speaker was traded to the Cleveland Indians.

Golden Shoe Award Given to the player with the most stolen bases in the major leagues.

Gold Glove Award Given to the best fielder at his position in each league, as determined by managers and coaches.

Good Field, No Hit Mike Gonzalez played major league baseball for seventeen years with a variety of teams. Born in Havana, Cuba, he had a lot of baseball knowledge but a not-too-effective command of English. It was during his time as a scout that a phrase that has become part of the popular language was first uttered by Gonzalez. He was asked to check on a minor league ball player and—as the story goes—to telegraph back his findings to the major league club that had shown interest. Gonzalez watched the young ball player for a few days and noted that he couldn't swing the bat but had defensive skills. And then Gonzalez, saving time, money, type, and English, sent his scouting report: "Good Field, No Hit."

Good Wood To make contact with the ball with the fat part of the bat, thus hitting the ball well.

"Goofy" ("El Goofo") Name earned by legendary pitcher Lefty Gomez for his wild antics.

"Gooneybird" Hurler Don Larsen's teammates called him that for his late-night behavior.

"Goose" Pitcher Richard Michael Gossage, for loose and lively style.

Gopher Ball A pitch that "goes for" a home run—not a very well-thrown pitch from the pitcher's point of view.

"Gorgeous George" ("Gentleman George") George Sisler earned these nicknames because of his looks and demeanor. Elected to the Hall of Fame in 1939, he starred for the St. Louis Browns.

Go with the Pitch To hit the ball where it is pitched and not attempt to overpower it.

"Grandma" This was not a nickname Johnny Murphy liked, but he was called that for his pitching motion, rocking chair style. Another story is that fellow Yankee Pat Malone pinned the name on him because of his complaining nature, especially regarding food and lodgings.

Grand Slam It is believed that baseball was the first sport to use this term, which is derived from contract bridge (the taking of all thirteen tricks). As used in baseball, the term denotes a home run that is hit with the bases loaded. In 1930 the term was used in golf to describe the four major-tournament victories of Bobby Jones—the winning of the British and United States open and amateur championships. His unique accomplishment was also called the "Impregnable Quadrilateral." The modern use of the term, which came into vogue after World War II, refers to the winning of the United States Open, the British Open, the Masters, and the United States Professional Golfers' Association Championship by one player in the same year. No golfer has ever won the modern Grand Slam. In tennis the term describes the winning of the singles events of the French Open, Australian Open, Wimbledon, and the United States Open by one player in the same year. Its origin is traceable to golf's Grand Slam.

Grandslammer A bases-loaded home run.

Grapefruit League Refers to major league teams who go to spring training in Florida.

Grass Cutter A powerfully hit ground ball that skips along the ground and "cuts the grass."

"Gray Eagle" Hall of Famer Tris Speaker played twenty-two years in the majors and had a lifetime batting average of .344. His nickname came about because of the unique manner in which he played center field. Tris would play very shallow and race back to swoop down on fly balls hit over his head like some mighty eagle going after its prey.

"Great Agitator" Yankee Billy Martin, self-explanatory and well deserved.

"The Great One" Late Pirate outfielder Roberto Clemente was that. His friends called him "Bobby" or "Bob." In his native Puerto Rico, Clemente was called "Arriba." The five-tool outfielder died in a plane crash on a mission of mercy to Nicaragua.

Greenberg Gardens Hank Greenberg closed out his illustrious major league career in 1947 as a member of the Pittsburgh Pirates. A power hitting right-handed batter, he blasted twenty-five homers that year—most of them into a section of the outfield that was dubbed Greenberg Gardens.

Griffith Stadium Located in Washington, D.C., it opened July 24, 1911, and closed September 21, 1961. The stadium was named for Clark Griffith who owned the team from 1920 until his death in 1955.

Groove To throw a pitch over the fat, middle part of the plate. To be in a good, flowing playing condition, such as a batting groove.

Grounder A ball that is hit along the ground.

Groundout A play in which the batter is retired at first base on a grounder to an infielder.

Ground Out To hit into a groundout.

Ground Rule A special rule governing the course of play that is put into effect because of the particular features of a ball park.

Ground-Rule Double The awarding of two bases (a double) to a batter who hits a ball into a special ground-rule situation—the batted ball, for example, bouncing into the stands.

Guess Hitter A batter who swings at a pitch that he guesses will be a strike, a ball, low, high, and so forth.

Gun Down To throw out a player with a strong throw, generally referring to an outfielder's or catcher's throw.

Hack Wilson A short, red-faced, gorilla-shaped man, Hack Wilson played for the Chicago Cubs from 1926 to 1931. In those years he was an American folk hero—the million-dollar slugger from the five-and-ten-cent store. In those years he drove in more runs than any other player except for Babe Ruth and Lou Gehrig. He set National League records that still stand for the most home runs and most total bases in a season and the major league record for runs batted in. The stock market crashed in 1929, but the "Li'l Round Man" soared in 1930: he smashed fifty-six homers, drove in 190 runs, and batted .356.

The Cubs purchased Robert Lewis Wilson in 1926 from Toledo for $5,000. Dubbed Hackenschmidt, after a famous wrestler of the time, he ripped by day and nipped by night. The Hacker was called the poor man's Babe Ruth because of the $40,000 he earned in 1931—a salary second only to the Babe's. Wilson's batting trademarks were parallel knuckles on a no-nub bat handle, and a booming voice that declared when rival players taunted him, "Let 'em yowl. I used to be a boilermaker and noise doesn't bother me." In 1932 Hack became a Brooklyn Dodger and finished out his career as a member of the so-called Daffiness Boys. It was a perfect climate for the man with so many nicknames, and with the Dodgers he was called the "Hacker." With all his accomplishments, with all the verve he exhibited, with all the fame he had—Hack Wilson was not admitted to the Hall of Fame until 1979.

"Hammerin' Hank" Four times he led the American League in home run hitting. In 1938 he blasted fifty-eight—and no man had hit more in a season up to that point except Babe Ruth. His name was Henry Benjamin Greenberg, but he was better known as Hank Greenberg. He played a dozen years for the Detroit Tigers and finished his career in 1947 with the Pittsburgh Pirates. Greenberg was admitted to baseball's Hall of Fame in 1956 (see Greenberg Gardens).

Handcuff A condition occurring when an infielder has trouble controlling a powerfully hit ball.

Hang To throw a pitch that does not break (Hanging Curve).

Hanger A pitch that does not break.

"Happy Jack" Former major league pitcher Jack Chesbro spent time before he hit the majors as an attendant at the state mental hospital in Middletown, New York, where he pitched for the hospital team and showed off a very pleasant disposition.

The Harmonica Incident Despite a string of four straight pennants, the Bronx Bombers were a bust throughout much of the 1964 season. Yogi Berra had succeeded Ralph Houk as skipper; there were reports that he got more laughs than lauds from his players. It was getting to be late August; the Yankees were in third place behind Baltimore and Chicago. The Yankees were on the team bus heading to O'Hare Airport on August 20, 1964, losers of four straight to the White Sox, winless in ten of their last fifteen games. A 5-0 shutout at the hands of Chicago's John Buzhardt had totally demoralized them.

Phil Linz, #34, reserve infielder, a career .235 hitter, was a tough, aggressive player who loved being a Yankee. But he was regarded by some to be un-Yankee-like along with teammates Joe Pepitone and Jim Bouton. I sat in the back of the bus," Linz recalled. The bus was stuck in heavy traffic. It was a sticky humid Chicago summer day. "I was bored. I pulled out my harmonica. I had the Learner's Sheet for 'Mary Had a Little Lamb.' So I started fiddling. You blow in. You blow out."

An angry Berra snapped from the front of the bus: "Knock it off!" But Linz barely heard him. When asked what their manager had said, Mickey Mantle said, "Play it louder." Linz played louder. Berra stormed to the back of the bus and told Linz to "shove that thing." "I told Yogi that I didn't lose that game," Linz related. Berra smacked the harmonica out of Linz's hands. The harmonica flew into Joe Pepitone's knee and Pepitone jokingly winced in pain. Soon the entire bus—except for Berra—was in stitches.

Another version has it that Linz flipped the harmonica at the angered Berra and screamed: "What are you getting on me for? I give a hundred percent. Why don't you get on some of the guys who don't hustle?"

Linz was fined $200—but as the story goes received $20,000 for an endorsement from a harmonica company. "The next day," Linz gives his version, "the Hohner Company called and I got a contract for $5,000 to endorse their harmonica. The whole thing became a big joke."

Actually, the whole thing changed things around for the Yankees. The summer of 1964 was Linz's most productive season. Injuries to Tony Kubek made the "supersub" a regular: Linz started the majority of the games down the stretch, and every World Series game at short. New respect for Yogi propelled the Yanks to a 22-6 record in September and a win in a close pennant race over the White Sox. A loss in the World Series to the St. Louis Cardinals in seven games cost Berra his job. But there were those who said he was on his way out the day of the "Harmonica Incident."

"Harry the Hat" Harry William Walker of St. Louis Cardinal outfielding fame was in the habit of adjusting his baseball cap between pitches and annoying those around him.

"Hawk" Ken Harrelson, baseball's "bad boy" in the 1960s, provided fans with a colorful character on and off the field. He wore long blond hair, love beads, bell-bottoms, Nehru jackets, and his own "Hawk" medallion.

Heavy Ball A pitch that a batter has trouble hitting for distance.

Hesitation Pitch A specialty of Leroy "Satchel" Paige, this pitch came out of a slow windup that had a hitch in it. The ball came at the hitter at various speeds, causing problems in the timing of a swing and helping Satchel to win many games.

High and Tight High Above the strike zone, and close to the batter, used to describe the location of pitches.

Highlanders The team began in 1901 as the Baltimore Orioles and then moved to New York in 1903. Originally called the Highlanders for its Hilltop Park location, in 1914, Jim Price of the New York Press is credited with coming up with a new name for the team—the New York Yankees.

High Pitch A pitch that is above the batter's strike zone.

"Highpockets" George Kelly played for the New York Giants in the 1920s. A 6' 4", 190-pound first baseman, he earned his main nickname for the way his uniform pants hung on his spindly build. He was also called "Long George" by the press, and "Kell" by teammates.

Historic Baseball The game as played in the nineteenth century and preserved by clubs and associations.

Hit and Run A play in which the batter swings at the ball and the runner on base breaks for the next base.

Hit 'Em Where They Ain't William Henry Keeler played nineteen years in the major leagues and finished his career with a .345 lifetime batting average. In 1897 Keeler batted an incredible .432. A reporter asked the diminutive batter, "Mr. Keeler, how can a man your size hit four-thirty-two?" The reply to that question has become a rallying cry for all kinds of baseball players in all types of leagues. "Simple," Keeler smiled, "I keep my eyes clear and I hit 'em where they ain't."

Hitless Wonders The 1906 Chicago White Sox had a team batting average of .230, the most anemic of all the clubs in baseball that year. The team's pitching, however, more than made up for its lack of hitting. The White Sox staff recorded shutouts in thirty-two of the team's ninety-three victories. The "Hitless Wonders" copped the American League pennant and faced the Chicago Cubs in the World Series. The Cubs of 1906 are regarded as one of the greatest baseball teams of all time; they won 116 games that year, setting the all-time major league mark for victories in a season and for winning percentage. The White Sox continued their winning ways in the World Series, however, trimming their crosstown rivals in six games.

Hit the Dirt A situation in which a batter drops to the ground to avoid being hit by a pitched ball or where a base runner jumps back to the base to avoid being picked off by the pitcher.

Hitting for the Cycle Hitting a single, double, triple, and home run in the same game, not necessarily in that order.

"Hiya Kid!" Babe Ruth had a great deal of difficulty in remembering names, and "Hiya Kid!" was his traditional greeting to make up for this shortcoming. However, he once was introduced to President Calvin Coolidge and improved on his traditional greeting by shouting, "Hiya Prez!"

Hold A relief pitcher enters a game with his team leading and leaves the game without giving up the lead. No win or save credit is given.

Hold on Base A condition in which a pitcher, by keeping an eye on the runner and sometimes throwing the ball to the defender stationed at that base, attempts to keep the runner from taking too big a lead or stealing a base.

Hole The space between two infielders.

Holler Guy A player who has a lot of enthusiasm and screams out encouragement for his teammates.

Holy Cow Former New York Yankee broadcaster Phil Rizzuto was an exuberant and excitable individual. Some accused him of rooting for the home team, but most everyone admitted that the Scooter watched and described baseball through the eyes of a fan. The phrase associated with Rizzuto underscored his amazement at the happenings on a baseball field and is generally his "last word" (see "The Scooter").

Home A short way of saying home plate.

Home Plate A slab of white rubber with five sides that the pitcher throws to; it is also the final base touched by a runner to score a run. It is 17 inches by 8½ inches by 12 inches, cut to a point at rear. The distance from home plate to the pitcher's box is 60 feet 6 inches, to second base 127 feet 3⅜ inches.

Home Run A hit that leaves the ball park in fair territory; it is worth one run, or more if there are men on base. The batter is allowed to trot around the bases uncontested (Belt, Big Fly, Dinger, Go Deep, Go Downtown, Go Yard, Four Bagger: Circuit Clout) (see Inside-the-Park Home Run).

"Home Run" Baker If there ever was a baseball player who became a legend because of a nickname, it had to be John Franklin Baker. Admitted to the Hall of Fame in 1955, he had a powerful image but not much in the way of home runs. Baker played thirteen years and collected a grand total of ninety-three homers. His best homerun year was 1913, when he popped twelve round-trippers. Baker's lifetime home run percentage was 1.6, compared to Babe Ruth's 8.5, Hank Aaron's 6.3, and Rocky Colavito's 5.8. Powerful press agentry or key home runs in crucial situations have to be the explanations for Baker's nickname. His home run hitting did not make him deserving of it.

But to be fair—there were some moments: for his day he was a good home run hitter. In the Dead Ball Era, Baker led or tied for the league lead in homers four straight seasons (1911–1914), including winning the home run title in 1913 with twelve. In the 1911 World Series, he hit game-winning home runs on successive days against the Giants' future Hall of Fame pitchers Rube Marquard and Christy Mathewson.

"Home Run Twins" Mickey Mantle and Roger Maris, phrase coined in 1961.

Home Stand A stretch of games played by a team at home.

Homestead Grays Negro League team out of Pittsburgh that played many of its games in Washington in the 1930s and 1940s.

Home Whites Uniform worn by a team playing in its home ballpark.

"Hondo Hurricane" He was 6' 5" and weighed 210 pounds. He came up from the minor leagues to the New York Giants in 1947 with a "can't miss" label. Clint Hartung batted .309 that first year, and this meshed with his Hondo, Texas, birthplace to earn him his nickname. Unfortunately, the hurricane blew itself out. Hartung batted only .179 in 1948 and .190 in 1949. His major league career lasted but six years, and Hartung left with a .238 career batting average, just fourteen big league homers, and thoughts of what might have been.

Hook Slide An action where a runner slides into the side of a base, hooking it with a bent, back-stretched leg as he passes the base.

"Hoop" A shortening of the surname of Harry Hooper, who with Duffy Lewis and Tris Speaker formed Boston's famous "Million-Dollar Outfield."

"Hoosier Thunderbolt" Hall of Famer Amos Rusie, out of Indiana, played for the Indianapolis Hoosiers (1889), New York Giants (1890–1895, 1897–1898), and Cincinnati Reds (1901). He paced the league in strikeouts five times and passed the three-hundred-strikeout mark three straight seasons.

Horse Collar Describes a situation when a player gets no hits in a game.

"Horse Nose" Nickname given to catcher Pat Collins by Babe Ruth, a reference to a facial feature.

"Horsewhips Sam" Sam Jones earned this because of his sharp breaking curve ball.

Hot Corner Third base; the term originated because of the number of hard-smashed balls that arrive there.

Hot Stove League Wintertime baseball doings and gossip.

The House That Ruth Built On April 18, 1923, "The House That Ruth Built" opened for business. The New York Yankees' first home opponent was the Boston Red Sox. No one back then was bold enough to predict the fabulous and outstanding moments the future held in store for the brand new American League park.

The press release first announcing the new stadium indicated it would be shaped like the Yale Bowl and that it would contain towering battlements enclosing the entire park so that those lacking tickets would not even be able to get a glimpse of the action. Built at a cost of $2.5 million, "The Yankee Stadium," as it was originally named, had a brick-lined vault with electronic equipment under second base, making it possible to have a boxing ring and press area on the infield. Yankee Stadium was the first ballpark to be called a stadium and the last privately financed major league park. It was a gigantic horseshoe shaped by triple-decked grandstands. Huge wooden bleachers circled the park. The 10,712 upper-grandstand seats and 14,543 lower-grandstand seats were fixed in place by 135,000 individual steel castings on which 400,000 pieces of maple lumber were fastened by more than a million screws.

A massive crowd showed up for the proudest moment in the history of the South Bronx. Many in the huge assemblage wore heavy sweaters, coats, and hats. Some sported dinner jackets. The announced attendance was 74,217, later changed to 60,000. More than 25,000 were turned away. They would linger outside in the cold listening to the sounds of music and the roar of the crowd inside the stadium. At game time, the temperature was a nippy forty-nine degrees. Wind whipped the two Yankee pennants and blew dust from the dirt road that led to the stadium. The dominant sound of the day was the march beat played by the Seventh Regiment Band, directed by John Phillip Sousa. Seated in the celebrity box were Baseball Commissioner Kenesaw Mountain Landis, New York State Governor Al Smith, and Yankee owner Colonel Jacob Ruppert.

At 3:25 in the afternoon, Babe Ruth was presented with an oversized bat handsomely laid out in a glass case. At 3:30, Governor Smith threw out the first ball to Yankee catcher Wally Schang. At 3:35, home plate umpire Tommy Connolly bellowed: "Play ball!"

Babe Ruth said: "I'd give a year of my life if I can hit a home run in the first game in this new park." His wish and that of the tens of thousands in attendance came true. The Babe came to bat in the third inning. There were two Yankee base runners. Boston pitcher Howard Ehmke tried to fool Ruth with a slow pitch. The Sultan of Swat turned it into a fast pitch, hammering it on a line into the right-field bleachers. It was the first home run in Yankee Stadium history; Ruth got his wish.

The huge crowd was on its feet roaring as Ruth crossed the plate, removed his cap, extended it at arm's length in front of him, and waved to the ecstatic assemblage—witnesses to baseball history. The game played out into the lengthening afternoon shadows. "Sailor Bob" Shawkey, sporting a red sweat-shirt under his jersey, pitched the Yankees to a 4-1 victory, making the first Opening Day at Yankee Stadium a matter of record.

Houston Astros In 1962, the team was named the Colt .45s, then renamed for the famous NASA Space Center in 1965.

How about That Former New York Yankee broadcaster Mel Allen must have uttered that phrase thousands of times in noting the spectacular fielding plays, long home runs, and superb pitching performances that he viewed during his long career. It was a phrase expressed in an excited Southern accent that almost made those who heard it want to respond to Allen and give their opinion of what he had described.

"Howdy Doody" Darrell Evans was called this or "Howdy" by his Braves' teammates because of his resemblance to Howdy Doody. The nicknames were encouraged by Atlanta team owner Ted Turner.

"The Human Rain Delay" Mike Hargrove, for his delaying tactics as player and manager.

"The Human Vacuum Cleaner" Brooks Robinson made a name for himself with Baltimore as one of the top fielding third basemen of all time.

Hurl To pitch (Chuck).

Hurler A pitcher (Chucker).

"Hurricane" For Bob Hazle, after the storm that hit the South Carolina coast in 1954. The Milwaukee Braves, locked in the 1957 pennant race, lost outfielder Bill Bruton to a knee injury. Hazle replaced him and responded to the chance. He joined the starting lineup on August 4, 1957, helping the Braves win the pennant as he batted .403 over the end of that season.

Idiots Boston Red Sox manager Terry Francona explained the name his players gave to themselves in 2004: "They may not wear their hair normal, they many not dress normal, but they play the game as good as you can."

"If It's under 'W' for 'Won,' Nobody Asks You How" As a player and a manager, Leo Durocher could invent more ways to tease and taunt and beat the opposition than virtually any other figure in the history of baseball. His was an aggressive, no-holds-barred approach to the National Pastime. The quote attributed to him reflects his attitude toward the game (see "The Lip").

"Ignitor" Paul Molitor had a long and distinguished career primarily with the Milwaukee Brewers and could be counted on to make things happen for his teams.

"I Lost It in the Sun" Billy Loes was a Brooklyn Dodger pitcher in the 1950s. Possessed with a great deal of natural athletic ability, Loes never achieved the success experts predicted should have come to him as a matter of course. At times he was quicker with a quip than with his glove. During the 1952 World Series, Loes ingloriously misplayed a ground ball hit back to the pitcher's mound. Later he was questioned by a reporter who wished to learn what had been the problem. Loes responded, "I lost it in the sun."

"I Never Missed One in My Heart" Long-time major league umpire Bill Klem's phrase was his attempt to explain how difficult the job of umpiring was and how objective he always attempted to be. Klem retired in 1941—according to him, after the first time he pondered whether he had correctly called a play.

Infield The positions of first baseman, second baseman, third baseman, and shortstop.

Infield Fly A situation that occurs when, with less than two men out and with either all three bases occupied or first and second bases occupied, a hitter pops the ball up to the infield; the hitter is automatically declared out and the runners may advance at their own risk.

Infield Hit A hit achieved by hitting a ball that does not leave the infield.

Infield Out The retiring of a batter on a ball hit in the infield.

Inning A period of play that consists of three outs for each team. A regulation game consists of nine innings.

Inside-the-Park Home Run A home run that takes place when the ball is hit and is in play and the batter is able to reach home plate before being tagged out.

Intentional Walk A situation in which a pitcher deliberately throws four balls to a batter in a strategic attempt to prevent the batter from hitting.

Interference Getting in the way of a runner or a fielder, or hindering and making it difficult for that player to perform unhindered action.

"In the Catbird Seat" Red Barber beguiled Brooklyn Dodger fans for years with his Southern voice, narrative skills, honest manner, and down-home expressions. His pet phrase to describe when someone was pitching, hitting, fielding, or just functioning well was a reference to that individual as being in the "catbird seat." Barber also used the phrase to characterize a team ahead by a comfortable margin and virtually assured of victory.

In the Hole On the infield at a location nearly exactly between fielders, used to describe location of batted balls.

"Iron Horse" Lou Gehrig, a.k.a. "Larrupin' Lou" and "Pride of the Yankees," earned his main nickname for playing in 2,130 consecutive games—a major league baseball record that stood until Cal Ripken, Jr., came along. Day in and day out for fourteen years, like a thing made of iron, Gehrig was a fixture in the New York Yankee lineup. He led the league in RBIs five times and thirteen years he drove in more than one hundred runs a season. The man they also called Columbia Lou—a reference to his Columbia University student days—was admitted to the Hall of Fame in 1939.

"Iron Man" Joe McGinnity pitched in the majors from 1899 to 1908. He started 381 games and completed 351 of them. He had a lifetime earned-run average of 2.64. McGinnity could pitch day in and day out like a man made of iron. In 1903 he pitched and won three doubleheaders. Winner of 247 games—an average of almost twenty-five a year—McGinnity was admitted to baseball's Hall of Fame in 1946. Cal Ripken, Jr., for breaking the consecutive games played in mark set by Lou Gehrig. Teammates called him "Junior," as a tip of the cap to Cal, Sr., who was in the Orioles' organization more than three decades.

"Is Brooklyn Still in the League?" At the beginning of the 1934 baseball season, New York Giant's manager Bill Terry teasingly asked reporters that question about his team's subway rivals. It was a natural if uncomplimentary query. The Dodgers were still in the league, but they had not done much in the past few years. The final two games of the 1934 season saw the Dodgers still in the league but long out of the pennant race. On the other hand, the Giants were tied for first place with the St. Louis Cardinals. Brooklyn's last two games were with the Giants. Brooklyn won those last two games, while St. Louis swept its final two games from Cincinnati to take the National League pennant. And Giants manager Terry learned the virtues of letting sleeping dogs sleep. Van Lingle Mungo, the Dodgers' star pitcher of that year, remembers the way it was: "Because of Terry's taunt, we wanted to win just a little more each time we played them that year. The fans were even more so; they'd boo Terry every time he'd stick his head out of the dugout." Mungo pitched more innings than any other hurler in 1934, but he especially remembers the last game he pitched and won against the Giants. "It was like a World Series to me. I never wanted to win a game as much. I think it was one of the best games I ever pitched and I pitched it for Bill Terry."

"It's Not Over 'til It's Over" This phrase, attributed to Yogi Berra, underscores the former Yankee great's long experience in the wars of baseball. Berra, as player, manager, and coach, has seen the game of baseball from many levels. A victim and victor of late inning rallies, of curious changes in the destinies of players and teams, his stoic attitude to the National Pastime is the view of a pro, even though it is expressed in perhaps not the most appropriate syntax.

Jackie Robinson Award Rookie of the Year award.

Jam the Hitter To pitch a ball close to a hitter so as not to give him anything good to hit and to keep him off balance.

Jarry Park The Montreal Expos ended their baseball history in the 2004 season in the seventy-thousand-seat Olympique Stadium, a futuristic leftover from the Montreal Olympics. The roots of the team reach back, however, to Jarry Park, their first home. Months before the Expos played their first baseball game, in 1969, a site for the team had not been determined. National League President Warren Giles, Commissioner Bowie Kuhn, Montreal Mayor Jean Drapeau, and Montreal Expos President John McHale came to Jarry Park "as the last thing to look at as a possibility," according to McHale. He continued, "There was an amateur baseball game going on. There was great enthusiasm. As we walked into the park, the people recognized Warren Giles, and they stood up. They cried out: 'Le grand patron. Le grand patron!' Giles said, 'This is the place. This is the place. This is the only place I've seen where we can play baseball in Montreal.'" The Expos expanded the amateur ball park from the two thousand seats that existed behind home plate to a facility that accommodated twenty-eight thousand. In the ninth year of their existence, the Expos left Jarry Park and its *toujours un beau coup* ("a hit every time") baseball for something new. The old park remains for the people of Montreal *une affaire du coeur* ("an affair of the heart").

"JB" ("Johnny B") Catcher Johnny Bench had a Hall of Fame career playing for the Cincinnati Reds 1967–1983.

"Jet" Sam Jethroe, for his tremendous speed on the bases. He was one of the first Negro Leagues players to break through baseball's color barrier, and the first black athlete to play for the Boston Braves.

"Joltin' Joe" Joe DiMaggio, for the jolting shots he hit.

"Juan Gone" Juan Gonzalez got this nickname for his home run skills.

Jug-Handle Curve A wide-breaking curveball.

"Jumping Joe" Joe Dugan earned his nickname for being AWOL from his first big league club as a youngster.

"Junior" The Los Angeles Dodgers dedicated the 1978 World Series to James Gilliam, who died at the age of forty-nine just before the series began, a victim of a cerebral hemorrhage. There have been many athletes over the years who have been called Junior, but Gilliam seemed to have a lock on the name as he had a lock on the emotions of all those associated with baseball. He was given the name when he performed as the youngest player on the Baltimore Elite Giants, a black baseball team. There were attempts to retire the name when Gilliam played for the Brooklyn Dodgers and the Los Angeles Dodgers and then coached the L.A. team, but the name endured. In the 1978 World Series, all the Dodgers wore on their uniform sleeve a round black patch with Gilliam's number nineteen on it. In the eulogy for the man who was proud he was a Dodger, it was said, "He went through all of his life without ever once getting his signals crossed." Gilliam was "Junior," but he was a big man. Also Ken Griffey and countless others.

"The Junk Man" Eddie Lopat was the premier left-handed pitcher for the New York Yankees in the late 1940s and through most of the 1950s. He recalls how he obtained his nickname: "Ben Epstein was a writer for the *New York Daily Mirror* and a friend of mine from my Little Rock minor league baseball days. He told me in 1948 that he wanted to give me a name that would stay with me forever. 'I want to see what you think of it—"the junk man"?' In those days the writers had more consideration. They checked with players before they called them names. I told him I didn't care what they called me just as long as I could get the batters out and get paid for it." Epstein then wrote an article called "The Junkman Cometh," and as Lopat says, "The rest was history." The nickname derived from Lopat's ability to be a successful pitcher by tantalizing the hitters with an assortment of offspeed pitches. This writer and thousands of other baseball fans who saw Lopat pitch bragged more than once that if given a chance, they could hit the "junk" he threw (see "Steady Eddie").

Junk Pitcher A hurler who throws slow and deceptively breaking pitches, or "junk."

K The scorecard symbol for a strikeout. A backward K denotes a strikeout looking while a forward K indicates a strikeout swinging.

Kansas City Royals The name Royals was chosen by the team's fans in 1969 after the home of the "American Royal," one of the largest livestock shows and parades in the USA. The name also in honor of the old Negro Leagues team in Kansas City, the Monarchs.

Kauffman Stadium The Kansas City stadium was originally named Royals Stadium but changed to Kauffman Stadium after original owner, Ewing Kauffman.

Kenesaw Mountain Landis Judge Landis was baseball's first commissioner. He ruled the sport with supreme authority until 1946. The first part of his name came from the place where his father had been wounded during the Civil War.

"Kentucky Colonel" Earl Combs came from Kentucky.

Keystone Second base.

Keystone Combination The second baseman and the shortstop.

"Killer" Harmon Kleberg played for the Washington Senators (1954–1960) and the Minnesota Twins 1961–1974). His nickname was a play on his surname and a tribute to his hitting skills.

"The King and the Crown Prince" Babe Ruth and Lou Gehrig.

"King Kong" Charlie Keller played major league baseball for thirteen years, all but two of those years with the New York Yankees. Keller was a solid ball player with a lifetime batting average of .286. He was a muscular 5' 10," 185-pounder, and his nickname came from the main character of the movie of the same name. Keller's given names were Charles Ernest, but there were many pitchers who believed it was King Kong who was hitting against them.

"Kitty" Hurler Jim Kaat played for quite a few teams during 1950s through the 1970s. His nickname was a play on his surname.

"Klu" Ted Kluszewski played fifteen years in the major leagues. He pounded out 279 homers and recorded a lifetime slugging average of nearly .500 and a career batting average of nearly .300. He was a favorite of the Cincinnati fans; at 6' 2" and 225 pounds, his bulging biceps were too huge to be contained by ordinary shirtsleeves. Kluszewski cut off the sleeves and started a new fashion in baseball uniforms—just as fans and sportswriters cut off part of his name to make for a nickname more easily pronounced and printed.

"Knight of Kennett Square" Pitcher Herb Pennock because he raised thoroughbreds and hosted fox hunts in his home town of Kennett Square, Pennsylvania.

Knock out of the Box To score runs against a pitcher in such a way that he is removed from the game.

Knuckleball An unusual pitch that flutters as it comes to the batter (Flutterball; Knuckler).

Knuckle Curve A combination knuckleball and curveball.

"Knucksie" Phil Niekro used his knuckleball to last twenty-four years and win 318 games, with 121 of those victories coming after he turned forty.

"Larrupin' Lou" Lou Gehrig, for his power ways on the baseball diamond.

Lay Down a Bunt The act of bunting the ball.

Lead The number of steps a base runner takes off a base. A short lead takes place when the runner is close to the base. A long lead describes a proportionately longer distance off the base.

Lead Off To bat first in an inning or in the team's lineup. When a base runner steps off the base in order to reduce the distance to the next base, before a pitch is thrown.

Leadoff Batter (Man) The first hitter in the team's line-up or in an inning.

League Championship Most Valuable Player Award given to player in each league for outstanding achievement during the League Championship series.

Leave Men on Base A situation at the end of an inning when a team has been retired and one or more base runners have been left on base, unable to score (Strand Base Runner[s]).

Left Field Viewed from home plate, the left side of the outfield.

"Lefty" Hall of Fame pitcher Steve Carlton was a private man who never talked to the press. He was a southpaw and a man with some odd habits.

Leg Hit A base hit awarded to a runner who beats out a ground ball to the infield by using his speed.

"Le Grande Orange" Rusty Staub played for the Montreal Expos in the years 1969–1971. "He came here as an unknown, and not only was he our first big star," Expo President John McHale remembers, "but he had a way of relating to the people and a sense of being a star. His reddish hair, his physical stature, his unselfishness made him an easily identifiable figure. He was a very important factor in those years in the success of the team." Staub's size, red hair, and personality all merged into the nickname the Montreal fans coined for him.

Letters Team name printed on the front of a jersey.

Letup Pitch A pitch from which something is taken off, generally speed, so that it comes in to the batter with less velocity than he expects (Change-up).

"The Line" Detroit Hall of Famer Al Kaline was called this as a tribute to his reliability and a play on his last name.

Line Out To hit a line drive that is caught for an out.

Liner A ball hit straight and solidly (Line Drive).

Line Score A printed summary account, inning by inning, of a game.

"The Lip" When he was an infielder for the St. Louis Cardinals during the 1930s, Leo Durocher was known as Screechy because of his high-pitched voice and bench-jockeying ability. As he moved through his seventeen-year playing span and twenty-four-year managing career with the Brooklyn Dodgers, New York Giants, Chicago Cubs, and Houston Astros, Durocher attracted the ire of umpires and the hostility of rivals with what they termed his motor-mouth. A tough, combative, at times profane individual, Durocher's nickname was an apt one.

Little League Baseball In 1939 Carl E. Stotz founded the first Little League in Williamsport, Pennsylvania. Within two decades, kids and parents all over the United States and other countries were competitively involved. Williamsport has been the site of the Little League World Series since 1947. And the enterprise begun by Stotz is a big-time sports phenomenon.

"Little Looey" Small in size, shortstop Luis Aparicio made his mark as a member of the Chicago White Sox in the 1950s.

"Little Napoleon" John J. McGraw came from the old Baltimore Orioles to take control of the New York Giants on July 16, 1902. He inherited a last-place team that had had thirteen managers since 1891. The man they called Muggsy immediately released half the players on the roster of the Giants. "With my team," he said, "I'm absolute czar." Driving, cajoling, innovating, McGraw moved the Giants from a last-place finish in 1902 to a second-place finish in 1903. He drove the New York team to a pennant in 1904. In his thirty years as manager, the Giants won ten pennants and finished second eleven times. McGraw's small physical stature contrasted sharply with the giant power that his gait, his face, and his name projected throughout the world of baseball. He was famous for such lines as "The only popularity I know is to win," "Do what I tell you, and I'll take the blame if it goes wrong," and "I do the hiring and the firing around here." He was little in size but had Napoleonic power, and these two traits merged into the nickname of the man who was one of the greatest managers in baseball history.

"Little Professor" Joe DiMaggio's younger brother, Dom, played center field for the Boston Red Sox for eleven years and compiled a lifetime .298 batting average. He wore glasses, was a keen student of the game, and was but 5' 9" tall and 168 pounds, and these characteristics supplied the reason for his nickname.

Live Ball A ball that, because of its alleged composition, will travel a long way when hit—as opposed to a dead ball (Rabbit Ball).

Load the Ball The illegal placement by a pitcher of saliva or some other foreign substance on the ball, to gain an edge by causing the ball to move about unpredictably.

Load the Bases An offensive team's placing of runners on each base (Bases Full).

"Lolo" Mickey Lolich, former pitcher for the Detroit Tigers, for his last name, and how low his leg drive was in his delivery.

"Lonesome George" Former legendary Yankee General Manager George Weiss, for his aloof ways.

Long-Ball Hitter A batter who hits the ball for distance.

Long Reliever (Long Man) A relief pitcher counted on to pitch approximately three innings or more.

Look For To come to bat expecting a certain pitch. (The term also covers many situations involving expectation, such as "looking for a player" to supply home run power.)

Look the Runner Back A situation in which a pitcher attempts to control a base runner by staring at him, implying a throw; the pitcher's gaze alone will most times convince a runner to stay close to the base.

Looper A batted ball that drops in flight.

Losing Pitcher The pitcher who is officially charged with a loss.

"Losing Pitcher" One year he won eight games and lost eighteen; another year he won ten games and lost twenty; in 1939 he lost sixteen, and in 1940 he led the National League in losses with twenty-two. These statistics earned Hugh Noyes Mulcahy his nickname. In a nine-year career, Mulcahy won forty-five games and lost eighty-nine.

Lou Gehrig's Disease Amyotrophic lateral sclerosis (ALS), named after the famed New York Yankee who had the disease.

"Louisiana Lightning" The ninety-five-mph speed he can put on a fastball and his Louisiana birthplace have earned for Ron Guidry of the New York Yankees his colorful and alliterative nickname.

Louisville Slugger This bat is named for the Kentucky city that was named for a French king, Louis XVI, in 1780. The Hillerich and Bradsby bat factory has been manufacturing Louisville Sluggers since 1884. One white-ash tree is needed to produce sixty bats. More than six million bats are manufactured annually. Major league ballplayers use 2 percent of the annual production, but each of their bats is built according to precise individual specifications. Babe Ruth's Louisville Slugger model weighed forty-eight ounces, while the one wielded by Wee Willie Keeler weighed just thirty ounces.

"Mad Dog" Pitcher Greg Maddux acted like one at the time. Also called "The Professor," because of his teacherlike appearance.

"Mad Hungarian" Al Hrabosky, who arrived in the major leagues with the St. Louis Cardinals in 1970, is a self-created image. Originally a clean-cut pitcher, Hrabosky allowed his hair to grow long and cultivated a beard and a moustache. He then developed a procedure on the pitching mound designed to annoy, frustrate, and sometimes anger batters. He would step off the mound, walk in the direction of second base, pound his glove, talk to himself, trot back to the mound, glower in to the catcher, and release his pitch. Pleasing to the crowds, an aid to, in Hrabosky's phrase, "psyching myself up," the image and the routine fattened the pitcher's paychecks. There are those who declare that Hrabosky may be Hungarian, but he surely isn't mad.

"The Mahatma" Branch Rickey (1881–1965) was one of baseball's most influential personalities. Inventor of the farm system, the force responsible for Jackie Robinson breaking baseball's color line, the master builder of the St. Louis Cardinal and Brooklyn Dodger organizations, he was elected to the Hall of Fame in 1967. Sportswriter Tom Meany coined Rickey's nickname. Meany got the idea from John Gunther's phrase describing Mohandas K. Gandhi as a "combination of God, your own father, and Tammany Hall."

"Mail Carrier" Fans at Louisville in the minor leagues where Earle Combs starred called him that because of his speed and base-stealing skills.

"Major" Ralph Houk, for rank held in the Armed Forces and his demeanor.

"The Man" ("Stan the Man") Stanley Frank Musial, St. Louis Cardinal immortal, batted .315 as a rookie in 1942, when he was twenty-one years old. In 1962, at the age of forty-one, he hit .330—1 point under his lifetime batting average. Musial is the all-time Cardinal leader in games played, runs, hits, doubles, triples, homers, and total bases. His twisted, crouched, coiled stance at the plate enabled him to slash the ball with power or stroke it with finesse to any part of the playing field. Musial was an especially successful hitter in the small confines of Ebbets Field. His specialty was slamming frozen rope doubles off the outfield walls. Dodger fans had difficulty pronouncing his name, sometimes calling him "Musical." Many of the black Dodger fans simply referred to Musial as "the Man" in tribute to the power and style he displayed. Eventually fans all over the league used this nickname—a reference not only to Musial but to the respect due his power and authority.

"M&M Boys" Mickey Mantle and Roger Maris.

"Mandrake the Magician" During the late 1940s and into the 1950s, Don Mueller of the New York Giants appeared to have a special gift with a bat in his hands. His lifetime batting average was a respectable .296, yet he never led the league in any hitting category. His nickname came from his expert bat manipulation and his ability to hit the ball where he wanted it to go.

"Man in the Iron Hat" Yankee owner Captain Tillinghast L'Hommedieu Hutson wore the same squished derby hat over and over again.

"Man Nobody Knows" Catcher Bill Dickey, Yankee immortal, because of his blandness.

"Man of a Thousand Curves" His nickname was a bit hyperbolic, but the major league batters who swung at his stuff and came up empty might not disagree with it. For Johnny Sain, talented star of the Boston Braves and other teams, curveball pitches were a trademark and the reason for his nickname. He allegedly had such pitching skill that his curves dropped, darted, hesitated, broke wide, broke fast, broke slow, broke twice. There may not have been a thousand curves, but there were enough variations on these curves Sain possessed that the effect on batters was the same (see "Spahn and Sain and Pray for Rain").

"Man o' War" Sam Rice was a fleet-footed outfielder and was called "Man o' War" after the famous race-horse of his era.

"Marse Joe" Hall of Fame Manager Joe McCarthy, for his commanding style.

"Marvelous Marv" Marvin Eugene Throneberry was perhaps born to be a New York Met. His initials spelled out the name, and his personality and limited skills underscored the characteristics of the 1962 New York ex-pansion team. Throneberry, who looked like Mickey Mantle batting but did not get the same results, labored through a seven-year, four-different-team major league career. The Mets were his last team. He is a gentle, fine-humored man, and sportswriters hung the nickname on him in good-natured jest. Throneberry loved it and went along with their efforts to depict him as a clown. Once a teammate dropped an easy fly ball. Mar-velous Marv smiled and shouted, "What are you trying to do anyway, steal my fans?"

"Master Builder in Baseball" Jacob Ruppert, and that he was.

"Master Melvin" Mel Ott was a power-armed right fielder for twenty-two years with the New York Giants. He smashed 511 home runs in a fabled career that saw him average better than a hit a game while com-piling a lifetime batting average of .304. Ott became a Giant at the age of sixteen, and that's how his nick-name came about. Ott's Hollywood-type beginning was recalled by Eddie Logan, Giants equipment man-ager, who was about the same age as Ott at the time and was sent to pick up the youth: "We had the 9th Avenue El at the time. Mr. McGraw had told him to ride the El to the last stop, which was the Polo Grounds. He took the El the wrong way and wound up at the Battery. I looked for the straw suitcase. I found him. I said, 'C'mon boy, let's go.' He got the biggest thrill riding back on the train." Labeled "Mc-Graw's baby," Ott was in only thirty-five games in 1926, then eighty-two in 1927. "He's too young to play big-league ball," McGraw said, "but I am afraid to send him to the minors and have a manager there tin-ker with his unorthodox batting style. The style is natural with him. He'll get results as soon as he learns about big-league pitching." And he did.

"Meal Ticket" Through the long Depression years, one of the great constants in the fortunes of the New York Giants was pitcher Carl Hubbell. The Hall of Famer possessed a left-handed screwball that he threw at dif-ferent speeds and blended with a dazzling change of pace. He could make the ball almost disappear, so so-phisticated was his pitching style. Hubbell won 253 games for the Giants in a sixteen-year career and notched a 2.97 earned-run average. His nickname came from his value to the Giants. He was a selfless performer. "In a close game, he'd go down to the bullpen and start warming up. He wanted to show that he was willing and ready, and he'd defy the manager not to put him in," recalled former Giant owner Horace Stoneham.

"Mechanical Man" A Tiger superstar in the 1930s, Charlie Gehringer was given that nickname by Yankee pitcher Lefty Gomez who said he was automatic.

Mendoza Line Batters hitting below .215 are referred to as below the Mendoza line, a reference to Mario Mendoza, lifetime batting average—.215.

"Merry Mortician" Waite Hoyt was a cheery soul and worked off-season as a mortician.

"The Mick" Short for Mickey (Mantle).

"Mickey Mouth" Mickey Rivers, for his motor mouth.

"Mick the Quick" Mickey Rivers, for his speed.

"Mighty Mite" Hall of Famer Miller Huggins played thirteen years in the major leagues and managed for seventeen more with the Cardinals and Yankees. A 5' 6", 140-pounder, his small physical stature and his outstanding playing and managing ability merged into the qualities that produced his nickname.

"Milkman" Former Yankee pitcher Jim Turner because of his off-season job delivering milk.

Milwaukee Brewers The franchise began as the Seattle Pilots in 1969, then moved to Milwaukee in 1970 and picked up its nickname for the famous breweries in the city.

Minnesota Twins Named for the "Twin Cities" where the team is located, Minneapolis and St. Paul. Franchise moved from Washington, D.C., as the Senators (1901–1960), to Bloomington, Minnesota, as the Twins (1961–1981), then to Minneapolis in 1982.

"Minnie" Minoso His real name was Saturnino Orestes Arrieta Armas Minoso, but everyone knew him as Minnie, which made it easier for typesetters, reporters, and fans. Born November 29, 1922, in Havana, Cuba, Minoso played fifteen years in the majors, from 1949 to 1964 (he also appeared in one game in 1977, while a coach with the Chicago White Sox).

Miracle at Coogan's Bluff Throughout the long history of baseball there have been poignant, exciting, dramatic moments. But very few can compare to what happened on October 3, 1951, at the old Polo Grounds in New York City. Some refer to that time as "The Miracle at Coogan's Bluff." Others, especially in Brooklyn, call it "Dat Day." But no matter what label is applied it was a time to remember.

It was a time when the Giants played at the Polo Grounds in Manhattan and the Dodgers entertained millions in their tiny Brooklyn ballpark, Ebbets Field. It was a time of tremendous fan devotion to each team. In July Brooklyn manager Charlie Dressen had bragged, "The Giants is dead." It seemed to aptly describe the plight of Leo Durocher's team. For on August 12 the Giants trailed the Dodgers by thirteen and one-half games in the standings.

Then, incredibly, the Giants locked into what has been called "The Miracle Run." They won thirty-seven of their final forty-four games—sixteen of them in one frenetic stretch—and closed the gap. "It was a once-in-a-lifetime situation," recalls Monte Irvin, who batted .312 that year for the Giants. "We kept on winning. The Dodgers kept on losing. It seemed like we beat everybody in the seventh, eighth, and ninth inning."

The Giants and Dodgers finished the season in a flat-footed tie for first place and met on the first day of October in the first game of the first play-off in the history of the National League. The teams split the first two games, setting the stage for the third and final game. Don Newcombe of the Dodgers was pitted against Sal Maglie of the Giants. Both hurlers had won twenty-three games during the regular season.

The game began under overcast skies and a threat of rain. Radio play-by-play filtered into schoolrooms, factories, office buildings, city prisons, barbershops. The Wall Street teletype intermingled stock quotations with play-by-play details of the Giant-Dodger battle. The game was tied 1-1 after seven innings. Then Brooklyn scored three times in the top of the eighth. Many of the Dodger fans at the Polo Grounds and the multitude listening to the game on the radio thought that the Giants would not come back. Durocher and the Giants never gave up. "We knew that Newcombe would make the wrong pitch," said Monte Irvin. "That was his history."

The Giants came to bat in the bottom of the ninth inning—only three outs remained in their miracle season.

Alvin Dark led off with a single through the right side of the infield. Don Mueller slapped the ball past Dodger first baseman Gil Hodges. Irvin fouled out. Whitey Lockman doubled down the left field line. Dark scored. With runners on second and third Ralph Branca came in to relieve Newcombe. Bobby Thomson waited to bat. Durocher said, "I did not know whether they would pitch to Thomson or not. First base was open. Willie Mays, just a rookie, was on deck."

Veteran New York Giant announcer Russ Hodges described the moment to millions mesmerized at their radios that October afternoon: "Bobby Thomson up there swinging. . . . Bobby batting at .292. Branca pitches and Bobby takes a strike call on the inside corner. Lockman without too big of a lead at second but he'll be running like the wind if Thomson hits one. Branca throws . . . there's a long drive . . . it's gonna be, I believe . . ."

The precise moment was 3:58 p.m., October 3, 1951.

". . . the Giants win the pennant!" Hodges screamed the words at the top of his voice, all semblance of journalistic objectivity gone. "The Giants win the pennant! The Giants win the pennant!" Hodges bellowed it out eight times—and then overcome by the moment and voiceless, he had to yield the microphone.

Pandemonium was on parade at the Polo Grounds for hours after the game. For almost half an hour after the epic home run, there were so many phone calls placed by people in Manhattan and Brooklyn that the New York Telephone Company reported service almost broke down. Bobby Thomson and Ralph Branca would play out their major league careers. But the moment they shared—as hero and goat that October day at the Polo Grounds—would link them forever.

"Miracle Braves" The year was 1914, the year World War I began. The Boston Braves marched from last place in July to the National League pennant by winning sixty-one of their last seventy-seven games. That accomplishment was only a part of what earned the Braves their reputation as a "miracle" team. In the World Series, the Braves were given no chance to defeat a powerful Philadelphia Athletics team that boasted such pitching stars as Chief Bender, Bullet Joe Bush, Eddie Plank, and Jack Coombs and what was referred to as the "$100,000 infield" of Baker, Barry, McInnis, and Collins. Boston manager George Stallings was confident. "We'll stop them. We're coming and they're going."

Behind their powerful pitching trio of George Tyler, Dick Rudolph, and Bill James, the Braves won the first game, shocking the baseball world, then the next three, to demolish a dynasty and become the first team in the history of baseball to win four straight World Series games.

"Miracle Man" The manager of the "Miracle Braves," George Stallings, piloted four different teams in a thirteen-year managing career. He won only a single pennant in all those years—with the 1914 "Miracle Braves"—but the accomplishment was good enough to earn him his nickname.

"Mr. Automatic" Mariano Rivera, for his unflappable behavior and skills as a Yankee stopper.

"Mr. May" George Steinbrenner's sarcastic jibe at Dave Winfield because of his postseason struggles compared to Reggie Jackson's successes. It was a taunt from the Yankee principal owner that Winfield did well in the month of May when there was no real pressure.

"Mr. November" Derek Jeter, for his World Series home run, November 1, 2001.

"Mr. October" In Game Five of the 1977 ALCS Billy Martin benched Reggie Jackson. In a comeback win against Kansas City, Jackson retuned to slap a single. Thurman Munson sarcastically called Jackson "Mr. October." The nickname would have taken on a different meaning, but Jackson fitted the nickname to his persona.

"Monster" His size (6' 6" and 230 pounds) and his pitching efficiency during his seven-year stint for the Boston Red Sox in the 1960s earned Dick Radatz his nickname.

Montreal Expos Nickname derived from the 1967 World Exposition staged in Montreal. It was held two years before the team's inaugural game. The fair ran for the entire year and drew approximately fifty million people.

"Mookie" Willie Wilson was given this nickname by his family because of the funny way he said "milk" when he was a child.

Moon Shot Home run hit high and far.

"Moose" Bill Skowron's grandfather as a joke called him Mussolini, but his family shortened the nickname to Moose. This is another version—that he was named "Moose" because of his resemblance to Mussolini. Pitcher Mike Mussina (Baltimore Orioles 1991–2000, New York Yankees 2001–present) earned this name for size.

Mound A raised surface in the center of the diamond on which the pitcher stands and throws to the batter.

Moundsman Another name for a pitcher.

"Muff" To misplay a ground ball or a fly ball.

My Writers Casey Stengel's phrase for journalists he was close to.

Nail The act of throwing out a runner.

"Nails" Lenny Dykstra, allegedly this former major leaguer was as tough as nails.

"Nasty Boys" Norm Charlton in 1990 split time between the starting rotation and the bullpen, where he teamed up with fellow relievers Rob Dibble and Randy Myers to form the "Nasty Boys"—a fearsome trio that Cincinnati rode all the way to a World Series sweep of the favored Oakland A's.

National Baseball Hall of Fame and Museum Located at Cooperstown, New York, the site where Abner Doubleday—as myth would have it—invented the game of baseball, the Hall of Fame, established in 1939, is the oldest institution of its kind in the United States.

"Naugatuck Nugget" Born Francis Joseph Shea on October 2, 1920, in Naugatuck, Connecticut, Frank "Spec" Shea won two games in the 1947 World Series as a rookie for the New York Yankees. His nicknames came from his place of birth and his poor vision.

New York Yankees The Baltimore Orioles franchise was purchased for $18,000 by well-known gambler Frank Farrell and former New York City Chief of Police William S. "Big Bill" Devery, who bragged that he had never read a book. Farrell and Devery owned hundreds of pool rooms and nearly as many politicians, and they knew their way around town.

The team was first called Highlanders both after a famous British Army regiment named Gordon's Highlanders and because Hilltop Park was their home ballpark located on a hilltop overlooking Washington Heights.

The name "Yankees" was used first by sportswriters Mark Roth of the *New York Globe* and Sam Crane of the *New York Journal,* the name appearing in print for the first time on June 21, 1904, in the *Boston Herald.*

"Nice Guys Finish Last" As baseball player and manager, Leo Durocher prided himself on his combativeness. He schemed, argued, and fought with the opposition—and sometimes with his own teammates. His feelings about "nice guys" as revealed in this quote, now almost a cliché attributed to him, expressed his baseball philosophy and underscored his attitude toward winning (see "The Lip").

Nickel Series Refers to old days when New York City teams played against each other and the tariff was a five-cent subway ride.

Nightcap The second game of a doubleheader.

"Nightrider" Don Larsen called himself that because it reminded him of comic book heroes he read about and it fit with his late-night bar wanderings.

Nine A baseball team (Starting Nine).

"Ninety-Six" William Symmes Voiselle was also known as "Big Bill" for his size. Born January 29, 1919, in Greenwood, South Carolina, he and friends were stymied on Sundays by the rules of the day—no baseball on Sundays. They would sneak over to a local creek area in Ninety Six, South Carolina, and play. Voiselle in the 1940s took his skills to the major leagues as a pitcher with the Pirates and the nickname from his early playing area.

No-Hitter A game in which a pitcher (or pitchers) on one team does not allow any hits to the opposition.

"Nomar" Nomar Garciaparra's "nickname" is unique. His first name (which is actually his middle name) is his father's name (Ramon), spelled backwards.

Number ⅛ On August 19, 1951, Eddie Gaedel, wearing number ⅛, came to bat for the St. Louis Browns against the Detroit Tigers. Gaedel, who was signed by Browns owner Bill Veeck, walked on four straight pitches and was then replaced by a pinch runner. The next day the American League banned Gaedel, despite Veeck's protests. Gaedel was a midget, only 3' 7" tall.

Numbers In 1929, the New York Yankees introduced identifying numbers sewn on the backs of player jerseys, the first time that uniform numbers were used on a full-time basis. For the record, here is the list of the "original" ten Yankee uniform numbers:

#1—Earle Combs
#2—Mark Koenig
#3—Babe Ruth
#4—Lou Gehrig
#5—Bob Meusel
#6—Tony Lazzeri
#7—Leo Durocher
#8—Johnny Grabowski
#9—Benny Bengough
#10—Bill Dickey

Oakland Athletics The former Philadelphia Athletics franchise from 1901 to 1954 was the Kansas City Athletics and then from 1955 to 1967, the team was the Oakland A's, in 1968 then the Athletics in 1987.

"The Octopus" Name earned by former Cardinal shortstop Marty Marion because of his unusually long arms. He was also called "Slats" for the gainliness of his appearance. He was an outstanding fielder.

Official Game A game that goes four-and-one-half innings with home team ahead or five innings with the visitors leading.

Official Scorer The person who records the score and statistics of a game and rules on whether a hit or an error, and so forth, should be charged to a player in a particular situation.

Off-Speed Pitch A pitch that is slower than usual, so that the difference in velocity affects the timing of a hitter.

"Oil Can" Former colorful hurler Dennis Boyd grew up and learned to play ball in the Deep South. He would get so thirsty that the beverage he drank was, in his phrase, "just like drankin' ole."

"Oklahoma Kid" The young Mickey Mantle came from Oklahoma.

"Old Aches and Pains" Luke Appling performed for two decades with the Chicago White Sox. A .310 lifetime batting average was just one of the reasons he was admitted to the Hall of Fame in 1964. His nickname stemmed from the numerous real and imagined illnesses he picked up playing in 2,422 games, while averaging better than a hit a game. Appling was born April 2, 1907, and in 1950 was still playing major league baseball, aches, pains, and all.

"Old Fox" Name given to pilot-manager Clark Griffith of the old Highlanders because of his cunning ways.

"Old Hoss" Charles Radbourne was known as Charles or Charley until his amazing 1884 season, when he pitched 678 innings and earned the nickname.

"Old Reliable" Tommy Henrich played for the New York Yankees from 1937 to 1950. His lifetime batting average was only .282, but the value of Henrich to the Yankees was in his clutch hitting. Time after time he would come up in a key situation and deliver. His nickname had its roots in his ability to function under pressure and to perform reliably with distinction.

"Ole Perfessor" Hall of Famer Charles Dillon Stengel was an original. Born on July 30, 1890, in Kansas City, Missouri, he played in the majors for fourteen years and managed for twenty-five more—with the Brooklyn Dodgers, the Boston Braves, the New York Yankees (ten pennants), and the New York Mets (four tenth-place finishes). He had seen it all, and in one of his more coherent statements, he said, "This here team won't win anything until we spread enough of our players around the league and make the others [teams] horseshit, too." The statement underscored the ineptitude of the early Mets. Loquacious, dynamic, vital, Casey could lecture on baseball and life for hours and hours, and that was just part of the reason for his nickname. Actually, in 1914 Stengel held the title of professor at the University of Mississippi, for he spent that year's spring training coaching baseball at that institution. That's how he really came by his nickname.

On Deck A term describing a player stationed in the batter's on-deck circle in front of the dugout, preparing to be the next batter to come up and hit.

"One and Only" Babe Ruth; he was.

"One-Armed" Pete Gray Born Peter J. Wyshner (a.k.a. Pete Gray) on March 6, 1917, Gray was a longtime New York City semipro star who played in seventy-seven games for the St. Louis Browns in 1945. He actually had only one arm and played center field with an unpadded glove. He had an intricate and well-developed routine for catching the ball, removing the ball from his glove, and throwing the ball to the infield. Gray hit .218 for the Browns, not bad for a hitter with only one arm.

One-Bagger (One-Base Hit) A single.

"$100,000 Infield" That was the price tag and the nickname given to Eddie Collins, "Home Run" Baker, "Stuffy" McInnis, and Hack Barry, the players who composed the infield for Connie Mack's 1914 Philadelphia Athletics.

Opposite Field The part of the field opposite the batter's box a hitter occupies. Thus, right field is the opposite field for a hitter who bats right, and left field is the opposite field for a hitter who bats from the left side of the plate.

Opposite Field Home Run One hit on the side of the plate opposite the side the batter stands on; for example, a home run over the right-field fence by a right-handed batter.

Opposite Held The part of the field opposite the batter's box a hitter occupies. Thus, right field is the opposite field for a hitter who bats right, and left field is the opposite field for a hitter who bats from the left side of the plate.

Out To be retired by the defense.

Outfield The playing area beyond the infield where outfielders are stationed.

Outfielder The positions of left fielder, right fielder, and center fielder (Picketman).

Outhit To get more hits than another player or team.

Outpitch To pitch better than an opponent.

Outside Corner Over the edge of home plate away from the batter, used to describe the location of pitches.

Outslug Usually, to defeat another team by displaying more extra-base power.

Overmanage To bother and hamper a team with excess strategy and suggestions—generally the suggestions and strategy come from the manager.

Overslide To slide into a base and then past it.

Palmball An off-speed pitch, not often used, for which a pitcher grips the ball between the thumb and the palm.

"Papa" ("Steady Edgar") Edgar Martinez was the Seattle Mariners' family man and father figure in the clubhouse.

Papi David Ortiz, Boston Red Sox. Called "Papi" by his teammates, a sign of respect for a Hispanic person.

Passed Ball An error charged to a catcher for a pitch he is unable to control, resulting in a runner advancing to the next base or a batter getting to first base on a strikeout.

Payoff Pitch One made when the pitch count is full.

Pebble Play In the twelfth inning of the final game of the 1924 World Series between the New York Giants and the Washington Senators, a ground ball that bounced over the head of Giant infielder Freddy Lindstrom led to a score for Washington that gave it the World Championship. It was claimed that the batted ball hit a pebble. "It was never written up the way I looked at it," observed former Giant and Hall of Famer George Kelly. "Now it did hit a pebble, but Fred backed up on it, inexperience. It was his rookie year. This gave the ball an extra hop—the ball played Fred, he didn't play it."

"The Peerless Leader" Frank Leroy Chance, the first baseman in the famous Tinker-to-Evers-to-Chance Chicago Cubs infield trio, was aptly nicknamed. In the years 1906–1911, he led the Cubs to four pennants and two second-place finishes. Functioning as both a player and a manager, Chance recorded 405 career stolen bases—a Cub record—and his clutch hitting and spirited play served as examples of his leadership.

"Pee Wee" Harold Henry Reese was also known as the "Little Colonel," for he hailed from colonel country in Kentucky, but almost everyone called him "Pee Wee." Various reasons have been advanced for his nickname—he liked playing marbles as a kid; he was small (5' 10", 160 pounds); he came up at the same time as Harold "Pistol Pete" Reiser, and writers sought to have the two paired with alliterative nicknames. Whatever the derivation, Reese was anything but small in his influence on the fortunes of the Dodgers. He could run, hit, bunt, field, steal, throw, inspire—and most of all win and influence his team's winning. And he was especially instrumental in easing the way for Jackie Robinson to break the color line in major league baseball.

When the 1947 season started, some opposing National League players gave Jackie Robinson a hard time. In Boston one day, Reese made a gesture of acceptance for all the world to see. He went over to

Robinson and simply put his arm around Jackie. This was at a time when even Robinson's own teammates staged a short-lived protest against having him on the team.

"I get a lot of credit and I appreciate it," Reese said. "But after a while, I thought of him as I would Duke Snider or Gil Hodges or anyone else. We never thought of this as a big deal. We were just playing ball and having fun."

Reese spent his entire sixteen-year career with the Dodgers, appearing in seven World Series. He played fifteen years in Brooklyn and followed the team to Los Angeles for one more season before retiring in 1958. His uniform number (1) was retired by Los Angeles on July 1, 1984.

One of the magical moments in Reese's career took place on June 22, 1955. It was a day after he had recorded his two-thousandth hit. "Pee Wee" was given a birthday party at Ebbets Field. It was the first and only night dedicated to a player up to that time when fans were asked not to contribute anything.

All they were asked to bring was cigars, cigarettes, lighters, candles— anything they could light up for Pee Wee who remembered, "When I came to Brooklyn in 1940 I was a scared kid. To tell the truth I was twice as scared on my birthday night at Ebbets Field." And then the moment arrived. Fans at that old Brooklyn ballpark watched the lights dim, lit up whatever they had brought, and sang "Happy Birthday" to Pee Wee with varying levels of competency.

There are those of a certain age who still remember Pee Wee Reese bringing the lineup card out to home plate, raising his right arm, leading the Dodgers onto the playing field. "Being Captain of the Dodgers," Reese recalled, "meant representing an organization committed to winning and trying to keep it going. We could have won every year if the breaks had gone right."

Peg A forceful throw (catcher to second baseman, for example) aimed at retiring a base runner.

"The Penguin" A Tacoma, Washington, native, Ron Cey of the Los Angeles Dodgers is one of major league baseball's top third basemen. His awkward movements when walking and, especially, when running have resulted in his nickname.

Pennant A pennant-shaped banner that symbolizes the winning of a league championship (Flag).

Pennant Race The battle for the pennant among contending teams.

"The People's Cherce" Fred "Dixie" Walker compiled a .306 batting average in an eighteen-year major league baseball career, with five different teams. From 1940 to 1947 he starred in the outfield for the Brooklyn Dodgers and won the affection of the fans at Ebbets Field. The team had bigger stars and more proficient players, but Walker somehow had a rapport with the fans that made him their favorite and earned for him his "Brooklynese" nickname.

"Pepi" Short for Joe Pepitone out of Brooklyn, New York, of brief major league fame with the Yankees and other teams.

Pepper Game Pregame warm-up action where a player chops the ball on the ground to teammates who field the ball and flip it back to him.

Percentage Player, Manager One who goes by past form or logical odds and acts on the basis of these considerations.

Perfect Game A no-hitter in which none of the twenty-seven opposing batters in a nine-inning game, for example, gets on base. The most famous of them all was Don Larsen's beauty on October 8, 1956.

The image of the Yankee right-hander casually tossing the ball from a no-stretch windup to Yogi Berra remains part of baseball lore. Larsen struck out Junior Gilliam on a breaking ball to start the game. Then the 3-2 count on Pee Wee Reese—and the strikeout. It all blended together—the autumn shadows and the smoke and the haze at the stadium, the World Series buntings on railings along the first- and third-base lines, the scoreboard and the zeroes for the Dodgers of Brooklyn mounting inning after inning.

The 6' 4", 240-pound hurler threw no more than fifteen pitches in any one inning against the mighty Dodgers Campanella, Reese, Hodges, Gilliam, Robinson, Snider, and Furillo. A second-inning Jackie Robinson line drive off the glove of Andy Carey at third was picked up by Gil McDougald. Out at first. Mantle's great jump on a fifth-inning line drive by Gil Hodges positioned him for a backhand grab of the ball. Hodges eighth-inning hot shot down the third-base line was converted into an out by Andy Carey. Sandy Amoros and Duke Snider of the Dodgers hit balls into the right-field seats—foul but barely so.

Just two seasons before Don Larsen, pitching for Baltimore, had one of the worst records ever (3-21). He became a Yankee in the fall of 1954 in a seventeen-player trade. "Nobody lost more games than me in the American League that year," Larsen said. "But two of my wins came against the Yankees. That's probably why I came to them." In 1956, "Gooneybird" (his teammates called him that for his late-night behavior) posted an 11-5 record. In his next-to-last start of 1956, Larsen unveiled his no-windup delivery. "The ghouls sent me a message," he joked, explaining why.

Larsen started Game 2 in the World Series against Brooklyn. He was atrocious, walking four, allowing four runs in one and two-thirds innings. There was no one more shocked than the big right-hander when he learned when he arrived at Yankee Stadium that he would be the starter in Game 5. Now he was finishing it. "Everybody suddenly got scared we weren't playing the outfield right," Stengel said. "I never seen so many managers." The Yankee infield of first baseman Joe Collins, second baseman Billy Martin, shortstop Gil McDougald, and third baseman Andy Carey was ready for any kind of play.

The Yankees were clinging to a 2-0 lead scratched out against veteran Sal Maglie, age thirty-nine. Gilliam hit a hard one-hopper to short to open the seventh inning and was thrown out by McDougald. Reese and Snider flied out. In the eighth, Robinson grounded back to Larsen. Carey caught Hodges's low liner at third base. Amoros struck out. The huge crowd of 64,519 cheered each out. The game moved to the bottom of the ninth inning. "If it was 9-0, Larsen would've been paying little attention," Berra remembered. "It was close and he had to be extremely disciplined. He was. At the start of the ninth I didn't say a thing about how well he was throwing. I went to the mound and reminded him that if he walked one guy and the next guy hit one out, the game was tied."

"The last three outs were the toughest," the Indiana native recalled. "I was so weak in the knees that I thought I was going to faint. I was so nervous I almost fell down. My legs were rubbery. My fingers didn't feel like they belonged to me. I said to myself, 'Please help me somebody.'" The 64,519 in the stands were quiet. Four pitches were fouled off by Furillo, and then he hit a fly ball out to Batter in right field. Campanella grounded out weakly to Billy Martin at second base. Left-handed batter Dale Mitchell pinch hit for Maglie. It would be the final major league at bat for the thirty-five-year-old lifetime .312 hitter. Announcer Bob Wolff called it this way:

"Count is one and one. And this crowd just straining forward on every pitch. Here it comes . . . a swing and a miss! Two strikes, ball one to Dale Mitchell. Listen to this crowd! I'll guarantee that nobody—but nobody—has left this ball park. And if somebody did manage to leave early, man he's missing the greatest! Two strikes and a ball . . . Mitchell waiting, stands deep, feet close together. Larsen is ready, gets the sign. Two strikes, ball one, here comes the pitch. Strike three! A no-hitter! A perfect game for Don Larsen!"

That final pitch—Larsen's ninety-seventh of the game that took just two hours and six minutes—was the only one that elicited controversy. "The third strike on Mitchell was absolutely positively a strike on the outside corner," Berra maintains to this day. "No question about it. People say it was a ball and that I rushed the mound to hug Larsen to make the umpire think it was a strike. Nonsense. It was a perfect strike."

Casey Stengel was asked if that the best game he had ever seen Larsen pitch. "So far," was the Yankee manager's response.

The rest of Larsen's fourteen-year career—with eight teams—consisted of unbroken mediocrity punctuated with flashes of competence. He finished with an 81-91 record and 3.78 ERA.

Named the MVP of the Series by *Sport* magazine for his epic feat, Larsen received a Corvette. He also earned about $35,000 in endorsements and appearances, including $6,000 for being on Bob Hope's TV show. He spent $1,000 for plaques commemorating the game and gave them to his teammates, Yankee executives, the six umpires, his parents, and close friends.

The man who the reached perfection also received many letters and notes including this one:

Dear Mr. Larsen:

It is a noteworthy event when anybody achieves perfection in anything. It has been so long since anyone pitched a perfect big league game that I have to go back to my generation of ballplayers to recall such a thing—and that is truly a long time ago.

This note brings you my very sincere congratulations on a memorable feat, one that will inspire pitchers for a long time to come. With best wishes,

> Sincerely,
> Dwight D. Eisenhower
> President of the United States

"I pitched for fourteen years with eight different clubs and won only eighty-one games," Larsen said. "Hey, I gave it my best shot and I tried and I wish my record had been better, but I was very pleased to get into the World Series and pitch the Perfect Game. And I guess that is what I will always be remembered for. I have been asked a million times about the perfect game," Larsen mused. "I never dreamed about something like that happening. Everybody is entitled to a good day, and mine came at the right time."

Pesky Pole The right-field foul pole at Fenway Park in Boston is only 302 feet from home plate. Its name allegedly came from former Sox infielder Johnny Pesky's proclivity in hitting dingers past the pole. The facts: Pesky hit only seventeen home runs in his entire ten-year career, and only a half-dozen of those were at Fenway Park. The name "Pesky Pole" is supposed to have been coined by Mel Parnell after Pesky hit a homer there that helped Parnell win a game. But the phrase didn't become popular until the late 1980s or early 1990s.

Philadelphia Phillies The nickname derived from "Philly," an inhabitant of the city. In the early days, also spelled Fillies. From 1943 to 1944, the team was known as the "Blue Jays," and there was a time it was also known as the "Quakers."

Pickoff The retiring of a base runner through a throw to the player covering the base, who tags the runner before he can get back to the base.

Pickoff Play A set play aimed at picking off a base runner.

"Pie" Pie Traynor may have received his nickname for his favorite childhood food.

Pilot Another name for a baseball manager (Skipper).

Pinch Hit To come up to the plate to hit for another batter.

Pinch Hitter The player who comes up to the plate to hit for another batter.

Pinch Run To function as a substitute runner for another player. The substitute takes the other player's place at the base that the player had occupied.

Pinch Runner A generally faster runner who comes into a game to take the place of a man on base and to run for him.

Pine Tar Cloth saturated with tar that is rubbed on a batter's hands or bat for better grip.

Pine Tar Game The 1983 season was an up and down one for the Yankees. But on July 24, things were on the upside. They were positioned to take over first place as they prepared to play the Royals of Kansas City at Yankee Stadium. The game that was played that day was fairly ordinary. As it moved to the top of the ninth inning, the Yankees had a 4-3 lead. The Royals came to bat in the top of the ninth. No one could have forecast what would come next.

There were two outs. Goose Gossage was one out away from the wrap-up of the Yankee victory. George Brett had other ideas—home run, into the stands in right field!

The Royal superstar ran out the homer that had apparently given his team a 5-4 lead. But just seconds after crossing the plate and going into his dugout, Brett saw Yankee manager Billy Martin approach home plate rookie umpire Tim McClelland. "I was feeling pretty good about myself after hitting the homer," Brett said. "I was sitting in the dugout. Somebody said they were checking the pine tar, and I said, 'If they call me out for using too much pine tar, I'm going to kill one of those SOBs.'"

McClelland called to the Royal dugout and asked to see Brett's bat. Then he conferred with his umpiring crew. Martin watched from a few feet away. Brett looked out from the bench. Then McClelland thrust his arm in the air. It was the signal that indicated George Brett was out—excessive use of pine tar on his bat. McClelland had brought forth rule 1.10(b): "A bat may not be covered by such a substance more than 18 inches from the tip of the handle." The umpire ruled that Brett's bat had "heavy pine tar" nineteen–twenty inches from the tip of the handle and lighter pine tar for another three–four inches.

The home run was disallowed. The game was over. The Yankees were declared 4-3 winners. Brett, enraged, raced out of the dugout. Then mayhem and fury took center stage. Brett, not your calmest player, lost it. At one point, umpire Joe Brinkman had Brett in a choke hold. That was the easy part for the Royal superstar. Next, he was ejected from the game and went berserk. Others did, too. Royals pitcher Gaylord Perry grabbed the bat from McClelland who tossed it to Hal McRae who passed it on to pitcher Steve Renko who was halfway up the tunnel to the team clubhouse. Then Yankee Stadium security guards grabbed him and grabbed the bat which was then impounded.

The Royals lodged a protest of the Yankee victory. The Yankees went off to Texas where they won three games and took over first place for the first time that season. The almost comical mess was debated by baseball fans all over the nation. The media couldn't get enough of it. "Why a .356 hitter like George Brett," *Time* magazine commented, "would lumber along with a Marv Throneberry Model (lifetime .237) is the sort of paradox that, scientists say, has trees talking to themselves."

Eventually American League president Lee McPhail overturned McClelland's decision. Acknowledging that Brett had pine tar too high on the bat, McPhail explained that it was the league's belief that "games should be won and lost on the playing field—not through technicalities of the rules." Yankee owner George Steinbrenner was miffed. "I wouldn't want to be Lee MacPhail living in New York!" he snapped. The Brett home run was reinstated. The Royals' protest was upheld. The contest was declared "suspended." Both teams were told to find a mutually agreeable time, continue playing the game, and conclude it.

The date was August 18. Play was resumed for the last four outs of a game that had begun on July 24. The Yankees, strangely anxious to make a few more bucks, announced they would charge regular admission for the game's continuation. There were fan mumblings of protest. The Yankees quietly changed the charging admission idea. It was too late and to no avail. Only twelve hundred fans showed up.

The atmosphere was bizarre. To show their rage and annoyance at the whole turn of events, the Yankees for the final out of the top of the ninth played pitcher Ron Guidry in centerfield and outfielder Don Mattingly (a left-hander) at second base. Guidry played center field because the Yankees had traded away Jerry Mumphrey, who had come into the game for defensive purposes. New York's George Frazier struck out McRae for the third out. In the bottom of the ninth Royals' reliever Dan Quisenberry was able to retire the Yankees in order. The "Pine Tar Game" belonged to history.

"Pistol Pete" Pete Reiser played only a decade of major league baseball, fewer than one thousand games, but Harold Reiser exploded like a pistol on the fans and players of baseball in the early 1940s. In his second season (1941), he led the National League in batting (.343), and twice he was the stolen-base leader. Tragic collisions against the outfield walls in St. Louis and then in Brooklyn damaged him, slowed his talent, and reduced his skills. There are those who still wonder how great he might have been if not for the pounding he took against those unpadded outfield walls.

Pitch around a Batter To consciously refuse to give a batter a good pitch to hit, out of respect for the ability of the batter. A base on balls is sometimes given so as not to allow the batter to see pitches that he might be able to hit.

Pitcher The player who is positioned on the pitcher's mound who throws the ball to the plate (Hurler; Moundsman; Chucker; Twirler).

Pitcher-of-Record A pitcher officially liable to be charged with a win or loss even though he has been removed from a game. This condition prevails until or unless the score is tied and a new pitcher-of-record is established.

Pitcher's Duel A tough, low-scoring game, highlighted by effective pitching on both sides (Squeaker).

Pitcher's Mound Located on a line between home plate and second base, this raised surface is the area a pitcher operates on.

Pitcher's Plate twenty-four inches by six inches.

Pitcher's Toe Attachment to the front of a pitcher's shoe on the pivot foot, used to protect the top of the shoe and made of leather or plastic.

Pitching Chart A record; a complete statistical accounting of a pitching performance in a game, usually kept by the pitcher who is scheduled to start the next day.

Pitching Symbols:

Avg A Batting Average Against (Hitter's batting average against that pitcher) H/AB
BB Bases on Balls (Walks)
BF Batters Faced
BF/9 Batters Faced per Nine Innings
BK Balks
CG Complete Games
ERA Earned-Run Average (Earned Runs/Innings times Nine)
G Games
GB Ground Balls
GF Games Finished
GS Games Started
H Hits
HBP Hit by Pitch
HR Home Runs Allowed
IBB Intentional Bases on Balls
IP Innings Pitched
K Strikeouts

L Losses
R Runs
Sho Shutouts
Sv Saves
W Wins
WP Wild Pitches

Pitch Out To throw a pitch that is so far outside it can't be hit. The catcher catches the pitch standing to allow a quick throw to try picking off a runner.

Pittsburgh Pirates Pittsburgh entered the National League in 1887, assuming the Kansas City, Missouri, franchise. Regaled in garish, striped baseball uniforms at the start, the team was called the "Potato Bugs," "Zulus," "Smoked Italians," and "Alleghenies." The franchise was called the "Innocents" until 1891 when it signed second baseman Lou Bierbatter. His old club, the Philadelphia Athletics, and its fans weren't at all happy about the way Bierbatter was "obtained" and dubbed his new club the "Pirates" because they "pirated" the star player away from them. Not much happened after that as far as Bierbatter was concerned—he hit .206 that year—but he was the "loot" that earned the Pittsburgh franchise the name Pirates.

Pivot A second baseman's turning maneuver as he touches the base with one foot and whirls about to throw to first base to complete a double-play attempt.

Plate Umpire The home plate umpire.

Platoon To alternate players at one position.

Playoffs Postseason competition to determine league entry into the World Series.

PNC Park Ceremonial groundbreaking for PNC Park took place on April 7, 1999, and opening day took place just two years later on April 9, 2001, with a sellout crowd of 36,954 at the new home of the Pirates named after PNC Bank, which paid in excess of $30 million for the naming rights.

Pole the Ball To hit the ball with power.

Polo Grounds During the 1880s, the National League baseball team was known as the New Yorkers. There was another team in town, the New York Metropolitans of the fledgling American Association. Both teams played their season-opening games on a field across from Central Park's northeastern corner at 110th Street and Fifth Avenue. The land on which they played was owned by *New York Herald Tribune* publisher James Gordon Bennett. Bennett and his society friends had played polo on that field and that's how the baseball field came to be known as the Polo Grounds. In 1889 the New York National League team moved its games to a new location at 157th Street and Eighth Avenue. The site was dubbed the New Polo Grounds and eventually was simply called the Polo Grounds. Polo was never played there.

"Pop" Eddie Popowski didn't take the field in the major league as a player, but "Pop" spent sixty-five years as a member of the Boston Red Sox franchise. He first joined the Red Sox organization in 1937, spending time as a player.

Pop Fly, Pop It Up, Pop-Up, Pop All signify a short fly ball.

Pop-Foul A short, foul fly ball.

Pop Out To be retired on a short fly ball.

Popping the Ball The act of a pitcher throwing the ball so hard at the catcher that it can be heard "popping" into the catcher's mitt.

"Pops" Hall of Fame outfielder Willie Stargell led the Pittsburgh Pirates family for twenty-one years.

Porky Former slabman Half Reniff, a bit on that side.

Power Alley An area in the outfield that a particular player can hit to with power; the areas between center field and right field, and center field and left field, where many home runs are hit.

Power the Ball The ability to hit or throw the ball with force.

"Pride of Penacook" Former Yankee third baseman Red Rolfe's nickname came from the little town he hailed from in New Hampshire.

"Pride of the Yankees" Lou Gehrig was that.

"Prince Hal" Charismatic, elegant Hal Chase had a royal quality about him.

"Prince of the City" Derek Jeter, for his good looks and almost elegant bearing.

"Principal Owner" George Steinbrenner, no doubt here.

Protect the Plate The defensive behavior of a batter swinging at pitches that he thinks may be called strikes.

Protect the Runner The act of a hitter swinging at any pitch in a hit-and-run or steal situation to attempt to hamper a catcher's throw aimed at putting out the runner.

"Pud" Galvin was also known as "The Little Steam Engine" and "Gentle Jeems." "Pud" was short for "pudding."

"Pudge" Hall of fame catcher Carlton Fisk was called by this nickname for his chunky physique as a youngster and teenager.

"Pudge" ("I-Rod") Ivan Rodriguez as a youth earned the nickname not due to comparisons with catching great Carlton Fisk, but in reference to his weight.

Pull Hitter One who pulls the ball.

Pull the Ball The act of a hitter swinging in such a way that the ball will be hit to the same side of the field from which he bats: a right-handed hitter pulls to left field, a left-handed hitter pulls to right field. This situation is the reverse of hitting to the opposite field.

"Push Button Manager" Joe McCarthy, for his by-the-book ways.

Putout The actual act of retiring a player; the first baseman who catches the ball thrown by a shortstop to retire the runner streaking down the first base line gets credit for a putout, for example.

"Rabbit Maranville" Walter James Vincent Maranville's nickname was rooted in his slight size (he was 5' 5" and 155 pounds) and the way he scampered around the bases and sprightly played his shortstop position throughout a twenty-three-year major league career. Maranville averaged approximately one home run per year throughout his career, but he more than made up for his power deficiency by averaging nearly a hit a game. He stole 291 bases and scored more than 1,200 runs—part of the reason for his nickname and his Hall of Fame admission in 1954.

"Ragin' Cajun" Ron Guidry, for temperament and Louisiana roots.

"Rags" Dave Righetti, abbreviation for his name.

Rain Check Baseball games are cancelled for rain, but must be rescheduled.

"Rajah" Baseball Hall of Famer Rogers Hornsby had a lifetime batting average of .358 and was one of the few men in baseball history to bat .400 three times. Hornsby gained his nickname through what some claimed was a contemptuous pronunciation of his first name—a less-than-appealing reference to his petulant personality. One of the greatest hitters of all time, Hornsby would not go to the movies or read newspapers for fear of straining his keen vision and thus marring his ability to select the right pitches to swing at. He was a regal and special talent and personality.

"Rapid Robert" Hall of Famer Bob Feller pitched for the Cleveland Indians for eighteen seasons, winning 266 games. In his major league debut, on August 23, 1936, the Van Meter, Iowa, farm boy, then seventeen years old, struck out the first eight men to face him and then seven more, for a total of fifteen—one short of the then-league record. The blazing speed and power he was able to put on his fastball earned him his nickname. The twelve one-hitters and three no-hitters that Feller recorded in his career helped earn him his reputation as one of baseball's premier hurlers.

"Reading Rifle" Carl Furillo played fifteen years for the Dodgers and for most of those years was a virtual fixture in right field. He was born in Stony Creek Mills, Pennsylvania, close to Reading, and this, coupled with the power of his throwing arm, earned him his nickname. He was also known as "Skoonj," a corruption of the word *scungilli*, which was a favorite dish of the Italian-American player.

"Red Rooster" Doug Rader, for red hair and roosterlike behavior.

"Reg-ger-oo" Name given by Howard Cosell to Reggie Jackson, an endearing reference.

"Rhino" Roy Hitt, a squat, 5' 10", 200-pound pitcher for Cincinnati in the early 1900s, whose shape reminded people of a rhinoceros.

Road Grays Away uniform, nonwhite these days.

"Road Runner II" Even nicknames have been protected by the law. The Atlanta Braves signed an agreement with Warner Brothers that granted the Braves the right to call one of their baseball players by this name after the cartoon character. The agreement made it illegal for any other athlete to use the name.

"Rocket" Roger Clemens, for the speed and power of his fastball.

Roof Shot Home run that lands in the upper deck of a ballpark.

"Root" Yankee owner Jake Ruppert's way of (mis)pronouncing Babe Ruth's surname.

Rhubarb Noisy or heated argument on the playing field.

Roberto Clemente Man of the Year Award Given annually to player for sportsmanship and community service.

"Rock" Tim Raines, for his rock-solid build and dependability. Earl Averill earned this nickname for consistent play and a solid physical build. "Popeye" and "Rockhead" were other Averill nicknames for his physical appearance.

Rolaids Relief Man Award Given to a relief pitcher in each league for outstanding performance; sponsored by Rolaids since 1976.

"Rooting for the New York Yankees Is Like Rooting for General Motors" During the 1950s the New York Yankees, powered by Mickey Mantle, Whitey Ford, Phil Rizzuto, Allie Reynolds, Jerry Coleman, Yogi Berra, Eddie Lopat, Elston Howard, Bill Skowron, and others, won eight World Series. They seemed to get better, to acquire more and more talent each year, to win with amazing regularity—even monotony. This line attributed to an anti-Yankee—and perhaps an anticorporate—Giant fan, underscored the mechanical, profitable winning ways of the New York team.

"Rubberarm" As a starter and reliever, 1915–1919, Alan Russell never turned his back on a chance to pitch.

"Rube" Rube Waddell earned this nickname because he was a big, fresh, country kid as a rookie. "Rube" was a term used to refer to farmboys. The left-handed hurler went on to become a Hall of Famer.

"Running Redbird" Lou Brock earned this for his base-stealing skills as a member of the St. Louis Cardinals.

"Ruppert Rifles" The Yankees during owner Jake Ruppert's tenure.

"Ruthville" Bleachers in right-center where Babe Ruth hit home runs.

"The Ryan Express" Nolan Ryan, star fastballer, picked up the nickname from a movie of that name in his era. A tremendous work ethic was another. Nolan had 992,040 votes to rank first among all pitchers on the All-Century team. He was followed by Sandy Koufax (970,434), Cy Young (867,523), Roger Clemens (601,244), and Bob Gibson (582,031). That's elite company. One can only wonder what went through Nolan's mind out there on the field next to Bob Gibson, Hank Aaron, and Sandy Koufax. Aaron was one of Ryan's idols in his growing-up years, and Koufax was a pitcher he truly admired.

In his autorbiography *Throwing Heat*, cowritten with Harvey Frommer, your faithful scribe, he reminisced, "One Sunday between my junior and senior years in high school we went to see the Houston Colt .45s play the Los Angeles Dodgers. Sandy Koufax was pitching, and I was a big Koufax fan. It was the first time I had ever seen Sandy pitch. I was truly amazed at how fast he was and how good a curveball he had. I think he was the most overpowering pitcher I had ever seen."

The all-time strikeout record belongs to Nolan now. But once upon a time, and for a long period, it belonged to Walter Johnson, who finished in sixth-place in the voting for pitchers with 479,279 votes. One day early in the 1969 season, Nolan was sitting in the Mets' dugout when Jim Bunning recorded his 2500th strikeout. He asked Tom Seaver what the all-time record for strikeouts was and was told that it was 3,508 and held by Walter Johnson.

"That Johnson record will probably stand forever," Ryan told Seaver. Baseball fans know it didn't. Nolan broke it and is the all-time strikeout leader with 5,714. That Ryan record will probably stand forever, as will a few other records Nolan picked up along the way. He holds the record for most strikeouts in a major league season with 383, which he set while playing for the Angels in 1973. He struck out one hundred in a season twenty-four times, another record. He also set the record for most consecutive seasons with one hundred or more strikeouts, doing it twenty-three times in a row. Ryan holds the record for most career no-hitters with seven.

"Ryno" For Ryne Sandberg, former star of the Chicago Cubs, a variation of his given name and an acknowledgment of his grit.

Sack Base (Bag).

Sacrifice A bunted ball that advances a teammate, or a ball hit to the outfield that enables a runner to tag up and score. The player committing the sacrifice does not reach base, but he also does not get a time at bat charged against his batting average (Sacrifice Bunt; Sacrifice Hit; Sacrifice Fly).

"Sad Sam" Jones The former pitcher earned the nickname "Sad Sam" or "Sad Sam the Cemetery Man" for his somber demeanor.

Safety Base hit, single.

Safety Squeeze Takes place when the runner waits to see how effective the bunt is.

"Sailor Bob" Bob Shawkey spent most of 1918 in the Navy as a yeoman petty officer aboard the battleship *Arkansas.*

San Diego Padres For the Spanish word for priest, inspired by the padres of the Roman Catholic Mission San Diego de Alcala.

Sanitaries Athletic hose.

"Satchel" The immortal pitcher Leroy Paige received his nickname when he was seven years old. Back then he carried passengers' small bags, known as satchels, at the local railroad station in his hometown of Mobile, Alabama. Paige was a longtime star in the Negro Leagues—there are estimates that he pitched for thirty-three years and won more than two thousand games. Traveling all over the world to play baseball—by car, by bus, by train, some days also by horse and carriage—wherever there was a game, the lanky hurler was there. His nickname came from the fact that most of those years he lived out of his "satchel" or suitcase. Paige was proud of his nickname and even wore it on his uniform.

A bone-thin 6' 3" with size 12 flat feet, he billed himself as "The World's Greatest Pitcher." Paige claimed that his real secret of success stemmed from the fact that "even though I got old, my arm stayed nineteen." He was vigorously opposed to exercise. "I believe in training," he joked, "by rising up and down gently from the bench." Paige's rules for successful living were: 1) avoid fried meats which angry up the blood; 2) if your stomach disputes you, lie down and pacify it with cool thoughts; 3) keep your juices flowing by jangling around gently as you move; 4) go very gently on the vices such as carrying on in society—the social ramble ain't restful; 5) avoid running at all times; and 6) don't look back, something might be gaining on you. Through all the long and difficult years in the Negro Leagues, Paige hungered for a shot at the majors. The Cleveland Indians needed extra pitching, and their owner Bill Veeck was interested in Paige. As the story goes, Veeck wanted to test Paige's control before signing him to a contract. Allegedly Veeck placed a cigarette on the ground—a simulation of home plate. Paige took aim. Five fastballs were fired—all but one sailed directly over the cigarette. Paige got his contract!

On July 9, 1948, Leroy Robert Paige arrived on the major league baseball scene as a rookie pitcher for the Cleveland Indians. He gave his official age as "42???" to owner Bill Veeck. His exact age was always clouded in mystery and rarely did he answer questions about it. And when he did, he quipped: "Age is a question of mind over matter. If you don't mind, it doesn't matter." But he definitely was the oldest rookie ever to play in the majors.

In 1948, Satchel won six games and lost only one, compiled a fine 2.48 earned run average, and helped pitch the Indians to the pennant and World Series victory that year. Three years later Veeck was reunited with Paige, this time with the St. Louis Browns. Satchel passed the time away relaxing in his personal rocking chair in the bullpen when he was not pitching. There were appearances in the All-Star games of 1952 and 1953. And then he was done—for a time.

In 1965, a year that would have made him fifty-nine years old based on his "official birthday" (July 7, 1906, in Mobile, Alabama), he pitched three shutout innings for the Kansas City Athletics to become the oldest man to pitch in a major league game. It was the last time he took the mound. In 1971, on what he called the proudest day of his life, Leroy "Satchel" Paige was elected to the National Baseball Hall of Fame. He was the first player ever elected from the Negro Leagues.

Satchel Paige passed away on June 8, 1982, in Kansas City, Missouri. But stories of what he said and did have grown through the years, as the man has become both a myth and a legend. It is like the big fish story—the size of the fish caught grows bigger with each telling of the tale. Nevertheless, Paige had the right stuff, hyperbole notwithstanding.

Satchel reportedly began his professional career in 1926 and was an immediate gate attraction with his dazzling variety of pitches, and words for every occasion. He played baseball year-round, often pitching two games a day in two different cities in the Negro Leagues.

Joining the Pittsburgh Crawfords during the early 1930s, Satch was 32-7 and 31-4 in 1932 and 1933, respectively. But his time with the team was always interrupted by salary disputes. In those instances, Paige would go on barnstorming gigs for more money and compete against all levels of competition including top major league players.

He played in the Dominican Republic and then Mexico, where he developed a sore arm. In 1938, he signed with the Kansas City Monarchs and his arm was better than ever. With the Monarchs, Paige had his complete pitching arsenal on display. He had a wide breaking curveball, and his famous "hesitation pitch" that came out of a windup that looked like slow motion. He also had a "bee-ball," a "jump-ball," a "trouble-ball," a "long-ball," and other pitches without names that he made up as he went along.

Satchel pitched the Monarchs to four straight Negro American League pennants (1939–1942), accentuated by a clean sweep of the powerful Homestead Grays in the 1942 Negro Leagues World Series. Satchel won three of the games in that series. In 1946, he helped pitch the Monarchs to their fifth pennant during his time with the team. Satchel also pitched in five East-West Black All-Star games.

In his time he graced, and dressed up, the rosters of the Birmingham Black Barons, the Baltimore Black Sox, the Cleveland Cubs, the Pittsburgh Crawfords, the Kansas City Monarchs, the New York Black Yankees, the Memphis Red Sox, and the Philadelphia Stars. His career spanned five decades. In his time he was acknowledged as the greatest pitcher in the history of the Negro Leagues. It was a time when he had a string of sixty-four consecutive scoreless innings, and a stretch of twenty-one straight wins.

It was also a time when some saw Paige bring his outfielders in and have them sit behind the mound while he proceeded to strike out the other side, and when some commented on how he intentionally walked the bases loaded so that he could pitch to Josh Gibson, black baseball's best hitter.

It was a time when there were the "out-of-thin-air-you-had-to-be-there" stories: Paige and his habit of striking out the first nine batters he faced in exhibition games; Paige and his firing twenty straight pitches across a chewing gum wrapper—a very mini home plate; Paige throwing so hard that the ball disappeared before it reached the catcher's mitt.

The man they called "World's Greatest Pitcher" had a lot to say about his craft. "I never threw an illegal pitch. The trouble is, once in a while I would toss one that ain't never been seen by this generation. Just take the ball and throw it where you want to. Throw strikes. Home plate don't move." "They said I was the greatest pitcher they ever saw. . . . I couldn't understand why they couldn't give me no justice." Joe DiMaggio called him "the best and fastest pitcher I've ever faced."

Save Credit given to relief pitcher for protecting team's victory.

"Say Hey" Both a greeting and a nickname—and also a condition—this term belonged to Willie Mays. Regarded by many as the greatest player baseball has ever known (and in 1979, voted into the Hall of Fame), Mays pounded 660 homers and over three thousand hits (better than a hit a game), scored over two thousand runs, drew nearly fifteen hundred walks, drove in nearly two thousand runs, and compiled a lifetime batting average of .302. The image of Mays in a Giants uniform stealing a base, hitting the ball out of the park, racing back to make a sensational catch running out from under his cap—all underscore the verve of the man they called the "Say Hey Kid." Willie Howard Mays was born on May 6, 1931, in Westfield, Alabama. The New York Giants called him up on May 15, 1951, from Minneapolis in the American Association. He was bating .477 after thirty-five games.

Garry Schumacher, publicist for the Giants at that time, recalled the first time he ever saw Mays. "The Giants were on their way from Chicago to Philadelphia to conclude the last three games of a road trip," Schumacher said. "I was by the front door of the Giants' office on Times Square. Suddenly, this kid comes in. There were always a lot of kids coming around; some of them wanted tickets and some wanted tryouts. He was carrying a few bats in one hand and a bag in the other that contained his glove and spikes. He was wearing the most unusual cap I ever saw, plaid colored. When I found out who he was, we bought him some clothes and then sent him to Philadelphia to join the club. He was wearing the new clothes when he left, but funny thing—he refused to take off that funny cap."

Mays made his major league debut with the Giants on May 25, 1951. But his start in the majors after just 116 minor leagues games was a shaky one. He was hitless in his first twelve at-bats, cried in the dugout, and said, "I am not ready for this." He begged manager Leo Durocher to send him back down to the minors.

Baseball

But "Leo the Lip" refused to listen to the pleas of the rookie center fielder just as another Giant manager, John J. McGraw, had refused to send a youthful Mel Ott to the minors. "You're my center fielder as long as I am the manager of this team," Durocher said. "You're the best center fielder I have ever seen."

Mays's first home run was off the great Warren Spahn. He hit it over the roof of the Polo Grounds. "We had a meeting of the pitchers," Spahn recalls. "We knew Mays was having trouble. I'll never forgive myself. We might have gotten rid of Willie forever if I'd only struck him out."

In Pittsburgh's old Forbes Field, Rocky Nelson blasted a drive 457 feet to deep dead center. Galloping back, Mays realized as his feet hit the warning track that the ball was hooking to his right side. The ball was sinking and Mays could not reach across his body to glove the drive. So just as the ball got to his level, Mays stuck out his bare hand and made the catch. It was an incredible feat.

Durocher told all the Giants to give Mays the silent treatment when he returned to the dugout. But Pittsburgh's General Manager Branch Ricky sent the Giant rookie a hastily written note: "That was the finest catch I have ever seen . . . and the finest I ever expect to see."

There is that catch and so many others. There are also the images of Mays playing stickball in the streets of Harlem with neighborhood kids, running out from under his cap pursuing a fly ball, pounding one of his 660 career home runs, playing the game with a verve, a gusto, and an attitude that awed those who were around him.

"Willie could do everything from the day he joined the Giants," Durocher recalled. "Everybody loved him," notes his former teammate Monte Irvin. "He was a rare talent. Having him on your team playing center field gave us confidence. We figured that if a ball stayed in the park, he could catch it."

Mays was "The Natural." He led the NL in slugging percentage five times. He won the home run crown four times. Twice, he won the NL MVP Award. "He lit up a room when he came in," Durocher said. The superstar of superstars, the man they called the "Say Hey Kid," was on the scene for twenty-two major-league seasons. He is all over the record book and in the memory of so many baseball fans.

"Say It Ain't So, Joe" This often-repeated sentence, used frequently in song and story, had its origins in the emotions of a little boy. After the 1919 Chicago "Black Sox" World Series scandal, a lad walked up to Shoeless Joe Jackson, one of the accused players, and made the plea to his idol (see Black Sox and "Shoeless Joe").

Scatter the Hits The yielding by a pitcher of a good number of hits that are spaced over several innings to hamper opposition scoring.

"Schnozz" ("Bocci") His given name was Ernesto Natali Lombardi, but all knew him as Ernie. The Hall of Fame catcher had a big nose and liked to play bocci.

"Schoolboy Wonder" Waite Hoyt made his major league debut in 1918 when he was a teenager. He struck out two of the three batters he faced.

"The Scooter" Phil Rizzuto pedaled about at shortstop for thirteen years as a member of the New York Yankees. His small stature (5' 6", 150 pounds) and his agile ways in the field earned him his nickname coined by Mel Allen. The first time Allen saw the little man run he said, "Man, you're not running, you're scootin'". (see "Holy Cow").

Score The amount of runs each team achieves or is achieving at a given moment in a game; to drive in a run; to cross the plate and tally a run.

Scoreboard A highly visible board, generally beyond the outfield, that gives information about the score, the batting orders, the pitchers, other games in progress, or scheduled coming events.

Scorecard A program purchased at ballparks by fans, who use it to keep score of the game in progress.

Scoring Position Location on the bases (generally second or third) from which a player can score on a hit or a fly ball.

"Scrap Iron" Former Houston player, then manager, Phil Garner, for his feisty ways.

Scratch for Runs To have difficulty in scoring.

Scratch Hit A questionable hit that barely enables a runner to reach base safely.

Screen A wire barrier covering the area in the stands behind home plate to prevent fans from being hit by foul balls.

Screwball A seemingly straight pitch which unexpectedly swerves to the right, when thrown by a right-handed pitcher, or to the left, when thrown by a left-handed pitcher (Scroogie).

Seattle Mariners The franchise name reflects the nautical heritage of Washington state.

Second Base The base midway between first base and third base and lined up with home plate (Second).

Second Baseman A fielder positioned, normally, to the right of second base. This player is a key man in double plays and in covering the area around his position and between first and second base.

"Second Place Joe" Joe McCarthy's three straight second-place finishes prompted the nickname before the Yanks won four consecutive world championships, 1936-1939. The name was also used when he was manager of the Cubs and had some disappointing second-place finishes.

"Senator" Steve Garvey projected his Mr. Clean image to the nation in a television interview before the 1974 World Series when he explained that his nickname, "Senator," referred to his postbaseball political aspirations.

Set Down in Order To retire a side in order with no hits, no walks, no errors, and no runs.

Set Position A pitcher's stance assumed after a stretch—the ball is held in front of the body, with one foot positioned on the rubber.

Set the Table Get on base before more powerful batters.

Setup Man A relief pitcher who is consistently used immediately before the closer.

Seventh-Inning Stretch A baseball custom that enables fans to stand and to stretch a few moments before the half of the seventh inning that the team they are rooting for comes to bat.

Shade The act of defensive players moving slightly toward the side of a position they expect a batter to hit to.

Shagger One who collects balls on the field during batting practice.

Shake Off a Sign A situation where a pitcher will not accept a sign for a pitch given by a catcher and will indicate this by head or glove movement.

Shea Stadium On October 17, 1960, the National League awarded a New York City baseball franchise to a team that would be known as the Mets. That October day was the culmination of the efforts of a special mayoral committee appointed to find a way to return National League baseball to New York. Attorney William Shea headed the committee. The Mets' stadium, located in Flushing Meadows, Queens, near the site of the old World's Fair, is named for the man who was instrumental in acting as the godfather of the New York Mets.

Shell a Pitcher To get quite a few hits and runs off a pitcher, generally in a brief period of time.

Shift To move players from traditional defensive positions to other locations to compensate for a hitter's pattern.

"Shoeless Joe" Joseph Jefferson Wofford Jackson was born to a poor family on July 16, 1889, in Greenville, South Carolina. School was never a part of his life, for at the age of six he was already working in the cotton mills as a cleanup boy. By the time he was thirteen he was laboring a dozen hours a day along with his father and brother. His sole escape from the backbreaking work, the din and dust of the mill, took place out in the grassy fields playing baseball. He was a natural right from the start, good enough to be noticed and recruited to play for the mill team organized by the company.

One hot summer day Jackson played the outfield wearing a new pair of shoes. They pinched his feet, so he took them off and played in his stocking feet. A sportswriter who saw what he did dubbed him "Shoeless Joe." The name stuck even though that was the only time Jackson is reported to have played shoeless.

He despised the name, for he felt it reinforced his country bumpkin origins, and the fact that he could not read or write. Perhaps that was why when he played for the Chicago White Sox after stints with the Philadelphia Athletics and Cleveland Indians, he wore alligator and patent leather shoes—the more expensive the better. It was as if he were announcing to the world: "I am not a 'Shoeless Joe.' I do wear shoes. And they cost a lot of money!"

He was the greatest ballplayer ever from South Carolina, one of the top players of all time. His lifetime batting average was .356, topped only by Ty Cobb and Rogers Hornsby. Four times he batted over .370. Babe Ruth copied his swing claiming Jackson was the greatest hitter he ever saw. Ruth, Cobb, and Casey Stengel all placed him on their all-time, all-star team. He was such a remarkable fielder that his glove was called "the place where triples go to die."

In the National Baseball Hall of Fame at Cooperstown one can find Jackson's shoes. His life-size photograph is there. But he is not there, even though others with far less credentials and far more soiled reputations are. Shoeless Joe had to leave the game in disgrace, one of the members of the "Black Sox" accused of throwing the 1919 World Series.

He was asked under oath at trial:

"Did you do anything to throw those games?"

"No sir," was his response.

"Any game in the series?"

"Not a one," Jackson answered. "I didn't have an error or make no misplay."

In fact, Shoeless Joe was understating his accomplishments, which included the only series home run, the highest batting average, and the collecting of a record dozen hits, while committing no errors.

It took the jury a single ballot to acquit all eight accused players of the charges against them. But the very next day baseball's first commissioner—Judge Kenesaw Mountain Landis—issued a verdict of his own. He banned all eight players from baseball for life. Landis was brought into organized baseball in the fall of 1920 with a lifetime contract and a mandate to clean up the game using whatever methods he saw fit. He had the reputation of being a vindictive judge, a hanging judge—and he was all of that.

Every baseball commissioner since Landis has refused to act on Shoeless Joe's behalf.

Commissioner Faye Vincent said: "I can't uncipher or decipher what took place back then. I have no intention of taking formal action." Commissioner Bart Giammatti said: "I do not wish to play God with history. The Jackson case is best left to historical debate and analysis. I am not for re-instatement."

Public pressure keeps increasing year by year. But the ban still remains. It is a story that won't go away, like a riddle inside a jigsaw puzzle inside an enigma. It is a story about a great baseball injustice—a talented player caught at a crossroad in American history, who became a victim, a scapegoat, so that the sport of baseball could offer up a cleaner image.

Shoestring Catch The grabbing of a fly ball by an outfielder just as it is about to hit the ground.

Shorten Up the Infield A defensive move in which infielders move in closer to the plate.

Short-Hop To grab a batted ball by charging in at it and seizing it before it bounces high.

Short Porch The right-field stands in Yankee Stadium.

Short Reliever A relief pitcher who pitches for a brief time (Short Relief; Spot Reliever; Short Man).

Shortstop A player positioned between third base and second base, closer to second, who has double-play responsibilities as a main part of his job.

Shot A hard-hit ball.

Shotgun Arm A powerful throwing arm.

Shot Heard 'round the World (Dat Day; Miracle at Coogan's Bluff) On October 3, 1951, at 3:58 p.m. in the Polo Grounds in New York City, in the last game of the play-off's last inning, Bobby Thomson pounded a one-strike fastball thrown by Ralph Branca. The ball went out on a low and curving line and landed 315 feet away from home plate in the stands. The Polo Grounds exploded with frantic fans and excited ball players. On the radio, New York Giants announcer Russ Hodges screamed out eight times in a row, "The Giants win the pennant!" Not only had the Giants come from thirteen and one-half games back in mid-August to this moment, they had beaten their archrivals, the great Brooklyn Dodgers, by scoring four runs in the bottom of the ninth inning. On the streets of New York City, the word went out. In Brooklyn there was sadness, and comedian Phil Foster referred to the time as "Dat Day" in his best alliterative Brooklynese. Others called it the "Shot Heard 'round the World," while Giant fans were content to savor the moment as the miracle that took place at Coogan's Bluff, the geographical region where the Polo Grounds was located.

Shutout A game in which a pitcher holds the opposition scoreless.

Sidearmer A pitcher who throws the ball to the plate from a sidearm position, as opposed to overhanded.

"Silent Bob" Name given to Bob Meusel because of his aloofness.

"Silent One" Name given by Howard Cosell to Chris Chambliss, for his taciturn manner.

Silver Slugger Award One given to the best offensive player in each league for each position.

"Singer Throwing Machine" Bill Singer's time as a pitcher in the major leagues, from 1964 to 1973, saw him compile a record of eighty-nine wins and ninety losses. His nickname was a play on words with the Singer sewing machine.

Single A one-base hit.

Single in a Run To score a runner by hitting a single.

Sinker A pitch that drops as it nears the plate.

Sinking Liner A line drive that drops as it gathers distance.

Skimmer A batted ball that rapidly glides across the ground.

Skip Rope A quick, jumping movement by a batter to get out of the way of a pitched ball that is coming too close to him.

Skull To bean or hit a batter in the head with a pitched ball.

Sky Out To hit the ball high in the air and have it caught (Rainmaker).

Slab The pitcher's rubber.

"Slammin' Sammy" Sammy Sosa, former Cub hero, for his power feats.

Slash the Ball To hit the ball sharply to the outfield.

Slice Foul When a fly ball or line drive starts out over fair territory, then curves into foul territory due to aerodynamic force caused by spinning of the ball, imparted by the bat.

Slice the Ball To hit the ball so that, for example, it veers left when batted by a left-handed hitter.

"Slick" Whitey Ford used a spitter to strike out Willie Mays in the 1964 All-Star Game. That was just one of the reasons for the Yankee star's nickname.

Slide The action of a base runner hitting the ground and coming into a base head or feet first. A belly slide is a variation in which a player flops on his belly with hands outstretched toward the base.

Slider A hard breaking pitch with less overall motion than a curve ball.

"Sliding Billy" He played from 1888 to 1901, and in that time stole 912 bases. A 5' 6", 165-pounder, William Robert ("Billy") Hamilton three years in a row stole over a hundred bases. His steals and his slides earned him his nickname. His reputation coupled with a .344 lifetime batting average was good enough to get him admitted to baseball's Hall of Fame in 1961.

Slip Pitch A dropping pitch that comes toward the plate with off-speed velocity.

"Slow" Joe Doyle, New York Highlanders, because of his time-consuming pace.

Slugger A player who gets long extra-base hits.

Slugging Average The ratio of total bases achieved to number of times at bat, which indicates the extra-base capability of the batter.

Slugging Duel A game with many hits and many runs scored (Slugfest).

Slump A period of ineffectiveness for a team or an individual.

Smash A powerfully hit ball.

Smoking It The throwing of pitches with top velocity—throwing "smoke."

Softball The sport was originally called kittenball when it was played indoors with an oversized baseball in 1895. Lewis Robert, a Minneapolis firefighter, is credited with making the first softball—a softer and larger version of the ball used in baseball. It is alleged that firehouse spare time inspired Lewis to innovate what was at first an indoor game that was played on a field with a diamond about two-thirds the size of the normal baseball diamond. By the turn of the century, the sport had moved outdoors and had a distinctive rule requiring that pitchers throw underhand. In 1933 the sport was given a new name, "softball," and was a featured part of the Century of Progress World's Fair in Chicago. Its new name came from the softness of the ball and, indeed, there are today those who refer to baseball as "hardball," to distinguish the two sports.

Soft Liner A line drive that is hit without much force.

Softly Hit Ball A ball that is hit without much force.

"Solid Citizens" The name Hall of Fame manager Joe McCarthy gave to players he relied on.

Solid Contact The act of hitting the ball and getting "good wood" or the fat part of the bat into contact with the ball.

Solo Clout A home run with no one on base.

"Sooner with Spooner" In 1954 Karl Benjamin Spooner, left-handed pitcher, joined the Brooklyn Dodgers. He pitched two complete games, yielding no runs and a total of only seven hits, and amazingly he struck out a grand total of twenty-seven batters. The Brooklyn fans switched from their traditional slogan of "Wait 'til next year" to one that had more immediate promise, "Sooner with Spooner." Sadly, as has occurred with so many baseball phenomenons, Spooner soon faded. In 1955 he won eight games and lost six, and by 1956 he was through as a major leaguer.

Sophomore Jinx The tendency for players to follow a good rookie season with a less spectacular one.

"Soup" Clarence Campbell, who hit three home runs in the major leagues, died on February 16, 2000. He played in 104 games for the Indians in 1941 and hit .250 with three home runs and thirty-five RBI.

Southpaw To avoid the sun shining into the eyes of a batter during the afternoon, ball fields were built with center field due east of home plate. A right-handed pitcher's throwing hand would thus point north as he faced a batter. That was how a left-handed hurler became a "southpaw."

Southpaw Slants The pitching style of a left-handed pitcher.

"Space Man" Bill Lee, former pitcher, always was a bit "spacey."

"Spahn and Sain and Pray for Rain" The Boston Braves of the late 1940s were a pretty successful baseball team. A large part of their success resulted from the efforts of pitchers Warren Spahn and Johnny Sain.

In 1947 the dynamic duo accounted for forty-two wins between them. The following year they won a total of thirty-nine games and powered the Braves to the National League pennant. "There was more than Spahn and Sain," remembers former Braves traveling secretary Don Davidson. "There were a couple of guys named Bobby Hogue and Nelson Potter, but hardly anybody remembers them." The "Spahn and Sain" slogan was actually a throwback to "Tyler, James, and Rudolph"—a slogan of the 1914 "Miracle Braves." George Tyler, Bill James, and Dick Rudolph were the winning pitchers in sixty-nine of the club's ninety-four victories. Day after day for sixty straight games, the trio alternated as pitchers for that 1914 Boston Braves team (see "Miracle Braves").

Spaldeen The name of the bouncing rubber ball that is part of the memory of most Americans is a shortened or "sweetened" form of Alfred Goodwill Spalding's name (see Spalding).

Spalding Alfred Goodwill Spalding (1850–1915) is a member of baseball's Hall of Fame. In 1871 he won twenty-one games. Then he went on to post records of 36-8, 41-15, 52-18, and 56-5. At the age of twenty-six, in 1876, Spalding managed the Chicago White Stockings to the pennant and helped his own cause by winning forty-six games. In 1880 he packed it in as an active major leaguer and founded a sporting goods firm that made a fortune—and made his name part of the language. His rigid specifications for the manufacture of baseballs gave stability and uniformity to the balls used in the sport up to that time. His name became a synonym for a baseball (see Spaldeen).

Spear a Liner To catch a line drive by running it down and catching it with the arms fully extended.

Spike To inflict injury on another player with the spikes of baseball shoes—in sliding situations, for example.

Spikes Metal projections on the bottom of the shoes worn by baseball players, cleats.

Spitter An illegal pitch that involves a pitcher placing saliva or some other moist substance on the pitch to make it break oddly as it comes to the batter (Spitball; Moist Pitch; Wet Pitch).

"Splendid Splinter" He was also nicknamed the "Thumper," because of the power with which he hit the ball, and the "Kid," because of his tempestuous attitude—but his main nickname was perhaps the most appropriate. Ted Williams was one of the most splendid players who ever lived, and he could really "splinter" the ball. The handsome slugger compiled a lifetime batting average of .344 and a slugging percentage of .634. Williams blasted 521 career home runs, scored nearly 1,800 runs, and drove in over 1,800 runs. So keen was his batting eye that he walked over 2,000 times while striking out only 709 times. In 1941 he batted .406—the last time any player hit .400 or better. One of the most celebrated moments in the career of the Boston Red Sox slugger took place in the 1946 All-Star Game. Williams came to bat against Rip Sewell and his celebrated "eephus" (blooper) pitch. Williams had already walked in the game and hit a home run. Sewell's pitch came to the plate in a high arc, and Williams actually trotted out to the pitch, bashing it into the right-field bullpen for a home run. "That was the first homer ever hit off the pitch," Sewell said later.

"The ball came to the plate in a twenty-foot arc," recalled Williams. "I didn't know whether I'd be able to get enough power into that kind of a pitch for a home run." There was no kind of pitch Williams couldn't hit for a home run (see Eephus Pitch).

Spot Starter A pitcher called into action to start games as the team needs him, as opposed to a regular starting pitcher.

Spray Hitter A batter who is able to hit the ball to all fields.

Spray the Ball To hit the ball to all fields.

"Springfield Rifle" Former star Yankee hurler Vic Raschi, after his birthplace, Springfield, Massachusetts.

Spring Training The conditioning and exhibition season of professional baseball teams, which generally starts in late February in a warm-weather location and lasts until a few days before the start of the new season.

"Spud" The nickname for Yankee star hurler Spurgeon Ferdinand Chandler was easier for everyone.

Square Around to Bunt A batter's movement out of a normal batting stance into a position facing the pitcher, with the bat extended parallel to the batter's feet, which point toward the infield.

Squeeze Play An offensive strategy move in which a team with less than two outs and a man on third base will have a batter bunt the ball, hoping the runner will be able to score.

"Squire (or Knight) of Kennett Square" Herb Pennock came from historic Kennett Square, Pennsylvania, an area of horsemen and fox hunters. Pennock himself was an expert rider and a master of hounds.

Start An opportunity given to a pitcher to begin a game. To be the pitcher who begins a game.

Starter A pitcher who starts a game (Starting Pitcher).

Starting Rotation The order in which starting pitchers perform on a continuing basis—every fourth or fifth day as a starter is the general rule, which would mean that a team has four or five starters.

"Steady Eddie" Eddie Murray who played for the Baltimore Orioles (1977–1988, 1996), Los Angeles Dodgers (1989–1991, 1997), New York Mets (1992–1993), and Cleveland Indians (1994–1996), before finishing his career with the Baltimore Orioles, Anaheim Angels, and Los Angeles Dodgers (1996–1997).

New York Yankee broadcaster Mel Allen invented this rhyming name for pitcher Eddie Lopat. A hard working, consistent performer, Lopat led the Yankee pitching staff five years in a row in earned-run average (see "Junk Man").

Steal To run from one base to the next, attempting to get there safely by catching the other team off guard when a pitch is thrown home.

"Stengelese" The late and great Hall of Fame manager Casey Stengel could say a mouthful. Herewith, a sampler:

"Butcher boy": A chopped ground ball

"Embalmed": Sleeping

"Green pea": Rookie or unseasoned player

"He could squeeze your ear brows off": A tough player

"Hold the gun": I want to change pitchers

"Ned in the third reader": Naiveté

"Plumber": A good fielder

"Road apple": A bum
"Whiskey slick": A playboy
"Worm killers": Low balls

A Stengelese monologue—Spring training, 1955:

And now we come to Collins which may be an outfielder. He played centerfield at Newark and also played right field for me in the World Series. You can look it up, but he had Novikoff on one side of him and someone else whose name I have forgotten on the other but you can look it up. That should prove he's a great outfielder in order to do it with them guys on either side of him.

There's a kid infielder named Richardson who was in our rookie camp which he doesn't look like he can play because he's as stiff as a stick—but whoosh—and the ball's there and he does it so fast it would take some of them Sunshine Park handicappers with the field glasses on to see him do it so fast does he do it. He never misses. As soon as he misses a ball, we'll send him back home.

We started out to get us a shortstop and now we got eight of them. We don't fool, we don't. I ain't yet found a way to play more than one man in each position although we can shift them around and make them maybe outfielders outa them or put 'em all at ketch like we done with Howard.

You ask me what kind of ball club I want, one with power or one with speed, well a lot of power but not too much, and a lot of speed but not too much. The best club is the versatile club, the one that has a homer hitter here and a bunter there, a fast ball pitcher here and a change-of-pace pitcher there. That way, the other team never knows what's going to hit it next.

At the Congressional hearings on baseball's Reserve Clause, July 19, 1958:

In Kankakee, Illinois or someplace like that, I tore my suit sitting in the stands . . . now they've got good seats.

I got a little concern yesterday in the first three innings when I saw the three players I had gotten rid of, and I said when I lost nine what am I going to do and when I had a couple of my players I thought so great of that did not do so good up to the sixth inning I was more confused but I finally had to go and call on a young man in Baltimore that we don't own and the Yankees don't own him, and he is doing pretty good, and I would actually have to tell you that we are more the Greta Garbo type now from success.

We are being hated, I mean from the ownership and all, we are being hated. Every sport that gets too great or one individual—but if we made 27 cents and it pays to have a winner at home, why would you have a good winner in your own park if you were an owner?

That is the result of baseball. An owner gets most of the money at home and it's up to him and his staff to do better or they ought to be discharged.

Step Up to the Plate To get into the batter's box in preparation to hit.

"Stick" Long time baseball "brain" Gene Michael, when at Kent State playing basketball, had a lean and long appearance.

Stirrup Sock Without a heel or toe and designed to be worn over an athletic sock, usually of a color that matches the player's uniform.

St. Louis Cardinals Originally, during the Gay Nineties, the St. Louis National League baseball entry was known as the "Browns." Then they were known as the "Perfectos." That was a misnomer, for in the years 1892–1999 they finished twelfth three times, eleventh three times, tenth once, ninth once, and eighth once. In 1899 their owner, Chris Von Der Ahe, decided that perhaps a new look in uniforms might help. The team was outfitted in flashy new fabric accentuated with red trim and red stockings. From the new look came the new name—the "Cardinals."

Stolen Base A successful steal of a base by a runner.

Stop To bring a batted ball under control by knocking it down or slowing its movement so as to be able to play it.

Stopper A consistently effective starting pitcher.

"The Stork" Gangly George Theodore, reserve outfielder for the New York Mets in the early 1970s.

Straightaway To be lined up with an outfielder's position—a hitter can bat the ball to straightaway center field, and a fielder can play straightaway center field, for example.

Stranded A term that describes a runner or runners left on base at the end of an inning, unable to be brought in to score by other hitters on their team (Left on Base).

Stretch A modified windup used by a pitcher when runners are on base that enables the pitcher to keep closer check on runners.

"Stretch" ("Big Mac") Willie McCovey was a huge star for the San Francisco Giants. His size was the reason for one of his nicknames and the other was an abbreviation of his surname.

Strike A pitch in the strike zone or one that is swung at and missed or fouled off. A highly accurate outfielder's throw.

Strikeout The act of retiring a batter by getting three strikes on him.

Strike Zone The imaginary area that extends over home plate from the batter's knees to his armpits; a pitch thrown in the strike zone will be a strike on the batter unless he hits it into fair territory.

Stroke To hit the ball smoothly, and consistently well, to the outfield.

Stuff The movement and liveliness a pitcher is able to impart to the pitches he throws to a batter—a pitcher having his "good stuff" is throwing well.

"Sub" Former Yankee and Red Sox hurler Carl Mays, born in 1891 in Liberty, Kentucky, threw to the plate with an underhanded or submarine motion.

Subway Series The term originated for New York City baseball when players and fans traveled by subway to games. Back in 1889 the *New York Times* observed: "The competition between Brooklyn and New York as regards baseball is unparalleled in the history of the national game."

The competition may have been unparalleled, but it was also unequal. Throughout most of their history the Dodgers of Brooklyn were a sad sack team. The Yankees were the royalty of baseball.

It was not until 1941 that the rivalry between the two franchises reached fever pitch in the first Subway Series. The results were predictable. The Yankees won. There was another Brooklyn-New York Subway Series in 1947—same result. In 1949—same result. In 1952, in 1953—same results.

In 1955, it was again a Subway Series—Dodgers versus Yankees. Brooklyn had lost all seven series it had played—five of them to the Bronx Bombers. Casey Stengel's Yankees took the first two games. Since no team had ever won a seven-game World Series after losing the first two games, Yankee fans were getting ready to celebrate. And once again Dodger fans were trotting out their poignant slogan: "Wait 'til Next Year."

But 1955 was Next Year! The Brooks pushed the Yankees to a seventh game. And Johnny Podres threw a 2-0 complete game shutout to give the Brooklyn Dodgers their first and only World Championship. The precise moment was 3:43 p.m. on October 4, 1955. Brooklyn streets were clogged with celebrating fans. Honking car horns, clanging pots and pans, and shredded newspaper all punctuated that one singular moment. There was joy in Flatbush. The hated Yankees had been defeated.

However, all the celebrating was short-lived and bittersweet. For in 1956, the last time there was a Subway Series, it was Yanks over Dodgers in seven games. And in 1957 the Dodgers of Brooklyn moved to Los Angeles.

Pretenders to the throne of "Subway Series" have sprung up since then—Yankees versus Los Angeles Dodgers in a transcoastal World Series. Even the "Shuttle Series"—the World Series of 1986 between the Boston Red Sox and New York Mets. The name derived from the two cities that were linked by commuter air-shuttle routes and shameless commercialism by shuttle operators Eastern and Pan American.

The meeting between the Yankees and Mets in October 2000 was the only real Subway Series for purists since 1956.

Suicide Squeeze Takes place when the runner breaks the instant the pitch is released.

"Sukey" Working with Branch Rickey, Clyde Sukeforth went to scout Jackie Robinson as he played for the Kansas City Monarchs in 1945. Robinson did not play in that game, but Sukeforth set up a meeting between Robinson and Rickey. And the rest led to the breaking of the color line in baseball.

"Sultan of Swat" One of the nicknames given to Babe Ruth—Swat was once a principality but today is part of Pakistan (see "Babe").

Sunday Best A term describing a pitcher throwing his most effective pitch(es).

"Sunday Teddy" In 1939, White Sox manager Jimmy Dykes started to use Ted Lyons, who was thirty-eight years old, only on Sunday afternoons. This pattern was maintained through the 1942 season, with the veteran starting twenty-one, twenty-two, twenty-two, and twenty games each year. The veteran right-hander posted a fine 52-30 record for that span, with a 2.96 ERA (he led the American League in ERA at the age of forty-one in 1942, with a 2.10 mark). Fans took to calling him "Sunday Teddy," and belying his age, Lyons completed seventy-two of his eighty-five starts over those years.

Superchief Most major league baseball players of Indian descent somehow have been tagged with the nickname Chief. Allie Reynolds, whose glory years were 1947–1954 with the New York Yankees, was no ordinary pitcher, but he was of Indian descent. Thus the man born in Bethany, Oklahoma, was nicknamed Superchief.

Superjew Born April 4, 1943, in the Bronx, New York, Mike Epstein played for five different teams in an eight-year major league baseball career. His religion and his size (6' 4", 230 pounds) were the roots for his nickname.

"Super Sub" Chico Salmon spent nine years in the major leagues as a utility infielder. His first four seasons were with the Indians, where he played several different positions.

"Swamp Baby" Charlie Wilson, born in Clinton, South Carolina, appeared in fifty-six games over four seasons in the major leagues. Wilson supposedly earned the nickname after he flooded a baseball field so that he could get a day off. This prank was immortalized in the film *Bull Durham.* In 1931, Wilson hit one home run and drove in eleven runs for the Boston Braves.

Swat the Ball To hit the ball with power and for distance.

Sweep a Series To win all the games in a series played with another team.

Swing To move the bat in an arc motion to hit a pitched ball.

Swing Away To take a full cut (full swing) at a pitch.

Swing for the Fences To swing with maximum force in an attempt to hit a home run. (Swing from the Heels; Go for the Downs.)

Swinging Bunt A half-swing, half-bunt.

Swish An expression describing a batter swinging hard at a pitched ball and not making contact.

Switch Hitter A batter who can hit from either side of the plate.

Tab To select a player for a certain performance—for example, to "tab a pitcher to start the first game of the World Series."

Tag Out To touch a base runner with the ball when he is off base, thus making him out (Tag).

Tag Up A situation in which a runner stays on base until a fly ball is caught. He then has the option to run to the next base, attempting to beat the throw.

Take a Pitch To allow a pitch to come over the plate without swinging at it.

Take Off The opening move in the running of a player from one base to another in an attempt to steal a base. A condition where a pitch suddenly deviates in its motion as it comes to the plate (usually refers to a ball that rises sharply).

Take-Out Play A situation where a base runner slides into a fielder, attempting to knock that player off balance and prevent his making a play.

Take Sign A signal from a manager or coach to a batter to not swing at a pitch.

"The Tall Tactician" Cornelius Alexander McGillicuddy, also and better known as Connie Mack, was a major league baseball manager for fifty-three years. He ranks first in games managed, games won, and games lost. A lean, 6-foot-plus individual, his size and the millions of managing decisions he made between 1894 and 1950 earned this Hall of Famer his alliterative nickname.

Tampa Bay Devil Rays The franchise was granted on March 9, 1995. A "name-the-team competition" resulted in seven thousand entries. The winning entries were Manta Rays and Devil Rays, the same fish. But more than fifty thousand votes later, "Devil Rays" became the name of the team.

"Tanglefoot Lou" Lou Gehrig, for his awkward early days as a player.

Tap To select a player for a specific task.

Tape-Measure Home Run An exceptionally long home run.

Tapioca Sky Milky white roof of the Metrodome in Minneapolis that sometimes causes problems for out-fielders.

Tee Off To hit a pitcher especially hard.

Texas Rangers From 1961 to 1971, the team was known as the Washington Senators.

"Thayer Mask" First catcher's mask, patented by Fred Thayer in 1878. The idea for a baseball catcher's mask was borrowed from fencing masks.

Third Base The base on the left side of the infield, as viewed from home plate (Third).

Third Baseman The player whose position is third base and who defensively covers mainly the area between third and shortstop (Third Sacker; Hot Sack Guardian).

Thread the Needle A pitcher's ability to get a pitch over a particular part of the plate where the batter is not able to effectively make contact with the ball.

Three-Base Hit A triple (Three-Bagger).

"Three Finger" Brown Hall of Famer Mordecai Peter Centennial Brown had a mangled right hand as a result of a childhood accident—and that was the reason for his nickname. It was also, according to Brown, the reason for his success as a pitcher for the Chicago Cubs and others. "It gave me a bigger dip for my pitches," he said. Brown's dip helped him record fifty-eight lifetime shutouts and average more than twenty-four wins a year in the 1906–1911 period, while allowing barely a run a game in the 1906 and 1909 seasons. Admitted to the Hall of Fame in 1949, Brown's lifetime earned-run average was an astonishing 2.06, the third lowest in baseball history. Incidentally, his penultimate name, Centennial, reflected the fact that he was born in the centennial year of the United States, which was also the first year of the National League.

Three-Hundred Hitter A batter who hits .300 or better.

"$3 Million Man" Nickname placed on Catfish Hunter when he signed with the Yankees as a free agent for that sum in 1974.

Thrower A pitcher not distinguished by his thinking ability.

Throw Out a Ball A situation where an umpire discards a ball that has become not playable because it is scuffed, matted, or dirtied.

Throw Out a Runner The act of throwing a ball to a fielder who tags out a base runner.

Time the Pitch A situation where a batter swings at a pitch, making contact with the ball as a result of good timing.

Tinker to Evers to Chance A synonym for making the double play in baseball is the expression "Tinker to Evers to Chance." Yet the Chicago Cub trio, during the peak years of their careers (1906–1909), averaged fewer than fourteen double plays a year. What they did on the field was romanticized in the famous poem written by Franklin P. Adams:

These are the saddest of possible words—"Tinker to Evers to Chance."
Trio of bear cubs, and fleeter than birds—"Tinker to Evers to Chance."
Ruthlessly pricking our gonfalon bubble—Making a Giant hit into a double—
Words that are weighty with nothing but trouble:
    "Tinker to Evers to Chance."

Tommy John Surgery Elbow surgery for pitchers, named after Tommy John, a pitcher and the first professional athlete to successfully undergo the operation.

"Tom Terrific" Tom Seaver made his mark as star pitcher for the New York Mets from 1967 to 1977, and in that time he was "terrific." The media came up with his nickname "Tom Terrific," which used to be the name of a children's cartoon show.

Tony Conigliaro Award Annual award to the player who best exemplifies the character of former Red Sox slugger Tony Conigliaro for courage overcoming adversity.

Tools of Ignorance Catcher's equipment, so called because of the implication that only a dumb player would be willing to play such a tough position.

Top The first half of an inning. Also, to hit a ball above its center line so that its flight or roll has topspin.

"To Play This Game You've Got to Have a Lot of Little Boy in You" Hall of Famer Roy Campanella, for a decade a fixture with the Brooklyn Dodgers, was the originator of what is now a cliché about baseball. Campy had a lot of little boy in him, and a great deal of major league talent. He was a powerfully built catcher, a marvelous handler of pitchers, and a clutch-hitting slugger, but an automobile accident curtailed his playing career and tragically reduced him to remaining in a wheelchair for the rest of his days. His love of baseball is reflected in his insightful comment about the game.

Top of the Inning The first half of an inning, during which the visiting team bats.

Toronto Blue Jays So named in 1977 in a contest because of the blue in team colors.

Total Bases The adding up of the number of bases a hit is equal to: a single is one base, a double is two bases, a triple is three bases, a home run is four bases.

Touch 'Em All Describes the ritual of a player who homers, touching all the bases.

"The Toy Cannon" Outfielder Jimmy Wynn was small in stature at 5' 6", but his bat had a lot of pop.

Tracking It Down The running after and catching of a fly ball by an outfielder.

Trap a Ball To catch a ball the instant after it touches the ground on a bounce.

Triple A three-base hit (Three-Bagger).

Triple Crown The winning of the batting championship, home run title, and RBI crown by one player in the same season. A symbolic—and financially very rewarding—accomplishment.

Triple Play Three outs recorded on one play.

"Tug" Frank Edwin McGraw, Jr., left-handed relief pitcher, coauthor of a comic strip called "Scroogie," possessor of a wicked screwball, and in his own words, "a little bit of a screwball myself," was a baseball original. McGraw was a member of the New York Mets from 1967 to 1974. In back-to-back years, 1971 and 1972, his earned-run average was a glittering 1.70. He starred for the Mets in two World Series and coined the slogan of the team back then, "Ya Gotta Believe." His parents nicknamed him Tug because he tugged at so many things when he was a baby (see "Ya Gotta Believe").

"Tugboat" The late Yankee catcher Thurman Munson was known by this name as well as "Squatty Body" and "The Wall." All the names fit the gritty and determined athlete.

Twin Bill A doubleheader.

Twi-Night Doubleheader Two games, usually for the same admission charge; the first game takes place in early evening, and the second game immediately follows.

"Twinkletoes" George Selkirk ran with his weight on the balls of his feet, hence the nickname given to him by teammates at Newark in the International League.

Twirl To pitch.

Twirler A pitcher.

Two-Base Hit A double (Two-Bagger).

"Two Head" A negative nickname used by opponents to describe the size of Babe Ruth's head, which seemed gigantic to some.

Umpires Personnel who officiate at a game: the home plate umpire is stationed behind the plate and calls balls and strikes; other umpires are stationed near each base (Arbiters; Men in Blue; Umps).

Unearned Run A run scored as a result of a mistake made by the defensive team and not charged against a pitcher's earned-run average.

"The Unholy Trio" Billy Martin, Mickey Mantle, and Whitey Ford, for their fooling-around ways.

Uniform (Uni) Outfit identifying members of the same team.

United Nations Pitching Staff Ismael Valdes (Mexico), Ramon Martinez (Dominican Republic), Hideo Nomo (Japan), Pedro Astacio (Dominican Republic), and Chan Ho Park (South Korea) made up the Los Angeles Dodgers rotation in 1997.

Unofficial Game A game that goes four innings or fewer, or goes four and one-half innings when the home team is losing (or tied), is "unofficial." But if the home team is ahead after four and one-half innings, the game is official and the home team wins.

Up the Middle On the field very close to second base, used to describe the location of batted balls.

Velocity The speed of a pitched ball (Zip).

"Vinegar Bend" Wilmer David Mizell was born in Vinegar Bend, Alabama, and got his nickname from that. He made his major league debut in 1952 as a pitcher.

"Wabash George" ("Big George") Moniker for George Mullin because he played semipro ball in Wabash, Indiana. He hurled for the Detroit Tigers from 1902 to 1913, among other teams.

"Wahoo Sam" Sam Crawford, Detroit Tiger star and Hall of Famer, hailed from Wahoo, Nebraska.

"Wait 'til Next Year" A plaintive refrain echoed annually by the fans of the old Brooklyn Dodgers, this phrase was an expression of eternal optimism and faith in the ability of their beloved Bums to make up for all the failures and inadequacies of years gone by. It especially applied to the World Series. In 1941, for example, the Dodgers won the pennant but lost the World Series in five games to the New York Yankees. In 1947 the Dodgers won the pennant and lost again in the World Series, this time in seven games, to the New York Yankees. They lost in the 1949 World Series to the Yankees; they bowed in the 1952 World Series to the Yankees; they were defeated in the 1953 World Series by the Yankees—but 1955 was "next year." The series went seven games, and the Dodgers defeated the New York Yankees and became World Champions at long last.

Walk The receiving of a fourth pitch outside the strike zone by a batter, which allows him to move to first base (Pass; Base on Balls).

"The Walking Man" Eddie Yost played nearly two decades in the major leagues. His lifetime batting average was only .254, but that didn't keep him off the bases. Yost coaxed pitchers into yielding 1,614 walks to him—almost a walk a game through his long career—which places him fifth on the all-time bases-on-balls list.

Walk-off Home Run Game-ending home team home run in the bottom of the ninth inning or in an extra inning.

Wall-Scraper Home run when the ball hits the outfield fence above the home run line.

Warming Up The throwing of practice pitches in the bullpen by a relief pitcher who is readying himself to enter the game.

Warm-Up Pitches Practice pitches allowed a pitcher each inning before the opposing side comes up to bat.

Warning Track The area in front of outfield walls, composed of a surface different from the playing field, which serves to warn a player that he is nearing the wall.

"The Warrior" Paul O'Neill had this name pinned on him by George Steinbrenner as a nod to the Yankee outfielder's fiery ways.

Washington Nationals The Montreal Expos moved to Washington and became the Nationals in November 2004. Runnerup nicknames were "Senators" (the preference of commissioner Bud Selig, even though the Rangers held the rights to the name) and "Grays," but Mayor Anthony Williams objected to the appropriateness of the name "Senators" because of the District of Columbia's lack of representation in the U.S. Senate. "We don't have senators here," the mayor said. "Give us two senators, and I'll be happy to call them the Senators." Williams wanted "Grays" as a tribute to the Homestead Grays, a Negro League team that played many of its games in Washington in the 1930s and 1940s. But the real home of the Grays was Pittsburgh.

Washington Senators The original American League Senators played in the nation's capital from 1901 to 1960. Their nickname came from that of two National League teams in Washington in the late 1800s. The franchise moved to Minnesota becoming the Twins. The expansion Senators were in D.C. 1961–1971 before moving to Texas and becoming the Rangers.

Wasted Pitch A ball intentionally pitched out of the strike zone to get the batter to swing at it or set him up for the next pitch.

"The Weatherman" Mickey Rivers had a knack for predicting weather.

Webbing Laces that connect a glove's (or mitt's) thumb and fingers.

"Wee Willie" He was born March 3, 1872, in Brooklyn, New York. He died on January 1, 1923, in Brooklyn, New York. William Henry Keeler made his debut at the Polo Grounds as a member of the New York Giants on September 30, 1892. He singled off the Phillies' Tim Keefe for the first of his 2,926 career hits. The son of a Brooklyn trolley switchman, Keeler two years later became a member of the famed Baltimore Orioles.

A lefty all the way, he weighed only 140 pounds and was a shade over 5' 4". His tiny physical stature earned him his nickname, but pound for pound he was one of the greatest hitters baseball ever produced. Keeler played for nineteen years and recorded a lifetime batting average of .345, fifth on the all-time list. He collected 2,962 hits in 2,124 games, spraying the ball to all fields. Wee Willie's greatest year was 1897, a season in which he batted .432, recorded 243 hits and sixty-four stolen bases, and scored 145 runs. He swung a bat that weighed only thirty ounces, but as he said, he "hit 'em where they ain't"—and that was more than good enough to gain Keeler entry into baseball's Hall of Fame in 1939.

Keeler opened the 1897 season with two hits in five at bats against Boston. Then for two months the slight southpaw swinger slapped hit after hit, game after game—from April 22 to June 18—for forty-four straight games. His record stood for forty-four years until Joe DiMaggio came along and snapped it in 1941.

The Sporting News offered this mangled prose about Keeler as a fielder: "He swears by the teeth of his mask-carved horse chestnut, that he always carries with him as a talisman that he inevitably dreams of it in the night before when he is going to boot one—muff an easy fly ball, that is to say, in the meadow on the morrow. 'All of us fellows in the outworks have got just so many of them in a season to drop and there's no use trying to buck against fate.'"

In 1898, a year after Keeler batted that astonishing .432, he set a mark for hitting that will probably never be topped, notching 202 singles in just 128 games. He truly was hitting them where the fielders weren't. It was a season in which the left-handed bat magician recorded 214 hits. His batting average was .379, but the incredible number of singles amassed saw him register a puny .410 slugging percentage. That 1898 season Keeler came to bat 564 times in 128 games, walking only twenty-eight times without striking out. A slugger he was not. But, oh what a hitter!

William Henry Keeler played nineteen years in the major leagues and finished his career with a .345 lifetime batting average. Quite justifiably the little man was one of the first to be enshrined in the National Baseball Hall of Fame in 1939.

"Whale" Former Brooklyn Dodger hurler Don Newcombe was called this for his size and some would say slow manner. "Newk" was used too, a shortening of his surname.

"Wheeze Kids" The Philadelphia Phillies had some good teams in the 1980s that featured old timers like Steve Carlton and Pete Rose.

Whiff To swing at a pitch and miss it. To strike out.

"The Whip" A 6' 6" right-hander, Ewell Blackwell had a sidearm motion and a crackling fastball that terrorized National League batters in the 1940s and 1950s. The former Cincinnati star's right arm seemed to "whip" the ball in at the batter, and that's how his nickname came to be. Winner of sixteen straight games in 1947, he struck out almost a batter an inning during his ten-year career.

"White Gorilla" Former right-handed power pitcher Goose Gossage, for the way he looked.

"White Owl Wallop" Expression, in deference to cigar sponsor, that legendary Yankee announcer Mel Allen used to describe a home run.

"White Rat" Former manager Whitey Herzog earned the name for his blonde hair and scheming ways.

Whitewash To shut out a team (Blank).

"Whitey" William Frederick Wietelmann was given this nickname by Casey Stengel, his first manager. There have been a host of players given that nickname for their blonde hair, including Whitey Lockman, Whitey Herzog, Whitey Ford.

"Whiz Kids" There is no clear explanation as to how the 1950 Philadelphia Phillies baseball team earned its nickname. Some ascribe the name's derivation to the club's youth and newness: only one regular on that team, which won the National League pennant, was over thirty years of age. Some claim the nickname was a spin-off from the phrase "gee whiz," since the Phillies of that year seemingly came from nowhere to challenge and defeat the great Brooklyn Dodgers for the pennant. It was a team that because of its youth, its underdog role, and its past history of failure attracted national attention and fused its personality to its nickname.

Wide A pitch outside the strike zone.

"Wild Elk of the Wasatch" Heusser, who pitched in the National League from 1935 to 1948.

"Wild Horse of the Osage" Johnny Leonard Roosevelt Martin, better known as Pepper Martin, starred for thirteen seasons with the National League's St. Louis Cardinals. He could hit, he could run, he could field, he could throw, he could win—and he did all of these things with wild abandon, with an élan and a verve that earned him his nickname. If he couldn't stop a hard smash down to his third-base position with his glove, he would stop the ball with his chest. If he could not get into a base feet-first, he would leap into the air and belly-flop his way there. Martin took the extra base, risked the daring chance, played with fire and fury. Three times in the mid-1930s he led the league in stolen bases, and throughout that decade he functioned as the horse that led the Cardinal "Gashouse Gang" (see "Gashouse Gang").

Wild Pitch A pitch far outside the strike zone that cannot be handled by the catcher.

"Wild Thing" Mitch Williams, pitcher, would hit and walk a lot of batters, as well as throw a lot of wild pitches. He also had wild hair and a wild pitching motion. This nickname was also used in the movie *Major League*.

Wild Throw A throw to a defensive player that is so inaccurate it can't be handled.

"Willie the Wonder" Hyperbolic name pinned on Willie Horton who played for several American League teams in 1960s and 1970s and impressed people with his talent.

Windup Arm and leg motions by a pitcher that serve as preliminary steps for the pitching of a ball.

Winning Pitcher A pitcher officially given credit for a victory.

"Winny" Affectionate shortening of Dave Winfield's name.

Winter Ball Off-season, warm-weather baseball competition.

"The Wizard" Ichiro Suzuki of the Seattle Mariners is the first Japanese position player in the major leagues. In 2004, he broke George Sisler's eighty-one-year-old record for hits in a season. Called "The Wizard" in the United States for his skills and "Elvis" in Japan, Suzuki was an icon in Japan after winning seven batting titles there.

"Wizard of Oz" An abbreviation of his first name and tip of the cap to Ozzie Smith for his peerless fielding skills. No other shortstop could get to the ball as fast, and utilize the fielders around him, like Ozzie.

Work the Count A situation where a batter attempts to get the count in his favor by fouling off balls, taking pitches, and so forth.

World Series In 1903 the Pittsburgh Pirates of the National League won their third consecutive pennant. Owner Barney Dreyfuss was instrumental in arranging for a set of postseason games with the American League champion Boston Somersets (later Red Sox). The teams played a nine-game series, with Boston winning five of the games (one of their pitchers was Cy Young) and the World Championship. There was a one-year interruption in the competition, because the 1904 National League pennant winner was the New York Giants, whose owner, John T. Bush, refused to allow his team to oppose an American League entry. Part of the reason behind Bush's refusal was the existence of a rival American League team in New York City. By 1905 Bush had changed his mind and even helped shape the new format for the World Series—a best-of-seven competition—and behind Christy Mathewson, who pitched three shutouts, the Giants defeated the Philadelphia Athletics in five games. Dubbed the Fall Classic, the World Series year in and year out has become an integral, appealing part of the American sports scene.

World Series Ring The jeweled ring given to members of the team that wins the World Series.

Wrigley Field In 1916 William Wrigley, Jr., joined with a group of wealthy Chicagoans to purchase the Chicago Cubs. The National League team was thus wrested from the absentee ownership of the Taft family of Cincinnati. In 1921 Wrigley took over the major ownership of the team. By 1926 the old Federal ball park that the Cubs played in was given a new name in honor of its owner—Wrigley Field. The park was double decked, freshly painted, and renovated. And through the years, the ballpark and the Cubs have been synonymous with the Wrigley family. The past is as real as the present at Wrigley Field, on the North Side of Chicago. All the games are played in daylight on grass that is real and green. Ivy vines cover the redbrick outfield walls. Tall buildings crowd close to the little ballpark, serving as penthouse seats for the Cub rooters. There is no electric scoreboard, no advertising. The oldest stadium in the National League, the field and its mood have the stamp of the Wrigleys, as well as the name.

Wrist Hitter A player who gets good wrist action into his swing at a ball.

Wrong-Field Hit A hit to the field that is opposite to the one a batter is normally expected to hit to—a right-handed batter hitting to right field, for example.

"Ya Gotta Believe" In 1973 the New York Mets bolted from last place on August 30 to win the National League Eastern Division title on the final day of the season. Pitcher Tug McGraw had coined a slogan, "Ya gotta believe," which acted as the team's battle cry and motivation. Lacking a .300 hitter, a twenty-game winner, and a one-hundred-RBI man, the "believing" Mets swept by Cincinnati in the play-offs and battled Oakland to the seventh game of the World Series before finally losing (see Amazin' Mets).

"Yankee Clipper" Joseph Paul DiMaggio was one of nine children of a fisherman father who had emigrated from Sicily. It was all planned for Joe to become a fisherman like his father, but Joe could not abide the smell of fish and he often got seasick. His real passion was playing baseball.

In 1934, he was playing baseball about as well as it could be played when his contract with the San Francisco Seals of the Pacific Coast League was purchased by the Yankees. The deal contained the clause that the graceful outfielder be allowed to play one more season for the Seals. His 1935 season gave the people of San Francisco something to remember—he batted .398, recorded 270 hits, and drove in 154 runs.

Permission was granted for DiMag in 1936 to drive cross-country with fellow San Franciscans Tony Lazzeri and Frank Crosetti to the Yankee spring training camp in St. Petersburg, Florida. Lazzeri turned to DiMaggio after the trio had concluded one day of driving and said, "You take over, Joe." "I don't drive," DiMaggio answered. It was reported that these were the only words he uttered during the entire three-day automobile trek. As a Yankee he didn't do much talking either. His abilities on the playing field said it all.

He would step into the batter's box and stub his right toe into the dirt in back of his left heel. It was almost a dance step. His feet were spaced approximately 4 feet apart, with the weight of his frame on his left leg. Erect, almost in a military position, Joe Dee would hold his bat at the end and poise it on his right shoulder—a rifle at the ready. He would look at the pitcher from deep in the batter's box and assume a stance that almost crowded the plate. He was ready.

In DiMaggio's time—thirteen seasons with the Yankees—they won ten pennants. In 1951, the man they called the Yankee Clipper retired at age thirty-six. Management attempted to get him to perform in pinstripes for one more season. But he had too much pride, and too much pain. He knew it was over.

Joseph Paul DiMaggio left behind the memory of a player who moved about in the vast center field of Yankee Stadium with an almost poetical grace. He had played when he was fatigued, when he was hurt, when it mattered a great deal, and when it didn't matter at all.

"Joe was the complete player in everything he did," said his former manager Joe McCarthy. "They'd hit the ball to center field and Joe would stretch out those long legs of his and run the ball down. He never made a mistake on the bases and in Yankee Stadium, a tough park for a right-hander, he was a great hitter, one of the best." DiMag had a career average of .325, 361 home runs, eight World Series home runs, and two batting championships. He also won three MVPs and holds the record of fifty-six straight games with a hit.

"Those statistics don't even tell half the story," said DiMag's former teammate pitcher Eddie Lopat. "What he meant to the Yankees, you'll never find in the statistics. He was the real leader of our team. He was the best." Like the famed Yankee clipper ships that sailed the oceans riding the winds and the tides, DiMaggio moved across the reaches of the center field pastureland of Yankee Stadium flawlessly playing his kind of game—steady, stoic, dependable. His nickname accentuated his role and style. DiMaggio was also known as "Joltin' Joe" because of his power, and "Joe Di," an affectionate abbreviation of his name.

"The Yankee Clipper" Slap at George Steinbrenner who always has had a longing to see his players clean-shaven.

"Yankee Empire Builder" Former Yankee General Manager Ed Barrow was all of that.

"Yankee Killer" Willard Nixon, known as for his mastery of the Yankees during the 1950s, beating New York six games in a row during the 1954–1955 season.

"Yaz" Carl Yastrzemski played for the Boston Red Sox (1961–1983).

"Yogi" Baseball Hall of Famer and language guru Lawrence Peter Berra was given his famous nickname as a boy after his friends saw a film featuring a Hindu seated in a yoga position. It reminded them of how Berra seemed to always look awkward behind the plate. In his first few seasons with the Yankees, Berra was simply known as Larry. It wasn't until he began to earn a comic reputation that sports writers began calling him by his boyhood nickname.

"You Could Look It Up" Casey Stengel began his major league playing career in 1912, his managing career in 1934. He played for fourteen years, managed for twenty-five years. His baseball career ended in 1965 after stints with the Brooklyn Dodgers, Boston Braves, Pittsburgh Pirates, Philadelphia Phillies, New York Giants, New York Yankees, and New York Mets. Casey could talk for hours about baseball and life. And sometimes in the midst of animated conversation about a utility outfielder on the old Boston Braves, or a balk by a forgotten pitcher on the Pittsburgh Pirates, to emphasize that he was not relating fiction he would exclaim: "You could look it up!"

Youth of America Casey Stengel's beginning years as manager of the New York Mets were a time of trial and frustration for many. Afflicted with over-the-hill players and has-beens, Casey delighted in the potential of some of the younger Mets. Although not quite ready for prime-time baseball, they had promise and Stengel's feeling for them was revealed in this phrase, which he pronounced, "The yuth of America" (see "Can't Anybody Here Play This Game?").

"Yo-Yo" For small size and hyperactivity, Luis Arroyo.

Basketball

"The Admiral" Former San Antonio Spur star David Robinson was called this because of his Naval Academy roots and leadership skills on the court.

Air Ball An ineffective shot that completely misses the backboard and the rim.

"Air Jordan" Michael Jordan was a leaper literally hanging in the air. His own sneaker line underscored his nickname.

Alley-Oop Shot An acrobatic shot made by a player who goes high in the air and shoots the ball as he is falling to the ground.

"All-World" Lloyd Free, National Basketball Association (NBA) free soul, who learned his basketball on the sidewalks of New York, gave himself this nickname. Free was a little man in a world of giants who considered his "rainbow shot," which went high in the air and down at the basket, worthy of the nickname he dreamed up.

Alternating-Possession Rule In college basketball the possession arrow changes direction after each subsequent jump ball, alternating the team gaining possession of the ball.

"Amoeba Defense" The basketball team at University of Nevada at Las Vegas coached by Jerry Tarkanian and featuring players like Larry Johnson had a smothering defense.

"The Answer" Allen Iverson of the Philadelphia 76ers has always been an offensive force with an answer to any challenge on the NBA court.

Anticipation A player's ability to sense ahead of time what an opponent or team will do.

Assist A pass by one player to another that results in the second player scoring a basket.

Atlanta Hawks From 1946 to 1951 the team was known as the Tri-Cities Blackhawks because of the area they played in which had been the site of a major part of the 1832 Black Hawk War. Home games took place in Moline, Illinois; Rock Island, Illinois; and Davenport, Iowa. The franchise relocated to Milwaukee (1951–1955), then St. Louis (1955–1968), where its nickname was shortened to Hawks. They became the Atlanta Hawks in 1968.

Backboard The rectangular structure, six feet by three and a half feet, that the basket is attached to (Glass).

Backcourt The part of the court that contains the basket. There are actually two backcourts, as one team's backcourt is the other team's forecourt, depending on whether the team is playing offense or defense.

Backcourt Foul Foul against an offensive player in his own backcourt.

Backcourt Violation A professional rule that states a team must move the ball out of its backcourt within ten seconds after gaining possession. Failure to do this awards the ball to the other team.

Back Door A situation where an offensive player goes behind the defense under his own basket to receive a pass.

"Bad Boys" The rough and tough style of play of the Detroit Pistons coached by Chuck Daly in the late 1980s to early 1990s that included Isaiah Thomas, Bill Laimbeer, Joe Dumars, John Salley, and Dennis Rodman, who earned the team that name.

Ball Weight of ball: not less than twenty ounces nor more than twenty-two. Circumference of ball: not greater than thirty inches and not less than twenty-nine and a half inches (College).

Bank Shot To use the backboard to make a shot via an angular carom of the ball into the basket, as opposed to shooting straight into the basket.

"The Baron" A strong-minded individual whose Kentucky teams rank among the greatest in the history of college basketball, Adolph Rupp's nickname came from his imperial manner and his record of success. "I know I have plenty of enemies," he once said, "but I'd rather be the most hated winning coach in the country than the most popular losing one." Rupp's teams made more appearances in the NCAA tournament than any other coach's; he produced more than two dozen All-Americans, and he ranks on top of the list of all-time winning college coaches.

Baseline The shorter boundary lines at either end of the court behind the basket.

Basket Attached to the backboard, an eighteen-inch-diameter metal ring from which a fifteen-to-eighteen-inch corded net is suspended and through which the ball must go for a field goal worth two points or a free throw worth one point (Hoop; Hole).

Basket-Hanger Also known as "hanger," a player who stays back under his basket while the other team is on offense; a quick pass to him from a teammate potentially makes for an easy basket. The problem with this strategy is that it leaves the basket-hanger's team shorthanded on defense.

Beat the Defender When an offensive player, with or without the ball, gets past an opponent guarding him.

"Big Aristotle" ("Diesel") Shaquille O'Neal, for his size and alleged philosophical bent.

"Big Country" Bryant Reeves, for his rural roots and size.

"Big D" Former New York Knick Dave DeBusschere never backed down from a challenge and played bigger than his 6' 6" frame.

"Big Dipper" His full name was Wilton Norman Chamberlain. He was born in 1936 in Philadelphia and grew up to be 7' 1" and 275 pounds. Voted in as one of the fifty greatest NBA players of all time, he was elected to the Basketball Hall of Fame in 1978. And he named his Los Angeles mansion Ursa Major, the astronomical term for the Big Dipper constellation. There was a retractable roof over Chamberlain's bed— Big Dipper watching Big Dipper.

"Big E" At 6' 9" and 230 pounds, Elvin Hayes was an intimidating performer in the NBA. The former University of Houston All-American, a fine shooter and rebounder, earned his nickname for his size, performance, and appeal.

"Big Fella" Kareem Abdul-Jabbar had this nickname because of his size. Others were "Cap" and "The Captain" for his leadership.

"Big Game James" The former L.A. Laker star James Worthy rose to the occasion in prime-time moments.

"Big Nasty" Corliss Williamson, longtime NBA player, tough-minded and all business.

"Big O" Oscar Robertson was big at 6' 5" and 205 pounds, but the nickname all of basketball knew him by came more from his big skills than his size. Robertson was a great shooter, a great passer, and a tremendous defensive player. Former Boston Celtic coach Red Auerbach once remarked, "He's so great he scares me. He can beat you all by himself and usually does." Robertson was selected to the All-Star team each year of his playing career and that was just another reason for his nickname—the "Big O" stood not for zero, but for oh!

"Big Smooth" The large Sam Perkins played for several NBA teams—always with grace and ease.

"Big Ticket" Kevin Garnett came into the NBA as a teenager and was called "Da Kid." His more permanent nickname derives from the skills and showmanship he displays game after game for Minnesota.

Blind Pass A pass from a ball handler who estimates where his intended receiver should be.

Blocked Shot A situation where a defensive player legally gets his hand on the ball held by an offensive player to hamper the shot.

Blocking Illegal movement of a defensive player into path of an offensive player to interfere with free movement.

Bomb A shot at the basket taken from long range.

Bonus (Free Throw) An extra foul shot awarded when a team uses up its allowance of fouls in a quarter of play. A fouled player in pro basketball gets two attempts for a one-shot foul, three attempts for a two-shot foul. High schools and colleges award the bonus for one-shot fouls; if the free throw is successful, there is another free throw awarded (Penalty Shot).

Bonus Situation After a team has used up its allowable fouls in a period, the bonus or penalty situation is applied.

Boston Celtics Nickname originated in 1946 by Walter Brown, the founder of the franchise. "We'll call them the Boston Celtics," he said. "The name has a great basketball tradition, especially when you think of the original 'Celtics' team, the legendary barnstorming team, and an American Basketball League franchise in the 1920s–1930s. Boston is full of Irishmen; so we'll put the players in green uniforms and call them the Boston Celtics after their Celtic ancestors."

Bounce Pass The passing of the ball on one bounce from one offensive player to another.

Box Out To position the body in front of another player in jockeying for rebounding position.

Bucket A field goal (Hoop).

Buzzer Shot One that scores a basket just as time elapses in a quarter.

Cager Another name for a basketball player.

Center Pivotman, generally the tallest member of a team, who in the past always played with his back to the basket on offense.

Center Circle A four-foot circle located in the middle of the court and intersected by the division line. This marked-off area is used for the center jump at the start of each half.

Center Jump A procedure used to begin play in each half that involves opposing centers jumping at the ball tossed up in the air at the center circle by the referee. Each center attempts to tap the ball to a teammate.

Charging A personal-foul violation committed when an offensive player runs into a defensive player who has established his position on the court. If the defensive player had moved into that position to interfere with the offensive player, the defensive player is guilty of blocking, and there is no charging violation.

Charity Line The free-throw line (Charity Stripe).

Charlotte Bobcats Began NBA play in 2004–2005 season. Other nicknames considered included "Dragons" and "Flight."

Charlotte Hornets Originally, the Charlotte team was named the "Spirit," but that didn't go over too well. A contest was launched among fans to come up with a new name. Runner-up names included the Charlotte "Gold," the Charlotte "Knights," and incredibly the original name—the Charlotte "Spirit."

Chicago Bulls Some people think that the Chicago Bulls got their name because of the stockyards that exist in that windy city. But the Bulls actually received their moniker in 1966 from their first owner, Richard Klein, who admired bulls because of their toughness and looked forward to having a team that had that quality.

Chick-isms Chick Hearn was a legendary L.A. Laker announcer who had a way with words. His original descriptive phrases and more famous calls have found their way into NBA lingo.

"Air-Ball" A shot that draws nothing but air.

"Bunny Hop in the Pea Patch" Traveling.

"Caught with His Hand in the Cookie Jar" Reaching foul.

"Charity Stripe" The free-throw line.

"Didn't Draw Iron" A shot missing the rim, but hitting the backboard.

"Finger Roll" A shot taken when ball rolls off the fingers of the shooter.

"Frozen Rope" A shot with a very flat trajectory.

"Garbage Time" Playing out the remainder of a game that has already been decided.

"Heart-Brrrreak!" A shot that appears to go in, but rattles off the rim and misses. Sometimes "it went in so far you could read the commissioner's name from below."

"No Harm, No Foul (No Blood, No Ambulance, No Stitches)" A noncall by an official when insignificant contact has occurred.

"Not Phi Beta Kappa" Simply put, not a smart play.

"This Game's in the Refrigerator, the Door's Closed, the Lights Are Out, the Eggs Are Cooling, the Butter's Getting Hard, and the Jello's Jiggling!" When the Lakers were defeating an opponent so badly a game was basically over.

"Since Hector Was a Pup" A very long time.

"Chief" Robert Parrish starred for the Celtics and took charge, hence the nickname. He had a stern, no-nonsense look on his face, reminding teammates of the Indian chief from the movie *One Flew Over the Cuckoo's Nest.*

"Chocolate Thunder" Darryl Dawkins played in the NBA for fourteen seasons. He was a ferocious performer.

"Clark Kent" Kurt Rambis wore safety-type glasses à la Superman's alter ego, hence the nickname. He was also called "blue-collar Kurt," for his lunch-pail work ethic.

Cleveland Cavaliers Alliteration was probably one of the reasons for the name "Cavaliers" winning out in a Cleveland newspaper competition back in 1970. But that name in recent years has been de-emphasized in favor of "Cavs." Other entries were Jays, Foresters, Towers, and Presidents. From 1970 to 1974 in Cleveland, Ohio, then moved to Richfield, Ohio, in 1974.

"Clyde" During the late 1960s and early 1970s Walt Frazier of the New York Knickerbockers of the NBA epitomized the cool, calculated precision of a daring basketball player. During his prime, the movie *Bonnie and Clyde,* about a bank-robbing duo, was popular. Frazier's facial hair, his elegant dress off the basketball court, his flashy car and mod ways earned for him the nickname "Clyde." He would steal the basketball, pass brilliantly, perform best under pressure, display an unruffled manner—all of which were the sporting counterparts to the characteristics of the movie antihero Clyde.

Cold Lacking the ability to score points (Cold Streak).

"Cornbread" Current Boston radio color commentator Cedric Maxwell played eight years with the Celtics and also led UNC Charlotte to the 1977 Final Four. He had a fondness for that type of bread.

Court A 94' x 50' area bounded by two sidelines and two end lines. A basket is located at each end.

Court Vision Ability of a player to see everything on the court during play.

Crossover Dribble Player dribbles ball across his body from one hand to the other.

Cylinder Imaginary area directly above the basket where goaltending or basket interference can occur.

D Defense.

Dallas Mavericks In 1980, a Dallas radio station sorted out many suggested names in a name-the-team contest and picked "Mavericks," thinking it had Texas flavor. Samuel A. Maverick was a Texan who neglected to brand his cattle.

Dead Ball A nonlive ball. Occurs after each successful field goal or free-throw attempt, after an official's whistle, or if the ball leaves the court. Play is stopped, then continued by a jump ball, throw-in, or free throw.

Defense Preventing the offense from scoring; the team without the ball.

Defensive Board The backboard guarded by the defense.

Defensive Rebound A rebound off the defensive board.

Denver Nuggets When the Denver Rockets of the American Basketball Association (ABA) came into the NBA, they had to change their name because the Houston Rockets already existed. So the Denver franchise took the "Nuggets" name of an original NBA franchise, which was appropriate for an area with a history of gold and silver mining.

Detroit Pistons The Pistons came into being early on in NBA history, 1948. They were known then as the Ft. Wayne Zollner Pistons. It was a case of an owner naming a team for himself and the business that he ran. Fred Zollner owned a huge piston-manufacturing company. In 1957, the team moved to Detroit (1957–1978), and the Pistons name moved right along with it. There were moves to Pontiac, Michigan, 1978–1988, then to Auburn Hills in 1988.

Division Line The midcourt line dividing the court in half (Timeline).

"Dollar Bill" Born July 28, 1943, in Crystal City, Missouri, Bill Bradley was a fine athlete almost from the start. An incredible high school basketball player, he could have probably gone to any college in America on a basketball scholarship. But he chose Princeton and paid his own way since Ivy League schools did not offer athletic scholarships. He led Princeton to three Ivy League titles, averaged 30.1 points per game, and was a two-time All-American. The only junior, he was the captain of the 1964 gold medal–winning U.S. Olympic team.

His contract with the New York Knickerbockers called for $500,000 for four years' work, but the nickname given Bill Bradley was not for the money he earned but for the money he saved. While other NBA stars drove flashy cars and sported ever more lavish wardrobes, Bradley lived simply and dressed even more simply. His apartment, one friend said, "looked like a Holiday Inn room before the maid shows up."

Bradley reportedly used paper clips when his cuff buttons gave out. There was a precedent for his behavior. While a Rhodes scholar at Oxford for two years, Bradley lived out of what was called "a large and appallingly messy suitcase." He had more important things on his mind than style and consumer comforts. Bradley led New York to NBA titles and was the toast of New York. But in his time as a Knick, Bradley never did a commercial. He was very conscious even then of his image. He even had a special clause in his contract that said he did not have to do any endorsements.

The urbane and sophisticated Bill Bradley, whose name and image dominated headlines some years back as he sometimes pursued the Democratic Presidential nomination is, in many ways, the same person he was when he starred for the New York Knickerbockers of the NBA.

Double Double Generally, a player scoring and rebounding in double figures in the same game.

Double Dribble A violation that gives the ball over to the other team; it is caused by a player starting his dribble, stopping, and then starting it again.

Double Figures The scoring of more than nine points in a game by a player.

Double-Team The guarding of one offensive player by two defensive players.

Downcourt The area of the court opposite that where the action is taking place.

Downtown Shooting at the basket from an area that is a long distance from the backboard.

"Downtown" Freddy Brown, for his three-point shooting.

Draft Method NBA teams use annually to select college or foreign players for their franchises.

Draw a Foul To deliberately maneuver oneself so as to be fouled; to be fouled.

"Dr. Dunkenstein" Darrell Griffith, so named for his dunking exploits while at the University of Louisville.

"The Dream" Hakeem Olajuwon, who starred for the Houston Rockets, was a big man who dominated on both sides of the court with a combination of power and finesse. He is the all-time leader in blocked shots.

Dream Team Media name for basketball team that won the gold medal at the 1992 Barcelona Olympics; it was the first time nonamateurs were permitted to represent the USA in basketball. The members of this team were Charles Barkley, Larry Bird, Clyde Drexler, Patrick Ewing, Magic Johnson, Michael Jordan, Christian Laettner, Karl Malone, Chris Mullin, Scottie Pippen, David Robinson, and John Stockton. In the 1996 Olympics, the U.S. team was called Dream Team II and in 2000, Dream Team III, and so forth.

Dribble To bounce and control the ball with one hand and walk or run with the ball at the same time.

Dribble-Drive A player drives to the basket while dribbling.

Drive To dribble with speed toward the basket in a scoring attempt.

"Dr. J". Agile and talented Julius Erving, one of the premier stars first of the ABA and then in the NBA, could do tricks with a basketball. Neither his first nor his last name conjures up images of a driving, talented, cool basketball player. Thus, the "Dr." stems from what he can do with a basketball and an ailing team, and the "J" is a more relevant sounding abbreviation for his first name.

Dunk To leap high in the air and, with hand(s) above the rim, drop the ball through the basket for a score (Slam Dunk, Stuff).

"Dunkin' Dutchman" Rik Smits, former NBA star, for his Dutch roots and seven-foot-plus size.

"Easy Ed" A lean 6' 8", 190-pounder, Ed Macauley ranks as one of the top centers in NBA history. A three-time All-Star in a nine-year playing career during the 1950s, Macauley specialized in a smooth, almost unstoppable hook shot and driving layups. His temperament and his performing skills were characterized by an ease and a grace that was reflected in his nickname.

Elbowing A player excessively swings his elbows.

End Line Boundary line behind each basket.

Established Position A defensive player's stance with both feet firmly planted on the floor before an offensive player's head and shoulder get past him. An offensive player running into that defender is charged with a foul.

Fadeaway Jump(er) A jump shot at the basket in which the body of the player falls backward in getting the shot off.

Fake (Feint) Deceptive move to throw a defender off balance and allow an offensive player to shoot or get a pass.

Fast Break A quick breakaway downcourt to their basket by the team on offense.

Feed To pass the ball to another player, who then shoots it.

Field Goal A basket scored from the floor and worth two points (Hoop).

Field-Goal Percentage Ratio of shots taken to field goals scored.

Final Four In college basketball, the four regional champions (West, East, Midwest, and Southeast) remaining from the sixty-four college teams that compete in the NCAA Tournament. They play one another to determine the national champion.

Finals, NBA Annual championship series of the NBA's postseason.

"Fire and Ice" Chris Corchiani and Rodney Monroe of North Carolina State. One was the Pack's fiery point guard refusing to lose, and the other was an ice-cold marksman once hitting nine three-pointers in a game. Corchiani is one of three NCAA players to have one thousand assists.

Five-Second Rule An amateur rule that bans players from holding ball in their forecourt for more than five seconds without making a move. Violation results in a jump ball at midcourt.

Flagrant Foul Unnecessary or excessive contact against an opponent.

Floor Area of the court within end lines and sidelines.

Floor Violation Player's action that violates rules but does not prevent an opponent's movement or cause him harm; penalized by a change in possession (Violation).

Follow Up A situation where a player follows up a rebounded shot with another shot.

Force (Forcing) the Shot The act of a player shooting at the basket even though he is being defended effectively or does not have a good opportunity to make the shot.

Forecourt The part of the court nearest the basket.

40 Minutes of Hell For the University of Arkansas, Nolan Richardson's nonstop pressure defense earned Arkansas a national championship in 1994 and got them to the championship game in 1995.

Forwards Two taller players who generally play in the corners on either side of their pivotman.

Foul Actions by players breaking rules but are not floor violations; these are penalized by a change in possession or free-throw opportunities. See "Personal Foul" or "Technical Foul."

Foul Lane Painted area bordered by the end line and the foul line, outside which players must stand during free throws; also the area an offensive player cannot spend more than three seconds at a time in.

Foul Line Line fifteen feet from the backboard and parallel to the end line from which players shoot free-throws.

Foul Out To use up the allowed number of fouls and be forced to leave the game. In pro ball, six is the limit; in college, the limit is five.

Four-Point Play A three point shot followed by a successful free-throw.

Franchise Player Star player around which a franchise is built.

Free Agent, Restricted An NBA player whose contract has expired and who has received a "qualifying offer" from his current club providing a salary level predetermined by the collective bargaining agreement. While this player is free to negotiate an offer from a new team, his current team has a right of first refusal to match that offer, thereby obligating him to remain with his current team.

Free Agent, Unrestricted NBA player who has completed his third NBA season (or fourth season, if his current team exercised its "option" to have him play for a fourth year) and is free to negotiate a contract with other NBA teams without his current team having a right of first refusal.

Free Throw An unguarded shot worth one point taken by a player from the free-throw line for personal or technical fouls (Foul Shot).

Free Throw Area The part of the court that includes the free-throw line, the free-throw lane, and sometimes the free-throw circle.

Free Throw Circle Located at either end of the court, these circles are bisected by the free-throw lines.

Free Throw Lane Bordered by the end line and the free-throw line, this lane is nineteen feet long and sixteen feet wide in pro basketball (Three-Second Lane; Three-Second Area).

Free Throw Line Parallel to the end line and fifteen feet in front of the backboard, this twelve-foot-long "charity stripe" is the line players must stand behind in taking free shots.

Free Throw Percentage The ratio of free throws made to free throws taken.

Front To attempt to deny the ball to a player by taking a defensive stance in front of him.

Frontcourt Area between the midcourt line and the end line closest to the offense's basket.

Frontcourtmen The two forwards and center.

Frontline The three players who are frontcourtmen.

Full-Court Press Defensive guarding all over the court from the time the ball is inbounded by the team on offense.

Game Clock The clock that indicates playing time used.

Garbage Shooter A player who specializes in taking and making easy shots close to the basket.

"The General" A moniker for controversial college basketball coach Bob Knight for his overbearing ways.

Get the Roll A phrase that describes a player's touch at the basket as the ball he has shot rolls on the rim and through the hoop.

"The Glide" Clyde Drexler's role model was Julius Erving. "He seemed to fly. I wanted to be like him," said Drexler, who earned the nickname "Clyde the Glide" for his own swooping moves.

"The Glove" Gary Payton, the all-time scoring leader at Oregon State, made a name for himself with the Seattle Supersonics on the other side of the ball—as a defender.

Goal Shot from the field worth two points (Basket).

Goaltending A violation caused by a player interfering with the ball before it begins its downward movement in an imaginary funnel over the rim.

Go Baseline A phrase that describes a player on offense driving with the basketball along the baseline under the basket.

Golden State Warriors In 1925, there was a Philadelphia Warriors team in the American Basketball League. In 1946, when Philadelphia joined the NBA, it took its nickname from that old team. The Golden State Warriors are a descendant of the old Philadelphia Warriors. They've gone through a couple of geographical shifts. Philly became the San Francisco Warriors, San Francisco became the Oakland Warriors, and Oakland became the Golden State Warriors.

"Granmama" Larry Johnson, who played for the Knicks and other teams in the NBA—even when he was young he looked grandmotherly.

Guarding The act of following an opponent around the court to prevent him from getting close to the basket, taking an open shot, or making easy an pass.

Guards Positions generally played by smaller players adept at ball handling and dribbling; they usually operate on the perimeter of the offensive and defensive zones.

Gunner A player who shoots the ball whenever he can (Chucker).

Hack To hit an opponent's arm with the hand—a personal foul.

"Hack-a-Shaq" Primitive defensive scheme designed to try to stop the most unstoppable man in the NBA—Shaquille O'Neal. Fouling him puts him on the foul line where his skills are subpar.

Half-Court (Set Offense) A team takes the time to develop a play in its frontcourt, such as the give-and-go or a screening play; opposite of Fast Break.

Hand Check The action of a defensive player who places his hand(s) on the body of the ball handler.

Hanger A defensive player who stays back under his offensive basket while his team is on defense and awaits the opportunity for his team to go on offense so that he is positioned for an easy shot.

Hang in the Air A phrase that describes a player's ability to remain airborne for a brief moment—while taking a jump shot, for example.

Hang on the Rim The act of illegally placing the hands on the rim of the basket and hanging from that position.

Held Ball A situation where two opposing players simultaneously have possession of the ball, causing a jump ball.

Helping Out To assist a teammate in defensive coverage.

High Percentage Shot One likely to go in the basket, such as a layup.

High Post Imaginary area outside either side of the foul lane at the free-throw line extended.

"His Airness" Michael Jordan seemed to fly in the air and also his play had a touch of royalty about it for some, hence the nickname.

Hole The basket. Also, an area deep in the pivot area under the basket.

Hook Pass A pass made by a player who raises his arm high over his head and arcs the ball to a teammate.

Hook Shot A type of shot in which a player positions the ball high over his head in the outstretched hand of his outstretched arm and arcs the ball at the basket.

Hoop A basket.

"Horse" Harry Gallatin starred for the NBA New York Knickerbockers during the 1950s. Though just 6' 6", his bulk and power enabled him to out-rebound much taller opponents. In the 1953–1954 season Gallatin pulled down 1,098 rebounds, an average of 15.3 per game. His strength and stamina earned him his nickname.

"Hot Dog" Dennis Rodman, master rebounder and man of many hair colors and show-off ways.

Hot Hand A player or team on a streak of effective shooting.

Houston Rockets The Houston Rockets were once the San Diego Rockets (1967–1971). When the franchise moved to Houston in 1971, the name went along and fit in a city linked to space programs and industries.

"The Human Eraser" Marvin Webster of the New York Knickerbockers in the NBA earned his nickname for his shot-blocking ability. At seven-foot-plus, Webster's size and timing has enabled him to wipe out scoring efforts of opponents by simply batting the ball away from the hoop.

"Human Highlight Reel" Dominique Wilkins—passing was not his game but spectacular offensive moves were.

"The Iceman" George Gervin was locked into this name for his cool and calm demeanor on the NBA court. One thing he could do was finger roll. The Iceman was the man in the ABA. He was so good that the Spurs stole him from the Virginia Squires through a harsh court battle.

"I Love Waltah" Tommy Heinsohn, Celtic broadcaster, started the unofficial Walter McCarty fan club, coining the catch phrase and creating a national fan club for the likable reserve Celtic forward who was traded to Phoenix in 2005.

Inadvertent Whistle One blown by an official by accident.

Inbounds The area within the end lines and sidelines of the court; also the act of bringing the ball into this area by means of a throw-in.

Inbounds Play A situation where the ball is put into play after it has gone out of bounds or play has been stopped.

Incidental Contact Minor contact usually overlooked by officials.

Indiana Pacers When the Indiana franchise came into existence in 1967 in the ABA, the owners said they named the team Pacers because they intended to set the pace in professional basketball. There was also the matter of the famous Indianapolis 500 Raceway. And when Indiana joined the NBA in 1976, the name Pacers went along.

Inside Shooting Shots taken by a player near or under the basket.

Intentional Foul A deliberate foul generally committed late in a game to stop the clock, giving the opposition a chance at free throws in hopes that the shots will be missed and the fouling team will gain ball possession.

In the Paint Being in the foul lane area, which is painted a different color from the rest of the court.

"Jellybean" Joe Bryant is the father of Kobe. He played eight seasons in the NBA for the Philadelphia 76ers and other teams. The elder Bryant had a fondness for jelly beans.

"Jones Boys" K. C. and Sam Jones were the great Celtic backcourt in the 1960s. K. C. was "Mr. Defense," while Sam was "Mr. Offense."

Jump Ball A situation where two opposing players leap up at a ball thrown by the referee and each attempts to tap it to his respective teammates; used at the start of the half and when disagreement as to who has the right to possession of the ball occurs.

Jump Pass A type of pass where the player leaps in the air and passes the ball to a teammate.

Jump Shot A type of shot that involves a player jumping in the air and releasing the ball from a position over or behind his head.

Keepaway Game Tactic used (more so in college games) by a team that is leading near the end of the game to keep the ball from its opponents to prevent them from scoring while using up time off the game clock (Freezing).

Key, Keyhole The area at each end of the court consisting of the foul circle, foul lane, and free-throw line; named for the shape it had years ago.

"Kobe" L.A. star Kobe Bryant was named after a "Kobe" steak listed on the menu of a Japanese restaurant or, as the story goes, for a Japanese restaurant itself.

"Larry Legend" Boston Celtic superstar Larry Bird could do it all on the basketball floor and was most deserving of this nickname.

Layup, Layin A shot taken after driving to the basket by leaping up under the basket and using one hand to drop the ball directly into the basket (layin) or to bank the ball off the backboard into it (layup).

Leading the Receiver Passer throws the ball where he thinks a receiver is headed.

Lead Pass A pass ahead of a teammate, who runs for the ball.

Leaper A player with top jumping ability.

Line Drive A shot with no arc.

Live Ball As soon as a ball is given to a free-throw shooter or a thrower on a throw-in, it is live, but the game clock does not restart until the ball is alive.

Loose Ball One that is alive but not in the possession of either team.

Loose-Ball Foul In professional basketball, a personal foul by a player trying to get control of a loose ball. It is charged as a team foul, with the opposing team awarded possession of the ball via a throw-in—except during a penalty situation, when two foul shots are given to the fouled player.

Los Angeles Clippers In 1971, the city of San Diego lost its NBA franchise when its team moved to Houston and became the Rockets. The franchise that was originally the Buffalo Braves, from 1970 to 1978, moved to San Diego. The owners weren't too thrilled with San Diego Braves as a name. So one of those name-the-team contests was staged, and the winning entry was, you guessed it, "Clippers." That was because, once upon a time, lots of beautiful clipper ships passed through the great harbor of San Diego. In fact, the *Star of India* was still harbored in San Diego. In 1984 the franchise moved to Los Angeles and the name Clippers came along.

Los Angeles Lakers The Minneapolis Lakers made the move to L.A. before the 1960 season and took with them their nickname that comes from the state of Minnesota's motto: "The Land of 10,000 Lakes."

Low Post Imaginary area outside either side of the foul lane near to the basket.

Lower Percentage Shot One less likely to go in the basket, such as one thrown by a player who is off balance or outside his shooting range.

Lowest Scoring NBA Game The 1950–1951 season saw the NBA go from an unwieldy seventeen-team league to eleven teams in a two-division setup. It was also a season that included the lowest-scoring game in NBA history. On November 22, 1950, the yawner of all yawners was played. The game pitted Fort Wayne against Minneapolis and was played on the home court of the Lakers, who enjoyed a great home advantage. Their court was shorter and narrower than normal size. Their team was big, bulky, and slow—all of which were perfectly suited for a slowdown game.

In the game, the two teams combined for just thirty-one shots. When it was over, Ft. Wayne had creaked out a 19-18 triumph in a painful and boring example of how dull a stalling contest could be. The game started serious talk throughout the NBA about ways to prevent those kinds of contests from taking place.

Then on January 6, 1951, a very cold night in Rochester, the Royals played against the Indianapolis Olympians in what has gone down as the longest game in the annals of the NBA. The game lasted a grand total of seventy-eight minutes and included six overtimes. Some of the loyal Rochester fans booed, and hundreds of others walked out of the old Edgerton Park Arena. They just couldn't abide the slow-down stalling tactics of both teams. In the half-dozen overtimes, just twenty-three shots were taken. At the start of each overtime, the team that earned the tip just held on to the ball for one last shot. Players just stood around gaping and staring at each other. One player dribbled or held the ball and looked around hoping to make the smart pass for a high percentage shot. Indianapolis finally won the game, 75-73.

Red Holzman recalled: "I played seventy-six of the seventy-eight minutes in that opus. And although I was in great shape, my tail was dragging when the historic marathon was over." That game and the bore that was the 19-18 contest made players and coaches see the need and the urgency to speed up the game. It was these two games, and others like them, that set the stage for the creation of the twenty-four-second clock—and the salvation of the NBA.

The clock was first used in the 1954–1955 season, and scoring jumped an average of fifteen points a game as a result. The new NBA era was under way. In 1951, after the 19-18 game, Red Holzman claimed he got the idea for a shot clock and told some of the owners about it. They dismissed him as "a young squirt." But someone must have been listening.

"Magic" Earvin Johnson of Los Angeles Lakers' fame had this nickname pinned on him for his "wizardry" on the court.

"Mailman" Former great Utah star Karl Malone always seemed to deliver.

Man-to-Man Defense Defensive style where each defensive player is responsible for guarding one opponent.

March Madness Three-week-long NCAA basketball competition leading to a national championship is held during March (see also Final Four).

Match-Ups Players on opposing teams who guard each other.

Memphis Grizzlies Franchise started as an expansion team in 1995 and moved to Memphis in 2001. Originally known as Vancouver Mounties but changed after the objections of the Royal Canadian Mounted Police to "Grizzlies," because grizzly bears are part of the scene in British Columbia. The animal is also part of the mythology of the area.

Miami Heat Miami in 1988 held a name-the-team contest and received more than five thousand entries. Some of the names that didn't make it included: "Flamingos," "Waves," "Palm Trees," "Beaches," "Suntan," and "Shade." "Heat" beat them all out. One clever team official explained: "When you think of Miami, heat is what comes to mind." The Miami Heat mascot appropriately enough is called "Burnie."

"Michelangelo" Hall of Fame North Carolina coach Dean Smith, an artist as a coach with more wins than any other collegiate coach.

"Microwave" Vinnie Johnson was a member of the "Bad Boys" teams of the late 1980s to early 1990s Detroit Pistons. A sixth man who came off the bench and "heated up" in seconds, he was nicknamed "The Microwave" by Danny Ainge.

Middle The part of the court near the free-throw line.

Milwaukee Bucks A guy named R. D. Treblicox of Whitefish Bay, Wisconsin, got himself a brand new car for coming up with the name "Bucks" back in 1968 for Milwaukee's NBA team. He reasoned that "bucks are spirited, good jumpers, fast and agile." His pick beat out names like "Stags," "Skunks," and "Stallions." Treblicox knew both his bucks and his basketball.

Minnesota Timberwolves Over six thousand entries were submitted for the Minnesota nickname in 1989. The choice came down to "Timberwolves" vs. "Polars." "Timberwolves" easily won. That animal is native to Minnesota, and no other professional sports team ever thought to use the name.

Mismatch A situation where a tall player by accident or missed assignment gets matched against a smaller player and gets a height advantage or vice versa.

"Mr. Clutch" Hall of Famer Jerry West was that.

Naismith Memorial Basketball Hall of Fame Dr. James Naismith (1861–1939), a physical education instructor at Springfield College in Massachusetts, invented basketball in 1891. Naismith's chairman gave him the task of organizing some type of game to fill the time between fall football and spring baseball for the class the doctor taught. The only restriction was that the game had to be played indoors, for the students balked at outdoor activities. Naismith at first attempted to adapt outdoor games such as soccer, lacrosse, and rugby to indoor play. This did not work too well. The sports were unsuited to a confined area and resulted in broken windows and damaged players. Naismith finally settled on the idea of a noncontact sport in which players were not allowed to run with the ball. He got the janitor at the college to string peach baskets on the balconies at each end of the gym.

Dividing his eighteen students into two teams, he gave them a soccer ball to play with, posted his original "Thirteen Rules" on the gym's bulletin board, and thus solved his problem of a winter game for the students at Springfield College. There were suggestions that the game be called Naismith Ball, but the good doctor was too modest for this. He coined the name basketball for the game he invented. In February 1968 the Basketball Hall of Fame was officially opened on the campus where the game was introduced, and its name honors the man who was the father of basketball.

National Association for Intercollegiate Athletics (NAIA) Focused on the needs of small and medium-size institutions, the NAIA's roots reach back to 1937 and an organization called the National Association of Intercollegiate Basketball. In 1940 the NAIB expanded its focus to include most college sports and changed its name to the present NAIA.

NCAA Tournament An annual competition between sixty-four college teams of the National Collegiate Athletic Association focused on crowning a national champion (see March Madness).

"Never Nervous" Pervis Ellsion starred for the Louisville Cardinals where he was clutch in pressure situations.

New Jersey Nets The Nets began life in the ABA and were known as the New Jersey Americans. In 1968, the team left New Jersey and moved to Commack, Long Island, and were renamed the New York Nets. The reasoning was that since the New York metropolitan area had the football Jets and the baseball Mets, why not the basketball Nets? Just before the 1977–1978 season, the franchise moved back across the Hudson River to New Jersey. Then Brooklyn beckoned.

New Orleans Hornets Since 1988, originally located in Charlotte, where the nickname got its name, which has been continued in New Orleans. During the Revolutionary War, General Cornwallis remarked about the resistance met in North Carolina, "There's a rebel behind every bush, it's a veritable nest of hornets!" The franchise moved to New Orleans in 2002.

New York Knickerbockers The name "Knickerbockers" dates back to when New York was New Amsterdam, and Dutch settlers had trousers bunched up at the knee known as "knickers." The Knicks and the Celtics are the only teams still playing in the NBA in their original cities.

NIT (National Invitational Tournament) The oldest college tournament, in which thirty-two teams not selected to the NCAA Tournament compete each year.

Offense Team with possession of the ball.

Offensive Foul A personal foul committed by a member of a team on offense.

Offensive Rebound A rebound taken by offensive team.

Officials The crew chief, referee, and umpire who control the game, stop and start play, and impose penalties for violations and fouls.

Off the Dribble Shot taken while driving to the basket.

One-and-One A bonus shot given in amateur ball if first free shot is successful. In pro ball, the bonus shot is taken whether or not the first shot is made.

One-on-One A man-to-man offensive and/or defensive action.

Open Man (Open) Offensive player free to receive a pass with a chance to take a good shot.

Opportunity Shot A shot at the basket made available through luck or a defensive team's lapse.

Orlando Magic The "Orlando Sentinel" sponsored a name-the-team contest in 1989. The final choices were "Magic" and "Juice." Orlando general manager Pat Williams explained why "Magic" won out: "Magic is synonymous with the Orlando area. We have the Magic Kingdom in Disney World, and the tourism slogan here is 'Come to the Magic.'"

Outlet Pass A quick, long, downcourt pass generally made immediately after a rebound.

Out of Bounds A situation where a ball is no longer in play after touching or going over sidelines or baselines.

Out-of-Bounds Play A strategy used by a team in putting the ball back in play.

Out-Rebound To rebound more effectively than another player or team.

Outside Shooting Shots taken from the perimeter.

Over the Limit When a team commits five or more team fouls per NBA period (four in each overtime); eight or more per WNBA half; seven or more per half in college; this team is also said to be in the penalty.

Overtime (OT) The extra period(s) played after a regulation game ends tied.

"Owl without a Vowel" Bill Mlkvy played forward for the Temple University Owls basketball team. Since his last name does not contain a vowel, he became "the owl without a vowel."

Palming Turning the ball over with a palm-twisting motion while dribbling—a violation that gives possession of the ball to the other team.

Pass A player throws the ball to a teammate; used to start plays, move the ball downcourt, keep it away from defenders, and get it to a shooter.

Passer Player who passes the ball to a teammate.

Passing Lane An imaginary aisle between offensive players through which passes are made; the defense tries to protect against passes going through the passing lanes.

"The Pearl" A slick, smooth ball handler and imaginative shotmaker, Earl Monroe (also known as "Mr. Magic") earned his nickname with his spectacular moves on the basketball court.

Penalty Shot A bonus free throw.

Penalty Situation The condition of a team being in the bonus situation.

Penetration The ability by a player or team on offense to get in very close to the basket.

Percentage Shot A shot at the basket that has a good chance to succeed.

Perimeter area Beyond the foul circle, away from the basket.

Period Any quarter, half, or overtime segment.

Personal Foul Illegal physical contact by one player with another, such as charging, hacking, and so forth.

Philadelphia 76ers In 1963, the old Syracuse Nats were sold and became the Philadelphia 76ers. The Philly franchise got its name from American history.

"Phi Slamma Jamma" The 1983 Houston Cougars dunked several times a game and were a top college basketball team. Hence, the dunking fraternity label.

Phoenix Suns In 1968, the new Phoenix franchise offered a cash prize and a couple of season tickets to the winner of a name-the-team contest. "Suns" was the winning name. Runner-ups included "Scorpions," "Rattlers," and "Dust Devils." There were almost thirty thousand names submitted.

Pick A maneuver where an offensive player, by standing motionless, screens out a defensive player.

Pick-and-Roll A play where a pick is set and then the player moves off the pick and sprints toward the basket, anticipating a pass.

Picked Off A defender who has been successfully prevented from reaching the ball handler by an offensive screener.

Pick-up Games Played by players who get together informally.

Pin To temporarily stop the ball on the backboard by pressing it there with a hand.

"Pistol Pete" From 1967 to 1970 Louisiana State University's Pete Maravich, a skinny guard with floppy socks, was the leading collegiate basketball point scorer in the United States. He scored nearly four thousand points, averaging almost forty-five points a game, during his varsity career. Press Maravich, his father and also his LSU coach, gave him his nickname. It was a reference to the young Maravich's quick-trigger shot release and his scoring ability. Pistol Pete continued his illustrious career with the Atlanta Hawks and then the New Orleans Jazz of the NBA. Scoring, passing the ball between his legs or behind his back, showing off a bewildering variety of shots, Maravich became one of the top guns in pro basketball. He was immortalized in "The Ballad of Peter Maravich," written by Woody Jenkins:

> Maravich, oh Maravich, Love to fake, love to score,
> Love to hear the people roar. Just a boy of twenty-two,
> You made a name at LSU.

Pivot To turn on one foot while keeping the pivot foot stationary.

Pivot Center The foot that must remain touching the floor until a ball handler who has stopped dribbling is ready to pass or shoot.

Pivotman A player who performs in the pivot or center position.

Playing Court College: ninety-four feet long by fifty feet wide (desired dimensions). High School: eighty-four feet long by fifty feet wide (desired dimensions).

Playmaker The point guard who generally sets up plays for his teammates.

Podoloff Cup A trophy awarded annually to the National Basketball Association's Most Valuable Player, it is named in honor of Maurice Podoloff, the first commissioner of the NBA, who was, curiously, just five feet tall.

Point Guard A player who plays the guard position and directs his team's offense, generally from behind his team's offensive foul line.

Point-Shaving Illegal practice where players intentionally win a game, but by fewer points than the point spread; led to two major college scandals (involved thirty-two of the biggest stars in the 1950s, then twenty-two colleges in 1961).

"Pop" Longtime San Antonio Spurs' head coach Greg Popovich, a shortening of his surname and tip of the cap to his longevity.

Portland Trailblazers Since 1970, named from a contest; the name "Chinooks" was considered, but "Trailblazers" was chosen in the end.

Position The place on the court occupied by a player; good position is related to effective scoring, rebounding, and defense.

Possession In control of the ball.

Possession Arrow In college, used to determine which team's turn it is to inbound the ball to begin a period or in a jump ball situation.

Post The pivot position: the high post is near the foul line for an offensive player; the low post is near the basket.

Post Position Location of a player standing in the low post or high post.

Power Forward A strong rebounding and defensive forward.

Pull Up To drive to the basket with the ball, stop short, and, most times, shoot from this stopped position.

Pump Fake To feign shooting the ball at the basket. A Double Pump Fake involves feigning a shot twice.

Pure Shooter A player who generally scores baskets cleanly and effortlessly.

Push Off To illegally use the hands to push an opponent.

Put the Ball on the Floor To dribble the ball.

Quadruple Double Double-digits scored in four categories.

Rebound To gain control of the ball as it comes off the backboard or rim after a missed shot.

Rebounder One who rebounds.

Receiver Player getting pass.

Referees The two or three officials who supervise all aspects of a basketball game. A Trail Referee is the one who follows the offensive flow of the game down the court. An Alternate Referee is in attendance in pro basketball games to replace one of the three referees in case of an emergency or illness.

Regulation Game Four twelve-minute quarters in the NBA or two twenty-minute halves in college; a game that ends without overtime periods.

"The Rens" Their full name was the Renaissance Big Five, and in the period 1932–1936 there was no better basketball team in all the United States. Organized in 1922 in Harlem by Bob Douglas and disbanded in 1948, the Rens were an all-black, independent team that consisted of Clarence "Fat" Jenkins, Bill Yancey, John "Casey" Holt, James "Pappy" Ricks, Eyre "Bruiser" Saitch, Charles "Tarzan" Cooper, and "Wee" Willie Smith. Both Yancey and Jenkins were also great stars in Negro Leagues baseball.

They played one-night stands, traveled and slept in their own bus, played all types of teams under all types of circumstances. In 1933–1934 they posted a record of eighty-eight straight wins and completed the year with a 127-7 record. In 1932–1936 the Rens won 473 games and lost only forty-nine. They existed before the Harlem Globetrotters and were a much different kind of team. The Globies clowned around; the Rens played to win and did they win! For their time there was no better basketball team in the world. Their home games were played on the dance floor of the Renaissance Casino Ballroom in Harlem. And when the games ended some of the Rens would stay around and dance with the ladies and enjoy the atmosphere.

There were times that they played two or three games in a single day as they barnstormed across the country. They had to set up command posts in places like Chicago and Indianapolis and return from as far away as two hundred miles after games because racial bigotry denied them hotel rooms. Their postgame meals were often cold cuts that they carried on the bus because so many places refused to feed or lodge them.

Their "road secretary" Eric Illidge carried a tabulator to personally count the number of fans at games because the Rens were generally paid a percentage of the gate. He also carried a pistol and told the guys, "Never come out on the court unless I have the money." It was the only way the Rens could survive.

The Rens disbanded in 1948, and in 1963 the entire team was elected to membership in the National Basketball Hall of Fame. The story of the New York Renaissance Five is a story of great success achieved in the face of bigotry, great odds, and tremendous sacrifice. Illidge, the man with the pistol, explained it all: "We would not let anyone deny us our right to make a living."

Reverse Dunk The act of dunking the ball from an over-the-head or -shoulder position opposite to the way the body is leaning.

Reverse English Reverse spin put on a shot.

"Rifleman" Chuck Person, from the TV show of the same name—a tribute to this former NBA player's marksmanship on the court.

Rim The basket's circular metal frame.

Rimmer A shot that rolls on the rim (Rims the Ring).

Roll To turn the body and move toward the basket.

Roundball Nickname for basketball ("Cage Sport"; "Hoop Game").

"Round Mound of Rebound" A reference to Charles Barkley's rebounding skills and not too svelte appearance in college and early NBA days.

Run The quick scoring of field goals by a team.

Run-and-Gun A high-powered running and shooting offense.

Sacramento Kings The Rochester Royals played in the NBA for nine seasons and then transferred to Cincinnati. The name Royals was kept. In 1972, the franchise moved to Kansas City, Missouri, and the name was dropped to avoid confusion in the Kansas City area as the Kansas City and the Omaha baseball teams both used the name Royals. The new name for the NBA basketball franchise became the Kansas City-Omaha Kings and, in 1975, simply the Kansas City Kings. A decade later, when the team moved to California, they became the Sacramento Kings.

Sag To position the defense around a particular player or area by moving defensive players from other positions.

Salary Cap An annual dollar limit that a single NBA team may pay all its players.

San Antonio Spurs Nickname came in a public naming contest. The team is actually a descendant of the old Dallas Chaparrals of the ABA. But when the Chaps moved in 1973 to San Antonio, their nickname became a footnote to history. Renamed the Gunslingers after moving from Dallas in 1967, and later renamed the San Antonio Spurs, 1973. Other entries were "Stampede," "Armadillos," "Defenders," and "Texans."

Save To keep a ball from going out of bounds.

Scoop Shot An underhand (running) shot taken close to basket.

Screen A maneuver where an offensive player gets stationary position in front of a teammate, thus acting as a human barrier or screen for his teammate to shoot over (Screener).

Seattle Supersonics The existence of a huge Boeing aircraft plant in Seattle inspired Howard E. Schmidt's name suggestion in 1967 for the Seattle NBA franchise.

"Secretary of Defense" Michael Cooper, former Laker star, for his skills as a defensive player.

Set Play Prearranged offensive move(s).

"Shark" When Jerry Tarkanian coached for University of Nevada at Las Vegas, he was called by that name for his winning and offensive ways.

Shooter One who takes a shot.

Shooter's Roll Ability to get even an inaccurate shot to bounce lightly off the rim and into the basket.

Shooting Range Distance from which a player is likely to make his shots.

Short A shot that does not touch the basket, but may touch the rim.

Shot Clock A clock that indicates the time left for shooting; in the NBA, players must shoot within twenty-four seconds.

"Showtime" The Pat Riley–coached L.A. Lakers, a team that featured "Magic" Johnson and others who put on a show.

Sidelines Two boundary lines that run the length of the court.

Sixth Man The first substitute usually used by a team—generally an excellent player.

"Sky" Kenny Walker was a leaper in his prime NBA days.

"Skywalker" In his prime especially in the ABA, it seemed David Thompson was doing that.

Slam Dunk A dunk that is forcefully jammed into a basket (Stuff).

"Sleepy" Eric Floyd played for Georgetown and the Houston Rockets. He looked that way.

Slough Off The act of a defender(s) leaving the player being guarded to aid in coverage of another opponent.

"The Spider" John Salley was a member of the Detroit Pistons, known for his small body, but long arms and legs.

Spot A favorite mark on the court from which a player shoots well.

Squaring Up When a player's shoulders are facing the basket as he releases the ball for a shot; considered good shooting position.

Stall A maneuver where an offensive team late in a game slows down the action and sometimes does not even shoot the ball, in an effort to control the game and the time (this tactic is not too feasible in professional basketball, with the twenty-four-second clock).

Steal A situation where a defensive player legally takes the ball away from an offensive player.

Steps Walking, traveling.

"The Stilt" Wilt Chamberlain, great NBA All-Star, was one man who could make heads turn upward. Over seven feet tall, he seemed to most of the opposition and the fans to be playing on stilts, and that's where his nickname came from. Chamberlain had a 30.1 lifetime scoring average. He was also known as "The Big Dipper," for many of his shots were simply "dipped" or dropped into the basket from above the rim. The greatest offensive player in the history of the game, Chamberlain's career began in the 1959–1960 season, at a time when there were not so many dominant big men playing. Thus, his "Stilt" nickname underscored his size.

There was probably no greater admirer of Wilt Chamberlain than the old New York Knicks head coach Red Holzman. When I was writing *Holzman on Hoops* in 1990, Red told me, "Wilt was taller than the seven-foot-one he was listed as. And he was a bull. He worked out mainly on his own with his own methods. He lifted a lot of weights and did a lot of running at the beach. Part of his strength was his ability to come back from injuries," Holzman noted. "Wilt would get hurt and come back so fast you couldn't believe it. An injury that would sideline another player for a month or more would lay up Wilt for just a week."

Knicks centers were given directions by Holzman: "Do not touch Wilt if he is under the basket going up in the act of shooting." Holzman went on to add, "Down under, there was no way Wilt would ever miss scoring no matter how hard he was hit. He was just so powerful."

The night of nights for Chamberlain on a basketball court took place March 2, 1962. The game was played in Hershey, Pennsylvania, of all places. Chamberlain's Philadelphia Warriors team was matched up against the New York Knicks. An exhibition game took place first between players from two professional football teams—the Philadelphia Eagles and the Baltimore Colts. Wilt was bigger and stronger than any of the guys on those teams.

In the first quarter of the game, Chamberlain was just warming up. He popped in twenty-three points, while the crowd chanted, "Give it to Wilt! Give it to Wilt!" In the second quarter, he scored eighteen points. Up to that game, the most points Wilt had ever amassed in a contest was seventy-eight, but he had sixty-nine points after the third quarter and seemed a cinch to break his own standard.

But no one expected him to do what he did. Although three Knicks each scored over thirty points in the game, no one cared. It was Chamberlain's night. With forty-two seconds to go in the game, Chamberlain received the ball under the basket and stuffed it in with two hands for his ninety-ninth and one-hundredth points. They had to hold up the game after he hit the century mark. Fans mobbed the court trying to get a piece of the man they called "The Big Dipper." All told, he hit thirty-six of sixty-three field goal attempts and made twenty-eight of thirty-two free throws for a grand total of 100 points. The magnificent performance was part of a 1961–1962 season, in which he averaged 50.4 points.

After the game Chamberlain told everyone who would listen, "I wasn't even thinking of hitting one hundred. After putting in nine straight free throws, I was thinking about a foul-shooting record." Foul shots were Chamberlain's obsession on the court—and only real weakness as well.

Streak Shooter One who makes a high percentage of his shots in spurts.

Stutter Step A quick, switching movement by a player from one foot to the other to fake out his opponent.

Substitute Player who comes into the game to replace a player on the court.

Sweep the Boards Rebound effectively.

Swing Man A player capable of playing more than one position well.

Swish A term that describes the scoring of a basket by getting the ball into the hoop without its touching the rim.

Switch To quickly exchange defensive assignments in the midst of play.

Tap In To tip a ball into the basket off a rebound from the rim or backboard.

Team Foul A foul charged to a team's quota for a period, which, when exceeded, allows the other team the bonus or penalty shot. The NBA allows four of these fouls per period, one in the final two minutes of a period, three in an overtime period.

Technical Foul A misconduct penalty for violations such as abusive behavior that gives a free throw plus possession of the ball to the other team ("T"). In the NBA, the offending team regains possession of the ball.

Ten-Second Rule A professional regulation that requires an offensive team, after putting the ball in play, to bring it over the midcourt line within ten seconds, or else lose possession of the ball.

Three-Point Arc Line from which players take long-range shots earning three-point baskets. The distance is twenty-two feet.

Three-Point Play A situation where a player who gets fouled while scoring a basket has the opportunity to score a third point on the play via a foul shot.

Three-Second Violation A regulation that bans an offensive player from remaining in the free-throw lane for more than three consecutive seconds.

Throw-in To put a ball in play.

"Throws Up a Brick" Player tosses up a particularly errant shot.

"Throws Up a Prayer" A wild shot that will need a miracle to score.

"Ticky-Tack" A foul called when very little contact has been made.

Timeout When play is temporarily suspended by an official or at the request of a team to respond to an injured player or discuss strategy; there are full timeouts (one hundred or sixty seconds in NBA, 120 seconds in WNBA, seventy-five or sixty seconds in college) and twenty-second timeouts (thirty seconds in college).

"Tiny" He was less than 6 feet tall, and for an NBA player that was something unusual. But Nate Archibald, a member of the Basketball Hall of Fame and the NBA's fiftieth anniversary all-time team, had the goods. He was the only player in NBA history to lead the league in scoring and assists in the same season, averaging 34 points and 11.4 assists per game with the Kansas City-Omaha Kings during the 1972–1973 season.

Tip-in A quick follow-up shot made when a player pushes or taps the ball into the basket without first gaining control of the ball.

Tip-off The initial jump ball that starts a game.

T-Mac Tracy McGrady, abbreviations galore.

Tommy Points Awarded by Boston Celtic announcer Tommy Heinsohn to players who hustle and show toughness and team play.

Toronto Raptors The NBA's twenty-eighth team, and its first expansion franchise outside of the United States, picked up its "Raptors" name in a name-the-team contest. Runner-up names were "Beavers," "Bobcats," "Dragons," "Grizzlies," "Hogs," "Scorpions," "Tarantulas," "Terriers," "Towers," and "T-Rex."

Touch A good feel for shooting the basketball.

"Tractor Traylor" Robert Traylor, a play on his girth and name.

Trailer An offensive player who trails the offensive flow and comes late into a play.

Transition The shift from offense to defense or vice versa.

Trap A situation where defensive players double-team a player with the ball in an attempt to gain control of it (Trap Press).

"Tricky Dick" One of the all-time greats in NBA history, Dick McGuire was one of the smoothest and most skilled of ball handlers. His behind-the-back passes, his ability to find the open man, his feinting virtuosity, and his excellent dribbling provided the reason for his nickname.

Triple Double A player who gets double figures in three statistical categories: points, rebounds, assists, steals, or blocked shots.

"The Truth" Shaq O'Neal created the nickname for Paul Pierce—some say to underscore the Celtic star's up-front manner on and off the court.

"Tsar of the Telestrator" Mike Fratello, for his alleged skills scribbling and explaining NBA game moves in his time as an announcer.

Turnover When the offense loses possession through its negligence.

Twenty-Four-Second Rule An NBA regulation that requires the offensive team to shoot within twenty-four seconds after gaining possession of the ball; failure to do so as indicated on the twenty-four-second clock awards the ball to the other team.

Utah Jazz The franchise came into being in 1979, when the New Orleans Jazz (1974–1979) moved there and kept their name and team colors.

Washington Wizards The present Washington franchise began life as the Chicago Packers in 1961, named by its owner after his packing company. A year later, the name was "Zephyrs." In 1963, the team was in Baltimore and was renamed the "Bullets" after the city's first basketball franchise that got started in 1946. That club picked up its "Bullets" name because it played its games near a foundry that made ammunition during World War II. In the 1973–1974 season, the franchise adopted "Capitol Bullets" when it moved to Landover, Maryland, in 1973, and took the name Washington Bullets in 1974. That nickname was viewed as politically incorrect. Washington owner Abe Pollin changed the name to Wizards in 1997.

Weakside Side of the court away from the ball.

Weave An arclike movement in a figure eight by offensive players aimed at freeing a player for an easy shot.

"White Chocolate" Jason Williams was given his nickname for being one of the flashiest white players in the NBA.

"Wizard of Westwood" Coach John Wooden worked his wizardry at UCLA in the Westwood area of Los Angeles.

World B. Free An NBA journeyman, Lloyd Free had his name legally changed to World B. Free to show his political involvement.

"X" Xavier McDaniel had some moments of glory for several different NBA teams.

"Yes" Broadcaster Marv Albert's signature call for a shot made.

"Z" Zydrunas Ilgauskas of the Cleveland Cavaliers is a 7' 3", $60 million investment with a name that for some is tough to pronounce.

"Zo" Abbreviation of longtime power forward/center Alonzo Mourning's given name.

Zone Defense A condition that involves each defender guarding an area, not a player—illegal in professional basketball.

Zone Press To press on defense in a particular area of the court.

Billiards

Angled (Snooker, pocket games) Pocket's corner prevents a player from shooting the cue ball directly at an object ball (see Corner-Hooked).

Angle Shot (Pocket games) Shot requiring cue ball to drive the object ball other than straight ahead (see Cut Shot).

Apex of Triangle (Pocket games) Position in the grouping of object balls that is located on the foot spot; the front ball position of the pyramid or rack.

Around the Table (Carom games) When cue ball in an effort to score makes contact with three or more cushions, usually including the two short cushions.

Balance Point (General) The cue point where it would remain level if held by a single support, usually about eighteen inches from the cue's butt end.

Ball On (Snooker) A colored (nonred) ball a player wants to legally pocket (On Ball).

Bank Shot (Pocket games) Object ball is driven to one or more cushions before it is pocketed. It is not an obvious shot and must be called in games requiring called shots (Kick Shot).

Baulk (Snooker) Space intervening between the bottom cushion and the Baulk-Line.

Baulk-Line (Snooker) Straight line drawn twenty-nine inches from the face of the bottom cushion and parallel to it.

Bed of Table (General) Playing area exclusive of the cushions; flat, cloth-covered surface of the table.

Billiard A count or score; successful shot.

Billiards The French word *billarts* or *billiard* ("cue stick") is the derivation of the sport's name. Billiards started as an indoor version of lawn bowling, a game the English played with a passion—only to have this passion frustrated when rain fell. The sport was moved indoors.

Blind Draw (General) Way to determine pairings or bracketing of players in tournaments that makes for totally random placement or pairing of contestants.

Bottle (Pocket games) Specially shaped leather or plastic container (Shake Bottle).

Bottom Cushion (Snooker) One that is located at the head of a snooker table—closest to the D.

Break (Snooker) Total scored in one inning.

Breaking Violation (Pocket games) A violation of special rules applying only to the opening break shot of certain games.

Bridge (General) The hand configuration holding and guiding during play the shaft-end of the cue (see Mechanical Bridge).

Burst (Forty-One Pocket Billiards) Scoring a total in excess of forty-one points.

Butt of Cue (General) Larger end of a cue, opposite the tip.

Called Ball (Pocket games) The ball the player has designated to be pocketed.

Called Pocket (Pocket games) The pocket into which a player has designated a ball to be shot.

Call Shot (Pocket games) Requirement that a player designate, before each shot, the ball to be made and the pocket into which it will be made.

Carom (General) To bounce off or glance off an object ball or cushion; a shot in which the cue ball bounces off one ball into another.

Carom, Scoring (General) Contact by the cue ball with object balls, the bottle, or cushions in such a manner that a legal score is made.

Center Spot (General) Exact center point of a table's playing surface.

Chalk (General) A dry, slightly abrasive substance that is applied to the cue tip for nonslip contact.

Chuck Nurse (Straight Rail Billiards) A scoring technique used when one object ball rests against the cushion and the second object ball is to one side away from the cushion.

Clean Bank (Bank Pocket Billiards) Object ball being played does not touch any other object balls.

Clear Ball (Carom games) All-white ball, devoid of any markings (Spot Ball).

Combination (Pocket games) A scoring effort shot where cue ball first strikes a ball other than the one to be pocketed, with the ball initially contacted in turn striking one or more other balls.

Combination On (Pocket games) Two or more balls positioned so that a ball can be driven into a called pocket with a combination shot (Dead Combo or; On Combo).

Combination On (Snooker) See Plant.

Contact Point (General) Precise point of contact between the cue ball and the object ball.

Corner-Hooked (Pocket games, Snooker) When the corner of a pocket prevents shooting the cue ball in a straight path directly to an object ball.

Count (General) A score; a successful shot.

The Count (General) Running score at any time during a player's inning.

Cross Corner (Pocket games) A bank shot rebounding off a cushion into a corner pocket.

Cross Side (Pocket games) A bank shot rebounding from a cushion and into a side pocket.

Cross Table Shot (Carom games) Scoring takes place by driving the cue ball across the table between the long cushion.

Crotch (Carom games) Corner area of a carom table in straight-rail billiards where player may score no more than three successive counts with the balls before driving at least one object ball out of the area.

Crutch (General) Slang for mechanical bridge.

Cue (General) Tapered, usually wooden device, used to strike the cue ball to execute carom or pocket billiard shots (Cue Stick).

Cue Ball (General) The white, unnumbered ball that is always struck by the cue during play.

Cue Ball in Hand (Pocket games) The cue ball may be put into play anywhere on playing surface (Ball in Hand).

Cue Ball in Hand behind the Head String (Pocket games) The cue ball may be put into play anywhere between the head string and the cushion on head end of the table.

Cue Ball in Hand within the Half-Circle (Snooker) When the cue ball has entered a pocket or has been forced off the table, the base of the cue ball may be placed anywhere within or on the half-circle. It remains in hand until the player strikes the cue ball with the tip of the cue or a foul is committed while the ball is on the table (Cue Ball in Hand within the D).

Cue Tip (General) Specially processed leather or other pliable material attached to the shaft end of the cue.

Cushion (General) Cloth-covered rubber border on the inside of the rails on carom and pocket billiard tables.

Cut Shot (Pocket games) Cue ball contacts object ball to one side or the other of full center, driving it in a direction other than the initial cue ball path.

D (Snooker) Semicircular area with straight side formed by the line drawn between the spot for yellow and the spot for green.

Dead Ball (Pocket games) Stroking a cue ball so that virtually all of its speed/spin is transferred to the object ball.

Dead Ball Shot (Pocket games) One with relative lack of cue ball motion after contact with object ball (Kill Shot).

Diamonds (General) Inlays/ markings on table rails for reference or target points.

Draw Shot (General) The striking of a cue ball below center with resulting backspin sending it returning toward the player after full contact with an object ball.

Drop Pockets (Pocket games) Pockets lacking automatic return of the balls to the foot end of the table.

Double Elimination (General) Player is not eliminated until he has sustained two match losses.

Double Hit (General) Cue ball in this shot is struck twice by the cue tip on the same stroke.

Double Round Robin (General) Tournament format where each contestant in a field plays each of the other players twice.

English (General) Sidespin applied to cue ball by striking it off center.

Feather Shot (General) The cue ball in this shot hardly touches or grazes the object ball.

Ferrule (General) Protective material (usually plastic, horn, or metal) at the cue shaft's end onto which the cue tip is attached.

Follow Shot (General) Cue ball is struck above center and the resulting forward spin causes it to roll forward after contact with an object ball.

Follow-through (General) After contact with the cue ball, movement of the cue is through the area previously occupied by the cue ball.

Foot of Table (General) End of a carom or pocket billiard table at which the balls are racked or positioned when game starts.

Foot Spot (General) The point on the foot end of the table where imaginary lines drawn between the center diamonds of the short rails and the second diamonds of the long rails intersect.

Foot String (General) A line on the foot end of the table between the second diamonds of the long rails, passing through the foot spot.

Force (General) Power applied on the stroke to the cue ball; it can possibly distort and alter natural angles and action of the ball.

Force Draw (General) A shot with extreme follow.

Force Follow (General) Applied to the cue ball, a follow shot with extreme overspin.

Foul (General) Infraction of the rules of play.

Foul Stroke (General) A stroke where a foul takes place.

Frame (Snooker) Equivalent of one game in snooker.

Free Ball (Snooker) After a foul, if the cue ball is snookered, the referee states "Free Ball." Should nonoffending player take the next stroke, he may nominate any ball as "on." For this stroke, that ball is regarded as, and acquire the value of, the ball on.

Free Break (Pocket games) Opening break shot where wide spread of the object balls is achieved without penalty.

Frozen (General) One ball touching another or cushion.

Full Ball (General) Cue ball's contact with an object ball at a contact point on a line bisecting centers of the cue ball and object ball.

Game Play starts when referee has finished racking the balls and ends at the conclusion of a legal shot which pockets the last required ball.

Game Ball (General) Ball producing victory in a game if pocketed legally.

Gather Shot (Carom games) Shot where appropriate technique and speed are used to drive one or more balls away from the other(s).

Grip (General) How the butt of the cue is held in the hand.

Gully Table (Pocket games) One with pockets and a return system delivering balls as they are pocketed to a collection bin on the table's foot end.

Handicapping (General) Changes in the scoring and/or rules of games enabling players of differing abilities to compete more equally.

Head of Table (General) Table's end from which opening break is performed; end normally marked with the manufacturer's nameplate.

Head Spot (General) Point on the head of the table where imaginary lines drawn between the center diamonds of the short rails and the second diamonds of long rails intersect.

Head String (General) A line on the head end of the table between the second diamonds of the long rails, passing through the head spot.

Hickey (Snooker Golf) Any foul.

High Run (14.1 Continuous) In specified segment of play, the most balls scored in one turn (inning) at the table.

Hold (General) English stopping cue ball from continuing natural roll course.

Inning (General) A turn at the table by a player.

In-Off (Snooker) A losing hazard; the cue ball enters a pocket.

In the Rack (14.1 Continuous) A ball that would interfere with reracking of the object balls.

Jaw (Pocket games) Cushion's slanted part cut at an angle forming the opening from the bed of the table into the pocket.

Jawed Ball (Pocket games) A ball failing to drop because it bounces back and forth against jaws of a pocket.

Joint (General) Screw-and-thread device on two-piece cues, permitting it to be broken down into two separate sections.

Jumped Ball (General) Ball that is stroked off the playing surface, or a ball that is stroked in a manner which causes it to jump over another ball.

Jump Shot (General) Shot where cue ball or object ball is caused to rise off the bed of the table.

Key Ball (14.1 Continuous) A rack's fourteenth ball—so critical in obtaining position for all important first (or break) shot of each re-racking of the balls.

Kick Shot (General) A shot in which the cue ball banks off one or more cushions prior to making contact with an object ball or scoring.

Kiss (General) Contact between balls (see Kiss Shot).

Kiss-out (General) Accidental contact between balls making a shot fail.

Kiss Shot (Pocket games) When the cue ball makes more than one contact with object balls.

Kitchen (Pocket games) Slang for area of table between the head string and cushion on the head end of table.

Lag (Carom games) Shot where cue ball is shot three or more cushions before contacting object balls.

Lag for Break (General) Process determining the starting player of the game. Each player shoots a ball from behind the head string to the foot cushion, trying to return the ball as closely as possible to the head cushion.

Leave (Pocket games) After a player's shot, the position of the balls.

Long (General) Usually refers to a ball which, due to English and speed, travels a path with wider angles than those that are standard for such a ball if struck with natural English and moderate speed.

Long String (Pocket games) Line drawn from the center of the foot cushion to the foot spot (and beyond if necessary) where balls are spotted.

Losing Hazard (Snooker) When cue ball is pocketed after making contact with an object ball.

Lot (General) Procedures used to decide starting player or order of play through flipping coins, drawing straws, drawing cards, or drawing peas or pills.

Masse Shot (General) Shot where extreme English is applied to the cue ball through elevating cue butt at an angle with the bed of the table anywhere between thirty and ninety degrees.

Match Play begins when the players are ready to lag and concludes when the deciding game ends.

Mechanical Bridge (General) Grooved device mounted on handle providing support for the shaft of the cue for shots difficult to reach with normal bridge hand (Crutch, Rake).

Miscue (General) Stroke resulting in faulty cue tip contact with cue ball.

Miss Failure to execute a completed shot.

Miss (Snooker) Referee's call if it is judged the player has not tried to hit the ball on.

Mr. and Mrs. (Pocket billiards) Generally played by a man and a woman. The man must shoot at the balls in rotation; the woman is given a handicap and may shoot at any ball.

Natural (Carom games) Shot with only natural angle and stroke required for successful execution; a simple and easily visualized and accomplished opportunity to score.

Natural English (General) Moderate sidespin applied to cue ball favoring direction of the cue ball path. This gives the cue ball a natural roll and a bit more speed than a center hit.

Natural Roll (General) Movement of cue ball with English being applied.

Nip Draw (General) Short, sharp stroke, used when a normal draw stroke would result in a foul due.

Nurses (Carom games) Balls kept close to the cushions and each other, creating a series of relatively easy scoring opportunities.

Object Ball (Pocket games) Specific object ball being played on a shot.

Object Balls (General) Balls other than the cue ball on a shot.

Open Break (Pocket games) Requirement in certain games that a player must drive a minimum of four object balls out of the rack to the cushions for shot to be legal (Break).

Opening Break Shot (General) The first shot of a game.

Peas (Pocket games) Small plastic or wooden balls numbered 1 through 15 or 16 (Pills).

Plant (Snooker) Position of two or more red balls allowing a ball to be driven into a pocket with a combination shot.

Position (General) Placement of cue ball on each shot relative to the next planned shot (Shape).

Pot (Snooker) Pocketing an object ball.

Powder (General) Powdery substance to facilitate free, easy movement of the cue shaft through the bridge.

Power Draw Shot (General) Extreme draw applied to cue ball (Force Draw).

Push Shot (General) Cue tip maintains contact with the cue ball beyond the split second allowed for a normal and legally stroked shot.

Pyramid (Pocket games) Positioning of object balls in a triangular grouping (with the front apex ball on foot spot), used to begin many pocket billiard games.

Pyramid Spot (Snooker) One marked midway between the center spot and the face of the top cushion (Pink Spot).

Race (General) Predetermined number of games necessary to win a match or set of games.

Rack Triangular equipment to gather balls into the formation required by the game being played.

Rails (General) Table's top surface not covered by cloth. Cushions protrude toward the playing surface. The head and foot rails are short rails, while right and left rails are the long rails, dictated by standing at the head end of the table and facing foot end.

Red Ball (Carom games) Red-colored object ball.

Rest (Snooker) The mechanical bridge.

Reverse English (General) Sidespin applied to cue ball influencing opposite direction of its natural path.

Round Robin (General) Tournament format where each contestant plays each of the other players once.

Running English (General) Sidespin applied to the cue ball making rebound from an object ball or a cushion at a narrower angle at a faster speed than it would if struck at the same speed and direction without English.

Safety (General) Defensive positioning of the balls minimizing opponent's chances to score.

Scratch (Carom games) Scoring a point largely by accident, due to unanticipated kiss, unplanned time-shot, and so forth.

Scratch (Pocket games) Cue ball going into a pocket on a stroke.

Seeding (General) Predetermined initial pairings; advanced positioning of players.

Set (General) Predetermined number of games necessary to win a match.

Shaft (General) The thinner part of a cue. On a two-piece cue, the shaft extends from the cue tip to the joint.

Short (General) Due to English and stroke, the ball travels a path with narrower angles than those for a ball struck without English.

Short-Rack (Pocket games) Games using fewer than fifteen countable object balls.

Shot An action that begins at the instant the cue tip contacts the cue ball and ends when all balls in play stop rolling and spinning.

Shot Clock (General) Timing device to gauge the time limit a player is allowed to play a shot. The timing device must have at least the functions of a stopwatch: reset to zero, start, and stop.

Single Elimination (General) Tournament format where a single loss eliminates a player from the competition.

Snake (Carom games) Use of English causes cue ball to make three or more cushion contacts, though utilizing only two different cushions (Double-the-Rail Shot).

Snookered (Snooker) Incoming player's cue ball position where he is unable to shoot in a straight line and contact all portions of an on ball directly facing the cue ball. This condition exists because of balls not "on" that block the path.

Split Double Elimination (General) Modification of the double elimination tournament format where field is divided into sections; one player emerges from each of the sections to compete in a single showdown match for the championship.

Split Hit Situation where it can't be ascertained which object ball(s) the cue ball contacted first, as a result of close proximity of object balls.

Spot (General) Thin, circular piece of cloth or paper glued onto the cloth indicating the spot locality. For example, head spot, center spot, foot spot (handicap expression).

Spot Ball (Carom games) White ball standing out from the clear by one or more markings: spots, dots, or circles.

Spot Shot (Pocket games) Player shoots a ball on the foot spot with the cue ball in hand behind the head string.

Spotting Balls (General) Replacing balls to the table in positions as mandated by specific game rules.

Stance (General) Body position during shooting.

Stop Shot (Pocket games) Cue ball stops immediately upon striking the object ball.

Striker (Snooker) The player who is about to shoot and has yet to complete his inning.

Stroke (General) Movement of the cue as a shot is executed.

Successive Fouls (Pocket games) Fouls made on consecutive strokes by the same player, (Consecutive Fouls).

Table in Position (General) Term used to indicate that the object balls remain unmoved following a shot.

Throw Shot (Pocket games) Shot where English alters the path of an object ball. Or a combination shot of frozen or nearly frozen object balls where rubbing of the first ball across second ball pulls the shot away from the line joining the centers of the two balls.

Time Shot (General) Cue ball usually moves another ball into a different position and then continues to meet one of the moved balls for a score.

Top Cushion (Snooker) Cushion at the foot of a snooker table—closest to the black spot.

Triangle (Pocket games) Triangular device used to place the balls in position for the start of most games.

UN (General) Total of consecutive scores, points, or counts made by a player in one inning.

Yellow Ball (Carom games) The spot ball has been replaced by a yellow ball in international competition.

Boating: Rowing, Kayaking, and Canoeing

Abaft Toward or at the stern of a boat.

Abeam At right angles to the boat's centerline.

Aft Toward the back of the boat; the stern.

Amidships The center of the boat, midway between the bow and the stern and between the sides.

Backing (of Wind) Directional wind change to a counterclockwise motion.

Backpaddle To paddle in reverse, from stern to bow.

Bail To scoop water out of a boat.

Bang Plate A protective device for the upright part of a canoe (stem) affixed to the bow.

Beam The widest part of a boat.

Bearing A direction in relation to a compass point.

Bear Off To push off or away from an object (Bear Away).

Beat To sail into or toward the wind (Beating).

Beaufort Scale Devised in 1805 by British Rear Admiral Sir Francis Beaufort, the scale that bears his name indicates wind strength. Forces range from 0 to 17. Force 0 signifies calm; Force 1, light air (1–3 MPH); Force 2, slight breeze (4–7 MPH); Force 3, gentle breeze (8–12 MPH); Force 4, moderate breeze (13–18 MPH); Force 5, fresh breeze (19–24 MPH); Force 6, strong breeze (25–31 MPH); Force 7, moderate gale (32–38 MPH); Force 8, fresh gale (39–46 MPH); Force 9, strong gale (47–54 MPH); Force 10, whole gale (55–63 MPH); Force 11, storm (64–73 MPH); and the numbers 12–17 represent hurricane forces (74 MPH and more).

Bell Buoy A buoy with a bell that rings as a result of wave movement.

Bend To secure one thing to another, usually ropes.

Blade A paddle, or the flat or curved end of a paddle.

Bollard A heavy post on a jetty to which lines can be tied.

Bottom The underwater part of a boat.

Bow The front part of a boat.

Bower The main anchor.

Bow Person The person who paddles from the front (bow).

Broach To swing sharply toward the wind, usually in heavy seas and/or winds.

Bulkhead Partitions that carry flotation.

Buoy A fixed marker in the water that indicates a chart point, navigable waters, danger, and so forth.

Buoyancy Flotation, usually made of styrofoam blocks, and often built into canoes by the manufacturer.

By the Head A condition characterized by a craft more deeply loaded forward than aft.

By the Stern A condition characterized by a craft more deeply loaded aft than forward.

Cable Rope or chain used for towing.

Canadian Canoe A craft powered by a person using a single paddle from a kneeling position.

Canoe A vessel with a pointed stern that is propelled by paddles.

Catch a Crab To unintentionally dip an oar into the water or have it struck by a wave on the recovery stroke in rowing.

Center of Buoyancy The center of underwater volume of a boat.

Center of Gravity That single point of a vessel to which every other part is gravitationally attached.

Chart A navigational map.

Childs Cup Regatta This rowing race originated in 1879 and was named for the trophy donated by George W. Childs, publisher of the *Philadelphia Ledger*. It claims to be the second-oldest intercollegiate fixture. Originally it was a contest among Columbia, Princeton, and Pennsylvania universities. The regatta was suspended in 1884 but was resumed in 1912 as a competition between Pennsylvania and Princeton over a course of $1\frac{5}{16}$ mile at different venues.

Chine The place where the sides and hull of a boat meet.

Coaming A raised frame for protection around the cockpit.

Cockpit The hole cut into the boat for the paddler to sit or kneel on.

Course Route of a boat.

Coxswain A nonrowing crew member who directs the race and sets the beat (Cox).

Crew A rowing team; the operators of a racing shell.

Crew Racing The sport of rowing.

Dead Reckoning Calculation of the exact position of a vessel.

Dead Water The water near the stern of a boat, which appears to be flat.

Deck The upper surface of a boat, which has openings to admit the paddler into the cockpit.

Displacement The amount of water displaced by the underwater volume of a craft.

Doggett's Coat and Badge In his will, English actor Thomas Doggett made provisions for the awarding of a trophy to the winner of a race of approximately 4½ miles on the Thames River between London Bridge and Chelsea. The race was first held in 1715, and its prize has been awarded annually to the winning crew of novice oarsmen. It is the oldest continually granted trophy in the world of sports. The trophy is actually an orange-colored livery (coat) and a badge that represents Liberty. The "coat," the "badge," and Doggett's name are combined in the title of the trophy.

Double Blade A canoe or kayak paddle with blades at each end that are generally positioned at different angles (Double Paddle).

Draft A boat's depth beneath the water (Draught).

Drag Resistance to forward motion, especially in shallow water.

Drift The carrying along of a vessel by currents in the water. Also, the rate of a current, measured in knots.

Ebb The tide falling.

Eddy A limited, circular movement of water.

Eight A racing shell with eight oars used in rowing.

Elite A rowing oarsman in a winning boat in a major championship competition. Also, an event for elite oarsmen crews.

Even Keel A craft that is evenly balanced.

Fairing A structure designed to reduce drag.

Fathom A measurement of the depth of water: one fathom equals six feet.

Feather To turn oars or paddles in such a way that there is a minimum resistance to their movement.

Feathered Double Paddle Maximizing paddling efficiency by having one blade pull while the other one recovers water.

Ferry Glide The movement of a canoe or kayak from one side of a stream to another by angling the stern against the current and back-paddling.

Finish The lifting of an oar from the water and the beginning of a recovery.

Flare The upward curve of a craft's bow or its top overhang.

Flood The rising or incoming tide.

Fore Forward.

Fouled Anchor An anchor that has a turn of its cable caught around it or that is stuck on something.

Four A four-oared racing shell or its crew (in rowing).

Fours Four-oared-shell competition (in rowing).

Gale A forceful and brisk wind of 32–63 mph.

Gear Canoe or kayak camping-trip equipment.

Girth Generally, the hull's circumference at its biggest section.

GRP Fiberglass (Glass-Reinforced Plastic).

Gunwale General reference to tops of the sides of a canoe (Gunnel).

Harmsworth Trophy This trophy was first given in 1903 by Sir Alfred Harmsworth. The event it commemorated was the first international powerboat race, which was run over a distance of 135 miles. Staged generally at Picton, Ontario, or Detroit, the race is usually held at intervals of several years.

Head-of-the-River Race A rowing competition in which the shells begin at different intervals (Head Race).

Heave To To maintain a minimum speed in a heavy sea.

Heel To tilt or tip.

Hitch To To make fast to another object by using a rope.

Hogged A term referring to when the center of a boat is higher than its ends. If this condition results from intentional design, it is called Reverse Sheer.

Hogging A convex strain on a craft through its fore-and-aft axis.

Hog To To thoroughly scrub.

Hold A canoeing stroke that stops the craft's forward motion; reverse paddling or holding the paddle in the water with its blade perpendicular to the canoe's movement are two versions of the hold.

Hull The containerlike lower part of a canoe, kayak, or shell.

Inboard To be within—generally near the center—of a craft.

J-Stroke A maneuver in canoeing that is used to adjust the trim or compensate for drifting sideways: a stroke that resembles the shape of the letter J is made as a variation after a normal stroke is completed.

Kayak An Eskimo canoe, originally composed of sealskins stretched over a wooden frame that cover the entire craft except for a little hole in the upper-center half, where the paddler sits.

Kedge A small anchor used by canoes and kayaks.

Keel The backbone of a boat. Also, a fixed extension at the bottom of a boat for greater stability.

King Plank A deck's center plank.

King Post A deck's vertical post.

Knees Angular pieces of frame or metal that frame a vessel (Elbows).

Knot A nautical measure of speed: "one knot" means one nautical mile per hour. (A nautical mile is equal to one minute of latitude or longitude and is about 1.15 statute miles.)

Lash To secure with a rope (Lashing).

Latitude Degree measurements north or south of the equator.

Launch To set a boat afloat.

LDR Long-Distance Racing.

Line Small length of rope used to tie or tow a canoe (Painter).

LOA Length Overall.

Longitude Degree measurements east or west of the prime meridian at Greenwich, England.

LWL The Load Water Line, which notes the length of the waterline along the hull when either empty or loaded.

Mold A method of manufacturing canoes through the use of two molds, one forming the hull and the other forming the deck; the mating of the two creates the craft.

Oarlocks Square holes or U-shaped devices that hold the oars in place (Rowlocks).

Oarsman A racing-crew member who pulls an oar (female: Oarswoman).

Open A boat without a deck.

Outboard An auxiliary engine over the side of a craft.

Outrigger A supporting frame that holds the oarlock out from a racing shell's side.

Pooped A condition in which large waves break onto a craft's rear.

Port The left side of a boat.

Portage A place where a canoe is carried over land to avoid an obstruction.

Portaged The act of carrying a canoe overland.

Pram A dinghy of Norwegian style, generally with a flat bottom and square ends.

Punt A long, flat-bottomed English boat.

Quadruple Sculls Four-man sculling competition, in rowing (Quad).

Race Disturbed and generally fast running water.

Rapids Swiftly moving stretch of water.

Recovery The raising, feathering, and bringing toward the boat's bow of the blade after a stroke is completed and just before the next one is begun.

Regatta A series of rowboat, sailboat, or speedboat races.

Ride At anchor or on moorings.

Rowing The propelling of a boat by one oar with both hands.

Rowing Tank A big tank of water containing a simulated shell where rowing strokes and techniques are practiced.

Sculling The simultaneous pulling of two oars positioned on opposite sides of the boat.

Shooting Going over falls and rapids.

Skeg The rear part of a keel; the metal socket that supports the rudder's bottom.

Skin The outer covering of a hull.

Slap Support A corrective stroke used to stabilize a canoe or kayak in which the flat of the paddle blade strikes the water.

Sliding Seat A racing shell's seat, positioned on wheels that slide on metal tracks attached to the shell's frame; this enables an oarsman to maximize the strength of his limbs and back.

Sounding A measuring of the depth of the water by paddle, pole, or weighted line.

Spray Cover A sealing device fitted around the cockpit's raised frame and the paddler's waist (Spray Skirt).

Spray Deck An artificial canvas deck used to keep the spray out of the canoe's hull.

Square A rowing maneuver in which the paddle blade is moved vertically at the beginning of a stroke in anticipation of entry into the water.

Starboard The right side of a boat.

Stem The upright part of the front of a canoe.

Stern The rear of a boat.

Stern Person The person paddling from the stern in canoeing.

Sternpost The upright part of the back of a canoe.

Strike To put the oar in the water to start a stroke. Also, to row at a specific rate.

Stroke To push or pull a paddle or oar to propel a boat. Also, the person who paces the other crew members and sits in the sternmost seat in rowing (Coxswain).

Sweep A long oar used by racing shells.

Sweep Stroke A canoeing stroke that turns the craft by sweeping the paddle through the water.

Telemark A turning stroke executed when the boat is moving forward by leaning on the paddle and pivoting quickly about.

Tight Watertight.

Tippy A condition of instability on the part of a craft.

Topsides The sides of a boat above the waterline.

Tow To pull a canoe or kayak.

Transom A broad, nearly vertical stern.

Trim The balance of a boat.

Tumble Home A feature that helps canoes stay dry where the beam is narrower at deck level than at the waterline.

Under Way The condition of moving through the water.

Veer A clockwise wind change.

Wake Disturbance in the water caused by the drag or resistance of a vessel as it passes through water (Wash).

Wake Hang To surf on the bow wave or wake of a boat (Wash Hang; Wake Surfing).

Wash To illegally move ahead of another rowing shell, making the other crew row in the wake of the offending craft.

Waterline The dividing line between a boat's topsides and underbody.

Wherry A narrow exercise rowboat operated by one person with sculls.

Bobsledding and Snowboarding

Articulation Joint connecting bobsled's front section to its rear.

Belly A curve's bottom section.

Billy Fiske Memorial Trophy The most desired trophy in bobsledding, it is named for one of the most famous American competitors in the sport. Billy Fiske enlisted in the Royal Air Force in 1939, when World War II began. He died from wounds he suffered while flying a mission. The award in his name is for the National AAU four-man competition. Fiske is remembered for his driving a five-man U.S. team to triumph in the 1928 Winter Olympic Games and then repeating this feat four years later at Lake Placid, New York.

Block Piece of wood at the start line where the brakeman places his feet to get a better start.

Bobsled Large sled composed of two sections linked together. There are two sizes, two-man and four-man. The frame is metal, the shell of fiberglass or like material.

Bo-Dyn Trademarked name for a kind of sled, designed by NASCAR driver Geoff Bodine.

Brakeman Person in the last seat of a sled, who applies the brakes at a run's end.

Braking Straight (Braking Stretch) Long, straight section of track, after finish line, where after brakes are applied, and sled is slowed.

Bumpers Fins on front and back of sled used by crew members when they're loading (Bunks).

Cowling Front part of sled covering.

Crew Three sliders seated behind the driver in four-man bobsled.

D-Rings Handles that steer the sled, named for their shape.

Descent Trip down track (Run).

DNF Did Not Finish.

DNS Did Not Start.

Down Time Length of time for a run.

DQ Disqualified.

Driver Front person, responsible for steering.

Finish curve Last curve before finish line.

Gouge Large scratch on a runner.

Grooves Guide channels cut into ice at starting area, allowing a sled to follow straight line in process of pushing and loading.

Handles Bars at the back of two-man sled that brakeman pushes to start it on the descent.

Harold Monahan Trophy Like Billy Fiske, Harold "Bubs" Monahan was a World War II enlistee and a war casualty. He was a promising bobsled pilot who was shot down in his plane over Italy. The trophy in his name is awarded annually to the National AAU two-man bobsledding champions (see Billy Fiske Trophy).

Interval Time Time taken to cross specific section of the track.

Kriesel Corner containing 270 or more degrees of arc.

Labyrinth Series of rapid, short left and right curves.

Loading Driver and crew or brakeman getting into the sled.

Number 2 Person sitting immediately behind the driver in a four-man bobsled.

Number 3 Person sitting immediately behind Number 2 in front of the brakeman in a four-man bobsled.

Omega Corner containing between 180 and 270 degrees of arc.

Push Bars Located on each side of four-man sled, bars gripped by driver and crew during the push start.

Push Time Amount of time needed to push a sled over first fifty meters of a run.

Push Track Where teams practice pushing the sled.

Roof Top part of a curve, where ice is overhanging the run.

Runner Carrier Device holding a runner, located on the bottom of the sled.

Runner Gauge Implement used by officials that measures the thickness of a sled's runners.

Runners Four steel ice skates that a bobsled rides on.

Sanding The preparing of a sled for a run.

Scabbards Wood or metal guards used to protect the runners while sled is being transported.

Shades Canvas covers protecting a track from the sun and debris between races.

Slider An athlete who participates in "sliding sports"—bobsled, luge, skeleton sledding.

Speed Suit Skin-tight rubber suit worn by a slider.

Start Shoes While pushing on the ice, these shoes provide traction.

"Terrorizer" Tara Dakides, pro snowboarder, picked up her nickname for the way she terrorizes the slopes with her big air and crazy tricks.

Transition Track area that changes from a straight into a curve.

Travel Runners Temporary runners put on a sled so it can be transported from storage to track.

Bocce

Advantage "Pallino advantage" allegedly belongs to the team throwing the pallino (see below) since they place the pallino where they want it, to have a clear shot to place the first bocce ball.

Backboards Shorter court walls at each end of the court (Endboards, Backwalls).

Banking The act of throwing the bocce ball to hit and bounce off the sideboards toward the pallino.

Bocce Sometimes spelled bocci or boccie, the pronunciation is bä-che (phonetically "botchee"). It is the plural of the Italian word *boccia* that means "ball." The proper name of the sport is bocce (never "bocce ball").

Bocce Balls Eight larger balls of two distinct colors, four of each color, about 4¼ inches in diameter. They are rolled toward the pallino to score points.

Captain One designated to coach and make all team decisions.

Coin Toss Initial flip of a coin at the start of a game determining the team to throw the pallino the first time. The coin toss winner chooses the color of the team's bocce balls.

Court Rectangular playing area defined by a backboard at each end and two sideboards. The playing surface is level and smooth.

Court Bocce Played on a standard court.

Dead Ball During a frame, one removed from play.

End Captain One who coaches and makes team decisions at the team's end of the court.

Footwear Shoes with smooth soles, like sneakers.

Forfeit Action against a team that does not have at least two players to begin a game at designated start time or a team that refuses for any reason to complete a game.

Foul Act committed by a thrower violating game rules.

Frame (Giro) Playing of all the bocce balls in one direction. After points are awarded, a new frame starts in the opposite direction. Frames are played until enough points are accumulated to win the game.

"Go" Direction by referee to the team designated to throw the next ball.

Half Court Marker Line marked on the sideboards/court surface exactly midway between two backboards.

Hitting (Spock) An underhand bowling-type hard throw that is declared. It is sent directly at the balls on the court to purposely hit and move an opponent's ball or the pallino (Spocking, Shooting, Bombing, Raffa).

Hitting Foul Line Second foul line marked on the sideboards/court surface ten feet from each backboard behind which the bocce balls are thrown with force to hit and move other bocce balls or the pallino. A running delivery to gain momentum on the ball is allowed.

Illegal Movement Legally thrown ball moved from its resting position by a player or referee.

In Information given by the referee to players as to which team has the "In" ball (red or green).

In-Bound Lines Lines marked on the sideboards/backboards/court surface defining the twelve-inch boundary for the initial pallino throw.

In Team Team with closest bocce ball to the pallino.

Interference Legally thrown ball interfered with by someone or something not on the playing surface before the throw.

Kiss When bocce ball touches the pallino (Baci).

League Group of bocce teams playing a prescribed number of matches or games over a set time period. Records are kept to determine a winning team.

Live Ball Bocce ball legally in play on the court's surface.

Measure Measuring the distance between the pallino and the bocce balls to determine which team's balls are closest.

No Point or Tie Situation where the closest ball of each team is equidistant from the pallino. The team delivering the last ball must throw again unless all balls have been played, in which case no points are awarded for that frame.

Opponents The two teams competing against each other.

Out Team The team that does not have the closest bocce ball to the pallino.

Pallino Small ball used as a target ball for throwing the bocce balls (Object Ball, Jack, Pill, Cue Ball, Bullet, Pallina).

Penalty Action taken against a team or player for violating game rules.

Pointing Underhand throwing action of a player to roll the bocce ball as close to the pallino as possible to score points. Throwing styles vary from player to player. Pointing is sometimes called "Punto" or "Puntata."

Pointing Foul Line The first foul line marked on the sideboards/court surface six feet from each backboard behind which the pallino and bocce balls rolled for point must be released. Sometimes called the "Throwing," "Pitch," "Punto," or "Puntata" foul line.

Referee Official who enforces all game rules, directs play, determines the "in team," makes measurements, and determines team points each frame.

Scoreboard Numbers 1 through 12 arranged similar to the face of a clock with an arrow pointing to the score for the red or green team.

Sideboards Longer court walls parallel to the direction of throwing.

Social Bocce Group of people getting together in temporary teams.

Spock (Hitting) Declared underhand bowling-type hard throw to purposely hit and move an opponent's ball or the pallino (Spocking, Shooting, Bombing, Raffa).

Substitute Replacement on the team or on the league roster who replaces a regular player.

Team Four players maximum, two players minimum, each player throwing two balls. One or more substitute players are on the team.

Tournament Group of bocce teams playing matches or games over a set time period with losing teams eliminated until a single winning team remains.

Volo High arcing throw of a bocce ball beyond the court's center line.

Bowling

Aiming A bowler's focusing on the roll of the ball: a right-handed bowler will aim for the pocket of space between the 1 and 3 pins; a left-handed bowler will attempt to hit the 1 and 2 pins.

All Events A reference to a bowler who manages the highest score in all three competition divisions.

Alley A lane 62', 10$\frac{3}{16}$ inches long and 41–42 inches wide down which a ball travels to the pins. Also, a building that contains many lanes.

Approach The sixteen-foot-long part of the lane that leads to the foul line, where the bowler moves forward to release the ball. Also, the stance, steps, and motion used by a bowler in releasing the ball.

Average The total number of pins plus bonuses credited to a bowler divided by the total number of games played during a specific time period.

Baby Split A split where either the 2 and 7 pins or the 3 and 10 pins are left upright.

Backup A ball that veers to the same side as the hand that delivers it and hits the pins from the opposite side.

Back Wall A surface that is used to stop the pins (Ball Cushion).

Balk To cross the foul line without delivering the ball.

Ball Circumference, not more than 27.002 inches; weight, 16 pounds maximum.

Ball-Return Track The surface the ball moves on as it returns to the bowler.

Bedpost A split resulting in the 7 and 10 pins still standing.

Big Ball A powerful enough delivery so that a strike can be accomplished virtually anywhere the ball hits the pins.

Big Fill Following a spare, an effective pinfall on the first ball bowled.

Big Four A split resulting in the 4, 6, 7, and 10 pins still standing.

Blind Score Additional score granted a team for a game where a player has been disqualified or is absent— generally the noncompeting player's average minus ten.

Blow Inability to make a spare. Also, an error.

Bonus A spare bonus is the number of pins downed with the first ball of the next frame. A strike bonus is the number downed with the next two balls. Bonuses count in the frame in which they take place, as well as being added to the previous frame's spare or strike.

"Boomer" Leanne Barrette, for her powerful shot.

"Bosco" Don Carter, from his favorite drink.

Bowler's Thumb Muscle strain in the thumb as a result of the stress on the thumb as it leaves the thumbhole on the ball.

Bowling Judging from the enthusiasm and passion of today's bowlers, it is not surprising that the sport began life as a form of religious observance. In fourth-century Germany, peasants fastidiously set up small clubs that they called *kegels* in the cloisters of neighborhood churches. The peasants then enthusiastically rolled rounded stones at these *kegels* with the aim of knocking them down. A *kegel* symbolized a nonbeliever. The knocking down of all the *kegels* was a sign of arranging for good luck. Eventually the practice became a sport and spread to other nations. Bowling Green in New York City owes its name to the sporting efforts of the Dutch *keglers* of the seventeenth century who brought the German fourth-century religious practice along with them to America.

"Bowling's Golden Voice" That was an apt name for Chris Schenkel who announced national network bowling shows for more than four decades.

Box Score-sheet square that represents a frame.

Brooklyn A strike made when a right-handed bowler's ball hits the left side of the headpin or a left-handed bowler's ball hits the right side of the headpin.

Bucket Leaving the 2–4–5–8 or 3–5–6–9 pins in a spare cluster. The former is left by a right-handed bowler and the latter by a left-handed player.

Carry Knocking down one or several pins.

CC A 200 game.

Cherry An error that takes place when the ball knocks down only the front pins.

"Chesty" Joe Falcaro was not a big man but was a proud and forceful competitor, a pioneer in conducting exhibitions and executing trick shots.

Christmas Tree A split that leaves standing the 3, 7, and 10 pins (by a right-handed player).

Cincinnati A split that leaves the 8 and 10 pins standing.

"Clown Prince of Bowling" Andy Varipapa, known as perhaps the greatest trick shot artist. He credited Joe Falcaro with leading the way.

Convert To use the second ball to successfully knock down the remaining pins and get credit for a spare.

Count After a spare or strike, the number of pins downed with the first ball of a frame; it is employed as a method for giving the bonus for the previous mark. Also, not knocking down the greatest number of pins in a frame.

"Count" John Gengler, perhaps the best bowling hustler of all time, was known mainly as Gengler. His nickname came from his style of dressing and courtly manners.

Creeper A ball that is rolled slowly.

Curve A ball that sweeps in its roll to the other side of the alley from which it first made contact.

"Deadeye" Walter Ray Williams, Jr., world champion horseshoe pitcher and an incredible winning bowler, known for accuracy in hitting the strike pocket and converting spares.

Dead Mark The rolling of a strike or spare with the last ball in the tenth frame.

Dead Wood Pins that remain in the alley after being downed.

Dodo Split A split in which the headpin and either the 7 pin or the 10 pin are left standing.

"Doomsday Stroking Machine" Earl Anthony, consistency in rolling strikes spelled death for his opponents.

Double Two consecutive strikes.

Double Pinochle A split that leaves the 4, 6, 7, and 10 pins.

Doubles Two players are paired against two other players.

Double Wood Leaving one pin standing behind another.

Duckpin Bowling The sport and its name were both invented in 1900 through the efforts of baseball Hall of Famers John J. McGraw and Wilbert Robinson. At the time both men were partners in the Diamond Bowling Alleys in Baltimore. Seeking a variation on the bowling game, they had the tenpins transformed into smaller pins in conformity with the six-inch ball used for bowling in a game of that time called 5-back or cocked hat. When they watched their first set of little pins fly helter-skelter, the baseball immortals, both expert duck shooters, claimed it looked as if the pins were a flock of flying ducks. It was actually Bill Clarke, a Baltimore sportswriter, who stuck the label duckpins on the new pins and the new game. Clarke allegedly coined the term after the comments of McGraw and Robinson.

Dump Impeding the hook of a ball by releasing with the thumb and fingers at exactly the same time.

Dutch 200 A 200-point game during which the bowler alternates strikes and spares throughout the ten frames (Dutchman).

Error Failure to convert a spare leave.

Fast A lane that is finished in such a way that before beginning to hook, the ball slides a greater distance than on another surface.

Fence A row of pins standing after the first roll.

Fill The number of downed pins on the next ball after a spare.

Foul Line A ⅜ to 1-inch-wide line on the alley that is 60 feet away from the headpin. It separates the alley from the approach.

Foundation A ninth-frame strike.

Four Horsemen A 1–2–4–7 or 1–3–6–10 leave.

Frame One tenth of a game or a player's turn; or one of the ten squares on the score sheet for indicating a player's continuing score.

Full Roller A ball that slows up in its roll and the rotation placed on it makes it hook into the pins. The delivery is executed by a player holding his fingers at the side of the ball and giving a sharp lift to the ball when releasing it.

Full Spinner A ball that spins down the alley like a top because of the snapped-wrist release by a player.

Golden Gate A double pinochle—the 4, 6, 7, and 10 pins remain standing in this split.

Grip Most bowlers use the thumb, middle finger, and ring finger (three-finger grip). Some use a two finger grip—thumb and middle finger. The Conventional Grip has the thumb and fingers placed in the holes to the second joint. The Fingertip Grip puts the thumb completely in the hole, while the fingers are inserted only to the first joint. The Semifinger Grip is a compromise—fingers go into the holes halfway between the first and second joints.

Groove A path on the alley that has become slightly worn as a result of many balls rolling down it.

Gutter Ball A ball that rolls into the alley and is dead (Channel Ball).

Gutters Shallow grooves that run along each side of the alley to catch balls that are improperly aimed.

Half Worcester A split in which the pins left standing are either the 3 and 9 or the 2 and 8.

Headpin The pin closest to the bowler; the 1 pin.

Heads The first sixteen feet of a lane, composed of maple boards.

High-Low-Jack A split in which the pins left standing are the 1, 7, and 10.

Holding A lane whose surface gives more than the usual amount of skid to a ball before it hooks.

Hole Pocket: the spot most likely to create a strike.

Inning A frame.

"Iron Man" Harry Steers, first bowler to roll in fifty ABC Tournaments.

Kegler Another and more fancy name for a bowler.

Kingpin The 5 pin.

Lane A wooden surface, generally 62', 10¾₆" long and between 41 and 42 inches wide, that is the alley on which the bowler rolls the ball toward the pins at the far end. The surface is composed of pine wood, except for the first 16 feet and the last 3', 10", which are made of maple wood.

Leave Pins not knocked down after the first delivery of a frame.

Lift A method of adding spin or special roll to a ball that is accomplished by a player releasing the ball with a quick snap up of the fingers.

Light Hit Hitting the pins just off the pocket so that a strike is generally not possible.

Lily The 5, 7, and 10 pins are left standing after this split.

"Lindy" Alfred Faragalli, an admirer of Charles Lindbergh.

Line A complete game of ten frames (String).

Loft To throw the ball into the air and thus drop it onto the alley beyond the foul line.

Maples Pins.

Mark Ten-point value for a strike or spare.

Match Direct competition between two bowlers.

"Medford Meteor" Marshall Holman hailed from Medford, Oregon, and was like a meteor in the bowling world.

Miss To not make a spare when there is no split (Blow).

Mixer Rolling the ball so that the pins are hit in such a way that they will cause a chain reaction of spinning pins to make contact with and down other pins.

Mother-in-Law The 7 pin.

"Mumbles" Bill Lillard, a top all-time competitor, had a habit of talking to himself under his breath.

Nose Hit Flush headpin contact with a rolled ball.

Off-Spinner A player who uses off-spin on the ball.

One in the Dark A condition where one pin remains standing obscured behind another pin.

Open Bowling One person bowling alone.

Open Frame When a bowler does not succeed in downing all the pins: a nonstrike, nonspare frame.

Out and In A sweeping hook that goes toward the gutter and then hooks back to the pocket. This delivery is generally released near the middle of the foul line.

Outroll To triumph over the competition in a series.

Pacer A noncompetitive bowler who varies bowling turns with a tournament participant to allow the latter to complete his string along with other players. The pacer's score is not counted and he also helps the competitive bowler obtain rest breaks between frames.

Perfect Game A score of 300 on twelve straight strikes.

Pick a Cherry To be unable to down an easy leave's remaining pin(s) (Leave a Cherry).

Picket Fence A split in which the 1, 2, 4, and 7 or the 1, 3, 6, and 10 pins are left standing.

Pick Up To turn over a spare.

Pin Bowler One who generally aims at the pins.

Pinch To clench the ball too tightly.

Pin Deck The alley surface, made of maple boards, that the pins stand on.

Pinfall Those pins downed by one ball, or the aggregate total of pins downed by a bowler in any sequence of play.

Pins Made of maple, and either all wood or plastic-coated, they are 15" high and 4.75" wide. They weigh from 3 pounds, 6 ounces to 3 pounds, 10 ounces, and are numbered from 1 to 10.

Pinsetter The method (or person) by which (whom) pins are set.

Pit The dropped section behind the pin deck into which knocked-down pins go.

Pitch The ball's finger-hole angle.

Pocket The space between the 1 and 3 pins or the 1 and 2 pins—for right-handed and left-handed bowlers, respectively—that is the best spot from which a strike may be scored.

Pocket Split A split that includes the 5 and 7 pins or the 5 and 9 pins and that takes place after the ball hits the pocket.

Provisional Ball The rolling of another ball that results from an inability to immediately resolve differences about a previous pinfall.

Provisional Frame The rolling of another frame that results from an inability to immediately resolve differences about a previous frame.

Pumpkin Meager pinfall.

Railroad Split A difficult split of two or more pins that are not close to each other.

Red-Posts The 7–10 split (Goal Posts).

Roll-off Playoff contest.

Roundhouse A curve that sweeps wide.

Running An alley surface that causes an earlier hook or greater curve than on other surfaces.

Runway The approach area.

Semiroller (Spinner) An effective and popular delivery that ranks between the full roller and the spinner.

Series Three straight games, the grand total of which figures in league play toward the team's score.

Setup The arrangement of the pins, all ten in a triangular formation.

Shadow Ball A practice ball rolled down a lane. Most times, there are no pins set up.

Short Pin A pin that rolls but does not knock down a standing pin.

Sleeper Pin One pin hidden behind another in a leave (One in the Dark).

Slow Surface A lane finish that slows the ball and creates a condition where a ball hooks earlier than on another surface.

Small Ball A relatively ineffective delivery of the ball because of limited action on it.

Sour Apple The 5, 7, and 10 pins are left standing in this split.

Spare The knocking down of all ten pins with two balls in the same frame.

Split The leaving of two or more pins standing after the ball is delivered. The pins are generally not close together (Railroad).

Spot Guide marks—dots, triangles—about sixteen feet in front of the foul line in the lane, sometimes used to aim a delivery of the ball at the pins.

Spot Bowler One who uses the spots consistently to aim the ball, as opposed to aiming the ball at the pins.

Spread Eagle A split in which the 2, 3, 4, 6, 7, and 10 pins are left standing.

Squash An ineffective, actionless delivery.

Stiff Surface A lane finish that holds the ball, is fast, and holds back the tendency of the ball to hook.

Straight Ball A ball that goes down the alley and does not hook or curve; the bowler's fingers are held behind the ball, which moves down the alley with a rotation toward the pins.

Strike To knock down all ten pins with the first ball delivered in a frame.

Strike Out To complete a game with three straight tenth-frame strikes.

String A complete game (Line).

Sweeper An effective hook, downing most of the pins.

Tandem A leave of two pins, one of which is positioned behind the other.

Tap An apparently perfect hit in the pocket that leaves a single pin standing.

Thin Hit A hit near the side of the pocket away from the headpin.

Three Hundred A perfect game.

Topspinner A player who uses a lot of topspin in his delivery.

"Tornado in a Miniskirt" Paula Carter, Don Carter's wife, probably received more publicity than any other woman in bowling history. She had bowling skills, speaking skills, wit, and a sense of style.

Turkey Three strikes in a row in one game.

"Twisted Sister" Michele Feldman, for the action she is able to get from her ball.

Washout Similar to a split, except that the headpin is left standing: the 1, 2, and 10 pins—and on occasion the 4 pin—are involved for a right-handed bowler. A left-handed bowler leaves the 1, 3, and 7 pins—and on occasion the 6 pin.

Wood Pins.

Woolworth A split that leaves the 5 and 10 pins standing.

Worcester A split in which all pins but the 1 and 5 are left standing.

Working Ball A ball that has movement and action so that the pins scatter on contact.

"Wrongfoot" Lou Campi, only right-handed star of his era to finish his approach on his right foot.

Boxing

"Ambling Alp" Allegedly the inspiration for the book and movie *The Harder They Fall* by Budd Schulberg, Primo Carnera was also allegedly discovered functioning as a strongman in a touring European circus. He was nearly three hundred pounds of man and at 6' 6" was an impressive fighting figure. However, he was more of a human punching bag than a pro boxer. Carnera was knocked down eleven times in eleven rounds by Max Baer and suffered similar losses to other fighters. The fights he won were allegedly fixed. His nickname came from his size and his lack of any style or movement in the ring.

Apron That part of the floor of the ring that extends beyond the ropes.

Bandages Gauze protective wrappings placed over the boxer's hands and taped at the wrist.

Bantamweight In the 1880s, when organized boxing was young and innocent, the smallest competitors were called "little chickens" or "bantams," after the fowl of the same name. These fighters could go at each other for hours at a time and although they were bantams, they were anything but little chickens. The original bantamweights weighed 105 pounds, then 112, 116, and today, 118.

"Bayonne Bleeder" Chuck Wepner came from Bayonne, New Jersey, and when hit and cut tended to bleed more than most.

"The Bigger They Are, the Harder They Fall" Bob Fitzsimmons was one of the most unusual physical specimens ever to perform in a boxing ring. He had a heavyweight's torso, a lightweight's head, and a middleweight's legs. During his career he was at different times middleweight champion of the world, light-heavyweight champion of the world, and heavyweight champion of the world. The size or shape or reputation of an opponent did not faze him—he fought all comers all over the world. John L. Sullivan called him "a fighting machine on stilts" and marveled at his ability to knock out men many pounds heavier than he.

Fitzsimmons defeated Gentleman Jim Corbett for the heavyweight championship and chose Jim Jeffries as the first man to fight in defense of the crown. When critics wondered about the choice—Jeffries would outweigh Fitzsimmons by about fifty pounds and was thirteen years younger—Fitz responded, "The bigger they are, the harder they fall." Those words had worked for the English-born boxer all his life, but this fight would be different. They fought on June 9, 1899, at the Seaside Sporting Club in Coney Island, Jeffries in his famous crouch, Fitzsimmons boring in but unable to land any telling blows. In the fifth round Fitzsimmons scored with his famous solar plexus punch—the punch that had destroyed Corbett. Although the blow was delivered with great force right to the pit of the challenger's stomach and Fitzsimmons moved back to give Jeffries room to topple—nothing changed. Jeffries kept on fighting. But finally, the dead-fatigued champ went down and out. Bob Fitzsimmons, who had fought his first match when Jeffries was five years old, was king of the hill.

"Big Smoke" In 1908 Jack Johnson became the first black heavyweight champion of the world. A little over six feet tall, a little over two hundred pounds, a little too flashy for his time—he wore mod clothes and drove yellow racing cars at high speed—Johnson was continually in trouble with the law because of brawling in public and reckless driving. His nickname was a grudging label for what he was. The "big" referred to his size. The "smoke" was that era's slang expression for a black person.

"Black Assassin" ("Michigan Assassin") Stanley Ketchel was a ferocious fighter; his black hair and Michigan roots were where his names came from.

"Black Uhlan of the Rhine" German heavyweight boxer Max Schmeling, for his black hair and where he hailed from. Born September 28, 1905, in a little town in the state of Brandenburg, he grew up to become one of the top heavyweights of his time and is best remembered for two legendary battles Joe Louis.

Their first fight was on June 19, 1936, and Schmeling knocked out the previously unbeaten Louis in the twelfth round. The Nazi regime in Germany propagandized that victory as a sign of "Aryan supremacy." The rematch scheduled at Yankee Stadium on June 22, 1938, was billed as the battle of evil against good. President Franklin D. Roosevelt invited Joe Louis to the White House, exhorting the black athlete to beat Schmeling for America. The man they called the "Brown Bomber" did just that, sending the German to the canvas four times, knocking him out in two minutes, four seconds of the first round to retain his world title.

By many accounts, the depiction of Schmeling as a Nazi tool was inaccurate. For the 1936 Olympics in Berlin, Schmeling was able to get Hitler to promise that all U.S. athletes would be protected. The German boxer hid two Jewish boys in his Berlin apartment during Pogrom Night in 1938, when the Nazis burned books in a central square, rampaging through the city, setting synagogues ablaze. Schmeling also allegedly used his influence to save Jewish friends from concentration camps. The end for Max Schmeling came on February 4, 2005. He passed away at age ninety-nine.

Block To ward off a punch by using the arms to receive a blow.

Bob and Weave To shuffle from side to side and up and down in order to unbalance an opponent.

"Body Snatcher" Mike McCallum, for his powerful poundings of midsections of opponents. A former junior middleweight and middleweight world champion, his career record was 49-5-1 with 36 knockouts.

"Bonecrusher" James Smith, this boxer was all of that.

"Boom Boom" Ray Mancini; one punch from this lightweight and out went his opponent's lights.

"Boston Gob" Jack Sharkey was world heavyweight champion, 1932–1933. He was a sailor from Boston.

"Boston Strongboy" John L. Sullivan hailed from that city and he was powerful.

"Boston Tar Baby" (**"Boston Terror"**) Sam Langford is considered to be the greatest fighter to never win a world boxing championship. One of the most avoided fighters in the history of boxing, despite being outweighed by twenty to fifty pounds in many of his fights, Langford scored more knockouts than George Foreman and Mike Tyson combined. Fighting from lightweight to heavyweight, Sam Langford took on all the best fighters of the first two decades of the twentieth century. He spent the last years of his fighting career virtually blind where the bulk of his losses occurred, although he still won a number of fights impressively by knockouts.

Bout A match between two boxers.

Break Referee's command for boxers to separate from a clinch.

"Brighton Boy" Tom Sayers was one of the great English champions often fighting much larger men. A skillful pugilist, he packed a powerful wallop. Sayers was elected to the Ring Boxing Hall of Fame in 1954. His name came from where he was born on May 25, 1826, Brighton, Sussex, England.

"Brockton Blockbuster" Born in 1923 in Brockton, Massachusetts, from which part of his nickname derived, Rocky Marciano (his real name was Rocco Marchegiano) was heavyweight champion of the world from 1952 to 1956. Marciano won all of his forty-nine pro fights, forty-three of which were knockout victories, including eleven KOs in the first round. The power of Marciano's punches and the devastating effect they had on opponents was the reason for the second half of his nickname. Marciano was killed in a light-plane crash in 1969 on the eve of his forty-sixth birthday.

"Brown Bomber" This famous nickname for Joe Louis, heavyweight boxing champion of the world from 1937 to 1948, was derived from the color of his skin and the power of his punches. Louis won sixty-eight of seventy-one fights—fifty-four of them by knocking out his opponents.

Buckhorse This term is a British slang expression for a punch or a blow that became popular in 1850. Its origin lay in the actions of the famous English boxer John Smith, whose ring name was Buckhorse. For a few shillings, he would allow an individual to punch him on the side of the head as hard as possible. Ultimately, the blow became known as a buckhorse.

Bummy Davis Albert Abraham Davidoff was a Jewish boxer in the 1930s and 1940s. The popular explanation for his nickname is that he earned it as a result of the rough-and-tumble tactics he used as a boxer. Another and more interesting explanation is the Americanization of his Yiddish name, which went through stages from the original "Ahvroom" to "Boomy" and then "Bummy." Davis suffered a violent death. He attempted to break up a holdup in a Brooklyn bar. Fighting with the holdup man, Davis broke the man's jaw in two places. The holdup man then shot Bummy in the throat. Though mortally wounded, Davis still managed to chase the gunman into the street. But the gunman got away and Davis died of his wounds.

Bum of the Month Club In 1941 Joe Louis fought six bouts in six months, defeating all challengers. His victims were referred to as not-so-exclusive members of the Bum of the Month Club, a disparaging comment on their skills and the easy wins Louis had over them. Actually Louis did not seek out easy bouts. In his rule as heavyweight champ of the world—eleven years, eight months, and twelve days (the longest reign of any heavyweight king)—the Brown Bomber risked his title twenty-five times and fought more often than any other champ.

Buttoning Using the top of the head as a striking surface against an opponent; an illegal move.

Canvas The floor (mat) of a ring.

Cards Score sheets used by officials to evaluate a fight. Also, the series of bouts slated for a specific day or night at a particular arena.

Caution An admonition from the referee but generally not for serious infringements of the rules by the boxer. A warning is issued after three cautions.

"Cincinnati Flash" Heavyweight Ezzard Charles had flash and hailed from the Queen City.

"Cinderella Man" James J. Braddock earned his nickname climbing from poverty to the heavyweight championship of the world. He was born in New York City and turned pro in 1926. His greatest moment took place on June 13, 1935, in Long Island City when as a 10-1 underdog he defeated Max Baer to win the title.

Class Weight divisions in which boxers traditionally fight.

Clinch To hold an opponent's arms, making it difficult for him to strike a blow.

"Clones Colossus" Heavyweight boxer Kevin McBride was born in the town of Clones, Ireland, in January 1973. McBride was 6' 7" and 255 pounds. That explains the second half of his nickname.

Club Fighter A local or neighborhood boxer; a fighter skilled in the ability to take punishment.

Combination Punches Blows delivered quickly, one after the other.

Corners Each ring has four corners: two are occupied between rounds by each fighter and his trainers; the neutral corners are not occupied. When one fighter is knocked down, the other is required to move to the farther neutral corner.

Count The act of a referee calling out numbers one through ten after a fighter has been knocked down.

Counted Out When a fighter is unable to get back to his feet before the referee reaches "ten" in the calling of the count.

Counterpunch The throwing of punches by a fighter to counter those thrown by an opponent.

Covering Holding the hands high in front of the face to keep the opponent from landing a clean punch.

Cross (Right Cross) A sharp blow that gets its power from a boxer quickly turning his waist and shifting his weight directly over a straight left leg.

Cut Man An aide, stationed in the boxer's corner, who is skilled in taking care of cuts.

"The Deaf One" ("Deaf") James Burke (1809–1845) was boxing champ in England and the first of his countrymen to fight on U.S. soil. He had learned to box while working as a waterman on the Thames River. His nickname came from his hearing problems.

Decision The awarding of a win to a fighter for taking the most rounds or getting the most points in a fight that goes the scheduled amount of rounds.

Down A situation that occurs when any part of a boxer's body, with the exception of his feet, touches the canvas or makes contact with the canvas; he is then subject to being counted out by the referee.

"Drummer Boy" Sonny Liston beat opponents like a drummer drums his drum.

"Easton Assassin" Larry Holmes was born in Cuthbert, Georgia, but has spent the majority of his life living in Easton, Pennsylvania. As a heavyweight champion, he won his first forty-eight professional fights, threatening to break Rocky Marciano's record of the most fights undefeated for a world champion (49-0). His final record was in sixty-nine bouts that included just six losses.

"Executioner" Bernard Hopkins; the Philadelphia fighter's grim demeanor made the nickname appropriate.

Featherweight A class division with a maximum allowable weight of 126 pounds for professionals and 125 pounds for amateurs.

Feint A faked punch designed to fool an opponent.

"Fighting Marine" Gene Tunney was all of that.

Five-Point Must System A method of scoring that awards the winner of a round five points and the loser less than five.

Five-Point System A method of scoring where the loser is given any number of points less than the amount (up to five) awarded to the winner.

Flatten To knock out an opponent.

Floor To punch an opponent so that he is knocked down.

Flyweight A class division with a maximum allowable weight of 112 pounds.

Footwork Movement of the feet for better offensive or defensive positioning.

Foul An unsportsmanlike action. In essence, an infringement of boxing rules, including: hitting below the belt; hitting with any part of the body other than the knuckles; leaning against the ropes; head-butting; not breaking on the referee's command; hitting the back of the opponent's neck, head, or torso; hitting an opponent who is down; throwing a punch while in a clinch; holding and hitting; offensive language; assaulting or acting aggressively toward the referee; spitting out the mouthpiece; passive defense (not trying to avoid a punch by covering up); tripping; or kicking.

"Galveston Giant" ("Lil' Arthur") Jack Arthur Johnson hailed from Galveston, Texas, and was a giant. He became heavyweight champion of the world in 1908, defeating Tommy Burns in fourteen rounds, becoming the first black heavyweight boxing champion. Johnson's decade of being unbeaten ended in 1915 when the man they called the "Great White Hope," Jess Willard, finally defeated him.

"Gentleman Jim" During the late-nineteenth century, the sport's popularity rose in the U.S. because of him. Corbett was a scientific boxer from a middle-class background who had attended college. The majority of Corbett's fights were gloved bouts under the Marquis of Queensberry Rules.

The first of the modern world heavyweight champs, James J. Corbett defeated John L. Sullivan on September 7, 1892. It was the first match staged in the United States under Queensberry rules and with five-ounce gloves. The bout ended in the twenty-first round, when Corbett kayoed Sullivan, culminating a fight that pitted a scientific boxer against a slugger. Sullivan retired after the defeat. Corbett's nickname had its roots in his stylized manner of dress, his pompadour hair comb, and his intelligent, articulate, mannered behavior His other nicknames included "Handsome Jim," "Pompadour Jim."

"Ghetto Wizard" Benny Leonard, a Jewish boxer born Benjamin Leiner, turned pro at age fifteen. He won the World Lightweight Championship at age twenty-one and held it for nearly seven years between 1917 and 1925 when he retired unbeaten as champion. He was one of the top pound-for-pound fighters ever. He was dubbed "The Ghetto Wizard" because he came out of the ghetto and was a fleet-footed wizard of a boxer with a strong punch.

Glove A boxer's mitt which is padded as a protective cushion for both boxer and opponent and laced at the inside of the wrist. In professional fights, not less than eight-ounce gloves generally are used. For U.S. boxing: 10 ounces for boxers 106–156 pounds; 12-ounces for boxers 165–201+ pounds. For international competition: 8 ounces for lighter classes; 10 ounces for heavier divisions.

"Golden Boy" Oscar de la Hoya said: "I want to be considered one of the great legends in boxing." Born on February 4, 1973, in East Los Angeles, California, de la Hoya's record during his amateur boxing career was an outstanding 223-5 with 163 knockouts—more than enough to make him a legend and earn him his nickname. He turned pro right after winning a gold medal at the 1992 Olympics in Barcelona.

Golden Gloves When this competition originated in 1927 under the sponsorship of the *New York Daily News*, it was strictly an amateur boxing competition for fighters in the New York City area. Today the competition is both national and international. Arch Ward, former sports editor of the *Chicago Tribune,* was mainly responsible for making the event international. He set up All-American and All-European title fights. Many top fighters got their start in the Golden Gloves: Sugar Ray Robinson, Joe Louis, Barney Ross, Tony Zale, Rocky Marciano—all world champs at one time or another.

"The Greatest" (**"Louisville Lip"**) Muhammad Ali. That he was!

"Great White Hope" After Jack Johnson defeated Tommy Burns on December 26, 1908, to become the first black heavyweight champion, a frenzied search began for the white boxer—the white hope—who could defeat him. An arrogant, sophisticated type, Johnson's exploits with the law and with white women prodded the "white hope" advocates. They even talked Jim Jeffries out of a six-year retirement and got him to fight Johnson. It took the efforts of gigantic Jess Willard through twenty-six rounds in the heat of Havana on April 15, 1915, to knock out Johnson and claim the heavyweight championship of the world and the title of the "Great White Hope."

"Grizzly Bear of the West" Legendary James J. Jeffries came out of the West and to those who came up against him it was like a battle with a grizzly bear.

"Hammerin' Hank" ("Hurricane Henry," "Homicide Hank," "Human Buzz Saw," "Little Perpetual Motion") Henry Armstrong was one of the best all-around fighters ever. His nicknames are a testament to that.

Handler A boxer's second; one who trains a boxer.

"Hands of Stone" Roberto Duran, for hitting so hard.

Haymaker A ferocious punch.

Headgear (Headguard) A protective covering over the ears and forehead of a boxer that is generally used in practice sessions.

Heavy Bag A large stuffed training bag that is usually suspended from the ceiling and is used by a boxer to develop punching force.

Heavyweight A class division with any weight over 175 allowed.

"He Can Run But He Can't Hide" Joe Louis and Billy Conn fought twice for the heavyweight championship of the world. Conn, the former light-heavyweight champion, had resigned his title to be able to box in the heavyweight division. He met Louis in 1941. Conn, a sleek 174 pounds, was a sharp contrast to the burly Louis. At the end of the twelfth round, Conn was leading Louis on points. An overconfident Conn then tried for a knockout in the thirteenth round, but he was knocked out instead as Louis unloaded a rapid combination of punishing blows. World War II intervened and both men served in the army. Their second bout was scheduled for Yankee Stadium on June 19, 1946. Conn bragged that he would easily win the fight, that his speed would be too much for Louis, whom he claimed would not be able to catch up to him. "He can run but he can't hide" was the quiet and confident reply of the Brown Bomber. A crowd of 45,000 paid $1,925,564—making for the second largest payday in the history of boxing to time. For seven rounds Conn ran. He circled, he danced, he countered, he stayed away from Louis. The crowd booed so much that at times the two boxers had difficulty hearing the bell ring at the end of a round. In the eighth round, coming out of a clinch, Louis landed a left hook to Conn's jaw. He followed up quickly with a barrage of lefts and rights. Conn stumbled, staggered, fell. He was unable to run or to hide—he couldn't get up, and Louis prevailed.

"Hitman" Tommy Hearns. That he was, as well as "The Motor City Cobra"—for his roots and strike ability.

Hook A short, powerful blow that has the weight of the entire boxer's body behind it; the elbow is bent and kept rigid and the blow is delivered in an arc.

"Hurricane" Rubin Carter was one of several boxers with this nickname, a tag that made reference to frenetic fighting ability.

Infighting Boxing at close range.

"Iron Mike" Mike Tyson's nickname was as plain as his style and fitted him perfectly. In his prime he was just black trunks, black shoes, and intimidation.

"Italian Stallion" The fictional Rocky Balboa (*Rocky*) was Italian and was as strong as a horse.

Jab A stinging, straight blow generally delivered to the head.

Jack Johnson During World War I the German 5.9-inch howitzer was used against the Allies, and its sound, its power, and the thick black smoke that it gave off reminded people of the boxer Jack Johnson.

"Jersey Joe Walcott" His real name was Arnold Cream. But he came from Jersey and the alliterative moniker had a certain swagger to it.

"The Jew" Considered the father of scientific boxing, Daniel Mendoza held the English boxing crown from 1792 to 1795. He called himself "Mendoza the Jew" with pride in his Portuguese Jewish origins.

Kayo A knockout, when a fighter takes the count of ten without being able to regain his feet (KO).

"Kid Blackie" He first appeared as Jack Dempsey in 1914. His nickname came from his place of birth and ferocious style of fighting.

"Kid Chocolate" (**"The Cuban Bon Bon"**) His name was Eligio Saldana. He was a top boxer in the 1930s, and very fond of the night life and good times. When he retired from boxing, he lived a quiet life in Cuba. Fidel Castro recognized his achievements in the late 1970s and settled the Kid in a state mansion. Chocolate passed away in 1988.

Kidney Punch An illegal punch at the small of the back.

Knock Out To score a kayo or knockout.

Knockout Kayo.

Land a Punch To hit another fighter.

Lead The first blow in a series of punches.

"Leg Iron Mike" When he was imprisoned, some referred to Mike Tyson by this nickname, but not when he was around. When Tyson was defeated by Buster Douglas, some called him "Aluminum Mike."

Light-Heavyweight A class division with a maximum weight allowance of 175 pounds.

Light-Middleweight An amateur class division with a maximum weight allowance of 156 pounds.

"Lights Out" James Toney was an accomplished and skilled boxer who kayoed quite a few of his opponents.

Lightweight A class division with a maximum allowable weight of 135 pounds.

Light-Welterweight An amateur class division with a maximum weight allowance of 139 pounds.

"Living Death" (**"Sweet Swatter from Sweetwater, Texas"**) Lew Jenkins was raised in Depression-era Texas, and that's how he got one nickname. Lightweight champ of the world, he doled out much punishment to opponents, and that is how he got his main nickname.

The Long Count The first meeting between Jack Dempsey and Gene Tunney saw a record crowd of more than 120,000 jammed into Philadelphia's Sesquicentennial Stadium on September 26, 1926. Dempsey, in defense of his title for the first time in three years, lost.

The rematch was on September 25, 1927, before 104,000 plus at Soldiers Field in Chicago. Dempsey was paid a record $711,000 for the first fight, $450,000 for the second. Tunney got $200,000 and then $990,000. With fifty seconds elapsed in the seventh round, Dempsey decked Tunney and then stood as close to his opponent as possible. Referee Dave Barry motioned Dempsey toward the neutral corner, then walked over to Dempsey and half pushed him there. Meanwhile, Tunney sat on the canvas. Instead of picking up the timekeeper's count at six, the referee shouted "One." Tunney lifted his head and looked at Barry but did not get up until the count reached nine.

It was the birth of the "Long Count" controversy. Tunney was able to recoup and take control of the fight, boxing his way to another ten-round unanimous decision. Jack Dempsey explained why he did not go immediately to a neutral corner: "I couldn't move. I just couldn't. I wanted Tunney to get up. I wanted to kill the S.O.B."

Dempsey retired from boxing after that fight. To this day what happened that September 22, 1927, remains one of the most controversial subjects in all of sports. Dempsey supporters claim the "long count" gave Tunney four extra seconds, for the referee delayed the count, under the rules, until the Manassa Mauler went to a neutral corner. Tunney claimed that "at the count of four I came to and was in good shape. I had six seconds to go. Without the long count I would have had two seconds to go. Could I, in that space of time, have got up? I'm quite sure I could have."

Low Blow A below-the-belt punch.

"Macho" Hector Camacho, to rhyme with his name and glorify his machismo.

"Madcap Maxie" Max Baer was a skilled fighter who loved to have a good time.

"Manassa Mauler" William Harrison "Jack" Dempsey was born June 24, 1895. The son of a poor timber and mining family from Manassa, Colorado, he did little stray the public opinion of boxing as a brutal sport. After Jack Dempsey began fighting at the age of 17, few opponents could claim they were left standing after a full bout with him. At 16, Dempsey began hopping on trains and travelled west to fight as a professional, and his exact record is not known because he sometimes used the name "kid blackie" to book himself into fights. He first appeared as Jack Dempsey in 1914.

Mandatory Count A regulation generally followed in amateur boxing that stipulates that, in the event of a knockdown, the fight does not continue until a mandatory count of eight has been called.

"Marvelous" Marvin Hagler He made the middleweight division glamorous again. This terrific boxer nicknamed himself and changed his legal name to "Marvelous."

Middleweight A class division with a maximum allowable weight of 160 pounds.

"Mighty Atom" ("The Ghost with a Hammer in His Hand") In a thirteen-year career Jimmy Wilde lost only four of 149 fights. He was born in Wales. Working in the coal mines shaped his enormous strength— all 108 pounds. Wilde, the greatest flyweight of all time, was inducted into the World Boxing Hall of Fame in 1959 and the International Boxing Hall of Fame in 1990.

Million-Dollar Gate This phrase describes the amount of money that comes in through the turnstiles, or gate, to witness a live match. There have been several of these mammoth moneymakers over the years, but it took the promotional genius of Tex Rickard and the contrasting images of Jack Dempsey and Georges Carpentier to create the first one. On the afternoon of July 2, 1921, in Jersey City, New Jersey, 80,000 people paid $1,789,238 to see the rough and crude Manassa Mauler clash with the suave and sophisticated French military hero. It was a press agent's dream fight. It was also the first championship bout that was broadcast on the radio. Carpentier was outweighed by Dempsey by sixteen pounds and outclassed in fighting skill, but the crowd was for the underdog they called "Gorgeous George" and the "Orchid Man." Though advised to give the fans a show, Dempsey grew impatient in the fourth round, and after landing a few heavy blows on the Frenchman, knocked him out (see Gorgeous George, Manassa Mauler).

"(Old) Mongoose" Archie Moore was perhaps the greatest light heavyweight of all time. He had an incredible 140 knockouts in a career that ran from 1936 to 1963. In 228 recorded bouts, Moore lost just seven times. His nickname was fitting—he had the heart of a champion and a mongoose.

Mouthpiece A rubber (plastic) guard placed in a boxer's mouth to prevent cut lips and damage to the teeth.

Neutral Corner One of two corners that are not designated to either boxer.

"The Old Master" Joe Gans, lightweight champion of the world, 1902–1908, was one of the most dominant fighters ever. Gans was a defensive whiz and a devastating puncher.

One-Two A punching combination that generally consists of a left lead followed by a right cross.

"The Orchid (Man)" Born in 1894 Georges Carpentier was a professional prizefighter from the age of thirteen, a champ at age sixteen, a decorated war hero, and a man idolized by the French people. He was handsome and aristocratic, graceful and continental, and a lover of orchids ("Gorgeous George").

Outfighting Boxing at long range.

Outpoint To win a decision on points.

Penalty Loss of points or a fight by a fighter for illegal blows or behavior.

Preliminary Bout A fight by less-experienced boxers that precedes a main-event match.

Pug Slang term for a boxer, derived from the word "pugilist."

Pugilism Sometimes used as a more erudite word to describe the sport of boxing, this term is derived from the Latin *pugil,* meaning "one who fights with his fists." The shorter version of the word is "pug," which describes a boxer. Pug-nosed also comes from the same root.

Pulling a Punch To deliberately soften the force of a blow.

Puncher A fighter known for slugging ability rather than for style and finesse.

Punching Bag A term that applies to either a heavy bag used to develop power or a speed bag used to develop timing.

Purse A fighter's share of the gate receipts.

Put Away, Put Out To finish off an opponent via a knockout.

Queensberry Rules The eighth marquis of Queensberry, John Sholto Douglas (1844–1900), a boxing fan, collaborated with lightweight boxer John Graham Chambers to devise some rules to make the sport they loved a bit more humane, for the England of their time featured bare-knuckled, brutal boxing brawls that caused scores of deaths and many injuries. They produced a set of twelve rules that mandated the use of boxing gloves, the ten-second knockout count, three-minute rounds, and the banning of gouging and wrestling. Codified in 1867, generally in effect in all matches by 1875, and made standard in 1889, the dozen rules became known as the Queensberry Rules. Modern boxing is largely regulated on the basis of the Queensberry Rules. And to this day, the name for the rules drawn up with the help of the marquis of

Queensberry are words synonymous with fair play and playing by the rules in all sports. The original rules were as follows:

1. To be a fair, stand-up boxing match in a 24-foot ring, or as near that size as practicable.
2. No wrestling or hugging allowed.
3. The rounds to be of 3 minutes' duration, and 1 minute's time between rounds.
4. If either man falls through weakness or otherwise, he must get up unassisted, ten seconds to be allowed him to do so, the other man meanwhile to return to his corner; and when the fallen man is on his legs, the round to be resumed, and continued till the 3 minutes have expired. If one man fails to come to the scratch in the ten seconds allowed, it shall be in the power of the referee to give his award in favor of the other man.
5. A man hanging on the ropes in a helpless state, with his toes off the ground, shall be considered down.
6. No seconds or any other person to be allowed in the ring during the rounds.
7. Should the contest be stopped by an unavoidable interference, the referee to name the time and place as soon as possible for finishing the contest, so that the match must be won and lost, unless the backers of both men agree to draw the stakes.
8. The gloves to be fair-sized boxing gloves of the best quality, and new.
9. Should a glove burst, or come off, it must be replaced to the referee's satisfaction.
10. A man on one knee is considered down, and if struck is entitled to the stakes.
11. No shoes or boots with springs allowed.
12. The contest in all other respects to be governed by revised rules of the London Prize Ring.

Rabbit Punch An illegal back-of-the-glove shot to the base of an opponent's skull or the back of his neck.
"Raging Bull" Jake LaMotta—the name described this fierce fighter very well.
"Real Deal" Evander Holyfield, three time heavyweight champion, was.
The Real McCoy Norman Selby was his real name, but he advertised himself as Charles "Kid" McCoy. Welterweight champion from 1896 to 1899, McCoy's lifetime record was eighty-one wins (thirty-five of them by knockouts), six losses, and eighteen draws. There are a few versions as to how the term "The Real McCoy" came into being. One version explains that when the Kid was in his boxing prime and sipping away quietly in a barroom, he heard a bragging voice shout, "I can lick any of the McCoys around, anytime, any place." McCoy took the braggart up on his boast and kayoed him. Awakened some time later, the now-subdued braggart said: "I meant I could beat any of the fighters around using the McCoy name—not the real McCoy himself." Another story runs along the lines of a drunk challenging the Kid in another barroom scene, yelling, "If you're the real McCoy, prove it with your fists." The Kid proved it. The drunk went down for a long count. When he awakened, he allegedly said, "That's the real McCoy, all right." In

most of his fights, the advertisements always promised that "the real McCoy will appear," and although he was really Norman Selby, he was indeed the Real McCoy.

Ring Pro matches take place in an area not less than eighteen nor more than twenty-four feet square including the apron. Enclosed by four covered ropes, each not less than one inch in diameter, the ring has a floor with a twp-inch padding of Ensolite (or equivalent). For USA Boxing or Olympic-style boxing, there is not less than sixteen nor more than twenty feet square within the ropes. The floor has to extend beyond the ring ropes not less than two feet. Ring posts are connected to the four ring ropes.

Ring Names/Real Names Boxing is a form of show business. Some would say that it is *all* show business today. Nevertheless, over the years boxers, like show business personalities, have changed their real names to more dramatic, more easily remembered, and more pronounceable ring names. Some significant examples follow:

Ring	*Real*
Lou Ambers	Louis D'Ambrosio
Henry Armstrong	Henry Jackson
Tommy Burns	Noah Brusso
Kid Chocolate	Eligio Sardinias
Jack Delaney	Ovila Chapdelaine
Tony DeMarco	Leonard Liotta
Jack Dempsey	William Harrison Dempsey
Jack ("Nonpareil") Dempsey	John Kelly
Joe Dundee	Samuel Lazzaro
Johnny Dundee	Joseph Carrora
Vince Dundee	Vincent Lazzaro
Jackie Fields	Jacob Finkelstein
Tiger Flowers	Theo Flowers
Joe Gans	Joseph Gaines
Kid Gavilan	Geraldo Gonzalez
Joey Giardello	Carmine Tillelli
Rocky Graziano	Rocco Barbelo
Beau Jack	Sidney Walker
Jack Johnson	John Arthur Johnson
Stanley Ketchel	Stanislaus Kiecal
Benny Leonard	Benjamin Leiner
Battling Levinsky	Barney Lebrowitz
Joe Louis	Joe Louis Barrow
Rocky Marciano	Rocco Marchegiano

Joey Maxim	Joseph Beradinelli
Kid McCoy	Norman Selby
Archie Moore	Archibald Wright
Willie Pep	William Papaleo
Ray Robinson	Walker Smith
Jack Root	James Ruthaly
Barney Ross	Barnet Rasofsky
Jack Sharkey	Joseph Paul Zukauskas
Dick Tiger	Dick Ihetu
Gene Tunney	James Joseph Tunney
Jersey Joe Walcott	Arnold Raymond Cream
Chalky Wright	Albert Wright
Tony Zale	Anthony Zaleski

Ringside The area close to the ring.

Ringside Physician A doctor who checks the condition of competitors before the bout, evaluates if a dazed boxer can continue, and has the authority to stop a bout at any time.

Ringside Seats Seats close to the ring.

Roadwork Outdoor running exercise done by a boxer as a form of conditioning.

Rope-a-Dope This name and technique, both allegedly invented by Muhammad Ali, denoted a style of boxing in which Ali would alternately fight toe-to-toe with an opponent and then rest against the ropes, taking the opponent's punches. The strategy behind this maneuver was to give Ali a chance to rest and to make the opponent "dopey," or arm-weary, from throwing punches that did little damage to Ali.

Ropes Three or four strands of rope surrounding the ring that are covered with soft material.

Round A three-minute period in professional competition during which the actual fighting takes place; each round is followed by a one-minute rest period.

Roundhouse A wide sweeping hook punch.

RSC (Referee Stops Contest) An official result that follows when a boxer is outclassed, has been hurt, or reached the standing-eight count limit. In the official results the winner's name is given followed by RSC and the round the bout was ended. For example: John Smith, RSC (4).

RSCH (Referee Stops Contest Head) A variation on RSC, which results when a referee ends a bout because a boxer has taken too many blows to the head.

"Ruby Robert" Bob Fitzsimmons was boxing's first triple-crown champion gaining the world's middleweight (1891–1897), light-heavyweight (1903–1905), and heavyweight (1897–1899) crowns during a thirty-four-year career. He was a real ruby of a fighter.

Scorecard The form used by a judge or a fan to keep a round-by-round score of a fight.

Scoring Blow Punch landing cleanly on the opponent's head or torso and struck with the knuckles, signified by the white stripe on the glove. Three judges agreeing within a one-second window that the blow was clean gets a point for the boxer.

Second A person aside from the coach giving aid or advice between rounds to a boxer.

Shadow Boxing A training procedure involving sparring with an imaginary opponent.

"She Be Stinging" Laila Ali, with apologies to her dad.

"Six Heads" Andrew Lewis is a fighter of many skills. His nickname comes from the fact that other boxers generally see six of him when he connects.

"Smokin'" Joe Frazier, heavyweight par excellence, full of fire and fury and smoke.

Sparring Partner A training partner with whom a boxer works in preparation for a bout.

Split Decision A decision agreed to by a majority but not all of the officials.

Stance The position a boxer takes in facing an opponent.

Standing-Eight Count When a boxer is in difficulty or has been knocked down the referee stops the action, counts to eight, and determines if the boxer can continue. If a boxer takes three standing-eights in a round or four in a fight, the bout is stopped and the opponent is declared the winner.

"Star of David" Dmitriy Salita is a talented Jewish welterweight who came from Odessa to Brooklyn. When not training, he is generally in a small brick building on Ocean Avenue in Flatbush, where he reads Torah along with a Lubavitcher rabbi.

Stop To kayo an opponent.

Stop the Fight An action by a referee that halts a bout in progress, generally because one of the fighters, in the referee's judgment, is unable to continue.

"Sugar" Ray Robinson's real name was Walker Smith. He turned pro in 1940 and won his first forty fights before losing to Jake LaMotta. After that loss, Robinson did not lose for another eight years. His career covered three decades. Thought of as the best fighter in history, pound-for-pound, he earned the nickname "Sugar Ray" when a newspaper reporter described him as "sweet as sugar."

Ray Leonard had speed, firepower, and charisma, filling the boxing void left when Muhammad Ali retired in 1981. Leonard was named Fighter of the Decade for the 1980s. He won five world titles in five weight classes. His nickname derives from that of Ray Robinson.

Sunday Punch A boxer's most effective punch.

"Sweetpea" Pernell Whittaker, for a baby face, a sweet feeling for boxing, and small stature.

Take a Dive To fake being knocked out.

Technical Knockout The winning of a fight by a boxer as a result of a referee's decision that the victor's opponent is physically unable to continue the match (TKO).

"They Never Come Back" Just who uttered what is now a phrase associated with the heavyweight division of boxing is unknown. Its rationale is clear, though, for throughout history there have been examples of boxers—dethroned, damaged, defeated, retired—who attempted to make a comeback. Rusty, aged, out of condition, after their time, lacking motivation, these fighters, goaded by the desire for one more big paycheck, one more fling in the spotlight, almost always disappointed themselves and their fans. Thus the expression—almost a cliché—is well rooted in boxing. Such figures as Muhammad Ali have weakened the generalization. Ali came back not once but twice to claim the heavyweight championship of the world.

"Thrilla in Manila" Muhammad Ali versus Joe Frazier in the capital of the Philippines on October 1, 1975. Some boxing fans call it the greatest fight ever. Ali and Frazier seemed to honestly dislike each other—they had already split two fights between them. Ali won this one.

"Tipton Slasher" William Perry hailed from Tipton, England, and was a slashing type of fighter.

Trainer A person who conditions and cares for a fighter.

Uppercut A punch thrown up from the waist with a bent arm and generally aimed at an opponent's head.

Warning Given by the referee to the boxer who commits a serious foul or receives three cautions. When the referee signals a warning, the ringside judges can decide whether to give a point to the opponent. Three warnings in a bout mean disqualification.

Weaving Eluding punches by turning and twisting movements.

Weigh-in The official weighing of two boxers who will compete against each other—in most cases, that same day.

Welterweight Boxing Division The word "welter" was originally used to describe a weight class in English horse racing. About 1792, English boxers who weighed around 145 pounds referred to themselves as "welters." Paddington Tom Jones was the first "welterweight" champion; from 1792 to 1795, Jones triumphed in matches against all challengers.

"Whitechapel Whirlwind" Boxing immortal Jackie "Kid" Berg was born Judah Bergman, a Cockney Jew from East London who exploded upon the American boxing scene. His nickname came from his home neighborhood and his ferocious manner in the ring.

"Wild Bull of the Pampas" Luis Angel Firpo was a 6' 3", 220-pound boxer from Argentina. His wild hair, his bobbing head as he sprung from his corner to start a round, and his Argentinean ancestry prompted the nickname given to him by writer Damon Runyon. Firpo and his nickname are both especially remembered as a result of his September 14, 1923, Polo Grounds battle with Jack Dempsey. The epic slugfest lasted only to the fifty-seventh second of the second round. Up to that point, Dempsey had been downed twice by Firpo, while the Manassa Mauler had pounded Firpo to the mat six times. Firpo fought in a fury, like a wild bull, like a wild and maimed bull. The fight ended when Dempsey put him down for the seventh and final time.

"The Wisp" Willie Pep, for his slightness.

"Yama Bahama" William Hohalis Butler, Jr., was born on February 16, 1933, in Bimini in the Bahamas. When Yama turned twenty he moved to Florida and started training at the Miami Beach Gym. When the young middleweight was set to turn pro, Lee Evans of the *Miami Herald* got an idea for a nickname for the boxer looking at the boat owned by Butler's manager, George Lyon. Masking the last name of it first, he changed the first letter of the new first name M to Y. William H. Butler, Jr., became "Yama Bahama."

Cricket

All-Rounder One who bats and bowls equally well.

Arm-Ball A ball bowled by a finger spinner that moves straight but later in flight drifts outwards.

Bail An old word of French describing a movable horizontal part of the little gate, or "wicket," that served as the entrance to a sheep pen, used as the target for bowling in early versions of the game.

Barter This English cricket term has its roots in the skilled performance of Robert Barter, warden at Winchester College (1832–1861). Barter was famous for his half-volley hits—the shot that the term bearing his name denotes.

Bat An Old English word meaning a stick or club. Earliest types of bats were somewhat like a hockey stick—long, heavy clubs curved outward toward the bottom.

Beamer Full-toss delivery that travels shoulder-to-head-high at the batsman.

Blocker Batsman who plays too defensively.

Bosey This Australian cricket term originated in England and was taken from the name of the English bowler B. J. T. Bosanquet. He made famous the technique known as the "googly" when he toured Australia in 1903–1904. Bowled with leg-break action, the googly is an off-break ball. Bosanquet's "bosey" thus is named for its inventor and one of its leading practitioners.

Boundary Line denoting the edge of the playing area.

Box Genital protector, incorrectly called abdominal protector.

Chinaman This politically incorrect term derives from the 1929–1930 series between England and West Indies. The West Indian left-arm wrist spinner, Ellis Achong, of Chinese descent, bowled a ball that Walter Robbins missed and was stumped. As the story goes, Robbins returned to the dressing room and exclaimed, "Fancy getting out to a bloody Chinaman!"

Cover Term's origin allegedly was that the fielder in this position was called "The man who covers the point and middle wicket."

Creases A crease is a furrow in the surface. They were originally cut in the turf. This method of marking lasted until painted white lines were introduced.

Cricket Cricket gets its name from the Anglo-Saxon word *cryce*, a term used to describe a wooden stick used to hit a ball. The earliest recorded cricket match took place in 1697.

Duck The origin is the old description of a batsman who failed to score as having made a "duck's egg"—the shape resembling the figure 0.

Ferret A terrible batsman, so poor that he is called after an animal that rabbiters send into the burrows after the rabbits!

Fishing A batsman playing and missing outside of stump.

Flannels The term came from the white knee breeches of the eighteenth-century game, originally made out of thick warm flannel, aptly suited to the English game and that country's predominantly chilly summer climate.

Four Number of runs awarded to the batsman when striking the ball which lands within the playing area, but travels over the boundary.

Full-Toss Ball reaching the batsman without bouncing.

Googly The origin of this term is that the delivery mystified the batsman so much it made eyes "goggle." It is a ball bowled by a wrist spinner that turns the opposite way.

Gully The name is from the more general meaning of gully, suggesting a narrow channel or "gorge" between point and the slips. Gully is a fairly recent term for the position formerly called short third man or backward point. After the development of off-theory attack toward the end of the nineteenth century, it became a position in its own right.

Half-Volley Ball pitching about a yard in front of the batsman.

Hat Trick Originating from an old custom giving a hat or cap to a bowler who achieved the feat of taking three wickets in a row.

Jaffa Unplayable ball which the batsman has no idea about.

Leg Break Bowler A right-arm wrist spinner who spins the ball away from a right-handed batsman.

Long Hop Short-pitched delivery.

Lost Ball The rule was introduced in 1809 when a lot of cricket was played in sheep meadows and lost balls happened regularly.

Mankad Comes from the Sydney Test between Australia and India when Indian spinner Vinoo Mankad ran out Australian opener Bill Brown in this way without warning. Mankad's name is for any act regarded as highly unsportsmanlike.

Mid-On, Mid-Off Contractions of the earlier position "middle wicket off" and "middle wicket on." Manuals and illustrations of the early-nineteenth century depict middle wicket as one of the standard fielding positions of the game then. Middle wicket was an offside fielding position between extra cover and the bowler. However, an equivalent leg-side position was also sometimes, thus the two "middle wicket" positions as middle wicket off (Mid-Off) and middle wicket on (Mid-On).

Mid-Wicket Ancient cricket term receiving its current meaning only in the 1930s. Prior to that "mid-wicket" or "middle wicket" was simply another name for mid-off. The position currently called mid-wicket in earlier times would have been called "forward square leg" or perhaps "extra mid-on."

Off-Break Bowler A right-arm finger spinner who spins the ball into a right-handed batsman from outside the off stump.

Pads These came into cricket only with the advent of roundarm and overarm bowling, which were sufficiently fast to injure the legs of batsman. Early cricketers did not consider it sporting to defend their wickets with their legs, so there was no need for pads.

Pair Batsman who has two "ducks" in both innings.

Pick-up How a bat feels to a particular batsman. Bats of the same weight can feel different.

Pitch A 22-yard strip on which the ball is bowled (Wicket).

Plank Bat which performs poorly, give vibration in the batsman's hands.

Point From early cricket when the position was called "point of the bat," this indicates that the fielder stood very near to the end of the striker's bat (hence the even older name for this position was "bat's end").

Popping Crease Originates from the popping hole that was cut in the turf. This hole played a major part in early cricket rules; the batsman had to place his bat in this hole on completion of a "notch" or run. To get the batsman out, the wicketkeeper needed to put the ball in the hole before the batsman could reach it with his bat. Serious hand injuries resulted and this procedure was ultimately replaced by the batsman being required to touch a stick held by the umpire. Ultimately, in the modern game, the popping hole was represented symbolically by a popping crease for the purposes of scoring a run.

Roundarm Bowling Allegedly developed by Christina Willes, the sister of Kent player John Willes, in the early-nineteenth century because she had problems bowling underarm around her voluminous skirts. She got around this difficulty developing a higher action.

Seam Bowler (Seamer) A bowler whose main goal is to move the ball off the pitch by landing it on the seam.

Six Number of runs awarded the batsman when striking the ball over the boundary without landing within the playing area.

Slips An early description of the long stop, who "is required to cover many slips from the bat," gives insight into how "skips" came to be. Early cricket writers identify two slip positions: a short-slip, which was equivalent to the modern-day first or second slip position; a long-slip, equivalent to the modern-day short third-man or fly-slip position. By the turn of the twentieth century an attacking field generally had two slips (in the modern sense) which were called "first slip" and "cover-slip" or "extra-slip."

Slogger Batsman who hits the ball across the line generally in the air.

Slow Left Arm A left arm off-break bowler.

Square Area in the center of a cricket ground specially prepared and rolled forming the pitch.

Swing Bowler One whose main aim is to move the ball in the air.

Tail-Ender (Rabbit) One lacking skill as a batsman who comes in at the bottom of the order, thus "tail."

Third Man Position that was beginning to come more in vogue with the spread of overarm bowling and the development of off-theory attack to supplement the more established close offside fielding positions of point and short-slip. New fieldsman was thus the third man up.

Top Spinner A top spinner bowled by a wrist spinner which goes straight on.

Umpires The term derives from the Middle English term *noumpere,* a "nonpeer" or "unequal," indicating an "odd man" or third party called in to adjudicate. Two umpires have always been in effect, presumably dating back to the origins of the double-wicket game.

Wicket Set of three stumps and two bails (Pitch).

Yorker Purpose of a good "yorker" is to deceive the batsman through pitching the ball at his feet. Derived from a eighteenth- and nineteenth-century regional slang kink between the words *Yorkshire* and *york* and the notion of cheating and deception.

Croquet

Alive In American play, a ball that has cleared a wicket but has not roqueted another ball is alive on that ball. In British game, all balls are alive at the start of each player's turn.

All-Around Break Running all wickets in one turn.

Angle of Divergence One where balls part when a croquet shot is made.

Angle of Split The angle between two lines, along which the two balls travel.

Aunt Emma Conservative player seeking to advance from one wicket to the next who wastes talent through dull play.

Back Peel Peeling a ball through its wicket, right after running that wicket.

Ball in Hand One that has to be picked up and moved, either before taking croquet or because it has gone out of bounds.

Baulk-Line In British play, starting lines. On each of the short sides of the yard-line are other unmarked lines, approximately twelve yards in length.

Beefy Shot A long, hard shot.

Being off Color Not hitting true.

Bisque Shot able to be replayed from its original position with no penalty.

Bisque Extraction Strategy of getting an opponent to use up his bisques ineffectively or for defensive purposes only.

Break Extending one's turn by using one or more of the other balls.

Break Down To make a mistake involuntarily, making one's turn end during the course of a break.

Cannon Shot Making a roquet on the same shot as a croquet.

Carrying Through Following through with your arms leading.

Center Style Traditional stance with mallet between one's knees.

Clips Color of each ball, the clips are placed on the next wicket. The clips are placed on the top of the wickets through the first six wickets and on the sides for the six back wickets.

Cold Ball The roque, last ball played of your opponent.

Condoning Failure of a player to claim a foul within the limits of claims makes the play in question valid. A foul is not charged to the striker.

Contact Touching or making contact with another ball. A foul when one's mallet contacts another ball and the turn ends.

Continuation Stroke Extra stroke earned by running a wicket; stroke after making a croquet.

Corner To hit a ball or croquet another ball into a corner for defensive purposes.

Corner Cannon Shot combination of rush and croquet stroke; croqueting a ball after taking croquet from another ball in the corner.

Corner Flags They are situated at the four corners of the course.

Corner Pegs They are located a yard on each side of the corner flags.

Croquet Around 1300 the French played a game called Paille-Maille, which was the grandfather of croquet. The French word *croche*, a reference to a crooked stick, is the origin of the name for the sport of croquet. Most people associate the sport with England because of its nineteenth-century popularity on wide English lawns perfectly suited for the playing of the game.

Croquet Shot One made after a roquet. The ball of the striker is placed in contact with the roqueted ball and in taking croquet both balls are sent off to their desired positions.

Cross Peg A leave where opponents' balls are left straddling the peg thwarting the desired shot by the opponent.

Cross Wire A leave where opponents' balls are left on each side of a wicket, preventing a desired shot by the opponent.

Crown Top part of a wicket.

Crush Shot Employed to jar a ball lying against the wicket through it.

Cut Rush A shot played so that the rushed ball moves off at an angle to the direction of the stroke.

Deadness A striker's ball hits another ball preventing him from using that ball until going through the next wicket. The striker is dead on the other ball, after taking the croquet shot.

Deadness Board Equipment used to keep track of deadness throughout the game.

Delayed Triple Peel Temporarily abandoning a triple peel and resuming later in the turn.

Destroy Shot One taken with great force to send a croqueted ball the furthest distance possible.

Double Banking Playing two separate games simultaneously on the same course because of time or space restrictions.

Double Elimination Two losses before being eliminated.

Double Peel A ball knocked through two wickets in the same turn, not necessarily on the same stroke.

Double Roll Shot where striker's ball rolls the same distance as the roquet's ball.

Double Tap A fault, striker's ball is hit twice in the same shot.

Drive Shot By hitting slightly down on the striker's ball during croquet, the croqueted ball travels about three times the distance.

Emma Peel An avenging play.

Fault Stroke that is a foul or unacceptable one.

Feather-Off Light take-off shot.

Foot Shot Croquet shot taken with the foot on the ball.

Forestall Foul is committed, but opponent does not stop play before the next stroke to claim a misplay. Penalty is not assessed, foul is forestalled.

Four-Ball Break Backbone of the game. Ideally, all four balls are used to go around the course in a single turn.

Free Shot One which, if missed, will not have negative consequences. The more advanced the play, however, the less chance there is for free shots. Even on the first wicket one shot can mean the difference between winning and losing.

Golf Style Style of swing in which the mallet is swung cross the body like a putter.

Go to Bed with Bisques Losing in a handicap game with one or more unused bisques.

Half-Jump Shot By hitting down on the ball, striker sends both obstructing and striker's ball through the wicket.

Hitting True Hitting the ball with a level swing, as opposed to hitting up or down.

Hong Kong Archaic term for taking croquet.

Hoop English term for wicket.

Hoop-Bound A swing hindered by a wicket.

Hoop Doc Therapist or psychiatrist consulted by a player suffering anxiety associated with wicket-shooting errors.

Hoop-Running Shot One through the proper wicket.

Irish Peel Roll stroke similar to the half-jump shot, both balls going through their wickets.

Irish Style Akin to center style, but using the Irish grip.

Is For The next wicket a ball is headed for.

Jam Illegal shot when a ball lies against the wicket made with unlawfully prolonged contact between the ball and the arch.

Jaws Wicket entrance.

Join Up Playing the ball near its partner.

Jump Ball Through hitting down on the ball, the striker can make the ball jump over an obstructing ball.

Kiss Cannon Like a corner cannon, shot with the added element of hitting a third ball with the croqueted ball, as well as roqueting the intended target with the strikers ball.

Knocking Up Hitting practice balls for a feel of the course.

Laying a Break Positioning balls at future wickets for setting up a break.

Lay Up A long, reckless, wild shot to escape from a dangerous position.

Leave Position of the balls after a shot.

Level Play Nonhandicapped competition.

Lift A ball-in-hand either after the roquet or going out of bounds is lifted for repositioning.

Limit of Claims Time during which a fault can be called; otherwise invalid (Forestalling).

Next-Two Leave Striker leaves his partner with a rush to the wicket and the opponent's ball at each of the next two wickets.

No Brainer A lucky shot.

Non-Playing Side Area on the other side of the wicket that is being played.

One-Ball Shot One in which only one ball is hit.

Pass Roll A croquet shot where the strikers ball goes farther than the croqueted ball.

Peel Making another ball to make the wicket.

Peg-Down Interrupting a game, marking the position of the balls and clips, intending to resume later.

Pegged-Out Game One where at least one ball has pegged out.

Penultimate Next-to-last wicket.

Pilot Ball One off which a wicket is made in a four-ball break.

Pioneer Ball The ball in a three- or four- ball break sent forward to the wicket after the one the striker is going for.

Pivot Ball Middle ball in a four-ball break.

Playing Side Area in front of wicket being approached.

Predominance A hand or a foot leads the wing too much, common error.

Pseudo-Cannon Shot Three-ball croquet shot, the croqueted ball moves just a little way out of the corner.

Pull Tendency for the ball to curve inward from the line of aim.

Push Keeping the mallet on the ball for a bit of time.

Quadruple Peel Four-wicket peel.

Qualifying Shot One that begins a turn.

Questionable Stroke Play of dubious legality, one with chance of a foul.

Quintuple Peel A five-wicket peel.

Reverse Palm Grip Most popular grip, made with the lower hand's palm facing away from the body, upper hand's palm facing toward the body.

Right of Choice After a lag or coin toss, winner has the choice of starting position or choice of balls.

Rigor Mortis The condition of being dead on all balls (Three Ball Dead, Three B D).

Roll Stroke A striking-down croquet shot used to add distance to the striker's ball as well as the croqueted ball.

Roquet Striker's ball hits another ball, followed by a croquet shot and a continuation shot.

Rover Ball One that has passed through all the wickets but has not yet pegged out.

Rover Wicket Final wicket before the peg.

Rush (Long or Short) A roquet shot sending the roqueted ball in a given direction.

Rush Line Imaginary line along which a ball is roqueted on a rush shot.

Rush Line Principle Shot made before an intended rush shot. It should be taken from a spot on or near the rush line.

Scatter Shot played only as a last resort; separates balls that lie too close together.

Sextuple Peel Part of a plan to complete a game in two breaks, similar to a quadruple peel.

Shepherding Illegal stroke of guiding the ball through the wicket with the mallet.

Side Technique where ball is not struck with the center of the mallet.

Spin Angular momentum that a moving object has is determined by mass, size, and spin.

Split Shot Croquet shot where the two balls go off at different angles.

Stalk Approaching the ball along the line where it is to be sent in order to insure proper aim.

Stepping Stone Placement of a ball in an advantageous position near a wicket or the peg.

Sticky Wicket Having a difficult approach to the wicket; being stuck in the wicket.

Stop Shot Delivering an upward shot to the striker's ball during a croquet. The croqueted ball is sent a considerable distance, while the striker's ball hardly moves.

Straight Croquet Shot where striker's ball goes half the distance of the croqueted ball.

Straight Triple Peel Doing three peels with backward ball making the same three wickets.

Strike Actual hitting of the ball with the mallet.

Striker Player whose turn it is. Turns determined by the color of the balls: blue, red, black, yellow (green, orange).

Stroke Movement of the mallet beginning with the backstroke and ending with the follow-through whether or not the ball is hit.

Stymie Ball blocking the intended path of the striker's ball.

Take-off Shot Croquet shot where striker's ball travels a great distance, but the croqueted ball moves very little.

Thick Take-off Croquet shot where croqueted ball moves further than on a simple take-off and goes a good distance.

Three-Ball Break Break using three balls, the cornerstone of the pegged-out game.

Tice Shot placing a ball in a position that entices opponent to shoot at it, but at a sufficient distance that the shot will likely be missed.

Two-Ball Break Break using two balls; the most difficult of all breaks, involving shots of the greatest distance.

Upright Style Another name for front style of swinging the mallet.

Vectors Lines defined by moving objects. For example, when red is struck, the line that red travels is its vector.

Waive Passing up one's turn.

Wicket Metal upright through which the balls are played.

Willis Setting Basis for the six-wicket, one-peg game, introduced in 1922.

Winter Wickets Thin wire wickets for use when the ground is frozen.

Wired Ball One behind the wicket or peg that because of the obstruction cannot be hit by the striker's ball or other ball.

Cycling

Accessories Add-ons to the bike or rider: lights, mudguards, helmets, and so forth.
Alloy Steel alloy in frames and rims.
ATB All Terrain Bicycle.
Barbag Luggage fitting on handlebar.
Bar Ends Handlebars extension.
Bars Handlebars.
Base Layer "Wicking" garments worn next to the skin for comfort and warmth.
Big Ring Biggest of the front chainwheels.
Block Cluster of sprockets, or cogs, on back wheel.
Bosses Brazed-on mounting points on a bike's frame (Braze-ons).
Bottom Bracket Axle linking the two cranks.
Brake Shoe Sleeve the brake pad is fixed to.
Bunny-Hop Jumping off the ground on the bike.
Butted Tubes Frame tubing with thin walls at center, reducing weight (Double-Butted).
Cadence Pedaling rate.
Cager Car driver, slang.
Captain Person who sits at the front of a tandem.
Chainset Cogs or chainwheels attached to cranks.
Chainstay Tube running from bottom bracket to rear of the frame.
Chainwheel The cog, or cogs, attached to cranks.
Clearance Amount of space between ground and bottom bracket.

Cleats Mechanism screwed to sole of the shoe to fit clipless pedal.

CoolMax Technical fabric made from polyester used for jerseys and base layers.

Cordura Heavy-duty nylon used in panniers, boots, and rucksacks.

Crank Pedal arm.

Cro-Mo, Chrome-Moly Abbreviations for chrome-molybdenum, which is a high-tensile steel alloy used for cycle frames.

Damping Cushioned spring associated with suspension systems.

Derailleurs Mechanisms to change gears at the rear of the bike (rear mech), or at the front (front mech) if more than one chainring is there.

Dish(ing) The degree of asymmetry of the spoke arrangement on either side of a wheel.

Down Tube One running from headtube at the front of the bike to bottom bracket.

Drop Handlebars On-road racing bikes and tourers, they curve down in an s-shape.

Drop Out Place where wheel is attached to the fork at the front or the frame at the rear.

Elastomer Suspension Spongelike plastic that compresses and expands to provide damping.

Frameset Frame and forks.

Freewheel Cogs at the rear of the bike.

Gore-Tex Waterproof breathable fabric.

Granny Ring The smaller of the front chainwheels. In the granny ring you spin very fast and can climb steep slopes.

Groupset Refers to components of a bicycle: brakes, hub, chain, cranks, chainset, freewheel, and gears.

Halogen Type of cycle light filament bulb that emits a bright, white light.

Headset The sleeve inside the frame that links the stem to the front fork.

Head Tube Contains headset.

Honking Pedaling out of the saddle, placing much weight and power onto the pedals, usually uphill.

HPV Human-powered vehicle; pedal-driven cycles with untraditional appearances.

Hybrid Cross between road bike and a mountain bike.

IBD Independent Bicycle Dealer (LBS).

Knobblies Deep-tread tires.

Lacing Weaving spokes together forming a wheel.

LBS Local Bicycle Shop (IBD).

LED Light Emitting Diode; lights that flash.

Lugs Sleeves joining two frame tubes together.

Mitts Short-fingered gloves.

MTB Mountain bike, abbreviation.

Nipple Bolt securing a spoke to the rim.

Pannier Racks Framing fitting onto front or rear of a bike that carries luggage.

Pertex Windproof, water-resistant lightweight, nylon fabric.

Polartec Polyester fleece fabric.

Presta Valve On the inner tube, found mostly on road, touring, city, and hybrid bikes.

Quick Release (QR) Skewers securing wheel through the hub that can be tightened and released quickly without tools.

Rake Curvature in a pair of front forks that spring a little.

Rear Triangle Seatstays and chainstays; back end of the bike.

Recumbent HPV bike where one sits reclining in a bucket seat.

Rim Part of the wheel where the tire runs around and where the spokes are attached.

Rip-Stop Method of preventing windproof fabric from tearing.

Roadies Those preferring road riding to mountain biking.

Roadster European style bikes.

Sag Wagon Luggage-carrying van or truck which follows cyclists.

Sam Browne Belt Fluorescent sash worn by cyclists and motorcyclists to make other road users aware of their existence. Belt was invented by General Sir Sam Browne VC (1821–1901), a veteran of the Indian Mutiny.

Schraeder Valve On an inner tube, mainly found on mountain bikes.

Seat Post (Seat Pin) One attached to saddle which can be set up or down in the seat tube suiting rider's height.

Seatstay Frame tube running from the top of the seat tube to the rear of the frame.

Semi-Slicks Tires with partial or shallow tread.

Shifter Gear-changing lever.

Skewer Rod pushed through the hub securing the wheel to the drop-outs.

Slicks Tires lacking tread.

SPD Shimano Pedaling Dynamics; term for Shimano clipless pedals.

Sprocket Cog in the freewheel.

Stem Attaches the handlebar to the frame via the headset.

Stoker One who sits at the back of a tandem.

Toe-Strap One fitted to a pedal, keeping the foot in position so power can be added to the upstroke not just the downstroke.

Top Tube Frame tube running along top of the frame (Crossbar).

Track-Stand Balancing bike in one place with both feet on the pedals.

Trike Tricycle term.

Truing Straightening a buckled wheel.

Twist Shift Changing gear by twisting part of the grip on the handlebar.

Ventile Traditional, tough, windproof, waterproof cotton fabric.

Wheelbase Distance between the wheel axles.

Wicking Clothing that draws moisture, or sweat, away from the body to the outside of the garment.

Darts

Aces Double ones.

Angel Dart Shot missing the target but still producing a good score, such as a triple 18 by a player who was aiming for triple 20.

Annie's Room Score of one.

Baby Ton Score of ninety-five, especially if attained with five 19s.

Bag o' Nuts 45 points on a throw.

Bail-out Dart Third dart of a throw, hitting target after the first two have missed (Barn Dart, Hail Mary Dart).

Barrel Metal area of the dart, gripped by the shooter.

Baseball American Game of nine innings and the target number is the number of the inning being played.

Basement Double 3s.

Bed Specific target area; for example, double 20 (see Three in a Bed).

Bed and Breakfast Scoring twenty-six points in one throw with a 20, a 5, and a 1. The name comes from the fact that in England, the traditional bed and breakfast price was two pounds and sixpence.

Black Dog Double bull.

Black Eye Center area of the bull's-eye, worth fifty points.

Black Hat Hitting three double bulls in one throw, name comes from "hat trick."

Bombs Very large or heavy darts (Bombers).

Bones When a shooter needs a double 1 to get down to zero.

Bricked Player failing to hit a single mark in a round of cricket is in this position.

Bucket of Nails When all three darts land in the 1s.

Buckshot When three darts in a throw are scattered over the board.

Bull Bull's-eye.

Bull and Cork Center of the bull.

Bull Out Winning a game with a double bull.

Bull's-eye Centermost area of the board, composed of the single bull and double bull.

Bull Up Throwing at the bull to decide which player throws first.

Busted Having scored too many points attempting to finish a 01 game.

Century A score of one hundred or more points in one round.

Chalk To keep score.

Chalker The scorekeeper.

Championship Board A dartboard where double and triple rings and the bullseye are half the size of a normal board, many times used for practice.

Checkout Shot hit to win the game.

Chips Feat of scoring twenty-six points in a throw (Classic).

Chucker Shooter throwing at board without aiming at any particular number.

Clickity Click Score of sixty-six on a throw.

Clock Dartboard.

Convertibles Darts with interchangeable tips, for playing steel-tip or soft-tip (electronic darts).

Cork The bullseye.

Crack To hit a single when aiming at a double.

Cricket Team game whose object is to hit three each of the numbers 15 through 20 and the bullseyes.

Dartitis Malady preventing a player from releasing the dart.

Dead-Eye Hitting three double bulls in one turn.

Diddle for the Middle ("Dibble," "Piddle") Preliminary act of throwing a single at the bull to determine which player will throw first.

Dinky Doo The twenty-two.

Dirty Darts Questionable tactics, like scoring excessive points in Cricket.

Double Bull Center portion of the bullseye, worth fifty points.

Double Cork Same as double bull.

Double In (DI) Hitting the double area of a number to start a 01 game.

Double Out (DO) Hitting the double area of a number to win a 01 game.

Double Ring Outer ring of the dart board, worth double the designated number.

Double Top The double 20.

Downstairs Bottom area of board.

Easy In, Easy Out Said of a game where a double in or double out is not required.

Fall Out To score with a dart while aiming for another number. For example, hitting a 16 in cricket when aiming at the 19 (Scud).

Fat Large area of a number, between double and triple rings, worth a single score.

501 Game where player starts with 501 points and attempts to get down to zero; almost always double-out.

Flat Tire Dart landing in the black ring around the board, outside scoring area.

Flight The feathers of dart.

Foot Fault Stepping or touching beyond the throw line when delivering a dart.

Game On Request for silence at game's start.

Game Shot The potential winning shot.

Garden States Score of eighty-eight.

"Goldfinger" Maureen Flowers was an excellent dart thrower. At one time, she was the best in the world.

Good Group Three darts in a close grouping.

G-O-T An urging to a player to get mentally focused; abbreviation for "Get on Top."

Half a Crown Score of twenty-six (slang from the former British coinage, when two shillings and sixpence equaled half a crown).

Happy Meal Score of sixty-nine.

Hat Trick Feat of hitting the bull with all three darts.

Heinz Score of fifty-seven, derived from Heinz's 57 varieties (Varieties).

High Ton Score between 150 and 180 in a 01 game.

Hockey Throw line.

Island Dartboard's playing surface, inside the outer double wire; darts landing outside the island do not count.

Knurl Patterned or grooved area on the barrel of the dart, for better gripping.

Leg One game of a match.

Load Score of 180.

Low Ton Score of 100 to 149 in an 01 game.

Lower Class Score of twenty-nine.

Mad House D-Hitting a double 1 to win a 01 game.

Mark A scoring dart in a cricket game.

Match Series of games, usually best two-out-of-three.

Money Dart Winning dart in a cash prize tournament.

Mugs Away Announcement that losers of the latest game go first in the next game.

Nice Spread Sarcastic reference to widely scattered shots.

Nines The 19s in cricket.

Oche Throw line, pronounced "ockey," like the cockney version of "hockey."

On Your Knees Comment to a player needing a double 3, because it's on the bottom of the board.

Oxo Score of zero in a round.

Perfect Game One that's won with the minimum number of darts; six darts in 301, eight in cricket, nine in 501.

Phat Closing the bull's-eye in cricket through hitting a double and single after missing with the first dart.

Piddle Same as "diddle for the middle."

Pie A scoring area of the dartboard.

Plastic Darts Soft-tip darts used to play electronic darts.

Point Monger (Monger) Someone scoring excessive points in cricket.

Poor Man's Triple (PMT) Hitting three singles of the same number.

Popcorn Three darts so closely grouped together that one or more flights are knocked off.

Rail Wire on a steel-tip board; plastic separators on an electronic board.

Right There Exclamation when a player just misses number being aimed for.

Robin Hood Feat of sticking one dart into the back of another that's on the board.

Rock Short dart; speed dart.

Rotation A game.

Round A single turn where a player shoots three darts.

Round of Nine (RO9) A round in which a player hits three triples.

Round the Clock Game where object is to hit each number on the board, in numerical sequence.

Route 66 Score of sixty-six points on a throw.

Rubber Last game in a three-game match.

Sergeant Feat of scoring three successive numbers in a round to win a free turn in a game of Round the Clock.

Sevens The 17s in cricket.

Shaft The part of the dart behind the barrel that holds the flight.

Shanghai Hitting a single, double, and triple of the same number.

Shelly Shot Hitting a triple 19 with the first dart in cricket.

Sheriff Darter with the lead in a game.

Shit House Score of 111 points with three darts.

Shut Out Winning a 301 game before opponent has doubled in (Whitewash, Skunk).

Single Bull The outer ring of the bull's-eye, worth twenty-five points.

Single-In (SI) An 01 game; a player doesn't have to double in.

Single-Out (SO) A 01 game, a player doesn't have to double out.

Six Dart Out Perfect 301 double-in, double-out game, accomplished by winning with minimum of six darts.

Sixes The 16s in cricket.

Slice Wedge representing a particular number; for example, the 20 wedge.

Slip Shot Score of twenty-eight.

Slop Scoring with a dart—despite missing its intended target.

Small Pie Small area representing a single number, between bull and triple ring.

Soft Tip Descriptive of the electronic version of darts, which uses plastic rather than steel-tip darts.

Spider, Spider Web Wire assembly on the dartboard marking off target areas.

Splash Throwing two darts at the board simultaneously as an alternative to diddling for the middle. Player with the higher score goes first.

Split the 11 Throwing a dart between the two digits of the 11 on the number ring.

Steady A score of 60.

Straight-Off A 01 game where it's not necessary to double out.

Straight-On A 01 game where it's not necessary to double in.

Sunset Strip Score of seventy-seven points in a throw.

301 Game where player starts with 301 points and tries to get down to zero.

Three in a Bed (Chubby Darts) Three darts located in the same scoring area. For example—three triple 15s.

Tin Hat No score.

Toe Line The hockey.

Ton Score of 100 points in a round; often combined with other numbers like Ton-80.

Ton-Eighty Three triple 20s (worth 180 points).

Tops A double 20.

Triple Ring Inner ring of the dartboard, worth triple the designated number.

Trombones Score of seventy-six points in a round.

Two and Six Score of twenty-six points in a round; also known as bed and breakfast.

Two Fat Ladies eighty-eight points in a round.

Umbrellas Seventy-seven points in a round.

Upstairs Upper area of the board.

Wet Feet Player who commits a foot fault is said to have wet feet.

White Horse Scoring three triples in one round of cricket.

White Moment Time when a player clearly has the psychological edge in a game.

Widdy Wooden steel-tip darts with a feather flight used in most American-style darts; name derives from the Widdy Manufacturing Company.

Winger Dart One that scores after ricocheting off a dart that's already in the board.

Wire To bounce a dart off a wire.

Wood Area around the target, outside the scoring area.

Woody Dart landing in the wood.

01 Game Generally, games of 301 and 501; there are also similar games like 101, 401, 601, and 1001.

Diving

Approach The method of getting into position to dive.

Armstand Dive A dive accomplished from a starting handstand position, back to the water, at the platform's end.

Back Dive Takeoff from end of board with back toward water.

Back Flip A backward somersaulting dive.

Back Header A backward dive with the head hitting the water first.

Backward Dive A dive in which water entry is feet first facing the board, or headfirst facing away from the board; the starting position is facing the board (Back Dive).

Balk An illegal movement by the diver.

Belly Whopper A dive in which the front of the body (especially the stomach region) makes flat contact with the water.

Cannonball The act of jumping feet first off the board and into the water with knees tucked under the chin and arms wrapped around the legs.

Compulsory Mandated by the rules to be performed; a diver may choose from a list of compulsory dives.

Degree of Difficulty A method of determining a diver's final competitive score by assigning a number that indicates the relative difficulty of each of his preliminary and optional dives. The preliminary and optional dives are multiplied by this number.

Diving Well A deep area under a diving platform that has enough depth so that the diver cannot hit bottom as he or she dives.

Entry The moment of entering the water as a dive is completed.

Flying Describes dive where diver assumes a straight position from takeoff, or after one somersault in a 115C, before executing the remainder of the dive.

Forward Dive A dive in which water entry is headfirst facing the board or feet first facing away from the board; the starting position faces away from the board (Front Dive).

Free Position Combination of straight, pike, or tuck positions.

Front Header A forward dive headfirst into the water.

High Board A diving board positioned three meters (9.8 feet) above the water.

Hurdle Final segment of a diver's approach to takeoff.

Hyperbaric Describes increased pressure over the pressure in one atmosphere.

Inward Dive A dive in which water entry is headfirst away from the board or feet first facing the board; the starting position is toward the board, and the diver, by jumping away from the board, rotates his body forward to the board on his way to water entry.

Jackknife A dive with the body positioned in a jackknife pose, hands touching or close to the ankles, head entering the water first.

Judge Diving official scoring each dive on a scale of 0 (lowest) to 10 (highest).

Layout A diving position with legs together and held straight, arms positioned up and to the rear, and back arched.

Optional A move left to the judgment of the diver.

Pike A V-like diving position with arms held either straight out to the sides or in contact with the feet or the backs of the knees.

Pike Position Dive position where body is bent at the hips, legs straight at the knees, and toes pointed, feet held together.

Platform Stationary, nonbending diving platform, at least 20 feet long and 6 1/2 feet wide. The platform height used in competition is 10 meters (approximately 33 feet).

Points Ratings earned for approach, takeoff, maneuvers in the air, and entry.

Referee Manages competition insuring all regulations are observed.

Reverse Dive In this maneuver, the diver faces the water, jumps up, and rotates in reverse so that water entry is either feet first away from the board or headfirst facing the board (Gainer).

Somersault Movement where the diver rotates his body on an imaginary horizontal axis through the hips. This dive can be performed in a variety of combinations.

Springboard Adjustable diving board regulating "springiness."

Straight Position When body is straight without bending at knees or hips, feet together and toes pointed. Previously called the "layout" position.

Swan Dive A dive with legs extended to the rear, back arched, and arms stretched out like a swan; water entry is headfirst.

Takeoff The method of leaving the diving board.

Tower A platform for diving.

Tuck A diving position with knees bent, thighs pressed against the chest, and hands wrapped about the shins.

Twist Dive A dive in which at some point between the takeoff and entry the diver executes a twisting maneuver.

Unattached Diver competing in a U.S. Diving–sponsored event but does not represent a U.S. Diving club.

USAS (United States Aquatic Sports, Inc.) An organization representing all aquatic sports, including diving, swimming, water polo, and synchronized swimming.

Equitation (Horseback Riding)

Aids Methods of controlling and communicating with a horse: natural aids are the rider's body and voice and use of weight; artificial aids consist of all mechanical devices.

Balanced Seat A riding position distinguished by a body leaning forward, well-bent knees, legs touching the horse; most often used for hunting or jumping events (Forward Seat, Jumping Seat, Military Seat).

Ballast The use of the rider's weight to give balance to the horse.

Base of Support That portion of the rider's body that makes contact with the horse or saddle; one of the four basic elements of the seat.

Between the Rider's Hands and Legs Control of a horse is accomplished by the rider's hands directing the forward part of the horse and the rider's legs directing that part of the horse behind the saddle.

Bit The portion of the bridle that fits into the mouth of the horse.

Bridle Headgear on the horse consisting of a headstall, a bit, and reins by which a horse is guided by the rider.

Cadence The beat or rhythm of a horse's stride.

Canter A slow, three-beat gallop, at about ten–twelve miles per hour.

Change of Leg The changing of one lead foot for the other.

Collection The moving of a horse into erect posture with hind legs and hocks positioned under it to make for a rearward center of gravity.

Confirmed The act of a horse having been placed on a desired gait and speed and maintaining them without additional effort by the rider.

Dressage An event that demonstrates a horse's ability and training and the cooperation of the horse and rider as they perform a number of difficult maneuvers.

Equilibrium One of the four basic elements of the balanced seat; a means through which a rider helps the horse's balance by positioning his or her weight.

Equitation The act of riding on horseback; horsemanship.

Extension To move the horse into a full stride.

Flank Movements Quarter-turns made by a horse followed by riding straight forward in the new direction.

Fly Sheet A light blanket that fits over a horse's back to prevent flies from biting.

Free Schooling To work or train a horse without a rider.

Gait Sequential moves by a horse whose hooves move forward, hitting the ground in a steady pace.

Gallop A quick, three-beat gait in a leaping motion.

Girth A strap that is positioned under a horse's belly to hold the saddle in place.

Hackamore A bridle that exerts pressure on a horse's nose to aid in control.

Halter A strap or rope and headstall used to lead or tie up a horse.

Headstall The portion of the bridle that fits over the head.

Horn A knoblike projection from a saddle.

Jump Racing Competition over hurdles or other obstacles.

Jump Rider A steeplechase event rider.

Lead The foot used by a horse to begin a gait.

Leg The rider's leg, broken down into the categories of active or commanding, assisting, and holding (the placement of the leg against the horse to hamper its moving in that direction).

Lower Leg One of the basic elements of the balanced seat: that portion of the rider's leg not in contact with the horse. If needed, however, it can be brought into one of the three leg positions.

Near Side The left side of a horse.

Off Side The right side of a horse.

On the Aids The responding of a horse to natural or artificial aids.

Pace A two-beat gait, a bit quicker than a trot, in which the legs on the same side of the body move at the same time.

Rack A fast, smooth gait in which each foot is lifted and put down separately (Single Foot).

Rate The act of making a horse decrease or increase its gait and remain at the new rate.

Rein-Back The act of making a horse move backward.

Reins Narrow, long leather strips held at one end by the rider and attached at the other end to the bit.

Saddle A padded leather seat on a horse. Also, the act of putting a saddle on a horse.

Seat The rider's posture and stance in the saddle. Also, the flat part of the saddle.

Shoes Plates of metal fitted around the outside edges of a horse's hooves.

Steeplechase A horse race conducted on a course with obstacles such as hedges and ditches.

Stride The horse's movement from the time a leg leaves the ground until it returns.

Tack Riding equipment.

Tactile Sensitivity A rider's ability to sense what his or her horse is doing or will do.

Travers A dressage position in which a horse is led near a wall, its body angled approximately thirty degrees from the wall, and its head close to the wall and pointed in the direction its is moving.

Trot A two-beat gait at about nine miles per hour with the horse's front and hind legs at opposite sides of the body simultaneously hitting the ground.

Turn A 360-degree turn by a horse so that it winds up moving in the same direction in which it began.

Upper Body One of the four elements of the balanced seat, involving all parts of the rider's body above hip level including the hands.

Walk A four-beat gait at about four miles per hour, with each foot touching the ground at different intervals.

Fencing

Absence of Blade When fencers' blades are not in contact with each other.

Abstain To refrain from voting when an official is unsure whether a touch or foul has taken place.

Action on the Blade A maneuver that allows a fencer to make contact with the blade of an opponent.

Advance To move toward an opponent by stepping out with the front foot and bringing the other foot close to the front foot.

Advance Lunge An advance followed without pause by a lunge.

Adversary An opponent.

Aids Last three fingers of the sword hand.

A Partie Prise An attacking maneuver employed to disguise a defensive technique that an opponent is expecting to be used.

Assault A contest between two fencers.

Attack Movement(s) Movement(s) designed to score a hit.

Attack on Preparation An attack just before an opponent has launched an attack; an attack while an opponent is preparing an attack.

Attack on the Blade Movement(s) designed to deflect or attempt to deflect the blade of an opponent.

Attention Position taken by fencers just before the command to fence that involves the front foot pointed toward the opponent, a right-angled rear foot, and the sword held out and positioned at a forty-five-degree angle to the ground.

Backward Lunge An attack that ends up with the fencer in lunge position, but that is executed by sliding the rear foot directly backward.

Balestra Forward jump lunge.

Barette An attachment to the lower front of the mask for protection of the throat (Bib).

Barrage A tie, or fence-off, in a qualifying round.

Bayonet Type of electrical connector for weapons.

Beat A sharp blow against the middle or weak part of the opponent's blade, designed to open a line of attack or provoke a reaction.

Beat Parry A parry that forces the opponent's blade out of line by giving it a quick beat.

Benefit of the Doubt A cut or thrust so light that it is of questionable validity.

Bent-Arm Attack An attack executed without initially establishing right of way by taking a position in line.

Bind Attack forcing opponent's blade up, down, or sideways from one line into another as a result of the pressure exerted by the binder's blade (Liement).

Black Card Indicates most serious offenses in a fencing competition usually resulting in offending fencer being expelled from the event or tournament.

Blade That part of the weapon (sword) that extends from the guard to the tip.

Bout The personal combat between two fencers.

Break Ground To retreat.

Broadsword Military sword and fencing weapon popular in the eighteenth and nineteenth centuries, akin to heavy sabre.

Broken Time Change suddenly in the tempo of a fencer's actions to fool opponent into responding at the wrong time.

Button Protective pad on the end of a foil.

Cadence Fencing rhythm.

Cavation A technique used during a thrust that directs the hand motion slightly to the side while angling the point at the target by wrist or finger action.

Ceding Parry Parry against a thrust by yielding to its pressure, allowing the blade to be moved to a new line, and then blocking the opponent's blade from this new line.

Change Beat A beat executed immediately after a change of engagement.

Change of Engagement The act of engaging in a new line, of moving an opponent's blade into a new line.

Change of Time The intentional breaking of the rhythmic pattern of action in an attempt to confuse an opponent.

Class Categories of fencers, including prep, novice, intermediate, and senior.

Closed Stance A line that is blocked as a result of the arm or sword position of an opponent.

Close In To get into a clinch.

Close the Line To carry the hand, at the conclusion of a thrust, far enough to the side to block a direct counterattack.

Closing In Attacking or defending maneuver in which a fencer moves closer to an opponent to create problems for the opponent in executing a thrust.

Composed Attack An attack made with an advance.

Compound Attack An attack consisting of two or more movements.

Compound Parry A parry consisting of two or more movements used in combination.

Compound Return A riposte consisting of one or more feints (Compound Riposte).

Contraction Parry A simple parry and a circular parry combined.

Contretemps A parry riposte created as a result of second intention.

Conversation Back-and-forth play of the blades in a match, composed of phrases and also gaps of no blade action.

Corps-à-Corps Torso contact between the contestants that cannot immediately be broken—results in a halt being called; illegal in foil and sabre (Clinch).

Coulé Attack or feint sliding along the opponent's blade (Graze, Glise, Glissade).

Counterattack The stop thrust and the time thrust—an attacking maneuver that responds directly to the attack of an opponent.

Counter-Disengagement To disengage in the opposite direction, to deceive the opponent.

Counter-Parry A parry that describes a circle, picks up the opponent's blade, and brings it back to the original line of engagement; a parry of a riposte.

Counter-Riposte An offensive action made immediately after parrying the opponent's riposte.

Counter-Time A planned move that uses a feint to draw an opponent into a counterattack, which is parried in anticipation of the scoring riposte.

Coupé Attack or deception passing around the opponent's tip.

Covered A line of engagement is "covered" when the defender's weapon has closed the line to a straight thrust.

Croisé Action where opponent's blade is forced into the high or low line on the same side (Semi-Bind).

Cross Advance or retreat by crossing one leg over the other leg.

Cut A sabre-fencing scoring blow that is accomplished by striking an opponent with the edge of the weapon.

Cutover A form of changing the line of engagement that is accomplished by passing the blade over the point of the opponent's blade (Coupé).

Cutting the Line Parry that does not follow the normal lines of defense but cuts across them.

Deceive To manipulate the blade so that a defender's parry is avoided.

Derobement Deception of the attack.

Development The complete lunge from arm-extension to completion.

Direct Attack or riposte finishing in the same line in which it was formed, no feints out of that line.

Direct Attack An attack that involves one or more feints plus a final cut or thrust.

Direct Cut Ending with a blade-edged cutting move.

Director The official who starts, stops, and supervises, who analyzes movements, and who awards the touches in a bout (President).

Disengage An attack that changes the line of engagement by passing the blade under or over the blade of the opponent.

Disengage Circular blade movement deceiving the opponent's parry, removes blades from engagement, or changes the line of engagement.

Displacement Moving the target to avoid an attack.

Distance The space or distance between contestants at any given time.

Double An attack with two disengagements in the same direction followed up by a lunge.

Doublé Attack or riposte describing a complete circle around the opponent's blade.

Double Touch The act of two contestants making touches at the same instant.

Dry Fencing without electric scoring aids.

Elbow Guard A protective leather cup that is strapped to the elbow of the sword arm.

Electric Epée An electrical device that automatically, via bell or light, records the touches in épée bouts.

En Garde Fencing position; stance that fencers assume when preparing to fence (On Guard).

End Line Either line marking the extreme rear ends of the fencing area.

Engagement A crossing of the blades covering any of the four possible lines.

Envelopment Engagement sweeping opponent's blade through a full circle.

Epée A sword similar to the foil except that the guard is larger and the blade is less flexible and heavier.

Epée Ink A red liquid that is placed on the point d'arret (a little point that catches onto clothing) of the épée to mark the spot of a hit.

False Back edge of a sabre blade.

False Attack A simulated attack.

Feint A blade movement designed to resemble an attack, aimed to draw a reaction or parry.

Fencing Strip The area where a bout takes place.

Fencing Target Those parts of the opponent that may be legitimately contacted with the weapon to score a touch.

Fencing Time Time required to complete a single, simple fencing action.

FIE (Federation Internationale d'Escrime), the world governing body of fencing.

Fingering The act of controlling a weapon's movements through the use of the fingers and thumb without employing wrist, elbow, or shoulder.

Fleche A running attack generally executed from beyond normal lunging distance (Flash).

Flick A cutlike action that lands with the point, often involving some whip of the foible of the blade to "throw" the point around a block or other obstruction.

Florentine Fencing style where a secondary weapon or other instrument is used in the off hand.

Flying Parry (Riposte) Parry with a backward glide and riposte by cutover.

Foible The upper, weak part of the blade.

Foil Fencing weapon containing rectangular cross-section blade and small bell guard; a sword buttoned making it less dangerous for practice.

Forte The strong section of the blade.

French Grip Traditional hilt with slightly curved grip and large pommel.

French Style Utilization of mainly the thumb and forefinger in holding the weapon in attacking.

Froissement Attack displacing opponent's blade by a strong grazing action.

Gain A lunge of more than usual length.

Glide An offensive action against the blade of an opponent in which pressure is applied laterally while the fencer is moving forward (Graze; Coulé).

Grand Salute A ritualistic mock or simulated combat that is done as the opening exercise of a competition.

Guard Metal cup or bow protecting hand from being hit; defensive position assumed when not attacking.

High Lines Lines of attack and defense located above the hand.

High-Low A one-two attack where the disengages are below the high and low lines.

Hilt Handle of a sword, consisting of guard, grip, and pommel.

Homologated Certified for use in FIE competitions.

In Distance Close enough to an opponent to score a hit just by lunging.

In Line A condition where a fencer has his arm extended and the point of his weapon threatening his opponent's target.

In Quartata Attack made with a quarter-turn to the inside, concealing the front but exposing the back.

In Time When a stop-hit arrives a minimum of at least one fencing time before the original attack.

Indirect Attack or riposte that finishes in the opposite line to which it was formed, by means of a disengage or coupé.

Infighting Action so close that there is actual contact between the opponents.

Inside Lines Lines of attack and defense that are to the side leading to the front of the target.

Insistence Through the parry forcing an attack.

Interception Counterattack intercepting and checking an indirect attack or other disengagement.

Invitation Any defending blade movement designed to prompt an opponent into an attack.

Jury The four officials who look out for hits in a dry fencing bout.

Lamé Metallic vest/jacket for detecting valid touches in foil and sabre.

Line Main direction of an attack (high/low, inside/outside), compared often to parry that must be made to deflect the attack; also point in line.

Lines The theoretical area of attack and defense; there are inside, outside, high, and low lines, all of which are related to the hand and weapon positioning.

Low Lines Attacking and defending lines of attack located below the hand.

Lunge The classical method of reaching an opponent on the attack that involves extending the sword arm, stepping forward on the front foot, and a keeping of the rear foot in place.

Mal-Parry One failing to prevent the attack from landing.

Manipulators Thumb and index finger of the sword hand.

Maraging Special steel used for making blades.

March Attack An advanced lunge.

Marker Points Old method of detecting hits using inked points.

Martingale A strap that binds the grip to the wrist/forearm.

Match The aggregate of bouts between two fencing teams.

Measure Distance between the fencers.

Metallic Jacket A highly conductive lame jacket used in electric fencing that covers the torso or target area only.

Middle The middle third of the blade, between foible and forte.

Neuvième Unconventional parry (#9) sometimes described as blade behind the back, pointing down; other times similar to elevated sixte.

Octave Parry #8; blade down and to outside, wrist supinated.

On Deck The act of being in position to begin a bout after the one in progress is finished.

On Guard The basic position of a fencer facing his or her adversary.

Opposition Contact and pressure against the opposing blade to keep an opponent from scoring. Holding the opponent's blade in a nonthreatening line; a time hit; any attack or counter-attack with opposition.

Outside Lines The lines of attack and defense that are on the side of the hand and blade nearest the back and forward flank.

Parry A deflection of an opponent's blade. Parries are numbered one to eight. They are sometimes referred to by their traditional French names: prime (one); seconde (two); tierce (three); quatre (four); quinte (five); sixte (six); septième (seven); octave (eight).

Pass A cut that misses and continues past its target.

Passata-Sotto Lunge performed by dropping one hand to the floor.

Passé Attack passing the target without hitting; also a cross-step (see Cross).

Phrase Interval of continuous action between contestants.

Piste The surface fencers compete on (Strip).

Pistol Grip Modern, orthopedic grip, shaped slightly like a small pistol.

Plaqué Point attack that lands flat.

Plastron Partial jacket worn for extra protection; typically a half-jacket worn under the main jacket on the weapon-arm side of the body.

Point Valid touch; tip of sword; an attack made with the point, thrust.

Point in Line Extended arm and blade threatening the opponent.

Pommel Fastener that attaches the grip to the blade.

Preparation Initial phase of an attack, before right-of-way is established.

Presentation Offering one's blade for engagement by the opponent.

Pressure A lateral pressing upon the blade of an opponent, employed as a method of preparation for attack.

Prime Parry #1; blade down and to the inside, wrist pronated.

Principle of Defense Use of forte against foible when parrying.

Priority (in sabre) Superceded rules deciding which fencer will be awarded the touch in the event that they attack simultaneously; also used synonymously with right-of-way.

Prise de Fer Taking the blade; an engagement of the blades forcing opponent's weapon into a new line.

Pronation A grip on the handle of the sword with the back of the hand facing up.

Quatre Parry #4; blade up, to the inside, wrist supinated.

Quinte Parry #5; blade up, to the inside, wrist pronated. Blade in saber is held above the head to protect from cuts.

Rapier Long, double-edged thrusting sword popular in the sixteenth and seventeenth centuries.

Recovery The return to "on guard" position after a lunge.

Red Card Indicates repeated minor rule infractions or a major rule infraction by one of the fencers. A point is awarded to the other fencer.

Redoublement A renewed attack with a blade action.

Referee Director, president; mediator of the fencing bout.

Remise A renewed attack that is generally a replacement of the point in the original line of attack.

Reprise A new attack that takes place after the original attack does not work.

Retreat Step back.

Right-of-Way Rules for awarding the point in case of double touch in foil or sabre.

Riposte Attack made immediately after a parry of the opponent's attack.

Sabre Fencing weapon with flat blade and knuckle guard, used with cutting or thrusting actions.

Salle Fencing hall or club.

Salute A customary acknowledgment with the weapon of one's opponent and referee at the beginning and conclusion of the bout.

Seconde Parry #2; blade down and to the outside, wrist pronated.

Second Intention False action to draw a response from the opponent, opening the opportunity for the intended action that follows, generally a counter-riposte.

Septime Parry #7; blade down and to the inside, wrist supinated.

Simple Attack (or riposte) involving no feints.

Simultaneous In foil and sabre, two attacks—the right-of-way is too close to determine.

Single Stick A type of fencing with basket-hilted wooden sticks.

Sixte Parry #6; blade up, to the outside, wrist supinated.

Small Sword A light dueling sword popular in the eighteenth century, forerunner to the foil.

Stop Cut A stop hit with the edge in sabre, most times to the cuff.

Stop Hit Counterattack that hits: counter-attack whose touch is valid by virtue of its timing.

Stop Thrust A counterattack aimed at breaking up an attack just by thrusting into it.

Straight Thrust Direct and basic attack.

Supination A sword-hand position with fingers facing up.

Three Prong Type of épée body wire/connector; old-fashioned tip that would snag clothing, making it easier to detect hits in the pre-electric era.

Through Steel A cut lands only because flexible blade whips over the parrying blade.

Thrust Attack made by moving sword parallel to its length and landing with the point.

Tierce Parry #3; blade up and to the outside, wrist pronated.

Time Hit Old name for stop hit with opposition.

Time Thrust A closing of the line against an opponent by anticipating his final move and thus scoring (Time Hit).

Trompement Deception of the parry.

Two Prong Kind of body-wire/connector in foil and sabre.

Uncovered A position where a line is unprotected against a straight thrust.

Warning Line A warning marker line parallel to and one meter from each end of the fencing surface (piste) in foil competition and two meters from each end in sabre and épée.

Whip-over In sabre, a touch resulting from the foible of the blade whipping over the opponent's guard or blade when parried.

Whirl A cut executed by swinging the blade through a complete circle.

Whites Fencing clothing.

Width of Guard "On guard" position distance between the feet.

Willful Brutality Intentional roughness.

Yellow Card Indicates minor rule infraction by one of the fencers.

Yielding Parry Intentionally giving way to an opponent with the aim of finally gaining control of the attacking blade.

Field Hockey

Advance Pushing, shoving, advancing the ball in any way, using body, hands, or feet rather than the stick—a foul.

Attacker Player positioned on offense whose chief job is to score (Forward).

Back line One of two lines marking the field's lengthwise boundaries.

Ball Made of solid plastic, its circumference is $8^{13}/_{16}$ to 9 inches and weight between $5\frac{1}{2}$ and $5\frac{3}{4}$ ounces.

Blade Flat side of the stick's head, used to hit ball.

Bully Method of starting or restarting play; referee places the ball on the ground between two opposing players who tap flat sides of their sticks together three times before going for the ball.

Center Line Line dividing field into two halves.

Center Mark Middle of pitch where ball is placed for a bully.

Center Pass Pass from center of field, used to start a half or following a goal.

Cover Positioning oneself between opposing player and the ball.

D Goal circle, shaped like a D.

Dangerous Play Action capable of causing injury.

Defender Player positioned in defensive end of field (Fullback).

Dribble Controlling ball with short strokes of stick while on the move.

Field Hockey Hockey played on a field; two opposing teams use curved sticks to drive a ball into the opponents' net. Field hockey is the oldest known stick-and-ball game (perhaps apart from Irish hurling, which dates back to prehistoric times). Evidence of games played with a ball and stick go back over four thousand years to the Nile Valley in Egypt. The modern game of field hockey evolved in England during the nineteenth century and led to the creation of the sport's international federation, the Fédération Internationale de Hockey (FIH) in 1924. Field hockey has two thirty-five-minute halves in major contests.

Flick Raising the ball from the ground into the air with a quick movement of the stick. Ball must not rise more than eighteen inches above the playing surface.

Free Hit Play awarded for any infraction outside goal circle. All opposing players must stand at least five yards away from the place it takes place—at or near the spot of the infraction.

Goal Field hockey goal is a net seven feet high, twelve feet wide, and four feet deep.

Goal Circle D-shaped area composed of two quarter-circles, measured sixteen yards out from each goalpost and joined by a short straight line (Shooting Circle, Striking Circle).

Goalkeeper Player that protects the goal and is allowed to use the kickers, leg guards or the stick to propel the ball. Hands may also be used to stop the ball, but not to grasp it.

Green Card One issued by referee to warn for a minor rules violation.

Halfback One who plays both offense and defense, patrolling the field's middle area (Midfielder).

High Stick Stick raised above shoulder level—a violation.

Hit Swinging movement of stick toward the ball.

Inner Forward who plays in or near the center of field (Wing).

Interchange Temporary switch of positions by teammates.

Jab Poking continually at the ball trying to make attacking player.

Kicker Protective equipment that covers the front and sides of the goalkeeper's shoes, allowing the kicking of the ball.

Link Midfielder.

Long Corner Attacking team is given possession if defending player unintentionally kicks the ball over the back line. Ball is put in play on the back line about five meters from corner flag.

Mark Guarding an opponent closely.

Misconduct Intentional violations, time-wasting, rough or dangerous play, or any bad behavior. Green, yellow, or red cards can be issued for misconduct.

Obstruction Sticks or bodies may not be used to prevent other players from hitting the ball. It's also obstruction if the goalkeeper lies on the ball.

Overtime Tie game results in sudden-death, ten-minute overtime period. Victory goes to first team scoring a goal.

Pass Back Center pass.

Penalty Corner Attacking team is awarded a penalty corner when a defending player deliberately hits the ball over the back line. Ball is placed on the goal line at least ten yards from the goal. An offensive player is allowed a free hit from that point.

Penalty Stroke Fouling of an opponent by a defending player in the goal circle results in a penalty stroke awarded. Ball is placed seven yards from goal. Only goalkeeper is allowed to defend.

Pitch The field hockey playing area, one hundred yards long by sixty yards wide, divided by a center line and two twenty-five-yard lines, one in each half of the field.

Push Moving the ball with a short, pushing movement of the stick, with both the ball and the head of the stick contacting the ground.

Push Back Center pass.

Push In Pass which puts the ball back into play after it has gone out of bounds.

Raised Ball Lifting the ball more than eighteen inches above the ground with a hit is an offense, known as a raised ball, if it is dangerous or likely to lead to dangerous play.

Red Card A player guilty of an intentional foul gets this card from the referee resulting in ejection from the game and suspension of the player for the team's next game.

Reverse Stick Turning stick and making blade point right, allowing a hit or push in that direction.

Scoop Player raises a stationary or slowly moving ball off the ground with a shovel-like movement of the stick.

Sixteen-Yard Hit Offense commits foul in the goal circle giving opponent free hit at the top of the circle, sixteen yards from the end line.

Stick Composed of wood or fiberglass with a curved head flat on one side, rounded on the other.

Stick Interference Using stick to hit an opponent's stick.

Tackle Attempting to take the ball away from the opponent, using the stick.

Third-Party Obstruction Positioning oneself between ball and opponent, allowing a teammate unobstructed access to the ball.

Time-Wasting Stalling to keep play from continuing or resuming within a reasonable period of time.

Trapping Stepping on the ball or covering it with the body—a violation.

Yellow Card An intentional foul that penalizes a player by suspension from the game for five minutes or more. Penalty is signaled with a yellow card presented by the referee.

Football

"Ace" Clarence McKay Parker was born in 1917 in Portsmouth, Virginia. At Duke, Parker became a great punter. But he went into baseball not football when he graduated. With the Philadelphia Athletics's he became the first man in American League history to hit a home-run as a pinch hitter in his first at bat. After ninety-five games as a major league baseball player, Parker returned to football in 1937 and became a triple-threat, two-way star. A member of the college and professional football halls of fame, Parker was an "ace" athlete all the way.

"Alabama Antelope" Don Hutson came from the Rose Bowl–winning University of Alabama football team to the Green Bay Packers of the National Football League (NFL) in 1935. He stayed for eleven seasons; nine times he was named All-Pro. Hutson's nickname came from his collegiate alma mater and the blazing speed and deceptive moves he was able to unleash as a pro. Named an all-time All-Pro in 1970, Hutson caught nearly five hundred passes in his pro career, and almost one out of five of those receptions resulted in a touchdown.

All-American Walter Camp's name is always identified with the idea of selecting college football All-Americans. However, credit for the original idea belongs to Caspar W. Whitney, a part-owner of *This Week's Sport* magazine, who approached Camp with the concept. Both Camp and Whitney chose the All-Americans for 1889 and 1890. *This Week's Sport* then ceased publication. Whitney joined *Harper's Weekly* and from 1891 to 1896 picked All-American teams for that publication. Camp picked the 1897 team for *Harper's Weekly.* In 1898 Camp began a long career with *Collier's,* selecting All-American teams until his death in 1925. While with *Collier's,* Camp listed the All-Americans from 1889 on and thus created the impression that he was the one responsible for the "All-American" concept, while Whitney actually deserves the credit.

American Football League (AFL) Existed from 1960 to 1969. There were three earlier, unrelated, and unsuccessful football leagues with the name American Football League (1926, 1936–1937, and 1940–1941). The AFL was founded by Lamar Hunt. Of all the leagues that have attempted to challenge the dominance of the NFL, it was the only one to be truly successful. In 1970, the NFL merged with the American Football League to form a single league.

"America's Team" The NFL granted the rights to its thirteenth franchise to Dallas and owners Clint Murchison, Jr., and Bedford Wynne on January 28, 1960. The team initially was going to be called the "Rangers," but "Cowboys" became the name of choice. Ultimately, the franchise's winning ways, attractive performers, and wide fan base earned the nickname.

Amos Alonzo Stagg Memorial Stadium Site of University of the Pacific women's soccer games, once known as Pacific Memorial Stadium, the 30,000-seat structure was renamed in 1988 for the man who was a legendary football coach late in his career at Pacific.

Area Blocking Blocking any opponent in a specific area instead of blocking a particular player (Zone Blocking).

Arizona Cardinals The Cardinals originally played in Chicago as a charter franchise of the American Professional Football Association (APFA). Owner-manager Chris O'Brien deemed the used, faded maroon jerseys he acquired from the University of Chicago "cardinal red." When the American Professional Football Association began in 1920—out of which the NFL grew—the team from Chicago was known as the "Cardinals." The team moved to St. Louis in 1960 and Phoenix in 1988.

Arrowhead Stadium The Kansas City Chiefs and St. Louis Cardinals played the inaugural game at Arrowhead Stadium on August 12, 1972. The name of the stadium is connected to the nickname of the Kansas City franchise.

"Assassin" Legendary Oakland Raiders safety Jack Tatum roamed the secondary from 1971 through 1979, a solid hitter and an intimidating force.

Astroturf Not all the artificial carpets that have taken root in ballparks and stadiums in the United States and around the world are produced by the Monsanto Chemical Company. Astroturf was the first, however, having been installed when the Houston Astrodome opened in 1965, and that's why the term has almost become a generic one for artificial sod. There is also Tartan Turf (made by Minnesota Mining and Manufacturing) and Poly-Turf (a product of American Bilt-Rite). Resistant to all types of weather, more efficient to keep up than grass, and better for traction than most other surfaces, synthetic "grass" has continued to "grow" throughout the world of sports, despite complaints that it results in more injuries for players.

Atlanta Falcons A contest in 1965 led to the nickname, making the proud, dignified, courageous bird the team symbol. There were 1,300 entries suggesting 558 different names. Although several entries in a fan contest suggested Falcons, a teacher was declared the winner because of her reason: "The falcon is proud and dignified with great courage and fight."

Audible Verbally changing a play at the line of scrimmage from the play originally called in the team huddle (Automatic).

"Baby-Faced Assassin" A member of the College Football Hall of Fame, an All-American in 1932 and 1933, guard Bill Corbus had a boyish appearance that belied his competitive furies as blocker and tackler for Stanford.

Back An offensive player who lines up most often 1 yard or more behind the line of scrimmage and whose duties include running with the ball, catching passes, and blocking (Offensive Back).

Backfield The four offensive backs: quarterback, two halfbacks, fullback. The names given to the various backfield members can change depending on the team formation.

Backfield Line A vertical plane one yard behind and parallel to the line of scrimmage that all backfield members except the quarterback must line up behind.

Back Judge An official positioned in the defensive backfield on the same side of the field as the line judge; he mainly checks for infractions on deep plays and makes out-of-bounds and field-goal rulings.

Backpedal A player's backing-up or running-backward movements to receive a kicked football.

"Bad Moon" Andre Rison—Indianapolis, Atlanta, Cleveland, Jacksonville, Green Bay. At every stop along Rison's journey through the NFL, he carried unwanted baggage and quickly wore out his welcome. Off-the-field incidents overshadowed NFL catches. Hence, the negative nickname.

Balanced Line An offensive line positioned with an equal number of players lined up on either side of the center.

Ballcarrier The player who runs with the ball.

Ball Control Maintaining possession of the football for long periods of time without allowing the opposition to get its chance on offense.

Ball Is Spotted The placement of the football on the ground, from which "spot" play will resume.

Baltimore Ravens After a twelve-year void following the Colts' move to Indianapolis, Baltimore again acquired an NFL team in 1996 when the Cleveland Browns relocated. Owner Art Modell allowed the Browns' name, colors, and history to remain in Cleveland. Baltimore then set up focus groups and fan polls to help secure a new nickname. "Ravens" won out over "Americans" and "Marauders." The name refers to Edgar Allan Poe's poem "The Raven." Poe lived and died in Baltimore.

"Bear" Paul William Bryant was born on September 11, 1913, in Moro Bottom, Arkansas, the youngest of eleven children. He earned the nickname "Bear" by actually wrestling a bear in a theater for a dollar a minute. He accomplished bigger things as the legendary coach at the University of Alabama and other stops where he posted a collective record of 323-85-17. He is enshrined in the College Football Hall of Fame.

Beat When a player gets past an opponent trying to block or tackle him.

"Big D" The city of Dallas, Texas, and the National Football League team that represents the city, the Cowboys, do things in a big way. Computer-dominated, adorned with colorful star players, bedecked with some weird fans and lovely and shapely females who function as cheerleaders, the Cowboys of the NFL tower over most teams in prestige and performance—earning them their nickname.

"Big Daddy" Lipscomb "I just wrap my arms around the whole backfield and peel 'em one by one until I get to the ball carrier. Him I keep." He played in L.A. from 1953 to 1955. From 1956 to 1960 he played for the Baltimore Colts and finished his career with the Pittsburgh Steelers, playing from 1961 to 1962. The 6' 6", 288-pound tackle was more than worthy of his nickname.

"Big Jelly" As a senior at Florida State, Nigel Dixon stood 6' 10" and weighed 340 pounds. He began his Seminole career at a robust 420 pounds but ended up dropping his waist size from 54 to 44 inches due to a diet of chicken, turkey, rice, and vegetables.

"Black Cyclone" Charles Follis was the first African-American to ink a professional football contract when he signed on with the Shelby (Ohio) Athletic Club, founded in 1904. One of his teammates was Branch Rickey. Follis later became a catcher for the Negro League Star-Light Champs (Cleveland) and Cuban Giants (New York). His name came from his race and his athletic verve.

Blackout When a regional network TV affiliate is banned from showing a non–sold out local game.

Blind Side The area a player (especially a quarterback) cannot see clearly; thus, if he is looking left, he may get hit on his right.

Blitz A furious charge by defensive players against a quarterback—most often a gambling maneuver performed when the defense anticipates a passing play (Red Dog).

Block A maneuver in which offensive players legally stop, interfere with, or off-balance the movements of defensive players by using the shoulders or body. Hands may not be used.

Blocker The player preceding a ball carrier who blocks to prevent the defense from tackling his teammate; blockers use their arms and bodies but may not hold an opponent.

Blown Assignment A mistake made by players in executing an assignment.

Bomb An especially long and generally spectacular forward pass.

Bootleg A situation in which a quarterback takes the ball on a handoff, hides the ball at his side, and sprints to that area of the field generally unprotected by blockers.

Bowl Game College football game played in late December or early January, after the regular season, between two successful teams.

"Broadway Joe" In 1964 the St. Louis Cardinals of the National Football League and the New York Jets of the American Football League, symbolizing the war of the leagues for star players and television attractions, battled over the right to sign Alabama quarterback Joe Namath. The AFL and the Jets won. Namath was signed to a four-year contract at $25,000 a season plus a $200,000 bonus. Scouting jobs were provided for his three brothers and a brother-in-law at $10,000 a year. A green Lincoln Continental plus other luxury features were included in the deal, which totaled approximately $427,000.

What was called the "Namath Effect" was now set. His skills on the playing field virtually assured the merger of the AFL and the NFL, and he paced the Jets and the AFL in 1969 to a Super Bowl III victory over the Baltimore Colts, the National Football League representative.

Off the field Namath was showcased with glamorous starlet types, with the Manhattan skyline as his backdrop and the saloons and penthouses of New York City as his resting places. An affable, charming, outgoing man, Namath attracted the ardor of women and the envy of men. He was well publicized, and his nickname was a well-earned appellation for him and for the mystique of the Big Apple.

"Bronco" Nagurski He came to the Chicago Bears in 1930 out of the University of Michigan, where he had been an All-American at both fullback and tackle. He went on to become one of the storied power runners in National Football League history. In the years 1933–1937, plus 1943, Bronislaw Nagurski led the league in yards rushing. His nickname came from his habit of running with his head down, like a wild bucking bronco.

Bronco Nagurski Trophy It has been awarded annually since 1993 to the best all-around defensive college football player.

"Bruiser" Hall of Famer Frank Kinard played for the Brooklyn Dodgers/Tigers (1938–1944) and the New York Yankees, 1946–1947 (AAFC). He was a skilled but "lightweight" tackle with a bruising style of play.

Buffalo Bills Buffalo's team in the All-America Football Conference (AAFC) in 1946 was the Bisons. In 1947, a contest was held to rename the team, which was owned by James Breuil of the Frontier Oil Company. The winning entry suggested Bills, reflecting on the famous western frontiersman, Buffalo Bill Cody. When Buffalo joined the new American Football League in 1960, the name of the city's earlier pro football entry was adopted. The franchise moved to Orchard Park, New York, in 1973 and kept the name.

"Bulldog" Clyde Turner was a poor unknown farm boy from western Texas yearning to get a football scholarship via tryout. He told coaches his name was "Bulldog," thinking that would make a good impression.

Bullet A pass that is thrown exceptionally hard and fast.

"Bullet" Bob The Dallas Cowboys' Bob Hayes helped change the game of NFL football with his world-class speed.

Bump and Run Defensive technique used by the cornerback who hits or bumps the receiver within five yards (one yard in college) of the line of scrimmage to slow him down and then follow, him to prevent him from catching a pass.

Burn To badly beat a defender by scoring or getting away from him.

"The Bus" Pittsburgh Steeler running back Jerome Bettis, big and powerful, decorated Black and Gold, just like a school bus.

"Butch Cassidy and the Sundance Kid" The Dolphins of Miami went through an undefeated and untied 1972 NFL season, capping their winning ways with a Super Bowl triumph. The following year Miami lost only two games and recorded another Super Bowl triumph. Running backs Larry Csonka and Jim Kiick plowed out the yardage for the mighty Miami team and functioned as a potent team in their own right. Csonka, for example, notched a record 145 yards rushing in Super Bowl VIII. Their nickname came from the popular movie of the time about a pair of western outlaws who were daringly efficient.

Buttonhook An offensive maneuver in which a receiver runs downfield quickly and then turns sharply in to face the passer.

Cadence The quarterback's signal-calling rhythm.

Call Instructs players to engage in a preplanned play.

Captains' Meeting A handshaking ceremony just before the start of the game during which the officials introduce the opposing team captains to each other.

"Cardiac" Cardinals The St. Louis Cardinals of 1975 and 1976 were an explosive, exciting team. They had Terry Metcalf, Mel Gray, Jim Hart, and others capable of making the big play. Game after game, in the waning minutes—and sometimes seconds—of play, a long pass or a breakaway run would power the team to victory. They might be losing by a touchdown or more, but with their offensive tricks and skills they were never out of a game until the final gun sounded. The frequency and the drama of their comebacks caused heart palpitations among their rooters and earned the team its well-deserved nickname.

Carolina Panthers The nickname for the 1995 expansion team was picked by team president Mark Richardson, the son of owner Jerry Richardson, who felt that there should be some "synergy" between the name and the team colors and also suggested the team colors of black, blue, and silver. That name was held just once before by an NFL team—the Detroit Panthers, 1925–1926.

Carpets In 1944 the National Football League witnessed the merger of the Pittsburgh Steelers and the Chicago Cardinals. The nickname for the merged team came from part of the name of each of the teams and was spelled and spoken as "carpet." The team's record underscored its name, for every club in the league walked over it.

Carry The act of running with the ball.

"Cash and Carry" Charles C. Pyle was one of the legendary promoters in sports. Dance marathons, six-day bike races, tennis exhibitions, and the contracting of Red Grange to play at $3,000 a game for the Chicago Bears were among his accomplishments. Pyle agreed with P. T. Barnum that "there's a sucker born every minute." Pyle ran his business affairs with money on an up-front basis, and that's how his nickname came about.

The Catch More than sixty thousand fans jammed San Francisco's Candlestick Park for the National Football Conference championship matchup between the storied and veteran Dallas Cowboys and the potential-filled 49ers on January 10, 1982. The season before, the 49ers were 6-10. Now with Joe Montana in his first year as the starting quarterback, they had a glitzy (13-3) best record in the NFL.

The game was a seesaw affair like two boxers going at each other through the opening rounds of a fight. In the fourth quarter Dallas clung to a 27-21 lead. With 4:54 left in the game, San Francisco moved down the field in a time-consuming, methodical, textbook drive. With 58 seconds left, the 49ers were on the Cowboys' 6-yard line—third down, three yards for a first. The ball was snapped to Montana, who rolled right trying to avoid a furious Dallas rush. A play had been drawn up to get the ball to Freddie Solomon but he was smothered. Losing his balance, going backward, Montana hurled the ball to Dwight Clark at the back of the end zone. The toss to the 6-foot-4 Clark was thrown very high. Defender Everson Walls gave up on the play, saying later that he thought Clark had no chance to make the catch since the ball was thrown so high. But a leaping Clark made the catch, grabbing the ball with his fingertips and coming down just barely in bounds for the TD.

Pandemonium prevailed at Candlestick. San Francisco held on for a 28-27 win, giving them their first Super Bowl berth. What Dwight Clark accomplished has gone down in football lore as "The Catch." There are those who argue that Joe Montana was trying to get rid of the ball and throw it out of the end zone and that Clark happened to get in the way.

"That's not true," Clark explained. "That was a play that we practiced over and over again." Two weeks after "The Catch," the 49ers trimmed Cincinnati, 26-21, in Super Bowl XVI in Pontiac, Michigan. That triumph was the first of a quartet of Super Bowl wins for Joe Montana and the 49ers in a span of nine years.

In his third season as head coach and general manager, Bill Walsh was named to all seven NFL Coach of the Year honors, while six 49ers were named to the Pro Bowl—WR wide receiver Dwight Clark, G Randy Cross, QB Joe Montana, DE Fred Dean, CB Ronnie Lott, and S Dwight Hicks. "The Catch" was the trigger that enabled San Francisco to become one of the dominant football franchises for a couple of decades.

Center An offensive lineman positioned in the middle of the line who snaps the ball to the quarterback.

Chain A ten-yard length of chain that measures the distance the football has to be moved forward for a series of downs. Both ends of the chain are fastened to a rod for easy movement.

Chain-Crew Officials' aides who move the chain and indicate the downs.

Check-off The act of calling an audible at the line of scrimmage to alter a play.

Chicago Bears The franchise began in Decatur, Illinois, in 1920 as the Decatur Staleys, named as the company football team of the A. E. Staley Corn Products Company. In Chicago from 1921, the Staleys were renamed the "Bears" in 1922. The Staleys played at Wrigley Field, the home of baseball's Cubs. Coach George Halas said that if the baseball tenants were Cubs, then his more rugged players should be known as the Bears.

Chicken-Fight A situation where an offensive player on a passing play continually blocks a defensive lineman from an upright position.

Chip Shot An easy, short-yardage field-goal attempt.

"Choo-Choo" After a successful high school career, Charlie Justice entered the Navy in 1943. He played for a Bainbridge, Maryland, team made up largely of pro players. It was there that his famous moniker was bestowed upon him.

"We were playing in a game," Justice remembered, "and an officer was sitting in the stands with Paul Minton, the editor of the *Baltimore Sun*. The officer said, 'Look at that guy run. He looks like a runaway train. We ought to call him Choo Choo.' Minton picked it up and used it in the paper."

He entered University of North Carolina at 170 pounds. In his first start, he gained 102 yards rushing in a 14-14 tie with Virginia Tech. By the end of his freshman season, he had amassed 943 yards while passing for 274.

Cincinnati Bengals Paul Brown chose this nickname for Cincinnati's 1968 AFL expansion team because there had been earlier football teams in the city called the Bengals.

Circle A situation where a receiver runs a pass pattern across the line of scrimmage and circles toward the middle of the field for the reception.

Circle Pass One thrown to a receiver running a circle route.

Cleveland Browns The Cleveland All-America Football Conference franchise conducted a fan contest in 1945 to name the team. The most popular submission was "Browns" in recognition of the team's first coach and general manager Paul Brown, who was already a popular figure in Ohio sports. Brown at first vetoed the choice and the team selected from the contest entries the name "Panthers." However, after an area businessman informed the team that he owned the rights to the name Cleveland Panthers, from an earlier failed football team, Brown pulled back objections and agreed to the use of his name.

The franchise moved to Baltimore in 1996 and became the Ravens, then started over as the Browns in 1999. The city of Cleveland retains rights to nickname, colors, and all memorabilia.

Clip Blocking an opponent (except for the ball carrier) by hitting or throwing the body against the back of his legs. This is a legal move within the clipping zone at the start of play.

Clipping A fifteen-yard penalty caused by a clip that takes place during a free-kick down or outside the legal clipping zone during a down from scrimmage.

Clipping Zone A zone where an opponent may be legally clipped, extending approximately four yards on either side of the line of scrimmage and three yards in front and behind the offensive center.

Clothesline (Tackle) To use the outstretched arm to strike and knock down an opponent; a tackle generally made with a forearm that contacts the head or neck area of a ball carrier and stops him in his tracks.

Coffin Corner Any of the four corners on the field formed by the intersection of the goal lines and the sidelines. Punters aim for these areas to hamper a return and to give the other team poor field position.

Coin Toss A procedure in which an official flips a coin at the start of a game or sudden-death overtime period, and the visiting team designee calls "heads" or "tails" to determine whether his team kicks off or returns the football, and which goalpost his team will defend.

Complete To throw a forward pass that is caught by a receiver.

Completion A forward pass caught by a receiver that is credited in the statistics to the quarterback or the player who threw the pass.

Conferences Groups into which teams are divided in professional and college football.

Controlling the Game Clock The use of tactics by an offensive team to either save or use up time on the game clock.

Conversion For a ball kicked over the crossbar after a touchdown, one point is awarded; in nonprofessional play, 2 points are awarded if the ball is run or passed over the goal line.

Cornerback A defender who performs three–ten yards off the line of scrimmage, plays outside the linebackers, defends against the sweep, and covers the wide receivers.

Counter An offensive move designed to confuse the opposition in which the ball carrier runs in the opposite direction of most of his blockers.

Cover (Coverage) To prevent a player from gaining yards; in pass coverage, a defender follows a receiver to prevent him from catching a pass; in kick coverage, members of the kicking team try to prevent a long kick return.

Coverage The way a defender or a defense as a whole guards; defensive responsibilities.

Crackback An illegal blind-side block thrown by a pass receiver on a linebacker or defensive back; the receiver starts downfield and then "cracks" (cuts) back toward the middle of the line.

"Crazy Legs" A star (1949–1957) for the Los Angeles Rams, Elroy Hirsch had a career that saw him go from success to tragedy and back to success again. So poignant and melodramatic was his life that Hollywood even made a movie based on it, *Crazy Legs: All-American.* He was just grooving into a successful career in 1948 when he suffered a fractured skull in a collision on the football field. There was a temporary loss of body coordination, and doctors told him he would never be able to play again. They were wrong. He went on to become pro football's first flanker and helped revolutionize the sport. His nickname came from the wild and almost uncontrolled way his legs splayed behind him when he ran, from his full-out running—head back, arms stretched out to grasp a flying football on his fingertips, legs churning out yardage and leaving defenders behind.

"Crimson Tide" University of Alabama, for its colors.

Crossblock Blocking a defensive lineman from the side—usually takes place when blocking assignments are switched.

Crossbuck The crossing of two running backs who have charged diagonally into the line of scrimmage; the quarterback fakes a handoff to one back and gives the ball to the other.

"Curly" Earl Louis Lambeau was for a time a star player and for thirty-one years the coach of the Green Bay Packers. The curly-headed guy also founded the team.

Cut A quick change of direction by a ball carrier to avoid a defender.

Cutback A ball carrier's sharp, unexpected upfield move or cut toward the middle of the line after a lateral run behind the line of scrimmage.

Dallas Cowboys Since 1960, named for the history of cowboys in the area. "Rangers" was actually the first name suggested. The club went with "Cowboys" since it was thought that "Rangers" might cause confusion—there was a local minor-league baseball team of the same name.

Daylight Open space in a team's defense vulnerable to the offensive team's running.

"Deacon" David Jones defensive end was the anchor of the Los Angeles Rams' "Fearsome Foursome" and never met a quarterback he liked. In fact, Jones is widely credited with inventing the term "quarterback sack."

Dead Ball Play is over and the football is dead; it becomes live as soon as it is snapped for the next play.

Deep Back A member of the receiving team on a kickoff or punt return who is positioned farther back than other players on his team.

Defensive Backs Generally, the two cornerbacks and two safeties, who usually play behind the linebackers and defend against the pass or the run.

Delay A momentary hesitation by a running back or receiver prior to taking the ball or running with it.

Delay of Game A 5-yard penalty given to a team that does not play the ball within a certain period of time and thus stalls the progress of the game.

Denver Broncos Nickname came through a contest in January 1960. "Broncos" was the winner, referring to Denver's Wild West heritage.

Detroit Lions Began in Portsmouth, Ohio, as the Spartans from 1930 to 1933, then moved to Detroit from 1934 to 1974, and to Pontiac, Michigan, in 1975. The Lions name was chosen by George A. Richards, the

Detroit radio executive who purchased the Portsmouth Spartans and moved the team to Detroit in 1934. "The lion is monarch of the jungle," a team spokesperson said, "and we hope to be the monarch of the league." Felines were already prevalent in Detroit. Baseball could claim the Tigers and a Detroit football team called the Panthers had folded after two years in 1927.

"Diesel" John Riggins of the Jets would tirelessly run the football thirty to forty times each game—over not around defenders.

"Disembodied Spirit" Walter Camp selected Frank Hinkey as a four-time All-American end from Yale because he was poetry in motion; he "drifted through the interference like a disembodied spirit," said Camp. Hinkey, who wore his hair long in the style of the day and was often likened to Hamlet, is often considered the greatest football player of his era. At only 157 pounds, when Hinkey tackled, he didn't just trip up a runner at the ankles. When Hinkey tackled, he seemed to explode into the ball carrier.

Division Subgroup within an NFL conference. A grouping of teams in college football, where Division I contains the most competitive teams and Division III the fewest.

"Doak" Doak Walker's real first name is Ewell; his middle name, Doak, is generally thought of as his nickname.

Dog Pound Home field end zone area occupied by rabid Cleveland Browns' fans.

The Doomsday Defense In 1966, the Cowboys increased the nation's awareness of their team. Tom Landry's exciting, multiple-formation offense was the NFL's best show. By 1970, the Cowboys were known for their stifling defense.

Double Coverage A situation where two defenders guard one offensive player.

Double Reverse An offensive play which results in the final ball carrier running in the original direction of play after a reverse with another handoff.

Double Wing A situation where two halfbacks are placed wide on either side of the offensive formation; additionally, there is a split end, and one of the halfbacks plays a slotback position.

Down One of four chances a team on offense has to gain ten yards; the state of a player who has just been tackled; a ball that a player touches to the ground in the end zone to get a touchback.

Down-and-In Offensive pattern in which a receiver sprints straight down the field, fakes, then cuts quickly to the inside.

Down-and-Out Offensive pattern in which a receiver sprints straight down the field, then cuts quickly to the outside.

Down Indicator A tall rod topped by numbered cards that is used at the sidelines to indicate the ball's position at the start of a down and the number of the down (1-4).

Downing Putting the ball on the ground to stop play.

Down the Field Team moves in the direction of the opponent's goal line.

Draft Bert Bell, former NFL commissioner and owner, came up with the idea of the draft, reasoning that it would give some help to weaker teams by providing them with first crack at top college players. Before that 1936 draft there was what was known as open signing—players being allowed to sign with any team.

That first draft was held at the Ritz-Carlton Hotel in Philadelphia, a hotel owned interestingly enough by Bell's family. The format had clubs selecting in reverse order of their finish, with the last pick going to the league champion no matter its record. The National Football League of 1936 had only nine franchises: Boston Redskins, Brooklyn Dodgers, Chicago Bears, Chicago Cardinals, Detroit Lions, Green Bay Packers, New York Giants, Bell's Philadelphia Eagles, and the Pittsburgh Steelers.

That first NFL draft had nine rounds, and eighty-one players were selected in total. Since the Eagles had the worst record in 1935, they got the first pick in the draft—Heisman Trophy (then referred to as the Downtown Athletic Trophy) winner Jay Berwanger, a halfback from the University of Chicago. However, Berwanger claimed he had no interest in playing pro football with the Eagles, so he was traded to the Chicago Bears, but George Halas could not convince Berwanger to play for the Bears.

The number two pick did sign and did play. He was Riley Smith of Alabama who was picked by the Boston Redskins. For the record, the other players picked in the first round of that first NFL draft were: Brooklyn—Dick Crayne, B, Iowa; Chicago Bears—Joe Stydahar, T, West Virginia; Chicago Cardinals—Jim Lawrence, B, TCU; Detroit—Sid Wagner, G, Michigan State; Green Bay—Russ Letlow, G, San Francisco; New York—Art Lewis, T, Ohio U.; Pittsburgh, Bill Shakespeare, B, Notre Dame.

The draft was a tribute to the visionary nature of those football owners who deeply believed in the concept of the greatest good for the greatest number, and what was good for the league. Those owners were men like Tim Mara, Curly Lambeau, George Halas, and Bert Bell, a man who even sold tickets on the street to push his Philadelphia franchise along. By the late 1940s the draft was increased to thirty rounds, but by the mid-1990s it was radically reduced to just seven rounds. From a struggling and limited organization, the NFL has grown and prospered through the decades. The draft is not the least of the influences that made the league thrive. It has been one of the most crucial ideas implemented by the NFL, keeping the league competitive and varied throughout its history.

Draw Play A running play disguised as a passing play; the quarterback at the last moment hands off to a back who usually has faked pass blocking and then runs straight ahead.

Drive A successful series of downs that generally result in a scoring play.

"The Drive" This term will forever be associated with quarterback John Elway who moved the Broncos ninety-eight yards in the closing seconds of the 1986 American Football Conference Championship Game against the Cleveland Browns. It tied the score at 20-20 in regulation time. The Broncos won the game on a field goal in overtime.

Drop Back The action of a quarterback stepping straight back from the line of scrimmage to get passing room.

Drop Kick Type of free kick where a player drops the ball and kicks it right after it hits the ground; rarely used today.

Eat the Ball A phrase describing a quarterback's allowing himself to be tackled instead of throwing an intentionally bad pass.

Eligible Receiver A player permitted by the rules to catch a pass; ordinarily, only the two ends and the backs are eligible.

Encroachment When, just before the ball is snapped, a player illegally places part of his body over the line of scrimmage or makes contact with an opposition player.

End Around A reverse play in which an end comes into his own backfield, gets the ball, and runs to the other end of the offensive line.

End Line Boundary line running width of the field along each end.

Ends Two players on each team who line up at the outer edge of the offensive and defensive lines.

End Zones Goal areas, ten yards deep, located at both ends of the field between the end lines and the goal lines—where touchdowns may be scored.

Extra Point A point after a touchdown is scored, accomplished by kicking the ball between the uprights of the goalposts.

Face Mask Infraction A penalty imposed for grabbing the face mask (protective cage attached to the front of the helmet) of a player.

Fade Back The action of a quarterback moving back a few steps from the line of scrimmage to throw a pass.

Fair Catch A catch of a punted ball in which the receiver raises an arm to signal he will not run after catching the ball.

False Start A violation that occurs when an offensive player, after getting into a set position on the line of scrimmage, moves before the ball is snapped.

"Father of American Football" Walter Camp introduced and pushed through many changes in the game of football that modernized the sport, and that earned him his nickname. Yale team captain from 1876 to 1881, Camp was a key member of the Intercollegiate Football Association rules committee from 1878 to 1925. It was he who convinced that important committee to cut a football playing squad from fifteen to eleven players and to delegate a center to hike the ball to another player who called the signals, thus creating the scrimmage. Camp also had a hand in other changes that laid the foundations of the game of football as we know it today.

"Fearsome Foursome" Lamar Lundy, Deacon Jones, Merlin Olsen, and Roosevelt Grier starred for the devastating line of the Los Angeles Rams in the 1960s.

Field Goal A three-point score made by kicking the ball through the goalposts and over the crossbar.

Field Judge An official positioned in the defensive backfield some yards from the line of scrimmage; this official helps time the game and covers deep pass and punt situations.

Field Position The position of the offensive team's line of scrimmage relative to the goal line.

50-Yard Line The midfield dividing line.

"Fighting Irish" Notre Dame teams, for their spirit and ethnic roots.

Firing Off the Ball A maneuver in which the offensive line surges forward to block the instant the ball is snapped.

First Down The first of a series of four downs; each time a team gets 10 yards or fewer in 4 downs (tries), a new first down is awarded.

Flag A weighted gold or red handkerchief dropped by an official ("flags flying") to indicate a penalty.

Flanker A halfback positioned wide in an offensive formation and generally used as a pass receiver (Flankerback).

Flanks The ends of a formation.

Flat The area directly to the left or right of the line of scrimmage in an offensive formation.

Flat Pass A pass into the flat to a receiver.

Fleaflicker A play in which a quarterback throws a long pass after getting the ball on a double reverse.

Floater A pass that stays up in the air (floats).

Flood To get more pass receivers into a section of the field than there are defenders available to cover these receivers; to overload an area with players.

Fly The running of a straight downfield pattern by a receiver.

"Flying Dutchman" Steve Van Buren was a man of many nicknames in his wonderful eight-year career in the National Football League—"Wham Bam," "The Bayou Boy," "Supersonic Steve," "Blockbuster" But the one he most favored was "The Flying Dutchman!" a tribute to his ethnic roots, speed, and agility.

Formation The pattern (or set) in which offensive or defensive players line up at the line of scrimmage at the start of play.

Forward Pass Pass thrown past the line of scrimmage so that it winds up further downfield than when it started; the passer must also be behind the line of scrimmage when he throws the ball.

Forward Progress Location to which a ball carrier has advanced the ball, even if he was pushed backward after getting there.

Foul Violation of football's rules by a team or player, punishable by a penalty.

"The Freak" Titans defensive end Jevon Kearse has "freaky" ability, with speed, quickness, tenacity, and a tackle-to-tackle wingspan.

Free Ball A ball "up for grabs," a live ball that is not in the possession of any player, and can be recovered by any player on the field.

Free Kick Type of kick taken to start or restart play after a team has scored, with no defenders nearer than ten yards away; includes a kickoff and a kick after a touchdown, a safety, or a field goal.

Free Safety A defender positioned generally about 10 yards deep on the weak side who is not responsible for specific offensive coverage and who can retreat for specific offensive plays.

Front The defensive line.

Front Four The two defensive tackles and two defensive ends.

"Four Horsemen" "Outlined against a blue-gray October sky, the Four Horsemen rode again. In dramatic lore they are known as Famine, Pestilence, Destruction and Death. These are only aliases. Their real names are Stuhldreher, Miller, Crowley and Layden." Those lines from a column written by Grantland Rice in the *New York Herald-Tribune* opened his description of how Notre Dame's football team defeated Army 13-7 in 1924. His romantic reference has become the very personification of the power and mystique of football in America, a reference to the backfield of 1922–1924.

Fullback An offensive back who is generally stationed behind the quarterback.

Fumble Ball carrier loses possession of the ball by dropping it or having it knocked away before a play ends; the first player to regain possession of the loose ball is said to make the recovery, and his team takes over on offense.

"The Future Is Now" When George Allen took over as head coach of the Washington Redskins of the NFL in 1971, he immediately traded for veteran players. Many of his trades involved giving up future draft choices to other teams for the immediate value of football players able to perform for Washington. Some criticized Allen, claiming he was mortgaging the future for the present. His response was that "the future is now" (see Over-The-Hill Gang).

"Gadabout Gladiator" Hall of Famer Bobby Layne played fifteen seasons in the NFL and made his mark with the Detroit Lions in the 1950s. He was a gladiator and a free spirit.

Gainer A play that advances the ball.

"Galloping Ghost" An All-American at the University of Illinois three straight years in the early 1920s, Harold "Red" Grange scored thirty-one touchdowns and gained 3,637 yards. His running skills and evasive techniques were so potent that he was able almost to "disappear" from opponents, and that's how his nickname came to be. Grange was also known as the "Flying Terror" in tribute to what he could do to the opposition. After signing with the Chicago Bears in 1925, Grange became such an attraction that some observers credit him with almost single-handedly establishing professional football.

"Red Grange of Illinois is three or four men rolled into one for football purposes," wrote Damon Runyon. "He is Jack Dempsey, Babe Ruth, Al Jolson, Paavo Nurmi and Man o' War. Put together, they spell Grange." If you dreamed up a football movie in which the star scores four touchdowns covering an incredible 262 yards in just 12 minutes—no one would believe it could happen. But that's what Grange accomplished against one of the best defenses in the country. That 1924 game against Michigan so inspired Grantland Rice to give Grange his nickname and write:

> A streak of fire, a breath of flame
> Eluding all who reach and clutch;
> A gray ghost thrown into the game
> That rival hands may never touch;
> A rubber bounding, blasting soul
> Whose destination is the goal.

Game Ball A football given to a coach or player for contributing to a winning effort.

Game Breaker A player capable of making a big play that changes the course of a game.

Gang Tackle A situation in which a few tacklers gang up on a ball carrier.

Gap An opening between linemen that a defensive or offensive player can "shoot" through.

"Getting a Tie Is like Kissing Your Sister" For Vince Lombardi of the Green Bay Packers, winning wasn't the only thing—it was the enjoyment of winning that also counted. A driven, dedicated coach, Lombardi hated finishing second. There were times during his career when his teams could have played it safe and settled for a tie rather than risk defeat. Lombardi's passion for victory and his apathy toward "no decision" is reflected in the above quote.

Goal Line Line drawn across the width of the field, ten yards inside each end line, which a team must cross with the ball to score a touchdown.

Goal-Line Stand An ordinarily furious battle close to the goal line, during which the defensive team tries to fight off the offensive team's scoring effort.

Goal Posts Two upright posts at each end line, approximately twenty feet high and crossed by a bar ten feet off the ground. College goal posts are twenty-three feet, four inches wide and H-shaped. Professional goal posts are eighteen and a half feet wide and in the shape of a squared Y.

Goal to Go A condition in which the attacking team is within ten yards of the goal line and can score a touchdown on the next play without getting a first down.

"Go for It" When a team facing a fourth down decides to try for a new first down, instead of kicking or punting.

"Grand Old Man of Football" The nickname was especially fitting for Amos Alonzo Stagg, who concluded his grand coaching career at Pacific, from 1933 to 1946, when he truly was the grand old man of football (Mr. Integrity).

Grantland Rice Award Given annually since 1954 to the college football national champion. The award is named for Grantland Rice (1880–1954), often referred to as the dean of American sportswriters.

"Greasy" ("The Coach") If Alfred Earle Neale had never coached the Eagles, he would still deserve a nickname. Born in Parkersburg, West Virginia, on November 5, 1891, he acquired his unusual nickname before he was ten years old. "I used to play with a boy who didn't take many baths. I told him one day he was dirty and he told me I was greasy. It stuck." It is highly appropriate that Neale's nickname be rooted in his outspokenness. That trait was to be his strength and his weakness throughout his career.

Green Bay Packers The National Football League's Wisconsin franchise was organized in 1919 by Curly Lambeau. The grand sum of $500 was contributed to the new Green Bay team for equipment and uniforms by the Indian Packing Company. And with the money came the team's nickname, the "Packers," and permission to use the packing company field for practice sessions.

Grey Cup Albert Henry George Grey, former governor-general of Canada, donated the cup in 1909. It is the championship trophy and the name of the championship game of the Canadian Football League.

Gridiron A name for the football field, so called because of the grid pattern formed by its numerous stripes.

Ground Gainer A player who gains yards by running with the ball.

Guards The two blocking offensive linemen positioned on either side of the center.

"Gus" Charles Emile Dorais, the Notre Dame quarterback and later a famous coach, got his nickname from a moderately famous French artist in the last century named Gustave Doré. "Doré" was pronounced the same as "Dorais"—hence "Gus."

"Hail Mary" Describes Roger Staubach's pass (an all-or-nothing heave) that led the Cowboys to a 17-14 win in the 1975 NFC playoff game. The phrase is also used to refer to all such attempts when the football is thrown a long distance with very little hope of its being caught.

Halfback An offensive backfield player generally positioned to the side of the fullback.

Handoff The giving of the ball to another player.

Hang Time The amount of time a punt stays in the air.

Hash Mark An in-bounds line marker.

Head Linesman Official who supervises the chain crew, checks for offsides, marks out of bounds, and so forth.

Hear Footsteps The loss of concentration by a player going for a pass as a result of anticipating that an opponent may be closing in.

"He Hate Me" The XFL took a fancy to players sporting nicknames on their jerseys. Dozens did, including Las Vegas Outlaws running back Rod Smart. There was never a cogent explanation for the popular nickname.

The Heidi Game The setting was the Oakland Coliseum on November 17, 1968. With 1:05 to play and the Jets leading their hated rival, the Raiders, 32-29, NBC threw the switch on the game on the East Coast to show the movie *Heidi*. Network executives had cut away, feeling New York's lead was safe with so little time remaining. But a 20-yard pass by Daryle Lamonica and a 15-yard penalty put the Raiders into Jets territory. Then, halfback Charlie Smith, isolated on Hudson's replacement, ran by the safety and hauled in a 43-yard touchdown pass with 42 seconds left to put Oakland ahead, 36-32. On the kickoff, Earl Christy of the Jets bobbled the ball. The Raiders' Preston Ridlehuber recovered. Touchdown. Oakland wins 43-32.

It was a shocker for the Jets. But nothing compared to the shockwaves that hit the NBC switchboard. Angry viewers phoned to complain about missing the fantastic ending of the game. NBC finally issued a public apology.

Heisman Trophy An annual award given since 1935 to the best undergraduate collegiate football player in the United States, the trophy gets its name from John W. Heisman. A coach from 1892 to 1928, Heisman was both an innovative figure and a fearsome competitor. Never content with just a winning effort, he once allowed one of his teams to trounce an opponent by scoring 220 points, and this earned him the nickname "Shut the Gates of Mercy."

Since the day in 1935 when Chicago's Jay Berwanger became the first Heisman Memorial Trophy winner, the award has become one of the most prestigious in all of sports. Its significance was underscored by Mike Garrett of the University of Southern California, who won the award in 1965. "If I wanted to be immortal, I figured I could do that by winning the Heisman."

Hike The center's snap of the ball to the quarterback.

Hitch An offensive play where the receiver sprints downfield a bit and then turns quickly to receive a pass.

Hit the Hole The action of a ball carrier who runs into an opening in the defensive line that was created by his blocker(s).

Holding A rules violation in which an offensive player uses his arms and/or hands to impede a defensive player, or a defensive player tackles or holds a player other than the ball carrier.

Hole A gap in the line, vacated by blocker, at which a play is aimed.

"Hollywood Henderson" Dallas Cowboy strong-side linebacker Thomas Henderson's nickname came from his flamboyant manner on the playing field and his outspoken comments off the field. When he scored, he dunked the ball over the crossbar—a technique that irritated the opposition and that he claimed to have originated. During the 1978 National Football League season, he created headlines by stating that the Los Angeles Rams did not have "enough class" to make the Super Bowl. Hollywood defended his actions: "I just had fun. I meant nothing personal about what I say. I didn't like to be dull, or just an old, ugly linebacker."

"Holy Roller" In the second game of the 1978 season, John Madden's last as Oakland's coach, the Raiders trailed the San Diego Chargers 20-14. On fourth down at the Chargers 14-yard line, linebacker Woody Lowe was charging Oakland quarterback Kenny "Snake" Stabler. Rolling away from the pressure, Stabler was hit, and the football came out of his hands. Running back Pete Banaszak knocked (or as some said later, pushed or rolled) the ball toward the end zone. Tight end Dave Casper eventually fell on the ball for a touchdown. The NFL Competition Committee after the season changed the rule about fumbling. From then on, an intentional fumble was considered a forward pass and incomplete. The league also decreed that no other offensive player can advance a fumble in the final two minutes of a game. Those rules somewhat ended "Holy Roller" plays.

Home Field Advantage Benefits a team gets by playing games in the area where it is based in its home stadium. Fan support, familiarity with surroundings, and lack of travel, are all advantages.

Hook An offensive play in which a receiver runs a bit downfield and then cuts back to the scrimmage line.

"Hopalong" Howard Cassady was the Heisman Trophy winner in 1955. At Ohio State, Columbus sportswriters said he hopped all over the field like the performing cowboy and the nickname stuck. Cassady made an impact on the Ohio State gridiron right from his first game as a freshman and went on to a highly successful career in the NFL.

Houston Texans After Houston became the NFL's thirty-second franchise on October 6, 1999, various focus groups considered nickname suggestions—"Apollos," "Bobcats," "Stallions," "Texans," and "Wildcatters." The Texans' name, colors, and logo were made known at a rally in downtown Houston on September 6, 2000.

Huddle A formation between downs in which players gather in a group to get signals straight for the next play; there is a defensive huddle and an offensive huddle.

"The Ice Bowl" The game-time temperature at Lambeau Field on December 31, 1967, was 13 degrees below zero. There were fifty thousand plus in attendance that New Year's Eve to watch their beloved Packers go up against the Dallas Cowboys. The Pack had an early 14-0 lead. But with 4:50 left in the game they were behind, 17-14.

Hall of Fame quarterback-to-be Bart Starr marched Green Bay down the field. With sixteen seconds remaining and the field a sheet of ice and two previous running plays ineffective and no time outs left, a completed pass was the only option. Even an incomplete pass would stop the clock for a field goal attempt to tie the game. Starr conferred with Packers coach Vince Lombardi. Back on the field Starr took the snap from center Ken Bowman and then dove over for the score. "We had run out of ideas," Starr said of the play. The Pack won the "ice bowl" 21-17.

I Formation An offensive formation in which two setbacks line up behind the quarterback and the third back is positioned as a wide receiver. The "power I" is a variation in which a fourth running back is stationed to the side of the other backs.

Illegal Motion A rules violation caused by line-of-scrimmage movement of lined-up offensive players before the ball is snapped.

Illegal Procedure A violation of rules dealing with technical infractions.

"Immaculate Reception" On December 23, 1972, a game that had perhaps the most fantastic finish in the history of professional football was played. It was the Pittsburgh Steelers against the Oakland Raiders in an American Football Conference divisional playoff game.

At the half, the score was 0-0. The game's first score did not come until Roy Gerela put the icing on a fifty-five-yard drive with an eighteen-yard field goal in the third quarter, lifting Pittsburgh up 3-0. In the fourth quarter, Gerela made the score 6-0 when he kicked another field goal from twenty-nine yards out. That field goal seemed to wake up the Raiders, triggering their best drive of the day. Ken Stabler, who had come in to replace Daryle Lamonica at quarterback, read a Steeler blitz, circled left end, and scampered thirty yards for a touchdown. Stabler gave the Raiders a 7-6 advantage with 1:13 to go. Pittsburgh quarterback Terry Bradshaw moved his team forward, completing two passes, but found himself facing a fourth down with ten yards to go from his own 40-yard line and but twenty-two seconds left in the game.

The play was designed with Barry Pearson as Bradshaw's first passing option. Running back John "Frenchy" Fuqua was the second. But "at first all that could go wrong with the play went wrong." Bradshaw recalled. One of things that definitely went wrong was that Bradshaw was flushed from the pocket. Franco Harris, spotting his quarterback in trouble, left his backfield slot and positioned himself as a potential receiver. Bradshaw fired the ball twenty yards downfield to Fuqua. The ball and Raiders' defensive back Jack Tatum hit Fuqua at the same time. "Frenchy" fell to the ground, and the ball flew in the air backward about 15 yards.

Seemingly coming out of nowhere, Franco Harris caught the ball just off his shoe tops and raced down the field on his way to the end zone. It was an incredible 42-yard run that completed a 60-yard scoring play. Bedlam was on parade in Pittsburgh as fans and players stormed out onto the playing field. There were still fifteen seconds left on the clock and a huge argument developed as to the validity of the Harris touchdown. Oakland argued that the pass was illegal because it bounced off Fuqua to Harris. The rule back then stated that a pass could not be tipped from one offensive player to another without a defensive player also touching the ball.

But referee Fred Swearingen's ruling was that Tatum had also touched the ball and that it was a legal catch and a touchdown. The game's final score: Pittsburgh 13, Oakland 7. The game would always be remembered for the Franco Harris catch—"The Immaculate Reception." More important to fans of the Pittsburgh Steelers, that game set in motion the groundwork for the rest of the 1970s, a decade in which the Steelers would win four Super Bowl titles. And Terry Bradshaw—to this day half in jest, half for real, says: "That was the play we had drawn up—Franco was the receiver all the way."

In Bounds The region of the field inside the sidelines and end lines.

Incomplete Pass Forward pass that touches the ground before being caught.

Indianapolis Colts In 1946, the Miami Seahawks of the All-American Football Conference were relocated to Baltimore. Charles Evans of Middle River, Maryland, won a name contest by submitting Colts. His reasoning? "Colts are the youngest entry in the league, Maryland is famous for its race horses." The franchise kept the name when it moved to Indianapolis in 1984.

Ineligible Receiver A player who is not allowed to catch a forward pass.

"Intellectual Assassin" Ron Mix had wit, intelligence, and a drive to succeed on the gridiron, hence the nickname. A unanimous choice as an offensive tackle on the all-time American Football League team chosen in 1969, Mix was surprisingly fast for a 6-foot-4, 255-pounder. After starting at the University of Southern California for three years, Mix joined the Chargers in 1960, the AFL's first season. The team moved from L.A. to San Diego in 1961. Mix was named to the All-AFL team nine years in a row, from 1960 through 1968. He retired after the 1969 season but returned to play a final season with the Oakland Raiders in 1971.

Intentional Grounding A violation occurring when a passer throws the ball to an area where it can't be intercepted, but where it is not possible for a member of his team to catch it.

Interception The act of a defensive player catching a pass that the opposing quarterback aimed at his pass receiver.

Interior Line The portion of the line between the ends that consists of the interior linemen: tackles, guards, center.

Iron Bowl One of the most heated of college football games, it pits University of Alabama against Auburn University. The name is traced to the fact that in the first half of the 1900s the schools played against each other in Birmingham, a major iron and steel manufacturing center.

"Ironhead" Craig Heyward earned this nickname because of his power and headstrong manner of play.

"It's Not Whether You Win or Lose, But How You Play the Game" This line from a romantic poem written by sportswriter Grantland Rice has very nearly become a cliché's cliché: some would say a rationale for losers. Rice was wont to philosophize about sports (especially football), likening games to the game of life.

Jacksonville Jaguars Jacksonville held a contest in 1991, two years before the city was awarded the NFL's thirtieth franchise. Jaguars claimed the majority of votes, besting a group that included "Sharks," "Stingrays," and (ironically) "Panthers."

Jim Thorpe Trophy The annual award to the most valuable player in the National Football League is named in honor of the great Native American athlete who starred in baseball, in track, and in the Olympics.

Thorpe gained national prominence in 1912 for his Olympic decathlon triumphs. In 1915 he was signed by the Canton Bulldogs of the NFL for the then-lavish fee of $250 a game. A 6' 1", 190-pound power runner, it was said of him, "When old Jim hits them, they rattle." Thorpe's value to football transcended what he did on the field. He was a gate attraction who enabled the sport to grow and prosper.

"Joe Cool" Former quarterback great Joe Montana, for his manner.

"Joe Pa" Abbreviation of the name of Penn State legend coach Joe Paterno.

"Johnny Blood" John Victor McNally picked up the name in 1924 when he and a friend wanted to try out for a semipro team in Minneapolis. They needed assumed names to play ball as pros since they both had some college eligibility playing time left. They passed a theater where the Rudolph Valentino movie *Blood and Sand* was playing. McNally told his buddy, "I'll be Blood and you will be Sand."

McNally entered the NFL with the Milwaukee Badgers in 1925. Four years later he joined the Green Bay Packers helping them win three straight championships 1929–1931. The 6-foot-1, 190-pound McNally had sprinter speed and great leaping ability. Though best known as a pass receiver, he was an outstanding all-around player. He is deservedly in the Hall of Fame.

Juke To feint an opponent out of position.

Kansas City Chiefs The AFL franchise began in 1960 as the Dallas Texans. When the team was moved to Kansas City in 1963, the new name was selected by a fan contest partly to honor Native Americans who had lived in the area and also to honor H. Roe Bartle, mayor of Kansas City, Boy Scout executive, and founder of the tribe of Mic-O-Say. His nickname was "Chief."

Keeper A deceptive offensive play where a quarterback fakes a handoff and then runs with the ball.

Key On To watch the moves of a specific opposing player to evaluate what he will do.

"The Kick" Back in 1899, Princeton trailed Yale, 10-6. A field goal would win the game, for they were worth five points back then. All the Princeton kickers had been injured. Arthur Poe, one of the Six Little Poes of Baltimore and one of the six football-playing great-nephews of the American literary giant Edgar Allen Poe, volunteered to kick. But he had never, as the story goes, kicked a field goal in his life. But kick he did and Princeton defeated Yale in an Ivy League moment known forever as "the kick."

Kickoff A ball kicked off by the offensive team—from the 35-yard line in professional football and the 40-yard line in college football—to the receiving team to start play in each half or after a field goal or touchdown is scored.

Kickoff Return An effort made by the kickoff-receiving team to run the ball back for better field position.

Kill the Clock To use up time via time-consuming plays; a team ahead late in the game often will use short running plays to kill the clock.

Lambeau Field It was dedicated on September 29, 1957, as Green Bay defeated the Chicago Bears 21-17. The field's original name was "City Stadium." It was rededicated on September 11, 1965, and renamed for Curly Lambeau, a legend in Green Bay football, following his death the previous June.

Late Hit The act of making contact with the quarterback after he has thrown the ball, or with a kicker after he has kicked the ball, or with a receiver after he has caught the ball.

Lateral An overhand or underhand pass in any direction except that toward the opponent's goal line. Also, a straight sideways movement by a runner.

Linebacker A defender usually positioned a couple of yards behind his line.

Lineman A player who starts each play within one yard of the line of scrimmage.

Line of Scrimmage An imaginary line drawn through the spot on the field the ball was carried to in its last play and running parallel to the goal posts on either side of the field; the next play begins from this point.

"Little Boy Blue" Albie Booth was a 5-foot-6, 144-pound sophomore Yale halfback. He came off the bench on October 26, 1929, with his team trailing Army 13-0. Scoring fourteen points, he put Yale in the lead and then returned a punt seventy yards, running through the entire Army team for a touchdown and a 21-13 victory. Newspaper reports dubbed him "le Boy Blue."

Live Ball The football is live as soon as it is snapped or free kicked (as in a kickoff); it is the opposite of a dead ball.

Long Count The action of a quarterback in making a longer signal count in order to unbalance the opposition.

Looper A short pass thrown in a fairly high arc.

Loose Ball One that is not in possession of either team, such as after a fumble or a kickoff; it can be recovered by either team.

Loss of Down A penalty for a violation that makes a team lose a down.

"L. T." Lawrence Taylor was probably the best defensive player in NFL history. His nickname is his initials.

"Mad Stork" Ted Hendricks was one of the greatest defensive players in college football history. The 6' 8" Hendricks was a three-time All-American at Miami and a big star in the NFL.

Man in Motion An offensive back's movement parallel to or away from the line of scrimmage before the ball is snapped.

"Manster" Randy White got the nickname as in half-man, half monster. He was a 6' 4", 257-pound defensive tackle who could single-handedly dismantle game plans. He entertained Dallas fans for fourteen seasons.

Man-to-Man Coverage A defensive strategy in which specific defenders are assigned to specific potential pass receivers.

March A long drive by a team toward the opposition's goal.

"Mercury" Eugene Morris was one of the more colorful figures in NFL history. A star and speedy running back with the Miami Dolphins, he had personality and speed and also an appropriate nickname.

Miami Dolphins Named for the popular mammal of the coastal area in a fan contest in 1966 that drew 19,843 entries to name the AFL expansion team. A total of 622 contestants suggested "Dolphins." Team owner Joe Robbie said he liked the name because "the dolphin is one of the fastest and smartest creatures in the sea."

Michie Stadium The home of Army football was constructed in 1924 on meadowland. It was formally dedicated to the memory of Dennis Mahan Michie, instrumental in starting the game of football at the U.S. Military Academy in 1890.

Middle Linebacker A position in the middle of the defensive line.

Midfield The 50-yard line, which divides the length of the field in half.

Million-Dollar Backfield In 1947 the Chicago Cardinals, the oldest team in the National Football League at that time in terms of continuous operation, won their first championship. The Cardinals were paced by a backfield of Paul Christman (Missouri), Pat Harder (Wisconsin), Charlie Trippi (Georgia), and Elmer Angsman (Notre Dame)—a quartet that because of their worth to the franchise was valued at $1 million, big money in that era. Christman had seventeen touchdown passes and more than 2,000 yards in the air in 1947.

"Minister of Defense" Reggie White, formerly all-time sacks leader in the NFL, had a nickname derived from the fact that he was an ordained minister and a terrific defensive player, one of the greats in NFL history.

Minnesota Vikings The franchise was located from 1961 to 1981 in Bloomington, Minnesota, then moved to Minneapolis in 1982. The nickname is a tip of the hat to the Nordic roots of the area's population. Bert Rose, the first general manager of the Minnesota team that began NFL play in 1961, selected the Vikings name because so many people in Minnesota and the surrounding area traced their heritage to Scandinavia.

Miracle in the Meadowlands A 1978 game between the Giants and the Eagles was truly deserving of its label. All the Giants had to do was sit on the ball with the lead—there was less than a minute to go in the game. Instead there was a running play to Larry Csonka, and a fumble when attempting the hand-off from Joe Pisarcik. Herman Edwards recovered the fumble for the Eagles and ran it in for a score, enabling Philadelphia to win the game.

Monday-Morning Quarterbacking The American custom of second guessing a football team's performance.

Monster Park Candlestick Park, home of the San Francisco 49ers NFL team, was renamed in 2004 in a $6 million deal with electronics cable company Monster Cable Products, a Bay Area company.

Mousetrap To lure a defensive lineman into the offensive team's backfield and then block that player from the side.

Move off the Ball Quick movement by a player or players from a set position as the ball is snapped.

Moving Pocket A protective screen of blockers for a quarterback that moves to shield him from opponents.

"Mr. Inside and Mr. Outside" In the years 1944–1946 the Army football team never lost a game. A major reason for its success was the running abilities of Felix "Doc" Blanchard and Glenn Davis. The duo scored eighty-nine touchdowns between them and averaged a collective 8.3 yards per carry for the Black Knights of Army. Blanchard was possessed of bull-like power and made most of his runs into the inside of the line; he was known as Mr. Inside. Davis used his blazing speed running the ball time after time to the outside of the line; he was known as Mr. Outside.

"Mr. Integrity" Amos Alonzo Stagg coached for forty-one years at Chicago, still one of the longest head-coaching tenures in the history of college football. He also coached track for thirty-two years, baseball for nineteen years, and basketball for one year. He died in 1965 at the age of 103, a legend, a man of his word through all the decades (Grand Old Man of Football).

Necessary Line Imaginary line the offense must cross to achieve a new first down.

Neutral Zone An area that extends along the line of scrimmage for the width of the spotted football; no one except the center may be in the neutral zone when the ball is about to be put into play at the beginning of a down.

New England Patriots The team, originally located in Boston, was named the Patriots because of the area's heritage as the birthplace of the American Revolution. A group of New England sportswriters picked "Patriots" as a tribute to Patriot Day, which celebrates Paul Revere's ride.

New Orleans Saints Named for the famous song "When the Saints Go Marching In," the franchise was awarded on All Saints Day, November 1, 1966.

New York Giants In 1925, Tim Mara purchased New York's first professional football team. Mara decided on Giants because his team would play at the Polo Grounds, the home of baseball's New York Giants.

New York Jets In 1963, the team name was changed from the New York Titans to the Jets. On the same day they hired Weeb Ewbank, the owners announced that they were changing the team's name to Jets. It sounded like New York's baseball Mets and LaGuardia Airport was nearby.

New York Titans New York Titans' owner Harry Wismer opted for the name for it was in his phrase: "Bigger than a giant." And his football team competed (unsuccessfully) with the New York Giants. But at least the nickname was a bigger deal, to him.

"The New York Sack Exchange" Mark Gastineau, Joe Klecko, Marty Lyons, and Abdul Salaam—starting front four on the Jets' defense, they made life miserable for opposing quarterbacks in the early 1980s.

NFL (National Football League) The major professional football league in the U.S.; headquarters are in New York.

NFL Championship Game held from 1933 through 1965 to decide the champion of professional football; renamed the Super Bowl in 1966.

Nickel Defense A fifth defensive back replaces a linebacker on the field, increasing pass coverage.

"Nigerian Nightmare" Christian Okoye hailed from Nigeria and was a load for defenders as a 260-pound running back for six seasons when he gained 4,897 yards for the Kansas City Chiefs.

"Night Train" Lane A standout National Football League cornerback in the years 1952–1965, Dick Lane played with a daring ferocity and verve. He was a "hitter," and his nickname had its roots in the locomotive explosiveness with which he went after the ball and the ball carrier. The rhythm of the big-band arrangement of "Night Train" by Buddy Morrow fused with the rhythm that Dick Lane harnessed his playing engine to.

No-Name Defense The Miami Dolphins of the National Football League breezed through an undefeated and untied 1972 season and a Super Bowl win over Washington to become the first professional team ever to go through a complete season with all wins. The heart of that team was a defense that allowed the fewest points in the NFL. None of the Miami defenders had any sort of fame or reputation, but they functioned as a team, and that's how the nickname came to be. Interestingly enough, the five interior offensive linemen—Norm Evans, Wayne Moore, Bob Keuchenberg, Larry Little, and Jim Langer—all had been cut by other teams.

The No Namers were:

LDE	Vern Den Herder
LDT	Manny Fernandez
RDT	Bob Heinz
RDE	Bill Stanfill
LLB	Doug Swift
MLB	Nick Buoniconti
RLB	Mike Kolen
LCB	Tim Foley
RCB	Curtis Johnson
SS	Jake Scott
FS	Dick Anderson

"Norse Nightmare" Gary Larsen was a star for the Minnesota Vikings at left defensive tackle. A blond, mustached, big former marine, his nickname came from his Nordic background and the hits he put on the opposition.

Nose Guard A defensive lineman who plays opposite the offensive center and between the defensive tackles (Middle Guard).

Oakland Raiders In 1960, Oakland held a contest to pick a name for its AFL team. The fans chose Señors. Oakland management chose Raiders. The origin of the name is not known.

Odd Front An alignment of a four-man line in which one defensive tackle is positioned directly opposite to the center, as in a five-man line.

Offending Team Team committing a foul.

Offside A violation that involves having any part of one's body beyond the scrimmage line as the ball is put into play on a scrimmage down or beyond the restraining line on a free-kick down. The center, however, is permitted to be in the neutral zone while preparing for the snap during a scrimmage down, provided he is not beyond the neutral zone and his feet are behind the ball. The kicker or the holder in a free-kick down may have part of his body beyond the restraining line.

"O. J." ("The Juice") His name is Orenthal James Simpson. His teammates originally believed that his initials stood for "orange juice."

"Old Indestructible" Mel Hein was a charter inductee into the NFL Hall of Fame in 1963. He never missed a single game in fifteen-year pro career with the New York Giants.

"The Old Man" William Alexander had the tough task at the age of thirty of replacing the legendary John Heisman as the coach of Georgia Tech in 1920. A disciplinarian on the field, Alexander rooted loudly for the underdog. His players affectionately referred to him as "The Old Man," a kind of mocking reference to his youth.

"Old 98" Tom Harmon wore jersey number 98. An All-Star football player at the University of Michigan, he played halfback/defensive back for the Los Angeles Rams (1946–1947).

On Downs Describes a team's loss of possession for failure to reach the necessary line on a fourth-down play.

Onside Kick Offensive strategy when kicking team intentionally kicks "short," hoping to recover the ball, which must travel at least ten yards to be in play.

Open Field The part of the field beyond the defensive line where defenders are spread and offensive players can run in the open.

Open Receiver Player who has no defender closely covering him.

Option Play An offensive play in which a player can choose to either run or pass; quarterback and halfback options are examples.

Orange Crush The 1977 Denver Broncos NFL team wore orange-colored uniforms, and its fierce and determined defensive tactics were aimed at throttling the opposing team's offense all over the field. The site of the Orange Crush soft drink manufacturing plant, Denver the city could be identified with soda pop, just as the Broncos could be identified by the way they popped the opposition. It was a perfect marriage, a team that wore orange and a soda pop that had the color in its name.

Outland Trophy The annual award to the best interior lineman in college football is named in honor of John Outland, University of Pennsylvania All-American guard in 1897 and 1898. The trophy originated in 1946, and its winners have included Dick Modzelweski (1952), Alex Karras (1957), Merlin Olsen (1961), Bobby Bell (1962), Ron Yary (1967), and Randy White (1974).

Out of Bounds Region of the field touching or outside the sidelines and end lines; as soon as a ball carrier or the ball itself touches out of bounds, the play is over.

Over-the-Hill Gang In 1971 George Allen took over as head coach of the National Football League Washington Redskins and immediately obtained players who by pro football standards were aged, washed up. But they transformed the Redskins into a contending team. Allen's pickups included Billy Kilmer, Roy Jefferson, Boyd Dowler, Clifton McNeil, Vernon Biggs, Ron McDole, Diron Talbert, Jack Pardee, and Speedy Duncan. These players and others reached back to the days of their prime, playing aggressive, opportunistic football. The team reached the Super Bowl in 1973, only Allen's second season at the helm.

"Ox" Owen Lloyd Parry went 6' 4" and weighed 230, a pretty good size for that era of the 1930s with the New York Giants.

"Papa Bear" George Halas, a founder of the National Football League, spent forty-eight years of his life coaching the Chicago Bears, the team he owned since its founding. His age and his tenure with the team earned him his nickname. In his time he won nine divisional titles and five World Championships. When he retired from coaching in 1968, he said: "I won't miss the detail work, the game analysis, the short list—

but the sidelines, the excitement, the decisions—that's what I love." He was a familiar sight at Wrigley Field on Sunday afternoons, jabbering with players and officials, at times virtually transcending the game on the field.

Pass-Block Blocking protection for a passer.

Pass Defender A defensive player who covers an opposing receiver.

Passing Game A strategy that uses a passing offense as opposed to a running offense.

Pass Interference A violation caused by unfairly interfering with the attempt of a receiver to catch a forward pass.

Pass Patterns (Pass Routes) Predetermined paths receivers follow to help the passer quickly locate them so he can more easily get the ball to them.

Pass Protection Blocking by offensive players to keep defenders away from the quarterback on passing plays.

Pass Rush The charging of the passer by the defensive line.

Paul Brown Stadium The stadium is approximately five blocks west of baseball's Great American Ballpark and is named for one of the legends of Cincinnati Bengals football.

Peeling Tacklers A situation where a runner causes tacklers to fall off him as he runs with the ball.

Penalty The loss of downs or yardage charged against a team that is guilty of a violation of the rules.

Penetration Movement into the opposition's portion of the field.

"Pepper" Thomas Johnson, New York Giants football player, was given this nickname by his grandmother. As a child he loved pepper so much he added it to everything he ate.

Personal Foul One that might cause injury; punishable by a fifteen-yard penalty.

Philadelphia Eagles Bert Bell established his NFL franchise in Philadelphia in 1933 at a time the United States was suffering through the Great Depression. New president Franklin D. Roosevelt had introduced his "New Deal" program through the National Recovery Administration, which had the Blue Eagle as its symbol. Since Bell hoped his franchise also was headed for a new deal, he picked Eagles as the nickname.

Picked Off A football that is intercepted.

Pigskin Nickname for the football.

Piling On Defenders jumping on a player after he has had his forward motion stopped on a play—an illegal move.

Pit Kind of war zone in the middle of the offensive and defensive line where the "battle in the trenches" takes place.

Pitchout An underhand lateral toss by one back to another, generally made behind the line of scrimmage.

Pittsburgh Steelers Team was founded in 1933 and dubbed the "Pirates" to complement the baseball team in Pittsburgh. In 1940, owner Art Rooney changed the name to "Steelers," reflecting the city's ties to the steel industry. Chicago Cardinals and Pittsburgh also merged for one season and became Card-Pitt in 1944.

Placekick Act of kicking a ball that is in a stationary position on the ground, a technique used for kickoffs and attempted field goals.

Platoon Unit trained especially for offense or defense.

Play A spurt of action that begins with a snap and ends with a dead ball.

Play-Action Pass A maneuver in which a quarterback fakes a handoff and then passes.

Playbook Team's strategy and play manual.

Play Clock Clock displayed above each end zone that limits the time teams may take between plays to forty seconds (thirty in college); the ball must be snapped before the clock runs down to zero.

Playoffs The postseason tournament that determines the NFL champion.

Plunge Back's lunge into defensive line for short yardage.

Pocket area behind the offensive line, where the quarterback is protected by his blockers.

Poes of Princeton In 1899, the Princeton football team had a half-dozen players who answered to the name of Poe. All of them were great-nephews of poet Edgar Allan Poe.

Point-after-Touchdown (PAT) After a touchdown, the scoring team is allowed to add another point by kicking the football through uprights of the goalpost (Extra Point).

"Polish Rifle" Quarterback star Ron Jaworski, for the power of his arm and ethnic background.

Pop A short toss for safe yardage.

"Pop" Glenn Scobey Warner (1871–1954) played the game but made his name as the developer of stars like Jim Thorpe and some nifty innovations in the gridiron game. Warner is credited with introducing the double-wing formation, the practice of numbered plays, and dummy scrimmaging. He was a father figure to many.

Possession To be holding or in control of the football.

Post A pass route that sends a receiver downfield and then cutting toward goalposts (Post Pattern).

Power Block A blocking maneuver in which an offensive lineman attempts to force a defensive lineman straight back or sideways.

Power Play A play in which a ball carrier follows blockers who attempt to power-block and clear a path for him.

Prevent Defense A defensive strategy usually used late in a game against a team that is trailing; the team that is winning puts in extra pass defenders to prevent a quick score, realizing that running plays will not be of much help to the opposition.

Previous Spot Where the ball was snapped to begin the last play.

Primary Receiver The main receiver on a particular play.

"Prime Time" Deion Sanders always put his money where his mouth was as a talented and dynamic performer (Neon Deion).

"Pudge" William Walter Heffelfinger was a three-time all-American at Yale, 1889–1891. He was a "lineman's lineman." Called "Pudge" by his friends because of his six-foot, two hundred-pound plus frame, and "One-

Man Army" by the opposition, the Yale standout had the speed and power to enable him to single-handedly break up play after play.

Pull Offensive blocking out led by pulling guards and tackles to create room for the ball carrier; a line play that sees a guard (or tackle) pivot into his own backfield to lead a running play around an end of the scrimmage line.

Punt When a player ten yards behind the center catches a snap, drops it, and kicks it before it hits the ground; an opponent tries to catch and advance it the other way.

"Purple People Eaters" ("Purple Gang") The Vikings' defensive line was so good in the late 1960s and during the 1970s. Like other good defenses, the Vikings tackled quarterbacks and runners for losses, but they went a step further. They used a "big play" defense that could turn a game from defeat into victory in one spectacular play. The Purple People Eaters did not consider it a day's work unless they intercepted passes, forced fumbles, blocked punts and field goals, and ran back loose balls for touchdowns. Jim Marshall, Alan Page, Carl Eller, and Gary Larsen comprised the front four of the Purple People Eaters. The Purple People Eaters earned a record four trips to the Super Bowl with Eller, Page, and Marshall starting in every one of them.

Pursuit The chasing effort of a defender against a ball carrier.

Pylon A short orange marker at each of the end zone's four corners.

Quarterback An offensive back whose responsibilities include calling signals and directing the offense; he initiates the offensive action on a play from the line of scrimmage; positioned behind the center in the T formation, he receives the ball directly from the center.

Quarterback Draw A fake pass followed by a quarterback sprint past onrushing tacklers up the middle of the field.

Quarterback Sneak A situation in which, having the ball snapped to him, the quarterback immediately runs with it.

Quick Count The opposite of a long count, a hurried and shortened signal-calling by a quarterback to unbalance the opposition.

Quick Kick A surprise maneuver where a punt is made on a first, second, or third down from a passing or running formation, aimed at getting a team a better field position.

Quick Opener Running back heads straight at a hole in the defensive line after getting a quick handoff from the quarterback.

Reading the Blitz A situation where a defensive team's potential blitz is anticipated by the offensive team.

Reading the Defense Recognition by the quarterback of the defensive formation, sometimes prompting him to call an audible to adjust the offense.

Receiver An offensive player who catches or attempts to catch a forward pass.

Reception Pass catch.

Recovery Gain or regain possession of a fumble.

"Red" Harold Grange came out of the University of Illinois into the National Football League with the Chicago Bears in 1925. Some observers noting the drawing power of Grange credit him with single-handedly establishing professional football. His nickname came from the color of his hair.

Red Dog The defensive charging of passer, usually via a linebacker blitz.

Red Shirt Designation given to a college player who did not play in any games during a particular year due to injury or coach's choice; such a player is permitted to practice with the team during that season and is granted an additional year of eligibility.

Red Zone Imaginary area between the defense's 20-yard line and its goal line, from which the offense is most likely to score points.

Referee The main official, positioned in the offensive backfield in plays from scrimmage; he oversees the game flow by starting the clock, placing the ball in play, and so forth.

"Refrigerator" William Perry was as big as a refrigerator. He astonished his teammates on the Chicago Bears with the amount of food he could eat.

Release Time The time needed by a quarterback to throw the ball.

Return An attempt by a player who has just caught an interception, punt, or kickoff to advance the ball the other way.

Reverse A play that is run in the opposite direction from the blocking pattern; a back moving in one direction hands the ball off to a teammate, who passes by him moving in the opposite direction.

"Rocky" Football star Robert Patrick Bleier was always better known as "Rocky." The son of an Appleton, Wisconsin, bar owner, Bleier explained how he got his nickname: "Our living quarters were in the back section of the ground floor, just off the dining room. . . . In my first few weeks, Dad would bring some of his customers back to the bedroom to take a peek at his son. . . . 'Son of a bitch looks like a little rock,' my dad would whisper proudly. So I was Rocky before I ever departed the crib."

Bleier, out of Notre Dame, was the 417th player drafted in the 1968 draft and went on to become Pittsburgh's inspirational leader and their "rock."

Rollout An offensive play in which the quarterback takes the snap from the center and runs to one side of the field behind his line with the option to run, pass, or hand off to a running back.

Rose Bowl The Tournament of Roses has been celebrated every New Year's Day since 1890 with floats and pageantry in an idea inspired by the Battle of Flowers at Nice—a feature of that city's Carnival festival held in the last days before Lent. On January 1, 1916, Pasadena, California, held a football game to tie in with its Rose Festival. The game was staged in the Pasadena Bowl, where Washington State trimmed Brown, 14-0, to give American collegiate football what has been called the "first of the Bowl Games." (Actually, the first bowl game took place in 1902; Michigan trounced Stanford, 49-0.) The event was known as the Tournament of Roses Association Game until 1923, when the Rose Bowl stadium was erected and given its name by Pasadena's Harlan W. Hall.

Roughing the Passer A violation committed when a defender, after a pass has been thrown, runs into or manhandles the quarterback.

Rozelle Rule National Football League Commissioner Pete Rozelle is credited with instituting this rule, which bears his name. It requires a team that signs a free agent who has played out his option to give the player's former team mutually agreed-on compensation. If this is not possible, the commissioner of the league determines the compensation.

Running Game The offensive strategy of running instead of throwing the ball for yardage.

Rush To charge a passer. Also, to get yards by running with the ball.

Sack The downing of a quarterback before he can throw the ball.

Safety Two points given to a defensive team for downing an offensive player carrying the ball in his own end zone.

Safety Blitz Safetyman's charge through the line aimed at sacking the quarterback.

Safetymen The two defensive backs who position themselves off the line of scrimmage to cover downfield passes and long runs.

Safety Valve A secondary receiver, usually positioned in the backfield or just over the scrimmage line, who serves as an optional target for the quarterback if the other receivers are covered.

San Diego Chargers The Los Angeles American Football League franchise held a contest in 1960. Three reasons for choosing "Chargers" have been offered—it sounded dynamic; the club's new stationery featured a horse; and owner Baron Hilton had recently instituted the Carte Blanche card. The team kept the name when it moved to San Diego the following year. Baron Hilton agreed after his general manager, Frank Ready, picked the "Chargers" name when he purchased an AFL franchise for Los Angeles. The Chargers played in Los Angeles in 1960 and moved to San Diego in 1961.

Sandwiched Ball carrier hit at the same time on different parts of his body by defenders.

San Francisco 49ers The name was adopted when San Francisco obtained an AAFC franchise in 1946. San Francisco owner Anthony J. Morabito chose 49ers for his All-America Football Conference squad because it reflected San Francisco's link to the California Gold Rush. The 49ers kept the name when they joined the NFL in 1950.

Scatback Quick and tricky ball carrier.

Scramble Technique used by a quarterback after a pass play has failed that involves running and dodging with the ball to avoid tacklers.

Screen Pass A pass into the flat to a receiver who has several blockers in front of him, accomplished by offensive linemen who allow defensive players to charge through the line and then create a screen ahead of the receiver.

Scrimmage Any play that starts with a snap from the line of scrimmage.

Seattle Seahawks Named for the birds and totem poles native to the area of Seattle. The nickname came as result of a fan contest that drew 20,365 entries and suggested 1,742 different names. "Seahawks" was suggested by 151 entrants and judged by the team ownership to be the best choice.

Secondary The defensive backfield, composed of two cornerbacks and the two safeties, whose main task is pass coverage.

Series The four downs a team has to advance ten yards.

Setback A back lined up usually behind the quarterback.

Shank To kick improperly with the wrong part of the foot so that the ball travels a short distance.

Shift The legal changing of position after lining up for the snap by members of the offensive team.

"Shipwreck" John Kelly arrived at the campus of University of Kentucky in 1928 via a chauffeured vehicle. He starred there and then went on to pro football with the Brooklyn Dodgers, married a millionaire, owned the Dodgers, then went on to make millions in Florida real estate. He was a man who went undercover for the FBI during World War II. He truly earned his nickname.

Shoot Defensive players rushing through an opening between linemen to get at the player with the ball (Rush, Charge, Blitz, Shoot the Gap).

Shotgun Offense A formation in which the quarterback gets the snap from the center not from a direct handoff, but from a position several yards behind the line of scrimmage, as in a punt formation.

Sideline Boundary line running the length of the field along each side; a ball carrier or ball that touches or crosses the sideline is out of bounds.

Sideline Pass An offensive play in which the receiver goes straight down the field and then quickly sprints to the sideline for the pass reception; used to stop the clock many times, as the receiver can step out of bounds after he catches the ball.

Single Elimination Tournament where a team is eliminated after one loss.

Single Wing An unbalanced line offensive formation: the strong side of the line has a back just outside the end; the quarterback functions behind the line as a blocker; and the tailback or fullback can get the center snap directly from their positions approximately five yards behind the line.

Slant An angular run toward the goal line.

"Slash" Kordell Stewart played many positions when he first entered the NFL with the Pittsburgh Steelers: quarterback/punt returner/wide receiver. He was a slasher wherever he played.

Sled A training device for blocking practice that has padding over a steel frame and slides on the ground as players push and pound against it.

"Slingin Sammy" Sammy Baugh came out of Texas Christian University, after having tossed a record 599 passes in three seasons, to join the Washington Redskins in 1937. Six times he led the NFL in passing; six times he was chosen All-Pro. Baugh's nickname derived from his highly accurate, rubber-armed passing over a sixteen-year pro career.

Slotback A player positioned behind the gap between tackle and end.

"Snake" Quarterbacks Kenny Stabler, Jake Plummer, and others—for their shifty moves.

Snap The act of a center passing the ball back between his legs to an offensive back.

"Sonny" Christian Adolph Jurgensen III (no wonder he was called "Sonny") was transformed into a legend in 1964 when he came to the Washington Redskins in a trade with the Philadelphia Eagles. Over the next eleven seasons, Jurgensen shattered records, completing 1,831 passes for 22,585 yards and 179 touchdowns. The Hall of Famer-to-be threw the football overhead, sidearm, or even behind his back.

Special Teams Squads that enter the game especially to make or return kicks and punts, to gain short yardage, and so forth.

Spike To slam the ball to the ground in an emotional manner, usually performed by a player in the end zone after scoring a touchdown.

Spiral Ball passed or kicked with a spin which propels it further with more accuracy.

Split End A receiver positioned at the end of the line of scrimmage, some yards away from his teammates.

Split the Uprights An expression for making an extra point or field goal that describes what the ball in flight does as it passes over the crossbar.

Spot Location on the field, determined by an official, to mark forward progress or the place of a foul.

Square Out An offensive play in which a receiver goes about fifteen yards downfield, slants outside, and sprints to the sideline parallel to the scrimmage line.

Squib A kickoff that is purposely short and difficult to handle for the receiving team (Squibbler).

Statue of Liberty Play A play in which the quarterback raises his arm, faking a pass, and has the ball taken by a teammate positioned behind him who then can run or pass.

"Steagles" Philadelphia and Pittsburgh merged for the 1943 season and became Phil-Pitt.

"Steel Curtain" Used to describe the Pittsburgh Steelers defensive unit for almost a decade, starting in the mid-1970s. Four players from those teams are in the Pro Football Hall of Fame: "Mean" Joe Greene, Jack Ham, Jack Lambert, and Mel Blount. Others linked in the public eye with the "Steel Curtain" include: L. C. Greenwood, Dwight White, and Ernie Holmes. The nickname was a play on the nickname and a tip of the cap to the defensive skills of the players.

Stickum A type of glue placed on a receiver's hands to help him catch passes.

St. Louis Cardinals A football club on the southwest side of Chicago was formed in 1898. The team was known as the "Normals" until 1901, when founder Chris O'Brien secured some hand-me-down jerseys from the University of Chicago. The jerseys were actually maroon but had a faded look. The team became the Racine Cardinals, and the nickname stuck as the club moved from Chicago (1922) to St. Louis (1960) and, finally, to Phoenix (1988).

St. Louis Rams In 1936, Cleveland's new AFL franchise took its name from one of the top collegiate teams of the era, the Fordham Rams. The Rams name has survived through moves to Los Angeles (1946), Anaheim (1980), and St. Louis (1995).

Stop-and-Go A pass route in which the receiver stops short and then goes deep downfield for a pass.

"Stout Steve" Steve Owen was a hefty and imaginative coach of the Giants in the 1930s.

Straight Arm (Stiff Arm) The action of a ball carrier using his extended arm as a way to shed a tackler.

Strip To pull the ball from the hands of an opponent.

Stripe Marking for a yard line.

Strong Safety The tight defensive safety positioned opposite the strong side of the offensive line.

Strong Side That part of an unbalanced line containing more players.

Stunt A maneuver that involves defensive players jumping in and out of line to unbalance the offense.

Succeeding Spot Where the next play starts if no penalty is called.

Sudden Death Professional football's extra period of play to determine the winner of a tied game; the first team to score wins (Sudden Victory).

Sugar Bowl After World War II the state of Louisiana led the United States in the production of cane sugar and earned the nickname the "Sugar State." The state's massive sports stadium, the Sugar Bowl, located in New Orleans, and the collegiate invitational bowl game that usually includes one team from the Southeastern Conference derive their common name from the state's nickname.

Super Bowl The merger of the American Football League and the National Football League led to the need for a championship game. The first contest was played on January 15, 1967, and although officially it was known as the National Football League championship game, its unofficial name, the Super Bowl, was used in the media, by the fans, and by the players—and the name has stuck.

One theory for how the high-sounding name came about is that at an owner's meeting centering on a discussion of what to call the game, one of the moguls had in his pocket a Superball that he had taken away from his youngster earlier that day. The owner was not too taken with the long and ordinary-sounding suggestion for what would become pro football's ultimate game. Squeezing the ball, he suggested the name Super Bowl, but the name was not received with much enthusiasm. Nevertheless, he mentioned the name to a reporter and as they say in sporting circles, "The rest is history."

The first Super Bowl saw the first dual-network color-coverage simulcast of a sports event in history and attracted the largest viewership ever to witness a sporting event up to that time. The Nielsen rating indicated that seventy-three million fans watched all or part of that game on one of the two networks, CBS or NBC. In actuality, the game was a contest between the two leagues and the two networks, for the CBS allegiance was to the NFL, and the NBC allegiance was to the AFL, which it had virtually created with its network dollars.

The Super Bowl from the start has been designated with a Roman numeral rather than by year—a move on the part of NFL Commissioner Pete Rozelle to give the contest a sense of class and, at the same time, of continuity.

Sweep The act of a ball carrier following his blockers around either end of the line, as opposed to going through the line.

"Sweetness" Hall of Famer Walter Payton was all of that.

Swing Pass A quickly thrown pass to a back on either side of the backfield positioned roughly parallel with the quarterback.

Tackle Eligible A legal maneuver in which the tight end gets into the backfield before the snap and technically becomes a back, thus allowing the tackle beside him to function as an end and an eligible pass receiver.

Tackles Offensive linemen positioned just outside the guards; defensive linemen positioned just inside their ends.

Tackling Making contact with a ball carrier causing him to touch the ground with any part of his body except his hands, thereby ending the play.

Tailback A running back positioned the greatest distance from the line of scrimmage.

Tampa Bay Buccaneers Named for the pirates and buccaneer history of the area, the nickname defeated more than four hundred entries in a radio-sponsored competition, held one month after Tampa was awarded the first of two expansion franchises on April 24, 1974. "Buccaneers" beat out competitors like "Buzzards," "Sea Horses," and "Mafia."

"Taxi Squad" Art McBride, original owner of the Cleveland Browns, owned several Cleveland-area taxi-cab companies in the 1940s, a time when NFL rosters were set at thirty-three players. Players cut by the Browns drove McBride taxis, allowing him to replace injured players immediately with well-skilled taxi drivers. The term has become interchangeable for players on a reserve list.

Tennessee Titans The franchise was originally in Houston and known as the "Oilers." They moved to Memphis in 1997 as the Tennessee Oilers. The name was changed to Titans when the franchise moved to Nashville.

Terrible Towels Fans of the Pittsburgh Steelers wave the golden "schmatas," celebrating their team and taunting opponents.

T Formation Resembling the letter T, this formation has the quarterback positioned just behind the center, the fullback about five yards behind the quarterback, and halfbacks spread slightly ahead on either side of the fullback.

Third-and-Long When the offense faces a third down and is more than a short running play away from a first down; usually third-and-five or greater.

"Three and Out" When a team has first, second, and third down and has to punt.

Three-Point Stance Player position before the snap: legs spread wide and one hand touching the ground, body leaning forward.

Tight End A blocking and pass-receiving offensive end generally positioned close to the tackle.

Tightrope The act of a runner gingerly running along the sidelines, trying to avoid stepping out of bounds.

Time of Possession The amount of time an offensive team controls the ball.

"The Toe" Lou Groza's kicking foot produced 1,343 points, on 234 field goals and 641 extra points, during his National Football League career. His coach, Paul Brown, said: "Lou Groza shortened the field from 100 yards to 60 yards." Perhaps the greatest place-kicker of all time, the 6' 3", 250-pound Groza was the hub of the Cleveland Browns during most of the 1960s. His kicking foot was the hub of his performance skills and it earned him an apt nickname.

"Tombstone" Rich Jackson terrorized (hence his nickname) opponents, particularly quarterbacks, from 1967 to 1972. Many considered him the best defensive end in football during his prime, and in 1970 he became the first Broncos' player to be named to the All-NFL first team.

"Too Tall" Ed Jones created havoc in the center of the field for quarterbacks and kickers, standing so much taller than his teammates.

Touchback A downed ball in the end zone after a punt or kickoff is brought out to the 20-yard line for a first down for the receiving team; a touchback is also awarded if his opponent kicks the ball across the end line.

Touchdown (TD) When an offensive team crosses the opponent's goal line with the ball, catches a pass in the opponent's end zone, or recovers a loose ball in the opponent's end zone; earns a team six points.

"Tuffy" Tailback and Hall of Famer Alphonse Leemans as a kid played with the bigger and tougher boys, and he truly earned that name. He grew to 5' 9" and 210 pounds and was really tough.

Turn In A receiver's pattern composed of a short downfield run followed by a cut to the middle of the playing field.

Turn Out A receiver's pattern composed of a short downfield run followed by a sideline cut.

Turnover Involuntary loss of possession of the ball during a play, either by a fumble or by throwing an interception.

Two-Minute Warning A signal that stops play with two minutes left in each half for an official timeout.

Two-Point Conversion When a team that just scored a touchdown starts a play at the opponent's two-yard line (three-yard line in college) and crosses the goal line to earn two points; when successful, it looks just like a touchdown. It was introduced to the NFL in 1994.

Umpire An official stationed in the defensive backfield in plays from scrimmage who checks holding, the positions of linemen on passing and kicking plays, the players' equipment, and so forth.

Unbalanced Line An unequal number of players on either side of the center.

Unnecessary Roughness A penalty situation that takes place when one player uses undue force against another.

Unsportsmanlike Conduct Behavior that is contrary to the ideal of good sportsmanship, such as fighting, abusive language, or unfairly assisting a player; generally it is penalized by a team's losing fifteen yards.

Up Back In the I formation, the ball carrier closest to the quarterback.

Washington Redskins George Preston Marshall acquired an NFL franchise in 1932 and named it the Boston Braves after the city's major league baseball team. However, after a financially devastating and poorly attended season in 1932, Marshall abandoned the "Braves" name in favor of the "Redskins." The Redskins name was retained when the team was moved to Washington in 1937.

Weak Safety A safety positioned on the same side of the field as the offensive line's weak side.

Weak Side That part of the unbalanced line with fewer players.

Wedge A group of blockers set up in front of the man who receives the kickoff and are positioned in a wedge-shaped formation.

"White Shoes" Everybody imitated the patented dance of Billy Johnson. It was a celebratory ritual from the end zone by a receiver who it was said never got his shoes dirty.

"Whizzer" The 1939 Pittsburgh Pirates, who became the "Steelers" a year later, signed Byron White for the unheard of salary of $15,000. He had been given his nickname for his scholar/athlete accomplishments. An All-American, he played one season for the Pirates, won the league's rushing title, and then sailed for England and his Rhodes scholarship. Then he returned to pro football and later made an even bigger name for himself as associate justice of the U.S. Supreme Court.

Wide Receiver A flankerback or split end in an offensive formation.

Wild Card A team that makes the NFL playoffs by having one of the two best records among nondivision winners in its conference.

"Winning Isn't Everything—It's the Only Thing." In 1959 Vince Lombardi took over as head coach of the Green Bay Packers. The year before, the Pack had lost ten games, tied one, and won one. Lombardi announced, "I'm in command here." He moved Green Bay in his first season as coach to a record of seven wins and five losses. By 1960 Lombardi, pushing, driving, scheming, inspiring, steered the Green Bay team to the Western Division National Football League title. In 1961 the Packers recorded their first World Championship in seventeen years. There was another championship in 1962, another in 1965, and another in 1966. The first Super Bowl ever played was a personal victory for Lombardi, as his Green Bay team demolished Kansas City, 35-10, on January 15, 1967. The following year, in Super Bowl II, Green Bay triumphed over Oakland, 33-14, in Lombardi's final game as Packer coach. Lombardi transformed the Packers from chronic losers into perennial winners during his nine glorious seasons as their coach, and he made his slogan into a way of life for the players and the fans of Green Bay (see "Getting a Tie Is like Kissing Your Sister").

"Win One for the Gipper" Storied Notre Dame football player George Gipp died at the age of twenty-three, at the height of his powers. Famed Notre Dame coach Knute Rockne related how Gipp in his deathbed speech said, "Sometime, Rock, when the team's up against it, when things are wrong and the breaks are beating the boys, tell them to go in there with all they've got and win just one for the Gipper." Rockne used that story to psyche up his Notre Dame players again and again. The phrase has become part of the language of inspirational sports expressions.

Wishbone Resembling a wishbone in appearance, this formation, which is popular in college play, has the quarterback close behind the center, the fullback about five yards behind the quarterback, and the halfbacks behind and to the sides of the fullback.

"Wrong Way" Riegels An astonished crowd at the 1929 Rose Bowl watched Roy Riegels, University of California, run seventy yards to his own end zone before he was finally brought down by a teammate. Riegels, who forever will be known as "Wrong Way" Riegels for his odd run, maintained, "At least I was trying."

Year of the Runner During the 1972 National Football League season, for the first time in history, ten runners rushed for 1,000 yards or more. That year in pro football was named for them, and later rules changes stemmed from their domination of the sport that year.

Golf

Ace To complete a hole with one stroke (Hole in One).

Address To take a stance and be positioned to hit the ball.

Approach Shot A fully stroked shot hit from the fairway to the putting green.

Apron Close-cut grass area surrounding the putting green.

"Arnie's Army" Excitable yet restrained when they must be, loyal but at times critical, those fans who through the years have followed golfer Arnold Palmer over hill and dale have earned their nickname. Some have even said that their presence has at times lent an extra dimension of support to Palmer's game.

Away The ball estimated to be farthest from the hole and to be played first.

Back Nine The last nine holes on an eighteen-hole course.

Ball A golf ball weighs no more than 1.62 ounces, is no more than 1.68 inches in diameter, and is covered with a rubber dimpled surface.

Best Ball A competition where the lower score of either one of two partners is counted for the match.

"Big Bertha's Paradise" Mallorca is one of those great places for golf 365 days a year. The island is a paradise for "Big Bertha" and everyone else.

"Big Easy" Ernie Els, for an elegant and relaxed swing, a big slow-motion arc.

"The Big Weasy" Michelle Wie, the teenage American talent; her nickname is a play on her size and name.

Birdie One stroke less than par for a hole.

Bisque A handicap used by a player on a hole(s) that is put into effect as long as the player requests it before beginning play on the hole.

Bite The backspin on a ball that causes it to stop sharply.

"Black Knight" ("Mr. Fitness") A very fit Gary Player, always dressed in black on the golf course, won his first major title in 1959 at the British Open. He is regarded as the best bunker player of all time. He won over 160 titles worldwide.

Blast To hit a ball out of a sand trap.

Blind Hole A hole that a player cannot see when attempting an approach shot.

Bogey In England around the turn of the century, a popular music-hall song exclaimed: "Hush! Hush! Hush! Here comes the Bogey man! So hide your head beneath the clothes, he'll catch you if he can!" At the Coventry Club in 1890, each hole on the golf course was given a scratch value—a ground score above par. The bogey man of the song became the bogey on the golf course—something to watch out for. In the United States, "bogey" eventually came to mean one stroke over par for a hole, "double bogey" to mean two strokes over par for a hole, and so forth.

"Boom Boom" In the nineties, when Fred Couples was at the top of his game, he truly hammered the ball a long distance.

"Boozie" ("Boozy Woosie") Veteran Welshman Ian Woosnam, for fondness of pints and other drinks: Early on in tour he traveled in a camper lacking scratch. His main food was beans and beer.

Borrow The degree of swerve off a direct line of a ball on a sloping putting green; a method of putting to compensate for the slope of a green.

"Boss of the Moss" Loren Roberts, one of the world's best putters.

Brassie This old term for the number 2 wood evolved from the brass plate that was affixed to the sole of the old wooden club. The plate's function was to offer protection to a club when a player used it from a bad lie.

Break of Green The slant or slope of the green.

Break Par To complete the playing of a hole under par.

"Bulldog" Corey Pavin, grit and determination personified, the former U.S. Open and Colonial champion player, earned his nickname.

Bunker Sand trap hazard.

Bunkered A situation where a golfer's ball is in a sand trap.

Bye Holes In match play, the holes that remain after the match result has been decided; these holes are not played if a player has a lead greater than the number of holes left.

Caddie The French had a hand in the insertion of this word into the language of sports. In eighteenth-century Scotland, a "caddie" (from the French word *cadet*) was a young fellow who ran around on errands or functioned as a porter. Eventually the young fellow and some older ones functioned as porters and ran around on errands looking for golf balls on courses, and they became known as caddies, persons who help a player with clubs and otherwise provide assistance in accordance with the rules.

"Calamity Jane" Jane Burke was a Wild West character of song and story who was quick on the draw and noted for always prophesying calamities. Golf great Bobby Jones had a putter characterized by a slightly lofted blade and a hickory shaft that had been broken in two places and bonded together again. Jones had great success with the putter he called "Calamity Jane," especially in 1920 when it helped him win the British and American open and amateur championships.

Callaway System A method used frequently by golfers who play infrequently and who have no established handicap; by applying the score a player makes to a predetermined formula, a handicap is arrived at.

Card To get a specific score on a hole or a round.

"Carnac" Jack Nicklaus, so called after the old Johnny Carson character "Carnac the Magnificent," who always knew the answers before one could ask the questions.

"Carnac, Junior" Tom Watson; like Nicklaus and "Carnac the Magnificent."

Carry The distance the ball stays in the air before it hits the ground.

Cart A metal holder with wheels to carry clubs and golf bag.

Casual Water A temporary collection of water not meant to be played as a permanent accumulation of water, such as a water hazard.

"The Cat" ("El Gato") Eduardo Romero, for his habit of whipping victories from other people's noses.

"Chachi" Billy Andrade, called that to honor the dark-haired, baby-faced *Happy Days* character.

Cheat Sheet Course diagram of the distances of holes.

"Chief" To rub it in, the nickname is a bit off-color. Dennis Paulson played with brother Dean in a tourney at the Valencia Country Club in the mid-1980s. He had a very poor swing at water following a poor chip and wound up covered with moss and mud. His brother said he resembled an Indian with his sun-reddened face. The nickname stuck.

Chip Shot A short and low approach shot to the green.

Closed Clubface A stance in which the right foot is pulled back from an imaginary line across the toes and parallel to the line of flight.

Clubface A golf club's face.

Clubhouse A building where equipment is kept and where golfers can change clothing and relax.

Concede The act of acknowledging in advance that an opponent will make a shot, which permits the opponent to get credit for making the shot without the bother of having to take it.

Course The playing area for golf.

Cup The hole in the putting green that the ball enters.

Curtis Cup British sisters Harriet and Margaret Curtis were excellent golfers who between them won the U.S. Ladies Golf Championship four times. In 1932 they presented the Curtis Cup for competition. Teams of women golfers representing each country compete for the cup annually, with the site alternating between Great Britain and the United States.

Designated Tournament A tournament that a golfing association requires all of its top players to perform in.

Deuce Two strokes scored on a hole.

Dimple Little craters on a golf ball that aid the accuracy of flight and the roll of the ball.

Divot Golfers become part-time gardeners as they replace the piece of sod ripped out by their clubs. The piece of sod is referred to as a *divot*, which is a Scottish word meaning a piece of turf.

Dogleg A fairway bend that crooks in a similar manner to the hind leg of a dog.

Dormie In golf, a player is in this condition if he is as many holes up as there are holes remaining to be played. Apparently the term evolved from the French word *endormi* ("asleep"). Thus, a player who is dormie up "can go to sleep," for there is not much purpose for further exertion.

Double Bogey Two over par for a hole.

Double Eagle Three under par for a hole (two strokes used to make a par-5 hole).

Down The number of holes or strokes that a player trails an opponent by.

Downhiller A putt that has to roll down a green that slopes in the direction of the cup.

Draw A shot that curves slightly from right to left with a slight hook.

Driver The number 1 wood club, used most often from the teeing-off area.

Drop To drop a ball in another spot away from an unplayable lie (Free Drop).

Dub An ineffective golfer; a poor shot.

Duffer A player lacking skill.

Eagle Two strokes below par for a hole (except for par-3 holes).

Eisenhower Cup Named for former president Dwight D. Eisenhower, who presented it, this cup originated in 1958. It symbolizes a golf tournament for teams of four amateurs from each competing country. It is also known as the World Cup.

"El Niño" Sergio Garcia was given this nickname by Spain's Jose Manuel Lara who maintained the idea came at the Dubai Desert Classic. It means "the boy" or better "the naughty boy." Lara explained: "I gave him the name when we were playing on the Spanish amateur team. He was rushing around the course, and I told him he was like El Niño."

Even Par A score of par on a hole or round.

Exempt Player One not required to qualify for a tournament.

Explosion Shot A forceful shot hit in a sand trap that powers the ball up and out of the trap and moves out quite a bit of sand (Blast).

Face The flat contact surface of a golf club (Clubface).

Fade A shot that curves in the air to the left or right.

Fairway An area of short, mowed grass between the teeing-off area and the putting green.

Fat The putting-green area away from the shot.

"Fat Jack" ("Whale Boy") Jack Nicklaus won the U.S. Open Championship, and with that arrived on the world stage. The press was not endeared to him though, viewing him as a young upstart challenging the huge popularity of Arnold Palmer. His bulky physique was the root of his nicknames. Gradually though, Nicklaus won over critics with the sheer excellence of his golf.

Fat Shot A swing in which the clubhead hits the ground before the ball, thus cutting down the distance of the shot.

Flag A marker placed on the green to indicate the location of the cup; it consists of a thin pole with the number of the hole printed on a flap attached to its top (Flagstick, Pin).

Flat Swing A technique for swinging at the ball in which a less-vertical and more-horizontal swing than usual is used.

Flight The path of the ball while in the air.

"Fluff" Mike Cowan, the old caddie for Tiger Woods, because of his mustache.

"Fore" This traditional shout to other golfers or bystanders to caution them that they may be hit by a ball is apparently an abridged version of the cry "Beware before."

Form A player's stance.

Foursome Four golfers playing together, hitting their own balls and keeping their own scores. In match play, two partners on each side playing one ball per side and sharing turns hitting the ball.

Front Nine The first nine holes on an eighteen-hole course.

Gallery The spectators at a tournament.

"Gene the Machine" Gene Littler, because of his perfect swing and consistent ball striking.

"Gentle Ben" Ben Crenshaw had this ironic nickname because he was known for his furious temper.

Gimme A putt so easy that it is conceded to an opponent.

"Golden Bear" Jack Nicklaus because of his blonde hair and bearlike stature. He was called "Ohio Fats" until he lost weight in his thirties.

Golf The "modern" birthplace of the sport of golf is the fabled St. Andrews course in Scotland, which was established in 1552. The Honourable Company of the Royal and Ancient Club—the Society of St. Andrews Golfers—in 1754 formulated the "thirteen articles" that form the bedrock of rules of the sport to this day. The actual word "golf" is allegedly derived from the Scottish word *goulf* which meant to "strike" or "cuff." As a noun, *goulf* referred to a "blow."

Many generations before the Scots, a form of golf existed. The Roman sport of *paganica* or the "country game" involved players swinging away with a club at a leather-covered ball that was stuffed with feathers. Frenchmen and Belgians knocked away at a wooden ball in their games of *crosse, chole,* and *jeu de mail.* The clubs they used came in all sizes, shapes, and textures. Sometimes in the game of *chole,* a leather ball stuffed with hay served as the replacement for the traditional wooden sphere. In other sections of the world, other national groups had games that were primitive versions of golf.

Golfing Irons/Woods Once upon a time the names of golfing irons and woods were more picturesque, but also more confusing. Why the names changed was mainly for convenience, but for the record here are the approximate matchups:

Modern Name	Old Name
No. 1 iron	Driving Iron
No. 2 iron	Midiron
No. 3 iron	Driving Mashie
No. 4 iron	Mashie-Iron

No. 5 iron	Mashie
No. 6 iron	Spade Mashie
No. 7 iron	Mashie Niblick
No. 8 iron	Lofter
No. 9 iron	Niblick
No. 10 iron	Wedge
No. 1 wood	Driver
No. 2 wood	Brassie
No. 3 wood	Spoon
No. 4 wood	Cleek

Grand Slam In 1930 the term was used in golf to describe the four major-tournament victories of Bobby Jones—the winning of the British and U.S. open and amateur championships. His unique accomplishment was also called the "Impregnable Quadrilateral." The modern use of the term, which came into vogue after World War II, refers to the winning of the U.S. Open, the British Open, the Masters, and the U.S. Professional Golfers' Association (PGA) Championship by one player in the same year. No golfer has ever won the modern Grand Slam.

"Great White Shark" Greg Norman, for his hair, attitude, and skills. He dominated the golf world for much of the 1980s and early 1990s with his aggressive game and charismatic demeanor. He was labeled the "Great White Shark" by a newspaper columnist during the 1981 Masters Tournament (White Shark).

Green An area of short, mowed grass at the end of a fairway that contains the hole the ball must go into (Putting Green).

Greens Fee Monetary charge for playing a course.

Greenside At or close to the green.

Grip The position of the hands on the club. Also, the rubber or elastic material on the hand position of the club.

"The Grip" John Ed Fiori had a powerful grip.

Ground In addressing the ball, to touch the head of the club to the ground in back of the ball.

"Haig" ("Sir Walter") Walter C. Hagen was a flamboyant figure and one of the top golfers in the Golden Age of sports—the winner of eleven national championships. Between 1914 and 1929, he won the PGA Championship five times. His nickname was an affectionate shortening of his last name. Hagen was the world's first full-time tournament professional, winning so often and in such lavish style that he single-handedly ushered in the time of the playing pro. Golf's greatest showman, he was a flamboyant and extremely talented player.

Handicap A certain number of strokes allowed to a golfer competing against a more skillful opponent; this handicap is deducted from the weaker player's final score.

Hazard Creeks, ditches, ponds, rivers, sand traps—features built into a course to offer extra challenges to a golfer.

Hit a Ball Fat To swing at a ball and get the clubhead low so that the shot goes high but short.

Hole The cup: the four-inch-diameter, usually four-inch-deep target the ball is aimed at. The term also refers to the total playing area from the tee to the hole—the eighteenth hole, and so forth.

Holeable An easy shot to make.

Hole High An approach shot that stops at one side of and generally even with the hole.

Hole in One Hitting the ball from the tee into the hole in one stroke (Ace).

Hole Out To hit the ball into the hole.

Home Hole The final hole in a round or on a course.

Honor The right or privilege to tee off first.

Hook To hit a ball that veers in the opposite direction (a right-handed golfer's hook would go left; a left-handed golfer's hook would go right).

Hooker A golfer who has a tendency to hook the ball.

Indian Express Jyoti Randhawa, for background and skills.

Irons Clubs made of steel and numbered 2–9 that have thin, bladelike heads and in most cases provide greater accuracy and loft than do woods.

"Ivan the Terrible" Ivan Gantz, a club pro from Indiana who played part-time on the PGA Tour, was famous because of his spontaneous outbursts.

"The King" Arnold Palmer, probably did more to promote golf than anyone else. In his time as a great player, golf first appeared on television and Palmer became a hero. Fans loved his aggressive play and risky shots.

"Laughing Dutchman" Robert-Jan Derksen, because of a smiley manner.

"Lawrence of Arabia" Zimbabwe's Tony Johnstone gave himself a nickname for his expertise in bunkers and style.

Lay Up Hitting a ball and getting it to stop ahead of time to avoid its going into a hazard.

Lie Where the ball comes to rest after being stroked. Also, an angle between the blade and the stick shaft.

Like As We Lie A term describing the playing of a hole or holes in the same number of strokes as a competitor.

Line The path a ball is going to travel as a golfer plays a hole.

Links A golf course with stretches of flat, undulating land along the seashore, covered with short grass.

Linksman A golfer.

Lip The rim of the golf cup; to get the ball to hit the rim but not drop into the cup.

"Little Easy" Retief Goosen, of mild character and easy, smooth swing.

Loft The angle of a club's face away from vertical. Also, the lifting of a ball into a high arc.

Lofting Iron The number 8 club, which has characteristics that enable it to loft the ball.

Long Game Long drives and shots make up this playing strategy or need.

Long Iron Long-distance irons: 1, 2, 3.

"Long John" ("The Wild Thing") Wild driving, wild drinking, and wild gambling John Daly.

Loose Impediment Not fixed or growing, or unnatural, objects that can be removed in order that the ball may be played.

"Lord" Byron Nelson.

Lost Ball Competitive regulations state that after five minutes of search, a ball that is not found is lost; another ball can be substituted for it and the player takes a one-stroke penalty and replays his shot.

Marker Scorer. Also, a coin or small, flat object placed on the ground to mark the position of a ball that is lifted by a golfer.

Mashie There are quite a few interesting theories as to how the club that today is called a number 5 iron got its original name. The Scottish kitchen utensil employed to make mashed potatoes did not resemble the club in appearance, but one theory states that what the club did to a golf ball when used by golfers lacking skill had the same "mashing" effect. Another explanation for how the term got its name was provided by J. H. Taylor, a golfer skilled in the use of the club. Taylor claimed that when the mashie was first used in 1888, it took its name from the "mashers" of the time—sophisticated, modern males who had a way with the ladies. The club, also new and also sophisticated, took its name from the play on words off "mashers," he explained. The simplest explanation for how "mashie" came to be is it evolved from the French word *massue* (club).

Mashie-Iron The number 4 iron.

Mashie Niblick The number 7 iron.

Masters Tournament The leading U.S. international golf tournament originated in 1934 at the Augusta National Golf Course in Georgia. Entry into the tournament is restricted to those invited by the club. Generally participants are picked on the basis of winning a major tournament during the previous year. The Augusta National Club was the creation of golfing great Bobby Jones and his colleague Clifford Roberts. The site of the course formerly was a famous horticultural nursery that covered some 365 acres. The location was ideal for a golf course, with its numerous trees and shrubs and its fertile land. Construction work on the course began in 1931, guided by Jones, who hit hundreds of shots to set up the best positions for hazards, tees, and greens. The first Augusta National Invitation meeting was held in 1934 and was restricted to the current and past winners of tournaments. From this policy came the name "Masters." Bobby Jones considered the name too high sounding, but others liked it and it has remained.

Match Foursome A competition where one ball is alternately shared by two partners pitted against another set of partners who also share one ball.

Match Play Scoring in this competition is tallied after each hole; the winner of the most holes wins the competition.

"Mechanical Man" Famed golfer Byron Nelson was given this alliterative title because of his smoothness and machinelike efficiency on the golf course.

Medalist Tournament medal play's low scorer.

"Merry Mex" Lee Trevino, for his ethnic background and demeanor.

"Mighty Mouse" Jerry Bruner, Seniors Tour star; a very small man who hits very long.

Miss Higgins A major obstacle to women golfers in the early days was their skirts. Billowy and bulky, they made it very frustrating for women to view the ball on the ground, especially with any kind of wind blowing. The problem was solved by an American golfer named Miss Higgins, who devised an elastic encirclement that could be slipped down from the waist to put the skirt in its place. This piece of elastic ingenuity was named after its innovator.

"Mr. November" Mike Weir won million-dollar tournaments in November 2000 and 2001. He was winless in other months.

Mulligan An extra or free shot granted in a friendly game to a player whose last shot was ineffective.

"Nacho" Ignacio Garrido from Spain; an easier reference especially for newspaper headlines.

Nassau Three matches in one: one point is scored for the first nine holes, another for the next nine, and another for the total eighteen.

Neck A position on a golf club's head close to the point where it leads into the shaft.

Net The score that remains after the handicap is deducted.

Niblick The number 9 iron.

Obstruction An artificial interference that may be legally removed.

Odd A stroke that, after a golfer hits it, becomes one more than his opponent needed to win a specific hole. Also, a handicap stroke.

Open A tournament open to amateurs and professionals.

"Open Doctor" Golf architects Robert Trent Jones (1906–2000) and his son Rees Jones designed, redesigned, or improved many courses where U.S. Opens have been played. The Jones philosophy: "Hard par, easy bogey."

Out The first nine holes, as contrasted to the second (back) nine.

Out of Bounds Out of the area defined by the boundary markers; a ball hit here can be replayed with a one-stroke penalty from a spot as close to where the ball went out of bounds as possible.

Outside Agency One forbidden to give advice to a golfer during a match (partners and caddies are permitted).

Par The number of strokes that course officials have judged necessary for a ball to be hit into a hole or for the total holes on a course. (Below Par is to use fewer strokes than have been deemed necessary.)

"Peanut" South Korea's Mi Hyun Kim, only 5-foot-1.

Penalty The adding of an additional stroke for a player who has to drop his ball from a hazard or put another ball in play.

Penalty Stroke A situation where a violation of playing rules adds an extra stroke to the score of a player.

"Phil the Thrill" Phil Mickelson, a chance taker and a thrill seeker.

Pin Another word for the flagstick.

Pitch and Run To play a shot so that part of the desired distance is covered by the roll of the ball after it strikes the ground.

Pitch Shot A lofting shot to the green, generally hit with backspin.

Play Through Move ahead of another golfer or group that plays slowly.

"Popeye" Australian Craig Parry has this moniker. He is chunky, small, and a fighter.

Pro-Am The pairing of a pro golfer with an amateur.

Provisional Ball A ball that is substituted for a lost ball.

Push A straight-line stroke angled to the side of the player's dominant hand.

Putt A soft stroke of the ball with a putter on the putting green, usually aimed at sinking the shot.

Putter The last-used club, used for rolling short and accurate shots on the green and into the hole. Also, a player who is putting.

Putting for Par A shot that, if made, assures par to the golfer.

"Queen of Mean" Danielle Ammacapane, nickname self-explanatory.

"Radar" Mike Reid, one of the straightest drivers on tour, has a resemblance to the character in *M*A*S*H*.

Ryder Cup American and British golf pros competed unofficially against each other in 1926. The British team won thirteen matches, lost one, and tied one. The "American" team included three Britishers and one Australian. And despite the lopsided score, the competition was well received. Samuel Ryder, a prosperous seed merchant, agreed to donate a gold cup to symbolize a competition to be held every two years between the United States and Great Britain. Valued at £750 back then, the cup and the competition named for Samuel Ryder have grown much in value since that time. The first Ryder Cup matches were held at Worcester, Massachusetts. The United States won nine matches, Britain two, and one match was tied. During his lifetime Ryder, the man, was known not only for the cup he donated but also for his generous aid for the expenses of the British teams.

"Seoul Sisters" Koreans Mi Hyun Kim and Hee-Won Han, and Se Ri Pak and Gloria Park.

"Silver Scot" Despite the loss of sight in one eye as a result of a World War I gas attack, Tommy Armour stands as one of golf's legends. His silver hair and the fact that he was born in Scotland led to his nickname.

"Slammin' Sammy" Sam Snead is one of golf's immortals. His alliterative nickname sprang from the verve of his personality and his style of play. An easygoing, likable man, Snead claimed he kept all his prize money in tin cans that he buried near his West Virginia home, ("The King of Swing," "The Slammer," "West Virginia Hillbilly").

"Slick" Davis Love III, is not quite.

"Smiling Assassin" Shigeki Maruyama from Japan, known on the U.S. tour as amiable but dead on game.

"Spade" In his early years as a golfer, Byron Nelson was called by that nickname. Nelson explained that when he walked to the tee he was at ease for it was all about a 6-iron shot. A spade then was a 6-iron.

"Spec" David Goldman (1909–2001), amateur golfer who was triumphant in more than two hundred tournaments, picked up his nickname for his freckles.

Square Tied up, having the same score.

"The Squire" Gene Sarazen was called by that name, a reference to his love for farming.

Stroke A swing at the ball that is charged to a player even if no contact with the ball is made.

Stroke Hole A hole where the handicap stroke is awarded.

Sudden Death A method of breaking a tied match: the first player to win a hole wins the match.

"Sunshine" Paul Goydos's nickname was pinned on him because of his ability to find the dark cloud in every silver lining.

"Tank" Laura Davies, for her huge body and great power.

"Tank" K. J. Choi, the first Korean-born player to earn a PGA Tour Card, as a youth was a power lifter. He was able to squat 350 pounds as a ninety-five-pound thirteen-year old.

Tee A wooden or plastic peg that raises the ball a bit off the ground to aid a golfer when he or she tees off (drives the ball).

Teeing Ground The driving area from which a ball is hit at the start of play on a hole.

Tee Off To start play on a hole by hitting the ball off the tee.

Tee Shot A long shot; a shot hit off the tee.

Tee Up To put the ball on the tee.

Three-Putt To take three putts before sinking a shot (the formula for par for a hole mandates two putts).

Through the Green The conditions affecting play from the time the ball is hit from the tee until it reaches the green; hazards, but not the rough, are exceptions.

"Tiger" The living legend Eldrick "Tiger" Woods was named after one of his father's friends, a soldier in Vietnam.

"Tigress" ("Webby") Karrie Webb's nickname from Tiger Woods derivation.

"Tommy Thunder Bolt" ("Tommy Terrible Bolt") Thomas Henry Bolt, for his temper tantrums and throwing or breaking clubs. In 1957, he broke a 4-wood against a pipe. Hitting two shots into the water in the 1960 U.S. Open at Cherry Hill, New Jersey, made Bolt throw his driver into the lake.

Top To hit the ball above its center.

Trap Shot A shot executed from a sand trap.

Triple Bogey Three strokes over par on a hole.

Vardon Grip Named for golfing great Harry Vardon and also known as the overlapping grip, this is the grip employed by most top golfers. Vardon's actual description of what he did is as follows: "The right hand is brought up so high that the palm of it covers over the left thumb, leaving very little of the latter to be seen. The first and second fingers of the right hand just reach round to the thumb of the left and the third finger completes the overlapping process, so that the club is held in the grip as if it were in a vice. The little finger of the right hand rides on the first finger of the left" (see Vardon Trophy).

Vardon Trophy Golf's award for the performer with the lowest average each year on the pro tour is named for Harry Vardon, six-time British Open winner and one-time U.S. Open champ. The first Vardon Trophy winner was Sam Snead in 1950 with a 69.23 average, which to date has not been beaten (see Vardon Grip).

Waggle To move the club in a rhythmic manner back and forth over the ball to get coordination and concentration before actually hitting the ball.

Walker Cup George A. Walker, former president of the United States Golf Association, donated a trophy for an international annual golf competition. The newspapers called the trophy the Walker Cup. Walker's plan evolved into a British-American golfing competition that, after being held annually in 1922, 1923, and 1924, became a biennial event.

"Walrus" Craig Stadler's nickname is derived from his famous moustache.

Water Hazard A hazard with water in it.

Wedge An iron effective for lofting the ball from an area near the putting green.

"Wee Ice Mon" Ben Hogan was called this because of his strong and silent play when he won the British Open in 1953.

Wood Clubs with hardwood heads that are numbered 1–5, used for long-distance shots.

Yip To hit the ball poorly when putting and so that it does not go into the hole.

Yips Pressures (real or imagined) that affect a golfer's quality of play.

Gymnastics

Aerial A procedure in which a gymnast turns over completely in the air and does not touch the floor with his or her hands.

Air Sense Awareness and a feel for position in the air.

All-Around Gymnast One who participates in all events.

Amplitude The maximum possible upward and outward extension or lift.

A-Part Lower-value movement.

Apparatus Gymnastic equipment.

Arch Position A position in which the body is bent backward in a curved and overextended position.

B-Part Intermediate-value movement.

Circles A movement in which the gymnast keeps both legs firmly together while rotating his or her body around the pommel horse.

Code of Points International book of rules for gymnastic competition.

Combination An exercise's construction; the correct sequence of moves and requirements throughout a routine.

Compulsories Required routines that are prearranged and have specific moves.

C-Part Superior-value movement.

Crash Pad A soft mat used in practice for safety.

Difficulty A movement's difficulty and risk.

Difficulty Rating A value assigned to a movement for its risk and effort.

Dismount The movement from a piece of equipment to the floor, the final procedure in a routine.

Dorsal Grip Movement executed with high bar gripped behind gymnast's back.

Emery Cloth A kind of sandpaper used to take off excess chalk that builds up on equipment.

Execution The style of performing movements.

Fall An accidental or unintentional landing on the mat.

Floor Mats Soft and padded mats, generally one to two inches thick, used to cushion landing impact.

Form A position in which the feet and toes are pointed and the legs are kept straight and tightly together.

Full Difficulty Meeting all the requirements in addition to risk.

Grips Handguards.

Gymnastics In conquering Greece the legions of Rome discovered the gymnasiums—places where the Greeks exercised (*gymna-zein,* "to exercise naked"). The Romans modified the Greek exercises into supplements to their military training and thus indirectly advanced the sport of gymnastics.

Hanging Position A position in which a gymnast hangs by his or her hands from the equipment.

Height How high a trick is performed above the floor or the apparatus.

Hop An action that takes place during the landing part of a dismount that involves stepping forward with two feet in an attempt to regain balance.

Intermediate Swing An extra swing of no value.

International Style The appropriate method of executing a maneuver.

Inverted Position A position in which the feet are placed directly over the head.

Kip The movement from a hanging position (under the equipment) to a support position (above the equipment).

L-Position A condition in which the body is bent forward ninety degrees at the hips.

Landing The final mat position after finishing a dismount.

Landing Mat A mat approximately four inches thick, generally found in the landing area for dismounts from the apparatus.

Layout Position A position in which the body during a movement is kept straight or arched to a degree; a still position.

Leg Work The legs are kept apart during these movements on the pommel horse (Single Leg Work, Scissors).

Lineup A list of participants for each event.

Mount Getting up and onto equipment; the first movement of a routine.

"Old One Leg" Nicolai Andrianov, Russian gymnast, could keep his legs straight and together during extremely difficult exercises, making it look as if he had only one leg.

Optionals Freestyle routines or movements chosen by a participant.

Parallel Bars A set of wooden bars, generally about eleven and a half feet long, five and a half feet high, and sixteen inches apart, upon which gymnastic movements such as balances, somersaults, and swings are performed.

Part A single skill or movement.

Part of No Value A skill so basic and simple that it does not even deserve an A-part rating.

Pass Sequential floor exercise moves in one direction.

Pike Position A position in which the body is bent forward at the hips, with the legs held still.

Pommel Horse A structure upon which swings and balancing feats are performed in men's gymnastics topped with two pommels (grips) approximately sixteen inches apart.

Pommels The wooden handles positioned on the top side of the pommel horse.

Postflight An interval in the vault from the horse to the landing mat.

Preflight An interval in the vault from the springboard to the horse.

Repulsion The pushing of the hands to lift a gymnast off the body of the horse in a vault.

Requirements Prescribed positions, skills, and releases for a routine.

Rip Skin torn off the palm of the hand.

Rosin A substance placed on slippers for improved traction.

Routine The full set of skills executed in one event.

Runway The approach aisle for running into a vault.

Sequence A series of movements.

Somersault A complete circular movement of the body in the air.

Split The movement of spreading the legs as wide apart as possible.

Spotter An aide stationed near the apparatus to guide or help a gymnast who falls.

Springboard A takeoff board (Ruether Board).

Stop Position A momentary hesitation in the performance of a movement.

Straddle Position Spreading the legs sideways as wide as possible.

Strength Part A movement executed with strength.

Superior Difficulty A rating assigned to a movement of extreme risk and tremendous effort.

Support Position A position in which the body weight is supported by a gymnast's hands and arms, which are positioned above the equipment.

Swinging Part A movement executed with a swinging motion of the body.

Trajectory The curving line of a vault.

Trampoline American George Nissen formally named this gymnastic apparatus in 1926, but its name stretches back to the circuses of the Middle Ages, in which similar devices were used. The word *trampoline* is derived from the Italian word for "stilt"—and stilts were what acrobats used back then on makeshift trampolines.

Transitions The connecting parts linking men's floor-exercise tumbling sections.

Trick Movement; skill.

Tuck Position Bent knees and legs held tightly against the chest with the hands characterizes this position.

Vaulting Horse A structure which is used for vaulting feats in gymnastics; it is a leather-covered rectangular form and is vaulted from end to end by male gymnasts and side to side by female gymnasts.

Vaulting Zones The three sections on the horse body indicated for hand placement.

Handball

Ace Flawless serve that cannot be returned by an opponent.

Avoidable Hinder Interference that is illegal because a player either gets in the way of another, not allowing a shot at the ball, or positions himself so that he is struck by a ball hit by his opponent.

Backcourt An area between the short line and the back wall.

Back-Wall Shot A shot made off a ball that rebounds off the back wall.

Bottom-Board Kill A powerfully hit shot struck very low so that as it rebounds from the front wall it does not even bounce (Flat Kill, Rollout).

Ceiling Shot A shot that hits the ceiling before striking the front wall—a defensive tactic.

Center Court A position near the short line in the middle of the court.

Changeup A slow serve performed with a sidearm stroke at half speed.

Corner Kill A shot hit with much force at one of the front corners that strikes two walls prior to bouncing on the floor.

Court The playing area, which is twenty feet wide, twenty feet high, and forty feet long, with a twelve-foot or higher back wall.

Court Hinder The striking of a court construction (a door latch, for example) by the ball, which constitutes an automatic hinder.

Cross-Corner Kill A corner kill shot hit on a diagonal across the court to the front corner opposite the hand that strikes the ball.

Crotch Ball The striking of two surfaces by a ball at the same time.

Cut Off To hit the ball as it rebounds from the front wall just before it bounces on the floor (Fly Ball).

Cutthroat A game of handball played by three players.

Dead Ball A ball out of play without penalty.

Defensive Shot A shot hit to move an opponent into a position near the back wall.

Dig To get to a low shot just before it bounces for the second time.

Doubles A game that involves two players on each side.

Doubles Box An area next to the side walls in the service zone where a player must stay until the moment his partner's serve has crossed the short line.

Drive A powerful shot against the front wall that causes the ball to rebound quickly.

English Spin given to the ball to make it hook.

Error A player's inability to legally return a ball after having gotten his hand on it.

Fault A ball that is illegally served, causing a penalty.

Fist Ball A ball struck with a closed fist.

Foot Fault A server's fault caused when one or both feet are outside the service zone during the serve.

Four-Wall Handball A game played inside an enclosed four-wall court—the most popular style of handball.

Freeze Out A doubles strategy that sees both players on one team attempt to get all their shots to one of the players on the other, thus keeping the allegedly more-skilled partner out of the action.

Front Court The area of the court between the front wall and short line.

Game The player or team that is the first to score twenty-one points wins.

Handout A doubles-team player who serves first and loses the service.

Hinder Accidental interference with an opponent or the ball that does not involve a penalty.

Hit To strike the ball.

Hook The breaking to the left or right of a ball after it hits off the front wall and strikes the floor (Hop).

Inning The period of time service is held by a player or team.

Inside Corner Kill A corner kill shot in which the ball strikes the front wall first.

Irish Whip A stroking motion in which the ball is hit close to the body with an underarm technique.

Kill A low scoring shot against the front wall that prevents an opponent from making a legal return.

Left-Side Player A doubles player responsible for the left side of the court.

Lob A shot that is hit high and softly against the front wall and then drops severely and takes a high bounce to the court's rear.

Long A serve that initially strikes the front wall and then rebounds to the back wall before making contact with the floor (Short Serve).

Match The winning of two of three games.

Natural Hook A ball hit with the right hand that breaks to the left after rebounding from the front wall and hitting the ground; the ball will break to the right if hit with the left hand.

Offensive Position Stance taken by a player who is positioned with his feet set and is able to stroke the ball sidearm or underarm.

One-Wall Handball A type of handball played on a court that has just one wall.

Out Loss of service.

Outside Corner Kill Ball strikes side wall prior to hitting the front wall in this corner kill shot.

Overhand Stroke Generally a defensive shot in which a player hits the ball from a shoulder-high or higher position.

Pass Shot Shot that scores as a result of being struck at an angle, causing it to rebound out of reach of an opponent.

Point The serving side's tally.

Rally The playing of the ball by both sides after the ball is served and until one of the sides is unable to make a legal return.

Receiver(s) The player or players the ball is served to.

Referee The official in charge of a tournament match.

Reverse Hook Opposite of a natural hook.

Right-Side Player A doubles player responsible for the right side of the court.

Scotch Twist An angled serve aimed at striking close to the front-wall corner and then striking the side wall and rebounding diagonally toward the opposite side wall close to the back wall.

Semiglass Court Part of the side wall(s) and/or back wall is made of glass on this type of handball court.

Serve To put the ball in play.

Server The person who puts the ball in play.

Service Line A line parallel to and fifteen feet from the front wall.

Setup An easy opportunity for a player to make a scoring shot.

Shadow Serve Ball that is illegally served because it passes too close to the server, making it impossible for the receiver to see the ball until it is too late for him to make a return; no penalty is involved.

Shoot An attempt at a kill shot.

Short A serve that is illegal because of a "fault" or penalty by the server.

Short Line A line on a one-wall handball court that is sixteen feet from the wall and parallel to it.

Three-Wall Return A defensive shot that hits three walls (side wall, front wall, side wall) before hitting the floor.

Trap Shot A ball that is struck very close to the floor immediately after it bounces.

Hockey

Alternate Captain A player who is given the captain's duties when the official team captain is off the ice.

Amateur A performer in an amateur league who is paid and may also be given room and board.

Anaheim Mighty Ducks Named for the *Mighty Ducks* Disney movie starring Emilio Estevez. The team was owned by Disney after it joined the National Hockey League (NHL) as an expansion team in 1993. In 2005, Disney sold the team to private interests.

Art Ross Trophy The National Hockey League's award for the leading point scorer, it was presented to the league in 1947 in the name of former Boston manager-coach Arthur Howie Ross.

Assist Credit for helping in the scoring of a goal, generally given to the two players who last handled the puck prior to a score.

Atlanta Thrashers Named after the state bird of Georgia, the brown thrasher.

Attacking Zone The area of the rink that extends from the opposition's blue line to the goal line.

Avco World Trophy The World Hockey Association's best-of-seven-games championship series was named for Avco Financial Services, the league's major sponsor and donor. The first championship, in 1973, was won by the New England Whalers.

"Babe Ruth of Hockey" Eddie Shore of the National Hockey League Boston Bruins played for almost two decades, picking up nearly one thousand stitches in a brawling, no-holds-barred career. A defenseman who skated the length of the ice when the occasion demanded it, a crowd pleaser on his home ice, and a target for fans on the road, Shore was a seven-time All-Star and four-time Most Valuable Player. He made people notice hockey in the same way Babe Ruth made people notice baseball, and that was part of the reason for his nickname. Former Boston trainer Hammy Moore offered another reason: "Eddie was the only player I ever saw who had the whole arena standing every time he rushed down the ice . . . when he carried the puck you were *always* sure something would happen. He would either end up bashing somebody, get into a fight, or score a goal."

Back-Check Quick maneuvering against an offensive rush by a player skating back to defend the goal.

Backhand Passing or shooting with the back striking surface of the hockey stick; the name comes from the control exerted on the stick with the back of the lower hand.

Back Line Defenders.

Back-Skating Skating backward while facing an oncoming opponent.

Bad Goal A score that results from a defensive lapse, generally by the goaltender.

Banana Blade A hockey stick's very curved striking surface.

Beat the Defense To get by one or both defensemen.

Beat the Goalie Outwitting the goalie to score a goal.

Behind the Net Area of ice behind the goal cage.

Bench Penalty A penalty resulting from illegal behavior by members of a team's bench, including a coach; any team member may be designated by the coach to serve this two-minute penalty.

"Big Bird" His size and weight earned him the nickname as well as his tenacious defensive play. Larry Robinson is remembered best for his time as a Montreal Canadien, a team he won six Stanley Cup championships with. The Hall of Famer set records for appearing in the postseason twenty consecutive years.

Bill Masterton Memorial Trophy The National Hockey League's award for perseverance, sportsmanship, and dedication to hockey, it was presented to the league in 1966 to honor the name of the Minnesota North Star player, who died that year.

Blade The hockey stick's striking surface.

Blind Pass To pass the puck without looking.

"Blinky" This indelicate nickname was given to National Hockey League immortal Gordie Howe because of the slight facial tic an old injury gave him. In later years Howe was dubbed "Old Blinky."

Blocked Shot An attempt to score that is blocked before it gets to the goal.

Blueliner Defenseman.

Blue Lines Lines one foot wide and sixty feet toward the center from each goal line; mainly used to determine offsides, they divide the rink into the defensive, attacking, and neutral zones.

The Blues In 1885, the Oxford University Ice Hockey Club was formed, as the story goes, by Canadian students from Montreal who brought the new, exciting game with them. The OUIHC is the world's second-oldest club.

Board Check Illegally knocking an opponent into the walls surrounding the ring by hard checking (Boarding).

Board Pass Using the boards to pass the puck off to a teammate.

Boards A continuous wooden wall forty-two inches high that functions as a rink enclosure.

Body Checking The legal use of the upper part of the body to block an opponent by hitting him above the knees from the side or front after using no more than two strides to reach the opponent.

"Boom-Boom" Bernie Geoffrion invented the slapshot in ice hockey. His stick hit the puck so hard, it made a boom sound.

Boston Bruins When Charles Adams became the owner of the Boston hockey franchise in the mid-1920s, the colors for the team were more important for him than the team's name. Adams was president of Brookside Stores, whose colors were brown with yellow trim. He required the same colors for his team. The name Bruins was selected under contest guidelines: "The name chosen should preferably relate to an untamed animal whose name was synonymous with size, strength, agility, ferocity, and cunning; and in the color brown category."

Box Defense A formation used by penalty killers to defend against a power play.

Break A chance to begin a rush when defending players are caught out of position.

Breakaway A sudden rush at an opponent's goal before the defense has a chance to get set, leaving only the goalkeeper to beat for a goal.

Breaking Pass A timed pass to a teammate who skates into position to receive it.

Breakout Offensive strategy to move the puck from the defensive zone of a team.

Broad Street Bullies Teams that came to play the Philadelphia Flyers teams hated to arrive at Broad Street and enter the Spectrum, where they had to come against a very aggressive style of play.

Buffalo Sabres The name came via a contest where the franchise owners sought a variation on "Buffalo" or "Bison."

Butt Ending An illegal move: hitting an opponent with the butt end of the hockey stick.

Calder Memorial Trophy The National Hockey League's trophy for a top rookie, it is named after former NHL President Frank Calder.

Calgary Flames The franchise was originally located in Atlanta from 1972 to 1980 and was also called "Hot Lanta" for the historic burning of Atlanta in the Civil War. The name was kept after the Flames moved to Calgary in 1980, with the flaming "A" on the front of the players' jerseys being replaced by a flaming "C." By 1988 the name took on a new meaning from the 1988 Calgary Olympics flames.

Carolina Hurricanes Team name was a nod to hurricanes that often hit the Carolinas. Franchise was Hartford Whalers in the WHA in 1972; it moved to NHL in 1979 and to North Carolina in 1997.

Carom Rebound of the puck off the boards or any other object.

Carrying the Puck Advancing the puck via stick handling.

Catching Glove The goaltender's glove, used to catch high or on-ice shots.

Center The position of center on the line (Centerman).

Center Face-Off Circle A thirty-foot-diameter circle at midrink where the opening face-off and every face-off after a goal is scored takes place.

Center Ice The area between the blue lines; the neutral zone.

Centering Pass Pass from an attacking player toward the middle of the ice to a teammate with a better angle at the goal.

Center Line Red, twelve-inch-wide line across the ice midway between the two goals.

Challenge the Shooter A situation where the goaltender does not yield his position to a shooter.

Changing on the Fly Making player substitutions while the game is in progress.

Charging Illegally running into an opponent by taking more than two strides before hitting him.

Checking Close guarding of a player.

Checking Line A defensive-specialist forward line that checks the highest scoring forward line of the opposition.

Chicago Blackhawks Since 1926, named for the Army regiment of the owner, and the historical Chief Black Hawk. In 1986 Black Hawks changed to Blackhawks. Other nicknames: WHA Cougars 1972–1975.

"Chicoutimi Cucumber" Georges Vezina, Montreal goalie (1917–1926), was born in Chicoutimi, Quebec, in January 1887. Part of his nickname derived from his birthplace. The "cool as a cucumber" playing style used by Vezina explained the other half of his nickname. Overall, Vezina's nickname made for amusing alliteration and good sports copy, but it drove proofreaders wild (see Vezina Trophy).

"Chief" Hall of Famer George Armstrong was a huge star for the Toronto Maple Leafs. He spent his childhood in the small town of Falconbridge, near Sudbury, Ontario. He was born of Irish and Algonquin heritage–leading to his nickname. Johnny Bucyk was of Native American descent and had the same nickname.

"China Wall" Johnny Bower grew up very poor in a family of nine children. His goalie pads were from an old mattress, his pucks from "cow pies" (horse manure), his sticks from crooked tree branches shaved by his dad. The young Bower grew up into a terrific hockey player, a fearless goalie. Maskless, he never shied away from attacking any player and in fact patented the most dangerous move a goalie can make—the poke check. Diving head-first into the skates of an attacking player at full speed, he lost virtually every tooth in his mouth from sticks and pucks. Bower was one of the best goalies of all time, a true Hall of Famer. He was like the Great Wall of China on the ice—impenetrable.

Clear The act of a goaltender or a defenseman in passing the puck away from their defensive goal.

Colorado Avalanche This franchise began in 1972 as the Quebec Nordiques. It moved to Colorado in 1995 and took its nickname from the snow avalanches that come out of the Colorado mountains.

Columbus Blue Jackets The name is based on Ohio's pride and patriotism during the Civil War as both the state of Ohio and the city of Columbus were significantly influential for the Union Army. Ohio contributed more of its population to the Union Army than any other state, while many of the uniforms worn by the Union soldiers were manufactured in Columbus.

Conn Smythe Trophy The National Hockey League's playoff Most Valuable Player award, first presented in 1964, this trophy is named after the former Toronto coach-manager-owner.

Corner Any of the four rounded corners of the rink toward the back of the goals.

Cough Up the Puck To lose the puck because of defensive pressure.

Cover Player keeping close to an opponent to prevent him from receiving a pass or making an offensive play.

Cover the Points To hinder the opposing point men's offensive maneuvers by close checking at the blue line.

"Cowboy" Bill Flett was born in Vermillion, Alberta, in July 1943. Flett started playing hockey at the age of five. Bill's father, C. M. Flett, played professional hockey in Los Angeles and Spokane in the old Western League and again with Baltimore of the Eastern League. While growing up in Okotoks, Alberta, Bill started riding in rodeos. And that's where "Cowboy" originated. He played for Los Angeles, Philadelphia, Toronto, Atlanta, and Edmonton. In 1974, Bill won a Stanley Cup as part of the famous Broad Street Bullies.

Crease A rectangular, four-by-eight-foot area in front of each net where goaltenders stand; it is off limits for offensive players without the puck.

Crossbar The goal net's metal-frame top.

Crosschecking Illegally hitting an opponent with the stick held off the ice in both hands.

Crossing Pass An across-the-ice pass.

"CuJo" Curtis Joseph's nickname was a shortening of his first and last names. He was one of the "money" goalies of the 1990s.

Cupping To place a hand over the puck to grip it.

Curved Stick A stick that is concave in shape, not flat.

Cutting Down the Angle The movement of a goaltender out of the net to give a shooter less of a target.

"Cyclone" ("The Listowel Pistol") Born June 23, 1885, Fred Taylor grew up in Listowel, Ontario, and became the grandest star of his era. His nicknames derived from his place of birth and unmatched speed on the ice. His daring ice rushes gave Ottawa and Vancouver fans much to cheer about as he helped bring Stanley Cup championships to both cities.

Dallas Stars From 1967 to 1993 the franchise was in Bloomington, Minnesota, as the "North Stars." In 1978, the Cleveland Barons merged with the Minnesota North Stars and the franchise remained in Minnesota. It moved to Dallas in 1993, as the "Stars."

Dead Puck One that exits the rink or that a player has caught in his hand.

Defensive Defenseman A defenseman whose main responsibility is defense, not offense.

Defensive Forward A forward whose main responsibility is checking rather than offense.

Defensive Line Two defensemen.

Defensive Zone The area extending from either end of the rink to the nearest blue line in which a team defends its own goal.

Deflection A pass or shot that bounces off a player, his stick, or his skate and may go into goal for a score.

Deke A puck handler's faking move.

Delayed Offside The interception of the puck by a defensive player immediately after it crosses the blue line into the attacking zone that causes a delay in calling an offside (when an offensive player loses control of a puck as he is crossing the blue line, an offside is called immediately).

Delayed Penalty If a penalty would result in a team having fewer than four players on the ice, the penalty is temporarily put off. Also, a situation where the team that would benefit from a penalty has a good opportunity to score, in which case the referee will not call the penalty until a goal is scored or the team loses control of the puck.

Delay of Game Minor penalty imposed on any player who purposely delays the game in any way, such as shooting or batting the puck outside the playing area or displacing the goalpost from its normal position.

Detroit Red Wings The Detroit hockey franchise has existed since 1926 and was originally the "Cougars." The name was changed to the "Falcons" in 1929, then to the "Red Wings" when the franchise was purchased by James Norris. He had once played for a team in Montreal known as the "Winged Wheelers" and based on that decided to name his new team the "Red Wings" with a winged wheel as the logo. The logo is a natural fit for Detroit, also known as "The Motor City."

Digging for the Puck Battling for puck control in a crowd of players, generally in a corner of the rink.

"Dipsy Doodle Dandy from Delisle" Max Bentley earned his nickname for his fancy skating and superb stick handling. Youngest of the three NHL Bentleys (Doug and Reggie were the other two), Max grew up on a farm, one of thirteen children, six of whom were boys. All of the kids played hockey. That was his foundation and led him to success with several NHL teams. When Max Bentley retired, he had scored 245 goals—second among active players only to Maurice Richard.

"Dit" National Hockey League Hall of Famer Audrey Victor Clapper was always better known by his nickname, "Dit." For twenty years he wore the number 5 on the back of his Boston Bruins uniform. He explained his nickname this way: "When I was a child, my parents called me Vic. I couldn't say Vic. I'd lisp the name, and it came out Dit. The name stuck, sort of."

Dog a Man To tightly guard an opponent.

"The Dominator" Dominik Hasek won the Hart and Vezina Trophies, and he did it in the same season. The Sabres' defense was always better with "The Dominator" in net.

Double Minor Minor penalty given for certain accidental infractions that result in an injury to another player or for certain deliberate attempts to injure an opponent that are unsuccessful; penalty time of four minutes is served, double that of a normal minor penalty.

Double Shifting To utilize a player on more than one forward line.

Down a Man A situation where one or more of a team's players are in the penalty box and fewer than six men are skating.

Draw A face-off.

Dribble To use the end of the stick to control the puck while maneuvering it on the ice.

Drop Pass The leaving of a puck by the puck carrier for a teammate trailing the play.

Dump the Puck To shoot the puck into the other team's defensive zone from center ice.

Dynamite Line Cooney Weiland, Dutch Gainor, and Dit Clapper powered the Boston Bruins to the 1929 National Hockey League championship. The explosive scoring and checking power of this line earned it its nickname (see "Dit").

Eat the Puck A situation where a defenseman falls on a loose puck or throws his body at a shot at the goal.

Edmonton Oilers Since 1972, named for the once-flourishing oil industry in Alberta. Originally the Alberta Oilers of the WHA.

Elbowing The illegal use of elbows or arms to check an opponent.

Empty-Net Goal A score made into a net that has been left empty because a goaltender has been replaced in the waning moments of a game by an extra skater, in hopes of providing his team with more offense.

Endboards The boards located at the ends of the rink.

Endzones The areas from blue lines to boards behind the goal that constitute the attacking or defensive zones.

Enforcer The "policeman," a strong and tough player who inflicts punishment on opposing team members.

"E-Train" "E" for Eric and "train" for the power and speed of Eric Lindros, center for the New York Rangers.

Extra Man The player sent into a game to replace a goaltender.

Face Mask Protective mask worn by the goalie.

Face-Off The dropping of the puck by the official between the sticks of two opponents to start or resume play (Draw).

Face-Off Circles Five circular areas centered on the face-off spots at center ice and in the end zones and inside which only the official and the two facing-off players are permitted during face-offs.

Face-Off Spots Nine round spots that serve as face-off locations when play is continued in a different zone of the rink or when the action has to be moved from where it was stopped to another point in the rink.

Falling on the Puck Minor penalty taking place when a player other than the goalie closes his hand on the puck, deliberately falls on it, or gathers the puck under his body (Holding the Puck).

Fan on the Puck To miss the puck with the stick in a scoring, passing, or defending move.

"Fast Eddie" Ed Giacomin was one of the most successful and popular players ever to wear the uniform of the New York Rangers. His fiery nature and wandering style on the ice endeared him to the demanding Madison Square Garden supporters. Giacomin also gained fame by taking Jacques Plante's wandering style an extra step further by trying to skate up-ice and hit a teammate with a pass.

Feed the Puck To pass the puck.

"Fiery Phil" Phil Watson of the Rangers was the second player in their history to wear uniform number 7, and he was very instrumental in sparking his team for twelve memorable seasons. Always rough and ready, Watson was a key man on the 1939–1940 Stanley Cup team, centering the "Powerhouse Line" with Lynn Patrick on left wing and Bryan Hextall on the right—one of the most formidable trios in club history.

Fighting Major penalty occurring when two or more players drop their sticks and gloves and fight; if a referee deems one player to be the instigator, that player also receives a minor penalty and a misconduct penalty; the minor penalty for a less severe pushing and shoving match is called "roughing."

Finish-off Play Scoring a goal.

Flat Pass The puck slides flat along the ice in this type of pass.

Flip Pass The puck is lifted off the ice in this type of pass.

Flip Shot The puck is flipped through the air in this shot, which requires good wrist motion.

Floater An offensive player who slips into the center zone behind the attacking defensemen (Hanger).

Flopper A goaltender who frequently falls to the ice to make saves.

Florida Panthers Since 1993, named after the panthers in the state.

"The Fog" Freddie Shero of Philadelphia Flyers fame had a tendency to drift off in thought. Three days after winning his first cup, he spent three weeks in the Soviet Union to study Russian techniques.

Forecheck To check opponents in their own zone while attempting to regain puck possession.

Forehand Pass or shot taken from the right side of a right-handed player or from the left side of a left-handed player.

Forwards The forward line: center, left wing, right wing.

Foul Any rules infraction drawing a penalty.

Freeze the Puck To attempt to stop play by pinning the puck against the boards with stick or skate and thus force a face-off.

Full Strength A team with its full complement of six players on the ice.

Garbage Collector A player who looks for and gets easy goals.

Garbage Goal An easy goal from right in front of the goal mouth.

"Gertie" George Gravel was a National Hockey League official in the late 1940s. His unusual nickname was inspired by the Dick Tracy comic strip character Gravel Gertie.

Getting the Jump Moving quickly and getting a good start on the opponents.

Giveaway Losing possession of the puck because of an error.

Glove To knock the puck down with the hand.

Glove Save The act of a goaltender stopping a shot on the goal with his catching glove.

Glove Side The side of a goal cage closest to the glove hand of the goaltender.

Goal A point scored when the puck is sent into the opposition's goal and passes entirely over the red goal line.

Goal Cage Tubular steel frame six feet wide by four feet high, consisting of a cross bar and two goalposts to which a net is attached.

Goal Crease A rectangular, eight-foot-wide, four-foot-deep box outlined on the ice in front of the goals; it is off-limits to offensive players except when the puck is in the crease or the goaltender is not in the crease.

Goal Judges Officials seated in the stands directly behind the goals who indicate when a goal has been scored.

Goal Line A red line that extends across the surface of the ice in front of the goals in the offensive and defensive zones.

Goal Mouth The opening immediately in front of the goal.

Goalposts Metal bars framing area to which the net is attached which rests on the center of the goal line and between which a puck must pass to score a goal.

Goaltender A position played by a player who guards the net to prevent goals (Goalie; Netminder).

"Golden Hawk" Bobby Hull joined the Chicago Black Hawks as an eighteen-year-old during the 1957–1958 season. He concluded his amazing hockey career in 1979–1980. He was born Robert Marvin Hull, Jr., in

Point Anne, Ontario, Canada, on January 3, 1939. By the age of three Hull was skating; as early as age ten he was being tagged as a sure-fire NHL star. In 1960–1961, he led the team to the Stanley Cup championship—Chicago's first title since 1938. Possessor of probably the hardest shot in ice hockey, Hull was also one of the fastest skaters in NHL history. A ten-time NHL All-Star, a seven-time goal-scoring leader, and a three-time winner of the scoring championship, he was the first player in the NHL to score fifty goals in a season more than once (he had fifty in 1961–1962, fifty-four in 1955–1956, and fifty-two in 1956–1957). It is an understatement to call Hull a scoring machine. Hull was a fiery competitor who would not back away from a fight. His dental bills were a testimony to that part of his game. Most of his teeth were lost during his time in the NHL, and he played part of the 1968–1969 season with his mouth wired shut after having his jaw broken. At times Hull's nose was so shattered and battered that he could barely breathe through it.

Along with Boom-Boom Geoffrion, Hull was instrumental in popularizing the slap shot. With his Chicago teammate and good friend Stan Mikita, Hull first began to use the curved blade that made his own slap shot, and that of others, more deadly and elusive. Hull has been called the fastest player on ice—he was clocked at 29.7 miles per hour when in his prime.

"Golden Jet" The world of hockey was shocked on June 27, 1972, when Bobby Hull jumped to the new World Hockey Association in a ten-year deal reportedly worth $2.75 million. A contract dispute with Blackhawks' management prompted his move to the upstart league. He became hockey's first millionaire, and the WHA gained instant credibility. It was the greatest loss in Blackhawks history—his departure allegedly cost the franchise close to one billion dollars over the next ten years due to declining attendance. In the WHA Hull picked up a new nickname—"the Golden Jet." This time the "golden" referred to the money he was making, and the "jet" to the Winnipeg Jets where he performed. After the 1971–1972 season, Hull became player-coach of the Jets.

The man most regard as the best left wing in ice hockey history returned in 1979–1980 to the NHL as a member of the Hartford Whalers. In 1983, Bobby Hull was enshrined in the Hockey Hall of Fame.

Good Goal A shot too effective to be stopped by goaltender.

Good Penalty A wise penalty risked or sustained by a player to prevent an opposition score.

"The Great One" Wayne Gretzky was perhaps the greatest hockey player ever and a true ambassador for the sport.

"Grim Reaper" Stu Grimson is not a legendary figure, but his wielding of his stick like a scythe earned him the nickname.

"Gump" Worsley Goalie Lorne Worsley, also known as the "Gumper," was a National Hockey League star for the New York Rangers, Montreal Canadiens, and Minnesota North Stars. A tough, gritty performer, Worsley was given his nickname by a childhood friend who claimed that Worsley resembled the comic strip character Andy Gump. "Gump" had a highly successful twenty-one-season NHL goaltending career.

"Hammer" Dave Schultz earned this nickname for his hands, which were like hammers when he took off his gloves to land punches.

Hanging Back The act of a player staying back, hoping an interception by a teammate will set him up with a breakaway pass.

Hart Memorial Trophy The National Hockey League trophy awarded to a player who is judged most valuable to his team, this honor originated in 1960, when the original Hart Trophy was retired to hockey's Hall of Fame. The trophy gets its name from Cecil Hart, former Montreal manager-coach.

Hat Trick The scoring of three or more goals in one game by a player.

Head for the Hole The skating of a player into the open ice for a pass.

Head Man To pass the puck to a teammate closer to the opposition goal during a rush.

Headmanning the Puck Offensive, never retreating hockey; a combination of quick forward passes to teammates.

Heavy Shot A powerful and quick shot that sinks as it approaches the goal.

Heavy Traffic A battle for the puck in front of the goal.

High Sticking Illegally hitting an opponent with a stick raised higher than shoulder level in professional play or four feet in amateur play.

Hip Check Body checking an opponent off stride through the use of the hip.

Hit A body check that makes an opponent lose control of the puck or forces him out of a play.

"Hitman" Bret Hart, one of hockey's tough guys, hence the nickname.

Hitter A player highly skilled in body checking.

Hockey Many historians say the roots of hockey go back more than five hundred years in northern Europe where field hockey was a popular summer sport. All kinds of romantic and fanciful stories exist about the early days of hockey. In the seventeenth century, an ice game known as "kolven" was popular. It spread to the English marshland community of Bury Fen in the 1820s. The game there was called "bandy." Local players scrambled around the town's frozen meadowlands and swatted a wooden or cork ball, known as a "kit"or "cat," with sticks made from willow tree branches.

When the ponds and lakes froze in winter, many athletes took to the ice to engage in another version of their summer sport. Youngsters in little villages and hamlets of Canada played on frozen lakes and ponds with sticks made from the branches of trees, and pucks formed from frozen "horse apples." Eventually, the sport became an indoor game but its true origins can be traced to youth passing wintertime away outdoors. Many believe hockey got its name from the French word *hoquet,* which means "shepherd's crook" or "bent stick." The term "ice hockey" first appeared in newspaper accounts of a contest held at Montreal's Victoria Skating Rink in 1875. Hockey was strictly a sport for amateurs until 1904. That year the first professional league was created—strangely enough, in the United States. It was called the International Pro Hockey League and was located in Michigan's Upper Peninsula iron-mining region. That first league lasted for just three years.

The earliest North American games were played in Canada in the 1870s. British soldiers stationed in Halifax, Nova Scotia, allegedly organized contests on frozen ponds. At about that time in Montreal students from McGill University began skating against each other in a downtown ice rink. North America's first hockey league, a four-team affair, was launched in Kingston, Ontario, in 1885, and the hockey boom was on. Games soon were played on a regular basis among teams from Toronto, Ottawa, and Montreal.

A very interested onlooker was the English governor-general of Canada. In fact, Lord Stanley of Preston was so impressed that in 1892 he purchased a silver bowl with an interior gold finish and announced that it would be presented each year to the best amateur team in Canada. And that was how the Stanley Cup—awarded today to the franchise that wins the National Hockey League playoffs—came to be.

When hockey was first played in Canada, the teams had nine men per side. But by the time the Stanley Cup was introduced, it was a seven-man game. The change came about due to a late 1880s miscue. A club playing in the Montreal Winter Carnival showed up two men short. Its opponent was obliging enough to drop the same number of players on its team to even the match. In time, the smaller squad was preferred.

That number became the standard for the sport. Each team had a goaltender, three forwards, two defensemen, and a rover, who could move up ice on the attack or fall back to defend his goal. In the beginning, skates consisted of blades that were attached to shoes; sticks were made from tree branches. The first goalie shin- and kneepads were derived in design from cricket.

In 1910, the National Hockey Association (NHA) came into existence and was followed by the Pacific Coast League (PCL). There was a transcontinental championship series played by the two leagues, with the winner awarded the highly sought-after cup of Lord Stanley.

It took World War I to throw all of pro hockey into a state of suspension. One of the many products of peace was the creation of the NHL. As the years moved on the primitive quality of gear improved to some degree. Players wore protective gloves. Shin guards were used, but the early ones were not that effective in softening blows from a puck or stick. So some players stuffed newspapers or magazines behind them for extra protection.

For many years the blades on sticks were completely straight, but New York Rangers star Andy Bathgate began experimenting with a curve in the late 1950s. The idea caught on around the league. Players didn't begin wearing helmets with any sort of uniformity until the early 1970s. In the years before, only players recovering from a head injury or those embarrassed about being bald wore helmets. An NHL rule passed prior to the start of the 1979–1980 season mandated that anyone who came into the league from that point on had to wear a helmet. By the early 1990s there were only a few players left who went unprotected. The last one was Craig MacTavish, who retired after the 1996–1997 season.

Hockey Stop A stopping maneuver in which a player rapidly turns both feet perpendicular to his angle of travel, causing his skates to scrape the ice and stop his motion.

Holding Minor penalty which occurs when a player grabs and holds onto an opponent (or his stick) with his hands or arms to impede the opponent's progress.

Hook Check Side-sweeping the stick close to the ice in an attempt to snatch the puck from the opponent's stick.

Hooker A player skilled in hooking opponents.

Hooking Illegally using the stick to hold or trip opponents.

"Hound Dog" Bob Kelly, out of Oakville, Ontario, was an important piece in the Philadelphia Flyers' Stanley Cup championships of 1974 and 1975. He was part of the Broad Street Bullies, a fighter as well as a scorer. His nickname came from his aggressiveness as a winger.

Ice Time The amount of time a player spends on the ice during a game or a season.

Icing the Puck Shooting the puck from behind the center (red) line to beyond the opposition's goal line—a legal maneuver only when a team plays shorthanded; at other times, a face-off is held in the shooting team's defensive zone.

In Alone A phrase describing an offensive player who slips behind the defense and has only the goaltender to beat for a score.

In Deep A phrase describing a skater with a puck who manages to get in close to the net.

Inside Move An attempt to stickhandle by a defender on the side toward the rink's middle, away from the boards.

Interference A minor penalty for illegally impeding or checking an opponent who does not have possession of the puck.

Intermission Fifteen-minute recess between each of the three periods of a hockey game.

Intimidator A player who is rough-and-tumble and poses a physical threat to opposing players.

James Norris Memorial Trophy The National Hockey League's trophy for the top defenseman, this award was created in 1953 to honor the former president and owner of the Detroit Red Wings.

Jump Stop A stop from a jumping-and-sideward turn that puts the skater's blades perpendicular to the line of movement.

Keep the Puck In A concentrated effort to play the puck in the opponent's defensive zone.

Kick Save A goaltender's kicking away a shot heading for the net.

Kill To use up the time of a penalty.

"King" Defenseman Francis Clancy was just 5' 7" and 155 pounds, but he left a mark on the NHL as a player and person. King Clancy was known for his off-ice antics and his colorful personality as much as for his on-ice talent. Born in Ottawa, he was a fan favorite throughout his career as a player, coach, referee, and team executive. His nickname fit.

King Clancy Memorial Trophy The King Clancy Memorial Trophy is an annual award given to the player who best exemplifies leadership qualities on and off the ice and who has made a noteworthy humanitarian contribution in his community.

Kneeing Illegally checking an opponent with the knee.

"Knuckles" Chris Nilan was not averse to using his fists or knuckles, hence the nickname. The hard-working right-winger was in nearly seven hundred NHL games for three different NHL teams.

"Kraut Line" During the late 1930s and early 1940s, Bobby Bauer, Milt Schmidt, and Woodrow Wilson ("Woody") Dumart formed a potent line for the Boston Bruins of the National Hockey League. Their collective nickname came from their shared German heritage.

Lady Byng Memorial Trophy The National Hockey League's award for best sportsmanship combined with a high standard of playing ability, the trophy originated in 1925 and was named for the wife of the then governor-general of Canada.

Lead Pass One sent ahead of a moving teammate designed to meet the player at the location to which he is headed.

"Le Gros Bill" Jean Beliveau weighed 210 pounds and was 6 feet, 3 inches tall. His heft and height made him stand out in the scaled-down world of the National Hockey League, and this was just one reason for his nickname. His bigness is also seen in his Hall of Fame membership, his leading Montreal to ten Stanley Cup championships, his 507 goals in eighteen seasons, and his instinctively correct moves all over the rink.

Lester Patrick Trophy The National Hockey League's award for outstanding service to hockey in the United States, it was presented to the league in 1966 by the New York Rangers and named after that team's former coach and manager.

Lie The angle made by the shaft of the stick and the blade.

Lift Pass A long pass that is flipped into the air.

Lift Shot A flicked-wrist shot that lifts the puck into the air; used most effectively against a goaltender sprawled in front of the net.

Line Change The replacement of a whole forward line with three new skaters.

Linemate A forward who plays on the same line with a teammate.

Linesmen The two officials on the ice, one toward each end of the rink, responsible for rules infractions concerning offside plays at the blue lines or center line and for any icing violations; the linesmen conduct most of the face-offs, advise the referee regarding penalties, and separate players who are fighting. They are on skates and wear black pants and an official league sweater.

Los Angeles Kings The name came from a contest.

"Lunch Pail Gang" The Boston Bruins of the late seventies were a tough minded-bunch with a no-nonsense work ethic. Individual nicknames galore existed: Coach Don Cherry was "Grapes." Rick Middleton was their star right-winger and was dubbed "Nifty." The smooth center was "Ratty" (Jean Ratelle).

Major Penalty A five-minute penalty for a serious infraction, such as fighting; it mandates that an offending player report immediately to the penalty box and that his team play shorthanded.

Match Penalty A violation that suspends a player for the remainder of a game and leaves his team shorthanded for either five or ten minutes.

Match-Ups Offensive and defensive pairings in a game.

Mid-Ice The neutral or middle part of the rink.

Minnesota North Stars Fans in Minnesota chose "North Stars" because the Minnesota state motto is "Etoile du Nord," French for "Star of the North."

Minor Penalty A two-minute penalty, the kind most often imposed.

Miracle on Ice "Morrow, up to Silk, five seconds . . . do you believe in miracles, yes?!" That was the call uttered by Al Michael who had never broadcast hockey before that Olympics, but he captured the moment when the U.S. Olympic hockey team made us believe in miracles. The young Americans' upset of the mighty Soviets in the 1980 Winter Olympics remains one of the great moments in sports history.

Misconduct Penalty A ten-minute penalty for improper behavior that is charged against a player, not a team; substitution is permitted.

Missing a Check A defensive lapse allowing an opponent to get free for a pass or a shot.

Montreal Canadiens Since 1909, named for the team location in Canada (*Canadiens* is French for Canadians). The team was born eight years before the NHL began. The "C" and "H" in the logo represent the name "Club de Hockey Canadien."

Montreal Maroons Played in the National Hockey League from 1924 to 1938. Aliteration and uniform color equaled nickname.

Moving the Puck Effective offensive techniques that keep an attack flowing.

"Mr. Hockey" Gordie Howe—great player, great ambassador for the game, great in the community.

"Mr. Zero" Frank Brimsek began his pro hockey career in 1938 and ended it in 1949. Through all those years except one he played for the Boston Bruins. The Hall of Famer was a truly outstanding goalkeeper. His abilities in the net earned him the nickname "Kid Zero" when he was a youth, and "Mr. Zero" as he got older. It was said of Brimsek, "If all the pucks stopped by 'Frigid Frankie' were stuck together . . . they would make a solid rubber hose 3 inches in diameter, long enough to reach from Boston to his home town in Eveleth, Minnesota." Brimsek had forty career shutouts and a 2.73 goals-against average. Twice he recorded shutouts in three consecutive games.

Nashville Predators Name came from a contest and was chosen to show power and drive.

National Hockey League (NHL) On November 22, 1917, the league was organized in Montreal. Delegates present at the organizational meeting represented the Montreal Canadiens, Montreal Wanderers, Ottawa, and Quebec. Those four clubs, plus the Toronto Arenas, were admitted into the league. Quebec opted not to compete in the first NHL season of 1917–1918.

The league's first game was played on December 19, 1917. Playing a twenty-two-game schedule, the NHL picked up on a rule change put into place by the old NHA. It dropped the rover and employed only six players per side. Toronto was the champion of that first NHL season. In March 1918 it competed against the Pacific Coast League champion Vancouver Millionaires for the Stanley Cup. Toronto won the series three games to two. The Pacific Coast League went out of business, and by the beginning of the 1926 season the NHL held hockey's center stage all by itself. It divided its ten teams into two divisions and took control of the Stanley Cup.

Netkeeper Goaltender.

Nets The goal cage.

Neutral Zone Center ice area between the blue lines; neither an attacking nor a defending zone.

New Jersey Devils As legend has it, the "Jersey Devil" is a half-man, half-beast who has roamed New Jersey's Pine Barrens for over 250 years.

New York Islanders The name came from a suggestion made by original co-owner Roy Boe's wife. Instead of naming the team the Long Islanders, she suggested calling the team the New York Islanders in an effort to win over some unhappy New York Ranger fans.

New York Rangers The team's first owner in 1926 was Madison Square Garden president G. L. "Tex" Rickard. Fans and sportswriters referred to the new squad as "Tex's Rangers," and the name eventually stuck.

Offensive Defenseman An offensively skilled defenseman who skates and shoots well and is a good puck handler.

Offensive Zone The area from the blue line to the goal a team is attempting to score into.

Officials Two referees and two linesmen on the ice call infractions and hand out penalties. Off-ice officials include two goal judges, the game timekeeper, the penalty timekeeper, the official scorer, the statistician, and the video goal judge.

Offside An infraction caused when an attacking-team player crosses the blue line into the offensive zone before the puck; the play stops and a face-off takes place in the neutral zone.

Offside Pass A forward pass by an offensive-team player to a teammate in another zone. Defending team players are permitted to receive passes from their own defensive zone to the center red line.

Off Wing Reversing of positions by right or left wings during a play.

Onside A player is onside when he is positioned behind a puck passed or brought into attacking zone.

On-the-Fly Player changes or substitutions while play is under way.

Open Ice A section of the rink free and clear of opponents.

Ottawa Senators Since 1992, named for the capital city of Canada where the Senate is located.

Outside Move An attempt by a player to stickhandle away from the middle of the rink and toward the boards.

Overtime Additional period of play used to break a tie (see Sudden-Death Overtime).

Overtime Loss The statistical result for a team that loses a game in overtime after being tied after regulation; this category was created starting with the 1999–2000 season. It is worth one point in the standings.

Pads Bulky protective equipment worn by players, generally made of rubber and encased in fabric.

Pad Save The use of the leg pads by a goaltender to block a shot.

Passing A player uses his stick to send the puck to a teammate.

Passing Lanes Clear lanes on the ice for passes to teammates.

Passout An attempt to set up a shot by passing the puck to the front of the net from behind the goal cage or from the comers.

Patroling the Wings Two-way hockey played by right or left wings on their side of the ice.

Penalty A rules violation for which a player may be sent off the ice into the penalty box for two, five, or ten minutes or for the duration of the game.

Penalty Box A small bench located in the neutral zone across from the players' benches and set off from the stands and the playing area by a partition (Sin Bin).

Penalty Killers Players used mainly when their team is shorthanded on the ice; they usually attempt to play defense and use up time.

Penalty Shot A rare free shot on a goal defended only by the goaltender; granted to a player fouled from behind while carrying the puck past the center red line on a clean breakaway.

Periods There are three twenty-minute playing intervals separated by two intermissions.

Philadelphia Flyers Since 1967, named from a contest, with the winning entry submitted by a youngster, spelling it "Fliers," but the committee chose "Flyers," because it went phonetically with Philadelphia.

Phoenix Coyotes Named the "Coyotes" (common to the area) in a name-the-team contest. Started in Winnipeg as the Jets in 1972, moved to Phoenix in 1996.

"Pie" Former NHL stalwart Johnnie McKenzie went by several nicknames. As a youth in Alberta he was known as "Cowboy" to his friends for he was a rodeo rider. He joined the NHL in 1958–1959, and he brought a nickname along with him that he was never happy about. "There used to be a chocolate bar in Canada," he recalled. "It was called 'Pie Face.' The logo had a little, wee body with a larger head." A "Pie Face."

Pin the Puck To stop the puck's movement by pressing it on the ice against the boards (Freeze the Puck).

Pipe A goalpost. Goaltender plays "between the pipes."

Pittsburgh Penguins Since 1967, named after their home arena, the Civic Arena, which is nicknamed "The Igloo" because of its igloo shape.

Pivot The offensive position of the center in front of the opposition's goal.

Play the Man To check an opponent, forcing him to lose possession of the puck.

Plus and Minus Statistical evaluation of a player's team value; a plus is awarded a player on the ice when his team scores, a minus when opposition scores.

"Pocket Rocket" Henri Richard was Maurice Richard's younger brother. Maurice was born on August 4, 1921, and Henri on February 29, 1936. Henri, younger and smaller than his famous brother, who was called "Rocket Richard," was a "pocket" or lesser version of Maurice but then there were very few National Hockey League players who weren't. The nickname "Pocket Rocket" was one he did not like. Henri Richard was one of the best all-around players in the NHL. His name was inscribed on the Stanley Cup eleven times (see "Rocket").

Points Positions taken by defensemen just inside the offensive zone blue line.

Poke Check A fast one-handed thrust of the stick by a defensive player aimed at knocking the puck away from an opponent.

Policeman An aggressive and tough player who counterattacks if the opposition plays too rough.

Positional Play Skillfully positioned performances by the five skaters on a team, during which they avoid bunching together and execute plays effectively.

"Powerhouse Line" Phil Watson at center with Lynn Patrick on left wing and Bryan Hextall on the right formed one of the top trios in New York Rangers history.

Power Play The offensive thrust of a team that has a numerical advantage over the defending team because of a player or players in the penalty box. Generally, four forwards are put on the ice along with one defenseman to increase scoring ability during a power play.

"Production Line" Ted Lindsay, Gordie Howe, and Sid Abel are remembered in Detroit and throughout hockey as the trio that teamed up on the same line to produce many goals and seven league titles in a row in the late 1940s and early 1950s. Their scoring and title-producing play gave them their nickname.

Puck A vulcanized rubber disc one inch in thickness, three inches in diameter, and approximately six ounces in weight.

Puck Control Similar to ball control: maintaining possession of the puck through good skating, handling, and passing.

Pulling the Defense A faked shot by an offensive player in an attempt to draw a defenseman near him—then stickhandling around or passing the puck by the defender.

Pulling the Goalie Replacing the goaltender with a sixth skater when a team is behind late in a game.

Pull the Trigger To quickly shoot at the goal.

"Punch" George Imlach never did excel as a player but went on to become one of the more successful coaches in NHL history. A Hall of Famer, he made his mark directing some highly successful Toronto teams. His nickname came from the force he put into his work.

"Punch Line" The Montreal Canadiens of the National Hockey League finished first four straight times in 1944–1947 and took the Stanley Cup championship in 1944 and 1946. A big part of the team's success was the scoring power and playing ferocity of the line of Maurice Richard, Elmer Lach, and Toe Blake. The line had clout, and that was the reason for its nickname.

Ragging the Puck Maintaining puck possession by skating away from the opposition in center ice in circlelike moves (used especially when the team is trying to kill a penalty).

"Rat" Ken Linseman, it was said, looked and played like a rat during his time in the NHL.

Rebound A shot on goal that bounces back into play.

Red Light A light located above the boards behind each goal that is lit up by the goal judge to indicate a goal scored.

Red Line The midrink, one-foot-wide dividing line.

Referees Chief officials in a hockey game, distinguished from the other officials by a red armband. They wear black pants and an official league sweater; they are also on skates.

Referee's Crease A ten-foot-radius semicircle where the referee consults with the penalty timekeeper; no one else is permitted there.

Rink Iced area inside the boards where game of hockey is played; it is two hundred feet long by eighty-five feet wide with rounded corners.

Rising Shot A shot that starts at ice level but rises as it approaches the goal.

River Skater A strong, tireless skater.

"Roadrunner" Yvon Cournoyer was born November 22, 1943, in Drummondville, Quebec. He went on to play for the Montreal Canadiens from 1963 to 1979 and established himself as one of the game's premier forwards. Nicknamed for his tireless energy.

Rockered Blades Used by professional ice hockey skaters, the gentle curve in a very sharp blade of an ice skate produced by rounding the toe and heel of the blade to make it easier for hockey players to turn quickly.

"Rocket" Maurice Richard fused blinding speed and brilliant goal-scoring ability, earning him the nickname "The Rocket" as well as the adulation of Montreal fans through a spectacular eighteen-year National Hockey League career that saw him score 544 goals in 978 games.

Richard was named eight times to the NHL's first All-Star team and six times to the second. It was just last season that the NHL created the Rocket Richard Trophy for the player scoring the most goals in a season.

On the ice, Richard performed like a man possessed. Former star goalkeeper Glenn Hall recalled: "What I remember most of all about the Rocket was his eyes. When he came flying toward you with the puck on his stick, his eyes were all lit up, flashing and gleaming like a pinball machine. It was terrifying."

Roughing Unnecessarily physical play that results in a penalty.

Rush The attacking surge of a team on the opposition's goal.

"Russian Rocket" Pavel Bure, a nickname showing off his nationality and his speed.

San Jose Sharks Several shark research facilities are in the area, and part of the Bay Area is known as "Red Triangle," due to its shark population. The franchise began in San Francisco 1991–1993, then moved to San Jose in 1993.

Save A shot on goal stopped by a goaltender.

Scramble A close-range battle for the puck by several players from both teams.

Screen Shot A shot on goal from behind a screen of players who block the goalie's line of vision.

Set Up To get the puck positioned so that a teammate may have a shot at the goal.

Shadow To guard an opponent very closely throughout the game.

Shift That part of the game during which a player is on the ice without substitution.

Shinny Poor or disorganized play.

Shoot To drive the puck to the other end of the ice in a clearing attempt.

Shooting Angle The stance a player is in as he shoots from an angle at the goal.

Shorthanded A term describing a team that has a player or players in the penalty box and is thus at a disadvantage to the opposing team.

Shorthanded Goal A situation where a shorthanded team scores a goal.

Short-Shifting Frequent changes in the lineup by a team, aimed at keeping fresh players in action.

Shot on Goal A shot that either enters the goal for a score or is saved by the goaltender; used for statistical evaluation.

Shoulder Check The act of body checking with the shoulder.

Shoulder Deke A quick move of the shoulder in one direction and the player in another to fake out the opponent.

Sideboards The boards along the sides of the rink.

"Silver Fox" Former coach and manager of the New York Rangers, and cofounder of hockey's Pacific Coast League, Lester Patrick came by his nickname because of the whiteness of his hair and his crafty ways. A member of the Hockey Hall of Fame, Patrick also was honored by the naming of an entire hockey division after him.

Sin Bin Another name for penalty box.

Skate-Off To make continual contact in skating against another player; to push him away from the puck and out of the action.

Skating Club A team with excellent skaters.

Slap Pass A pass made by a player of a puck he does not have full control of.

Slap Shot A maneuver in which a player raises his stick and shoots at the goal by bringing the stick down with force just behind the puck.

Slashing Illegally swinging a stick at an opponent.

Slot The area between the end-zone face-off circles where attacking forwards have good opportunity shots at goal.

Smothering A goalie's maneuver to stop the puck by falling on it.

Snap Pass A quick pass made without backswing, accomplished by snapping the wrists forward to project the stick.

Soft Goal A slow shot that manages to get by the goaltender for a goal.

Solo A breakaway of a player down the ice in an attempt to score.

Spearing Illegally jabbing at a player with the point of the stick.

Speed Team A club with swift skaters.

Split the Defense A situation where a player skates between two opposing defenders for a shot on goal.

Stalling Delaying the game.

Standing Up at the Blue Line Defensemen awaiting the opposition's rush at their blue line instead of retreating into their own zone to defend.

Stand-up Goalie A goaltender who remains erect in attempting the majority of his saves.

Stanley Cup Frederick Arthur, Lord Stanley of Preston, Canada's governor-general in 1893, offered a trophy in his name to be awarded to the amateur hockey champs of Canada. The cost of that original trophy was $48.67. (He never saw a Stanley Cup game, for he returned to his native England before the first one was played, on March 22, 1894.) The successor of that cup is now awarded to the National Hockey League champion, and "Stanley Cup" describes the league's playoff series. Lord Stanley, incidentally, was the son of the Earl of Derby, who lent part of his name to the English Derby and the Kentucky Derby. The Stanley Cup is the oldest of all the North American competitive professional trophies.

Stick A wooden device used to play the puck; the thin handle is connected to a blade, which is the part of the stick that hits the puck.

Stickhandling Controlling the puck with the stick while skating.

Stick Mitt Goaltender's glove worn on the hand with which he grips his stick.

Stick Save A save executed by a goaltender with his stick.

Stick Side A shot at the goal directed toward the side of the net guarded by the goalie's stick.

St. Louis Blues Named by the owners for their feeling for the famous song by W. C. Handy. City famous for its "blues" music heritage.

"Stosh" Stan Mikita was called this, a kind of ethnic shortening of his first name. He was born Stanislaus Guoth in Sokolce, Czechoslovakia, and came to Canada in 1948 as an eight-year-old with his aunt and uncle, taking their family name, Mikita. By 1961–1962, Mikita was in the upper echelon of NHL skaters as a member of the Chicago Black Hawks. That year he was on the NHL First All-Star Team. He was the first player in NHL history to win the Art Ross, Hart, and Lady Byng trophies in the same season. Election of Mikita to the Hockey Hall of Fame came in 1983.

"Stratford Streak" National Hockey League Hall of Famer Howie Morenz of the Montreal Canadiens was the sport's dominant figure during the Roaring Twenties. A speedy center with a devastating shot, Morenz scored 270 goals in his career. He had a whole collection of nicknames, as fans and the media strained to characterize him. The "Stratford Streak" title was coined for his speed and for what some thought was his birthplace, Stratford, Ontario. Actually Morenz was born in Mitchell, Ontario. Thus he got a new nickname, "The Mitchell Meteor." He was also called the "Marvel of Hockey" and the "Canadian Catapult"—both referring to his skills on the ice. Quebec's French-speaking fans dubbed him "L'homme éclair" (Top Man). The prime of his career included eleven exciting years with Montreal. He was then traded to Chicago, and later to the New York Americans. The Canadiens got him back in 1936. On the comeback trail with Montreal, he suffered broken bones in his leg and ankle, was hospitalized, and tragically, after five weeks in the hospital, slipped and fell and died of a heart seizure. He was only thirty-four years old. Funeral services were held at center ice in the Montreal Forum, and thousands cried for the man they also called "Le Grande Morenz."

Substitution Taking place at any time, a player leaves his bench replacing a player leaving the game; play need not stop.

"Sudden Death" Mel Hill He would have gone through his National Hockey League career as a relative unknown, for Mel Hill, who played in the years 1937–1947 for Boston and Toronto, was a journeyman forward. But he was touched with greatness in the Stanley Cup playoffs as a member of the 1939 Boston Bruins team. In the opening game of the final series, Boston was tied, 1-1, with the New York Rangers, with only thirty-five seconds left in a third overtime (sudden death) period. Speeding down the right side, Hill snared a pass from teammate Bill Cowley and shot the puck into the Ranger goal. Hill scored another sudden-death goal in the second game. The score was tied in the nineth minute of the first overtime when Hill got off a thirty-foot shot that evaded Ranger goalie Bert Gardiner. The series moved to a seventh and decisive game. The two teams battled through regulation time, through the first overtime, the second over-time. At approximately one o'clock in the morning, eight minutes into the third sudden-death period, Hill struck again. Positioned ten feet in front of the Ranger goal, he smashed the puck in for Boston's winning score. Thus Hill scored goals in three different overtime (sudden-death) games, including the seventh game's third overtime period.

Sudden-Death Overtime Overtime period ending when one team scores a goal, determining the winner and terminating the game.

"Super Mario" Mario Lemieux, Pittsburgh Penguin center, one of the greatest players of all time. He has won two Stanley Cups, six scoring titles, and the Most Valuable Player award three times. He is among the top ten all-time in goals, assists, and points. His nickname fits.

Sweep Check To extend the stick virtually flat on the ice and sweep it toward the puck.

Take a Check To absorb a body check from an opponent and not lose control of the puck or be put out of a play.

Taking a Run Intentionally skating from some distance away into an opponent's path.

Tampa Bay Lightning Frequent lightning storms in the area, hence the nickname.

Telegraphing Looking directly at a teammate before making a pass.

"Terrible Ted" "I stopped counting the scars when they reached 400," Ted Lindsay once said. He was called "Terrible" and "Scarface" by the opposition, but there was always a grudging respect for the 5' 8", 160-pound Detroit Red Wing Hall of Famer. A vicious body checker, handy with his stick or his fists if the occasion demanded it, Lindsay was a slashing, driving, frenetic performer who made it "terribly" tough for the opposition.

Third-Man-In Rule The third man in a fight receives a game misconduct penalty and is out of the game for its duration. The rule was created to discourage players from jumping into a fight.

Three-on-One A type of break when three attackers come in on one defenseman.

Three-on-Two A type of break when three attacking players skate against two defensive players.

Tie Up a Player To effectively check an opponent and take him out of the play.

"Toe" Born August 21, 1912, in Victoria Mines, Ontario, Hector Blake came up through the amateur system in Sudbury, a breeding ground of talent. He earned his nickname from childhood friends who called him "Hectoe" for a while, then "Toe." While Blake's ranking as a great NHL coach is a given, often not noticed is his career as a top player. Blake, inducted into the Hockey Hall of Fame as a player in 1966, was on three Stanley Cup teams.

Toronto Maple Leafs Since 1916, originally named the "Arenas," renamed the "St. Patricks" in 1919 to draw the Irish fans. Then, in 1926, renamed by the owner for an old Toronto team called the "East Maple Leaves." The name was then changed for the Maple Leaf regiment of the First World War, and for the maple leaf on the Canadian flag.

Trailer An offensive player who lags behind a puck-carrying teammate, awaiting a backward or drop pass.

Tripping Illegally using the stick to trip a player.

"Turk" Walter Broda was called "Turk" not because he was Turkish—he was actually of Polish extraction— but because in his childhood in Brandon, Manitoba, his freckles made the other kids think of a turkey egg, or because his neck turned red when he angered. He grew up to become a Hall of Fame goalie for the Toronto Maple Leafs.

Derek "Turk" Sanderson, of the late-1960s Boston Bruins, was a fine forechecker, tough, a killer/scorer on the ice, and a tough guy off it, too. His nickname fit.

Two-Line Pass Type of offside violation occurring when a player passes the puck from his defending zone to a teammate across the red center line; play is stopped for a face-off (Offside Pass).

Two-on-One A break with two attacking players skating against a lone defensive player.

Two-on-Two A break with two attacking players skating against two defensive players.

Unassisted Goal A goal scored by a player without receiving a pass from a teammate.

Underled Pass A pass behind or to one side of a teammate, making it difficult for him to control the puck.

Vancouver Canucks Canadian folk hero, Johnny Canuck was a great logger, skater, and hockey player in his spare time. "Canuck" means Canadian.

Vezina Trophy The National Hockey League's award for the leading goalkeeper was first presented in 1926–1927 by the owners of the Montreal franchise, in honor of their former star goalkeeper, Georges Vezina (see Chicoutimi Cucumber).

Waffle Pad Large rectangle attached to the front of the stick hand of the goalie.

Wandering Goalie A goalie who often moves quite a distance from his goal cage to clear the puck.

Washington Capitols (Caps) For a team playing in the nation's capital, a good choice for a name.

Wash-out A hand signal by an official that can indicate a goal disallowed, no icing, or no offside.

Wheels Slang expression for legs.

Wide-Open Hockey Fluid and fast shooting, passing, and skating by both teams.

Winger Positions of left and right wing.

Win the Draw To win a face-off.

Wrist Shot A quick shot resulting from a player's coordination of snapped wrists and a short backswing of the stick.

Zamboni Brand of machine used to clean the ice.

Zones Areas made up by the two blue lines: the attacking zone is the area farthest from the goal a player is defending; the neutral zone is the central area; and the defending zone is the area where a player's goal is (the goal where his team's goalie is stationed).

Ice Skating: Figure Skating, Freestyle, Ice Dancing, Pair Skating

"American Ice Master" Jackson Haines revolutionized the sport of ice skating, and because of his contributions he was given his nickname. A U.S. ballet master, Haines went to Austria when the Civil War began. In Vienna he fused the Austrian interests in skating and in the waltz into a new form of ice skating. Haines invented dancing on ice, teaching and demonstrating how skaters could glide, spiral, twist, and synchronize their moves with music. He also introduced all manner of novelty gyrations on skates, including skating on stilts. In 1875, after his death, Finland erected a monument that paid tribute to Haines as the "American Skating King."

Arabesque A position in which a skater balances on one leg, with the other leg raised horizontally, the body leaning forward, and the back arched.

Axel A maneuver performed by a jump off the forward outside edge of one skate followed by one and a half turns in the air and a landing on the back outside edge of the other skate.

Axis An imaginary straight line around which skating curves are grouped in a symmetrical fashion.

Back That part of the body which is pressing away from the direction the skating toe is pointing.

Back Inside Edge The curve created when a skater moves backward leaning over onto the blade's inside edge.

Back Outside Edge The curve created when a skater moves backward leaning over onto the blade's outside edge.

Back Outside Three A one-footed turn from a curve on a back outside edge to a curve on a forward inside edge.

Barrier The structure surrounding an ice rink, usually three feet high and generally made of wood.

Blade The thin metal strip on the bottom of a skate that glides on the ice.

Bunny Hop A short jump from one skate to the toe of the other skate followed by a quick step onto the first skate.

"Burner" Cathy Turner, short track speed skater, won the gold medal in the women's 500-meter event in the 1992 and 1994 Winter Olympics. Her rhyming nickname was given to her by Olympic speed skating legend Eric Heiden as a tribute to her speed.

Camel A spin executed with the body in the arabesque position.

Canasta Tango A dance on ice to a tango tempo.

Center The intersection of the long and short axes that constitutes the beginning and ending point of a figure.

Center a Spin To keep a spin rotating on a fixed point.

Change of Edge To rock from edge to edge on one foot.

Chasse A maneuver performed by bringing the free foot alongside the skating foot and shifting one's weight to the free foot while the skating foot is lifted slightly off the ground.

Cheat To finish part of a turning jump after landing, instead of while still in the air.

Check A movement aimed at controlling the natural rotation of a turn.

Choctaw A graceful, fancy ice-skating step, this term is derived from the name of an Indian tribe of southern Mississippi. The Choctaws, one of the Five Civilized Tribes, got their name from the Spanish *chato* ("flattened"), because of the custom the Indians had of flattening the heads of male infants. How the actual skating maneuver—a half-turn from forward to backward or vice versa and a switch from one leg to the other that takes in a change of edge—is in reality related to the name of the Indian tribe is a matter of speculation.

Closed A position in which the body goes in the direction of the skating foot.

Closed Position An ice-dancing stance where partners face each other (Waltz Position).

Crossover A movement begun on the outside edge while the free foot crosses over the skating foot and lands on the inside edge.

Cross Roll A movement executed by crossing the free foot over the skating foot and positioning it to the inside of the roll.

Cross Stroke An ice-dancing term for when the feet are crossed and momentum is gathered from the outside edge of the foot that will become the free foot.

Dance Steps A freestyle term indicating a combination of edges and complex turns, skated to music, that forms a link between movements.

Deepen an Edge To cause the curvature to increase while skating an edge.

Edge Either of the two sharp sides of the skate's blade. Also, the curve caused by a skater leaning so that an edge cuts into the ice.

Eight Two circles started and finished at a specific point on the ice and both having a diameter about three times the height of the skater.

Figure An officially recognized design based on two- or three-circle forms.

Figure Skate A skate used for freestyle and figure skating that is slightly curved from front to back with small spikes (toe picks) at the toes.

Figure Skating Skating that involves the tracing of geometric patterns on the ice: pair skating, freestyle skating, ice dancing.

Forward That part of the body that is either in front of the skating toe or pressing in the direction in which the skating toe is pointing.

Forward Inside Edge The curve created when a skater moves forward leaning over the blade's inside edge.

Forward Inside Three A one-footed turn from a forward inside edge to a back outside edge.

Forward Outside Edge The curve created when a skater moves forward leaning over the blade's outside edge.

Forward Outside Three A one-footed turn from a curve on a forward outside edge to a curve on a back inside edge; the foot turns in the natural direction of the edge.

Free That part of the skater's body on the side of the leg in the air.

Free Foot (Leg) That foot (leg) that has just completed the push and is in the air.

Freestyle Jumps, spirals, spins, dance steps, and other movements (Free Skating).

Hand-in-Hand Position An ice-dancing position where both partners face front with arms extended and hands clasped (Extended Hold).

Hayes Jenkins Spiral The spiral used in men's figure skating, it is named for the American who was the first person to execute it.

Hipping A fault (common to forward-outside-edge skating) in which the skating hip presses into the circle.

Hockey Stop A stop favored by hockey players in which both heels are thrown to the right, the knees are bent, and the blades are turned at right angles to the line of travel.

Hollow The groove between a figure skate's two edges.

Ice Dancing A form of ballroom dancing on ice executed by a male and female duo that is classified as figure skating.

Inside Edge The skating-blade edge closest to the body's midline; the curve skated on this edge.

Key Positions The four shoulder and free-leg positions that make up basic combinations.

Kilian Position A dance competition stance in which the partners face in the same direction, with the woman on the man's right.

Kilian Position Reversed A dance-competition stance in which the partners face in the same direction, but with the woman on the man's left.

Lobe A semicircle.

Loop A movement performed on a single edge that starts with a semicircle, is followed by a quick rotation in the same direction, and is finished off with another semicircle, thus completing the circle.

Loop Jump A full-turn jump in which the skater takes off from a back outside edge, turns once in the air, and lands on the same back outside edge.

Master Tooth A spike at the front of a figureskate blade generally used as a pivot for spins (Master Pick).

Matched Set A combination of a skate and a boot attached to each other.

Mazurka A jump from a back edge that involves striking of the free toe into the ice, making a half turn in the air, and landing on the other toe and gliding onto a forward edge of the other foot.

Mohawk A turn from forward to backward or vice versa, or from one foot to the other. Variations include the Open or Inside Mohawk, in which the heel of the free foot is placed opposite the instep of the skating foot, the turn is made, the feet are changed, and the now free leg is behind the heel of the skating foot; the Closed Mohawk, in which the instep of the free foot is placed at the heel of the skating foot, the turn is made, the feet are changed, and the now free leg is passed in front of the skating leg; the Mohawk Jump, which involves landing after the turn on the corresponding edge of the other skate and continuing the curve in the opposite direction; and the Drop Mohawk, which is a mohawk followed by a change of feet, with the entire movement continuing in the original edge's curve.

Natural Rotation A skater's normal body flow created by the curve of an edge.

Neutral Position A position in which the skater's body is squared in the direction of travel with neither shoulder, arm, nor hip ahead of the other.

One-Foot Snowplow A skating stop in which one foot is placed "pigeon-toed" in front of the body.

One-Foot Spin A spin performed on one foot.

Open A position in which the skater's hips or shoulders are turned away from the skating foot and the free leg is a bit behind the skating foot.

Outside Edge The blade's edge nearest the outside of the foot. Also, the curve skated on this edge.

Pair Skating A figure-skating category of lifts, spins, and freestyle movements performed simultaneously by a pair of skaters.

Paragraph Three A figure-eight pattern performed on one foot in which there is a turn within the circle so that the skater finishes in the direction opposite to that in which he or she began.

Pattern An ice-dancing design for which edges and steps are laid out on the ice.

Pick A figure skate's sharp projection that functions as a grip on the ice in some spins and jumps (Toe Pick, Toe Rake, Tooth).

Pivot A freestyle movement where the toe pick is positioned on the ice and the skater spins around it.

Prepared Position The correct body position just before a turn.

Progressive A movement where the free foot is passed in front of the skating foot, usually landing on an inside edge (Run).

Radius The curve of a blade of a figure skate from front to back.

Roll A half-circle performed on the outside edge and generally followed by another half circle performed on the other foot's outside edge.

Russian Split Jump A straddle split leap in which the skater gets his legs slightly forward and extends his hands to his feet.

Salchow Swedish skater Urich Salchow was the first to execute this skating jump that bears his name. It is basically a leap from the back inner edge of one foot and a full turn in the air to a landing on the back outer edge of the other foot.

School Figures A group of sixty-nine distinct figures skated in two- or three-circle figure-eight patterns (used in skating competition).

Scissor Jump A jump in which the skating foot crosses behind the other foot in the air—a variation of the mazurka.

Sculling Movement off the heels and toes from an outer to an inner edge as a means of maneuvering oneself backward or forward.

Sit Spin A squatting-position spin off one skate generally performed with the other leg extended in front of the skater (also known as the Haines or Jackson Haines spin for the U.S. skater who made it popular).

Snowplow Stop A stop where both toes are turned in ("pigeon-toed") and cause the skater to stop by scraping the ice.

Speed Skate Designed for racing, this skate has a thin blade that protrudes a bit ahead of the toe's boot and has no curve from front to back.

Spin To make several circular moves in the same place on one or both skates.

Spiral A freestyle body position generally taken in skating an edge: a woman approximates an arabesque, while a man stands up with his free leg crossed in back of his skating leg and held close to the ice's surface and with his arms outstretched, skating a circle in this position in a decreasing radius.

Split Jump A jump from the backward edge of one foot into a half turn in the air, with the legs snapping out almost parallel to the ice surface (splitting) and a return to the forward edge of either foot.

Spread Eagle A gliding maneuver with arms positioned to the sides and skates positioned heel against heel in a straight line.

Spread-Eagle Mohawk A variation of the mohawk in which the free foot is placed on the ice just before the turn and lined up with the skating foot—an old-fashioned and cumbersome move.

Stanchion A supporting section of a skate connecting the blade to the heel or sole plate.

Strike The act of moving body weight from one foot onto the foot that becomes the new skating foot. Also, a mark on the ice or a position on the ice where a strike takes place.

Stroke A thrusting push to move across the ice.

Superimposition In figure skating, the tracing of one figure on top of the preceding one in as exact a manner as possible.

Swing Moving of a free leg past the leg that is the skating leg.

Swing Dance A basic ice dance to 4/4 tempo.

Swing Mohawk Any mohawk in which the free foot is swung past the skating foot prior to its being brought back into place to make the turn.

Swing Roll An ice-dancing edge position that is held for several beats while the free leg swings past the skating leg before its return into position before the new strike.

Takeoff The maneuver that enables a skater to leave the ice in performing a jump; the thrust in figures from one foot to the other to begin or sustain a figure.

Three Turn A turn from backward to forward or vice versa; the change to the opposite edge takes place along with rotation in the direction of the edge being skated (Three).

Thrust Momentum gained by pushing the blade against the ice surface to start from rest or to pick up speed.

Toe Loop Jump A jump from a back outside edge that involves striking the free foot's toe into the ice and the execution of one turn in the air; the landing is on the original back outside edge (Cherry Flip; Loop Jump).

Trace A white mark or figure made on the ice by the blade (Tracing).

Tracing Foot The foot on which a skater is standing.

Travel To move across the ice while rotating.

T Stop A stop that produces a skid because the free foot is placed behind and at right angles to the skating foot on the ice.

Tuck A slight crossing of the rear foot behind the skating foot on the final step of a forward progressive (Tucking).

"Tuffy" Former Canadian star Christine Hough earned this name for her love of dangerous skating maneuvers.

Turn A fast reverse of direction made in a flowing movement while skating an edge.

Upright Spin A spin in a standing position.

Walley A jump from the back inside edge of one foot into a full turn in the air, returning to the back outside edge of that same foot; upon landing, the skater curves in the opposite direction from the turn's rotation.

Waltz Jump A jump from a forward outside edge followed by a half turn in the air and a landing on the back outside edge of the other skate (Three Jump).

Waltz Three A three turn from a forward outside edge in which the free foot is positioned on the surface and continues the curve (Drop Three).

Wilson A jump from a back outside edge followed by a full turn in the air and a landing on the back outside edge of the other foot; it begins a curve in the opposite direction.

Jai Alai

The Basque language supplied the name of this sport that is appealing to many Latins. *Jai alai* in Basque means "merry festival," and that literally is what the sport is for many—especially for those who bet on the contests and win. The term "jai alai" denotes a fronton (or open-walled arena) used to play a variety of pelota called *cesta punta*. The term more broadly refers to the game itself.

The signature of the game is its fast pace—a 125-gram ball (or pelota) covered with parchment skin can travel faster than 180 mph. The ball is placed into play and volleyed by players wearing a wicker-basket glove approximately sixty-three to seventy centimeter long. Invented in the nineteenth century, the glove, *cesta punta* (in Spanish) or *xistera* (Basque), was invented by the French Basque Gantchiqui Diturbide (also Gantxiki Iturbide).

In countries such as France, Spain, and Mexico, jai alai is very popular. It is in some regions played in almost every town and city. In the United States, jai alai enjoyed some popularity as a gambling alternative to horse racing and remains popular among gamblers in Florida, where the game is used as a basis for pari-mutuel gambling.

Judo

Ashiwaza Foot-throw techniques.

Belts Professor Jigoro Kano, founder of judo, originated the system of belts to clarify rankings in the sport. The black belt symbolizes an expert, the white belt is given to a beginner, and other colors reflect the intermediate skills of judo practitioners.

Black Belt A belt worn by an expert.

Dan Degree.

Dojo Practice or exercise hall.

Gatame Mat-work holding technique.

Gi The judo or karate uniform.

Ippon One full point in a competitive match.

Jigo Tai A defensive stance or posture.

Judo Judo is an outgrowth of ju-jitsu, which came into being in Japan thousands of years ago. At first only samurai warriors were permitted to study the sport. By the 1850s different ju-jitsu schools existed all over Japan. Each one went its own way and seemed to have its own secrets.

Professor Jigoro Kano, a man frustrated by the different approaches and by what he saw as the violence of some of the schools, founded what we know today as judo. Kano did this in 1882, calling the new sport "judo," which means "the gentle way." Out went the dangerous moves such as foot and hand strikes, and in came some of the old ju-jitsu methods together with some new techniques.

Many trace judo's start in the United States to President Theodore Roosevelt. A believer in a keen mind and a strong body, Roosevelt witnessed a judo contest and was so impressed that he imported his own Japanese judo instructor.

Judoka One who practices judo.

Kaeshiza Techniques for counterattack.

Kake Technique application.

Kappo A system of artificial respiration.

Kata Training techniques consisting of formal, prearranged movements.

Kodokan The administration center of world judo, located in Tokyo.

Koshiwaza Hip-throw techniques.

Kuzushi The moment of completely breaking an opponent's balance.

Kwansetuwaza The art of locking an opponent.

Kyu A degree for a pupil.

Mattai A sign of submission; literally, "enough" or "I surrender."

Mundansha A judoka who is below black-belt rank.

Nage Waza Throwing techniques.

Newaza Groundwork.

Nippon Den Kodokan Judo The formal and full name for recognized world judo.

Osae Komi Waza Hold-down techniques.

Randori Free play; fighting practice.

Rei Bow.

Samurai A feudal Japanese warrior.

Sensei A teacher or instructor.

Shiai A contest or competitive match.

Shihan A master.

Shintai Advancing and retreating.

Shumewaza Strangulation or choking techniques.

Suri Ashi Sliding foot movements.

Sutemiwaza Sacrifice throws.

Tachiwaza Techniques of throwing.

Tatami A straw mat for practicing judo.

Techi Rei Bow from a standing position.

Tori One who applies judo techniques; the thrower.

Tsukuri The technique of breaking an opponent's balance.

Uke The person to whom techniques are applied; the one thrown.

Ukemi Breakfalls; the art of falling.

Waza Technique.

Waza Ari The half-point in competition.

Waz Ari Awasete Ippon Two half-points that equal an ippon (one full point) and determine a contest winner.

"Yawara-chan" Her nickname comes from the name of a popular cartoon character and is also derived from the first Chinese character used to write the word judo. Ryoko Tamura has won four world championships and an Olympic medal. She is a national hero in Japan.

Yudansha One holding a black-belt degree.

Za-Rei A bow from the sitting position.

Karate

Black Belt A belt worn by an expert.
Budo The way of the warrior.
Chosi Rhythm.
Do The way.
Dojo Karate school.
Fudo-Dachi An immovable stance.
Gi Karate uniform.
Hachiji-Dachi The natural stance.
Hyoshi Timing.
Jiyu Kumite Free sparring.
Jutsu Technique.
Kamae Fixed position or stance.
Karate Daruma, an Indian monk, introduced the skills of a martial art to the monks of the Shao Lin monastery in China thousands of years ago. It was taught as a way of developing strength and endurance. Daruma studied animals' fighting positions and blended these with other combat techniques. He taught the Shao Lin monks so effectively that they became the most fearsome fighters in all of China. A system of instruction was developed to keep the sport fairly secret but at the same time allow it to be passed on to those to whom the monks wished to teach it. The system was based on kata—set pieces and techniques—of the martial art that Daruma originated. In the 1600s the feudal lords on the island of Okinawa banned the use of all weapons. The martial art that Daruma developed then spread to Okinawa. It was called "Chinese hand," in tribute to the country where it was first developed.

Modern karate was introduced to the Japanese public in 1922 by Master Funakoshi Gichin. He gave it the name "karate," which means "open hand." Today shotokan ("Shoto" was Funakoshi's nickname) is the most widely practiced and taught approach to karate in the West.

Kata Set pieces and techniques; forms.

Keiko Practice.

Keirei Bow.

Keiri Striking.

Ki Vital energy.

Kime The point of focus; the maximum concentration of force.

Kumite Sparring.

Nagewaza Techniques of throwing.

Rei The ceremonial bow.

Reigi Politeness, courtesy.

Renshu Training.

Sensei A teacher or instructor.

Suki An opening.

Tsuki Punching.

Uchi Striking.

Uke Blocking.

Yoi The ready posture.

Lacrosse

Attackman A player with an offensive responsibility; there are three attack players and three midfielders (who attack and defend).

Ball A solid-rubber white or orange ball that weighs 5–5½ ounces and has a 2½-inch diameter and a circumference of 7¾–8 inches. Also, a call by a teammate that indicates he is going to get the ball and that another player on his team should bodycheck the player from whom the ball is being taken.

Bodychecking The act of legally blocking another player with the body, if that player is in possession of the ball, is a potential receiver, or is within fifteen feet of the ball.

"Break" A shout by a goalie indicating he has made a stop of the ball and wants his defense to break out for a clearing play.

Brush-off An offensive move that involves running an opponent into a teammate in order to gain freedom of movement (Pick).

Center A position occupied near midfield on both offense and defense by a player who usually participates in face-offs.

Charge A legal run into an opponent aimed at throwing him off balance.

Checking Hitting the stick of an opponent to dislodge the ball or hamper his passing or receiving of the ball.

Clearing The mounting of an attack by the defensemen the instant they intercept or stop the ball in their defensive area.

Close Attack The three attackmen: first attack, out home, in home.

Close Defense The three defensemen: point, cover point, first defense.

Cradle To maintain the ball in the pocket of the stick, or crosse, by rocking the crosse in a backward and forward motion.

Crosschecking Using the portion of the stick between the butt (bottom end) and the throat (the point at which the head of the stick begins) to stop an opponent with or without the ball—an illegal maneuver except when used against an opponent who is within fifteen yards of the ball.

Crosse The implement used to play lacrosse; it may not be less than seven inches nor more than twelve inches wide and must be between forty and seventy-two inches long—except for the goalkeeper's crosse, which may be any length desired (Stick).

Defenseman A player assigned to the defensive zone or position other than the goalkeeper.

Dodging The act of an offensive player's getting away from a defensive player by faking a move in one direction and then moving away with the ball in another direction. There are four main dodges: face, force, toss, and change-of-pace.

End Zones Areas at either end of the field behind the goal.

Expulsion Foul A three-minute penalty and ejection from the game charged against a player who has tried to hit a member of the other team, an official, or a coach; the ejected player is replaced by a substitute after the three-minute penalty time is completed.

Extra Man A situation where a team has an extra attacker, either as a result of a dodge or because the other team is shy a player because of a penalty.

Face-off A method of putting the ball into play in the middle of the field at the start of the game, the start of each quarter, after each score, and when the official cannot decide which team caused the ball to go out of play. Two players face each other with their backs to their respective goals, their sticks flat on the ground, and the ball positioned between their sticks, and they attempt to gain possession of the ball or to pass it.

Flick The act of shooting or passing the ball after a catch without stopping to cradle the ball.

Forcing The act of making an attacking player in possession of the ball retreat so as to be unable to execute a pass.

Free Play The act of restarting play by the referee that involves placing the ball in the stick of an opposition player at the point closest to where the ball was lost out of bounds by the other team.

Hen Hawk An underhand shot.

Home The attacking players—two in men's play, three in women's play.

Indian Check A gambling check that is aimed at jarring an opponent's stick to spring the ball loose.

Indian Pendants The stick's head end strings that can be manipulated to change the pocket's depth.

Lacrosse Pierre de Charlevoix, a French cleric, gave the sport of lacrosse its name in 1705. The Algonquin Indians were happily playing a game of their favorite sport, *baggataway,* and the Frenchman was an especially interested spectator. The webbed stick used by the Indians was a particular source of interest to de Charlevoix, who saw in the stick a resemblance to a bishop's *crozier* ("cross"). Ultimately, the French adopted the sport the Indians played and changed the name from "baggataway" to "lacrosse."

Midfielders The three players who perform on both offense and defense: second defense, center, second attack.

Penalty Box An area where players put out of the game because of infractions must stay until the expiration of their penalty time.

"Pick-up" A goalie's call directing a teammate to take an opponent.

Poke Check The act of keeping an opponent at crosse's length by poking at the butt of his crosse.

Riding An action by a team after losing the ball or attempting a shot that is aimed at preventing the defense from clearing the ball to its attackers.

"Right (Left) Back" Calls by a goalie to indicate the position of the ball to his teammates when the ball is behind the goal.

Scooping the Ball The act of getting the ball off the ground and into the crosse.

Screen An attacking player positions himself so that the goalie has difficulty seeing the shot on goal.

"Shift" A goalie's call that indicates a man has been dodged and that the entire defense should shift toward the ball.

Slashing The illegal use of the crosse on the arm or hand of an opponent.

Luge

Artificial Track One that is refrigerated.

Base Weight Maximum weight carried by the luge slider, typically seventy-five kilograms for women's singles, ninety kilograms for men's singles.

Block Portion of the start when the athlete places the sled into a forward rock; followed by compression.

Bootie Racing shoe of a luger. The bottom is smooth, rounded.

Box A hollowed-out section of the kufens (sled runners) that holds the gummies and bridge legs.

Bridge A section of the sled connecting the kufens and carrying the pod. There is a front bridge and rear bridge on each sled.

Bridge Bolts Bolts passing through the boxes holding the bridges to the kufens.

Clear A track that is free of obstacles.

Compression Portion of the start when the sled is placed into a final rearward motion; followed by the pull.

Control Steel A steel instrument measuring the control temperature mounted along the track.

Crank To steer extremely hard.

Crash Hitting the track's wall or going off the track entirely.

Diamond Paste A paste containing microscopic diamond particles used to polish the steels.

DNF Did Not Finish.

DNS Did Not Start.

Draw Random selection of names determining the initial start order for a race.

Drive Controlling the sled in its run down the course.

DSQ Disqualified. Athlete entered race but was disqualified for a rule violation.

Expansion Joint Separated sections of track that allow for expansion or contraction because of changes in temperature.

G-Forces Gravitational forces exerted on the slider by acceleration, deceleration, and direction changes.

Gummy One of four cylindrical rubber pieces holding bridge legs, allowing them to move up and down and giving sled flexibility.

Handle Located on each side of the sled inside the pod, one of two metal grips used to push the sled during the start, and sometimes for steering during the run.

Handle Steer Pushing or pulling on the handles to steer the sled.

Hook Steer Steering the sled by hooking a toe under a kufen and lifting it.

Horn Curved area at the front of a kufen.

Kreisel A turn where the track crosses back upon itself.

Kufen (Cufin) One of the sled's runners.

Labyrinth Three or more curves following in rapid sequence.

Line Path followed by the sled down the track.

Loop Time-wasting line that, dipping in middle of a curve, rises near the exit.

Lose One's Head Head snaps back because of a curve's high g-forces.

Luge Name comes from the French word *luge,* which means "sled" and refers to one- and two-man sleds on which one sleighs supine and feet-first. Steering is done by shifting the weight or pulling straps attached to the sled's runners. "Luge" is also the name of the sport.

Mind Run Visualization technique where slider imagines a luge run in real time and practices all the actions.

Mouth Guard Rubber or plastic piece some sliders wear to reduce vibration of the jaw and chattering of the teeth.

Neck Strap Strap attaching the helmet to the body or legs helping the slider support the head against high g-forces.

Omega Curve Series of three curves alternating in direction; the second curve is much longer than the first and third.

Orthoplast Moldable plastic used by sliders to make thin, hard pads.

Outrun Portion of the track beyond the finish line where sleds slow to a stop.

Paddle To push a sled using spiked gloves on the surface of the ice.

Pod Aerodynamically shaped shell; athlete's seat (Shell).

Pull Portion of the start when the athlete pulls the sled forward preparing for the final push.

Push Portion of the start when the athlete pushes the luge forward to the start line using handles.

Roll Steering the slide with shoulder pressure.

Runner Guard Covering of rubber hose or molded fiberglass protecting the steel when the sled is off the course from scratches.

Runner Temperature Steels temperature. It cannot exceed a maximum, based on track conditions and race rules (Steel Temperature).

S-Curve Two connected curves in alternating directions.

Scraper Tool used to smooth the track surface.

Settle Portion of the start where the athlete lies back on the sled.

Shades Retractable covers shielding the track between runs from sunlight and sometimes from snow.

Shampoo Liquid to keep the visor from fogging.

Shave Shearing off a top layer of thin ice with steels.

Slider Luge or bobsled athlete.

Speed Suit Slider's skin-tight, aerodynamic outfit.

Spikes Metal protrusions worn on the slider's glove fingertips or the backs of the knuckles as aid's in paddling at the start.

Split Time The time it takes to cover a given section of the track.

Start Order Sequence for sliders taking their runs.

Start Time The time it takes to get from the start to the first intermediate point.

Steels Steel runners that are attached to the kufens.

Steel Work Polishing the steels.

Visor Rounded sheet of clear or tinted plastic attached to the front of the helmet protecting the face (Face Shield).

Weigh-in Determining via weighing how much additional weight an athlete is allowed to carry during the race.

Weight Vest Garment where additional weight can be carried.

Motorcycling

Ape Hangers Handlebars rising up very high to the handgrips.

Back It In To turn a motorcycle into a sideways slide, making it corner so that it looks as if the rear wheel is ahead of front wheel.

Berm A dirt bank created on an off-road course corner as a result of the turns of a great many motorcycles.

Binned It Crashed the motorcycle, virtually wrecking it.

Blow Off To skillfully pass another motorcycle.

Boinger Rear shock absorber.

Bus Stop Slow first-gear corner.

Buzz It To run an engine at an exceedingly high rpm.

Cafe Racer Street bike personalized with cosmetic features and, sometimes, performance features resembling a road racer.

Camber The degree of bank in a turn.

"Cannonball" One of the legends of motorcycling is E. G. "Cannonball" Baker. He was the earliest of the transcontinental riders, coasting from Los Angeles to New York in eight days, twenty-one hours, and sixteen minutes. That pioneer mark and most of the other speed and endurance records set by this man, who powered his machine as if it were a cannonball, have since been broken. Yet Baker remains in legend and in deed as perhaps the greatest at his craft that ever existed. He is best remembered for "cannonballing" back and forth between the coasts, setting and then breaking new records. In 1935 he crossed the nation on his motorcycle for the 106th time. In 1941, the year of his final major run, then sixty years old, Baker made it across the country in six days, six hours, and twenty-five minutes—"And I didn't break any laws," he said.

Clip-Ons Handlebars that are low and flat and attach directly to the motorcycle.

Crossed Up An airborne jumping maneuver with the front wheel angled to the direction of flight.

Detuned Situation when things are going badly.

Disco Mode When a cop is seen with his lights flashing.

DNF Did Not Finish; a condition where something was not accomplished.

DNS Did Not Start; a condition where a performer or object was not able to function.

Electrics Anything on a motorcycle involved with electricity.

Endo To go end-over-end.

Face Shield A plastic visor that is transparent and attached to the front of a safety helmet.

Fairing A streamlined shape that attaches to the front of a motorcycle to cut down wind resistance.

Fish Oil Fluids that do not function properly on a bike.

Friction Zone Area of the hand lever where the clutch engages.

Getting Off Leaving a motorcycle that is still moving before the rider had planned to do so.

Getting under the Paint An extreme technique used to cut wind resistance in which the rider crouches down as low as possible on the tank.

Grab the Binders Braking a motorcycle.

Grid A competition event's starting area.

Groove The line tracked through a corner by a motorcycle.

Hacks Passenger-carrying sidecar motorcycles (Sidehacks).

Hanging Off Reducing a bike's lean-angle by leaning from the seat in the direction of a turn.

Holeshot Quickly seizing lead as a race starts.

Hotshoe A skilled and quick rider.

Leathers Padded leather fabrics making up the rider's protective outer clothing.

Lid Motorcycle helmet.

Lightweight A performer lacking skill or staying power.

Moto One heat out of the two or three events that compose a complete motocross.

Motocross Motorcycle competition conducted over all-natural terrain courses (MX; Scramble).

Pegs Footrests on motorcycles.

Rear Sets Suitable for high speeds, pegs positioned farther to the rear of a bike than normal that accommodate laid-forward body positioning.

Red Line Upper limit of rpms for a motorcycle engine indicated by a red zone on the tachometer.

Rippin' Going very fast.

Sano Sanitary machine in appearance and production.

Sissy Bar Metal bar fastened to rear of the motorcycle seat that the passenger can lean against.

Slicks Tires lacking a tread pattern.

Slug A slow bike or rider.

Smoke To defeat someone convincingly.

Squid A rider whose comments about his riding abilities far exceed his performance (Street Squid).

Squirrelly Erratic riding ability.

Sweeper A broad high-speed turn.

Tear-offs Disposable plastic sheets that can be attached to the face shield and removed when insects, mud, and so forth, create reduced vision.

Topping Off Filling a fluid tank or receptacle to the limit.

Tranny Transmission.

Tucked In Buried into the motorcycle to cut down wind resistance.

Two-Up Carrying a passenger on the motorcycle.

Up on the Pegs Riding position where all the weight is placed on the foot pegs and the rider is standing up.

WFO Wide-open throttle.

Wheelie Lifting the motorcycle's front wheel off the ground.

Wind It Out To get an engine revved up to its red line or best up-shifting gear point for each speed.

Wobble A rolling and turning of the machine almost out of the rider's control.

Wrench A motorcycle mechanic.

Zap To pass another rider very quickly.

Motor Sports: Auto Racing, Drag Racing

Airfoil Device on the rear portion of a car utilizing wind to aid in handling.

"Alabama Gang" Home state originally of Bobby and Donnie Allison, Red Farmer, and Neil Bonnett. Later group included Bobby's son Davey; Donnie's son-in-law, Hut Stricklin; and native Alabaman Jeff Purvis, who drove for both Bobby and Neil at various times in his career.

Altered A drag-racing classification that describes a modified automobile body that generally does not have glass or fenders.

Autocross A driving competition of timed heats through a twisting course (Gymkhana, Slalom).

"Awesome Bill from Dawsonville" Bill Elliott hailed from Dawsonville, Georgia. Also called "Million Dollar Bill" for his triumph in the Winston Million in 1985.

Axle A pin on which a wheel revolves.

Back Marker A vehicle positioned on the final few rows of the starting grid.

Back Off To slow down on the throttle.

Bad Scene A not-too-pleasant situation.

Bank A turn's degree of incline (Banking).

Bend A generally shallow turn. Also, to damage a racing car.

"Bermuda Triangle" Pocono International Raceway in Pennsylvania, the only three-cornered track on the circuit.

Big Banger A big engine, generally with more than 305 cubic inches of displacement (Big Bore).

"Big Left Turn" Langhorne Speedway in Pennsylvania was used by NASCAR only from 1949 to 1957. It was an old one-mile dirt track built on swampland and underground creeks laid out in a perfect circle; no corners or straightaways, just a constant left turn. Just beyond the start-finish line, the track went downhill steeply and was known among drivers as "Puke Alley" ("The Track That Ate the Heroes").

Binders Brakes.

Bite Tire traction.

Black Flag A signal by racing officials requiring a driver to return to the pit the next time around the course.

Blend The mixture of methanol and nitromethane used in some cars.

Blip To race an engine in brief bursts.

Block A car's cylinder block.

Blower A supercharger.

Blown Engine One broken down or supercharged.

Blueprint To take apart an engine and rebuild it beyond the precision point of standard factory construction.

Body in White A car body just off the production line in its natural metal color.

Boss Outstanding.

Box Transmission; gear box.

Brain Fade A driver's mental mistake.

Brake Fade The loss of effectiveness of brakes because of overheating as a result of continued use.

Brake Horsepower (BHP) A measuring instrument for evaluating the horsepower of an engine.

"Brickyard" The Indianapolis Motor Speedway, an apt description.

BRM The designation given in 1950 to a series of British Grand Prix racing cars, including, after 1963, a gas turbine model. The initial letters of the last names of the designers—P. Berthon and R. Mays—are included in the name for the racing-car series.

Bubble A qualifying lineup's last position, in which a driver is vulnerable to being replaced by a faster driver.

"Buckshot" Ray Jones ran into a table as a child and did not complain. His grandfather said he was tough as a buckshot.

Bull Ring An oval track of a half-mile or less.

Buy the Farm To be killed in an accident (Buy It).

Caliper A clamping device that grips the disc in a system of disc brakes.

Cam A shaft formation that creates motion.

Camshaft A rotating shaft that indirectly activates cylinder valves.

Carb Abbreviation for carburetor.

Catch Fences Fences positioned at different spots off the course to catch cars and minimize danger.

CC (Cubic Centimeters) A measuring unit used to calculate the amount of engine displacement; 1,000 cc equals 1 liter.

Championship Car A racing car built especially for major competition—similar to formula racers but possessing a larger engine displacement.

"Chargin' Charlie" Charlie Glotzbach, over thirty years in NASCAR, took pride in the name—a salute to his aggressive driving.

Chassis The understructure of a racecar.

Checkered Flag Composed of black and white squares, this flag is used to signal the end of a race.

Chevrolet The car was named after Louis Chevrolet, who designed the first model in 1911. Louis was the brother of Gaston, winner of the 1920 Indianapolis 500. The car Gaston Chevrolet drove was built by Louis. Both brothers, who were Frenchmen, were especially skilled racing drivers.

Chicane A manmade obstacle, such as a comer or turn placed where racing officials desire to reduce the speed of cars.

"Chicken Driver" Cale Yarborough earned the name in running verbal battles with driver Darrell Waltrip.

Chief Steward An individual who runs the race and is the leading official.

Christmas Tree The light system mounted on a vertical pole that is used to count down to the start of a drag race.

Chute A straightaway.

CID Cubic Inches of Displacement.

Closed Course A road designed only for racing.

"Clown Prince of Racing" Joe Weatherly, for assorted high jinks on and off the track; also called "Little Joe" for his size.

Club Racing Amateur events.

Come-In Signal A signal (usually an arrow) used by a pit-crew member to call in the driver on his next lap.

Comingman A rookie driver with great potential (British term).

Compound Substance used to make racing tires, usually a blend of natural and synthetic rubbers with resin, carbon black, bonding agents, and other substances.

Consy Consolation race.

Crankshaft The shaft transmitting power from the pistons to the differential.

Crash Box A transmission that is not synchronized.

Cubes Cubic inches of displacement.

Dice A British term that describes very close racing between two or more cars with changes of position common; to engage in close racing.

Differential Engine power comes from this unit to the drive wheels.

Displacement Measure of an engine's size—the difference between the volume contained in the cylinders when the pistons are at the bottom of the stroke and the volume remaining when the pistons are at the top. It can be calculated by multiplying bore times stroke times 0.785 times the number of cylinders.

"D. J." Dale Arnold Jarrett.

DOHC Double Overhead Camshaft.

Downshift To shift in road racing from higher to lower gear to slow a car without any significant change in engine speed.

Drafting Trailing close behind another car and literally allowing that car to break through the air (Tow).

Drag Race A race that is generally restricted to a quarter-mile straightaway and based on acceleration speed.

Dragster An auto used for drag racing, characterized by having the driver's seat set behind the rear wheels.

Drift A maneuver used in cornering in which all the wheels slide as the car is accelerated through a turn.

Drive Shaft The drive train part that sends power from the engine to the driving wheels.

Drive Train The total system that carries power from the engine to the driving wheels.

"Duffle Bag" Doug Richert didn't stay in one place long. He was crew chief for Greg Biffle in the Roush Racing #16 Ford Taurus and for Rod Osterlund's championship winning team in 1980, with a young driver named Dale Earnhardt.

"D. W." Darrell Waltrip is terrific behind the microphone, but he was also a legend behind the wheel with eighty-four wins.

Dynamometer An instrument that measures engine output.

Eliminated Beaten in a drag race.

"Elmhurst Express" Hometowns have always been a popular part of nicknames. Fred Lorenzen hailed from Elmhurst, Illinois (See "Ford's Golden Boy," "Golden Boy").

Equipe French term for race team.

ERA This term is both the initials of the English Racing Association and the name given in 1934 to a series of racing cars designed by Peter Berthon.

Esses A sequence of continuous shallow left and right turns.

ET Elapsed Time.

E-Z A signal from the pit to "take it easy," generally given to a driver well in the lead.

Factory Team A squad of drivers and cars entered in a race by an auto manufacturer.

"Fireball" (**"King of the Superspeedways"**) Edward Glenn Roberts was a legendary daring driver. His main nickname came from his time as a baseball pitcher. It also decribed the way he was on the track. Roberts earned thirty-three career wins. He died in a crash during the 1964 World 600.

Fishtailing The weaving from side to side of the rear of a car.

Flat-Out At top speed (Full Bore, Full Chat).

"Flying Indian" Roy Tyner, for his Native American roots.

Flying Start The moving at high speed of a formation of racing cars as they take the starting line's green flag. In a Rolling Start, the cars move out at a relatively low speed.

Footprint The spot on the ground where a tire makes contact.

"Ford's Golden Boy" Fred Lorenzen was a carpenter from Illinois.He joined NASCAR in 1960 and started to defeat the biggest names at the biggest tracks. In 1963, Lorenzen became the first driver to win more than $100,000 in a season. His nickname is self-explanatory.

Formula Specifications detailed for open-wheel racing cars that have an open cockpit and a single seat.

Formula Libre Anything is possible; anything goes.

Four-Wheel Drive (4-WD) Engine power is transmitted in this system to all four wheels, rather than only to two.

Fuel Commonly some mixture of methanol and nitromethane.

Fuel Injection A technique in which fuel goes directly into the cylinders, as opposed to going through a carburetor (Full Bore, Flat Out).

Gasser A kind of drag racer.

Gear Box Transmission.

"Gentle Giant" Wylie "Buddy" Baker, on March 24, 1970, while testing his blue Dodge Daytona for the first running of the Alabama 500 at Talladega set a world closed-course record of 200.447 mph and became the first driver to exceed 200 mph on a closed course. He was gentle, but he was a giant among his peers in ability.

"Gentleman Ned" Ned Jarrett, for being so mannerly and for a graceful exit.

Get Sideways A spinning slide that moves the car on an angle to the traffic flow.

Go into the Country To unintentionally leave the racing circuit.

"Golden Boy" There was a moment that a young Northern-born driver Fred Lorenzen came south and took the Grand National Cup series by storm. That's how he got his nickname.

Gordon Bennett Cup Named for the famed American publisher who presented it, this cup symbolized the winning of an international auto race for teams of three cars manufactured entirely in the country that entered them in competition. The races were staged in the years 1899–1905 and were ultimately supplanted by the Grand Prix (see Grand Prix).

Grand Prix (Races) This term is French for "grand prize." It was first employed in 1863, as a designation for the one-mile, seven-furlong horserace for three-year-olds. Today's Grand Prix races denote the thirteen races for single-seater Formula I cars. Staged annually in thirteen different nations, the points earned are counted for the world championship for drivers.

Grand Touring Car A sports car that blends passenger features with racing potential.

Grid The starting lineup in road racing (Starting Grid).

Groove The best and most efficient racing route on an oval track.

Ground Clearance The space between the bottom of a car and the ground.

GT Grand Touring car.

Gymkhana Clocked competition around a twisting course involving cars that execute certain specified maneuvers.

Hairpin A very sharp turn (Switchback).

Hairy Exciting, wild, frightening.

Half-Shaft The axle shaft.

"Hat Man of NASCAR" Bill Brodrick, a tall blond man who for years served as Winner's Circle coordinator and assisted the drivers with donning the proper hats at the right time for photographs. He was employed by Unocal 76, once the "official fuel of NASCAR."

Hauler A very fast car.

Heel and Toe The use of only the right foot on the brake pedal and accelerator—an almost mandatory technique for racers.

"High Groove Harry" Harry Grant, for running on the high side of the track.

Hill Climb A race up a hill, with one car at a time racing against the clock.

Hobby A novice-type stock-car racer.

Homologation A manufacturing procedure that certifies a car for use in a given racing class.

Hot Dog A talented driver (Hot Shoe).

"Iceman" Terry Labonte, for his cool manner on the track.

Impound Area Enclosed inspection area that is utilized after a race.

Indianapolis 500 Staged annually since 1911, this event run in May at the Indianapolis Motor Speedway and sponsored by the United States Auto Club gets its name from its location and the number of miles autos must complete to win the race.

Infield The area enclosed by a road course or an oval track that is used for pits, parking, garages, and race watching.

"The Intimidator" Dale Earnhardt had moxie—when opponents saw his black number 3 car approaching, they felt the challenge. At the front he was virtually impossible to pass. He was also called "Ironhead" for his forceful ways, "One Tough Customer" from his Wrangler Jeans sponsorship, and "The Man in Black" from his black number 3 GM Goodwrench car.

"Jaws" Darrell Waltrip's nickname pinned on him by Cale Yarborough during D. W.'s six-win season in 1977.

Juice A racing fuel blend.

Jump To start before the signal is given, usually in drag racing.

"The King" ("King Richard") Seven-time champion Richard Petty, whose father Lee began family involvement with the sport and whose son, Kyle, carried on. Richard Petty also had a hometown nickname, "The Randleman Rocket," for his North Carolina roots.

"King of the Restrictor Plate" Sterling Marlin, because of his success on the super speedways.

Knock-offs A single-wing nut easy to put on and take off that is used to fasten a wheel to its hub; the nut is "knocked off" with a mallet.

Koni Type of shock absorber used in racing and sports cars.

"The Lady in Black" ("The Track Too Tough to Tame", "TTTTTT") The grand old lady, Darlington Raceway in Darlington, South Carolina. She was the first paved super speedway in NASCAR, opening her doors to racing in 1950.

Lap One complete circuit of the course. Also, to pass a slower driver and move into the circuit ahead of that driver.

Lay It On To get a car to go exceptionally fast.

Lead Foot Aggressive driver who always goes for the lead.

Le Mans Start A type of start in which the drivers, at the starting signal, run to their cars, start the engines, and begin racing.

Line The best and most efficient route in road racing around a circuit. Also, the manner or route in which a driver takes a specific turn.

Liter A metric unit measurement of liquid capacity—just a bit more than a quart.

"Little E" Dale Earnhardt, Jr., also long known as "Junior," but the nickname given to him by his father has the nicest ring—"June bug."

Lose It To lose control of a car.

Loud Pedal The accelerator.

Mag Wheels Magnesium-cast wheels.

Manifold A distributing or collecting chamber: the intake manifold distributes the mixture of fuel and air to the cylinders from the carburetor; the exhaust manifold collects gases from the cylinders and sends them to the exhaust pipes.

Mark One of a series of cars or products (Mark II would be the second in a line of cars, etc.).

Marshal A road-racing communications individual, such as a flagman.

"Master of the Restart" Ron Hornaday, the best at it.

Methanol A type of alcohol blended into the fuel in racing cars and in some drag racers.

Mickey Mouse Not to be taken seriously; a racing course with a great many turns.

Mod Up-to-date—as in a car with the latest modifications.

Monocoque A chassis that lacks a frame.

Moonshiners' Races Races for drivers who compete after filling out cards at local tracks.

"Mr. Excitement" Jimmy Spencer, whose driving style contributed much to the nickname.

"Mr. September" Harry Gant, for winning four consecutive races at age fifty-one in September 1991. He would have made the string five but suffered brake failure late in the race at North Wilkesboro and finished second to Dale Earnhardt.

Mule A car used for practice.

Nerf To bump lightly against another car, usually from behind and often on purpose. Very often the tactic is a warning or a bit of psychology. Very common in NASCAR racing.

Nerfing Bar A bumper that protects the wheels from making contact with each other.

Nitro An ingredient in the fuel blend used by racing cars and some drag racers (Nitromethane).

Nomex A brand of flame-resistant fabric that is popularly used in the clothing of racing drivers.

Normally Aspirated A nonsupercharged and nonturbocharged engine that gets air into combustion chambers via regular suction resulting from piston downstroke.

Out of Shape Any break or disturbance in the smooth line of movement of a driver's car.

Oversteer Inclination of a car to turn more sharply on a curve than the driver wishes.

Pace Car A car, generally a flashy convertible, that is positioned ahead of the pack to set the pace prior to the start of a race.

Pace Lap An oval-racing quick circuit of the track by all the cars, which follow a pace car so that when the starting line is reached, the cars are virtually up to maximum speed.

Pacer Driver Travels at pretty much the same speed throughout the race, conserving his car and hoping that those traveling faster will be forced to drop out with mechanical problems.

Paddock A work and parking area for cars in road racing.

"The Paperclip" Little Martinsville Speedway, located in southern Virginia, earned its nickname because of its long narrow shape.

Parade Lap A slow-moving formation of all the cars in the race, held prior to the pace lap for the benefit of the spectators.

Pieces Parts and/or engine components.

Pit(s) A service area for cars, generally located on the front straightaway and restricted to participants and officials (Working Pits).

Pit Crew Workers in the service area for cars.

Pit Road A path that leads in and out of the pits from the course (Pit Lane).

Pit Stop To get off the track for a stop in the pits in order to have the car serviced.

Planing The floating on a film of water by a car whose tires are unable to provide much traction on a wet surface (Aquaplaning, Hydroplaning).

Pole (Position) The number one position, because it enables a car to move flat-out without worry about banging into another car.

Pop Methanol and nitromethane fuel blend; any exotic fuel blend.

"Pops" Curtis Turner, for the noise that his right front fender made when it tangled with a competitor's left rear fender.

Production The manner in which a car is produced by a manufacturer.

Proto(type) A car that does not have to conform; one of a kind; a new car's test model.

Pump Gas The same quality of gasoline used by the public (Pump Fuel).

Qualifying Speed sessions before a race to determine the actual starting positions, with the fastest lap times resulting in the award of the pole position.

Raunchy Sloppy appearance of an individual or car, or improper behavior.

Red Flag A solid red flag used to stop a race.

Rev To gun an engine. As a noun, "revs" is short for "revolutions per minute."

Rev Counter A tachometer, which indicates an engine's revolutions per minute.

Ride A race car driving assignment.

Riding the Rails Taking the outside line around a turn.

Road Course A partial or total road-racing course that uses public highways.

Road Race A race held on a road course rather than an oval track.

"The Rock" North Carolina Speedway at Rockingham, North Carolina; the one-mile high-banked track that NASCAR closed.

Roll Bar A safety device composed of tubular steel fastened to the chassis above the driver's head; it is designed to protect the driver if the car rolls over.

Roll Cage Tubular steel surrounding a driver in a stock car or Transamerican sedan and designed to provide protection in a crash or turnover.

"Ronda Roadrunner" Robert Glenn "Junior" Johnson, named for the place where he grew up in North Carolina and still lives. Also called "The Wilkes County Wildman" for the same reason.

RPM Revolutions per Minute—the measurement of the speed at which an engine turns.

Run Out of Road To go off course during a maneuver by using up all the track area.

"Rushville Rocket" ("Smoke") Tony Stewart had the first part of his nickname for his hometown in Indiana and the second for speed.

Sandbag To hold back on showing all the speed a vehicle is capable of and thus give the opposition a false sense of security.

Sanitary A clean race.

Scrutineering A thorough inspection of a racing car for safety and conformity to the rules.

Scuderia Italian term for race team.

Shoes Tires.

Shunt A collision (British).

Shut-off In road racing, the moment just before a turn that requires a driver to decrease speed; personalized shut-offs are a blend of the equipment, skill, and the courage possessed by a driver.

Shut the Gate To block a car that is attempting to move ahead on the inside of a turn (Close The Gate).

"Silver Fox" David Pearson, lovingly known for years by this name—for early-graying hair.

Slalom A type of gymkhana in which drivers maneuver through a course marked by pylons.

Slicks Wide, flat-surface tires on drive wheels of drag racers.

Slide A skidding of the rear wheels.

Slingshotting A stock-car racing technique that involves following in the slipstream of another car and then passing (slinging) by that car.

"Smokey" Henry Yunick, from one of the first races he ever drove, when the old car he brought to race began smoking on the track and the announcer, unable to remember the youngster's name, called him "Smokey."

Speed Trap Area at the end of a drag strip where electric eyes measure a vehicle's speed at the end of its run.

Spin To lose control of a car by spinning out or spinning off the course.

Spoiler A device that enables a car to resist the tendency at high speed to lift off the ground—an air deflector.

Sports Car A vehicle that basically handles better and brakes better than an ordinary passenger car.

Sportsman A light-bodied stock car with engine modified in certain limited ways.

Stack(s) Pipe(s) affixed to the fuel injection system or the carburetor to pull in air (Velocity Stacks).

Stock Block Mass-produced engine block that is adapted for racing.

Stock Car A racing car that is basically unmodified from a standard production model.

Stroke To drive a car at a speed lower than its potential. Also, the distance a piston moves inside a cylinder.

"Suitcase Jake" Jake Elder, mechanic, who had trouble getting a long-term home with any one team.

Supercharger A mechanical device that enables a car to have a more powerful fuel-air mixture than normal atmospheric pressure can supply.

Switchback A maneuver that is close to a U-turn.

Tachometer Instrument measuring rpm.

T-Bone To smash broadside into another car.

Ten-Tenths Ultimate performance, as opposed to nine-tenths (nearly ultimate performance).

Time Trials Solo competitions against the clock; speed competitions before a race to establish starting positions.

"Timmonsville Flash" Darrell Waltrip, for his home town of Timmonsville, South Carolina.

"Tiny" DeWayne Lund, a play on his size, 6' 4" and 270 pounds.

Torque A rotating shaft's twisting force.

Torsion Bar Suspension system rod that operates like a spring.

Tow Drafting another car by a driver.

Tread Surface pattern of a tire. Also, width of a car measured between its tires' centerlines.

Turbocharger A supercharger driven by a turbine that, in turn, is driven by the car's exhaust gases.

"Turtle" Herman Beam raced from the late 1950s into the early 1960s. In seven years of racing Beam never wrecked anyone nor was he wrecked—he just occupied the lane that no one else wanted and went at his own speed.

Tweak To attempt to get even more power out of an engine by tuning.

Understeer A tendency by an automobile's front to take control of the vehicle and drag it along and out of control.

Unreal Exceptional.

Wheelbase Distance between a car's front and rear axles.

Windmill Supercharger.

Wing Spoiler.

Wires Wire wheels.

X-Car An experimental car.

Yellow Flag A signal that indicates there are dangerous conditions on the track (Yellow Light).

Yellowtail A rookie NASCAR driver; cars driven by rookies have yellow rear bumpers.

Mountain Biking

Acro-Brats Youngsters who use their bikes like pogo sticks, with pegs coming out the front axle.

Afterglow Hanging out after a race, discussing experiences.

Age Marks Holes in rider's apparel revealing age of the garment and how long the rider has been in mountain biking.

Air Space between tires and the ground.

ATB All-Terrain Bike or Biking.

Auger Crashing and involuntarily taking samples of the local geology, usually (Face Plant).

Babyheads Roundish rocks that pose problems to riders.

Bacon Scabs on a rider's knees, elbows, or other body parts.

Bag Fail to show.

Bagger A person who always agrees to show but rarely does.

Balance Blackout When a rider starts to fall and loses balance without reason.

Banana Scraper Low-hanging branches.

Betty Female rider.

Biff Crash (Wipeout).

Biopace Any uneven pedaling motion.

Boing-Boing Bike with full (front and rear) suspension.

Boink Run out of energy; grow exhausted on a ride (Bonk).

Bolt-on After-market bicycle parts that are literally bolted on.

Bomb Riding without regard to personal safety.

Bombers Earliest mountain bikes, converted from cruiser road bikes for going down mountains.

Bra Rubber strip inside the protecting tube from the nipples.

Brain Biking computer, usually featuring an odometer, speedometer, clock, and other "important" display modes.

Brain Bucket Helmet.

Brain Sieve Helmet featuring more vents than protective surface.

BSG Bike Store Guy.

Bunny Hop Lifting both wheels off the ground by crouching down and then exploding upward, pulling the bike along.

Burrito Rim braking surface bent inward toward the tube, forming a section looking like a rolled burrito.

Buzz Euphoric feeling.

Carve Riding with great speed around the corners of a twisting road.

Cashed Exhausted; bonked.

Chainsuck When the bike chain gets jammed between the frame and the chain rings.

Chi-Chi Parts used to dress up a bicycle to make it more impressive looking (Cyclephernalia).

Chunder Crash.

Clean Negotiating a trail successfully without crashing or dabbing.

Clipless Clips or cleats clipped onto the soles of special shoes. These replaced toe clips.

Cloon Slamming into the ground, resulting in delay in the action.

Clotheslined Having caught an upper body part on a low piece of vegetation.

Cob Clearer Lead rider who has to clear out spider webs for riders who follow (Spider Patrol).

Cockrotter One who allows bike to fall into disrepair.

Condom Little plastic or rubber item protecting the tube's valve stem from rim damage.

Corndog Becoming covered in silt.

Dab Putting a foot down to catch one's balance on a difficult section of trail.

Death Cookies Fist-sized rocks knocking the bike around.

Death March Truly exhausting ride (Epic).

Dialed In Bike has everything working correctly.

Dirt Bike Off-road motorcycle.

Dual Boinger Full-suspension bicycle.

Endo To fly unexpectedly over the handlebars, thus being forcibly ejected from the bike.

Engine The rider.

Enscarfment Food break at the edge of a cliff.

Face Plant Hitting the ground face first (Auger, Digger, Soil Sample, Spring Planting).

First Blood First rider in a group who crashes and starts bleeding.

Foot Fault Rider unable to disengage cleats from the pedals before falling over.

Fred One spending much money on a bike and clothing, but lacking riding skills (Poser, Barney).

FS, F/S Front Suspension, Full Suspension.

Gear Masher One riding in too high a gear.

Giblets Colorful parts and pieces to supplement a bike.

Gonzo Treacherous.

Granny Gear Lowest gear available on a bike, aimed at steep uphill climbing and very easy to pedal in on flat ground.

Gravity Check A fall.

Grinder Long uphill climb.

Grunt Very difficult climb, needing use of the granny gear.

Gutter Bunny Bicycling commuter.

Half-Track Narrow and/or overgrown trail.

Hammer Going fast and hard.

Hardtail Bike with front suspension but lacking rear suspension.

Hiker Log Obstacle put on the trail by those hostile to bikers.

Honk Vomit from exertion.

Horizontal Track Stand Foot fault that happens at a stop sign.

IMBA International Mountain Biking Association, an organization for trail advocacy.

Impedimentia Items on a bike impeding performance, looking bad.

Involuntary Dismount Crash.

Jet Accelerate; go very fast.

John Boy'ed A face covered with spots of mud, like "John Boy" on *The Waltons*.

JRA Just Riding Along.

Kick-Out Rider pushes the back tire to one side in a bunny hop.

LBS Local Bike Shop.

Lid Helmet.

Line Desirable path or strategy to take on a tricky trail section.

Mo Momentum.

Mojo Charm a biker wears or attaches to his bike.

MTB Mountain Biking; mountain bike itself.

Mud Diving What happens when a bike slows abruptly in the mud, throwing the rider into wet goo.

Nirvana To be in tune with bike, trail, and physical well being (The Zone).

NORBA National Off-Road Bicycling Association.

OHV Off-Highway Vehicle.

Organ Donor One who rides without a helmet (Metal Head).

ORV Off-Road Vehicle.

Panic Skid Trying desperately to prevent an impending stack by pushing heels deep into the ground.

Pirelliology Ability to identify tires from the tracks they leave.

Potato Chip Badly bent wheel.

Prang Hitting ground hard, usually damaging something.

Purple Ano Anodized purple aluminum.

Push-Push Pedaling motion of a novice involving alternately pushing each foot down, instead of spinning.

Redsocks Hikers who wear those funny red socks who seem to always block best singletracks.

Retro-Grouch Rider preferring old bike and components.

'Rhoid Buffing Butt touches rear wheel when bike goes down a steep hill.

Rigid Bike lacking suspension.

Roadie Rider favoring paved surfaces.

Rookie Mark Chain grease on a rider's pant leg.

Roost Accelerate quickly; stop suddenly.

Scream Dream ride; long, straight, and deceptively steep hill.

Shimano Techno-fad shifting system.

Singletrack Trail just wide enough for one person or bike.

Skid Lid Helmet.

Sky Jumping extremely high.

Snake Bite Double inner tube puncture.

Sneakers Tires.

Soil Sample Face plant.

Spin Smooth pedal motion.

Spudded Being unable to unclip, from spuds in time and crashing.

Spuds (SPD) Shimano Pedaling Dynamics, clipless pedals.

Stack Crash.

Steed Bike.

Stoked Euphoric feeling.

Superman Rider flying over the handlebars.

Tea Party Chatting group of riders.

Techno-Weenie Rider more aware of latest parts and techno-fads than about the trails.

Thrash Causing major ecological damage to a trail.

Three-Hour Tour Ride that at the start seems easy but turns out not to be. Derived from the theme song to *Gilligan's Island.*

Ti Titanium.

Toe Clips Clip-and-strap system connecting a rider's feet and toes to the pedals.

Trail Swag Stuff left by other bikers and found on the trail.

Tricked Out Bike with latest and hottest components.

Tweak Rider twists handlebars back and forth in midair.

Vultures Spectators present at dangerous obstacles hoping to see blood.

Washboard Soil surface undulations making for a very rough ride.

Wash Out Loss of front tire traction.

Wheelie Lifting front wheel off the ground.

Wheelie Drop Combining a wheelie and a jump to navigate large drop with little speed due to a limited run-out.

Whoop-De-Doos Up-and-down bumps.

Wild Pigs Poorly adjusted brake pads that squeal.

Winky Reflector.

Wipeout Crash.

Wonky Not functioning properly. "I bailed, and now my wheel is all wonky, and all I hear are wild pigs."

Wrench Working on a bike; to adjust or repair; bike shop mechanic.

Yard Sale Horrendous crash leaving water bottles, pump, tool bag, and so forth, scattered.

Zone Out State of mind of not paying attention to riding needs.

Mountaineering:
Hiking, Climbing, Rock Climbing

Abseil (German) descending by sliding down a rope; rappelling.

Active Protection Spring loaded devices used by traditional and aid climbers.

Adze The broad, sharp edge on the back of an ice axe/ice tool used for chopping ice.

Aid Climbing Moving up a rock face by hanging on fixed or placed protection like pitons or nuts. Also known in the United States as Sixth Class Climbing.

Aider Webbing ladder used for aid climbing (see Etrier).

Aid Route Route that can only be ascended using aid climbing techniques.

Alcove A recessed belay ledge surrounded by vertical rock on all sides.

Alpine Butterfly Butterfly knot.

Alpine Rock Climbing Rock climbing performed at altitudes requiring mountaineering skills.

Alpine Start A predawn start to a climbing day.

Alpine Style Modern, light, and fast mountaineering where members of a small team without fixed ropes carry everything on their backs at one time, moving continually toward the summit.

AMGA American Mountain Guides Association, a nonprofit organization.

AMS Acute Mountain Sickness; relatively mild disorder caused by the body's inability to rapidly acclimatize to altitudes in excess of 8,000 feet (HAPE, HACE).

Anchor Two or more anchor points equalized by rope or webbing.

Anchor Point Rope attached to the rock using a fixed or placed piece of protection.

Anchor Rope Climbing rope portion that is tied from a belayer to a nearby anchor point.

Arête Narrow ridge.

Ascenders Devices for ascending a rope that slide freely when pushed up the rope but stop in place when weighted (Jumars, Prussik Knot).

ATC Air Traffic Controller.

Avalanche A snow- or icefall down a mountain slope.

Backstepping Advanced face-climbing technique using outside edge of a shoe with bent knee pointing toward the ground.

Bail To give up on a rock climb or a summit attempt because of advancing bad weather.

Balance Climbing Movement up slopes and cliffs too steep to walk up.

Barn Door To lose balance on one side of the body causing the climber to swing like a barn door.

Base Camp Lowest and largest fixed camp during a mountaineering ascent.

Bashie See Copperhead.

Belay To secure a climber by holding the other end of the rope.

Belay Betty, Belay Bob The girlfriend or boyfriend of an addictive rock climber.

Belay Device Rope threaded through this device provides a mechanical advantage to the belayer.

Belayer One at a belay station securing the climber by holding the other end of the rope.

Belaying Braking action, playing, paying out, or taking in of a rope tied to a climber.

Belay On Climber by the belayer when they are ready to belay.

Belay Point Spot selected by a belayer to secure himself; an object used for belaying.

Belay Slave Nonclimbing friend of an addicted rock climber.

Belay Station Safe stance—anchor, a rope, and a belayer.

"Below" Call used by British climbers warning of impending impact with objects coming from above (e.g., falling rock).

"Berg Heil!" A German greeting at the summit.

Bergschrund Top crevasse in a glacier where moving ice has separated from the main rock wall and/or static ice ("shrund").

Beta Insider information about a climb.

Beta Flash To lead a climb on the first try without problems.

Big Wall Long and sustained aid climb taking more than one day to ascend (Grade VI).

Biner Short for carabiner.

"Bird" Trad and aid climber Jim Bridwell, famous for pioneering countless hard routes in Yosemite National Park and Alaska's Ruth Gorge.

Birdbeak Tiny hooked piton.

Bivouac (Bivi) An uncomfortable sleeping place in the middle of a route.

Bivy Sack Lightweight and waterproof cocoonlike shell fitting over a sleeping bag and used instead of a tent.

Black Ice Old ice, very hard and difficult to climb.

Blast To climb quickly.

Bleausard One who frequents "Bleau" (or Fontainebleau), the site of some excellent bouldering near Paris.

Blue Ice Extremely dense ice with a watery hue and a few air bubbles.

Bolt A metal bolt, usually one quarter inch in diameter, that has been drilled into the rock (Sport Climbing, Coffin Nail).

Bomber Something that is exceptionally solid like an anchor or a hold.

Bombproof Wrong feeling that anchor is infallible.

Bonehead A novice climber.

Bong Older style of extra-wide piton.

Bootie Found gear left behind on a climb by a previous party.

Bouldering Unroped climbing done near the ground with an emphasis on hard, technical movement.

Bounce To crater from an extreme height.

Bowline Sailing knot, not recommended for climbing, unless backed up with a second knot.

Brain Bucket Helmet.

Brake Hand Hand that never loses contact with the rope while belaying.

Bucket A large, confidence-inspiring handhold (see Jug).

Buildering Climbing buildings as if they were boulder problems.

Bulge Short section of rock that is steep or overhanging.

Bust a Move Successfully execute a hard crux move.

Butterfly Knot Loop in the middle of a rope, often used in glacier travel.

Buttress Shallow ridge projecting from a mountain's main face.

Cairn Marker usually made of stacked rocks indicating trail or other path of travel.

Cam Family of spring loaded camming devices (SLCDs), such as friends, camalots, aliens, and TCUs, used as protection in traditional rock and aid climbing.

Campus An inefficient and strength-intensive technique from training on campus boards where one does pull-ups moving from one hold to another.

Campus Board Wooden board with finger ledges used for strength training.

Carabiner Oval rough-shaped aluminum device with a gate that can be opened that is used to link objects like ropes, protection, and bolts together.

Chalk White powder used to keep hands from sweating (Antigravity Powder).

Chalk Bag Small pouch filled with chalk carried around the back for dipping one's hands into while climbing.

Chausey Poor rock conditions (Chossy).

Cheese Grater To fall or slide down a slab while scraping the knees, hands, and face.

Chest Harness Bra-like harness used in conjunction with a waist harness while carrying a heavy backpack.

Chickenhead Protruding lump of rock often found on otherwise smooth granite—makes for excellent hand- and foothold.

Chimed Exhausted.

Chimney A generally vertical opening through which a climber can move.

Chimney Climbing technique used to ascend chimneys that requires placing the feet against one wall and the back against the other.

Chipped Hold Hand- or foothold created with a hammer and chisel.

Chock Passive wired protection devices, nuts and stoppers, used in traditional and aid climbing.

Chockstone A wedged stone that blocks a chimney.

Chossy Loose rock conditions.

Chute An opening that is usually wider than a chimney. A very steep and narrow snow gully (see also Couloir).

Cirque Alpine valley ringed on three sides by precipitous mountains.

Class Yosemite Decimal System (YDS) designating overall character of the climbing on a route.

5.0 to 5.4	Two hand- and two footholds for each move; holds become progressively smaller as the number increases.
5.5 to 5.6	Two hand- and two footholds are there, evident to the experienced, but not as a matter of fact to beginner.
5.7	Move missing one hand- or foothold.
5.8	Move missing two holds of the four, or missing only one but is extremely difficult.
5.9	Move with but one reasonable hold that may be for either a foot or a hand.
5.10	No hand- or footholds. Choices are to pretend a hold is there.
5.11	Obviously impossible move occasionally accomplished.
5.12	Vertical and smooth surface. No one has ever made this move. A few claim they have.
5.13	Identical to 5.12 but located under overhanging rock.

Clean Completing a trad climb without using aid techniques or yarding on protection. To remove the protection from a route placed by the leader. Climbing without falling or dogging.

Clean Aid Aid climbing without hammering pitons or placing other similar gear which damages the rock.

Cliff A (larger) piece of rock good for climbing (Crag).

Cliffhanger Hooking device used while aid climbing to hang on small ledges and pockets.

"Climb Away" Final command given by belayer to climber to acknowledge they are actually belaying the climber ("On Belay").

"Climbing" Belayer to climber when they are about to begin climbing.

Climbing Competition Sport-climbing contest usually held in climbing gyms where amateur and professional climbers compete in categories of difficulty and speed.

Climbing Gym For indoor climbing year-round.

Climbing Shoes Foot apparel for rock climbing made from smooth sticky rubber, with a tight, performance-oriented fit.

Climbing Wall Specific wall within a climbing gym.

"Climb When Ready" Belayer signal to the climber that is it safe to begin climbing.

Clip To place the rope through a carabiner.

Clove Hitch Easily adjustable climbing knot usually used to tie the rope into a carabiner.

Coffin Nails Older generation, untrustworthy bolts one eighth inch in diameter and often rusted.

Col Steep high-mountain pass.

Committing Term for a climb that cannot be safely down-climbed or retreated from easily (Run Out).

Continuous Climbing Sequential climbing in distances of less than a rope length by two or more people connected by a rope; all climbers on the move at the same time.

Copperhead Aid climbing protection made of soft copper placed in cracks only a few millimeters in diameter and then hammered into place (Head, Bashie).

Cord Thin static rope (5–7 mm).

Cordelette Loop of cord between twenty and thirty feet long used to equalize anchors.

Corn Snow Unconsolidated granular snow often found on high mountains during late spring and summer that has gone through a short freeze/thaw cycle.

Corner Inside corner or outside corner where two rock walls meet (Dihedral).

Cornice Overhanging lip of snow or ice forming on the leeward side of a ridge because of wind loading.

Couloir Cleft between two rock walls often serving both as a direct path of ascent and a dangerous funnel for falling rock and ice.

Crab Abbreviation for carabiner.

Crack Gap or fissure in the rock varying in width from fingernail- to body-width or more.

Crag Small climbing area.

Crampons Strapped-on frames for shoes and boots that have spikes to facilitate moving on ice or hard snow.

Crank To pull on a hold with much strength.

Crash Pad A large, thick foam pad that is placed beneath boulder problems to soften falls and prevent injury.

Crater To fall or to hit the ground.

Crest Very top of a ridge. To climb to the very top of a ridge or arête.

Crevasse A glacier surface opening.

Crimper Very small hold accepting only the finger tips.

Crux Part of the climb requiring the hardest moves.

Cuff A steep and high face.

Cwm The Welsh spelling for coombe or cirque.

Daisy Chain Sling sewn with numerous loops which can be tethered to protection at a variety of different lengths.

Deadpoint Dynamic move; next hold is grabbed at very top of the motion.

Death Wobbles Jittery legs. (Elvis, Sewing Machine Leg).

Deck To hit the ground during a fall.

Deep Water Soloing Free soloing high above a large body of deep water.

Demigod Highest form of life in the climbing universe.

Descender Device used for rappelling.

Dihedral Area where two vertical sections of rock join at roughly ninety degrees to form a corner.

"Dirt Me" Slang uttered by climber to the belayer for lowering from the top of a climb.

"Doctor Death" Mountaineer Mark Twight gained fame for his cavalier attitude about climbing rigorous ice/snow/mixed routes in Alaska.

Dog To rest on a rope in free climbing.

Double Fisherman's Knot Two ropes of similar diameter tied together.

Down-Climbing Descending vertical rock.

Dry Tool Mixed climbing where one ascends a rock section using ice tools to hook small ledges.

Dude Generic name for climber.

Dynamic Belay Belayer either jumps or allows a limited amount of rope to slip through the belay device while stopping a long lead fall, reducing shock of the fall upon the climber and the anchor system.

Dynamic Rope Nylon kermantle rope for climbing designed to stretch when weighted.

Dyno Dynamic lunge toward a distant hold.

EB Famous brand of sport climbing shoes that began free climbing revolution.

Edge Small but sharp ledge on a rock face often suitable for crimping.

Edging Using edge of the climbing shoe underneath the ball of the foot to stand on small footholds.

Elvis Leg Someone climbing at a limit where the climber's leg begins shaking like Elvis Presley's (Sewing Machine Leg).

Epic Experience of having a well-planned climb turn into an unexpectedly grueling adventure.

Etrier French word for webbing ladder used to aid climbing.

Expedition Style Group goes slowly up a mountain by utilizing fixed ropes. Opposite of Alpine style.

Exposure Feeling while climbing that one is very high above the ground, surrounded only by air.

Face Unbroken vertical front on a cliff or mountainside.

Face Climbing Sport and traditional climbing.

Fall Dynamic retreat from a climb.

Fall Factor Measurement of forces placed on the belay and anchor systems.

"Falling" Shouted when a climber is falling or about to fall.

FecoFile A PVC tube for storing solid human waste on big walls (Shit Tube).

Feet Footholds (slang).

Fifi Hook Open hook tied to harness.

Figure 8 Metal rappelling and belaying device shaped like an 8.

Figure-Eight Knot Most popular knot used to tie a climbing rope into harness.

Fingerlock Jam where one wedges and then twists into a crack.

Firn Old, well-consolidated snow, close to ice in density.

First Ascent First to complete a new climb, considered a special honor.

Fisherman's Knot Safety knot often used in conjunction with a figure eight-knot (Grapevine Knot).

Fixed Line Long ropes established and then left in place on the steep and difficult sections during an expedition-style siege of a large mountain to expedite movement of climbers between camps.

Fixed Pro Bolts, pitons, stuck nuts, cams, tied-off chock stones, irremovable protection.

Fixed Rope One fastened to a secure object helping climbers in ascending or descending movements.

Flail To climb unsuccessfully and with great difficulty.

Flake Thin section of rock that detached from the main face.

Flapper Piece of skin torn off hand, creating bloody wound.

Flare Crack or chimney not secure to climb because the two sides of the rock are not parallel with each other.

Flash To successfully lead a climb on the first try. Variations: on-sight flash (climber has never seen the climb before) and beta flash (the climber has studied the climb before or has seen someone do the climb).

Following Climbing after the leader has finished and cleaning the protection he placed.

Free Climbing Moving up a rock using only hands, feet, and natural holds, unaided by ropes.

Free Solo Free climbing alone without a rope or protection.

Front Pointing Used in steep snow and ice climbing where the climber stands entirely on the two forward facing points of his crampons.

Gate Carabiner part that opens.

Gendarme Pinnacle difficult to circumnavigate rising directly from the top of a ridge.

Gerry Rail A hold large enough for the most senior climbers.

Glacier Slow-moving river of ice formed by snowfall that exceeds the rate of summer melt-off.

Glissading Skiing down a snow slope without skis by simply standing up and sliding.

Gnarly Difficult, sharp, hard hold or move.

Goomba Novice climber who thinks he knows it all.

"Got Me?" A check-in call to the belayer used to warn him that you are about to hang on the rope.

Grade Number denoting the length of time required by an average climber to ascend and descend a route.

Gravical Adrenaline high felt when there is much air between climber and ground level.

Grease Unable to grip a particularly slick hold due to the presence of sweat, lactic acid, or sand.

Grigri Belay device that automatically stops the rope when a climber falls.

Gripped Paralyzed, scared.

Grounder A fall where kinetic energy is not absorbed by the rope and protection, but by earth. Can be painful.

Gully A narrow ravine.

Gumby Inexperienced rock climber.

HACE High Altitude Cerebral Edema, leading to altered states of consciousness and possibly death.

Half Rope Belaying system where the climber is belayed on two independent small-diameter ropes (usually 8 or 9 mm) which are clipped into different pieces of protection.

Hand Jam Entire hand is wedged within a crack.

Handle Big banana-shaped hold often found in indoor gyms.

Hangdog To rest on the rope while free climbing (see Dog).

HAPE High Altitude Pulmonary Edema; an advanced form of altitude sickness in which liquid accumulates in the lungs and the climber experiences wheezing, coughing, and difficulty breathing (HACE).

Hardman, Hardwoman Climber with alleged extraordinary strength; survivor of epics.

Harness Matrix of two leg loops and a waist belt made of nylon that provides the connection between the rope and the climber.

Haul Bag Large tubular bag made of heavy-duty nylon for carrying food and supplies hauled via a rope by aid climbers on multiple-day big-wall climbs.

Head Abbreviation for copperhead.

Headwall Where mountain face steepens dramatically.

Hex Abbreviation for "hexentrix," a type of nut with an eccentric hexadiagonal shape. Works for wedging and also for camming.

Hip Belay Old-fashioned belay technique that does not require a belay device where the climber brings the rope around the back of his hip to provide friction and stopping power.

HMS Caribiner with one wide side for belaying with a munter hitch.

Hold A support for a hand or foot on a rock.

Hook A generic term used to describe a variety of aid climbing gear designed to precariously hang onto rock ledges as small as the edge of a dime.

Horn Spike of rock protrusion making for a good handhold or foothold (Chickenhead).

Horror Show A frightening route to lead due to inadequate protection.

Hueco Naturally occurring pocket formed within volcanic rock by gaseous bubbles trapped when the rock cooled.

"Ice!" Yelled to those below when a climber has dislodged ice (see "Rock!").

Ice Ax A picklike device that is used for cutting holds in ice and snow and as an aid to balance (Ice Tool).

Ice Climbing An increasingly popular genre of climbing where one ascends vertical or near-vertical ice pillars by using ice tools, crampons, and ice screws.

Ice Fall Steep section on a glacier where the ice becomes extremely broken and unstable.

Ice Screw Very sharp threaded tube capable of being screwed into hard ice, used for protection while ice climbing.

Italian Hitch Munter hitch knot or HMS knot.

Jam To wedge a finger, hand, fist, knee, or foot within a crack.

Jamming Techniques used to ascend cracks by placing jams.

Jug To move up a rope using ascenders while aid climbing.

Jugs Gear used to ascend a rope while aid climbing; slang for "Jumars."

Jumar Popular brand of rope-ascending devices.

Jumar To ascend a rope using Jumars or other ascending devices.

Karabiner British spelling of carabiner.

Kernmantle Rope Modern climbing rope with bundles of continuous nylon filaments (Kern) surrounded by a braided protective sheath (Mantle).

Knife Edge Extremely narrow and exposed ridge with big drops on both sides.

Knotted Cord Piece of cord with knot tied into the end used for protection.

Krab Carabiner.

Largo Start A climb or bouldering problem where the first move starts with a jump for high holds. Named after John Long (or "Largo").

Laser Cut A crack, usually found on sandstone, which has two sides that are very straight and parallel to each other (Splitter).

Lead To ascend a climb from bottom up by placing protection or clipping fixed protection with the rope.

Leader First person in upward climbs; one in charge.

Ledge Flat bit on a rock.

Lieback Climbing technique based on counterforce. One pulls with hands, pushes with feet. Upward progress gained through a shuffling motion.

Locking Biner Carabiner where gate can be locked in closed position.

Lock-off Strenuous position where one holds onto the rock with one bent arm and uses other arm to reach up for the next hold, or to place or clip protection.

Lowering Descending something or somebody.

"Lowering!" Call from the belayer to the climber when the latter is leaning on the rope and about to be lowered to the bottom of the climb.

Manky Marginal quality or old protection, not safe to rely upon.

Mantle Climbing technique where the climber presses down with his hands in order to get a foot onto the same hold as his hands. Used when there are no higher handholds within reach.

Mixed Climb Route requiring combination of different styles of ascent—mixed free and aid climbing, mixed rock and ice climbing, and so forth.

Moat Gap between snow and ice on a rock wall.

Mountain Walking Going across rocky terrain on foot.

Multipitch Climb A climb consisting of more than one pitch.

Munge Dirt and vegetation sometimes found in cracks (Choss).

Munter Hitch Knot used for belaying or rappelling in place of a belay device.

Nailing Aid climbing with a hammer and pitons.

Needle Rock formation with a pointed shape (Pinnacle).

Névé Consolidated granular snow formed by repeated freeze-and-thaw cycles.

Notch Small pass.

Nut Metal wedge for protection in cracks generally less than an inch across.

Nut Tool Metal hook used to help clean nuts stuck in the rock due to a fall or poor placement.

Objective Hazard Natural environment hazard classification: crevasses, weather, exposed terrain.

"Off Belay" Climber's yell after the finish of a climb or pitch when a belay is no longer needed. The belayer then removes the rope from the belay device.

Off Width Crack too big for fist jams, too small for chimneying. Often difficult to climb and frequently avoided.

"On Belay?" Climber's yell to belayer, starting a dialog which checks that both are ready to safely begin.

On-Sight (Flash) Successfully leading a sport or trad climb on the first try without possessing beta about it or having seen anyone climb it before.

Open Book Two vertical rock walls coming together roughly at ninety degrees, forming the inside of a corner.

Overcam To compress a cam to absolute minimum size during placement; cleaning becomes extremely difficult or impossible.

Overhand Knot Simple, multiple-purpose knot.

Overhand Loop Simplest type of knot possible.

Overhang Rock (or ice) that is more than vertical.

Over-Kilned Boilerplate or flaky rock.

Party Climb The act of several individuals roped to each other to climb a cliff.

Pass Lowest passage between two mountains.

Passive Protection Nuts and hexes, used by trad climbers, that are wedged into cracks; unlike active protection, they are not mechanical devices with springs.

Pendulum To swing on the rope.

Picket Two- to three-foot-long aluminum device hammered into hard snow or buried within soft snow creating an anchor point.

Pig Haul bag using for big wall climbing.

Pillar Outside corner.

Pink Point Redpoint a climb where the pro and runners have been preplaced.

Pinnacle Rock formation with a characteristic pointed shape; also called a "needle."

Pitch A section of climb between two belays and no longer than the length of one rope—check your topo. A treacherous and steep part of a mountain.

Piton An iron spike that is hammered into cracks and used as an aid in climbing technique.

Piton Hammer A hammer that is used to hammer pitons.

Plunge Stepping The climber walks down a steep snow slope by kicking heels into the slope while keeping toes up and weight forward.

Pocket Hold formed by a small depression in the rock.

Portaledge Foldable hanging platform used for sleeping on big wall climbs without ledges.

Postholing Exhausting process of walking through deep snow, named after shape left by the climber's footprints.

Problem A rated and named route up a boulder.

Protection (Pro) Equipment placed while lead climbing and connected to the rope through quickdraws or slings to shorten the length of a potential fall.

Prusik Sliding knot to ascend a rope, named after its inventor, Dr. Karl Prusik.

Pumped Overworked muscles, particularly the forearms.

Pumpy Climb that makes the climber pumped.

Quick Draw Short sling with carabiners on either side for clipping the rope to a point of protection.

Rack To organize the rack before climbing.

Rally To climb exceptionally well, especially on normally difficult climbs.

Ramp Low-angled ascending ledge.

Rappel (Rap) To descend by sliding down a rope.

Rappeler One who enjoys sliding down ropes instead of climbing up rocks.

Rappel Point The object a rappel rope is fastened to.

Rating Number denoting technical difficulty of the climb.

RDS Rapid Deceleration Syndrome; military term for very sudden illness happening at the end of a long fall.

Redpoint To lead a sport climb without falling or hangdogging. Unlike on-sighting, it is common to practice a hard sport climb many times before it is successfully redpointed (see Pink Point).

Resident Protection Fixed pro.

Resin Alternative to chalk. Can do permanent damage to the rock and is not allowed anywhere in the United States for that reason.

Rest Step Pacing technique for climbing low- to mid-angled slopes; pausing downhill, with legs and knees straight, heels down, in between each step.

Rib A slender buttress on a mountain similar to an arête, but on a much larger scale.

Ridge High divide extending out from a peak.

Ring Large ring cemented in the rock as a bolt.

"Rock!" Warning to those below that something is heading down toward them.

Roof A more or less horizontally overhanging part of a climb.

Rope Long and round nylon fabrication climbing rope generally between ten and eleven millimeter in diameter. "Half ropes" are between 8.5 and nine millimeter in diameter.

"Rope!" Warning when the climber is about to throw a rope down to the base of a crag, usually before rappelling.

Rope Soloing Climbing alone, using a rope for safety.

Route Particular path up a rock formation or mountain.

Runner Length of nylon with a carabiner at each end used to connect the rope to protection.

Running Beta Being told beta continually while attempting a climb.

Run Out Climb with long distances between pieces of protection.

Saddle A pass between two mountains.

"Safe" British equivalent of "Off Belay."

SAR Search and Rescue.

Schwag Horrible rock conditions.

Scrambling Easy climbing a that can be done unroped.

Screamer A very, very long fall; also, a piece of equipment resembling a quick draw that is clipped to protection of marginal quality.

Scree Small loose rocks covering the slope below a cliff that are often slippery and frustrating to ascend (Talus).

Screwgate Type of locking carabiner using a screw mechanism.

Scrube Hammer-in, screw-out type of ice screw.

Second Climber who follows the leader.

Self-Arrest Using an ice ax to stop a sliding fall down a snow slope.

Send To climb a route with ease.

Serac Large, unstable block or tower of ice found within icefall of a glacier.

Sewn Up Traditional route has so much gear placed on it that the crack looks as if it has been sewn shut.

Sharp End End of a rope tied to a leader.

Short Roping Two climbers tie into the middle of a rope relatively close to each other and then climb simultaneously.

Side Pull Handhold that can be pulled only horizontally.

Simul-Climbing Quick progress over relatively easy ground where both climbers climb at the same time instead of belaying each another. They are tied together with a rope and place protection as they go.

Simul-Soloing Resembles simul-climbing except that no rope is used. Using no rope is justified by the belief that the available protection is inadequate in quality to catch the climbers, thus a fall by one will pull the other to his possible death.

Sit Start Bouldering problem started in a sitting position.

Sketch Pad Cushion used for bouldering.

Skyhook Type of hook used for aid climbing.

Slab Low-angled rock often so smooth and featureless that smearing is required in order to climb. Dreaded by many climbers.

"Slack" Call from climber to the belayer when more rope is needed.

SLCD Spring-Loaded Camming Device.

Sling Nylon length with a carabiner at each end used to connect the rope to protection (Runner).

Slingshot Rope is preclipped into an anchor at the top of the climb in a top rope setup. Climber starts from the ground, goes up the anchor, and then is lowered down to the ground again.

Sloper Insecure handhold slanting downward.

Smearing Foot technique most often used on low-angle rock in which the sole of the climbing shoe is used to generate as much friction as possible.

Snow Bridge Thin layer of freshly fallen snow concealing a crevasse underneath.

Snow Pit Hole dug in a snow slope to assess avalanche stability.

Softman, Softwoman Formerly "Hardman" or "Hardwoman" able to accomplish epic climbs in comfortable style.

Soloing Climbing alone, but not necessarily unroped.

Splitter A crack with a consistent width for a long distance, thus "splitting" the rock face into two sections.

Sport Climbing Climbing emphasizing gymnastic movement; falling is relatively common because leaders clip relatively closely spaced bolts or other fixed protection.

Spray To brag or gloat.

Static Climbing Climbing conditions where the belayer is always above the climber and where there is always one rope-length or less of height.

Static Rope One which does not stretch when weighted and is generally not used for lead climbing or following.

Stem To bridge the feet between two holds, often on different rock walls, in order to take weight off the arms.

Step Kicking Climbing a snow slope by creating miniature platforms for the feet through a kicking motion.

Sticht Plate A belay device consisting of a plate with two slots in it. An original creation by Franz Sticht.

"Stick It!" Slang for "Reach for it and hold on!"

Sticky Rubber Soft and smooth rubber specially designed for climbing shoes that generates a high degree of friction when placed upon rock.

Stoked Fired up, wanting to finish a particular climb.

Stylin' Looking good, climbing well.

Summit Top of a mountain or rock. To reach the summit.

"Take!" Call from climber to the belayer for extra rope to be taken in so he can weight the rope and rest.

"Take In" British equivalent of "Up Rope."

"Taking In!" Call when climber is off belay and about to pull up the slack between him and the belayer.

Talus Large rocks and boulders on the slope below a cliff.

Tape Knot Threaded overhand knot. Solid but not fail proof (Water Knot).

Tarn Small alpine lake.

Ten Essentials Climbing gear necessities.

"Tension!" Call from belayer to climber when there is a need for extra rope to be taken in, in order for the rope to be weighted and then lowered.

Tension Climbing Climbing conditions where the climber is held by the belayer with tension on the rock.

Thank God Bucket A massive handhold when climber needs it.

"That's Me" Call from climber to belayer, usually on multipitch climbs, when all the slack has been taken in and the climber is ready to be put on belay.

Third Classing Climbing on easy ground without a rope.

Tick Marks Smears of chalk to help locate small holds when bouldering or sport climbing.

"Tight Rope" ("Tight") Serious request to belayer to take slack out of the system.

Timberline Elevation or line above which trees do not grow.

Toe Bottom of a buttress.

Topo A brief route drawing depicting locations of major crack systems, bolts, ledges, trees, belay stances, the location(s) of the crux(es), ratings, and other useful information.

Top-Rope In free-climbing a route, the safety rope is attached to the top of the climb.

Trad Abbreviation for traditional (climbing).

Trad Fall Leading a trad climb, the climber is caught by gear he placed.

Trad Rat A climber preferring trad climbing to bouldering or sport climbing.

Trail Markers Generally wooden markers placed on a route for identification purposes.

Traversing Zigzag pattern movement.

Tri-Cam Passive protection in rock climbing resembling a pyramid fixed atop a half-circle.

Tunnel Hourglass shape in rock allowing runner or cord to be fed through for protection.

Twin Ropes System for belaying that uses two smaller-diameter ropes similar to half ropes. Both ropes are always clipped through the same protection points.

Twistlock A style of locking carabiner in which the gate is locked with a spring-loaded clip.

UIAA Union Internationale des Associateions d'Alpinisme, the international body that sets standards for rock climbing and mountaineering equipment.

Undercling Handhold best gripped on its underside.

"Up Rope!" Climber's directions to the belayer when he wants slack taken in or a tighter belay.

Verglas Thin water ice on rock that makes climbing insecure.

Vôgen Great, terrific.

V Scale Open-ended system for rating the difficulty of boulder problems.

Warthog A roughened spike hammered into certain kinds of ice or frozen turf for protection.

"Watch Me!" Call from climber to the belayer when falling may be imminent.

Water Ice Very dense ice formed directly from water that generally looks light blue or clear, making for challenging ice climbing (see White Ice, Black Ice, Blue Ice).

Water Knot Most popular knot for tying webbing.

Webbing Flat and extremely strong material made of nylon that is hollow inside.

Weighting Delicate aid climbing test whereby the climber slowly hangs on a piece of protection to see if it will hold.

Whipper Very long and often scary fall.

White Ice Formed from snow that has partially melted and then refrozen multiple times, providing excellent climbing.

Wind Loading Wind transporting snow from the windward side to the leeward side of a ridge or pass.

Wombing A no-hands-rest.

Woodie Homemade climbing wall often made of plywood.

Yabo A "sit start." Named after John Yablonski, Southern California climber, nicknamed "Yabo."

Yard To pull up on a piece of protection at the crux of the climb when the climber cannot otherwise perform the move.

YDS Yosemite Decimal System, an open-ended system for rating the difficulty of climbs, developed by the Sierra Club.

Zawn (British) A deep and narrow fold or inlet in a sea cliff.

Zipper Aid fall, in which pieces of protection pull out one after the other and leader plummets out of control toward the ground. Often ends with a grounder (or a cardiac arrest).

Z-Pulley System Two pulleys that provide a 3:1 mechanical advantage used by mountaineers for hauling injured climbers; aids climbers for lifting heavy haul bags.

Olympics

According to historical records, the first ancient Olympic Games can be traced back to 776 BC. They were dedicated to the Olympian gods and were staged on the ancient plains of Olympia. They continued for nearly twelve centuries, until Emperor Theodosius decreed in AD 393 that all such "pagan cults" be banned.

The first Olympic footrace was run over a distance of 606 feet and 9 inches. This was a Greek unit of measurement called a *stadion,* and the race was named for the unit of measurement. The stands and the viewing area together with the site where the race was staged all eventually were referred to by the word *stadion.* And the site of the first Olympics, the *stadion* at Olympia, was the forerunner of all the world's stadiums.

The ancient Olympic Games were initially a one-day event until 684 BC, when they were extended to three days. In the fifth century BC, the games were extended again to cover five days. The ancient games included running, long jump, shot put, javelin, boxing, *pankration,* and equestrian events.

The famous marathon race did not exist in the ancient games. The starting pistol of the first Olympic marathon was fired on April 14, 1896, at 2:00 p.m.

Famous Greeks attended, and even participated in, the ancient Olympic Games: Socrates, Pythagoras, Plato, Aristotle, and even the father of medicine, Hippocrates.

Here is a list of all the Modern Olympic Games.

Olympic Summer Games:

Athens 1896
Paris 1900
St. Louis 1904
London 1908

Stockholm 1912
Antwerp 1920
Paris 1924
Amsterdam 1928
Los Angeles 1932
Berlin 1936
London 1948
Helsinki 1952
Melbourne 1956
Rome 1960
Tokyo 1964
Mexico City 1968
Munich 1972
Montreal 1976
Moscow 1980
Los Angeles 1984
Seoul 1988
Barcelona 1992
Atlanta 1996
Sydney 2000
Athens 2004

Olympic Winter Games:

Chamonix 1924
St. Moritz 1928
Lake Placid 1932
Garmisch-Partenkirchen 1936
St. Moritz 1948
Oslo 1952
Cortina d'Ampezzo 1956
Squaw Valley 1960
Innsbruck 1964
Grenoble 1968
Sapporo 1972
Innsbruck 1976

Lake Placid 1980
Sarajevo 1984
Calgary 1988
Albertville 1992
Lillehammer 1994
Nagano 1998
Salt Lake City 2002

Future Olympic Games:

Turin 2006 (Winter)
Beijing 2008 (Summer)
Vancouver 2010 (Winter)

Platform Tennis (Paddle Tennis)

Alley A two-foot-wide area between the side line and the alley line that runs the length of the court on either side.

Alley Line The line that marks the inside of the alley.

Alley Shot A shot straight down the alley area of the opposition's court.

Backcourt The playing court area between the service line and the baseline.

Backhand A stroke or grip in which the back of the hand faces the ball.

Backspin A backward spinning rotation applied to a ball (Underspin).

Baseline The end lines of the playing court.

Blitz A hard driving shot by a player on defense followed up by movement into a position close to the net.

Carry A condition where the ball fails to leave the paddle the instant it is hit.

Center Line A line that divides the right-center and left-center courts.

Chop Shot A downward, oblique stroke used for backspin shots.

Corner Shots Shots into the left or right corner of the screens that surround the court of the opponent(s).

Cross-court Shots Diagonal shots.

Deuce A scoring situation (when the game is at 40-40) when a team needs to take two straight points to win the game.

Fault An improper serve.

Foot Fault A fault as a result of a server's foot crossing or touching the baseline before he has served the ball.

Forecourt The area between the net and the service line, including the alley portions forward of the service line.

Forehand A stroke performed with the palm of the hand in the direction of the intended movement of the ball.

Let A point that must be replayed—for example, when a serve hits the top of the net and bounes into the proper service court.

Lob A stroke that lifts the ball high in the air into the opponent's playing area.

Off-the-Screen Shots Shots executed by hitting a ball after it has rebounded from the screens.

Overhead A stroke employed to drive a high ball down into an opponent's court.

Playing Court A marked-off area, twenty feet by forty-four feet, where paddle tennis takes place.

Rally A series of shots in which both sides are able to keep the ball in play to the conclusion of a point.

Receiver The player positioned in the service court who receives the serve.

Running around One's Backhand The action of a player who, in order to avoid making a backhand stroke, moves into a position to execute a forehand stroke (e.g., when a player moves to the left to avoid a backhand on a ball approaching on his left).

Screens Twelve-foot-high wire screening that surrounds the court.

Server The player who is serving.

Service The stroke that starts each point in a game and is the means of getting the ball into play.

Service Break The winning of a game by a receiver against the service of an opponent.

Service Courts The areas across the net where serving takes place, twelve feet deep by eight feet wide and marked off by the service line, the center line, the alley line, and the net.

Service Line The line that divides the service courts from the backcourt.

Side Line The line that marks the outside of the alley.

Slice A ball that spins sideways in its forward movement.

Strategic Spot A position on the court that enables a player to most effectively reach and hit the ball.

Topspin The spin of a ball in the same direction as its flight, caused by hitting up and behind it.

Volley To return a ball before it bounces.

Racquetball

Ace A good serve that the intended receiver is unable to return and that thus scores a point for the server.

Amoeba Man A very slow-moving player.

Apex The highest point which a ball bounces.

"A" Player A highly skilled player in tournament competition.

Around-the-Wall Ball A shot that strikes high up on the side wall, hits the front wall, then caroms to the other side wall, and finally bounces on the floor at three-quarter court.

Avoidable Hinder Resulting in the loss of a point or serve, an interference that causes problems in a rally's continuity.

Backcourt The area behind the short line.

Backhand Corner The juncture of the side and back walls on the same side as the backhand of a player.

Back-into-Back-Wall Shot A rear-wall drive that goes on the fly to the front wall.

Back Wall The rear wall.

Blinkus of the Thinkus To experience a mental lapse while playing.

Body Surf A diving, sliding move onto the court floor by a perspiring performer.

Bottom Boarder A flawless kill shot off the front wall's bottom board.

"B" Player A player of average skills in tournament competition.

Bull's-eye A front-wall target that when hit results in a perfect serve.

Bumblebee Ball Mis-hit ball that behaves like a wounded bumblebee.

Bumper Ball Mis-hit shot on the bumper (the protective racquet rim covering) that can cause a "bumblebee ball."

Control The consistent ability to hit the ball to the intended spots.

Controller A player who relies on a defensive and passing game.

Court Hinder An unavoidable hinder (a door latch, for example) that interferes with the ball and stops a rally, causing the point to be played over.

"C" Player The least skilled classification in tournament play.

Crack Ball A ball that is hit into the cracks between a wall and the floor.

Crotch The intersection of two playing surfaces.

Crotch Serve A serve that lands in the intersection of the front wall and the ceiling or floor and is a side-out.

Crowding Playing too close to an opponent and thus causing an avoidable hinder.

Die A ball that just makes it to the front wall and rebounds with little or no bounce.

Dig To get to a low kill shot just before its second bounce.

Donut No points scored in a game.

Drop Shot A softly lofted ball that hits low on the front wall (Dump Shot).

Error A misplay of the ball.

Exchange The end of a rally that effects a point or a side-out.

Fault An illegal serve.

Fishbowl A court composed of one or more glass walls.

Flat Rollout A kill shot in which the ball hits the front wall so close to the floor that it comes off with no bounce.

Floater A poorly hit ball or one with much backspin that floats toward the front wall.

Foot Fault Illegal move of a foot before or while serving.

Four-Wall Racquetball Indoor play on a court with four walls and a ceiling—the most popular form of the game.

Freak Ball A winning shot that is hit well from an unusual position.

Frontcourt The area in front of the short line plus the service box.

Game Twenty-one points equals one game.

Garbage Serve An off-speed serve that comes to the receiver at about shoulder level and is generally returned to the ceiling (Half Lob).

Garpike Serve A forehand crosscourt serve to the forehand of the opponent.

Gun Hand The hand that grips the racquet.

Half-and-Half The doubles-team procedure of dividing the court in half, with coverage responsibilities understood.

Hand-out A loss of service in doubles play by the first partner.

Head The racquet surface that strikes the ball.

I Formation A doubles team procedure in which one player covers the frontcourt and the other is responsible for the backcourt.

Isolation Strategy An effort in doubles play to hit the ball to one player while attempting to keep the other partner out of the game flow.

Kill A low shot hit off the front wall that rebounds so slightly as to make a return impossible.

Let A fault.

Long Serve A serve that hits the back wall on the fly.

Match The winner of two out of three games wins the match.

Mercy Ball Holding back on a swing to avoid having the ball or the racquet strike an opponent.

Off Hand The hand that does not grip the racquet.

Out An illegal serve that causes a loss of service.

Paddleball This hybrid racket sport was invented in 1930 by a physical education teacher at the University of Michigan. Earl Riskey peeled off the fuzz from a tennis ball that had been soaked in gasoline to create the first paddleball. He then created a variation of the paddle-tennis racket and the sport of paddleball was on its way.

Photon A powerfully hit shot (Bullet, Powder Ball).

Plum Ball A cinch setup.

Pushing Off Illegal contact with an opponent.

Racquet The Arabic word meaning "palm of the hand" is the origin of the term.

Receiving Line The five-foot line.

Rim A racquet's frame.

Roadrunner A player skilled in getting to the ball.

Rollout A flat kill shot that is impossible to retrieve.

Screen Ball The visual hindering of an opponent that results in the replay of the point.

Service Box The serving area, which is located between the front and short lines; the spot where the non-serving partner on a doubles team must be positioned when his partner serves.

Shoot the Ball To attempt a kill shot.

Short Line The line that a served ball must pass before striking the floor; it is parallel to and midway between the front and back walls.

Short Serve A serve that does not go beyond the short line.

Side-Out Loss of service by one side; points can be scored only by serving side.

Skip Ball A ball that strikes the floor prior to its getting to the front wall (Splinter Ball).

Straddle Ball A ball that comes off the front wall and goes through the legs of a player.

Target Area The area that the server wishes the ball to go to after a front wall rebound.

Thong A strap affixed to the racquet handle that has a loop that goes around the wrist of a player.

Three Quarters and One Quarter A diagonal division of court coverage by a doubles team in which the court is divided from one front corner to the opposite back corner.

Touch Fine control of the racquet.

Rugby

Advantage The referee's allowing of play to continue after an infringement if the nonoffending team gains a territorial or technical advantage.

Blind Side Generally the side closer to the touch line—the side of the field where the fly-half (stand-off half) has positioned himself at line-out, ruck, maul, and scrummage.

Crosskick An across-the-field attacking kick.

Dead Ball A ball not in play, blown dead by referee's whistle.

Defending Team The team in whose half of the field the stopping of play takes place.

Drawing Your Man Getting an opponent to commit to tackling the ball carrier instead of the man who is about to receive a pass.

Dribbling Ball control with the feet and the shins, a technique sometimes used by a pack of forwards who are advancing.

Drop Kick The kicking of the ball after it is dropped from the hands and just as it rebounds off the ground. A drop kick is made by the defending team from within the 25-yard line.

Drop-Out A method of restarting play, either after an unsuccessful conversion attempt, or from behind or at the 25-yard line, after an attacking player kicks, carries, passes, or knocks the halves and three-quarters that is closer to their opposition.

Dummy To fake passing the ball.

Fall on the Ball By turning his back on the opposition, a player drops on the ball to stop the opposition's foot rush.

Five-Yard Scrum After a defending player knocks, carries, passes, heels, or kicks the ball over his own goal line—and it becomes dead because it was touched down or went outside the playing field—the attacking team is given a scrum five yards from the goal line and opposite the spot where the ball went into the in-goal area.

Fly Kick A wild and unplanned kick (Hacking).

Foot-Up A penalty given to any member of either team in the front row of a scrum who advances a foot before the ball has touched the ground.

Free Kick If a score is being attempted, a free kick may be a dropkick or a place kick; if no score is being attempted, it is taken as a punt.

Garryown The roots for this term, which describes a high-lofted kick in rugby, come from the Irish rugby club of the same name. Employed as an offensive maneuver, this punt is used to gain ground, especially in those situations when forwards surge down the field.

Grounding the Ball Downward pressure applied to the ball by a player's hand(s), arm(s), or upper body to score a try.

Grubber Kick A punt designed to bounce along the ground.

Handling Game A phrase used to distinguish rugby football from association football (soccer) after 1823.

Knock-on Striking the ball with hand or arm toward the opposition's dead-ball line.

Line-Out A formation of at least two players from each team in single lines parallel to the touch line awaiting the ball thrown between them; it may extend from five to fifteen yards from the touch line.

Locks Set-scrum second-row forwards.

Loose-Head A position that is the front row forward nearest to the referee in a scrum.

Lying Deep A deep formation in an attack by the backs (halves and three-quarters) to get enough running room.

Lying Shallow A shallow formation in defense by the backs.

Mark A fair catch from a kick, a knock-on, or an intentional throw forward executed by a player with both feet on the ground who shouts "mark."

Maul A mob of players on both sides around a player in possession of the ball who shove and jostle each other to be able to get the ball when it is finally released.

No-Side The end of the game.

Offside Generally, a player is offside when in front of the ball played by another member of his team.

Pack The forwards.

Penalty Try A try granted by the referee to the attacking team if he judges that a try would have been scored if not for the defending team's foul play, misconduct, or obstruction; the try takes place between the posts and afterward a conversion may be attempted.

Place Kick A kick of a ball placed on the ground.

Player Ordered Off A player ejected from the game who may not return to play again in that game.

Punt A maneuver in which the ball is dropped from a player's hands and is kicked before it touches the ground—not a scoring kick, but one used to gain a tactical advantage.

Push-over Try A situation that occurs when the defending team is pushed from a scrum over its goal line into its goal-area by the attacking pack; a try is scored when an attacking member falls on the ball.

Ruck A loose scrum with the ball lying on the ground.

Rugby In 1823 a game of football (known to Americans as "soccer") was being fiercely played at Rugby College in England. One of the players, William Webb Ellis, broke a rule of the game by picking up the ball and running with it, thus creating one of the more historic moments in sports. The play was nullified, and Ellis was censured. Later, after much debate and discussion about what the youth had done, the school's officials decided that he had a good idea. Rugby College thus invented a new rule and a new game—rugby football. Close by the Rugby playing grounds is a tablet that celebrates the event. This stone commemorates the exploit of William Webb Ellis, who, with a fine disregard for the rules of football as played in his time, first took the ball in his arms and ran with it, thus originating the distinctive feature of the Rugby game.

Scrummage A play in which the forwards on each team lock arms and crouch over, the two sides meeting head-to-head and the ball being put into play in the tunnel between the front rows; three players must compose the front row of each side (Scrum).

Touch The ball is in touch after being carried on or over the touch line, or when it bounces on or passes over the touch line. A ball that passed over the touch line in the air and then is blown into play again by the wind is judged in-touch where it passed over the line.

Touch-Down A situation that takes place when a player 1grounds the ball in his own in-goal area—not a score.

Try A score worth four points accomplished by the grounding of the ball in the opposition's goal area by a member of the attacking team.

Up and Under A timed high kick within the field of play hit so that the kicker's teammates are positioned under the ball as it comes down.

Wheel A maneuver that takes place in a set-scrum, which is rotated when the ball is at the feet of the lock forwards; the players break to one side, advancing and dribbling the ball.

Sailing

Abaft Toward the stern.

Abeam At right angles to the boat's centerline.

Admiral's Cup Named for its presenter (the admiral) and other members of the Royal Ocean Racing Club (RORC), this cup originated in 1957. It is an international trophy for which teams of three boats from different nations compete when they participate in the Fastnet, Britannia Cup, Channel Race, and New York Yacht Club Race.

Aft Toward the back of the boat; the stern.

America's Cup The Royal Yacht Club of England in 1851 donated a trophy, originally called the Hundred-Guinea Cup, that was to go to the winner of a race around the Isle of Wight. The yacht race was a part of the ceremonies of the London Exposition of that year. Valued at about $500, the cup was won by a United States schooner named America, which defeated fourteen British yachts. The British were not too impressed with the American accomplishment and maintained that they would "in due time" get back the cup. As the competition evolved, the trophy was given to the New York Yacht Club for permanent and perpetual international competition and has been presented to the champions of a series of international races for twelve-meter yachts. The America's Cup still remains—as it always has—in the United States. More than $75,000,000 has been expended in attempting to win the cup named for the vessel named for the nation that originally won the trophy.

Amidships The center of the boat, midway between the bow and the stern and midway between the sides.

Backstays Lines from the mast to the stern which secure the mast.

Ballast Weight at the lowest point of the boat for purposes of stabilization. "Outside ballast" is lead or iron weight in keels. "Inside ballast" is movable weight inside the boat.

Batten A strip of plastic or wood that stiffens the roach in a sail's leech.

Batten Pocket The pocket that holds the batten.

Beam The width of the boat.

Bear Off Turning downwind, away from the wind.

Beat To sail windward.

Bend To make a sail fast to a spar through the use of knots, hooks, grooves, slides, and so forth.

Bermuda Race This sailing event originated in 1923 and is cosponsored by the Cruising Club of America and the Royal Bermuda Yacht Club. A race from New York to Bermuda, it alternates with the Fastnet, being held in even-numbered years (see Fastnet).

Bilge The turn of the hull below the waterline. Also, the area where water collects inside the hull.

Bitter End The free end of a rope, used for fastening.

Block Pulley.

Boom The spar at the bottom of a sail at right angles to the mast.

Bow The front end of a boat.

Bridle A length of wire fastened at either end and pulled at some point within its length.

Broach To swing sharply toward the wind when running, because of poor steering, heavy seas, or heavy wind.

Bumpers Devices on a boat's side for protection from docks, piles, other boats, and so forth.

Burdened Vessel A vessel that does not have right of way.

Centerboard A device located on the boat's centerline which can be lowered to navigate in shallow waters for boats with permanent keels or to secure against a sideward slip.

Centerline The center of a boat from bow to stern.

Chain Plates Metal plates bolted to the side of a boat to hold shrouds and stays.

Charts Nautical maps that contain navigation aids, water depths, landmarks, and so forth.

Chock A casting of metal or plastic through which lines are led to other vessels or to shore and which guide these lines against chafing.

Cleat A metal, plastic, or wood device that holds a line secure.

Clew The lower aft corner of a triangular sail.

Close-Hauled Sailing as close as possible to the wind with sails trimmed for beating (On the Wind, Beating, Strapped Down).

Coaming A raised protection around the cockpit.

Cockpit The portion of the boat for the crew to sail and sit in.

Cringle An eye of metal threaded into a sail for securing purposes.

Dagger Board A movable, stiff device used to avoid side slip.

Deck Plate A plate bolted to the deck, usually with an eye for shackles or blocks.

Downhaul A rope or rope/block that pulls down the boom to tighten the luffs.

Draft The deepest point of a sail from the depth of its curve to an imaginary line drawn from its tack to its clew (its two bottom corners). Also, the distance from a boat's waterline to the bottom of its hull or keel.

Ease To relieve the pressure on a sail by letting out the sheet.

Eye Splice A splice in which the end of a rope is made into a loop.

Fairlead An eye or casting that guides a line where a block is not needed.

Fastnet This major offshore race is sailed in August of every other year (alternating with the Bermuda Race) over a distance of 605 miles, from Cowes, Isle of Wight, to Fastnet Rock (off Cape Clear, in southwest Ireland), and back to Plymouth. The race originated in 1925. The name of the race is derived from Fastnet Rock.

Fetch To reach a goal without coming about. Distance free from obstruction of tide or wind.

Fly A masthead pennant or piece of yarn in rigging, used to indicate apparent wind.

Foot The lower edge of a sail.

Fore To the front (Forward).

Free Sailing with the wind anywhere from abeam to directly behind.

Freeboard The vertical distance from the waterline to the deck.

Furl To wrap a sail to a spar.

Gooseneck A joint-type fitting securing the boom to the mast.

Halyard A line for raising and lowering the sails.

Hard Alee Short for "the helm is hard alee," which is the signal for the movement of the rudder incident to turning.

Head The upper corner of a triangular sail. Also, a boat's toilet.

Headboard A wood or plastic stiffener used in the head of a sail.

Headstays Lines from the mast to the bow that secure the mast.

Head to Wind Sails shaking as the boat heads into wind; luffing.

Headway Forward motion.

Heave To throw or cast; to pull on a rope. As a noun, the rise and fall of a vessel.

Heel To tip or tilt.

Helm The lever used as a rudder. Also, the tendency of a vessel to steer relative to the wind; "weather helm" means tending to steer toward the wind.

Hull The body of a boat exclusive of rigging, centerboard, and so forth.

In Irons A condition where the boat faces the wind and has lost all headway (In Stays).

Jib A triangular sail in front of the mast.

Jibe To change tacks by turning away from the wind toward the sail.

Jib-Headed A triangular sail (Marconi, Bermudian).

Jibstay The stay that raises the jib.

Jumper Strut A device on the front side of the mast to increase stability of the upper part of the mast.

Keel The backbone of a boat. Also, a fixed extension at the bottom of the boat for greater stability.

Knot Friction devices to keep a line from slipping. Also, a nautical measure of speed: "one knot" means one nautical mile per hour. (A nautical mile is equal to one minute of latitude and is 1.15 statute miles.)

Lanyard A short, light line.

Lateral Plane The hull, keel, or centerboard—the area designed to offset drift or slippage.

Layline The line on which a boat can fetch a mark or buoy.

Lee Opposite to windward; the side of anything away from the wind. A lee shore is the shore at which the wind blows. "Leeward" means toward the lee side.

Leech The aft edge of a sail.

Leeway The distance slipped to leeward.

Lines Ropes or wires used in rigging.

List The leaning of a vessel to the heavier side.

Luff The fore edge of a sail. Also, the shaking of a sail when its head is toward the wind (luffing).

Mainmast The sole mast of a small boat; the principal mast of a larger boat.

Mainsail A sail rigged on the back of the mainmast.

Mainsheet A line used to control the mainsail.

Make Fast To tie up; secure.

Mast A vertical spar on which the sails are hoisted.

Moor To secure to a mooring.

Mooring A means of securing a boat in water while it is not sailing so that it is free to move in a complete circle.

Offshore Away from shore.

Off the Wind Sailing other than a close-hauled course.

On the Wind Sailing a close-hauled course.

Outboard Beyond the hull.

Outhaul A line used to secure the foot of a sail.

Overstand To go beyond the layline unnecessarily.

Pay Off To ease out a length of line or to turn away from the wind with the bow (Pay Out).

Pendant A short piece of line used for securing.

Pennant A length of line that fastens a boat to a mooring. A triangular flag.

Pinch To sail a boat inefficiently close to the wind.

Point To head high, close to the wind.

Port Left.

Port Side To sail with the wind from the port side.

Privileged Vessel A vessel with the right of way.

Quarter The boat's side between the beam and the stern.

Rail The outer edge of the deck.

Rake The inclination of the mast fore aft.

Reach Sailing a course between close-hauled and running.

"Ready about!" A spoken signal to prepare for tacking.

Reef To make a sail smaller or reduce sail area.

Reeve To pass a line through a block or fairlead.

Rig A boat's sail-plan and mast arrangement.

Rigging Spars, sails, lines, blocks, and so forth. "Standing rigging" is permanent; "Running rigging" can be moved about.

Roach The curve in the foot, leech, or luff of a sail.

Rode The anchor line.

Run To sail almost directly before the wind. Also, the aft underwater shape of the hull.

Sail Stops Lines used to tie a sail to a spar.

Seacocks Safety devices placed at or below waterline to control water flow in or out of a boat.

Seaway Sea area.

Shackle U-shaped metal fittings that join two objects.

Sheave The wheel in a block (Pulley).

Sheet A rope used to control a sail.

Slip A mooring or docking area between two small piers or floating booms.

Snap Hooks Hooks that spring closed.

Sole The floor of the boat's cabin.

Spar All poles.

Spinnaker Large, lightweight sail used for reaching or running.

Spreader A device used to spread rigging for increased strength in offsetting the tendency of a mast to bend.

Starboard The right side of a boat.

Stays Lines that support the mast.

Stem The foremost part of a boat.

Sternway Backward motion.

Stops Straps used to secure the sail to the boom.

Tack The forward corner of a sail; also, a forward course. To change from one tack to another.

Tender Lacking stiffness; lacking a tendency to heel. Also, a dinghylike craft used to transport supplies or people from shore to boat.

Tiller Wooden lever used to move the rudder.

Topsides The sides of a boat above the waterline.

Transom A broad, nearly vertical stern.

Traveler A track located near the stem and running horizontally. A slide runs on it that is fastened to the mainsheet. This enables the sheet to move from one side to the other when the boat is tacked, thus increasing sailing efficiency.

Trim To adjust a sail relative to wind direction and course of boat. Also, the balance of a boat.

Turnbuckle A threaded link that pulls two devices together and is used to adjust tension in stays and shrouds.

Wake Disturbances in the water caused by the drag or resistance of a vessel as it passes through water.

Waterline The dividing line between the topsides and the underbody of a boat.

Whisker Pole A light pole used to hold a jib windward to allow it to fill with wind.

Winch A small, drum-shaped device used to increase mechanical advantage for pulling in a line against tension; the line is wound clockwise, three turns or more.

Windward Toward the wind; the opposite of leeward.

Working Sails Ordinary sails, as opposed to light or storm sails.

Yachting The roots of this sport can be traced back to the Dutch word *jaght*, which means to "put on speed." Jaghtschips were speedy cargo boats that made their way over the Dutch canals and sometimes engaged in sporting races. In 1660 King Charles II left to take over the British throne and was given a yacht as a gift by the Dutch government. A couple of years later, King Charles II raced his yacht against one owned by the Duke of York. The king won the race, and the sport was on its way to winning the hearts of the seafaring English.

Scuba and Skin Diving

Absolute Pressure The true pressure, which takes into account both air pressure at the surface and water depth.

Abyss A depth of more than 1,000 feet.

Actual Bottom Time Total time in minutes from the beginning of descent until the beginning of ascent.

Ambient Pressure At any depth, the surrounding pressure of water (Liquid Pressure).

Apparatus All the parts and materials that create a breathing device.

Barotrauma Injury-producing pressure.

Breathing Air Compressed air inhaled by divers.

Buddy Breathing The sharing of air from the same cylinder by two or more divers.

Compressed-Air Demand Regulator A mechanism that gives off air to the diver whenever he inhales.

Cylinder A container for compressed gas (Bottle, Tank).

Decompression A technique that relieves a diver of pressure that has resulted from gases gathering in the body; the decreasing effects of water pressure felt by an ascending diver.

Decompression Sickness The forming of gas bubbles in the tissues of a diver as a result of decreased pressure.

Decompression Tables Charts noting where decompression should take place and how much time should be spent in decompression stops.

Ebb Tide A flowing out of the current from the shore.

Exposure Suit An outfit that is insulated to enable a diver to preserve body heat.

Fins Extensions attached to the feet of swimmers for more efficient speed.

Flood Tide The highest tide.

340

Gauge Pressure The difference between the surrounding atmospheric pressure and specific tank pressure being measured.

Group Designation Letter of the alphabet used in dive tables to designate the amount of Residual Nitrogen in a diver's body after a dive.

Hyperbaric Describes increased pressure over the pressure in an atmosphere.

Hyperventilating Taking a series of deep breaths.

J Valve An automatic shutoff valve on an air tank that is activated when pressure drops to 300 psi.

K Valve A valve on an air tank that does not accommodate a reserve air supply.

Mask A diver's window that is equipped with an air space between the eyes and the water to facilitate underwater vision.

Nitrogen Narcosis A kind of intoxication affecting a diver exposed to the effects of nitrogen and other gases.

Nitrox Combination of nitrogen and oxygen.

No Decompression Limits Maximum total bottom time which can be spent at a depth without decompression required.

Pneumothorax A painful condition that results from the expansion of compressed air from a ruptured lung; the ascending diver's chest cavity is affected, and sometimes the lungs and heart.

Recompression Treatment in a recompression chamber of a diver stricken with decompression sickness.

Regulator A device that enables a diver to receive air which has the same pressure as the surrounding water.

Repetitive Dive One made between ten minutes and twelve hours of a previous dive.

Residual Nitrogen Remains in body after a dive. Twelve hours are required to eliminate excess nitrogen.

Residual Nitrogen Time Amount of time, in minutes, added to the bottom time of a repetitive dive representing residual nitrogen of a previous dive. The amount is obtained from a table by using the group designation.

Rip Tide A powerful and dangerous current.

Runout An undertow that follows an outgoing tide from the shore current.

Safety Buckle A device allowing the use of one hand to fasten straps.

Scuba This term is an acronym for "Self-Contained Underwater Breathing Apparatus," which consists of an open-circuit compressed-air system and a closed-circuit oxygen rebreathing system. In 1943 the Aqua-Lung was first successfully developed and tested by Jacques-Yves Cousteau and Emile Gagnan. This independent breathing device enables a diver to obtain compressed air through a hose attached to a metal tank strapped to his back. The demand regulator, a valve, reacts to the breathing of the diver. The exact volume of air that is needed by the lungs is then fed to the diver to withstand increased pressure under water. Common usage incorrectly applies the label "scuba" solely to the Aqua-Lung.

Skin Diving A general term characterizing swimming on or under the water and using a snorkel or scuba equipment.

Skip Breathing A procedure involving the holding of breath or alternate breaths to conserve air.

Snorkel Diving Swimming with the use of a J-shaped rubber or plastic breathing tube that has a mouthpiece at the short end.

Speargun An underwater hunting tool.

Surface Interval The elapsed time between dives during which the diver is on the surface.

Surface Line A line attached to both diver and boat that is useful in aiding a diver seeking to find the way to the boat when ascending.

Total Bottom Time Sum of the residual nitrogen time and the actual bottom time of a dive, determining Group Designation after a repetitive dive.

Valve A device that regulates air flow in one direction.

Yoke A device that connects regulators to cylinders, or cylinders to other cylinders.

Skateboarding

Aerial Spin Leap off the skateboard followed by a turn in the air and then a landing on the board.

Airplane Four riders locked together and sitting on their boards execute a diamond-shaped downhill movement.

Air Tacking Lifting the front end of the board while it is in motion and maneuvering it left and right (Space Walking).

Arabesque A stunt that positions a rider with the waist bent, one foot on the board and the other leg extended back, while the arms are extended forward.

Backside Moving or turning away from the front foot's direction; an outside turn.

Base Plate A plate that joins the board, the hanger, and the suspension bolt.

Bearings Small, round steel balls that reduce friction and make skateboard wheels turn smoothly.

Blank The top of the skateboard; the riding surface.

Bongo An injury or bruise that results from a fall from a skateboard.

Buddy-Buddy Two or more riders sitting on their boards and holding hands while going downhill.

Burger A bad bruise.

Bushings The rubber rings around the kingpin that aid spring and cushion shock (Action Bushing, Cushions, Shocks).

Camber An arch toward the board's rear wheels.

Caravanning A stunt that involves a few skateboarders riding down a hill in a line and holding onto each other, usually in a sitting position.

Carving a Turn Turning sharply.

Catamaranning A stunt or trick that involves two skateboarders seated sideways with their feet on each other's boards.

Chassis A skateboard's board portion.

Chew It To fall badly.

Christie A move in which the skateboarder is crouched on one foot with the other foot extended to the side.

Coffin The act of riding on a skateboard while lying on one's back.

Composition A name formerly associated with the material used in old wheels—roller skates.

Comprehension The increased force felt on the body while making a turn.

Daffy The act of riding with each foot on a separate board, legs spread slightly forward and backward, while performing a wheelie on each board (nose-to-tail or tail-to-nose).

Doing a Run Long-distance skateboarding, generally downhill.

Flex The amount of flexibility in a board.

Free Exercise Gymnastic moves associated with skateboarding.

Freestyle Competitive events involving solo tricks and movements that are judged on the types attempted and poise in performance.

Geek An unskilled or clumsy skateboarder.

Gliding Moving forward with few or no turns.

Go for It Maximum effort, speed, or risk-taking.

Goofy-Footing An unorthodox riding position; riding with the weaker foot forward.

Gorilla Grip The act of jumping with the toes gripping the end of the board.

Gremmie A clumsy skateboarder or a child who gets in the way.

Hanger The plate that joins the blank and the axle assembly of the truck.

Hang Five The act of hanging the toes of one foot over a board's front end.

Hang Heels The act of extending both heels over a board's tail.

Hang Ten The act of extending the toes of both feet over a board's nose.

Having It Wired Being aware of precisely how a ride in a given area should be executed.

Heelie A tail wheelie.

Hodad An amateur or novice.

Hop A jump made in a crouched position with both hands holding the ends of the board, taking the board along with the jump.

Hot A skilled rider or an excellent place to skate.

Hot Dogging Trick skateboarding.

Inertia The inclination of a moving body to remain in motion and of a body at rest to stay at rest.

Inweighting Lightening weight on the board through lifting body weight off the board.

Jam A gathering of skateboarders for fun and racing.

Kick A type of raised tail on a skateboard.

Kick-out The act of stepping off the board to the right with the left foot, so that the right foot, which is in back, kicks the board into the air in a flashy manner.

Kingpin The main bolt that joins the truck to the base or hanger.

Leg Lift A free-exercise movement in which one leg is extended straight up and supported by an arm, while the other is on the board.

Long Board A board generally longer than four feet (Speedboard).

Long-Boarding Downhill racing.

Memory The tendency of a board to snap back to its original shape after flexing during weighting and un-weighting.

Nose A skateboard's front.

Nose Wheelie A wheelie where the tail is lifted off the ground.

One-Eighty (180 Degrees) A half-turn that pivots one end of the board.

Pearling Falling off the board (Spacing It).

Pivot The connector between the trunk's wheels that links up to the hanger or base.

Plank Riding Skateboarding (Sidewalk Surfing).

Pool Riding Skateboarding in empty swimming pools.

Power Slide A parallel turn mainly done on banks or at high speeds from a crouch position.

Pumping Side-to-side movements utilizing the skateboarder's weight for shifting from side to side—a means of moving along (Wedeling).

Pushing Along Scooter-type movement that involves one foot on the board and the other pushing off the ground.

Radical Any exotic position, maneuver, or terrain.

Road Rash Scraped skin resulting from falls.

Seven-Twenty (720 Degrees) Two or more complete spins executed without the lifted end touching ground.

Slalom A competitive downhill event involving bobbing and weaving between cones.

Slide Out A stopping maneuver executed by sliding the skateboard's rear end forward and skidding.

Spring Truck A truck assembly that uses springs instead of bushings as shock absorbers.

Stacked Board Riding on two boards, one atop the other, while holding them together with the hands and executing different tricks.

Stoked Excited or psyched up.

Super Session A contest or exhibition.

Switchbacking Skating zigzag, usually downhill.

Switchstance The act of jumping from a regular stance to one where the weaker foot is positioned forward, or vice versa, while in motion.

Tacking Zigzag, slowing-down motion.

Tail Rear of a skateboard.

Tail Wheelie A wheelie where the nose is lifted off the ground.

Tandem Two-on-one skateboard.

Terrain The land to be skateboarded; usually referring to its slope, curvature, and composition.

Three-Sixty (360 Degrees) A complete turn on a skateboard.

Tic-Tac-Toe Successive nose wheelies performed by touching the nose down to the left and the right, and variations of these moves.

Toe Tap A stopping maneuver executed by gently touching the toe of one foot to the ground repeatedly.

Truck Everything on a skateboard except for the blank and the wheels.

Tuck A deep crouch stance.

Walking the Board Taking small steps on the board while it is in motion (Walking the Plank).

Weighting Increasing weight on the board by crouching swiftly and slowly straightening up; more generally, the distribution of one's body weight on a board.

Wheelie Lifting either end of the board while keeping two wheels on the ground.

Wheelie Stop The act of stopping by executing a wheelie and lightly dragging the board's tail.

Wind Skating Skateboarding with a sail and mast attached to the board.

Wipeout A bad spill.

Wobblies Severe vibrations caused by speed.

Wonder Rolling Skateboarding.

Yoke That portion of the truck that contains the pivot, the kingpin, and the axle-support tube (the tube that joins the axle and the hanger).

Skiing

Abstem A turn that opens the tail of the lower ski into a V position.

Acrobatics Ski stunts or tricks.

Aerial Tramway An uphill ski lift that uses two aerial cabin cars, which move in opposite directions.

Airplane Turn An airborne turn off a large bump.

Alpine Concerned with downhill skiing.

Alpinist A downhill skier or one who competes in downhill events.

Angulation A body position that edges the skis into the hill with the knees bent toward the slope; the upper body is angled outward to compensate for this action (Comma Position).

Anticipation Upper-body rotation in the direction of the turn before unweighting and edge change.

Après-Ski Leisure-time activities after skiing.

Arberg Strap A leather strap fastened to the ski and wrapped around the boot to prevent the ski from running away when the binding releases.

AT "Alpine touring" or "Randonée"; a style of equipment used to ski in the backcountry.

Attack An all-out assault on a course.

Avalement The ability of a skier to absorb the irregularities in the terrain (bumps, dips, etc.) or to be able to turn quickly at high speeds; this is accomplished via knee-flex movement and by pushing the feet forward a bit.

Axial Motion Motion around the axis of the body that includes rotation and counterrotation.

Backcountry Skiing outside of ski areas.

Backward Lean Body positioning that places the skier's center of gravity behind the bindings.

Balaclava Protective knitted covering for the face and neck with openings for the eyes and sometimes the nose.

Banking The leaning of the entire body in the direction of the imaginary center of a parallel christie turn.

Base The running surface of a ski. Also, the amount of packed snow under the surface, a hill's bottom, or the bottom of a ski area.

Basket A ring around the ski pole that prevents the point from going too deeply into the snow (Snow Ring).

Bathtub A hole in the snow created by the body of a skier who has fallen down.

Benighted Forced to return from a ski trek as a result of darkness descending.

Binding A device that fastens the boot to the ski.

Bite To place pressure on ski edges to make them more effectively grip the snow.

Block Contraction of rotary body muscles to transmit the turning power generated in one part of the body to another portion.

Board A ski.

Boiler Plate A surface that is hard and frozen as a result of being exposed to a freeze after a warm period of rain.

Bomber A speed skier, as opposed to a skier who prefers turning.

Bounce A motion utilized to unweight skis.

Bowl A two- or three-sided valley popular for powder skiing often found in western ski areas.

Breakable Crust A hard skiing surface that is nevertheless not strong enough to support a skier's weight.

Bunny A novice female skier, generally overdressed and overly made up (Snow Bunny).

Bunny Hill A gentle slope for beginners (Bunny Slope).

Burn In Heating a base wax applied to a ski's running surface in order to turn the wax into a liquid that will penetrate the wood.

Carved Turn A turn in which the skier carves as finely as possible on the edges of the skis, making for a minimum of sideways slipping or skidding (Carved Edge).

Catching an Edge The accidental catching of the edge of a ski.

Chair Lift Uphill transportation on chairs suspended from a moving cable.

Change Up An arm-resting technique employed by cross-country skiers in which they skip alternate thrusts of the poles.

Chatter Ski-tip vibration as the ski turns on hard snow surface.

Check Any maneuver to slow down the skis.

Christie A contraction of the word "Christiana," a turn that places skis parallel to each other as the turn is completed.

Chute A steep, narrow descent.

Control Gates Sets of two flags positioned on a downhill course through which racers must pass; the purpose is to control and monitor potentially dangerous portions of the course.

Corn A type of snow occurring in spring or warm weather that is created from alternate freezing and thawing; easy turning is made possible for a skier by the honeycombed surface of this type of snow.

Cornice A ledge of overhanging ice or snow.

Counterrotation A turning motion of the upper part of the body that creates an equal but opposite reaction in the lower part of the body and takes place when skis are unweighted.

Course A racing route.

Cover A snow surface.

Critical Point The maximum distance point for a safe jump.

Crud Snow conditions that are not desirable, such as breakable crust (Junk Snow).

Crust Glazed surface atop snow caused by cycles of thawing and freezing.

Daffy Separating the legs at the high point of a jump as a stunt in freestyle aerial competition: one leg is in front and the other is in back, both legs are straight, and the skis are virtually vertical.

Deep Powder A foot or more of soft, dry, light, powdery snow.

Diagonal A ski-touring striding technique that combines a kick by one leg with a push off from a pole gripped in the hand opposite that leg.

Direct Parallel An instruction method that stresses parallel placement of feet and skis.

Dope Special wax preparations applied to skis, mainly used by California skiers.

Double-Pole To move forward by pushing off with both poles at the same time in ski touring.

Double Stem A running position in which both ski tails are pushed out into a V position (Snowplow).

Downhill The fastest and most dangerous of the three forms of Alpine racing—a race against time down a one- to three-mile-long course.

Downhiller A skier who participates in a downhill event.

Downhill Ski The lower ski; the one that becomes the lower ski in a turn.

Downhill Skiing Going down a slope after being towed to the top.

Down-Unweighting Reducing body weight on the snow by "dropping" the body sharply.

Drop Unweighting the skis by quickly lowering the body to make it easier for the skis to be turned.

Edge A full-length piece of steel on the running edges of the ski that aids in gripping the snow when the ski is edged or turned.

Edge Control The ability to turn or to put skis on edge.

Edge Set Edging the skis at the start of a turn.

Edging Controlling the skis' sideward slippage by settling them at an angle to the snow and getting them to "bite" the surface.

Egg Position Downhill-racing maneuver of crouching tightly, with head near knees and poles tucked under arms.

Extensions Rising body motion to unweight skis and start a turn.

Face The steepest part of a mountain; a slope's exposed front.

Fall Line The steepest line of descent on a hill.

Fat Ski Very wide ski designed especially for powder skiing.

Flush Slalom-race combination of gates that forces a racer into a series of tight turns on the fall line.

Foot Steering Changing the direction of the skis by turning legs and feet.

Forerunner A skier who checks out a course by skiing it just before a competition to detect any problems and to insure that the course is ready.

Forward Lean A skier's center of gravity is ahead of the bindings in this body position.

Free Skiing A skiing philosophy influenced by snowboarding; participant skis mostly in terrain parks concentrating on practicing acrobatic tricks.

Freestyle A competition evaluated on individual style and execution in three different events: downhill over rough land (mogul); gradual-slope stylized moves (ballet); acrobatic moves (aerial).

Frozen Granular Snow condition in which frozen granules are compacted into a hard, sometimes solid surface.

Garland A momentary side-step movement, performed while traversing a slope, that is followed by a straight traverse.

Gate Any arrangement of two poles or flags that a skier must pass through in the course of a race.

Gelandesrung A jump over an obstacle or bump in which the skier uses both poles for support.

Giant Slalom A combination of a slalom and a downhill race.

Glissade To slide down a snow slope without the use of skis, by squatting or keeping the feet straight.

GLM Graduated Length Method, a method of teaching that begins with using short skis and making parallel turns as the opening learning procedures.

Godile Linked parallel turns executed in the fall line.

Gondola An uphill ski lift that transports several skiers in a series of enclosed aerial cars that are suspended from a moving cable.

Grade The angle or pitch of a slope.

Groom To get a slope ready for skiing by snow packing or crust breaking.

Hairpin A slalom figure composed of two consecutive closed gates.

Half Sidestepping Similar to side-step climbing of a slope, except that the uphill ski is positioned ahead of the weighted one on each step and climbing takes place at an angle rather than straight up.

Helicopter A full-twisting freestyle aerial stunt.

Herringbone Climbing a hill with skis in the V position and with pressure weighted against the inside edges of the skis.

Hogback A bump that is sharply ridged.

Hospital Air Catching enough air from a jump so that injury is very likely.

Hot Dog A freestyle skier.

Huck Catching big air off a jump or cliff.

Inrun The steep slope, many times set on a high scaffolding, from which a skier generates speed prior to jumping.

Inside The side of the body near where a turn is being made.

J-Bar Lift A ski lift that carries a series of bars shaped like the letter J on a moving overhead cable; one bar is allocated to each skier.

Jet Turn In this parallel turn, body weight is farther back than normal as a result of pushing the skis forward.

Jump Turn An aerial maneuver that is employed when a skier is going at slow speed; essentially a complete turn in the air.

Kicker Large man-made jump within a terrain park or in the backcountry.

Kick Turn A 180-degree turn executed while moving one ski at a time on level ground.

Klister A sticky running wax employed by skiers on granular and crust surfaces in above-freezing temperatures.

Landing Hill Jumping-competition landing site.

Leverage A ski-turn effect created when a skier moves his other weight forward or backward in relation to the center of the skis.

Miniski A beginner's short ski.

Moebius Flip A full-twisting forward or backward flip in the air.

Mogul A bump that generally has been created by many skiers turning on the same spot and pushing snow into a mound.

Nordic Cross-country and ski-jumping competition.

Nordic Combined Cross-country and ski-jumping event scores are totaled to determine the winner of this competition.

Norm Point Landing-slope point in jumping competition where skiers are supposed to land.

Off Piste Skiing off trail.

Open Slalom Gate A gate set with both poles perpendicular to the line of descent.

Parallel Christie An advanced, very graceful version of the skidded turn: the skis are pressed together and throughout the entire turn are kept parallel.

Pasgang A touring maneuver: a kick is done at virtually the same time as a push, with the pole on the same side of the body.

Piste A ski trail.

Pivoting Twisting the ski in a different direction by turning the ball of the foot.

Poling Using the skis to move along over flat terrain by pushing with them.

Poma Lift A seat attached by a bar to an overhead moving cable.

Prejump The lifting of the skis into the air on the uphill side of a bump before a crest is reached.

Rail Metal Rail derived from staircase hand railings found in terrain parks for free skiers to slide on.

Release Binding A binding that releases the boot under preset pressure, as in the case of a fall.

Rotation Body motion around an imaginary axis in the direction of a turn.

Royal Christie An advanced turn executed on the inside ski, with the outside ski lifted off the snow.

Ruade A parallel turn performed by lifting the tails of the skis off the snow and pivoting around on the tips.

Running Wax Wax that holds the ski in position but allows it to move forward when gliding.

Schuss High-speed, straight skiing down the fall line.

Shaped Ski A ski whose tip and tail are dramatically wider than its midsection; they are much easier to turn and control, revolutionizing skiing.

Sidestepping Climbing by stepping skis sideways and at right angles.

Sitzmark A hole or indentation in the snow created by a skier's backward fall into the snow.

Ski Lift, Ski Tow A mechanism that takes a skier to the top of a slope.

Slipped Turn A turn made with the skis relatively flat throughout most of the maneuver.

Snaking The ability of the ski to follow variations in terrain fairly smoothly.

Snow Farming Maintaining and conditioning a ski slope's snow.

Snow Machine A mechanism that sprays misted water and creates man-made snow.

Snowplow To ski with the skis in an inverted V with tips close and heels apart in order to slow down or stop descent.

Snowplow Turn To use the snowplow position while turning, by weighting one ski in the turn and winding up where that ski points.

Spring Conditions A cycle of freezing and thawing creating moist and sticky snow surfaces.

Stack It In To fall badly.

Stem Opening the tail on one ski into a V position.

Stem Turn To execute a turn by stemming one ski into the V position and keeping it there until both skis are moved parallel as the turn is concluded.

Step Turn A turn executed by lifting one ski, positioning it to the sideward direction of the turn, then weighting it; the other ski is then brought alongside.

Swing A parallel turn at high speed.

Table Point The most distant point a skier is expected to land on a ski-jumping landing hill.

Tail The section of the ski behind the area where the boot is generally placed.

Take Off To leave the ground, as in a jump.

T-Bar Lift Intended to accommodate two skiers, a lift in which a collection of bars, each shaped like an inverted T, is suspended from moving overhead cables.

Telemark A style of skiing experiencing a recent revival where only the toe, and not the heel, is fixed in place. Originating from Norway, it is one of the oldest styles of skiing.

Terrain Park Designated trails on a ski mountain featuring jumps, half-pipes, rail slides, and other obstacles.

Touring Ski A ski that is light and narrow and turned up at the front.

Traverse Skiing diagonally across a slope.

Tuck Cutting down wind resistance in downhill skiing, for example, by squatting forward and placing poles parallel to the ground and under the arms.

Twin Tip A type of ski used by free skiers that can be skied forward or backward.

Twisting Turning the ski by pivoting the foot and lower leg.

Unweighting A method of reducing weight on skis just before turning, to make them move more easily.

Uphill Christie A turn in which the skis are swung uphill from a traverse, generally used for stopping.

Vorlage Forward body lean before a turn.

Wedeln A combination of close parallel turns made in the fall line with a minimum of edge set.

Wedge A common stopping position or slowing-down maneuver accomplished by digging the inside edges of the skis into the snow with the backs of the skis apart and their tips together.

Wide Track The act of skiing with skis parallel but feet positioned as much as one and a half feet apart.

Soccer

Active Resistance To use force in opposing another player.

Advantage When a team has possession of the ball, outnumbering opposition near the opposing goal.

Advantage Rule A regulation that mandates that play not be stopped for a violation if the offending team has not gained an advantage or if stopping play would place the offended team at a disadvantage.

African Passing the ball one way around a defender, running the opposite way, and retrieving the ball.

Air-Mail Shot or chip sent over the intended target.

Ambitious Ball Overly aggressive pass with slight chance of success.

American Football Phrase used by non-Americans to distinguish the U.S. sport of football from soccer, which they also call football.

Angle of Possibility The angle created by imaginary lines drawn from the ball to each upright of the goal within which the ball must enter to score a goal.

Anticipation Judging an opponent's action and moving into position to react accordingly and effectively.

Assist Pass leading to a goal.

Association Football The British name for soccer.

Attacker Any player in possession of the ball (Offensive Player).

Attacking Midfielder The most forward-playing midfielder, playing right behind the forwards.

Attacking Team The team in possession of the ball (Offensive Team).

"Ave It!" Expression meaning "Shoot already!"

"Away" Exhortation to a defender to get the ball out his end of the field.

Back Defender.

"Back" Instruction to pass ball straight behind a player.

"Back and Face" Following an attack, when midfield players are in advance positions, an instruction to them to return to their positions and face opponents prepared for the counterattack.

Back Door (British) Furthest goalpost from the ball.

Backdoor Burglar Player coming from behind and stealing the ball from the opponent.

Backfield Mainly defensive players: halfbacks, fullbacks, and goalkeeper.

Back Four In modern soccer, the four defenders.

Back Header Use of the head by a player to direct the ball backward.

Back of Square Player just behind a square ball allowing space in case of a bad pass.

Back Pass A pass by a player to a teammate behind him.

Back Up To play behind a teammate to strengthen the defense or to receive a pass.

Balance Concurrent presence of coverage by a team in important areas on the pitch.

Ball Carrier One in possession of the ball.

Banana Shot A forceful shot at the goal: the ball is kicked off-center and curves in flight.

Bangoo Crossed ball from end line sent to the penalty spot.

Beat To reach a ball before an opponent does, to outmaneuver an opponent through effective dribbling, or to get the ball.

Behind the Defender Area between a defender and his goal.

Bicycle Kick An acrobatic technique in which the ball is kicked overhead as the kicker lands on his back.

Book The recording by the referee of the name or names of players guilty of unsportsmanlike behavior; this action is a warning that the player might be removed from the game if the unsportsmanlike behavior is repeated.

Boot To kick the ball.

Booter A soccer player.

Bounding Board A goal-sized structure used for kicking, passing, and ball control drills (Kick Board).

Box The 18-yard box penalty area.

Break The quick advancing of the ball down the field by a team attempting to get its players near the opponent's goal before defense has a chance to retreat (Advantage).

Breakaway An attacker with the ball approaches the goal undefended and pits a sole attacker against the goalkeeper in a one-on-one showdown.

Bully Frenzied and confused action with several players trying to gain control of the ball, generally in front of the goal mouth.

Bump Goalkeeper's use of a fist to block a goal.

Bunch A situation where two or more players from the same team move into the same area of the field as another teammate.

Busby Babes The Manchester United football (soccer) team of the late 1950s was very young and was managed by Matt Busby, and these facts earned it its nickname. In 1958, eight members of the team were killed when the plane carrying the "Busby Babes" crashed on takeoff from the airport in Munich. Four of those killed were also top members of the English national team. Bobby Charlton, who survived the crash, became one of the best of the European forwards.

Bye A shot wide of the goal that crosses the goal line.

Cap To choose a player to compete for a national team in international competition.

Caps Recognition earned by a player for appearances for his nation in international games.

Carry(ing) A violation that involves a goalkeeper going beyond the four allowed steps without bouncing the ball.

Catenaccio System A lineup that has two strikers, three midfielders, and four defenders in the defensive side of the field, plus a sweeper positioned in front of the goalkeeper.

Caught Square When two or more defenders have been beaten by a through ball as a result of being positioned in a straight line or square to one another.

Caution A warning given by the referee to a player that involves the referee holding up a yellow card and writing the player's name in a notebook.

Center To pass the ball in the air from a sideline position back toward the center of the field and, if possible, in front of the goal of the opposition.

Center Circle Circular marking with a ten-yard radius in the center of the field from which kickoffs start or restart the game.

Center Half Central Defender.

Center Line A straight line dividing the field of play in half that runs from sideline to sideline.

Center Spot Small circular mark inside the center circle that indicates center of field where kickoffs are taken to start or restart the game.

Central Defender One guarding the area directly in front of his own goal in a zone defense; does not exist in a man-to-man defense.

Challenge To go after the player with the ball.

Charge To run into an opponent—legal if done from the front or side of the ball carrier, illegal against a player without the ball or from behind.

Charge the Ball To run up on the ball and take it from the opponent.

Charging Intentionally pushing an opponent away from the ball or throwing him off balance.

Check To come back and receive a ball from a teammate.

Check To Offensive player running toward the ball carrier and usually calling for a pass.

Chest Trap The act of trapping the ball with the chest in order to control the ball as it falls to the ground.

Chip Pass made by a stabbing motion of the kicking foot to the lower half of the ball to loft it over the heads of opponents (Chip Pass).

Chip Shot Kick lofted into the air to try to sail the ball over the goalkeeper's head and still make it under the crossbar into the goal.

Chop A deliberate change of direction with the ball, usually using the inside of the foot.

Clear (Clearance) A throw or kick, usually by the goalkeeper, that sends the ball out of danger from his end of the field.

Cleats The metal, plastic, or rubber points in the bottom of a soccer shoe used to provide a player with traction; term also used to refer to the shoes themselves.

Close Down Defender gets close to the attacker without letting the attacker get by with the ball.

Combination A play that involves two or more members of the same team who work together to outsmart the opposition.

CONCACAF The Confederation Norte-Centroamericana y del Caribe de Footbal, the regional organization of North American and Central American soccer under which World Cup qualifying matches are played; member countries include the United States, Canada, Mexico, and Central American and Caribbean countries.

Consolation Match A tournament game played between the losers of the two semifinal matches to determine the third-place team.

Contain To keep a player with the ball from beating you on the dribble.

Containment The act of keeping the opposition restricted to a certain area of the playing field.

Convert To successfully make a penalty kick.

Corner Arc Quarter-circle with a radius of one yard located at each of the four corners of the field; on a corner kick, the ball must be kicked from inside this arc (Corner Area).

Corner Flag Flage located at each of the four corners of the field, inside the corner area.

Corner Kick A direct free kick given the offensive team. The kick takes place from the corner of the field nearest the spot the ball went over the goal line after last being touched by the defending team.

Counterattack To begin an attack immediately after gaining possession of the ball.

Cover The act of staying very close to an opponent and hampering his ability to play the ball.

Creating Space When a player from the attacking team moves without the ball to draw defenders away from the ball carrier and give him space to maneuver.

Cross The act of kicking the ball from one side of the field to the other.

Crossbar Horizontal beam which forms the top of a goal and sits on top of the two posts; it is twenty-four feet long and supported eight feet above the ground.

Crossing Pass From an attacking player near the sideline to a teammate in the middle or opposite side of the field, this pass is used to give the teammate a good scoring opportunity.

Cut Back Pass back up the field, especially in front of a goal or where the defenders are running and therefore unable to quickly respond.

Cut Down the Angle Goalie comes out of the goal several feet to make himself closer and larger to an attacker, leaving the attacker less net to shoot at.

Cut Off Defensive player keeps his body between an attacker and the defender's goal, forcing the attacker out toward the sidelines.

Dangerous Play A play that the referee judges capable of causing injury to a player.

Dead Ball A ball no longer in play because it has gone out of bounds or the referee has stopped play.

Decoy Play A move designed to draw an opponent away from a certain area.

Defender A defensive player who aids the goalkeeper in protecting the goal.

Defending Team The team that attempts to gain control of the ball while defending its own goal.

Defense A team's function of preventing the opposition from scoring.

Defensemen The three or four players on a team whose primary task is to stop the opposition from scoring (Fullbacks).

Defensive Midfielder Player positioned just in front of his team's defense; often assigned to mark the opposition's best offensive player (Midfield Anchor).

Defensive Pressure One or more defenders closely mark a ball carrier to harass him into losing the ball.

Deflection Ricochet of a ball after it hits a player.

Depth An extra-man advantage that gives a player in possession of the ball several passing chances and additional support.

Direct Free Kick A kick, awarded for major fouls, that is a free kick from which a goal can be scored directly by the kicker.

Dispossess To take the ball away from a dribbler.

Dissent Arguing with a referee, which may result in a player being booked or sent off (ejected from the game).

Dive To deliberately fall down to try to fool the referee into giving a foul.

Diving Header Ball struck near ground level by the head of a diving player.

"Don't Dive" Directions to a defender to stay on his feet against a dribbler.

Draw A game ending in a tied score; also, to cause an opponent to leave the player being covered.

The Draw selection of World Cup teams, placing them into playing groups for the tournament; also, event surrounding this selection.

Dribble To advance the ball past defenders through a series of short taps with one or both feet while keeping the ball within one stride.

Dribbler Player advancing ball while controlling it with his feet (Dribbling).

Drive Hitting a hard, low shot on goal with the instep.

Driving the Ball Making a hard-hit shot at the goal or a long, well-hit pass.

Drop To pass the ball back to a supporting player.

Drop and Mark Movement by the defending team its goal, picking up and marking opponents.

Drop Ball A method of restarting play after temporary suspension of action whereby the referee drops the ball between two players who will both try to kick or otherwise gain control of the ball.

Drop In Support on defense.

Drop Kick Goalie dropping the ball from his hands and kicking it just after it hits the ground.

Dummy Allowing ball to go past or through a player's legs to a teammate.

Dummy Run A run by player without the ball to draw defender(s) away from the area under attack.

Earn Your Shirt Practice efforts to get to play in the game.

Ejection The banishing of a player from the game by the referee.

Eleven A soccer team (XI).

End Line The boundary line that marks the end of the field (see Goal Line).

English Football Association Founded in 1863 to set soccer rules, an association of English soccer teams.

Equalizer A goal that ties the score.

European Cup Winner's Cup Championship competition played by national champions of the European Football Association.

Extra Time Additional playing time at the end of a game that is caused by unusual delays during the game and for which there were no timeouts permitted (Stoppage Time).

F.A. Football Association, especially the English Football Association.

"Face Up" Face the direction of the ball and do not turn your back on the ball during stoppage of play.

F.A. Cup The postseason championship tournament and trophy of the English Football Association.

Fake Move(s) by a player meant to deceive an opposing player; used by a ball carrier to make a defender think the ball carrier is going to dribble, pass, or shoot in a certain direction when he is not (Feint).

Far Post Goalpost farthest from the ball.

"Fatty" One of the broadest fellows ever to take up space on a soccer field was William J. Foulke, an English goaltender. Foulke stood 6' 3" and weighed 311 pounds. He covered up a large part of the goal just by being there. Foulke once interrupted the progress of a game by jumping and then leaning too heavily on the crossbar, snapping it.

Feed Passing the ball to a teammate who can shoot for a goal.

Feint A deceptive move to mislead or confuse an opponent (Fake).

Field Rectangular area where soccer matches are played.

Field Goal Scoring play, when ball is blasted over the net.

FIFA Federation Internationale de Football Association, official governing body of international soccer since 1904, which established the World Cup tournament; helps set and revise (17 Laws) rules of the game.

FIFA World Cup Solid gold statue awarded to the champion of each World Cup tournament.

Fifty-Fifty Ball A loose ball that both teams have equal opportunity to bring under control.

Finish When a player shoots the ball into the goal using anything but an instep kick.

First-Time Kick Kicking a ball without trapping or controlling it.

Fisting Punching at the ball with the fist(s).

Flick Passing the ball with a strong, outside-of-the-foot movement (Jab Kick).

Flick Header Player using his head to deflect the ball.

Football Name for soccer everywhere in the English-speaking world except for the United States.

Foot Trap Player's use of the foot to control a rolling or low bouncing ball.

Formations Lineups on the soccer field. Players today are broken down into three groups: defenders, midfielders, and forwards. The goalkeeper is omitted, for no matter what the formation, that position is always the same.

Forward Mainly an attacking player whose job is to create and score goals.

Forward Pass Pass made toward the opposition's goal.

Fouling Illegally using the hands or body against an opponent, which can lead to a direct free kick for the opposition.

Foul Throw Illegally executed throw-in.

4–2–4 Formation that consists of four defenders, two midfielders, and 4 forwards.

4–3–3 Formation of four defenders, three midfielders, and three forwards; the most common formation used by teams.

4–4–2 Formation of four defenders, four midfielders, and two forwards.

Freeback A player not specifically designated to mark or guard an opponent (Sweeper, Libero).

Free Kick An unhampered kick of a stationary ball awarded a team when an opponent commits a foul.

Friendly (British) A game between two international teams before the beginning of regular international competition.

Front Header Striking of a ball in the air by a player's forehead; the most common type of header.

Front Tackle Attempt by a defender to kick the ball away from an attacker by approaching him from a head-on position.

Fullbacks Wide defenders playing flat with the central defenders in a "flat back four."

Full Time The close of the game.

Garrison Finish A last-minute, surprising victory.

Get Chalky Move to the outside of the field.

Get Stuck In To tackle.

"Get Up on That" Get up for a challenge in the air, and don't let the ball hit the ground.

Ghost Extra position. A situation where a player wanders around on his half of the field playing defense.

Give and Go Passing the ball to a teammate and running to a position to receive the return (Wall Pass).

"Give Him an Oscar" Faking injury.

Goal The target area, twenty-four feet wide by eight feet high. Also, the score made when the ball passes between the goalposts beneath the crossbar.

Goal Area A marked area in front of each goal that is twenty yards wide by six yards deep.

Goal Average The difference between goals scored and goals allowed by a given team during a set period; this statistic is used to break ties of teams with the same won-lost record and to determine which moves ahead in competition.

Goalkeeper The final line of defense and the only player permitted to use his hands within the field of play, with the restriction that this can only be done within the penalty area.

Goal Kick A type of kick performed by a defender when the ball last touched by an attacking player passes over the goal line without going into the goal; the ball must be kicked from inside the team's goal area and must go beyond the penalty area of the team.

Goal Line The boundary line at the ends of the field.

Goal Mouth The area immediately in front of the goal, between the goalposts and the crossbar.

Goalposts Usually wooden posts between four and five inches in width and depth.

Goal-Side Defender positioned between goal and offensive player.

Golas Foreign term for goal.

Golden Goal Score in overtime, ending match.

Good Out A well cleared ball by a defender.

Good Up Good attempt at an executed head ball.

"Got Me" Directions to a teammate: "I'm safe, kick me the ball."

Hack Someone who fouls way too much or an act of delivering a hard foul.

Halfback A defensive player who usually plays in his defensive half of the field between the forward line and his goal and whose job it is to guard opposing forwards. Halfbacks are designated by the part of the field they occupy: left, right, center. The halfback is not restricted to defense, however, and may initiate an attack (Midfielder, Linkman).

Halftime The end of the first forty-five-minute period of play.

Half-Volley Kicking the ball just as it rebounds off the ground.

Hampden Roar The name comes from the location—Hampden Park, the international soccer field at Glasgow, Scotland. An otherworldly noise springs forth from the mouths of the soccer zealots who attend games there. The sound envelops the huge stadium and does strange things to visiting teams. The roar is especially in evidence on the day of the Scottish Cup Final.

Handling Intentionally playing the ball with the hands, arms, or shoulders.

Hands Illegal act of intentionally touching the ball with any part of the hands or arms, which awards a direct free kick to the other team (Hand Ball).

Hard Tackle A fair but rough tackle.

Hat Trick Three goals in a game by a player.

"Have One" Encouraging player to take a shot at goal.

Header A shot or pass made by hitting the ball with the head.

Heading Hitting the ball with the front part of the forehead to pass, score, or control the ball.

Hedging A stalling action where the player backs up while containing an opponent with the ball so that the defense can recover its position.

Heel Backward pass with the heel of the foot.

Henri Delaunay Cup This trophy, originated in 1960, serves as the symbol of victory in the European Nations Cup, a soccer competition staged on the same elimination system as the World Cup and held every four years between the cycle of the World Cup. Henri Delaunay was a leading personality in French soccer and one of those instrumental in helping to create the World Cup.

Holding Obstructing a player's movement with hand or arm.

Hold the Ball Up Keep possession of the ball, or an instruction to do so.

Hole Space between opposition's defense and midfield; an offensive midfielder or defensive forward "plays in the hole."

Hook Curved trajectory of a ball due to spin a kicker gives it.

Hook Tackle A tackle made by dropping down to one knee and at the same time extending the other leg to hook the ball away from the opposing player (Sliding Tackle).

Hospital Pass One which could result in an injury to a teammate trying to reach it first.

Indirect Free Kick A kick awarded to a player for a less-serious foul committed by the opposition; the player kicks a stationary ball without any opposing players within ten yards of him. A goal can be scored on this kick only after the ball has touched another player.

Indirect Pass A pass that requires a player to move to a certain position to receive the ball.

Indoor Soccer A version of soccer played in an indoor hockey arena. The ice is replaced with a floor, and walls surround the playing area to contain the ball. There are six members to a team, including a goalkeeper. The goals are sixteen feet high and four feet wide. The game consists of three twenty-minute periods. Fouls are penalized by suspension for two–five minutes of the guilty player, during which time his team plays shorthanded.

Injury Time Time added to the end of a game to make up for time lost in the treatment and removal of a player who has been injured.

In Play A ball within boundaries of the field, not stopped by the referee.

Inside Forward Either of the two forwards who usually play between the wings and center forward.

Inside-of-the-Foot Kick A kick made with the inside edge of the foot, driving the ball to the side or diagonally forward.

Instep The part of the foot most often used for kicking, covered by shoelaces.

Instep Drive Straight shot taken with the instep of a player's foot; usually the most powerful and accurate of shots.

In-Swinger A corner kick or cross that swings the ball in the air toward the goal mouth.

Interception Gaining possession of the ball before it reaches the intended receiver of the other team.

Intermission Five-minute rest period between periods of a game.

Jockey Giving ground by a defender whose back is to the goal in order to gain time. No attempt to play the ball.

Juggling Keeping a ball in the air with any part of the body besides the hands or arms.

Jules Rimet Trophy One awarded to the World Cup winner 1930–1970.

Jump Kick A kick made by jumping into the air and kicking the ball while it is two or three feet off the ground.

Karaoke Moving in a fast motion sideways and crossing legs.

"Keeper" Warning shouted that the goalkeeper is coming out on the field.

Kick In Putting the ball in play when it goes out of play over the sideline. In women's soccer, a free kick at a stationary ball on the touch line after the opposing team has driven the ball into touch.

Kickoff A place kick executed from the center of the field at the start of the game, at the start of each period, and after each score.

Kick to a Stop Kicking the ball to an open area where a teammate can reach it before an opponent.

Killer Pass One splitting two defenders.

Kit A uniform.

Late Tackle One made after the ball was played by the offensive player.

Lateral Movement Movement from one sideline to the other.

Laws of the Game Seventeen main rules for soccer established by FIFA.

Lead Pass A pass aimed ahead of the intended receiver so that he can pick it up and drive on without breaking stride.

League Alliance of teams that organizes sporting competition.

"Leave It" Shouted direction not to touch the ball, let it roll by.

Let Allowing a pass to you go to your teammate.

"Let Him Know You" Shouted direction to make contact with the striker early in the match to try to put him off his game.

Libby A Massachusetts expression for a player faking injury.

Libero Italian expression for a sweeper who also goes forward to support or direct the attack.

"Line" Asking for a pass up touch line.

Lineman A forward.

Linesmen Two officials who are assistants to the referee and who primarily aid in indicating when the ball has gone over the sidelines.

Liniker Scoring with an unorthodox but legal body part, named after Garry Liniker.

Linkman Another name for a midfielder.

Liquid Catch Catching the ball with relaxed fingers and hands and arms drawn to the body.

Loft (Lob) A high, soft kick taken on the volley; usually a kick over the heads of the defense.

Long Ball A long pass.

Lunge To execute a long stride, putting weight on the foot that is moved.

"Man On" Shouted information that an opponent is approaching player with the ball from behind.

Man-to-Man Marking Following a player all over.

Marker A score.

Marking Covering and guarding an opponent so closely that it becomes very difficult for him to receive a pass.

Marking Back Fullback whose primary responsibility is marking one of the opposing forwards.

"Mark Up" Informing teammates to leave no one unmarked.

Match A soccer game.

Meg The dribbling or passing of a ball between a defender's legs (Nutmeg).

M Formation A formation resembling the letter M in which the five-player forward line assembles so that the outside forwards and the center forward play in a line relatively far from the goal, while the inside forwards lie close to the goal compare W Formation.

Midfield Field near the midfield line; the area controlled by the midfielders.

Midfield Anchor (Defensive midfielder).

Midfielder A player with both offensive and defensive responsibilities whose main job is to link up forwards and defenders (Linkman).

Midfield General Powerful (or just aggressive) central midfielder stamping authority on the game (Midfield Governor).

Midfield Line Line dividing field in half along its width (Center Line).

Miskick A poor kick.

MISL (Major Indoor Soccer League) Originated in the United States in 1977, playing games of six players per side in modified hockey rinks covered by artificial turf. In 1990, became the MSL.

Mobility Constant movement by players to create and use space.

Moving Dribbling.

Multiple Offense The movement of players allowing the creation of several offensive patterns.

"My Bad" One teammate to another, apologizing for a poorly played ball.

NASL (North American Soccer League) Outdoor league created in the United States in 1967. It attracted great international players including Pele and huge audiences in the 1970s but collapsed in 1985.

National Team One consisting of the best players in a nation chosen to represent it in international competitions such as the World Cup.

Near Post The post closest to the kicker.

Net Mesh fabric attached to and behind the goal, helpful in judging whether a goal has been scored.

New England Tea Men This North American Soccer League team made its debut in 1978. The Tea Men derive their name from the franchise owners, Thomas J. Lipton, Inc., the tea company.

Nutmeg Putting the ball between an opponent's legs (Meg).

Obstructing Intentionally blocking an opponent by standing in his path.

Offense Trying to score goals.

Official Game Clock Clock that referee carries on the field to determine when each half is over; it does not stop during the game, even when play does.

Officials The referee and two linesmen who work together to make sure the game is played according to the rules of soccer. They are responsible for stopping and restarting play, keeping track of the score and the time remaining, and citing violations of the rules, called fouls; they wear uniforms that distinguish them from the players on both teams.

Offside Violation called when a player in an offside position receives a pass from a teammate; indirect free kick is awarded to the nonoffending team. In women's soccer, a player is offside when she is in the attacking half of the field and there are fewer than three defenders between her and the goal.

Offside Line Either of two lines marked across the playing field parallel to and thirty-five yards from each goal line. These lines are used in American professional soccer in place of the halfway line to determine offsides and are analogous to the blue lines in ice hockey.

Offside Position Attacking player positioned so that two opposing defensive players (usually the goalie and one other defender) are between him and the goal he is attacking; a player is not offside if he is exactly even with one or both of these defensive players.

Off the Line Goalkeeper moving from the goal line to get the ball.

Olympic Goal Scoring a goal from the corner kick.

On Defense Team not in possession of the ball.

One Bounce A delayed game (for example, stadium lights go out) is resumed by the referee dropping the ball at midfield between two opposing players, where it is played after bouncing once.

"One More" To allow a crossing pass to go through or pass to the next teammate.

"One On" Requesting that only one defender pressure the ball.

One-Timer A goal scored on a cross or corner kick that is booted into the goal before it touches the ground.

One-Two A pass returned with the first touch; often where the first player continues to run and passes a defender while briefly without the ball.

"On Me Head" An invitation to a teammate to deliver the ball to one's head.

On Offense Team in possession of the ball.

Onside In a legal position with respect to the ball: being behind the ball when it is driven into the attacking part of the field, or having at least two defenders nearer the goal when the ball is being played by a teammate. Opposite of offside.

On the Carpet A pass on the ground.

Open An attacking player who does not have anyone marking him.

Open Goal A completely unprotected goal, with no obstacles between the ball and the goal at all.

"Open Up" A direction to use wingers and play wide.

Outlet Passes When a goaltender or defender passes the ball from close to his own goal toward the other team's goal; used to start a counterattack.

Out of Bounds A ball outside the boundaries of the field, having completely crossed a sideline or goal line.

Out of Play When a ball is outside the boundaries of the field or play has been stopped by the referee.

"Out of the Box" After a corner kick, the last player in the defense yells this to the rest of his team.

Outside Forwards The two forwards in a five-man forward line who usually play along the sides of the field.

Outside Halves The two halfbacks who usually play near the sides of the field.

Outside Left The left wing forward.

Outside Right The right wing forward.

Outstep The outer surface of the instep.

Out-Swinger Corner kick with a ball swinging away from the goal.

Overlap When a winger moves away from the sideline toward the center of the field to create space for a teammate to advance the ball undefended along the side of the field. The attacking play of a defender moving down the touch line past his own winger.

Over the Top Chipping a ball over the defense into space that the forwards run to.

Overtime Extra periods played after a regulation game ends tied, used in collegiate and championship international matches to determine a winner.

Own Goal A goal that a defensive player accidentally knocks into his own goal.

Pace Speed of the ball from a pass.

Parry A controlled and deliberate deflection by the goalkeeper, using the hands.

Pass To kick or head the ball to a teammate.

Pass-Back A pass made back to one's goalkeeper, usually in a pressure situation.

Passive Resistance Opposing with little effort.

Peel Cup The oldest soccer trophy in the United States, this cup was donated in 1909 by Peter J. Peel, a leading figure in Illinois soccer, as a fund-raiser for injured players. Today the Peel Cup is awarded to the amateur soccer champion of the state of Illinois.

"Pele" (Edson Arantes de Nascimento) Perhaps the most famous of all the nicknames in the history of sports is that of Pele. Strangely enough, even the man who is called by this name does not know how it originated or what it really means. Born October 23, 1940, in Tres Coracoes, Brazil, Pele's life with a soccer ball is the stuff of dreams. As a poor youth he learned to kick a "soccer ball" that was actually an old stuffed sock. Years later, after scoring his one-thousandth goal, he was awarded a four-pound soccer ball made of gold.

Charles de Gaulle made him a Knight of the Order of Merit. A company in Brazil named a coffee after him, which in that coffee-mad land became a bestseller. In 1960, after several European countries offered him $1 million to sign with their clubs, the government of Brazil declared him a national asset, making it impossible for him to leave Brazil without official permission. Pele's power and prestige was such that the Nigerian-Biafran war was halted for a day to allow Pele and his teammates to play a game and then depart without incident for more peaceful surroundings. Pope Paul VI told him, "Don't be nervous, my son. I am more nervous than you for I have been waiting to meet Pele personally for a long time." The Pope, like millions of others, knew Edson Arantes de Nascimento by his nickname.

The only player to have performed on three World Championship soccer teams—in 1958 (as a sixteen-year-old), 1962, and 1970—Pele averaged a goal a game in international competition and broke virtually every record in Brazil's soccer books. Ninety-three times he scored three goals in a game; thirty-one times he scored four goals in a contest; six times he recorded five goals in a match; and once he knocked in eight goals in a game. He scored more goals than any other player in the history of soccer. So valuable were his legs that they were insured for £20,000.

His signing of a three-year contract with the New York Cosmos on June 10, 1975, just 250 days after retiring from his Santos, Brazil, team, resulted in part from the efforts of former secretary of state Henry Kissinger. The secretary had told the Brazilian government that Pele's signing to play soccer in the United States would do much to improve international relations. Soccer's legend retired again on October 1, 1977, after his mission of giving the sport momentum in the United States was concluded.

He was called O Rei in Brazil, La Tulipe Noire in France, El Peligor in Chile, Il Re in Italy, O Vasilas in Greece, and King Pele wherever soccer zealots gathered. The power, passion, and personality of the man made most everyone forget his real name, Edson Arantes de Nascimento, and virtually everyone aware of his nickname, Pele.

Penalty Short hand for penalty kick; punishment doled out by referee for a violation of the rules.

Penalty Arc A semicircle whose center is the penalty spot and which extends from the top of the penalty area; it designates an area that opposing players are not allowed to enter prior to a penalty kick.

Penalty Area A portion of the playing field in front of each goal; a foul by a defending player within this area results in a penalty kick for the opposing player. In men's soccer, the penalty area is forty-four yards wide by eighteen yards deep and centered on the goal. A ten-yard arc extending from the penalty kick mark beyond the far end of the area serves to extend the penalty area during a penalty kick, since no player except for the kicker is permitted to stay within ten yards of the ball. In women's soccer, the penalty area is a semicircle with a fifteen-yard radius centered on the goal.

Penalty Goal A goal scored on a penalty kick.

Penalty Kick A direct free kick, taken from the twelve-yard spot in front of the goal, that is awarded for fouls committed by the defending team within their own penalty area.

Penalty Mark The spot twelve yards directly in front of each goal, usually indicated by a short line. It is from this mark that the penalty kick is taken (Penalty Spot).

Penetration Accurate and quick advancing of the ball in a scoring attempt.

Pinball A situation where the area of play is so congested that every attempt to shoot, pass, or clear rebounds from players.

Pitch British term for soccer field.

Pivot Instep Kick A kick made by swinging the leg around in front of the body, hitting the ball with the instep, and driving it to the side rather than straight ahead.

Place Kick A kick at a stationary ball placed on the ground.

Play To trap, dribble, kick, or head the ball.

"Playing around Them" Switching the ball from one side of the field to another with a succession of passes.

"Playing Feet" Passing a ball directly to a teammate's feet.

"Playing Kickball" Team using the system of just kicking the ball as far as it can with no regard to passing.

Playmaker Creative midfielder.

Playoff Tournament that takes place after the end of a season, used to determine a champion.

"Play On" A term used by referees signifying that no foul or stoppage is to be called, applying the Advantage Rule.

Play Space To push a ball into an open area of the field for another player to run on to, as opposed to playing to feet.

Play Them Offside A method of making offensive players move away from the goal.

"Play the Way You're Facing" Pass the way you are facing, then move to space.

Points Team statistic indicating its degree of success, calculated as follows: two points for a win (three in the 1994 World Cup), one point for a tie, zero points for a loss; also, an individual statistic for a player, calculated by totaling two points for each goal and one point for each assist.

Popeye Popping the ball off the goal causing it to come back at a player.

Poser Player who has style and looks good but lacks game.

Position The area of the field occupied by a player.

Possession Control of the ball.

Post Goalpost or the area near it.

Pressure A defender placing pressure on his opponent with the ball.

"Prince of Dribblers" Stanley Matthews retired from first-division English soccer five days after his fiftieth birthday, in 1965. During his prime, in the 1930s, Matthews's magic moves enabled him to run with the ball at will around any defender he came near. His passing, peerless footwork, and shifty moves with a ball seemingly attached to his foot by an invisible string earned him his royal nickname.

Professional Foul A deliberate foul to obtain an advantage: intimidation of the opposition, or prevention of a subsequent goal-scoring opportunity.

Pull To remove a goalkeeper when trailing late in a game and replace him with an additional offensive player to increase the chances of scoring.

Pulling the String A shot off a free kick that looks sure to go over the crossbar but at the last second dips into the goal.

Punt To kick a ball as it is dropped from the hands.

Push Pass A pass made by shoving the ball with the foot instead of kicking it.

"Push Up" A sweeper's directions to fellow defenders to stop lagging in the back; an attempt to draw the opposing team offsides, to get defenders in on the offensive transition.

Qualifying Draw The division of teams into groups for World Cup qualifying matches, held two years before the Draw.

Qualifying Matches Games played in the two years preceding the World Cup to determine which teams participate in the tournament.

Rainbow A player popping the ball up and flicking it over the head in a forward motion with the back of the heel.

Reading Anticipating and getting set for action that may take place; understanding and reacting to the strategy of the opposition (Reading the Game).

Receiver Player who gets a pass from a teammate.

Recovery The turning and sprinting of a beaten defender attempting to get between the ball and the goal.

Red Card A card used by the referee in international soccer to indicate that a player is being ejected from the game.

Referee The official responsible for the timing and control of the game.

Regular Season Schedule of games set before the season consisting of all games played before a playoff or tournament is held.

Regulation Game Two completed periods of a game, prior to any overtime or tiebreaker.

Riding a Ball A means of cushioning the impact of a ball, reducing its speed, and bringing it under control that is executed by a player giving at (or relaxing) the part of the body where the ball hits.

Roll Infield Switch positions with another player in the middle of the game.

Round A stage of a tournament where teams compete; the World Cup tournament has five main rounds.

Running off the Ball Player movements into pass-receiving positions.

Sag Off To move away from an opponent being marked.

Salamander A head-first dive at a ball in the air, in which a player heads the ball usually in an attempt to score.

Save The goalkeeper stopping an attempted goal by catching or deflecting the ball; any prevention of the ball from entering the goal.

Scissors Kick A kick made by jumping up and kicking first one leg into the air and then the other, which sends the ball above the head, usually behing the player.

Score Putting the ball into the net for a goal; also, the tally of goals for each team playing in a game.

Scorers Players scoring goals.

Scoring Chance An opportunity to take a shot at the goal.

Screening Keeping possession of and protecting the ball by placing one's body between the ball and the opponent.

Sell Succeed in fooling a defender or goalkeeper.

Sending Off The dismissal of a player from the game by the referee.

Set Play Planned strategy that a team uses when a game is restarted with a free kick, penalty kick, corner kick, goal kick, throw-in, or kickoff.

Set Up To kick the ball aloft and get it to land near the goal.

Shape Positioning of players on the field in relation to formation and ball location.

Shell Drop back past the midfielder with a shot and goal.

Shepherd To force an attacking player away from the front of the goal and into a corner or second defender. To maneuver opponents into less dangerous positions while retreating.

Shielding Ball carrier protecting the ball from a defender closely marking him or her, keeping his body between the ball and the defender (Screening).

Shin guards Pads that strap onto a player's lower leg protecting the shins.

Shooting Kicking the ball at the opponent's net in an attempt to score a goal.

Shorthanded Team playing with less than its full complement of eleven players.

Shot An attempt to score by kicking or heading the ball toward the goal line.

Shoulder Charge Minimal shoulder-to-shoulder contact by a defender against a ball carrier; the only contact allowed by the rules unless a defender touches the ball first.

Show Move from a position with an intervening defender to one with a clear line to the ball.

Shutout Preventing the opposition from scoring any goals in a game.

Side Foot A shot or pass made by kicking the ball with the side of the foot.

Sideline Line running along the length of the field on each side (Touchline).

Side Tackle An attempt by a defender to redirect the ball slightly with his foot away from a ball carrier running in the same direction.

Single Elimination A type of tournament where a single defeat eliminates a team from the tournament.

Skied A ball kicked needlessly high into the air.

Skinned Defender is turned inside out by a skilled dribbler.

"Skip" Shouted advice to allow ball to run to another player.

Sliding Tackle Attempt by the defender to take the ball away from a ball carrier by sliding on the ground feet-first into the ball.

Small-Sided Game Match played with fewer than eleven players per side.

Smoked Offensive player performed a terrific move, leaving defender in the dust.

Soccer Through the centuries, some type of football has been played. The first visitors to the Polynesian Islands found the natives kicking a ball made from bamboo fibers. Early callers on the Eskimos witnessed them kicking around a leather ball that was filled with moss. The Chinese, circa 400 BC, played *tsu chu*, a game in which players had to kick a ball through a hole in a silk net. "Ye Olde Football" is traced by some accounts to the Roman occupation of Britain and the British copying the Roman game of *haspastan*. As the English football game evolved, and then competed with rugby football, a need to codify and clarify it was evident.

On October 26, 1863, a historic meeting took place at Freeman's Tavern in London. That conference today is viewed as the birthdate of modern football, or soccer. The Football Association (F.A.) was formed. Its object was to confine itself exclusively to a kicking game, as distinct from rugby. The Football Association became and still is the ruling body of the game in England—and the only national association in the world that omits the name of its country in its official title.

Association Football became known as "association." Then it was abridged to "assoc." Ultimately the word was garbled into its present form, "soccer." To make things a bit more complex and confusing, the word "football" today is used in virtually every nation of the world to describe the sport that those in the United States refer to as "soccer."

Soft Touch Ability of a player to trap a pass sent to him at any speed or height.

Sold Him Like a Kipper Sent a defending player the wrong way with a turn.

Sole Kick A kick in which the sole of the shoe is put on top of the ball and the ball is pushed forcefully to the rear (Sole-of-the-Foot Kick, Sole Trap).

Space Open areas on the playing field that can be used by the offense.

Split Passing the ball between two defenders.

Split Tackle A tackle in which one foot is stationary and the other is aimed at the ball, as the tackler ends up on the field in a position resembling a split.

Spot Kick A stationary-ball kick; another term for the penalty kick.

Spun Like a Top Defender turned by a skilled dribbler.

Square Pass A pass pushed laterally across the field to a player moving forward, or by a player to a teammate running alongside him (Square Ball).

Stalemate Two players facing each other, each waiting for the other to make a move (Stand-off).

Stance The position of a player's feet.

Starter Player on the field to play at the start of a game.

Steal To takes the ball away from an opposing player.

"Step," "Step It" Directions to a defensive line to pull out for offside trap.

Stop A catch or deflection of a shot by a goalkeeper.

Stopper Defender who marks the best scorer on the attacking team, often the opposition's striker.

Stopper Back The back who plays near the center of the field, usually the center halfback.

Striker A central forward position whose major responsibility is scoring goals.

Strong Foot The foot a player is more skilled in using.

Substitution Replacing one player on the field with another player not on the field; FIFA rules allow only three substitutions per game.

Sudden Death A type of overtime where the first goal scored by a team ends the game and gives that team the victory; most overtime in soccer is not sudden death.

Suspended Ball A free-swinging ball that is employed as a training aid.

Sweeper Defender who plays closest to his own goal behind the rest of the defenders; a team's last line of defense.

Swerve Kick A kick with the outside of the foot that makes the ball curve in flight.

Swing It Change the side of attack by passing around the back.

Switch The act of one player exchanging places (position) with a teammate.

Tackle To attempt to kick the ball away from an opponent, to make him lose control of it, or to cause him to hurry his pass. Tackling takes place when both players are playing the ball with their feet.

"Take Ball" Pressure the dribbler.

Terrier An aggressive, tireless player.

Territory Half the field which a team defends.

Thigh Trap Use of the thigh by a player to slow down and control a ball in the air.

Three-on-One Break A type of break with three attacking players against only one defensive player.

Three-on-Two Break A type of break with three attacking players against two defensive players.

Through Pass A pass that goes past two opposition players to a teammate.

Throw-in The means of resuming play after the ball has gone out of bounds.

Tiebreaker When teams are tied after overtime in FIFA tournament play, a series of penalty kicks are taken by players from both teams, and the team that scores on more of them is declared the winner.

Tie Game When two teams score the same number of goals in a match; if the game ends tied, it is a draw.

Time Having enough time to control the ball before a defender can pressure.

Timekeeper Role of the referee, who keeps track of the official time and notifies teams and fans when each period is completed.

Touch Out-of-bounds area, outside of the touch lines.

Touch Line Boundary lines on the side of the field; the sidelines.

Touch-Line Kick A free kick from the touch line performed from the spot where the ball left the playing field.

Trailing Running behind another player.

Trapping A method of controlling the ball by stopping it with the feet, chest, thighs, or head.

Tripping Intentionally throwing or trying to throw a player.

Turnover Loss of possession of the ball.

Two-on-One Break A type of break with two attacking players against one defensive player.

Two-Way Midfielder Versatile midfielder, team leader, largely responsible for organizing play in the mid-field area.

Ungentlemanly Conduct Striking an opponent, for example, which can result in a player being dismissed from the game.

USSF (United States Soccer Federation) An organization formed in 1913 to govern soccer in America. It is America's connection to FIFA, providing soccer rules and guidelines to players, referees, and spectators nationwide.

USYSA (United States Youth Soccer Association) Official Youth Division that organizes and administers youth league competitions, establishes rules and guidelines, and stages clinics and workshops to support players, coaches, and referees.

Volley To kick a ball while it is in the air.

Wall A lined-up barrier of three–seven defenders positioned near the goal to help the goalkeeper in his defense against a free kick and to block as much of the kicker's view of the goal as possible.

Wall Pass A pass that is immediately kicked back to the passer so that it resembles a ball bouncing back from a wall (Give and Go).

Weak Foot One a player has less skill with.

Weak Side Side of the field without the ball.

Well Marshaled Tightly marked, defending and staying with a very good player with one or two designated players.

W Formation A five-man forward line formation resembling the letter W in which the outside forwards and the center forward play in a line close to the goal, while the inside forwards play far from the goal (compare M Formation).

"What a Cracker" Hard shot.

"What You See" Player with the ball has no one marking.

Wheel Man Central midfielder with primary duty for distributing the ball when his team is on the attack.

Width The holding of wide positions on the field by players to facilitate passing over the entire width of the field.

Win-Draw-Loss Record Summary of outcomes of a team's matches; for example, a team with a 3-1-3 record has played seven games and won three, tied one, and lost three.

Wing The area of the field near the touch line. Outside forward who plays to the sides of the strikers and whose primary task is to provide them with accurate crossing passes so they can shoot at the goal (Winger).

Wing Halfbacks The halfbacks on either side of the center halfback.

Win the Ball Winning control of the ball over an opposing player.

"With You" Call to let a teammate know of a player's availability.

World Cup Perhaps the ultimate in sports competition, soccer's World Championship eclipses baseball's World Series, American football's Super Bowl, hockey's Stanley Cup, and horse racing's Triple Crown. It is held at a different site every four years midway between Olympic years. More than one hundred nations today compete for up to two years to qualify for the finals, which are staged over a two- to three-week period in the summer. The host nation and the reigning World Cup champion automatically qualify. The fourteen survivors of the qualifying competition join with these two to complete the field of sixteen. Amateurs, professionals, and naturalized citizens of a country are eligible to participate. The concept of the World Cup was inspired by the dissatisfaction of some European nations, who claimed the Olympic Games placed them at a disadvantage in vying for a world soccer title. These nations reasoned that the Olympics were restricted to amateurs and their best players were professionals. Jules Rimet, a leading figure in French soccer and the president of Federation Internationale de Football (FIFA), the ruling body of the sport, together with Henri Delauney, another leading French soccer personality, conceived the basic outline and structure of the World Cup. Uruguay won the first World Cup, which was held in 1930.

Yellow Card A warning card held up by the referee to indicate that a player has committed a serious foul and is thereby being cautioned.

Zone Type of defense, assigning each defender to a particular area in front of or around the team's goal in which he is responsible for marking any attacker that enters; often used in youth league games but rarely in professional competition.

Squash

Ace A shot that an opponent cannot touch with his racket.

Alley Shot A shot hit straight along the wall (Rail Shot).

Backing on the Ball The backing up of a player to get a ball that has hit a side wall, then the back wall, and then breaks toward the middle of the court.

Boast In the direction horizontally across the court.

Boast for Nick A shot that is hit hard onto the side wall.

Corner Shot A shot that hits the comer and then returns.

Covering a Shot The position assumed by a player to physically block various returns by an opponent.

Crosscourt Shot A shot against the front wall hit in such a manner as to land across the court (V Shot).

Die The failure of a ball to bounce.

Doubles Squash played by four people (two on a side) in a larger court than singles (forty-five feet by twenty-five feet, compared to thirty-two feet by eighteen feet). A livelier ball with a red dot is used.

Drive A ball hit with power after it bounces.

Drop Shot A ball hit softly to the front wall.

Fault A service-rules violation that, if executed two straight times, results in loss of service and a point.

Gallery An area for spectators.

Get A scrambling return of a difficult shot.

Hall Volley A ball that is hit the instant after it bounces.

Length A term describing a ball that bounces twice or dies before it reaches the back wall.

Let A point that must be replayed.

Let Point A point awarded to a player who is deliberately interfered with by an opponent.

Lob A ball hit high on the front wall.

Lob Serve An underhand serve.

Midcourt The midpoint between the front and back walls.

Monkey Doubles Doubles played with a singles ball on a singles court with rackets whose handles have been cut down.

Nick A ball that hits the juncture of the floor and a side wall, or the floor and the back wall, in such a way that it rolls out and is almost impossible to retrieve.

No Set A call made optionally at 13-all or 14-all by the receiver who does not wish to lengthen a game by demanding that the player must win by two points (in both cases the game is won at 15).

Out Side The receiving side.

Philadelphia Shot A trick shot; a boast in reverse (Philadelphia Boast).

Putaway A shot that cannot be retrieved (Winner).

Quarter-Circle An area where, when serving, a player places his foot (Service Box).

Rally A series of shots.

Reverse Corner A cross-corner shot; a corner shot in reverse.

Service Line The line on the front wall that a ball that is served must hit above in order to be in play. The service line is 6½ feet off the floor for singles play and 8½ feet off the floor for doubles play (Cut Line).

Smash A hard, overhand swing at the ball that causes it to hit the wall with force.

T That area of the court just in front of the floor service line and the center service line—the best spot from which to hit returns.

Telltale A seventeen-inch-high rectangle of sheet metal positioned at the bottom of the front wall that gives off a ringing sound when hit by the ball (Tin).

Touch Finesse on the part of a player in hitting corner and drop shots.

Turning on the Ball The act of turning around to get a ball coming off the back wall.

Volley To hit a ball before it touches the floor.

Surfing

Above the Peak Along the line of highest point of a specific swell, to the left or right of the peak.

Axe Breaking of a wave on top of the surfer, knocking him off his board (Wipeout).

Backwash Water-flow off the beach incline that rushes back to the ocean after a breaker has washed up on shore.

Barge Big, clumsy surfboard.

Belly Surfboard bottom.

Belly-Board One less than three feet long used in body surfing.

Below the Peak Along the line of the swell.

"Big Kahuna" Duke Paoa Kahinu Mokoe Hulikohola Kahanamoku is generally regarded as the inventor of the modern surfboard. In his youth, Kahanamoku preferred an old-school board, constructed after the fashion of ancient Hawaiian *olo* boards. Kahanamoku easily qualified for the U.S. Olympic swimming team in 1912, breaking the record for the 200-meter freestyle in his trial heat for the 4 × 200 relay. He went on to win a gold medal in the 100-yard (91-m) in 1920. "Duke" was not a title, but a given name. His father was named "Duke" in honor of Prince Alfred, Duke of Edinburgh.

Big-Wave Board One with a pointed tail whose maximum width is in front; a surfboard used for conditions where there are big waves (Elephant Gun).

Blown Out Choppy water unsuitable for surfing.

Board Surfboard.

Body Surfing Surfing down the face of a breaker's incline by sliding along with the front part of the body.

Bouncing the Board Shifting the board's weight backward and forward to move the board's nose out of the water and then let it fall.

Chatter Sound of surfboard bending as it slides over choppy water.

Chop Rough water surface.

Clean-up Set Set of breakers bringing all surfers to shore.

Clean-up Wave Biggest breaker in a set.

Close Out A wave or waves breaking along the beach with no shoulder for the surfer to ride on (Closed Door).

Corner the Wave To be on the shoulder and away from the swirling water.

Crack the Wave To ride the wave.

Crashing Surf Fast surf.

Critical Wave that can break at any instant.

Crossover Walking the board by crossing one leg in front of another, moving either forward or backward on the board.

Curl Hollow part of a wave at the moment of its breaking (Hook, Tunnel, Tube).

Cut-Back Turning back into the breaking part of a wave.

Deck Top, or standing surface, of a surfboard.

Dig Paddle furiously.

Double-Ender Surfboard double-ended with a fin that can be fastened to either end without changing the ability of the board to perform.

Drop Steepest part of the wave.

Dumper Plunging or crashing wave.

Ebb Tide Flowing out of the current from the shore.

Exposure Suit An outfit that is insulated to enable a surfer to preserve body heat.

Face of the Wave Concave, steep part of a wave facing the shore.

Fast Condition affording fast surfboarding because the surf has a steep wave forming a wall.

Feather A noncrashing or plunging wave that holds up, with only the top part breaking (Spill).

Fetch The overall area in which the wind is able to catch the water to create swells; the length of the fetch generally has an effect on the height of the wave.

Flat Calm water where there is little or no surf, making surfing unsuitable.

Flood Tide Highest tide.

Glassy Nonchoppy, smooth water surface.

Go Behind Move past another surfer on the wave's seaward side.

Goofy Foot Most surfers stand with the left foot forward, not with their right (goofy) foot forward.

Green Back Swell that has not broken and is on the outside.

Gremlin Surfer who engages in objectionable and improper behavior.

Hairy When surfer's ten toes project over the surfboard's nose while a wave is being ridden (Hang Ten).

Hang Five When toes of one foot project over the nose of the surfboard while a wave is being ridden.

Head Dip Showing off.

Hold Up Holding together just a bit of a swell that is threatening to break at a critical point.

Hook Wave's concave portion (Curl, Tube).

Hook a Rail When rail of the surfboard knifes into the water to tip or capsize the board.

Hot Dog Show-off.

Hump Large wave.

Inside Wave's side that faces to the shore.

Island Giving up a ride by forcing the nose of the surfboard under the water (Island Pull-out, Nose Pull-out).

Kick Exert force on the surfboard's rear by stepping down on it while simultaneously raising the lead foot; this lifts the board's nose out of the water and makes it possible to pivot the board on its tail (Kick Out, Kick Turn).

Kook Beginner; a surfer lacking skills.

Late Takeoff To take off when a wave is very critical.

Line Fast surf: when the wave walls up with an open door and does not crash, enabling the surfer to ride onto the wave's shoulder (Line-Up).

Locked In When surfer finds a wave too steep to pull out of.

Log Clumsy and large surfboard, difficult to maneuver.

Make the Wave Moving across the wall before it breaks on the surfer and board.

Malibu Board Malibu Beach, about 25 miles west of Los Angeles, is one of California's top surfing areas. The finned fiberglass surfboard that virtually revolutionized surfing by making acrobatic gyrations possible from a standing position derives its name from Malibu Beach. Basic, highly maneuverable, lightweight, fiberglass-covered surfboard (Simmons' Board).

Noah A shark.

Open Door Breaking wave allowing surfer to ride away from the peak, out of hook, onto the shoulder.

Out of Control Big surf.

Outside Breaker's far side; to the seaward side of the swell.

Overstriding Making an error by positioning the weight too far forward and forcing the surfboard to nose underwater.

Rails Surfboard edges.

Reverse A kick-out that sees the rider and the surfboard turn in opposite directions.

Reverse (Skeg) Takeoff Stunt performed by catching the wave when the surfboard is in a reverse position with the skeg (fin).

Riptide Powerful and dangerous current.

Rock Dance Low-tide activity of surfers walking over rocks trying to recover their surfboards.

Rocker Amount of vertical curvature in profile of surfboard.

Roll Rocking or tilting from side to side of a board.

Runout Undertow following the outgoing tide from the shore current.

Safety Buckle Device making it possible to use one hand to fasten straps.

Scratch Paddle with force.

Section Part of a wave that walls up to break in a section of several feet.

Semipig Half Broad-tailed board.

Session Sequence of successive waves (Set).

Shape Surfboard's outline looking straight at the surfboard's deck or belly.

Shoot Ride a wave (Shoot the Wave, Shoot the Curl).

Shoulder Portion of a swell that is less steep than the part of the wave near the hook.

Showboating Showing off.

Shuffle Moving feet along the surface of the deck, thus moving weight backward or forward without crossing the legs.

Skeg Fin.

Skim Board Small disc-shaped or rectangular board used to skim over shallow water.

Slow Surf Gentle, sloping swells; feathering-crest surf conditions that hamper fast rides.

Soup Swirling and foaming water (Swash).

Soup Out Riding out the soup by moving straight off in a closeout.

South Bay Squared-off-at-the-end surfboard tail.

Spilling Surf Slow or feathering surf.

Spooky Conditions that are either hard to predict or difficult.

Stall To throw a board out of trim and stop its sliding.

Straight Off Riding a surfboard directly toward shore.

Surf Ski Wave-riding craft, long and hollow.

Train A session.

Trimming the Board Effective distribution of the rider's weight on the surfboard, positioning it flat against the water surface.

Trough Depression in front of breaker.

Tube Wave's concave face (Curl, Tunnel).

Turnaround Showboat maneuver in which a surfer turns around 360 degrees on the board.

Wall Instant large length of swell about to crash all at once; unsurfable beach (Wall Up, Wall Out).

Wax Paraffin.

Wedge Type of board with wood strips placed diagonally, joined at the nose.

Swimming

Anchor The final leg of a relay race.

Anchorman The participant who swims the final leg of a relay race.

Backstroke A swimming stroke in which the swimmer is on his back with legs alternately kicking and arms alternately pulling; one of the four primary competitive styles.

Breaststroke A stroke executed face down, with the legs executing the frog kick while the arms move forward and out symmetrically and simultaneously; the oldest stroke, and one of the four primary competitive strokes.

Butterfly A stroke in which the swimmer is face down, with the legs kicking in unison while the arms simultaneously move over and through the water; one of the four primary competitive strokes.

Circuit Training In-and-out-of-the-water training enabling a maximum number of swimmers to work out continually without wasting time.

Crawl Face-down swimming: the arms move independently of each other, and the legs kick individually; the most commonly used stroke in freestyle competition and the fastest competitive stroke (often synonymous with Freestyle).

Dead Man's Float Lying in a prone position on top of the water, with arms and legs extended.

Dolphin Kick The feet move up and down together in this butterfly-stroke kick that resembles the movement of a dolphin.

Flip A tumbling turn in which the swimmer bends and twists his body, pushing off the wall with the feet in a corkscrew movement.

Flutter Kick A freestyle kicking maneuver in which the swimmer's knees bend and straighten as each leg and foot presses down underwater; the legs alternately move, two or more times per arm stroke.

Freestyle The last leg of a medley race, in which a swimmer may select his stroke; however, the crawl, being the fastest stroke, is almost always used and has come to be synonymous with freestyle and is one of four primary competitive styles.

Frog Kick Similar to the movements of a frog's legs in the water, a kick in which the feet are drawn up behind the swimmer with knees bent, the legs then snapping open wide and together; a kick used primarily in the breaststroke.

Get on the Stroke Shortening a stroke.

Heat A qualifying competition.

Individual Medley (IM) A competition that requires swimming each leg with a different stroke; the order is generally as follows: butterfly, backstroke, breaststroke, freestyle.

In Phase Touching the wall at the finish as part of the downward motion of a final stroke.

Interval Training Procedure in which participants swim prescribed distances repeatedly with specific rest intervals (generally equal to the time of the swimming period).

Jamming the Pace Intentionally slowing down of the pace in the swimming of a portion of a race.

Jump In relays, leaving the starting block prior to his incoming teammate touching the wall—cause for a team to be disqualified.

Lap The length of a pool from one end to the other.

Leg One fourth of a relay swum by four different competitors.

Medley A competition in which a different stroke is used for each leg.

Meter A metric measure equal to 39.37 inches—a distance slightly longer than a yard (a 100-meter race is longer than a 100-yard race).

Overdistance Training Technique designed to build endurance in which swimmers swim longer distances than their normal racing distance.

Pace Swimming rate.

Peak A carefully planned procedure designed to round a swimmer's mind and body to top form before major competition.

Pulling Using only the arms while swimming.

Recovery A swimmer's sweeping arm movements over the water as they are placed in position to begin an underwater stroke (Return).

Relay A competition in which four team members perform either the same stroke or one of four different strokes in a specific order; a combined time score for each team determines the victor.

Scissors Kick A sidestroke kick in which one leg is bent and both legs swing open and shut like scissors.

Sidestroke A stroke in which a swimmer lies on his or her side, legs performing the scissors kick, the upper arm thrust out and bent to the chin, while the lower arm is thrust forward and bent to the chin.

Split A section of a race; in a 200-meter race, for example, there are four 50-meter splits.

Split Time The amount of time used up in swimming a split.

Sprint A short-distance competition.

Streamlining Stretching the body to minimize water resistance.

Stroke A particular combination of arm and leg movements and body position.

Time Trials Approximated racing conditions used to gauge swimming speed and sometimes employed for the selection of team members in a specific competition.

Wash A surge of water produced by a number of sprint swimmers turning at the wall at the same time.

Synchronized Swimming

Artistic Impression Judging category synchronized swimming involving choreography and movement that interprets the mood of the music.

Back Layout Position in which the body is extended with the face, chest, thighs, and feet at the water's surface.

Back Pike Body bent at hips forming a 45-degree angle or less, legs and trunk extended, with the back straight and the head in line.

Ballet Leg One leg extended perpendicular to the water surface, the body in a back layout position.

Ballet Leg Double Both legs extended perpendicular to the water surface, swimmer's face at the surface.

Boost Swimmer quickly rises from water, head first, bringing as much of the body as possible above the surface.

Cadence Action Individually and in rapid succession identical movements performed by all team members.

Combined Spin Descending spin of 360 degrees or more followed right after by an equal ascending spin.

Continuous Spin Descending spin with a rapid rotation through 720 degrees or more.

Crane Body extended upward, one leg extended forward at a 90-degree angle.

Deckwork Before swimmers enter the water, movements are performed on the deck of the pool; ten-second limit in international competition.

Degree of Difficulty For scoring purposes, a multiplier assigned to a raw score. For example: if the degree of difficulty is 1.2, and the raw score is 6, the final score is 7.2.

Descending Spin Beginning at the apex of the vertical position, a 180- or 360-degree spin that is completed when the heels reach the surface.

Dolphin Swimmer from a horizontal position on the surface submerges headfirst, swimming down and under, reemerging at the original location.

Dolphin Arch Body is arched with head, hips, and feet conforming to the arc.

Duet Two athletes swim together in an event.

Eggbeater Rapid rotary action of the legs supporting and propelling upper body while in an upright position, allowing the arms free.

Figure A specific combination of body positions and transitions, performed in a prescribed manner.

Figures Portion of competition where swimmers perform a series of highly technical movements.

Flamingo Position in which one leg is extended perpendicular to the surface while the other leg is drawn to chest. The lower leg is parallel to the surface and the face is at the surface.

Float On the water surface, a formation where two to eight swimmers are connected horizontally.

Free Routine Planned routine done to music choreographed by the competitors and their coaches, limited to five minutes plus or minus fifteen seconds.

Front Layout Position where the body is extended, with the head, upper back, buttocks, and heels at the surface.

Front Pike Position where the body is bent at the hips, forming a 90-degree angle, and the legs and trunk are extended, with the back straight, head in line.

Full Twist A 360-degree rotation of the body around its vertical axis.

Gel Swimmers use a specially formulated waterproof hair gel.

Grand Slam Winning first place in every event at a meet.

Half-Twist A 180-degree body rotation around its vertical axis.

Hybrid Figure Combination of different body positions and transitions with parts of figures.

Level Body location in relation to the water surface.

Lift Move in which one or more swimmers lift a swimmer or swimmers above the surface.

Nose Clip Device that holds nostrils closed to keep water out of the swimmer's nasal cavity while underwater.

Pattern Formation of team members in which all are in the same position or in alternating positions.

Pool Pattern Swimmer's path through the water.

Required Elements In technical routine, eight to ten fixed figures that must be performed.

Reverse Combined Spin An ascending spin of 360 degrees or more followed immediately by an equal descending spin.

Rocket Split Combination of thrust to the vertical position and a rapid leg split, followed by a return to maximum height in the vertical position.

Scull Continuous hand movements in the water to balance and support the body.

Spin Rotation while in the vertical position about the body's vertical axis.

Split One leg extended forward, the other backward, with the feet and thighs at the surface. Lower back arched, hips, shoulders, and head in a vertical line in the water.

Solo Individual swimmers compete against one another.

Surface Arch Lower back arched, hips, shoulders, and head on a vertical line. The legs are together and at the surface.

Synchronized Swimming The sport is regarded as a hybrid of swimming, gymnastics, and ballet. Competitors (individuals or teams) perform aesthetically pleasing and difficult movements while they hold their breath and keep afloat in the water. It became an Olympic sport open to women in 1984 but is still not open to men.

Team Ten swimmers compose a team; eight swim in a routine.

Technical Merit A category for judging synchronized swimming based primarily on the ability of the athletes to execute certain movements with precision.

Technical Routine Required elements must be performed in a specific sequence lasting two minutes and fifty seconds.

Thrust Swimmer begins in the back pike position, with the legs perpendicular to the surface, then moves the legs and hips rapidly upward, unrolling the body and assuming the vertical position.

Trio Three swimmers work together as a team.

Tub Legs are bent and together, the feet and knees are at the surface and parallel to it, the thighs are perpendicular, and the face is at the surface; the head is in line with the trunk.

Tuck Knees are brought nearly to the head, with the heels close to the buttocks and the back rounded.

Twirl A rapid 180-degree twist.

Twist A rotation of the body at sustained height.

Twist Spin A move combining a half-twist with a continuous spin, in rapid succession.

Vertical Position A position in which the body is extended perpendicular to the surface with the head down and the legs together. Head, hips, and ankles should be in line.

Walkout Front A move in which the swimmer starts in the split position, lifts the front leg in a 180-degree arc over the surface to meet the other leg, and then continues into the back layout position.

Tennis

Ace A point earned by serving a ball that cannot be returned.

Ad-In Advantage to the server.

Ad-Out Advantage to the receiver.

Advantage A point won by a player after deuce. If the player wins the next point, he wins the game; if he loses the next point, the score returns to deuce (Ad).

Advantage Court The left-handed service court, where the ball is served when an advantage belongs to one side or the other.

All A tie or equal score: "30-all," for example, refers to a tie at 30 in the game.

All-Court Game A player's ability to perform well from all over the court with all types of strokes.

Alley An area on each side of the singles court used to make the court larger for doubles play; the alley is out of bounds for singles play.

American Twist A serve in which the ball is struck with an upward motion, causing it to spin in flight and bounce to the left of the receiver when it hits the ground (Kick Serve).

Angle Games A playing style that uses the angles of the court, specifically the short angle at which a player hits a forehand shot crosscourt in order to land the ball inside the opponent's forehand sideline.

Angle Volley A volleying strike angled by an opponent.

Anticipatory Position A position a player takes while awaiting the opportunity to serve or return the ball.

Approach Shot A hard, deep shot into the opponent's court that gives the hitter a chance to move up to the net while putting the opponent on the defensive.

ATP Master's Race (Mercedes Super 9, ATP Super 9) Series of nine events in men's tennis in which a top-ten player is supposed to play eight of nine. Each tournament fields eight of the top ten players. This series concludes with the Tennis Masters Cup, a year-end round-robin tournament in which eight ATP players compete for the year-end title.

Australian Formation A positioning of players in a doubles game in which the server's partner stands on the same side of the court as the server (I Formation; Australian Doubles).

Backcourt The area between the baseline and the service line.

Backhand A stroke made with the playing arm and racket across the body and the back of the hand facing the direction the ball will be hit; a stroke played on the left-hand side of a right-handed player.

Back Room The space between the baseline and the court's backstop or fence (Runback).

Backspin Rotation on a ball resulting from a player hitting down behind it, making the ball spin in the opposite direction from its flight; when the ball hits the ground, it will stop short or bounce backward (Underspin).

Backstop A behind-the-court obstruction preventing the ball from rolling away.

Backswing The initial swinging of the racket backward in preparation for a forward stroke (Racquetback Position).

Bad Ball A ball that does not land in the playing area.

Ball The tennis ball: a hollow rubber sphere with a cemented, fuzzy, white or yellow cloth covering. Shall be more than 2½ inches and less than 2⅝ inches in diameter and weigh more than 2 ounces and less than 2⅛ ounces. Also, the word used for the effect of a stroke—for example, a "good-length ball" refers to a stroke that gets the ball to hit the ground near the baseline.

Ball Boy, Ball Girl One who retrieves the ball for the players.

Baseline The back line at either end of the court behind which a player must stand while serving.

Baseline Game A playing strategy in which a player stays close to the baseline and seldom moves into the forecourt.

Baseliner One who plays a baseline game.

"Beast" Max Mirnyi, the 6' 5" player from Belarus, for size and attitude.

Beaten by the Ball Arriving too late to have a good position from which to return the ball.

Best of Three (or Five) Maximum number of sets in any match. In "best of three" matches, players need to win two of the three sets. In men's tennis, most matches are "best of three."

Big Game A type of play emphasizing a big service and a net attack.

Big Point Crucial point deciding which player wins a set or important game.

Big Server A player who has a powerful serve.

Blocked Ball A ball returned by meeting it with a stiff wrist and stationary racquet (Stop Volley).

Bound The rising action of the ball off the surface of the court; the rising angle from a first and second impact on the court surface.

Break The unnatural bounding action of a ball as it leaves the ground after being hit with a cut or twist stroke.

Broken Service A game won by the server's opponent.

Buggy-Whip Extreme cross-court shot, generally hit on the run. A player follows through behind the head.

Bullet A ball hit with great force.

Bye A player in an elimination tournament who does not have to play in a round and automatically advances to the next round.

Call The score at a given time in a game.

"Canadian Doubles" Game played with three people, two against one. Alleys are considered good on the doubles side and out on the singles side.

Cannonball A serve that is extremely flat and fast.

Center Mark A short line projecting inward from the middle of the baseline that indicates the edge of the area a player must be standing in when serving ("hashmark").

Center Service Line A line that divides the service court in half and separates the right and left service courts.

Center Strop Used on some playing surfaces, a two-inch-wide piece of canvas that fastens the net at the center of the court.

Chalk White material marking lines on some tennis surfaces. A ball striking a chalked line will often raise white dust and tennis players talk of "seeing chalk," indicating their feeling that a disputed ball was in play because it hit the chalk.

Challenge Cups Trophies offered to winners of lawn tennis competition. The current holders are challenged by other entries for the right to hold the cup. Generally, the holder must compete against the winner of an event annually; a trophy won three times by the same player passes into his or her permanent possession.

Challenger The team or player that wins a preliminary competition for a challenge cup and thus has the right to challenge the champion for the trophy.

Challenge Round The final round in a challenge-type tourney. The champion nation of the previous year, for example, awaits the results of the challenging nation's elimination tournament. The winner of the eliminations automatically becomes the challenger pitted against the champion in the championship round.

Change of Ends Players change ends of the court during tennis matches. For example, after every "uneven" game (first, third, fifth, etc.) in a set (Change Over Changing Courts, Crossover).

Change of Length Shots made with varying lengths—a short shot, a deep shot, and so forth.

Change of Pace Changing speeds on shots or reversing spin on the ball.

Chip A short, angled shot, generally sliced and used to return a serve in a doubles match.

Chip and Charge A chip followed by an approach shot, generally on a return of serve.

Choke To grip the handle of the racket nearer its head, rather than toward the end.

Chop To give the ball a sharp backspin or underspin by chopping down and under the ball with the racket, used to return fast services, occasionally also for drop shots.

Circuit The different competitions and tournaments on a player's schedule (Tour).

Clay Court Court whose surface is made of crushed shale, stone, or brick. There are two sorts of clay courts at ATP Tour events: red clay, found mostly in Europe and South America, which is slower; and green clay (United States and United Kingdom), which is faster.

Closed-Face Racket A racket that has its face inclined in the direction of an oncoming ball.

Club Player One who plays regularly at a club rather than on tour.

Continental Grip Using the same grip for forehand and backhand (Service Grip).

Court A seventy-eight-foot-long by thirty-six-foot-wide rectangle that forms the playing area of the game of tennis. A three-foot-high net divides the court in half. Running parallel and four feet inside the sidelines are the service sidelines, which function as the boundary lines for the service courts and the sidelines for the singles courts. Parallel to the net and twenty-one feet on each side are the service lines, which are connected by a line that marks two service courts on each side of the net.

Types of courts: hard courts (asphalt, concrete, or tartan surfaces); cinder, sand, or shale courts; grass courts; carpeted courts; red or green clay courts.

Court Material The playing surface: grass, clay, hard, synthetic, and so forth.

Covered Court An indoor court, generally used for winter play, with a synthetic surface and a roof.

Crack Slang expression for an expert player.

"Crazy Croat" Goran Ivanisevic of Croatia at times shows off a hyperactive personality.

Crosscourt Shot A diagonal stroking of the ball from one side of the court to the other, either long or short. Long crosscourt shots are usually played from baseline to baseline, while short ones generally bounce near the opponent's service court line, often being played with topspin.

Curl Spin, cut, or twist placed on the ball as a result of a sharply cut stroke.

Davis Cup In 1900 Dwight Filley Davis (1879–1945) donated a silver cup designed to be awarded as a national trophy to the country triumphing in an international competition in lawn tennis. The donation took place while Davis was still an undergraduate at Harvard. From the start, all teams consisted of four amateur players. All Davis Cup contests include four singles matches and one doubles match. Davis was one of the more outstanding tennis players in United States history, as well as a high-ranking government official in the 1920s and 1930s.

Dead A ball out of play is dead—when a ball has struck the ground twice anywhere on court or once out of the court; when the ball has fallen into the net; when a player through a rules infraction has lost the point. A nonlively ball or one that has lost air pressure and lacks rebounding ability.

Deep A ball that is hit near the opposition's baseline or deep into his or her playing area.

Deep-Court Game A playing style that positions a player deep in the backcourt.

Default The loss of a tournament match by a player who fails to play; the opposition moves into the next round (Walkover).

Defensive Volley A volleying stroke made from below the level of the net (Low Volley).

Deuce An even score after six points of a game.

Deuce Court The ball is served into this righthanded court whenever the score is deuce.

Deuce Set After each side has won five games in the same set, a tie results; unless a tiebreaker is used, one side must win two consecutive games to win the set.

Dink A softly hit ball that falls just beyond the net (Softie).

Dipping Balls Balls barely clearing the net that drop quickly and short.

Double Elimination Tournament A competition in which a player is eliminated after losing two matches.

Double Fault Two successive misses (faults) in serving.

Double Hit To stroke the ball twice on the same play—an illegal action.

Doubles A game for four players, two on each side.

Doubles Alley Outside width of the court that is used only when playing doubles (Alley).

Down-the-Line Shot A ball that hits close to and parallel to the sideline.

Draft The roster of players entered in an event written out and bracketed in the order they will play.

Draw The organization of entrants in a tourney. For example, a traditional single elimination tournament will have each competitor's name placed on a separate card. The cards are then selected at random and the names on the cards are entered in the tournament chart as they have been selected. Seeded entrants are not involved in the process, since their positions have been determined beforehand.

Drive A hard-hit ball that usually travels quickly from one end of the court to the other.

Drop Shot A softly hit ball with backspin that just clears the net and lands with a low bounce close to the net.

Drop Volley A shot that resembles a drop shot, but instead of being executed as a ground stroke, it is executed as a volley.

Earned Point A point won because of the skills of a player rather than because of the error(s) of an opponent.

Eastern Grip Generally the most popular tennis grip in the United States: the palm is to the side of the handle when the racket's face is held in a vertical position, making a V between the thumb and forefinger at the top of the handle; in the backhand stroke, the V of the hand is toward the front edge of the handle as a result of the hand being placed forward.

Even Court The right court; whenever play is started here, an even number of points has been played in the current game.

Exhibition Matches Entertainment matches outside competitions. Players are rewarded with prize money, but no rankings points.

Face The strings of the racket; the hitting surface. A closed-face racket indicates that the top edge is turned forward, positioning the hitting surface down toward the ground. An open-face racket indicates that the top edge of the racket is positioned backward, making the hitting surface face upward.

Fall A shot that bounces twice without being returned.

Fault A serve that lands outside the proper service court; two straight faults cause a player to lose a point, but not the service.

15 The first point won by a player in a game.

Flat A racket-head position with the face perpendicular to the court and squarely facing the net (Square Face).

Flat Serve Without spin, following a low, straight trajectory, this serve can be effective. Generally better-suited for first serves.

Flub To miss an easy shot.

Follow-through Where a player swings the racket through in the direction of the stroke, even after the ball has been played. The follow-through affects the length, direction, and speed of the ball.

Foot Fault A violation that takes place when a serving player steps on or over the baseline; illegal movement of the feet is also a foot fault.

Forcing Shot A powerful attacking shot that is generally well placed, deep, and quickly delivered; it is designed to create a weak return or an error on the part of the opposition.

Forecourt Front part of court, between the net and the service line.

Forehand A stroke performed with the palm of the hand facing in the direction of the intended movement of the ball.

40 The third point reached in a game. If both players reach this score, deuce is called.

"Four Musketeers" English-speaking nations dominated the first twenty-six years of the Davis Cup tennis competition. In 1927 France broke through as a result of the efforts of Rene Lacoste, Henri Cochet, Jean Bototra, and Jacques Brugnon. The four Frenchmen were dubbed the "Four Musketeers," and they were responsible for keeping the Davis Cup in France for six straight years.

Gallery The spectators watching a game. Also, an area for spectators to watch the game.

Game Part of a set. Every set consists of at least six games.

Game Point A point that, if won, will clinch a game victory.

Grand Slam winning the four major tournaments in the same year:

U.S Open—Corona Park, New York (hard courts).
Australian Open—Melbourne Park, Melbourne (hard courts).
French Open—Roland Garros, Paris (red clay).
Wimbledon—All England Lawn and Tennis Club, London (grass).

Grass A grass tennis court.

Grip The way a racket is held in the hand.

Grooved Stroke A familiar stroke that a player performs automatically.

Ground Stroke A stroke in which the ball is hit after it has bounced.

"Guga" Nickname of Brazilian player, and two-time French Open champion, Gustavo Kuerten.

Hack To take a clumsy swing at the ball.

Hacker An ineffective player (Duffer).

Half-Court Section of the court close to the service line.

Half-Volley A defensive stroke in which a player hits the ball immediately after it has bounced.

Hard Court Court surface of asphalt, concrete, or a similar material.

Head The frame and strings of a racket.

Height of Net Center height is three feet, gradually rising to reach three-foot six-inch posts at a point three feet outside each side of the court.

Hold Service A situation where the server wins a game; holding service each time makes it impossible to lose a set.

I Formation o Doubles formation where the server and partner line up in the middle of the court and move to opposite sides only after the serve is played (Australian Doubles).

Kick Serve One with heavy spin, causing it to change direction or bounce unexpectedly when it lands in the service court (Twist Serve).

Kill A shot hit so hard that it is almost impossible to return (Smash, Putaway).

"Killing Kim" Kim Clijsters has this and several other nicknames. Born June 8, 1983, in Bilzen (Flanders, Belgium), she plays right-handed and has a two-handed backhand and adoring fans worldwide for the verve she displays—the reason for her nicknames (Kim Kong).

"King of the Nets" William Tatem Tilden II was one of the great stars of the Roaring Twenties. Tilden's unique style of play featured booming serves and long strides across the court that enabled him to stay back near the baseline. Seven times he won the United States Championship. Eleven times he was a Davis Cup team member. Tilden was the first American to triumph at Wimbledon. When he finally retired, he had won over seventy tennis championships and truly earned his nickname (Big Bill).

Left Court (Player) The partner on a doubles team who is served to in the left court; this court is also called the odd court, or backhand court, because a player with a stronger backhand is generally positioned there.

Let A serve that is done over again—for example, a serve that hits the top of the net before landing in the proper area. Also, a point interrupted by interference that is played over.

Line Ball A shot that hits the line.

"Little Miss Poker Face" Helen Wills won seven American championships, eight Wimbledon titles, and four French titles. Her behavior on the court was sphinxlike. She rarely spoke to an opponent but stared out from an expressionless face that was generally topped by a green-lined white eyeshade.

Lob A ball hit high in the air and deep into the backcourt of the opposition.

Lob Volley A shot similar to the lob but more advanced, since a player hits the ball just as it has bounced.

Longline Stroke played straight down the line, either along or adjacent to one of the sidelines.

Loop A ball hit with topspin, making it dip sharply.

Love A scoring term that represents zero.

Love Game A game in which the losing player does not score.

Love Set A set in which the losing player wins no games.

Lucky Loser In some knockout tournaments, one loss does not automatically result in a player being eliminated. Beaten players have the chance to play against each other. These players are known as "lucky losers" (Playback).

Match A game of tennis.

Match Point A point that will win the match if won by the player who is leading.

ME A term that describes the movement of a ball that scarcely bounces at all.

Mini-Break When the server loses the point during a tiebreaker, this is called a mini-break.

Mini-Tennis Players rallying short ground strokes from service line to service line, generally used to warm up.

Miss To fail to hit the ball, as in a missed swing.

Mixed Doubles A match in which a man and a woman form a team for a game of doubles against another man-and-woman team.

"Nasty" Ilie Nastase, Romanian player, reached number one in the 1970s; nickname for his unsportsmanlike behavior.

Net Ball A ball that hits the net and goes over, to remain in play (except on a serve).

Net Game A playing strategy in which a player stations himself in the forecourt.

Net Man The partner of the server in a doubles game, who positions himself in the forecourt near the net.

Netman A tennis player.

Net Play Action near the net.

No-Man's Land Midcourt area where players are especially vulnerable to balls bounced at their feet, forcing them to attempt demanding half-volleys.

Not Up A ball that bounces twice and cannot legally be played.

Odd Court The left court: when play is started in this court, an odd number of points in the current game have been played.

On the Rise An aggressive playing style in which the ball is returned by a player before it reaches the high point of its bounce; playing the ball "early" cuts down the reaction time for the opposition.

Opening A good offensive opportunity that if capitalized on, will enable a player to score a point.

Overhand A stroke in which the racket is positioned above the shoulder.

Overhead Smash A hard overhead stroke that resembles a serve and is used to counteract the lob (Smash, Overhead).

Overrule Umpire corrects a decision made by one of the judges.

Overspin Topspin.

Pace The speed of the ball.

Passing Shot Hitting the ball either down the line or crosscourt out of the reach of a net player—a technique used by a backcourt player when an opponent rushes the net.

Pat Ball Delivery A service that is soft.

Place To accurately hit the ball to a desired location.

Poach An advanced technique in doubles play that involves a net man vacating his position and crossing in front of his partner to take a ball that would have normally been played by the partner. Generally, a surprising aggressive shot.

Pop-up A high lob to the baseline that is made from close to the net.

Power Game Style of play that features hard smashes and serves.

Push To stroke the ball with the racket held flat so that no spin is placed on the ball.

Pusher Player who stays at the baseline just putting the ball in play by hitting moderate-to-easy defensive deep shots.

Putaway A shot hit so well that it is virtually impossible for an opponent to return it (Kill, Winner).

Qualifying Competition Tournament providing low-ranked players a chance to qualify for the tournament proper.

Quarterfinals The round in which eight players remain in a singles tournament, or eight teams in a doubles tournament (Round of Eight).

Rally Play after a serve to the conclusion of a point. Also, a series of shots during which both players are able to keep the ball in play.

Ranking The order players are ranked by associations, based on their quality of play.

Ready Position A short check-step, generally made just before or as the opponent hits the ball, that creates a neutral position for the feet allowing the player to move right or left, depending on the direction of the opponent's shot (Split-Step).

Receiver The player who receives the serve.

Registered Player One allowed to keep his amateur status even though he may register in an open tournament and keep any prize money won.

Retrieve To make a long run to return an effective shot made by an opponent.

Return To hit the ball back to an opponent; in general, this term applies to the return of a served ball.

Right Court (Player) The doubles-team partner who gets service in the right court (Even Court; Forehand Court).

Rough, Smooth Trimmings strings wound around racket strings near the tip and throat; a hitting surface can feel "smooth" or "rough" depending on the type of string winding.

Round Single-elimination tournament rounds are numbered up until the quarterfinal round: the first round is the first set of matches played; half the players are eliminated, and the others move into the second round, and so forth.

Round-Robin A competition in which each player or team plays every other player or team; the entry that wins the greatest number of matches is the victor.

Rush the Net A playing style in which a player, after hitting an approach shot, rushes the net to position himself more effectively to win a point.

Seeding Ranking teams or players on the basis of their ability or potential.

Semifinals The round in which four players remain in a singles tournament, or four teams in a doubles tournament; semifinal winners move ahead to the finals.

Serve Stroke which starts every point. Consists of toss and service "motion." Ball may not bounce on serve. Each point, the server gets a first serve and a second serve if the first is missed. Types of serves are flat, spin, kick, slice, underhand.

Serve and Volley A tactical approach where the serve (generally the first serve) is followed by a rush to the net to volley the return.

Server The player who is serving.

Service The served ball.

Service Ace A good serve that cannot be returned by the receiver.

Service Break The winning of a game by a receiver against the service of an opponent.

Service Courts The two areas on both sides of the court that lie between the half-court line and the service side line and extend from the net back to the service line.

Service Line The rear boundary of the service court, a line twenty-one feet away from and parallel to the net.

Service Sideline That part of the singles-court side line between the net and the service line that defines the side boundary of the service court in both singles and doubles play.

Set One of the major units into which a match is divided.

Set Point A point on which the player leading a set can win the game and the set at the same time.

Setup An easy shot that an opponent can hit very well and usually score a point on.

Short-Angle Shot A crosscourt shot directed near the juncture of an opponent's sideline and service line.

Sideline The line at either side of the court that marks the outside edge of the court's playing surface.

Sidespin The vertical spinning of a ball like a top.

Single Elimination Tournament A competition in which the loss of one match eliminates a player or team.

Singles A contest between two players.

Size of Court Rectangle one hundred and twenty feet long by sixty feet wide, marked off at seventy-eight feet long by twenty-seven feet wide (singles) and seventy-eight feet long by thirty-six feet wide (doubles).

Slice A groundstroke or volley hit with backspin; a ball that is served hit with sidespin. (Undercut).

Smash A powerful overhead swing at a dropping ball.

Stop Volley A stroke aimed at dropping the ball just over the net (Blocked Ball).

Stroke To strike the ball with the racket.

"Sweet Pete" Tennis great Pete Sampras, he was "Sweet Pete" but not to his competition.

Take the Net To move in close to the net.

Tape A canvas strip attached to the top of the net (Band).

Team Tennis Tennis performed by teams; a match equals five sets.

Tennis Numerous theories exist as to how tennis got its name. One theory holds that the French word *tenez* is the root for the word tennis. *Tenez*, originally spelled "tenetz," meant "to take heed," and in a broader sense, to play. Other theorists speculate that the word tennis derives from the ancient Egyptian city of Tanis in the Nile River delta. The Arabic word for the city was "Tinnis." The city of Tinnis was a booming locale for the making of fine linens, and the early tennis balls were created from light fabrics. Thus, once upon a time there might have been "tinnis" balls. And the old-fashioned term "tennist" is still used in some circles to describe one who plays tennis.

Tennis Elbow A painful injury to the elbow.

Tennis Grip The (Eastern) grip used to hold a racket.

Tennis Scoring The unusual scoring of a game in tennis—15 (one point), 30 (two points), 40 (three points)—originated with the recording of the progression of the rallies, or "rests," in real tennis. These were noted on a simple clock face positioned near the court. A player who won a rally would have his pointer moved through one quarter—the fifteenth minute. After the next rally, the pointer would be moved to 30, or to the next quarter on the clock. The next movement was to the three-quarter mark, or 45. Ultimately 45 was abbreviated to 40. When the pointer went around full circle, it was an indication that the conclusion of the game had been reached.

Tennist One who plays tennis.

30 The second point reached in a game.

Throat That part of the racquet just below the head.

Tiebreaker Rule for deciding sets when the score is 6-6. During tiebreakers, players are awarded points numerically. The first player with seven points is the winner of a set, provided he has a lead of two points. If not, play continues until this two-point advantage lead has been established. Score for the set is then recorded as 7-6.

Topspin The spin of a ball in the same direction as its flight, caused by hitting up and behind it.

Trajectory The flight of the ball, which varies according to the stroke used.

Twist The spin applied to curve a service ball; topspin.

Umpire The official who keeps score and is the decision maker as to which player has won a point. In major tournaments the umpire is assisted by a number of judges (e.g., line judges).

Undercut Hit the bottom of the ball to create a reverse spin (Chop).

Unforced Error One committed under no pressure from the opponent.

Unseeded A nonseeded player, one who is not favored to get through the early rounds of play.

Up and Back A doubles-play strategy in which one player is positioned near the net while the other stays in the backcourt.

Volley Return of a ball before it bounces.

Volleyer A player who is skilled in volley play.

Western Grip A grip in which the racquet is placed on the ground face down and the player simply picks it up with the "V" between the thumb and forefinger on the back plate. The player's palm is toward the bottom of the handle, and there is generally no hand shifting for a backhand stroke.

Wide-Breaking Shot A slice service with so much spin on it that the receiver is pulled into or beyond the alley.

Winner Shot winning the point outright. A "clean winner" is a shot that the opponent does not even touch with the racket (ACE).

Wood Shot A stroke in which the ball is hit off the wooden portion of the racquet. Today known simply as a "frame shot" or a ball hit off the frame ("shank").

"X Man" Nickname for Belgian player Xavier Malisse.

Track and Field

American Hop A body-positioning technique used for throwing the javelin.

Anchor The final or fourth leg (or runner) of a relay team.

Angle of Delivery The angle to the ground at which an implement is released.

Approach The adjustment(s) or run just prior to executing a throw or jump.

"Babe" Mildred Didrikson Zaharias was one of the true greats in women's athletics. Winner of two gold track-and-field medals at the 1932 Olympics, she had many nicknames: "The Amazing Amazon," "Belting Babe," "The Terrific Tomboy," "The Texas Tornado," and "Whatta-Gal Didrikson."

Baton A hollow cylinder passed from one member of a relay team to another.

Black Gazelle Wilma Rudolph is one of the most graceful black women the world of sports has produced, and from that characteristic came her nickname. Unable even to walk at the age of seven, she won three gold medals in the 1960 Olympics, in the 100- and 200-meter dashes and as the anchor runner in the 400-meter relay.

Blind Pass A pass of the baton to a relay-team member who is looking forward (Nonvisual Exchange).

Boston Marathon In 1897 the Boston Athletic Association inaugurated an annual international event that is staged each April. Individuals from all over the world compete in the 26-mile, 385-yard race that is run through the suburbs and city of Boston.

Box The container in which vaulters place their poles before taking off.

Break To leave the starting block before the gun sounds.

Breaking for the Pole Running to get the inside-lane position.

Break Mark A mark made in the landing pit by a performer.

Circle Competitive area for the discus, shot, hammer, and weight throws.

Clearance The space by which a performer clears an object such as a crossbar or a hurdle.

Closed Position The positioning of a shot or discus to the rear of the right shoulder and hip to get maximum power into the throw.

Crossbar A bar about sixteen feet long made of wood, plastic, or metal that functions as an obstacle for high jumpers or pole vaulters.

Curb A running track's inside border.

Cut-Down The dropping of the lead leg in clearing a hurdle.

Dead Heat A tie between two or more runners.

Decathlon A two-day, ten-event competition consisting of the following: day 1—100-meter dash, long jump, shot put, high jump, 400-meter dash; day 2—100-meter hurdles, discus throw, pole vault, javelin throw, 1,500-meter run. Competition is judged on the basis of points deducted from a maximum score based on an arbitrary standard of time.

Drive Leg One providing power for takeoff or stride.

Exchange Zone A twenty-meter-long area in which the relay baton must be passed (Passing Zone).

False Start A runner illegally leaving the starting block before the gun is fired.

Finish Posts Uprights to which the finish tape or string is attached.

Flat Ground that is level.

Flats Nonspiked track shoes, generally used by field-event competitors.

Flight A hurdles lane. Also, a round of trials.

"Flo Jo" Florence Joyner, the Olympic track star's nickname came from the first letters of her first and last names.

Flop A high-jumping procedure that involves going headfirst and backward over the bar and landing on the back ("Fosbury Flop").

Flyaway A pole-vaulting procedure that consists of leaving the pole at the peak of a vault.

"Fosbury Flop" Richard Douglas "Dick" Fosbury revolutionized the high jump using a back-first technique that became known as the "Fosbury flop." The American-born athlete began experimenting with a new technique at age sixteen in 1963 because he found available techniques too complicated. His new method involved diagonally sprinting toward the high bar, then curving and leaping backwards over the bar. There was initial skepticism from the high jumping community, but the "Fosbury flop" quickly caught on.

Foul Line A line that a contestant must remain behind in order to have a jump or throw qualify.

Foul Throw A throw that violates the rules; it is counted as a trial but is not measured.

Gather Composure intentionally created to generate increased effort, before a long jump takeoff, for example.

Guide Mark A mark on the track made by relay runners to assist them in recognizing the baton exchange zone.

"Gun Is Up" A verbal warning that the starter is about to begin the race.

Gun Lap The final lap in a race.

Hammer Throw A field event throw where a performer hurls a hammer with both hands from a throwing circle seven feet in diameter; the throw is aimed for distance and the hammer must land in a throwing sector which is bounded by two lines extending at a 60-degree angle from the center of the throwing circle.

Handoff The baton exchange between the incoming runner and outgoing runner in a relay race.

Headwind A wind blowing against an athlete's or runner's course.

Heat A preliminary contest that qualifies contestants for the final competition.

High-Jump Standards Supports that hold the crossbar for the high jump.

Hurdle An obstacle that runners must leap over in a hurdle race or steeplechase. As a verb, to leap over a barrier that is made of wood or metal.

Inside Lane The inside part of the track (Pole Position).

"Jesse" His real name was James Cleveland Owens, but as a youngster he told a teacher when asked that his name was J. C. The teacher misheard and called Owens "Jesse." It was Jesse not "J. C." who became most famous as a track star and for his participation in the 1936 Summer Olympics, staged in Berlin. Angering Hitler and thrilling free men everywhere, Owens won four gold medals.

Jog To run at a slow and even pace.

Kick To accelerate near the end of a race.

Kicker A runner who relies on his "kick" to win a race.

Lane Generally a four-foot-wide course marked out on a track on which a track athlete runs.

Lap A complete circuit around the track.

Lead Leg The first leg over a hurdle. Also, the first or kicking leg in jumping.

Lead-off Runner A relay team's first runner.

Leg A specified distance that must be run by a member of a relay team.

Marathon A race generally run over public roads—from which traffic has been banned—that is 26 miles, 385 yards long. In 490 BC the Greeks defeated a much larger Persian army in a very significant battle. The news of the Greek victory was brought to Athens by a messenger who ran the twenty-six miles from the field of battle at Marathon only to drop dead when he reached his destination. The ancient Greek event and the locale of the race give the modern event its name.

Mark A starting point for a race. A point of check during approach. The point where the long jumper, shot, or discus lands.

Medley A relay race in which the team members run different distances.

On the Mark A position taken by a runner directly behind the scratch line that is assumed at the command "On your mark," prior to the "Set" command.

Order A relay team's running sequence.

Pace A generally predetermined and consistent rate of speed used by a runner.

Pass A decision made by a contestant to decline attempting a jump or throw. Also, the exchange of a baton in a relay race.

Pentathlon A five-event contest that is usually part of women's track and field competitions consisting of the long jump, high jump, 200-meter dash, discus throw, and 1,500-meter run. Points are awarded according to the participant's positions on a scale based on arbitrary standards.

"Phantom Finn" Paavo Nurmi was one of the greatest of all long-distance runners in the history of sports. Allegedly the first man to run with a stopwatch in his hand, the athlete also called the "Flying Finn" set twenty-two world records in 1920–1931. His most outstanding achievements came in the 1920, 1924, and 1928 Olympics. A native of Finland, Nurmi's nickname derived from his ability to disappear from the rest of the field while excelling in long-distance competitions.

Pickup Zone An area eleven yards long in front of the passing zone in which the receiving runner in a relay race may begin running.

Pit A jumper's landing area, composed of cushioning material.

Pole Vault A field event where a competitor uses a pole to vault over a horizontal bar that is supported by two upright bars; each contestant must clear the bar in three opportunities; it is then raised to a higher position. The winner is the last contestant to clear the bar in its highest position.

Push-off A push up and away from the pole at the top of a pole vault.

Put The technique of pushing the shot in the air.

Recall The calling back of runners after a false start.

Receiver The relay runner receiving the baton.

Recovery Leg A runner's nondriving leg.

Relay A race in which several runners compose a team and each runner runs one leg of the competition.

Reverse The follow-through after a throw or put that involves reversing the feet.

Runway The approach area to the takeoff board in long jumping, or the scratch line in field competition.

Scratch Line A line that jumpers or throwers may not go over during a trial or that runners may not pass before the gun is fired.

Sector Lines Markings that section off where a fair throw must land in the discus throw or shot put.

Shift Moving the vaulting pole from the carry position to the vaulting box.

Shot A sphere made of iron or brass used in the shot-put competition that weighs eight, twelve, or fourteen pounds and is approximately five inches in diameter.

Shot Put To heave a shot.

Shuttle A relay in which the legs are run back and forth.

Sprint A race up to 400 meters (Dash).

Staggered Start Generally used in races around a curve, a starting alignment in which runners are positioned in a staggered manner in order to equalize the distance each must run.

Standing Broad Jump A jump for distance attempted without a running start.

Standing High Jump A jump for height attempted without a running start.

Starting Blocks Mechanisms generally anchored to the track against which runners place their feet as an aid in starting a race.

Steeplechase A race in which runners encounter hurdles and a water jump.

Stopboard A shot-put mechanism, usually a curved wooden block, anchored to the front edge of the throwing circle that acts to restrain the performer from stepping out of the circle. Also, a board that catches a vaulting pole at the start of a vault.

Straddle A high-jumping style in which the performer crosses over the bar on his stomach.

Straightaway The straight area of a track, as opposed to the curved portion.

Stride A step in running.

Takeoff The act of leaving the ground in a jump or vault.

Takeoff Board A board used for the takeoff by a running long jumper.

Takeoff Foot The foot that provides drive off the ground.

Takeoff Mark The spot from which the takeoff is performed in such competitions as the high jump and the long jump (Takeoff Spot).

Throwing Sector The specific arc where a thrown object must land.

Trailing Leg The rear or takeoff leg.

Trial An abbreviated term for field trial; an attempt made in a field event.

Triathlon A women's competition, consisting of three events.

Turn The portion of the track that is curved.

Tying Up The development of an inability to compete in a track and field event due to nervousness, muscle tightness, and so forth.

Visual Exchange A baton exchange in which the receiver has an eye on the incoming runner until the baton is passed.

Weight Man A competitor who throws or puts a weight.

Weight Throw A throw in a field event where a specific weight is thrown with both hands from a throwing circle seven feet in diameter. The weight must land in a throwing sector bounded by two lines extending at a 45-degree angle from the center of the throwing circle.

Western Roll A high-jumping style in which the jumper clears the bar while lying on his side.

Wind Sprint A short-distance sprint.

Trampolining and Tumbling

Arabian Handspring A handspring made with the legs positioned evenly or together throughout the technique.

Arch A bowlike position executed with hips thrust forward, spine bent backward, and toes pointed.

Arch Down A chest roll executed downward from a hand balance.

Arm Hook A quick bending of the elbow that snaps the arm across the chest in an upward slanting manner.

Arm Swing A quickly raised arm, generally with a straight elbow position.

Back Bend A backward arch that positions the hands below the head on the mat.

Back Flip A 360-degree turn backward from a springing start accomplished without the hands touching anything (Backward Somersault).

Back Handspring A springing movement off both feet into a backward arch with a pullover into a handstand that is completed with a spring to the balls of the feet (Flip-flop, Flic-flac).

Backover A variation of the back handspring that is executed slowly, with the legs allowed to move apart during the maneuver but not at the start or completion of the technique.

Back Roll A tuck off a backward roll that enables the body to perform a 360-degree turn and wind up positioned vertically (Backward Roll).

Baroni A half-twisting somersault that uses forward-to-backward momentum; a body-whipping somersault aided by a twist to the side to reverse the landing direction (Barani, Browny).

Bridge Support for the body by the head and feet, or head, hands, and feet—only in the positions of forward bent or backward arch.

Buck A diving stunt to the hands followed by a push away and snap back to a leaning-forward stance on both feet.

Bucking Bronco A series of quick bucks.

Butterfly A type of slanting cartwheel aerial.

Cartwheel Handspring to the side with arms and legs spread.

Cartwheel Handstand A cartwheel that is completed with the performer standing on his hands with his toes pointed upward.

Chest Roll A backward roll along the stomach and thighs until the toes touch, executed off a roll down from a handstand.

Cradle A trampolining maneuver that begins from a back drop that twists the gymnast half forward, with the final stage positioning the gymnast on his back.

Dead-Lift Jump A springing up from a crouch unaided by a previous movement's momentum.

Dive A roll forward after a headfirst leap in which the feet are cleared before there is hand contact.

Diving Handspring A dive onto the hands finished off with a front or back spring onto the feet.

Double Backward Somersault Two complete turns in the air.

Flange A body extension off a backward roll into a hand balance.

Forward Roll A roll forward with the body in a tucked position that moves the gymnast 360 degrees into a finish on both feet.

Front Bridge The positioning of the body only on the head, the toes, and the balls of the feet, looking down at the mat.

Front Handspring A running forward handspring from hands to feet.

Front Somersault Total forward aerial rotation from a takeoff from the feet to a landing on the feet.

Full Gainer A leaping forward run into a backward somersault, with body motion continuing forward.

Full Turn Total body rotation on the long axis.

Full-Twisting Backward Somersault A backward somersault that incorporates a full twist, with the body landing in the position it was in at the takeoff.

Gainer A reverse somersault executed with the body moving forward.

Hand Balance A position in which the body is poised vertically, the back is arched, the toes are pointed upward, and the performer is balanced on his hands (Handstand).

Handspring A forward or backward spring from hands to feet.

Headspring A springing movement from the head aided by leg swing that enables the performer to take off and land with both feet even.

Headstand A handstand with additional body support provided by the top of the head (Head and Hand Balance).

Jackknife A position with toes pointed, knees straight, hips flexed, and hands close to or touching the ankles.

Jump Through A maneuver executed from a face-down, body-and-arms-extended stance that enables the performer to "jump through" the stretched-out arms to a seated position.

Kickover A forward somersault initiated by a strong upward and backward kick from one leg and the other leg's spring takeoff.

Kip A projection of the body from a prone-back position to a vertical landing on both feet; a powerful hip snap and leg swing powers the move.

Layout A body extension into an overall arch, legs straightened together, arms up and back.

Lead-up Trick A basic move or trick that helps build skills for more difficult moves.

Leg Drive Extending the leg(s) to power the body up or forward.

Lunge A quick and powerful forward reaching movement.

Mule Kick A diving forward, into a hand balance, to a springing landing on the balls of the feet.

Neckspring A forward roll into a kip (Nip-up).

Novelty A nonstandard maneuver.

One-Hand Handspring A spring from a hand to either foot or both feet.

Pike A position with the body fully bent forward at the waist, the legs straight, the toes pointed, and the hands either extended to the sides or grasping the ankles.

Pike Full A forward somersault aided by a leg swing from a pike into a layout.

Press A steady pull that enables a performer to move into a hand or head balance.

Reverse Bridge A bridge accomplished with hips thrust up to arch the body with only the head and feet, or head, hands, and feet, touching the mat (Wrestler's Bridge).

Roll A turning maneuver in a tucked position, head over heels.

Routine A sequence of stunts generally performed in a straight line over a good part of the mat surface.

Shoulder Balance A body position in which weight is placed only on the shoulders and there is a reversed hand placement; the legs are positioned upward.

Sit Backward A fall backward to a seated position.

Snapdown A pushing-off and at the same time downward kick from a hand balance to a balls-of-the-feet, springing landing.

Somersault A feet-to-feet complete turn in the air.

Spot To help or guard a performer.

Spotter The performance of a move in a small area. Also, a takeoff and landing in almost the same spot.

Spring A thrusting movement from feet to hands to feet.

Swingtime The flow of one stunt into another in such a professional manner that it is difficult to note when one ended and the other began.

Throw A bending forward or arching backward to start a handspring or somersault.

Tigna A forward somersault after a tinsica landing.

Tinsica A half-twisting cartwheel move that enables the performer to finish by facing in the same position as he began.

Toe Point Full feet extension.

Trick A gymnastic maneuver.

Tuck A ball-like body position with knees bent, thighs drawn up tight against the chest, and hands clasping shins.

Twist A body turn on the long axis.

Walkover A handspring with legs spread wide and positioned for a walking stride on takeoff and landing.

Whip A forceful pullover to build momentum for a stunt.

Whipback A backward handspring.

Volleyball

Absorption A "giving with" the ball as it is hit by the passer.

Acceleration The application of forward momentum to the ball when passing.

Ace A serve that either lands untouched or is too difficult to return.

Attack Any procedure used to return the ball across the net.

Back Set An overhand pass employed in sending the ball in a backward direction.

Backward Roll A tumbling-type fundamental that permits a player to dive laterally for the ball, land without injury, and quickly assume a defensive position.

Block A defensive move by a player in which he or she jumps and reaches above the net to stop an offensive hit.

Bump A pass from one player to another hitting the ball with the wrists and forearms.

Catching the Ball A momentary coming to rest of the ball in the hands or arms of a player—a violation (Holding).

Change of Pace A spike that is softly hit to deceive the opposition.

Court Coverage Offensive and defensive court assignments of a player while the ball is in play.

Cut To come in between another player and the ball.

Cut Shot An offensive hit that results in a player slicing the ball barely over and parallel to the net, instead of hitting it with power.

Dig A defensive play to bring a spiked ball up into play.

Dink A soft hit that goes just over the net or beyond a blocker's hands.

Dive and Slide An advanced defensive technique enabling a player to spring forward to play a ball that is apparently out of reach.

Double Attack The ability to leap in the air and hit the ball with either hand.

Double Foul Simultaneous fouls committed by players on opposing teams; the play is done over, with the same team that was serving given a chance to serve again.

Double Hit The hitting of a ball twice in succession by a player.

Draw The position given in the bracketing of teams for competition that determines which teams a team will be matched against.

Dribbling The touching of the ball more than once by a player.

Fake A feigned spike swing at a ball by a player to keep the defense back.

Floater A spinless serve that performs like a baseball knuckleball.

Foot Foul A serving foul that takes place when a player steps on or over the backline.

Four-Two Offense A lineup in which there are four spikers and two setters.

Free Ball A ball that is easy to handle given by one team to another just to keep the ball in play.

Frontcourt The area between the net and the attacking line.

Front Line The front-row players lined up for a serve.

Half-Moon Defense A semicircular formation, as opposed to regular blocking.

Inside Closest to the center of the net.

Japanese Set A ball hit just high enough to clear the net.

Jump Set A play in which the setter jumps for a pass very close to the net.

Kill An unreturnable spike that scores a point for the offense.

Low Ball A ball that comes in below the waist.

Mystery Ball A ball that curves, floats, drops, zigs, zags.

Net A foul called when any player touches the net while play is in progress.

Net Antenna Vertical projections on both ends of the net that aid officials in judging whether the net has been touched during the playing of a game.

Net Ball The hitting of the net by a ball.

Off-Hand Spike A spike executed with the hand away from the setter.

Overset A set that goes over the net to the side of the defensive team.

Quick Serve A serve made before the opposing team is set.

Rotation The shifting of positions by players.

Roundhouse An overhand serve hit with topspin that makes the ball drop.

Screening The blocking of the view of a server from the opposing team members.

Serve To put the ball in play with a hand or arm strike.

Serving Order The order in which team members play their positions and then serve.

Set Placement of the ball near the net to facilitate spiking.

Set-up A method of setting the ball to another player on the team, who is positioned for such a play.

Shoot A two-handed set made usually as a dink over the net.

Sideout Failure of the serving team to score; the ball goes to the opposition.

Spike A forceful method of driving the ball into the opponent's court via a downward hit at the ball from a position above and close to the net.

Spiker A player positioned close to the net who is looking for hard, downward hits of the ball.

Stride and Flex A passing technique in which the upper body is moved into a position in front of the descending ball, even though the lower body does not reach this position.

Switch An after-the-serve strategy that has two players exchange positions, enabling a setter to move from the back line to the front line to get the pass and to set the ball for the spiker; a frontcourt-to-backcourt move, or vice versa, by a player.

Tape Shot A ball spiked or hit into the tape at the top of the net that continues on and over the net.

Technique Man A player skilled in spiking, setting, serving, and blocking.

Throw A mishandling foul when the ball is not set or hit cleanly.

Volleyball William G. Morgan, director of the YMCA of Holyoke, Massachusetts, and a Springfield College student, is credited with inventing the sport of volleyball and giving it its name. He actually originated a game that he called "Mintonette." In 1895 he began to experiment with variations of this game. Experiments with a net and a ball encouraged his students to volley the ball over the net, which led to their volleying the ball and resulting in Morgan's changing the name of the sport from "Mintonette" to "volleyball."

Wipe-off Shot A spike deliberately deflected off the blocker's hands.

Water Polo

Advantage Rule Refraining from calling a foul if the call would give advantage to the offender's team.

Attacking Team One with control of the ball.

Backhand Shot or pass flipped backward, over the shoulder or head.

Ball Pressurized sphere weighing 400 to 450 grams. For men's play, the ball is .68–.71 meters in circumference and inflated to 13–14 pounds of pressure. For women's play, the ball is .65–.78 meters in circumference and inflated to 12–13 pounds of pressure.

Ball Under Foul when player takes or holds the ball underwater while being tackled by an opponent.

Brutality Exclusion foul for very rough play, such as punching or kicking an opponent or official.

Bunny Goal scored on a hard shot near the goalkeeper's head (Donut).

Cap Caps numbered 1 to 13 are worn by players, with the goalkeeper wearing number 1 and a red cap. Team caps are generally white for one team and blue for the other.

Center-Back Defensive player whose prime role is covering the opposition's center-forward.

Center-Forward Chief attacking player, usually positioned directly in front of the opponents' goal between the two-meter and four-meter lines (Two-Meter Man, Hole Man, Hole Set).

Control of the Ball Player is considered in control if the ball is on the water in front of the horizontal plane of his shoulders.

Corner Throw Free throw awarded to attacking team if a defensive player touched the ball last before it went over the goal line.

Dead Time When the ball is dead, between the whistle for a foul and the restarting of play and the clock.

Dead-Time Foul Any foul committed during dead time.

Defensive Team The team that does not have control of the ball; opposite of attacking team.

Double Foul Simultaneous fouls by players.

Double Hole An offense stationing an attacker in front of each post of the goal (Double Post).

Dribble Swimming with the ball, usually while it rides on the wake in front of a swimmer.

Drive Quick move to the area in front of the goal by an offensive player who does not have the ball.

Drop Players drop back on defense protecting the center of the pool, attempting to block passes and shots.

Dry Pass One able to be caught above the water.

Eggbeater Alternating leg kick for treading water.

Exclusion Area Outside the field of play where a player must wait after an exclusion foul.

Exclusion Foul One resulting in the offending player being sent to the exclusion area for twenty seconds or until the opposing team has scored a goal. Afterward, the opposing team gets a free throw at the spot of the foul.

Field Measures twenty to thirty meters between the goal lines and ten to twenty meters wide with white buoys on each side of the pool indicating goal lines and the half-distance line. At each end of the pool colored buoys denote two-meter lines (red), four-meter lines (yellow), and seven-meter lines (green). Water depth is minimum of 1.8 meters. Preferred depth is two meters. Playing area extends a minimum of .3 meters behind the goal lines at each end of the pool.

Field Player Any player except goalkeeper.

Four-Meter Foul A foul by a defensive player inside the four-meter line directly aimed at preventing a goal. This results in the opposing team being awarded a penalty throw.

Four-Meter Line Imaginary line extending across the pool, four meters from each goal line.

Free Throw When play has to be restarted after the ball crosses a sideline or after a foul that does not result in a penalty throw. Player awarded the free throw may throw the ball or drop it into the water and dribble it before passing. Before a goal can be scored at least two players, from either side, must touch the ball.

Front Defending between center-forward and player with the ball.

Game A water polo game has four periods of seven minutes each, with a two-minute interval between periods. If the score is tied after the fourth period, two overtime periods of three minutes each, with a one-minute interval, can be played. If the score is still tied, a penalty shootout is used to determine the outcome.

Goal Two goalposts and a crossbar, from which a net is suspended. The goal posts are three meters apart and the crossbar is .9 meters above the surface of the water. A score is made by throwing or dribbling the ball so that it goes completely across the goal line, between the posts and under the crossbar.

Goal Judge There are two goal judges, one positioned on a side of the pool at each goal line. The goal judge's chief responsibility is to determine whether a goal has been scored and, if so, to signal the score by raising and crossing both arms.

Goalkeeper This individual must remain behind the half-distance line. The goalkeeper alone is allowed to stand or walk on the floor of the pool, to jump from the floor of the pool, to use both hands on the ball, and to punch the ball.

Goal Line Imaginary line extending across the pool at the mouth of the goal.

Goal Throw One taken by the defending goalkeeper from behind the two-meter line restarting play if an attacking player was the last to touch the ball before it went out over the goal line.

Greenie Quick shot taken by a player after receiving a pass near the goal; term was originally "guerrini."

Half-Distance Line An imaginary line, marked by white buoys, dividing the field of play into two equal ends.

Hold Lifting or carrying the ball, placing the hand over or under it, or pressing it beneath the water.

Hole Guard Defensive player who takes position in front of his own goal in order to guard the opposing center-forward.

Impeding Hindering the movement of an opponent who does not have possession of the ball.

Lane Press Defense where players are positioned in passing lanes, between the ball and the players they are guarding, rather than between the offensive players and the goal.

Live Time Clock is running.

Man-Down Period of twenty seconds when the defensive team is one player short because of an exclusion foul.

Man-Up Period of twenty seconds when the offensive team has one player more than the defensive team because of an exclusion foul.

Moving Pick When an offensive player swims in front of a player defending another offensive player, enabling that teammate to receive a pass or take a shot.

Natural Goal Scored from open play with both teams at full strength.

Neutral Throw One by a referee giving each team equal chance to reach the ball (Face Off).

Ordinary Foul An infringement that usually results in a free throw for the opposing team. Ordinary fouls include taking the ball underwater when tackled; playing the ball while standing or walking on the bottom of the pool; jumping from the bottom of the pool; hitting the ball with the fist; playing the ball with both hands at the same time; and deliberately impeding an opponent who doesn't have the ball.

Outlet Pass from the goalkeeper to a teammate beginning counterattack after a save.

Penalty Foul One that results in a penalty throw for the opposing team (Shootout).

Penalty Throw One taken from the four-meter line by a member of the attacking team the goalkeeper is the only defender (Penalty Shot).

Personal Foul Exclusion foul or penalty foul. A player who commits three personal fouls is permanently excluded from the game.

Point Offensive position farthest from the goal and approximately straight out from the goal.

Press Defense extended beyond its normal range.

Referee One is positioned on each side of the pool, the attacking or offensive referee, when the goal to his right is being attacked. The defensive referee remains at least as far back as the attacking player who is farthest from the goal. Referees together are responsible for calling fouls and declaring penalties.

Seven-Meter Line Imaginary line extending across the pool, seven meters from each goal line.

Shot Clock Clock displaying time remaining for a team to take a shot (Possession Clock).

Sink Pushing an opposing player under the water.

Splashing Deliberately splashing water in an opponent's face, an exclusion foul.

Stalling Failure to shoot or advance the ball within thirty-five seconds.

Stationary Pick Offensive player stops in front of a player who is defending another offensive player, allowing that teammate to receive a pass or take a shot.

Swim-off Method of starting a period. Players position themselves on their own goal lines. A referee blows the whistle, tosses the ball into the center of the pool, and players race for it (Sprint).

Team Seven players, including a goalkeeper, and a maximum of six substitutes.

Two-Meter Line Imaginary line extending across the pool, two meters from each goal line.

Two-Meter Violation Ordinary foul when a player is inside the opponent's two-meter line and not behind the line of the ball.

Weak Side Pool side opposite that where the ball is located.

Wet Pass One thrown so that it lands in the water.

Wet Shot One attempted by a player who is controlling the ball in the water.

Wing Area near the sideline.

Zone Defense where players defend an area, rather than a specific opposing player.

Weightlifting

Barbell A steel bar approximately six feet long to which circular weights are affixed at each end.

Bench Press The act of a weightlifter lying on a bench on his back and pushing a barbell out from his chest with arms extended, and then returning it to the chest position.

Clean To get a weight up to shoulder level by lifting it off the floor in one, nonstop motion.

Clean and Jerk The act of getting a weight to shoulder level, stopping, and then jerking the weight up over the head by shooting the arms straight up.

Dead Lift The lifting of a weight to hip level and then lowering it to the ground.

Dumbbell A short, barlike device that can be lifted with one hand and that has balls or discs attached at either end.

Incline Bench A 45-degree-angled bench used for pressing weights or for resting.

Jerk The thrusting of a weight over the head from a starting position at shoulder level.

Lifter Another name for a weightlifter.

Olympic Lifting International competition that involves only the snatch and the clean and jerk.

Power Lifting International competition that involves the bench press, the dead lift, and the squat.

Press A movement in which only the arms and the back are used to push a weight up from shoulder level to above the lifter's head (Military Press).

Snatch A lifting procedure performed in one continuous motion from the time the barbell leaves the floor until the arms are extended overhead; the lifter gets power into the move by squatting and then lunging upward with the barbell.

Squat A lifting procedure that involves moving from a squatting position to a standing position and placing the barbell behind the shoulder blades.

Standards Barbell-supporting posts.

Super Set Exercises for one group of muscles that are done just before a set of exercises for an opposing group of muscles.

Weight A disc that is attached to either a dumbbell or a barbell.

Wrestling

Anchor Firmly holding an opponent to prevent or restrict movement.

Armlock Holding an opponent's arm so that it cannot be moved.

Australian Tag-Team Wrestling Promoter Jack Pfeffer originated the idea of Australian tag-team wrestling during World War II. The aged, the out-of-shape, the inexperienced, and the unskilled wrestlers available for bouts during the war—for the able-bodied were taking part in the war effort—proved to be the inspiration for Pfeffer's promotion. Television helped fuel the public's interest and this hybrid version of wrestling is still popular today. It involves a fatigued wrestler being relieved by his partner if he is able to tag that partner, who is stationed at a corner of the ring.

Backheel A backward pull of an opponent onto the mat, accomplished by a wrestler getting behind his man, locking his hands around the waist, and positioning his feet against the heels of the opponent.

Bararm The gripping of an opponent's upper arm in the bend of a wrestler's elbow (Arm Bar).

Bodypress The positioning of a wrestler's total weight on top of an opponent who is lying on the mat under him.

Breakdown To strip away arm or leg support from an opponent on the mat and get him onto his side or stomach in preparation for pinning.

Bullfighter A technique used from a neutral standing position that incorporates movements similar to those of a matador avoiding a charging bull.

Counter To react to the moves of an opponent with the result that a wrestler is able to secure a hold.

Crab-Ride A hold that simulates the position of a crab: the wrestler is behind his opponent and has his toes locked behind the knees and his arms around the waist of the opponent.

Cradle A hold in which the opponent is held in a doubled-up position as a result of his head and one leg being caught between the interlocked hands of the other wrestler.

Cram A quick shove or jolt without follow-through, as distinguished from a push.

Cross-Ankle Pickup A takedown method in which the wrestler uses one hand to snatch his opponent's ankle and pushes with his body to move the opponent backward.

Cross-Body Ride While positioned generally to the back or behind an opponent, a wrestler locks one of the opponent's arms and scissors the other or opposite leg.

Crossover A takedown method in which a wrestler positioned to the rear of his opponent with arms locked about the opponent's waist, crosses one leg over another and, by dropping to the opposite knee, is able to pull the opponent down and over the outstretched leg.

Decision In the absence of a fall, a wrestler wins a match on the basis of the most points.

Defensive Position A stance assumed by a wrestler on his hands and knees; a coin flip by the referee determines which position—"offensive" or "defensive"—a wrestler assumes at the start of the second period, if no fall took place in the first period. Reversal of positions takes place in the third period if there was no fall in the second period.

Drag A takedown method that consists of the grabbing of the upper arm of an opponent and pulling him down.

Drill Dashing an opponent to the mat with much power.

Escape To recapture a neutral position.

Evident Superiority The scoring of at least eight points by a wrestler over an opponent, which is victory in a match.

Fall A match-ending situation in which a wrestler pins the shoulders of his opponent to the mat for one second in collegiate competition, or for two seconds in high school matches.

Far The side of the body farthest from the opponent.

Figure-4 Scissors A wrestler's encircling leg's foot locks behind the opposite leg's knee in this hold.

Fireman's Carry The gripping and placement of an opponent's arm over the wrestler's shoulder while positioning his other arm through the crotch region of the opponent, so as to bring the opponent up onto his shoulders in anticipation of a takedown.

Flatbacking A stance in which a wrestler leans forward with his back parallel to the mat surface.

Flying Mare Facing an opponent, a wrestler grips the wrist of the opponent, pivots, falls to one knee, and forces the opponent over his back and onto the mat.

Freestyle A mode of wrestling in which a wrestler may use his legs as scissors for gripping an opponent's arm or leg, but it is not legal to close the scissors around the head or body. Tripping and tackling is also permitted, but the rules ban injurious holds or ones that could cause an opponent much pain (Catch-As-Catch-Can).

Go-Behind To move around and behind an opponent.

"Gorgeous George" His real name was Raymond Wagner and his bleached-blond hair and outrageous manner in the wrestling ring during the 1950s turned on television viewers. Wagner's show-biz personality and his carefully coiffured tresses helped him earn more than $250,000 a year during his better years. It is believed that Wagner borrowed the nickname of Georges Carpentier, the elegant French boxer, for Wagner was anything but "gorgeous" in the ring.

Granby Roll An escape technique that resembles a cartwheel performed from a seated position.

Grapevine Intertwining leg hold.

Grappling The jockeying about on the part of wrestlers as they attempt to get holds on each other while on the mat.

Greco-Roman A style of wrestling that bans holds below the waist and the gripping of the legs of an opponent. Hooking, tripping, and lifting an opponent with the legs are also illegal. A wrestler's legs may be used only for support.

Ground Wrestling Mat wrestling (Sambo).

Guillotine A cross-body ride fall that winds up with a wrestler gripping the shoulders of the opponent to the mat and applying pressure to the far leg of the opponent.

Half Nelson The positioning of a wrestler's arm under the like arm of an opponent while pushing up against the back of the opponent's head at the same time, thus creating leverage in two directions. Variations of the "nelson" include full nelson, quarter nelson, three-quarter nelson.

Hammerlock The bending of an opponent's arm behind his back.

Headgear Protective ear covering.

Hiplock A combination of a headlock and a throw that pulls the opponent over the wrestler's hip.

"Hitman" Bret Hart grew up in Calgary with wrestling—his father, the famed wrestler and trainer Stu Hart, the Stampede Wrestling organization, and his large family of wrestling brothers. He became a champion wrestler and is much more than just a "hitman."

Hold The gripping of an opponent.

Hold-down The art of pinning an opponent on his back to the mat.

Lock A grip that completely immobilizes the part of an opponent's body that is being held.

Maneuver A planned movement.

Mat The sport of wrestling.

Match The actual wrestling contest: high-school matches in the United States consist of three two-minute periods; college matches begin with a two-minute period followed by two three-minute periods.

Matman A wrestler.

Mepham A gripping hold of the opponent's far arm when a wrestler stationed alongside and behind the opponent reaches with both hands around the opponent from either side.

Navy Ride A locking of an opponent's waist with one arm and his far leg with the other.

Near The side of the body nearest to the opponent.

Near-Fall A maneuver worth three points in collegiate wrestling, the conditions of which come close to an actual fall but do not meet the full criteria—holding an opponent's shoulders to the mat for one full second.

Offensive Position A stance assumed by a wrestler at an opponent's side, one arm placed around the waist of the opponent and a hand on his elbow. This position is given to a wrestler who has an advantage in a match. It is also determined by a referee coin toss.

Over-Arm Drag A swinging body movement from the mat that enables a wrestler to get his body around to the rear of an opponent.

Pancake A twisting, off-balancing throw of an opponent.

Penalty Loss of a point by a wrestler for illegal procedures or unnecessary roughness; two points are lost when these violations take place for the third time.

Pile Driver A professional technique in which a wrestler lifts his opponent and slams his head to the ground.

Pin A method of winning a match by hooding an opponent's shoulder blades to the mat for a full second in collegiate competition, or two seconds in high-school matches (Fall).

Points Ratings assigned wrestlers in evaluating their match performances: near-fall (3), takedown (2), reversal (2), predicament (2), time advantage of two minutes or more (2), time advantage of one minute (1), escape (1).

Post To firmly fix an arm to the mat surface for use as a support in the execution of a technique.

Predicament Outmoded term for near fall.

Princeton Lock A three-quarter nelson and leg lock combined.

Referee's Position Stances that begin the second and third periods of a match. The top wrestler is on offense while the other wrestler, on the bottom, is on defense. The ability to use an advantage or to escape from a bad position can then be evaluated.

Reversal The moving from a handicapped position to one of superiority over an opponent, for which two points are awarded a wrestler (Reverse).

Ride Like a "reversal," one of several ways a wrestler gains points via control of an opponent's moves. Basically, a ride implies control of an opponent while in an offense position—for example, gripping the ankle of an opponent to limit his ability to move about.

Scissors A locking of the legs about an opponent's body or head.

Set-up Originating a move that causes an opponent to react in an expected manner that helps the originator.

Sit-out A defensive move used many times by the bottom wrestler in the referee's position. The wrestler moves into the sitting position to attempt to escape holds or to get into an offensive position.

Snapdown A pushing movement used as an opponent jumps at a wrestler's feet, which results in the wrestler winding up behind the opponent for the application of a hold.

Stalemate A condition in which neither wrestler can maneuver himself into an advantage position.

Stand-up A method of escape that involves a crouched wrestler flexing his legs to assume a position above an opponent.

Stepover A method of escape that involves a wrestler using weight shifted to a leg placed over an opponent to his advantage.

Sugar Side The side of the wrestler that is exposed in his stance.

Switch A change from defense to offense through arm leverage.

Takedown The forcing of an opponent down to the mat.

Time Advantage The time one wrestler was in an advantage position over an opponent during the course of a match; sixty seconds or more entitles a wrestler to one point.

Total Victory A wrestler being awarded a win for application of a powerful submission hold or flawless throw.

Underhook A countering move that results in a wrestler hooking his arm beneath the arm or leg of an opponent.

Unlimited A weight class above 191 pounds.

Weight Class Categories of maximum allowable weights into which wrestlers are grouped.

International lb. (kg)	College lbs	High School lbs
105.5 (48)	118	98
114.5 (52)	126	105
125.5 (57)	134	112
136.5 (62)	142	119
149.5 (68)	150	126
163.1 (74)	158	132
180.5 (82)	167	138
198 (90)	177	145
220 (100)	190	155
over 100 kg, unlimited (minimum 75 lbs.)	unlimited	185

Whizzer A type of arm lock.

Wristlock The gripping of an opponent's wrist to create a hold.

About the Author

A celebrated sports journalist and historian, the author of thirty-five books on sports including the autobiographies of legends Nolan Ryan, Tony Dorsett, and Red Holzman, Harvey Frommer also authored the classics *New York City Baseball* and *Shoeless Joe and Ragtime Baseball*. Some of his other sports books include *Rickey and Robinson: The Men Who Broke Baseball's Color Line*, *The Yankee Encyclopedia*, *A Yankee Century*, and *Red Sox vs. Yankees: The Great Rivalry* with Frederic J. Frommer.

Together with Myrna Katz Frommer, he authored the critically acclaimed interactive oral histories *It Happened in the Catskills*, *It Happened in Brooklyn*, *Growing Up Jewish in America*, *It Happened on Broadway*, and *It Happened in Manhattan*.

He is a professor in the Master of Liberal Studies program at Dartmouth College.